COMPARATIVE URBANISM

IJURR-SUSC Published Titles

Comparative Urbanism: Tactics for Global Urban Studies
Jennifer Robinson

The Commodification Gap: Gentrification and Public Policy in London, Berlin and St. Petersburg
Matthias Bernt

Stolen Cars: A Journey Through São Paulo's Urban Conflict
Gabriel Feltran (ed.)

Classify, Exclude, Police: Urban Lives in South Africa and Nigeria
Laurent Fourchard

Housing in the Margins: Negotiating Urban Formalities in Berlin's Allotment Gardens
Hanna Hilbrandt

The Politics of Incremental Progressivism: Governments, Governances and Urban Policy Changes in São Paulo
Edited by Eduardo Cesar Leão Marques

Youth Urban Worlds: Aesthetic Political Action in Montreal
Julie-Anne Boudreau and Joëlle Rondeau

Paradoxes of Segregation: Housing Systems, Welfare Regimes and Ethnic Residential Change in Southern European Cities
Sonia Arbaci

Cities and Social Movements: Immigrant Rights Activism in the US, France, and the Netherlands, 1970-2015
Walter Nicholls and Justus Uitermark

From World City to the World in One City: Liverpool Through Malay Lives
Tim Bunnell

Urban Land Rent: Singapore as a Property State
Anne Haila

Globalised Minds, Roots in the City: Urban Upper-middle Classes in Europe
Alberta Andreotti, Patrick Le Galès and Francisco Javier Moreno-Fuentes

Confronting Suburbanization: Urban Decentralization in Post-Socialist Central and Eastern Europe
Kiril Stanilov and Luděk Sýkora (eds.)

Cities in Relations: Trajectories of Urban Development in Hanoi and Ouagadougou
Ola Söderström

Contesting the Indian City: Global Visions and the Politics of the Local
Gavin Shatkin (ed.)

Iron Curtains: Gates, Suburbs and Privatization of Space in the Post-socialist City
Sonia A. Hirt

Subprime Cities: The Political Economy of Mortgage Markets
Manuel B. Aalbers (ed.)

Locating Neoliberalism in East Asia: Neoliberalizing Spaces in Developmental States
Bae-Gyoon Park, Richard Child Hill and Asato Saito (eds.)

The Creative Capital of Cities: Interactive Knowledge of Creation and the Urbanization Economics of Innovation
Stefan Krätke

Worlding Cities: Asian Experiments and the Art of Being Global
Ananya Roy and Aihwa Ong (eds.)

Place, Exclusion and Mortgage Markets
Manuel B. Aalbers

Working Bodies: Interactive Service Employment and Workplace Identities
Linda McDowell

Networked Disease: Emerging Infections in the Global City
S. Harris Ali and Roger Keil (eds.)

Eurostars and Eurocities: Free Movement and Mobility in an Integrating Europe
Adrian Favell

Urban China in Transition
John R. Logan (ed.)

Getting Into Local Power: The Politics of Ethnic Minorities in British and French Cities
Romain Garbaye

Cities of Europe
Yuri Kazepov (ed.)

Cities, War, and Terrorism
Stephen Graham (ed.)

Cities and Visitors: Regulating Tourists, Markets, and City Space
Lily M. Hoffman, Susan S. Fainstein, and Dennis R. Judd (eds.)

Understanding the City: Contemporary and Future Perspectives
John Eade and Christopher Mele (eds.)

The New Chinese City: Globalization and Market Reform
John R. Logan (ed.)

Cinema and the City: Film and Urban Societies in a Global Context
Mark Shiel and Tony Fitzmaurice (eds.)

The Social Control of Cities? A Comparative Perspective
Sophie Body-Gendrot

Globalizing Cities: A New Spatial Order?
Peter Marcuse and Ronald van Kempen (eds.)

Contemporary Urban Japan: A Sociology of Consumption
John Clammer

Capital Culture: Gender at Work in the City
Linda McDowell

Cities After Socialism: Urban and Regional Change and Conflict in Post-Socialist Societies
Gregory Andrusz, Michael Harloe and Ivan Szelenyi (eds.)

The People's Home? Social Rented Housing in Europe and America
Michael Harloe

Post-Fordism
Ash Amin (ed.)

Free Markets and Food Riots
John Walton and David Seddon

COMPARATIVE URBANISM

Tactics for Global Urban Studies

JENNIFER ROBINSON

STUDIES IN URBAN AND SOCIAL CHANGE BOOK SERIES

This edition first published 2022
©2022 John Wiley & Sons Ltd

All rights reserved. No part of this publication may be reproduced, stored in a retrieval system, or transmitted, in any form or by any means, electronic, mechanical, photocopying, recording or otherwise, except as permitted by law. Advice on how to obtain permission to reuse material from this title is available at http://www.wiley.com/go/permissions.

The right of Jennifer Robinson to be identified as the author of this work has been asserted in accordance with law.

Registered Offices
John Wiley & Sons, Inc., 111 River Street, Hoboken, NJ 07030, USA
John Wiley & Sons Ltd, The Atrium, Southern Gate, Chichester, West Sussex, PO19 8SQ, UK

Editorial Office
9600 Garsington Road, Oxford, OX4 2DQ, UK

For details of our global editorial offices, customer services, and more information about Wiley products visit us at www.wiley.com.

Wiley also publishes its books in a variety of electronic formats and by print-on-demand. Some content that appears in standard print versions of this book may not be available in other formats.

Limit of Liability/Disclaimer of Warranty
The contents of this work are intended to further general scientific research, understanding, and discussion only and are not intended and should not be relied upon as recommending or promoting scientific method, diagnosis, or treatment by physicians for any particular patient. In view of ongoing research, equipment modifications, changes in governmental regulations, and the constant flow of information relating to the use of medicines, equipment, and devices, the reader is urged to review and evaluate the information provided in the package insert or instructions for each medicine, equipment, or device for, among other things, any changes in the instructions or indication of usage and for added warnings and precautions. While the publisher and authors have used their best efforts in preparing this work, they make no representations or warranties with respect to the accuracy or completeness of the contents of this work and specifically disclaim all warranties, including without limitation any implied warranties of merchantability or fitness for a particular purpose. No warranty may be created or extended by sales representatives, written sales materials or promotional statements for this work. The fact that an organization, website, or product is referred to in this work as a citation and/or potential source of further information does not mean that the publisher and authors endorse the information or services the organization, website, or product may provide or recommendations it may make. This work is sold with the understanding that the publisher is not engaged in rendering professional services. The advice and strategies contained herein may not be suitable for your situation. You should consult with a specialist where appropriate. Further, readers should be aware that websites listed in this work may have changed or disappeared between when this work was written and when it is read. Neither the publisher nor authors shall be liable for any loss of profit or any other commercial damages, including but not limited to special, incidental, consequential, or other damages.

Library of Congress Cataloging-in-Publication Data
Names: Robinson, Jennifer, 1963- author.
Title: Comparative urbanism : tactics for global urban studies / Jennifer Robinson.
Description: Hoboken, NJ : John Wiley & Sons, Ltd., [2023] | Series: IJURR
  studies in urban and social change book series | Includes
  bibliographical references and index.
Identifiers: LCCN 2021060402 (print) | LCCN 2021060403 (ebook) | ISBN
  9781119697510 (hardback) | ISBN 9781119697558 (paperback) | ISBN
  9781119697572 (pdf) | ISBN 9781119697565 (epub) | ISBN 9781119697589 (ebook)
Subjects: LCSH: Cities and towns--Study and teaching. | Sociology,
  Urban--Study and teaching. | Urbanization--Study and teaching.
Classification: LCC HT109 .R54 2023 (print) | LCC HT109 (ebook) | DDC
  307.76071--dc23/eng/20220224
LC record available at https://lccn.loc.gov/2021060402
LC ebook record available at https://lccn.loc.gov/2021060403

Cover image: Township-Wall by António Ole, III C 45608–A, Ethnologisches Museum, Staatliche Museen zu Berlin
  (photography by Martin Franken)
Cover design by Wiley

Set in 11/13pt AGaramondPro-Regular Integra Software Services Pvt. Ltd, Pondicherry, India

SKY10035291_071922

Contents

Series Editors' Preface   viii
Preface   ix

Introduction   1

Part I   Reformatting Comparison   23

1   Ways of Knowing the Global Urban   25
    Uncertain Territories, 'Strategic Essentialisms': Regions, the Global South and beyond   27
    The Disappearing City: Planetary Urbanisation and its Critics   35
    Decolonial, Developmental, Emergent: Different Starting Points, or Incomparability?   41
    Dimensions of a Comparative Urban Imagination   47
    Conclusion   50

2   The Limits of Comparative Methodologies in Urban Studies   53
    Some Analytical Limits to the 'World' of Cities: Beyond Incommensurability   54
    Conventional Strategies for Comparison in Urban Studies   57
    The Potential of Comparative Research   69
    Conclusion   76

3   Comparative Urbanism in the Archives: Thinking with Variety, Thinking with Connections   79
    Expanding the Comparative Gesture   80
    Thinking with Variety   83
    Stretching Comparisons: Thinking with Connections   91
    Conclusion   104

4   Thinking Cities through Elsewhere: Reformatting Comparison   107
    Thinking with Concrete Totalities   108
    Singularities, Repeated Instances, Concepts   119
    Genetic and Generative Grounds for Urban Comparisons   125
    Conclusion: From Grounds to Tactics   128

Part II Genetic Comparisons — 135

5 Connections — 137
- Connections as Urbanisation Processes — 138
- Connections Producing *Repeated Instances* — 146
- Every Case Matters — 154
- Conclusion — 159

6 Relations — 161
- Wider Processes — 164
- Urban Neoliberalisation, Comparatively — 171
- Connected Contexts — 186
- More Spatialities of the Urban: Topologies, Partial Connections, Submarine Relations — 191
- Conclusion — 195

Part III Generative Comparisons — 199

7 Generating Concepts — 201
- The Conceptualising Subject: Institutions, Horizons, Grounds — 204
- A Life of Concepts: Ideal Types — 217
- Thinking the 'Concrete' — 230
- Negotiated Universals: Concepts 'In-common' — 235
- Conclusion — 243

8 Composing Comparisons — 247
- Working with 'Conjuncture' — 249
- Conceptualising from Specificity — 263
- Thinking across Diversity — 271
- Conclusion — 276

9 Conversations — 279
- Shifting Grounds: Comparison as Practice — 280
- Comparison as Conversations — 284
- Theoretical Reflections — 292
- Mobile Concepts, or 'Arriving at' Concepts — 295
- Conclusion — 301

Part IV Thinking from the Urban as Distinctive	305
10 Territories	307
Thinking from Territories	308
Which Territorialisations?	312
Assembling Territories	320
Conclusion	325
11 Into the Territory, or, the Urban as Idea	329
Detachment	331
Suturing	336
Standstill	340
Ideas	346
Informality, as Idea	357
Conclusion	362
Conclusion: Starting Anywhere, Thinking with (Elsew)here	369
A Reformatted Urban Comparison	370
Conceptualisation	376
An Explosion of Urban Studies	383
References	*387*
Index	*441*

Colour insert between pages 132 and 133

Series Editors' Preface

IJURR Studies in Urban and Social Change Book Series

The IJURR Studies in Urban and Social Change Book Series shares IJURR's commitments to critical, global, and politically relevant analyses of our urban worlds. Books in this series bring forward innovative theoretical approaches and present rigorous empirical work, deepening understandings of urbanization processes, but also advancing critical insights in support of political action and change. The Book Series Editors appreciate the theoretically eclectic nature of the field of urban studies. It is a strength that we embrace and encourage. The Editors are particularly interested in the following issues:

- Comparative urbanism
- Diversity, difference and neighborhood change
- Environmental sustainability
- Financialization and gentrification
- Governance and politics
- International migration
- Inequalities
- Urban and environmental movements

The series is explicitly interdisciplinary; the Editors judge books by their contribution to the field of critical urban studies rather than according to disciplinary origin. We are committed to publishing studies with themes and formats that reflect the many different voices and practices in the field of urban studies. Proposals may be submitted to Editor in Chief, Walter Nicholls (wnicholl@uci.edu), and further information about the series can be found at www.ijurr.org.

Walter Nicholls
Manuel Aalbers
Talja Blokland
Dorothee Brantz
Patrick Le Galès
Jenny Robinson

Preface

Almost as soon as I had finished writing *Ordinary Cities* in 2005, people started asking me how such an approach could be operationalised. How exactly could all cities be treated on the same analytical plane as sites for thinking the urban? At times this seemed a ridiculous expectation, and the impossibility of bringing informality, for example, into a wider urban studies context provoked laughter in more than one job interview panel I sat in front of. As that book was finished at about the same time as my son was born, I didn't have an opportunity to discuss my emerging response to this (very good) question at great length for a while, and it took some years to bring my explorations on this topic to fruition. An early provocation to consider comparison as a starting point (presented at Durham in 2007) came to publication in 2011 (Robinson 2011), learning from assessments which had gone before and alongside (Pickvance 1987; Nijman 2007; Ward 2010; MacFarlane 2010). I have worked on this theme for over a decade now, alongside the growing up of my son, and in concert with some substantial empirical experiments in comparative research (e.g. Robinson et al. 2020).

I have enjoyed immensely puzzling over the issues which the reformatting of comparison for global urban studies entails. It has stretched me in ways which have been pure pleasure, including learning to read Gilles Deleuze and thinking with Walter Benjamin, returning to the feminist work which inspired the post-colonial critique of urban studies which crystallised for me in the 1990s in Durban, and engaging with a new generation of decolonial and feminist thinkers. My period of working at the Open University was inspiring and set in train the work for this book. As with others of us who came within the orbit of John Allen and the group assembled there in the early 2000s, we learnt to think spatially, to read widely, to 'theorise' and to build collegiality as a foundation for intellectual innovation. I owe John and my other colleagues at the OU a great debt. I am especially thinking at this time of the generosity and exceptional intellectual capacity of Clive Barnett, so sadly lost to us this year. His work and life will be an inspiration to many. He was a much valued colleague and friend.

At UCL I have benefitted from an amazingly rich environment of urbanists who are open to joining in with intriguing seminars and discussions, and where people who work on and come from so many different cities can find each other on a day-to-day basis. This goes just as well for colleagues across London colleges who work in a very close physical proximity, and form a fantastic community for expanding understandings of global urban experiences. The demands of the UK academy are a very long way from the pressured times of colleagues in so many places, including my alma mater in Durban. My colleagues there, Brij Maharaj (a long influence on my academic practice) and Orli Bass, teach with one additional physical geographer over 700 first-year students, and hundreds of senior students. The work loads are excruciating. The competitive and increasingly febrile environment in the UK notwithstanding (staff are overstretched and ambitious; students are customers with debt weighing heavily on their life plans), and despite the fact that after twenty years I feel that my 'home' is still Durban, I have been highly privileged in my career trajectory in the UK. At UCL I have found colleagues who are often kind, sociable and supportive in sharing tasks. I so value them, and particularly mention Pushpa Arabindoo, Andrew Harris, Ben Page and Tatiana Thieme, Ben Campkin, Clare Melhuish, Matthew Gandy, Charlotte Lemanski, Michael Edwards, Catalina Ortiz, Colin Marx, Barbara Lipietz, Fulong Wu, Jonathan Rokem. You made going to work a pleasure and have taught me much.

This book has been a long time in preparation – a rich decade of puzzling and practice, including some stimulating collaborations both in academia, with colleagues and students, and in the everyday politics of the urban, primarily in London and, for personal reasons – childcare! – to a much lesser extent than I would wish in Johannesburg and Cape Town. In the process I have incurred many debts and learnt much from others. I acknowledge them at the end of this preface. I was especially delighted to be a small part of the early days of the African Centre for Cities, and so excited to see all that has been achieved there. I count Edgar Pieterse, Susan Parnell, Vanessa Watson and Sophie Oldfield amongst the most influential and energising urban scholars, both in the wider world, and for me personally. Thank you. While UK academia is certainly a privileged place to find myself working when the music stopped on the mid-career roundabout, the last decade has involved an intense period of work, both at work and domestically, both physically and emotionally. Thank you to all those who have been so supportive in these years – and not least to my lovely neighbours in the midst of lockdown. For distanced coffees in the street, emergency shopping, accordion playing, and always a kind word, thank you!

In the UK academy publishing needs to happen sooner rather than later, despite whatever life brings along, and so in a strategy I learnt from my valued mentor at the Open University, John Allen, I have written this book in sections over this time. Luckily it has sustained a consistency of argument and analysis. Some readers might be familiar with the two core chapters – 2 and

4 – published in 2011 and 2016. But the book format gives an opportunity to build an extensive and wide-ranging argument over a lot of material, and to bring forward what I hope is a useful and perhaps distinctive approach to enlarging the comparative practice of urban studies, and to thinking the urban, globally.

Thanks, then, to those who have been companions and inspirations at different moments in what turned out to be a lifetime journey: Ola Söderström (who commented extensively on the book proposal), Ludovic Halbert, Matthias Bernt, Phil Harrison, Alison Todes, Fulong Wu, Maliq Simone, Filip de Boeck, Edgar Pieterse, Sue Parnell, Sophie Oldfield, Rob Morrell, Jane M. Jacobs, James Sidaway, Tim Bunnell, John Allen, Patrick Le Galès, Clive Barnett, Richard Ballard, Garth Myers, Oren Yiftachel, Juile Ren, Hanna Hilbrandt, Loretta Lees, Hyun Shin, Monica Degen … how lucky to be part of your generous worlds. Especially thank you to Phil Harrison and Fulong Wu for sharing in some comparative experiments, it was such a pleasure to work with you both, and it would not have been possible to write this book without your support. And to others who have embarked on new comparative initiatives, Evance Mwathunga, Wilbard Kombe, George Owusu and Sylvia Croese, thank you for taking the leap, and for enduring the challenges of working collaboratively in COVID times. To those students (and adopted students) at UCL whose comparative experiments inspired me so much – it has been a privilege to share an intellectual adventure with you all: Frances Brill, Alvaro Jimenez Sanchez, Susana Neves Alves, Aidan Mosselson, Astrid Wood, Hui-Chun-Liu, Shaun Teo, Rita Lambert, Azadeh Mashayekhi, Camila Saraiva, Ana McMillin, Gumeç Karamuk, Varvara Karipidou, Lubaina Mirza.

A number of people have commented on different elements of the book – thank you so much for your insights. I have also been lucky enough to have a few careful readers of the text. Garth Myers has been a consistent intellectual companion over many years, and I have learnt much from him for this book. Maliq Simone has read quite a few different draft papers – and commented within hours or days, in such a generous way. I can't always follow him on his often incandescent intellectual paths, but I am always so inspired and admiring. Talja Blokland read closely and commented in detail on a draft text – her responses coming from a different disciplinary direction were very instructive and also inspired me, although I was not able to do everything she suggested. Walter Nicholls as the series editor made extensive and very helpful comments across the entire text, thank you for your generous oversight of the process of producing this book. And the Editorial Board of the Studies in Urban and Social Change series were encouraging and enthusiastic all the way. Raphael de Kadt deserves a special mention for inspiring me to read and think when we were colleagues together in Durban. More practically, from his new ventures in photography in Johannesburg he kindly contributed one of the images in the text. Jacqueline Scott has been a steady, positive and supportive publishing partner at Wiley-Blackwell for the decade I have been involved with this series, and also for this book. It is always a pleasure to work with you, Jacqueline, and to explore Christmas markets and chat over a glass of wine. I also would like to thank Robert Rojek for his ongoing publishing support, although working together was not to be on this occasion.

I would like to acknowledge the funders of two research projects which supported the work for this book: the ESRC for an Urban Transformations grant ES/N006070/1, "Governing the Future City: A comparative analysis of governance innovations in large scale urban developments in Shanghai, London, Johannesburg" and the European Research Council (Advanced Grant 834999) for *Making Africa Urban: the transcalar politics of large-scale urban development*.

Throughout the writing of this book Christian Schmid has been an everyday intellectual interlocutor, perhaps in the Lefebvrian sense of the everyday as the fullness of all possibility, and a source of constant surprise. Christian has supported my own direction all the way, even when his own reference points might be different. His reading and comments were always kind, to the point, and astute – nudging me towards a better book. Thank you.

The book is written for the three people who gently tether me to life itself: my mother, Norma Robinson; my son, Ben Robinson; and my partner, Christian Schmid.

And dedicated to the three women in my north London village, without whom parenting and dancing would have been impossible: Lena Langer, Cécile Laborde and Brenda Lewis. Several operas, a few books and many tough projects have come to fruition alongside our children. Time to open that champagne…

Introduction

Urban studies has gone global – in the range of cities it considers, the scope of its theoretical ambition, and the breadth of practical concerns which now frame urban research. New topics, new subjects of theorisation and new centres of analytical innovation shape the field. The last decade has seen a significant transformation in the terms of the analysis of urbanisation and of the territories thought of as urban across the world. Many more places and processes are being brought into analytical conversation. Nonetheless, there is a keen awareness of the challenges of constituting a global field of urban studies. Shifts in the dynamic sites of rapid global urbanisation to Asia and Africa, along with the great diversity of forms of urban settlement, and the increasingly worldwide impacts of urbanisation processes, have led many urbanists to propose a renewal, if not a fundamental transformation, in urban theory. Many acknowledge this as a moment to confront head-on the impossible object of the city, whose boundaries are perhaps even more indistinct than ever. The traditional object of urban studies is arguably disappearing in the face of sprawling urban settlements and 'planetary' urbanisation processes. Cities, centres and suburbs become residual concepts, which must be used with circumspection and care. The field is in search of new vocabularies to engage with the extraordinary explosion and variety of urban forms – not just sprawling or extended, regional or mega, scholars reach for terms such as galactic and planetary to invoke the physical expansion and worldwide impact of urbanisation. There is much to think about here, and this book will contribute to how we can rebuild theorisations in engagement with these trends.

In this light, a series of methodological and epistemological dilemmas face all urbanists and require creative and new responses. How can concepts be reviewed, renovated, overthrown or invented across diverse urban outcomes? How can urban theory work effectively with different cases, thinking with the diversity of the urban world? How can the complexity of the urban be addressed with concepts which are necessarily always reductionist? Concepts are inevitably confined by those who articulate them to always begin somewhere, to be spoken always in some particular voice – and yet concepts must grapple with the inexhaustibility of social and material worlds. And what happens when concepts run aground, unable to speak to distinctive urban worlds?

A growing number of scholars from different persuasions and locations have set out their creative insights into how to approach these new objects of study – a globally diverse urban, and an expansive planetary urbanisation process. The field has proliferated with many different themes, theories and contexts being creatively drawn on to stretch understandings and challenge urban politics, policies and practices. Moreover, new theoretical optics, thinking with materialities, for example, or more insistent standpoints, from post- and de-colonial studies as well as black and critical race studies and feminism, impress the need for new thinking on the nature of the urban. But, if this is to be brought forward, the imperative is for new subjects and authors of urban theorising. The broadest provocation is to rethink the very terms on which the urban, its spatial forms and social and political meaning, might come to be known. This is a moment to relish a revolution in the field. At the same time, it is vital to consider the many challenges which urban studies faces in achieving this, including building insights across different language communities, and the severe resource-limitations on the participation of scholars in poor contexts. As a manifesto to think the urban from anywhere, comparative urbanism signals the urgent need for institutional transformation. This will be essential if scholarly practices which support revisable theory are to be undertaken by any scholar, anywhere, rather than entrenching authoritative voices from privileged institutions. A generous and generative community of scholarship will need to be crafted if new voices and new ideas are to find space to launch themselves into wider conversations.

In this whirlwind of theoretical, empirical and political exploration of the nature of the global urban, my personal hunch has been that the inheritances of comparative practice might offer a starting point for critical theory-building. Or, as I suggest, a more modest practice of conceptualisation. A comparative imagination could help to think the urban across its many diverse formations, and through its many interconnected outcomes. Both found and staged opportunities to bring different urban contexts into conversation could open up scope to explore this 'impossible' (and impossibly varied) object, urban. But as I delved more deeply into the archives of comparative urbanism I found a methodological tradition that was not fit for purpose. Comparative urban methodologies had hard-wired into their assumptions and procedures the field's (de)limitations and divisions. Over the last decades of the twentieth century, for example, comparative practice had come to reflect urban studies as a segmented practice in which studies of wealthier and poorer, 'northern' and 'southern', liberal democratic and socialist cities were diverted into different domains of academic endeavour. Walton (1981) concluded his review of comparative urban studies with the observation that while important theoretical advances had been made in urban studies, these had not really been comparative in nature, and were largely focussed on Europe and North America (p. 34). And, as David Slater (1978) noted, few comparative analyses had included 'third world' contexts. Such observations had of course been a starting point for my earlier proposal to treat all cities as 'ordinary', as an analytical clearing exercise to enable new analyses of the urban to emerge in the wake of these obsolete divisions (Robinson 2006). This book is the result of thinking through how that might be done.

If a comparative imagination is to support the endeavours of a current generation of scholars eager to transform urban studies, something very different in the way of comparative methods will be needed – a reformatted comparison, fit for the challenges of a twenty-first-century global urban studies. This book sets out the case for a comparative approach which specifically builds from the problematic and spatiality of the urban as a global phenomenon. It argues for a comparative imagination which is open and agile, drawing comparative practice back to its core features: thinking with elsewhere, to interrogate and change concepts. On this basis, the book proposes both new grounds and new tactics for comparison that emerge intrinsically from the spatiality and form of contemporary urbanisation. It establishes the basis on which one might draw different contexts into analytical encounters; and it sets out some specific tactics which can take forward a renovated and expansive process of concept formation, for global urban studies. I found a number of fellow enthusiasts for revising comparative practices, such as John Walton (1981), Chris Pickvance (1986), Janet Abu-Lughod (1999), Neil Brenner (2001), Jan Nijman (2007b), Kevin Ward (2010), Colin McFarlane (2010), Jane M. Jacobs (2012), Leitner, Peck and Sheppard (2019), Ren (2020) and many others we will discuss throughout the book.

These propositions sit alongside a range of new work on comparativism across the social sciences and humanities, inspired by global history, postcolonialism, and comparative literature, as well anthropologists revisiting the comparativism at its core (for example, Candea 2019; Friedman 2013; Lowe 2015; Scheffer and Niewöhner 2010). As with urbanists, these contributions have noted the potential afforded by a relational view of comparison informed by the wide-ranging interconnections which make of any context a starting point for charting wider insights rather than a stopping point of pure difference. However, I suggest that the spatiality of the urban means that urban studies also needs to account for variation and individuality – diverse and distinctive urban outcomes – and to consider what that might mean for thinking about a 'world of cities'. Stretched out social relations, to draw on Massey's (1994) evocative phrasing, while important to comparison, are not all that is needed to make sense of urbanisation processes and 'the urban'.

In proposing this reformulation, comparative urbanism emerges as much more than a method. Certainly, it indexes a thick and dynamic research practice which calls for careful attention to different contexts and concepts. It also indicates a mode of theorisation which sees concepts as strongly revisable. At its most expansive, comparative urbanism could be seen as itself a theory of the urban. In searching for ways in which a comparative imagination – thinking with elsewhere – might be formatted for the spatialities of the urban, a certain set of perspectives on the nature of the urban crystallised. Differentiated, diverse and distinctive - the forms of the object urban become apparent in the course of working out practical ways to come to know it. I was reminded of a childhood poem, The Thought Fox, in which Ted Hughes imagines a (thought) fox to suddenly appear from the depths of the forest, just like a thought might emerge at the end of a long night of writing ('Till, with a sudden sharp hot stink of fox/It enters the dark hole of the head'). In thinking through the messy practicalities and tangled starting points of method ('deeper within darkness', to borrow again from Hughes), something has revealed itself about the urban along the tracks of exploring how to come to know this (im)possible object.

Thus, through the course of this book, different spatialities of the urban come into view to convene the methodological experiments and conceptual innovations which a comparative imagination invites. The prolific circulating processes and interconnections that characterise the urban are an important starting point. These connections draw us to think across different urban contexts. Tracing these, the urban can be thought of as composed of a multiplicity of **differentiated** (repeated) outcomes. Urban outcomes, closely interconnected through a range of transnational processes, are part of repeated-but-differentiated formations within wider circulations and circuits of urbanisation and globalisation. For some thinkers the outcomes and wider processes are more closely tied together, as a form of 'variegation' (Peck and Theodore 2007). These different outcomes are good to think with and to compose comparative experiments. In a similar way, any concept of the 'urban' comes into being amongst emergent multiplicities (a virtuality, to follow Deleuze) of concepts and insights generated across different contexts and interconnected through public and scholarly circulations and conversations. After Walter Benjamin we might think of these as many partial and incomplete analytical 'constellations', or Ideas. Any concept of 'the urban', then, is emergent through the leaps and traces, the analytical and practical movements across space and time (Nyamnjoh 2017) needed to bring into view the multiplicity of whatever the urban might be.

However, the specific socio-spatial dynamics associated with urbanisation in particular locations constitute **diverse** urbanisation processes and varied outcomes evident across different regions and urban settlements. Thinking across this diversity can sometimes bring into perspective shared features of even very divergent urban experiences. These would not necessarily be connected to one another. But they might be related to specifically urban processes, such as competing land uses, mechanisms for capturing land value, or inherited spatial arrangements. Diverse outcomes might also be apparent in relation to coincidentally shared but varied aspects of urban social life, or mechanisms of social change. These, too, can ground comparative analysis - thinking through 'elsewhere' can inspire new reflections and insights.

In search of insights into the urban and urbanisation, then, it is helpful to think from and with both diversity (outcomes are specific in different places because of long historical trajectories of development and emergent socio-spatial dynamics) and differentiation (interconnected processes are associated with repetition and differentiation of elements of urban form and social process).

One further spatiality of the urban is relevant to comparative method. Whatever the urban is it only ever appears as **distinctive**, as specific territorialised outcomes of interconnections, urbanisation processes, spatial forms, sedimented practices, long histories, and the rich settings of experiences. The urban, we might suggest is always distinctive, we can only come to know it through its individuality. Schmid (2015) proposes that the urban is a 'specific' category. More emphatically, in the classic Hegelian triad (universal-particular-individual), the urban is the 'individual' which always interrupts and presents itself as the unruly ground to any effort to conceptualise. In this sense, the urban is characteristically spatial in the full sense of that term. It is opaque in its rich complexity and fullness, fundamentally hidden from interpretive view, revealing itself to us partially and becoming known to us through our always circumscribed, located and embodied efforts, often in the process of engaged and committed practices (Oldfield 2022) to shape urban futures.

This book rests on the core idea that as we need to begin again in thinking about the urban, we also need to begin again with thinking about comparative method. Where might new concepts come from? A reformatted comparative practice moves beyond a territorialised imagination of comparing delineated and pre-given places ('cities') and builds on a view of the urban as emergent from prolific circulations, trajectories, socio-material proximities and associational practices. Whatever the urban is or becomes in any given context, it can be seen as emergent from all these possibilities. In this sense, in the interests of critiquing, rebuilding and reinventing the conceptual repertoire of the field, comparative practices can respond to and work with the spatiality of the urban. A creative, open and critical perspective is crucial in comparative urbanism; not only is the urban a constantly changing, open historical formation but the terms on which we come to know it are also under constant debate and revision. The insight that the urban is a theoretical object (Brenner and Schmid 2014), or a conceptual proposition, stimulates revisable propositions about the urban and reinforces a practice of urban studies which keeps open conversations across the global urban world.

Building methodology from the spatiality of the urban – the full sociospatial worlds of territories; the interconnections that compose urban outcomes, differently each time; and from the practices of engaged, embodied and located researchers and urban dwellers in specific urban contexts – means that a comparative methodological wager signposts a process of theorisation, and the production of a theoretical object, the urban (Hill Collins 2019). The practice of comparative urbanism certainly aims to bring forward a set of conceptual propositions about the urban. But these will be concepts which, by virtue of the nature of the urban world, and by virtue of a comparative imagination, are situated, deeply revisable, contested, and provisional.

The point of a reformatted urban comparative practice is to provoke new conceptualisations, starting anywhere, with a strong orientation to revising existing concepts. And at the limit it suggests a 'theory' of the urban as interconnected and differentiated but diverse and specific; emergent and unstable as a concept or form, always slipping away from us, always somewhere else than we expect to find it (Simone 2011). Whatever the urban is, then, is open to the inexahustibility of the lived world; the diversity of the world of urban experiences; and to the vitality and revisability of concepts initiated by scholars and others in many different contexts.

The argument of this book is that any understanding of the urban is a double multiplicity – grounded in a multiplicity of experiences and observations; and existing alongside a potential multiplicity of conceptualisations. Certainly, this requires a new vision of theoretical practice – less assured, more likely to be dissipated than appropriated, but rather enlivened and mobilised (and also tripped up) in conversations across difference and along the tracks of the urban world. Any effort to come to understanding of whatever the urban is needs to confront also the limitations of this endeavour – and of course analyses of the world might set out to ask a different question than 'what is the urban'. Importantly, in a world constituted in the midst of violence, and in the wake of colonial and racist histories of erasure, whatever the urban is cannot only be seen through the lens of the multiplicity of conceptualisations, or the fullness of the urban world. US black and indigenous studies has strongly insisted on the absences, occlusions and silences which puncture violent and brutal histories of dehumanization, improverishment and slavery (Hartmann, 2008). This motivates methodologies actively crafting other starting points for scholarly practices in terms of subjectivities (McKittrick 2021), practice (Hill Collins 2019) and space itself (Brand 2018). This is potentially generative of an 'out of the outside' to dominant knowledges, as Moten (2018) articulates. Calls for different theoretical starting points arise in other contexts too. Doubling, spirit worlds, occlusions, ephemerality, cutting, fragmentations and displacements offer different starting points for thinking subectivitiy and knowledge, and the urban, in ways that operate in the wake of, and beyond, colonial power in Africa, for example (Simone 2001a; de Boeck and Baloji 2016; Mbembe 2017; Nyamnjoh 2017). Also in these contexts, producing new urban futures requires pragmatic engagement with the messy and opaque forms of actually existing urban politics and initiating inevitably compromised development initiatives (Parnell and Pieterse 2016).

If the term urban, then, is to open a conversation on aspects of social worlds across the world, it is as an (im)possible (virtual) object and an emergent, revisable conceptualisation. This book explores and expands ways to proliferate openings to new understandings of the urban.

Part I: Reformatting Comparison

The first part of the book interrogates the history and methodological principles of comparative urban practice. It makes the case for a reformatted urban comparative method, able to imagine starting to think the urban anywhere, in conversation with the multiple elsewheres of any urban situation.

Chapter 1 outlines the terrain of debates in urban studies which inform and form the backdrop to theoretical openings on the urban, providing a broad justification for the focus on comparativism, in relation to the landscape of contemporary urban studies. The potential of comparativism as a mode of imagining, practicing and theorising the urban emerges in close proximity with a range of different approaches. This chapter therefore outlines the need identified by urbanists for a renewed conceptualisation of the urban. The 'problem' of contemporary global urbanisation calls for new kinds of theoretical practice (more diverse, but also more embedded and engaged with the urban world), which have the capacity to draw ideas, skills and resources to address how cities might be liveable for people and survivable for the planet (Pieterse et al. 2018). Contemporary debates in the field therefore concern not just different theoretical approaches but, crucially, the politics of practice and positionality which arise in distinctive settings. Possible territorial divisions of urban analysis present themselves – the global South, regions, singularities. And scholars have proposed different ways of contesting the often parochial and power-laden claims to authorial voice which characterise the narratives conventionally identified as 'theoretical' in urban studies. Debates on positionality and identity might oppose 'theory-building' at all, or seek to disperse the conceptual object, 'urban' altogether. This chapter seeks to be critically respectful of a variety of kinds of 'urbanism' – a multiplicity of ways of coming to know and experience the urban. In a piece with Ananya Roy (Robinson and Roy 2015) we talked about 'genres of urbanism' as a way to catch a sense of theorisation as embedded in the production of the urban, as style, approach, orientation, practice, immersion, experience – indexing theory's place amongst a wide array of ways of making the urban. We are a long way from Wirth's (1938) definitive propositions about 'urbanism as a way of life', which offered only one way to identify the urban, and one way of urban life, subjugating in the process the lively diversity of urban experience.

My enthusiasm for comparative urbanism begins with the post-colonial ambition to interrogate, and to change, or invent new, concepts. Comparativism has a great track record of questioning and stretching concepts, and has something to teach urban scholars about how it might be possible to bring different kinds of urban contexts into conversation and to think with insights from elsewhere. The urban world currently presents many reasons and opportunities to do this. The imperative for strongly revisable theory is at the heart of comparative urbanism, as is the commitment to conceptualisation as enabling conversations beyond the single case. A comparative imagination exposes the possibility of real theoretical breaks, taking forward in a more expansive and determined way the 'small revolts' John Walton (1992, p. 126) identified as part of all research. This book looks to go further, though, in the spirit of a decolonial agenda, to explore how the process of conceptualisation itself might be established on new grounds.

Thus, while Chapter 1 sets the scene for how comparative urbanism might contribute to a range of initiatives to develop new approaches to understanding an expanding and diverse global urban world, Chapter 2 turns to consider how comparative urbanism might take forward the practice of global urban studies. I have been inspired by the potential of the comparative imagination but also mindful of the limits which have previously been placed on its scope. Both the inherited assumptions of urban theory (such as the segmentation of 'first' and 'third' world), and a reliance on a quasi-scientific formulation of criteria for case selection and causal analysis have significantly truncated its relevance to global urban studies. In **Chapter 2**, I therefore undertake an exercise in reviewing and critiquing this methodological inheritance. Defining comparability on the basis of territorially delimited 'cities', or according to features of the national contexts in which cities are located resulted in comparisons of only relatively similar kinds of cities. This placed significant limitations on the value of comparativism for global urban studies. Such tactics are also a poor fit with the spatiality of urbanisation. Thinking about causality through the rubric of isolating independent 'variables', for example, is at odds with the fullness and complexity of urban space. This chapter argues that in seeking to move 'comparative method' from restrictive formal methodologies to a more expansive kind of comparative imagination, it is helpful to pare comparison back to its core elements – thinking with elsewhere, to revise or generate new concepts. This has the effect of significantly expanding the repertoire for comparative tactics beyond the conventional variation-finding or encompassing methods prominent in urban studies (Brenner 2001; Kantor and Savitch 2005; Pickvance 1986), effectively putting the light touch 'comparative gesture' at the heart of the field to a more precise use. Counter to the ambitious scope and sometimes dominating authorial voice of a universalising theoretical practice, eager to draw 'elsewhere' in as evidence to support existing analytical agendas, a reformatted comparativism proposes a more agile theoretical practice. Such a practice would certainly engage with existing conceptualisations, but be committed to revisability, to thinking through a diversity of urban outcomes, and being open to starting to conceptualise anew from anywhere.

A very important analytical change in defining a new repertoire of comparative practice is to abandon the hopeless effort to apply a quasi-scientific rigour to case selection based on attempting to control for difference across cities, or defining comparability based on pre-given territories ('cities' or 'countries'). **Chapter 3** dives into the archives of comparative urbanism to explore how scholars have actually undertaken comparisons when faced with the conundrums of thinking the urban. What we see is that in many comparative studies although in their research design scholars are controlling for difference, restricting analyses to most similar cities, **it is precisely the variation across the cases that has provided the grounds for conceptual innovation and invention.** Perhaps, then, I suggest, we could just start with this variation, turning the conventional methodological advice around. Designing comparisons to stretch across a diversity of urban outcomes would be good for creative thinking about a phenomenon or process, stretching understandings and opening to new insights. Creating a comparator which allows analytical reach across difference and diversity (Deville et al. 2016), expanding the scope for the third term to bring divergent cases into conversation (Jacobs 2012), could inspire methodological experimentation. The chapter concludes that more loosely defined shared features, or repeated outcomes across different, even divergent, contexts, could form a good basis for exploring the diversity of urban experiences. Indeed, urban scholars have already pragmatically adopted such methodological innovations, increasingly diverging from the conventional approaches reviewed in Chapter 2: rather than trying to 'control for difference' we find writers thinking with the shared features of quite different urban contexts.

The archives of comparative urbanism also reveal a longstanding but growing repertoire of 'natural experiments' following the numerous interconnections amongst cities. Robert Park's prescient comments illustrate this long seam of interest, when he notes that 'every great commercial city today is a world-city. Cities like London, New York, San Francisco, Yokohama, Osaka, Shanghai, Singapore, and Bombay are not merely centres of a wide regional commerce. They are, by their position on the great ocean highway which now circles the earth, integral parts of a system of international commerce. They are way-stations and shopping centres, so to speak, on the main street of the world' (Robert Park 1952: 133–4). Since the 1970s, ideas about world and global cities, globalising urban processes and uneven and interependent development have been crucial in initiating a more global urban studies. This work, reviewed in Chapter 3, sets the scene for methodological innovations explored in Part 2 of the book.

Chapter 4 considers how to more formally ground urban comparisons on the basis of shared features and connections, variety and repetition. It also reflects on how to maximise the opening which comparative practice presents for theoretical revision. Resources for reframing concepts as highly revisable can be found in formal philosophical debates. The chapter engages with both Marxist and Deleuzian formulations to explore this. Marxist approaches which emphasise the relational constitution of social and economic life can ground a way of thinking the urban through connections (wider processes and relations). But inspired by the fullness of the 'concrete', and the inexhaustibility of social life, Marxist methods can also indicate an open horizon to understandings of urban life. Lefebvre's view of the urban as an open, concrete totality provides strong foundations for a comparative imagination oriented to revisable concepts. On a close reading of Deleuze's major philosophical contribution, *Difference and Repetition* (1994), which has been neglected by both urbanists and social scientists (Grossberg 2014), I find further inspiration to re-imagine comparison. Deleuze offers some manoeuvres which give scope for interrogating the meaning of a 'case' in relation to concepts. Rather than framing a case as a particular for a pre-given universal, in a representational or reflective idiom, his intervention invites us to revisit the dynamic processes by which phenomena come to be known, tracking the intertwined genesis (emergence) of both matter and ideas. We could then consider each urban outcome as distinctive, but possibly closely connected with many others through a shared genesis (in the processes of urbanisation). Thus, by tracing the prolific interconnections and wider processes which produce different urban phenomena, we are invited to place different outcomes in analytical relation. Deleuze's philosophical intervention recasts understandings of conceptualisation, inviting new ways forward for comparison. He offers us some new patterns for appreciating how concepts of things and the things themselves might be understood as entwined in the production of Ideas (concepts). For Deleuze, theoretical innovation might be conceived as a conceptual fecundity in active engagement with the world. Deleuze's formulations resonate with the committed engagement with the materiality, practices, experiences, empirical dynamics and politics of the urban which characterises much urban studies, across different perspectives.

On this basis, Chapter 4 outlines two grounds for comparative urban practice. These work with the intertwined production of the object urban through both material emergence (genesis) and a generative conceptual endeavor. Comparisons can then be developed on 'genetic' grounds, tracing the prolific interconnections and wider processes which produce the urban, and which constitute repeated or related but distinctive, urban outcomes. Different urban outcomes draw us to comparative analytical reflection, then, as we trace their genesis. Or 'generative' comparisons might emerge across shared features evident in the midst of the rich fullness and complexity of urban life. These provide an invitation to generate conceptual insights across diverse urban outcomes. Chapter 4 sets out these two grounds for urban comparisons, genetic and generative. Chapters 5 to 11 work through a range of comparative tactics which might be developed on these grounds across different theoretical traditions and draw on a wide range of examples of comparative urban research.

Part II: Genetic Comparisons

Part I of this book provides a critical perspective on different comparative traditions and resources which have been brought to explorations of a globalising urban world. It also establishes the potential of a reformatted comparativism for global urban studies. Chapter 4 offers explicit grounds for such a reformatted comparativism, working with the distinctive spatialities of the urban and philosophical accounts of the process of conceptualisation. Part II, and the rest of the book, presents a detailed elaboration of these grounds for comparative urbanism, and explores a range of tactics through which to operationalise these in research. I seek to cull insights from a wide range of, often divergent, perspectives, such as political economy or Deleuzian approaches, capital logic or Gramscian insights, critical realism, actor network theory, non-representational, post-structuralist, feminist or post-colonial and decolonial critiques. As well as being as clear as possible about their different potentialities and limits for the purposes of re-crafting comparison, where possible I will also seek to establish creative lines of conversation and shared insights across different traditions. The shared object of the urban, its spatiality, its complexity and its materiality, ground the many shared concerns of different intellectual traditions in urban studies, indicating that there are often few reasons for the a priori rejection of one or other theoretical persuasion where they are in fact grappling with many of the same problematics, albeit with different vocabularies, postulated objects and solutions. Urban studies can sometimes seem eager to demarcate differences in the interests of putative originality – perhaps driven by the accumulative logic of the western academy's citation and audit trails and reward systems. I seek to cultivate here an open engagement with different traditions in the interests of building creative new methodological approaches adequate to the global urban, while being clear where these approaches and thinkers diverge.

In Chapter 3, we culled methodological insights from suggestive comparative analyses conducted mostly in the twentieth century. The emphasis in Part II (and the rest of the book) is on some of the many experimental approaches emerging in recent decades. These allow us to consider a range of different tactics which might come to the fore within a reformatted comparative urbanism. Practically we consider in detail how a new repertoire of comparative urban practice can be (and has been) put to work. To some extent these examples inevitably reflect my own research interests and background. Empirical research has been essential for me to think through exactly how a reformatted comparative imagination might actually be put into practice. This will mean a somewhat focussed range of topics in the chapters to come, to some extent from the field of urban politics. Luckily this is one of the most traditional topics in comparative urbanism, concerning, for example, the politics of urban development, 'urban regimes', governing large-scale urban developments, policy mobilities, gentrification or suburbanisation. I also suggest some areas where a comparative imagination could enrich urban analyses by bringing together concepts usually reserved to distinct regions, such as bringing a UK-centric 'post-politics' into engagement with Latin American ideas of 'insurgent citizenship', or mobilising the African-centric term 'informality' to address questions of governance and the wider conceptualisation of the urban.

Chapter 4 drew on Deleuze's suggestion that when approaching the 'diverse' (an alternative term for the manifold, the fullness of all there is) we should not assume that it is given to us as 'diverse', that is, as composed of a diversity of pre-existing entities. He offers instead a philosophy of emergence, and some distinctive insights into how we come to know entities, to account for their individuation. Firstly, the virtuality of the material world indexes all the possibilities (say, of the urban) that might be realised in one instance; and secondly, the virtuality of Ideas opens to all the possible ideas there are to think with. The 'urban' might be seen then as (different(c)iated) phenomena which, insofar as they can come to be known, are emergent from both the shared genesis of the material urban world and the practices of knowing researchers. What there is to consider (agents, subjects, entities, assemblages, institutions, the urban) should not be presumed in advance, or simply associated with a search to reflect (or fail to reflect) a given reality in the mirror of representation. Following MacKenzie (2008) we might see analysis as an 'engine' of concept generation, rather than a camera on the world. However, while generating concepts might be the agile ambition of philosophy (Deleuze and Guattari 1994), for social science this depends on specifying certain agreed upon criteria for making acceptable observations and drawing relevant conclusions. What expectations and norms of the 'common concern' of scholarly enquiry can form a basis for designing and drawing insights from comparative experiments (Stengers 2011)? On what basis can we find 'sensible' ways (after Tilly 1984) to mobilise a comparative imagination? And where and on what terms might we lose patience with being sensible and propose more dissonant comparative experiments?

Part II develops responses to these questions in relation to the potential of comparative experiments on 'genetic' grounds. Chapters 5 and 6 indicate opportunities where the spatiality of the genesis or emergence of the urban draws the researcher towards reflections across different contexts. Thus, repeated instances are emergent from the vast array of interconnected processes which constitute all the possibilities that might give rise to 'any urban whatever' – to paraphrase Simone (2011). Starting points and directions for comparative reflection can be inspired by the profoundly interconnected nature of many different urban processes and outcomes. Following the tracks of the many urban phenomena which are interconnected and repeated across different contexts becomes a key comparative tactic. Similarly, repeated instances - emergent forms and processes distributed promiscuously across the urban world, for example, policy experiments, or satellite cities – are suggestive starting points for thinking the urban across different contexts.

A range of comparative tactics, on genetic grounds, are developed in Chapters 5 and 6. **Chapter 5** sets out to address the question, what exactly might be done with connections, comparatively? Here, tracing the flows of people, things and ideas that constitute urbanisation opens out to tactics including identifying and comparing different urbanisation processes; working comparatively with repeated instances in ways which might be empirically additive or analytically subtractive; or, working across instances to allow insights from each case to thicken understanding of others. **Chapter 6** considers connections through the lens of 'relational' approaches which are more characteristic of political economy analyses. Relational comparative approaches reinforce the invitation explored in Chapter 5 to think with the empirical interactions across different urban contexts, and also to mobilise the difference of any given place or concrete situation to interrogate existing conceptualisations (Leitner et al. 2019; Ward 2010). The analytical traditions which guide relational comparative practice open up different kinds of tactics from those which the 'repeated instance' invite. Most distinctively, in relational comparisons we are encouraged to work with the (translocal) social processes which link and jointly produce places and phenomena, especially in a globalised world. In this way, understanding of shared, extensive or wider processes is advanced. This chapter explores how comparative analysis can interrogate the nature of these processes as well as different contexts. An extended discussion of urban neoliberalism interrogates the idea of 'variegation' – that closely related sequences of outcomes in different contexts both constitute and transform a wider process. How can accounts of wider social processes be interrogated and questioned through comparative analysis of different outcomes? The chapter explores how cases which are entrained in the same wider processes might be considered comparatively. What can tracing specific relational connections between two places reveal of both? And as many different processes come together to shape any given context, resulting in a rich plenitude of social processes in any given place, how might a comparative imagination work with this? The chapter ends with reflections on a range of different ways in which 'relations' and 'connections' might be thought – including topological analyses which emphasise the spatiality of social relations rather than spatial flows or connections as such; and the partial and buried nature of connections which dominant histories and historiographies have erased.

Part III: Generative Comparisons

'Generative' grounds or reasons for bringing different cases or contexts into comparison, or thinking with elsewhere, lie in the curiosity and practices of the researcher to understand a phenomenon or problem. This can encourage researchers to design research which could help to think in a focussed way about the puzzles that specific contexts, or a number of diverse contexts and their shared features or divergences, present to analysis. Such initiatives could be grounded in practices of solidarity and collaboration, eager to transform urban life (Peake et al. 2021). Considering the variety of forms of a phenomenon raises questions about the limits of concepts available to understand them – perhaps their inability to stretch meaningfully across the different cases. For Deleuze, the field of available concepts constitutes a virtual series, the series of all possible ideas, which goes alongside and works with the virtual series of all the possibilities of the emergent urban world which present themselves to us, posing questions or 'problems', pressing at existing understandings. The intersection of these two series is the generative site in which new concepts might be produced, and old concepts reach their limits. Inspired by this formulation, Chapters 8 and 9 consider how comparative tactics emerge on generative grounds, through the agency of researchers crafting comparative analyses to review and generate concepts.

Firstly, though, **Chapter 7** considers in more detail how in comparisons on generative grounds, insights emerge from the practices of researchers, seeking to invent, expand, enrich and perhaps reach the end of the utility of a certain concept. In coming to know or seeking to transform the diverse urban world, concepts are inevitable. And the subjects of knowledge are irredeemably present. This is a crucial premise of this chapter and this book. Certainly, concepts of the urban are hard won across diversity, difference and the material world. Urban comparativists have found resources in different perspectives and practices to navigate this tricky terrain. It has become a commonplace to reference Merton's practical proposition to provoke theories of the 'middle range' (between empirical description and grand theories) as a positive outcome of urban comparisons (Leitner et al. 2019; Portes 2017; Ren 2020). But this is simply to point us towards the problem area which needs attention. How or on what grounds might concepts arise and be revised? How and why might concepts take hold and travel beyond the place where they were coined? What are we to make of the inevitable distance between concepts and things. Unfortunately, simply placing concepts in the 'middle range' is not a self-evident solution – all these questions remain valid for concepts which claim to stretch only so far, or to emerge in relation to specific situations or a delimited set of problems. This chapter rather considers what some paths towards the strongly revisable conceptualisations on which comparison depends might look like.

Generative comparative tactics, inspired by researchers' concerns and practices, pose the important question of who this researcher might be. I seek to sidestep the conventional figure of the Northern researcher and 'his' trajectories and travails across the urban world. The theorist I imagine, and sometimes am, starts out somewhere else altogether than this itinerary suggests, on the quest both for insight and to change 'her' world. Chapter 7 therefore draws inspiration from feminist, postcolonial and black studies. But in the spirit of post-colonial critique and decolonial ground clearing it also rifles critically through resources which might be salvaged from older configurations of the vitality of concepts (Weber) and the concrete situations that inspire theorisation (Marx). With Hannah Arendt, conceptualisation can be seen as a revisable and contestable horizon of collective understanding, inevitably mired in politics and power relations. But with Mbembe, the racialised terrain of the possibility of an emergent 'in-common' points to a scarred past and striated future for urban studies. Inspired also by Fred Moten, this chapter draws attention to scholars refusing racialised philosophies of knowledge and working against the fraught history of universals and euro-centric theories of subjectivity. The practice of generating concepts takes place on this fractured and flawed terrain. Resistant practices, and diverse lived experiences, inspire a search for quite other grounds for insight (McKittrick 2021).

For different theoretical traditions, then, the process of conceptualisation is bound to the embedded experiences and practices of researchers. The aim of Chapter 7, engaging critically with philosophers and social theorists who have been important in framing debates in urban studies, is to bring clearly to the fore the basis on which concepts can be treated as radically open to being revised, but to clarify that they are also forged in situated engagements with the urban world. Across all the different perspectives discussed, concepts are imagined to 'port' the social and material world in some way. With this in mind, Chapters 8 and 9 set out a range of ways in which comparisons on generative grounds might proceed and I bring in some insights from my own comparative and collaborative research.

Chapter 8 looks at the potential for comparisons to work with the dynamic virtuality of concepts. Such tactics of generative comparison are strongly influenced by the theoretical perspectives adopted by urban scholars, including how the urban is conceptualised. Different ways of thinking 'the urban' suggest distinctive formulations of the starting points and processes of conceptualisation, and so indicate different tactics for designing comparisons. This chapter considers in turn, then, ways of approaching the urban as contingent, as specific, and as diverse. Marxist-inspired perspectives describe the potential to think with extensive social processes and formations which stretch across many different urban settings, treating urban cases as sites where different social processes converge. This frames urban outcomes as 'contingent' or as 'conjunctures' (Leitner et al. 2019). However, with Lefebvre this could be seen as a rather one-sided or 'flat' view of the urban (as a convergence of social processes). A three-dimensional view of the urban as a full, inexhaustible space opens up comparative possibilities which treat the urban as a 'specific category', always distinctive (Schmid 2015). Emergent socio-spatial urbanisation processes (as opposed to the convergence of pre-defined 'social' processes) open up possibilities to think across diverse urban experiences (Schmid et al. 2018). This can be framed as thinking across shared features of urban processes, such as land-use dynamics, territorial pathways and the spatial form of urban contexts, which can ground comparative insights. But the chapter moves further in the direction of looser conversations across different, even divergent, urban contexts.

Thus, different theoretical vocabularies frame different possibilities for thinking the urban with a comparative imagination, with elsewhere: to work with 'contingency' posits different outcomes as framed within analyses of wider social processes, 'conjunctures' or totalities; to conceptualise from specificity indicates the generalised (spatial; inexhaustible) condition of the urban as distinctive and invites identification and analysis of emergent urbanisation processes; to think with diversity suggests the possibility to base comparative experiments on 'shared features' observed across different urban contexts or, more loosely, to initiate experimental 'conversations' across distinctive urban contexts in which each informs and enriches analyses of the others.

Chapter 9 explores a range of such experiments for maximising the potential to think with the diversity of global urban experiences. It also reflects on how concepts themselves might move beyond single cases. As concepts emerge in relation to different urban contexts, their circulation and mobility draws attention to the agency of researchers in putting ideas on the move – or drawing concepts in to their contexts, to generate insights and invent new ways of thinking the urban.

Part IV: Thinking from the Urban as Distinctive

While Part III of the book emphasises the generative creativity of scholars in conceptualising and engaging with the urban world, Part IV of the book explores comparative tactics which might emerge in response to the agency of the urban world. These comparative tactics embrace the potential for concepts to emerge in close entwinement with the materiality of urban life; and rely primarily on a view of the urban as **distinctive**. Chapters 5 and 6 consider the urban as 'differentiated' (tracing the genesis of the urban in its interconnections and/or starting from repeated instances), and Chapters 8 and 9 treat urban outcomes as 'diverse', with comparative experiments constituted across contexts brought into analytical relationship rather than being necessarily materially connected. **Chapter 10** opens to thinking with the fullness of urban territories to provoke comparative experiments. These could take shape across territories in a certain kind of relation to urbanisation ('suburbs', or 'peripheries' for example), or on the basis of the emergent territorialisations of the urban which make up the increasingly fragmented, dispersed and extensive urban forms of contemporary 'planetary' urbanisation. Treating these outcomes as territories, although certainly shaped by the prolific transnationalisation of urbanisation processes, draws attention to divergent urban experiences, and thus can be highly generative of new ways of thinking the urban. Generally, in the fullness of urban life which they index, territories offer dispersed and unpredictable starting points for analysis. They propose new grounds for conceptualisation within cities across the jumble of the material world, or in response to the unpredictable assembling of an archive of the production of space over long periods of time (Lefebvre 1991). Thinking in the midst of territories, even 'fragments' and 'fragmented' elements of urban life can inspire concepts and, to follow McFarlane (2019), offer 'lures' to elsewhere. Also, territories are not simply isolated fragments of the urban world, but intensely interconnected through multiple flows and networks with potentially world-wide reach, shaping an array of dispersed and fragmented territorialisations. The openings for thinking with elsewhere and for engaging in wider conversations are manifold, when starting from territories.

Treating urban outcomes as territories – as distinctive, or individual, with each outcome or element approached on its own terms – can liberate researchers from dependence on inherited concepts. Such a view of the urban constitutes arguably the most lively grounds for generating new concepts, for re-imagining the urban. Insights inspired by 'specific' or 'unique' urban places might be closely tied to a particular phenomenon or context, or only stretch to closely related experiences, any generalisation remaining close to the specificity (Lancione and McFarlane 2016). But the potentiality of new concepts to contribute in turn to the virtuality of ideas (all possible concepts) means that they point also outwards, perhaps being drawn on by others as circulating terms, with the potential to resonate with other emergent phenomena. Thus, concepts, emergent in particular contexts might be 'launched' into wider conversations, transforming urban studies from places and positionalities which have hitherto been treated as marginal to conceptualisation. Crucially, though, concepts are not innocent materialisations of the urban world: the researcher is not transparent, and the subjects of theorisation are differentially positioned in relation to powerful theory cultures and institutions. Chapter 10 justifies the potential to begin analysis of 'the urban' in any urban territory, and any urban outcome, seen as distinctive. This is extremely important for conceptual innovation. But the final chapter, **Chapter 11**, dives further 'into the territory', to interrogate the detailed way in which Ideas, or concepts might be imagined to form in the close entwining of emergent (material) urban worlds and the active agency of the researcher.

There are two interconnected puzzles here, which such a close-up perspective on urban life and the urban fabric poses. One concerns what can be said of/with the materiality of the urban. Does this mark a still point of transparency, in which the researcher is rendered invisible and matter speaks for itself? Or, is this a moment of conceptual darkness, in which there is no scope for analytical reflections or conversations beyond the immediate observation or intuition? If concepts fall away from experience (not just matter), or concepts are detached from each other, what hope is there for analytical conversations across the diverse and repeated empirical phenomena we are calling, the urban? The second puzzle arises as urban experience is released from representation through *universals*, and not given extensively as *generality*, nor derived as *conjunctures* from concrete-theoretical contradictions, relations and determinations, nor yet posited as the *specific* outcomes of theorised (if emergent and empirically derived) 'urban' processes. What possibility remains for conversations about the urban, or for thinking with elsewhere, if each urban outcome is treated as distinctive? Are we at the limits of comparison? This chapter addresses head on what it might mean to think from the urban as 'individual' outcomes, and to generate insights and Ideas drawing on unique observations of elements of the urban. We consider observations as 'singularities' – but as we will see these are not isolates, either empirically or conceptually. Deleuze invites us to consider their existence alongside 'neighbouring' singularities, and their place within a dynamic process of conceptualisation.

This chapter returns to Deleuze, then, and to the close affinities his philosophy has with Walter Benjamin's contributions to understanding urban experience. Especially important is the relationship between Benjamin's concept of 'dialectics at a standstill', and the formation of 'Ideas' in Deleuze. Here we find scope to explore Ideas or concepts (of the urban) as emergent and shifting constellations, alignments of singularities (observations) which express insights across the diversity and extremes of phenomena. These concerns are core themes of philosophy. But, in the spirit of thinking with the city, which has guided this book, I explore these through urbanists, of which Walter Benjamin was one. The chapter considers thinkers who start in the midst of urban territories, especially in contexts which have been marginalised in urban theory. Emergent and shared empirical observations, affinities and collaborations indicate highly creative, and urgently needed, dimensions to conceptualising the urban. The chapter begins with themes of occlusion and opacity as shadowing efforts to come to know the urban (Simone 2019). But as the argument unfolds, it becomes evident that across the range of comparative urban practices explored in this book, the scope for conceptual innovation is, perhaps ironically, most clearly apparent in these situations. Whatever 'the urban' might be, this chapter will reinforce, it is determinable only in its multiple emergent empirical and analytical constellations. Certainly, in this format, Ideas, or concepts of the urban, proliferate, present themselves as deeply revisable, emergent in relation to any urban context, and embedded in multiple elsewheres.

Across the chapters of Parts II to IV, it becomes clear that tracking genetic processes and embarking on generative explorations intertwine in the practice of comparing. Comparison is a challenging, slow and emergent research practice, in which the potential for comparison, the comparator, can be thought of as 'assembled' across the elements of cases, wider literature, individual researchers, evidence gathered, interlocutors, not least collaborators, residents, practitioners, who have their own productive 'wild' comparisons to put into the mix (Deville et al 2016). Chapter 9 begins with some reflections on this. Comparative tactics are part of a thick temporal field of emergent and processual method: the criteria, practices and phenomena which might initially stimulate or ground enquiries may disappear from view. The object and terms of comparison you start with might literally evaporate as the study unfolds. New concepts and entities might emerge along the way. And, in turn, these might morph into (new) good grounds for comparability. Formulating insightful comparisons on generative grounds can take a very long time!

But, whatever comparative urbanism might turn out to be – and however the urban might be conceptualised – this is over to you.

Conclusion

The point of a reformatted comparative practice is to provoke new conceptualisations, starting anywhere, with a strong orientation to revising existing concepts. Comparative urbanism seeks to contribute to innovative conceptualisation, displacing overweening 'theories' by composing analytical proximities across diverse urban contexts, tracing genetic connections across their differentiation in many urban contexts, or launching concepts starting from anywhere. Rather than seeking to prevent conceptual 'overstretch', a revised comparativism seeks to deliberately stretch concepts, perhaps to breaking point. This book builds comparative methodology from the spatiality of the urban: the full social worlds of territories; the interconnections that compose urban outcomes, differently each time; the diverse and emergent outcomes of urban processes, and from our practices as engaged, embodied and located researchers in specific urban contexts. After the fact, this methodological wager also signposts a process of theorisation of the urban. But one in which conceptualisations of the urban – new vocabularies of urbanisation – would necessarily be productively multiple. The conclusion to this book provides a summary statement on the contours of a reformatted comparative method for urban studies, and draws together the propositions of this book about conceptualising the urban. On this basis, global urban studies would become a field in which concepts are intrinsically highly revisable, where research is conducted in a modest authorial voice, and researchers are open to insights starting from anywhere. As a manifesto to think the urban from anywhere, however, comparative urbanism returns us to the urgent need for institutional transformation, and for scholarly practices which support revisable theory undertaken by any scholar, anywhere, perhaps in collaboration with other scholars or with urban dwellers. The conclusion reinforces this challenge. This book, then, is proposed in the name of the decolonisation of established agendas and voices, and in the hopes of stimulating thinking 'in-common' (Mbembe 2017) which embraces the lively differences of the urban world and opens to experiments which provoke new ways of thinking and practicing urban life.

The 'problem' of the urban in a Deleuzian sense indicates the presentation to us of something which requires a response, a conceptualisation. This book offers an ambitious and programmatic but also pragmatic response to the resulting question, how can we approach the urban, now? It is my hope that urbanists, and other scholars concerned with different urban places, from many different theoretical traditions, might find some resources here to generate the insights the urban world is demanding.

IMAGE 1.1 Township-Wall by António Ole, III C 45608 –A, Ethnologisches Museum, Staatliche Museen zu Berlin. (Photograph by Martin Franken)

IMAGE 1.2 Waiting for Bus by Dilomprizulike, 2003, at Africa Remix: Contemporary Art of a Continent, Hayward Gallery, London (2005). (Photograph by Marcus Leith)

PART I

Reformatting Comparison

The first part of the book interrogates the inherited practices of comparative urban studies. On the one hand, a review of comparative methods exposes a number of limitations: ideas about causality, cases and comparability are not a good fit with the demands of twenty-first century urban studies, and tend to restrict comparisons to very similar cities. This is the focus of Chapter 2. On the other hand, though, looking in detail at the actual comparative practices of urban scholars, some possibilities for different kinds of methods are evident. Designing comparisons based on the shared features of urban contexts, rather than waiting for these to emerge after imposing often confining criteria for determining comparable cases, opens up comparison to the world of cities. Chapter 3 considers this and also observes how urban scholars have come to think across the urban world, drawn by the many different processes which connect urban settlements in different regions and hemispheres. With these practices as inspiration, Chapter 4 explores some philosophical and methodological grounds to reformat comparative urbanism so that it might better suit analyses of the urban. This part establishes grounds for the book's ambition to promote more global theoretical conversations about the urban, able to start anywhere, thinking difference without assumptions of origin or copy, with a strong requirement for openness to revisability of concepts.

Two installations from an exhibition, Africa Remix, which I saw quite some years ago in London, led me to the image on the book's cover and have accompanied me as I thought and talked about this book. Dilomprizulike, the self-styled 'Junkman of Africa' from Nigeria (http://junkyard.good-craft.com/) composed a set of figures, 'Waiting for Bus', often photographed located on the side of a road running through an apparently un-built up area (Hayward Gallery 2003, p. 168; Image 1.2, p. 22; a colour version of this image can be found between pages 132 and 133 as Plate 6). And the Angolan sculptor, António Ole's vibrant 'Township Wall' gives a sense of the self-built settlements that characterise sub-Saharan Africa (Image 1.1, p. 22). Part of this installation forms the cover image; the full installation is reproduced in the colour insert between pages 132 and 133 as Plate 1. On António Ole, Luanda and urban theory, see Tomás (2022). In one version of the exibition, at the Mori Art Museum in Tokyo, Japan, these two installations were side by side in the gallery (Ogata 2007, p. 23). Staged like this, they provoke reflection on where urban dwellers are journeying, and on where the urban might be. Countryside and city are long interconnected through circular migration in the sub-Saharan African region. The urban is composed not only in the minds of the comparativist. The urban composes itself, is composed by urban dwellers, launching themselves into journeys, into the search for livelihoods, for connection, for shelter, for some kind of future. A key question for this part of the book is how urban scholars might follow the tracks and territories of the urban, and of urban residents, in crafting insights across the great diversity of urban experiences, and joining with others in shaping urban futures. Creative approaches to this abound, so Chapter 1 starts the book by drawing together the range of ways in which scholars have sought to come to know the urban world. Reflecting on how comparative urbanism might contribute to these efforts, the agenda is set for the rest of the book.

CHAPTER 1

Ways of Knowing the Global Urban

The vast extension of some urban settlements and a growing awareness of the impacts of urbanisation across the planet, including in remote places, alongside persistent growth in the urbanised population pose new challenges for urban studies. Divergent urban forms are fragmented and extended across often vast areas rather than spreading outwards from a putative central part of a 'city'. What kind of urban theorising might be relevant to this urban world? Research strategies more adequate to the complex spatiality of urban forms are needed. Theorisation of the urban has not only to respond to the changing geographies of global urbanisation but also to feminist, post- and decolonial critiques of urban studies, and to the substantial challenges of climate and development crises. At stake here are both the 'subjects' and geographies of theorising. Whose ideas count in shaping theorisation and how do different voices contribute to wider conversations about the urban? How might both the shared and the divergent concerns across wealthier and poorer cities inform theorisation? What difference does it make to think the urban in the midst of the interconnectedness of a globalised urban world? It is widely agreed that urban studies needs to embrace a much wider repertoire of urban contexts in building understandings of the rapidly changing forms of contemporary urbanisation. Parochial interpretations of the urban need to be revisited: but how exactly is this to be done?

Different scholars have set out on the project for global urban studies in a variety of directions. Pulling (some of) them together here, I invite readers to join me in being inspired by the creativity and range of work which supports global urban studies, and to take time to explore these different paths on their own terms. I review three sets of debates which have recently shaped urban studies, and which speak to the core concerns of theorising the urban. Each brings into the open, aspects of the emerging and persistent challenges

Comparative Urbanism: Tactics for Global Urban Studies, First Edition. Jennifer Robinson.
© 2022 John Wiley & Sons Ltd. Published 2022 by John Wiley & Sons Ltd.

of thinking the urban across the diversity of urban experiences. Together they help to ground practices of revisable theory building in urban studies. The chapter explores, first, different ways in which urban scholars propose to work with and across spatial difference. Here, regionally based scholarship, and the idea of the 'global South' have been prominent. Debates around these propositions signpost also the prolific interconnections which puncture such territorial containers. They alert urbanists to the diverse, (dis)connected communities of scholarship which make up urban studies. Globalised processes of capitalism and colonialism, and prolific circulations of money, ideas and people, establish that different forms of the urban across the globe – and ways of understanding these – are necessarily constituted in relationship to one another. A 'planetary' perspective prioritises such spatially extended processes of urbanisation, and seeks to dissolve the territorial container of the 'city' as a privileged starting point for urban studies. The second section considers how both proponents of Planetary Urbanisation and their feminist and postcolonial critics insist that theorisation of urbanisation processes must contend with spatial difference and specificity. Critics point to the need to rebuild urban studies through the diverse and divergent experiences that contribute to making urban life. Different positionalities of theorists matter, too, and the third section of the chapter explores how feminist critiques link with contributions from post- and de-colonial urban studies, black studies and critical race studies. Together with approaches inspired by materialities and 'assemblage' thinking, what comes to the fore here is the need to attend to the emergent distinctiveness of each urban context, as well as the opacity and unknowability of urban life. A range of wider epistemological issues are evident: whose voice counts in theorising the urban (and from where)? How is the process of coming to know urban worlds to be understood? The racialised and masculinist histories which scar the very terms on which the urban can be thought call for methodological renewal.

Across these different approaches, urban scholars face shared challenges of thinking the urban: an (im)possible object which is characterised by interconnections (differentiation), diversity (both spatial and social) and distinctiveness (specificity). The urban comes to be known from many different contexts and perspectives; but it is necessarily thought from somewhere. At the core of this book is the sensibility that such located knowledge of the urban is, however, inevitably shadowed by other urban experiences, by elsewhere(s). Given the nature and form of the 'urban question' in the twenty-first century, it is my proposition that to take forward all these different approaches, some kind of comparative imagination seems crucial – to think across diverse and interconnected urban experiences, and to build insights through engaging with the distinctive forms and inexhaustible complexity of urban life. What kind of comparative urbanism can provide methodological propositions for rebuilding urban theory in the midst of the empirical and conceptual revolutions shaping urban studies today? The final section provides an outline response to this question.

This chapter establishes how comparative urbanism emerges from and can align with, support and extend efforts to respond to the dual conceptual challenges presented, on the one hand, by the changing nature of urbanisation and, on the other hand, by calls to decentre and transform the practices of urban studies. The rest of the book then proposes how comparative urbanism might support a theorisation of the urban which works with and across the interconnections, divergences and distinctive outcomes which make up the global urban.

Uncertain Territories, 'Strategic Essentialisms': Regions, the Global South and beyond

In globalising urban studies, the challenges of difference arise in many different guises. Questions about how to distribute differences analytically within the global urban have been front and centre of debates about post-colonialising the field. Is the urban to be understood as varied by region, by the wealth of countries, or by common geopolitical categories? As scholars have searched for new ways of framing the urban, all these possibilities have been explored, with some suggestive implications for thinking comparatively about the global urban. But as we will explore here, the spatialities of the urban strongly undercut the spatial forms of 'regions' and the 'global South', even as these formulations have accumulated significant critical weight in reshaping the concerns of global urban studies.

Regions

To articulate the potential for new practices of theorising the urban from beyond the traditional Anglo-American heartlands of urban studies, post-colonial critics have sought to instigate new geographies of authority and voice. Surveying the key ideas about cities emerging from different regional contexts (Asia, Africa, South America), Roy (2009b) proposes a form of strategic essentialism as a grounding for this work. Certainly, it is an important starting point for post-colonial critique to insist on the space to speak back to arguably 'western' theory based on the best insights of scholars in different parts of the world. Formulating this as a 'strategic essentialism' acknowledges that territorialisations of knowledge production are only temporarily feasible.

The circulating and connected geographies of both knowledge production and the processes of urbanisation quickly puncture any straightforward area-based approach.

The 'strategic' epithet therefore indicates some of the limitations of this approach, but also its potentiality. For, certainly, new subjects of urban theory have emerged from embedded regional scholarship and regional circuits of theorisation which are productive and important in their own right (Bhan 2019; Pieterse 2013; Wu 2020). Cities, countries and regions support and produce communities of scholars (including their diaspora) whose concerns are distinctive, if internally sometimes highly differentiated. The 'region' as a ground for theorisation can be a substantively important and generative context for thinking, fostering scholarly networks, traditions and practices. Regions have shared histories and closer economic or political interactions which can frame careful and effective comparisons (Abu-Lughod 1976, 1999). However, both urban scholars and the processes they are interested in are open to influences from a wide array of different contexts and urbanisation processes which stretch across the globe (Bunnell 2013; Sidaway et al. 2014). Urban scholars are often both intimately driven by the situated histories and politics of a context, and connected to wider debate. Insofar as specific urban contexts are more than regionally determined, shaped by globalising processes, circulating policies and the re-iterations of urban forms which result from these prolific interconnections, the 'region' as a basis for theoretical voice is perforated. It might be claimed, momentarily, as grounds for distinctive conceptualisation but is quickly called into question through both internal differentiation and the disruptions of wider processes of globalisation. Cities are, as Mbembe and Nuttall have it, 'embedded in multiple elsewheres' (2004, p. 348), and the scholars of particular contexts are equally part of wider circuits of knowledge and concepts which trace multiple trajectories and histories.

This has animated scholars from former socialist contexts who have criticised the analytical 'territorial container' which the post-socialist epithet indexes (Stenning and and Hörschelmann 2008). Moves to de-territorialise post-socialism rather focus attention on how social processes are shaped by both historical continuities and reactive anti-continuities with socialist era formations, as well as extensive re-engagement with globalising processes (Sjöberg 2014). Thus, rather than a blanket categorisation of territories as post-socialist (Tuvikene 2016), 'post-socialism' becomes an analytic, or concept, to interrogate complex historical formations. This brings an awareness that the transitions with their epi-centre in the former Eastern Bloc have had massive implications for many other places too. With the demise of the Cold War the demilitarisation that followed had major impacts on cities like Los Angeles and opened new geopolitical frontiers implicating different urban contexts and regions (Tuvikene 2016). Post-socialism 'as process not container' is therefore suggestive of many opportunities for conversations with scholars in and of other contexts (Rogers 2010). These might be on the basis of being implicated in the same circuits and global connections. But opportunities for comparative insight across quite different historical processes also open up, for example, with places having undergone political and economic transitions in the same time frame, for example, from authoritarianism to democracy (Brazil, South Africa) or liberalising economies, such as India (Harrison and Todes 2014). A number of scholars have also been concerned to explore the parallels between initiatives to post-colonialise urban studies, and the need to foreground the voices of scholars of cities 'after transition' from socialism (Bernt 2016b; Chari and Verdery 2009; Müller 2020; Müller and Trabina 2020). Experiences of socialism and post-socialism can inform analyses of urban processes elsewhere. For example the intense culture of privatism driving distinctive forms of globally resonant micro-gating and hyper-postmodernism in the built environment of Sofia, Bulgaria (Hirt 2012); the rapid and extensive forms of suburbanisation with all its environmental implications, consequent upon rapid deregulation of land use management which have shaped urban experiences across former socialist countries (Sykora and Stanilov 2014); the marked informalisation of economy and society which ensued with economic liberalisation (Smith 2009); or the global flows of primary commodities which frame post-socialist economies and urbanisation (Gentile 2018).

Ferenčuhová (2016) is right, however, to counter such deterritorialising initiatives with the insistence that the historical divisions and resource-challenged institutional conditions of scholarly work in post-socialist contexts have shaped and limited the range of openings and wider theoretical conversations in urban studies from post-socialist contexts, both historically and today. Her concerns are shared by scholars writing in and about cities in Africa, where institutional resources are meagre and policy demands pressing. The call for a more methodologically diverse urban studies acknowledging the exigencies of different regional contexts is presented by Parnell and Pieterse (2016). They argue that in the African context more transversal practices are needed, embedded in practical terrains of often politicised forms of knowledge production. Stronger valorisation of research that involves the empirical documentation of less well known urban realities is also important. They insist that building insights from different regional contexts should have broader implications for urban studies: 'Either Africa must be ignored or the theory, method and data of urban studies must change' (p. 241). Importantly for our concerns here, they note that in a moment when the centres of urbanisation and urban studies are shifting globally, both African and post-socialist contexts face the possibility of being doubly marginalised, as Asian urbanisation and the growth of mega-urban regions overshadows interest in other contexts. But bringing China urban studies into wider conversations about the urban must also address the challenges of generating insights concerned with the specificities of that region, while insisting these also contribute to broader theorisations (Wu 2020). These shared concerns of scholars from very different regions perhaps signals the potential for cross-fertilisation, to support and inform one another and bypass the often obligatory 'northern' reference points of urban studies.

The scope for wider theoretical conversations is partly structured by different languages and segmented publishing realms (Slater 1992). Whereas some Asian, Indian and Anglophone African scholars might have closer access to and influence on hegemonic debates (Chatterjee 2004; Huat 2011; Mabogunje 1990; Tang 2021; Wu 2020), those from minor language communities, even in the European context, are often more fundamentally excluded (Sidaway et al. 2014; Vaiou 2004). Translations of key texts and stronger engagements with French and Spanish language literature as well as generational shifts in language learning priorities to favour English (for example in France and Germany) have opened up conversations with dominant Anglo traditions (Gintrac and Giroud 2014; Hasbaert 2013). Some of this is the result of the relocation of scholars from different regions to well-resourced northern institutions. The engagement is often one-directional, though, with English language speakers siloed by their limited language skills, and English language publishing norms dominating what is published as 'international' knowledge. The ongoing fracturing of intellectual endeavour presents a serious limit to wider conversations about 'the urban'. A patchwork of regionally and linguistically diverse theorisations sets the uneven and power laden terrain of 'global' urban studies.

Regionalisations of urban theory are to some extent inevitable, and productive, and provide many generative insights. They highlight the endemic classic challenge of theorising the global urban – seeking to build wider theorisations of the urban while always having to start somewhere. But regions are deeply entwined with a wider world (substantively and conceptually) and so their geographical delimitations are often artefacts of power and cartographic imagination rather than analysis. Building new subjects of urban theory on such essentialisms runs certain risks, potentially isolating new subjects of theorisation and preventing the emergence of new grounds for speaking more generally about the urban condition in ways that resonate with different regional experiences. Given the institutional and publishing landscape, this most likely preserves intact the authoritative analyses of the urban produced in the dominant heartlands of Euro-American scholarship. Strategic essentialism could re-establish earlier lines of incommensurability which saw urbanists disavow insights from geopolitically, developmentally and regionally different contexts (Robinson 2006). The dynamic strength of regional scholarship lies in its crucial importance to addressing the challenges of urbanisation in diverse contexts in different analytical registers. This needs to be balanced with attending to the range of historical trajectories, globalised relations and prolific interconnections which shape any urban context (Bunnell 2013). These can offer different pathways to launch emergent regionally based understandings into wider conversations. As Myers expresses: 'My goal is ... to point to the multifaceted urbanity in African contexts as of great value to global understanding of urbanism' (Myers 2011, p.7).

Global South

Some of the same challenges involved in deploying strategic regional imaginations as grounds from which to propose new accounts of the urban are evident in the idea of a 'southern' urban theory (Lawhon and Truelove 2020; Schindler 2017; Watson 2009). But the imagined geography of the south is even more complicated to work with than that of 'regions', which might have some substantive coherence in economic interconnection or political integration. On the one hand the idea of the 'global South' borrows an initially geopolitical (as 'third world' or non-aligned movement) and latterly developmental metaphor linking poorer nations beyond the capitalist heartland and western core. The concept has moved beyond the dividing line of 'poverty', though, which is the original meaning of the term formulated in the Brandt Commission report (1980), to describe a somewhat uncertain contour separating richer north and poorer south. Critically, its re-orientation as 'global' south makes sense of poor countries north of the equator, but also allows analysts to include experiences of poverty wherever it is found, including in wealthier contexts. The relational connections between poverty in the North and South, through migration, precarious working, deindustrialisation, and the wider restructuring of global capitalism, are important here.

As with thinking from regions, there might be good academic grounds for the imaginative delineation of distinctions between urbanisation in the global North and South to practically take forward postcolonial critiques. Raewyn Connell's (2007) path-breaking book, *Southern Theory* develops a *sui generis* analysis of the lines of exclusion of many parts of the world from the labour of (sociological) theorisation. She contests the positioning of some places as sources of data rather than theory, and insists on a reinvention of theory for a sociology 'at a world scale'. The appeal of the global south in academic analysis is only partly in the potential it offers for a critique of the uneven territorial distributions of poverty, wealth and power globally. Also key is its figuring of the ex-centric scholar or location, who/which can disturb or speak back to dominant knowledges in a radical idiom framed by their distinctive experiences (Comaroff and Comaroff 2012). In this vein, the idea of the global South is a highly suggestive tactic for global urbanism, and has inspired the articulation of distinctive approaches in urban studies. For example, the idea of thinking from the South is allied with calls for an engaged, politically committed research practice, informed by the inventive analyses emerging from city dwellers, international policy makers, states and other actors in some of the poorest cities which have been highly marginalised in urban studies to date (Bhan 2019; Pieterse 2013). Similarly, the desire to decentre analyses of the urban encourages new subject positions, with writers eager to recentre interpretations in new locations and sources of authority, based on the geographical metaphor of the South (Lawhon and Truelove 2020; Watson 2014b).

What defines the 'south' for urban scholars? As a baggy geopolitical category, it perhaps inherits the opportunism and potential indicated by the political non-aligned movement which lies behind the term, 'third world', whose mantle it inherited. 'Southern theory' might further be grounded on the global histories of colonisation which affect some contexts embraced by this term (Parnell and Oldfield 2014), or on a critique of the geopolitics of exclusion from knowledge production in the colonial present (Lawhon 2020). It might reflect the value of a theorisation from more peripheral capitalisms which perhaps constitute the leading edge of economic and political change (Comaroff and Comaroff 2012). The term 'global' South, though, permits a widening of attention to exploitation and poverty wherever it is found, across the 'north' and 'south' (Miraftab 2009). These overlapping ambitions for the term make of the 'global South' a highly dispersed spatial referent – and one which some propose to stretch further to encompass a putative global 'Southeast', acknowledging the shared analytical exclusions and political–economic marginality of both 'South' and 'East' (Müller 2020; Yiftachel 2006, 2020).

In their prescient critique of the concept, 'third world' city, Dick and Rimmer (1998) point to the many urban processes which connect cities across the developmental divisions which had fragmented twentieth century urban studies (Robinson 2006). To what extent does the concept of the global South potentially perpetuate such analytical divisions? Developmental differences now not only distinguish wealthier and poorer cities from one another along some important lines, but also tie cities together in new ways. For example, in extensive municipal collaborations to address global urban problems, as well as through the multiplicity of circuits of travel, trade, investment and imagination which shape urban policy and practice across the world (Lauermann 2018). In a globalised and interconnected urban world the analytical basis for maintaining a consistent conceptual separation between groups of cities is unclear.

In their collection *Handbook on Cities of the Global South* Parnell and Oldfield (2014) offer some nuanced reflections on defining the global south. They suggest that the 'spatial scope' of the term is not literal, and acknowledge the concept as fluid and contested. But this, they indicate, 'should not detract from the widespread concern to (re)view the global urban condition with a southern sensibility'. They motivate for a distinctive perspective in which the challenges of poverty and resourcing influence scholarship in and of the south. Research in such circumstances, they insist, has to be legitimate and to have local traction. They do, though, identify scope for contributions from the global south to understand problems of the global north, 'highlighting that resource limits, poverty, informality and growth are not the preserve of the south'. Indeed, they suggest that these challenges are found 'everywhere', and that 'much extant urban theory has a global application' (p. 3). Other authors agree that the demands, expectations and personal desire to address local problems through relevant research and identifying potential solutions, together with a broad commitment to 'praxis', often characterises the southern urban research experience (Bhan 2019). Helpfully, Lawhon and Truelove (2020) seek to 'disambiguate' what southern urban scholars are trying to achieve (although they don't interrogate the limits of the geopolitical container, the global south). They point out that scholarship from 'the south' emphasises empirical differences; seeks to respond to Euro-American hegemony that displaces the diversity of intellectual traditions which might be brought forward in the name of the South; and that practices and interventions in cities of the south seek to be relevant to those contexts. Seth Schindler (2017) proposes some specific tendencies and characteristics which southern cities might share, and sees these as distinctive kinds of 'cities' from those in the 'North Atlantic and Northeast Asia' (p. 60).

Given the imprecision and broad scope of the term, many theorists who have drawn on the geographical referent of the 'South' to propose a critique of metropolitan theory have hedged the term with numerous caveats. Connell (2007) embraces shifting geographical reference points in which the overlapping and imprecise markers of north–south, first world–third world, core–periphery must suffice to indicate 'the realities of global division' (p. 212), and where the limits of the geographical imagination underpinning the concept of south is clear – 'To use concepts like "periphery" is just the beginning of analysis, not the end' (p. 213). The Comaroffs' (2012) premise their analysis on the virtues of an 'ex-centric' viewpoint, and the assertion that the history of the present reveals itself 'more starkly in the antipodes' and is thus best investigated from that 'distinctive vantage' (p. 7). But their geographical imagination rests on a 'South' which is not only dialectically entwined with the North, but tied together through the 'labyrinthine capillaries' of transnational capital, with 'much North in the South, much South in the North'. At the end of the day, they suggest that 'the south' cannot be 'defined a priori but must be understood relationally', along a range of different processes: 'It is a historical artefact, a labile signifier in a grammar of signs whose semiotic content is determined, over time, by everyday material, political, and cultural processes, the dialectical products of a global world in motion' (p. 47). Perhaps this array of caveats and complex spatialities of analytical imagination and historical process might themselves be more promising as starting points than the idea of the global South. The question is, then, how to articulate hopes for new cartographies of knowledge production which might 'reshape the circuits through which social-scientific knowledge moves' and refit social science in both metropole and periphery for 'global dialogue' (Connell 2007, p. 227).

Efforts to locate and define urbanisation in and from the global south are drawn to move beyond the temptations of territorialisation given the instability of 'where' the global south might be, and what it might be characterised by. At base there is a significant mismatch between a territorialised imagination of 'south' and the crosscutting relational geographies of global urbanisation. Broader conversations about the nature of the urban also invite a move beyond the segmentations implied by 'southern' and 'northern'. Parnell and Oldfield (2014) motivate for the potential to think with the distinctive experiences of 'southern' urban contexts but they also find shared features across north and south which deserve analytical engagement. Comaroff and Comaroff (2012) track the basis for such engagement across global north and south to the wider circuits and connections of global capitalism. In his consideration of the implications of southern perspectives for 'rethinking urbanism' Myers (2020) traces 'subterranean' and forgotten relations across global south contexts but also between north and south. He follows Edouard Glissant to bring into view, from a de-centric positionality, the interrupted, fragmentary and forgotten relations which characterise the violent disruptions of ocean-borne slavery and island globalisations. Tracing the relations which proliferate from and across different contexts proposes analytical 'relations of equivalence' amongst diverse urban experiences. This links indigenous, settler and slave 'urbanisms' in Hartford, Connecticut, US, for example, through sometimes long-buried connections and flows, across continents, taking in both the Caribbean and the East coast of Africa. The stage is set to consider how the itineraries of global urban studies might proceed in the tracks of the interconnections and circulations which make up urbanisation, rather than on the unsteady territories of regions, the South – or, as the next section considers, the redundant territorial category, the city.

The Disappearing City: Planetary Urbanisation and its Critics

The idea of 'planetary urbanisation' draws on Henri Lefebvre's (2003[1974]) suggestive hypothesis of the 'complete urbanisation of society', and the potential impact of urbanisation (literally) anywhere. The sprawling extent and diverse forms of many cities, or even urban galaxies, as Soja and Kanai (2007) would have it, together with the proliferation of extensive urbanisation processes stretching amongst and beyond urban settlements, presents significant analytical challenges for urbanists (Brenner and Schmid 2014; Merrifield 2013). The globalisation of many urban processes has meant that flows and connections amongst cities are shaping the planet far beyond the physical extent of even these large urban settlements. If the 'urban' as such is in question and its forms and processes of formation are in such flux, building new theorisations, potentially starting anywhere (on the planet), seems imperative.

The core argument of Planetary Urbanisation is founded on an unobjectionable concern which has dogged urban studies almost since its inception – that the territorial referents of the term, 'city', do service for only a small portion of urban processes (Wirth 1938). Urban studies has always struggled to find the terminology which can keep pace with the expansion of territories seen as urban (Fawcett 1932; Gottman 1961). The search is once again on for new vocabularies of the urban to respond to its changing form, but also to replace the territorial shadow contained in the notion of the city. The Lefebvrian-inspired idea of planetary urbanisation has been highly suggestive in focusing attention on the processes of urbanisation, as opposed to 'cities' (Brenner and Schmid 2014, 2015). Theorising urbanisation at a planetary scale, however, must confront the challenge of approaching this across the great diversity of urban outcomes or territories, and the diversity of circulations and processes shaping the urban. What needs to be theorised as urban must therefore start with a multiplicity of forms, trends and interpretations of the urban condition around the world (Brenner and Schmid 2015). Lefebvre himself, as Goonedewarna et al. (eds) (2008, p. 297) observe, was generally sceptical of any 'premature intellectual totalisation', insisting on the necessary incompleteness of theoretical specifications of the urban, as both geographically varied and historically always in process.

Brenner and Schmid (2015) appropriately suggest, then, that urbanisation is variable, polymorphic and historically determinate and that what needs to be theorised as urban takes many different forms. They agree that the project of theorising urbanisation needs to think across a great diversity of urban processes and urban outcomes. In their seven theses on urbanisation Brenner and Schmid propose that:

urbanization under capitalism is always a historically and geographically variegated process: … (it) must be understood as a polymorphic, multiscalar and emergent dynamic of sociospatial transformation: it hinges upon and continuously produces differentiated, unevenly developed sociospatial configurations at all scales.

(Brenner and Schmid 2015, p. 175)

Some core questions of urban studies no longer admit a reasonable answer in this view: discerning where and what is the city has become an impossibility (Brenner and Schmid 2011; 2014; 2015; Brenner 2013; Merrifield 2013; Murray 2017; Keil 2017). The city, Merrifield (2013) insists, is a 'pseudoconcept'. Along with others taking this approach, we are invited to re-specify the theoretical content of the 'urban' and to develop new vocabularies of urbanisation in the face of the sense that the territorial term 'city' has become an inadequate starting point for theorisation (Brenner and Schmid 2015). These writers consider that **whatever the 'urban' might be, it can only be constituted in theory rather than on any a priori empirical grounds**. The earlier efforts of Wirth, Castells and Lefebvre to formulate such theorisations have become important reference points (Brenner and Schmid 2014; Angelo and Wachsmuth 2015). These three thinkers proposed (in turn) a conceptualisation of the urban within theoretical arguments about ways of urban life; forms of political mobilisation and institutions; and the form of urban space.

Here we might usefully pause to reflect on what these earlier theorists of the urban also have to teach us about the project of theorisation. Wirth's efforts to ground urban theory in ideas of size, heterogeneity and density were profoundly parochial (informed by the experience of particular – US and European – cities) and were widely criticised at the time and since by sociologists and anthropologists around the world for that reason (Robinson 2006). Castells' search for a mapping of theoretical concepts onto the city was motivated by his eagerness to displace the heterodox Marxist analysis which Lefebvre was offering to think the city with. In a strongly Althusserian argument he insisted that the 'ideological' conceptualisation of the city through a theorisation of space rather than class distracted from what he considered to be the proper focus on conjuncturally significant structural processes which had become aligned with the city – namely, collective consumption under advanced welfare state capitalism (Castells 1977; Stanek 2011). A spatially anaemic analysis of the urban ensued, and Lefebvre's contributions are only recently coming to be more fully appreciated after decades of inattention and misinterpretation (Goonewardena et al. 2008; Kipfer et al. 2012; Schmid, 2022). The implications for urban studies of the uneven engagement of Lefebvre and his interpreters with global urban experiences, or the colonialism which shaped European and post-colonial urban experiences, has only recently drawn some attention (Kipfer and Goonewardena 2013). In the meantime, and insufficiently acknowledged in the search for new vocabularies of 'planetary urbanisation', urban geographers have already attended most carefully to the dual spatialities of territorialisation and interconnection which shape this impossible, unbounded, fuzzy object of analysis (Massey et al. 1999; Ward 2010). It is worth noting, then, on the basis of these earlier theoretical initiatives, that theorisation of the urban has been shaped from particular locations, and from specific political and philosophical perspectives.

Provocations for a theorisation of planetary urbanisation have themselves been subject to critique along these lines. This includes the need to be alert to disclosing the locatedness of the inspirations for these theoretical propositions – the places and particular urbanisation processes which shape or dominate in contemporary theorisation. For Lefebvre, the main inspiration for planetary urbanisation, these were European. Through his life-time he was also influenced by a wide-ranging set of urban contexts and writers on diverse forms of urbanisation which he drew on in his analyses (Stanek 2011). But Lefebvrian theoretical vocabularies certainly rely on a critical engagement with European philosophical categories, if at times opaque and idiosyncratic sources across English, French, German and other languages (Goonewardena 2018; Schmid 2008, 2022). The repertoire of inspiration for thinking urbanisation as 'planetary' has its roots in European philosophy and the wider Euro-American academy and have been closely tied to (certain theorisations of) global capitalism based again on largely Euro-American perspectives (Brenner 2013; Merrifield 2013).

Criticisms of Planetary Urbanisation take off from these observations. Thinking from different urban contexts and experiences can bring into view a much wider range of processes shaping global, or planetary, urbanisation. Gendered inequality (Peake 2016) and diverse, black and indigenous urbanisms (Simone 2016) are important starting points for this critique and for initiatives to build new understandings of the urban. Developmental actors and policy-oriented interventions are crucial determinants of the urban and urbanisation in many poorer city contexts and may rely on a territorial imagination of the urban (Pieterse et al. 2018). Urban scholars across the world have long been concerned with the ways in which 'the city' and the countryside are woven together through an intricate range of (often transnational) 'extended' relationships. Circular migration, as a constituent and long-lasting feature of many Southern African urbanisms, for example, bears attention here (Potts 2010). Planetary urbanists can be criticised, then, for their excessive emphasis on capitalist processes in their opening statements (Brenner and Schmid 2014, 2015), and for occluding other social processes and analytical rubrics through which urbanisation, 'urban territories' or 'extended urbanisation' might be understood (Buckley and Strauss 2016; Ruddick et al. 2018).

This is particularly relevant to thinking 'the urban' as a spatial phenomenon, and suggests some lines of commonality between theorists of planetary urbanisation and some critics. Whatever the urban is, it indexes the rich fullness of spatial formations; conceptualisations of the urban need to build from the multiplicity of social worlds and materialities of urban space, and urban life. Lefebvre (2009) works closely with the idea of 'concrete totality' as a starting point for analysis – the replete fullness of the empirical world. If the urban is a spatial concept, in a rather recursive fashion anything which takes place in (or shapes) the spaces of urbanisation can be understood to be part of the category urban. This is a crucial point for the potential to post-colonialise and diversify theories of the urban. Whatever takes place in the urban, anywhere, defines the content and conceptualisation of the term. Thinking the urban from anywhere, and from any aspect of urban life, is a necessary potentiality of global urban studies, and a crucial expectation of comparative urbanism.

With the urban in view as a spatial phenomenon, the argument that 'ontological struggles around the everyday [are] connected to *but not wholly subsumed by* the processes of urbanization' (Ruddick et al. 2018, p. 5) requires some clarification. The suggestion that subjects are not fully determined by the urban context is of course, valid. But is it appropriate to draw the conclusion that these subjects are not (already fully) urban? This rests on the possibility that certain experiences and histories located in urban areas are not urban, or more strongly, do not belong in/to the urban. Across Southern Africa, and in many other colonial contexts, colonial administrators sought to exclude indigenous populations from urban areas. As a result, enforced circular migration drew towns and villages into 'one social field' (Gluckman 1961; Potts 2010). In this sense, subjects arriving in the urban (who might never have travelled to the city) were already strongly urbanised. And urban life was profoundly constituted through traditional practices, languages, customs and rule – often mediated by colonial interventions. On political grounds (whoever is in the city or connected to it is part of it and counts) as well as on theoretical grounds, the urban is transformed through its *constitutive* and already interconnected outside (Robinson 2006). Both a Lefebvrian account of space as the fullness of experience, and Massey's view of spatiality as the product of a 'simultaneity of trajectories', raise questions about the suggestion that some practices and experiences in urban areas do not belong in/to the urban. This offers an alternative post-colonial reading of the 'urban' question. Whatever urban subjects bring to the city, whatever their trajectories and journeys to urban contexts might be, it is quite important to acknowledge that they are already both of and in the urban. In that sense, the 'subjects' invoked by Ruddick et al. (2018) matter, but not to contain the scope of urbanity or urbanisation processes. Rather, it is to insist on the changing and varied nature of the urban, and to place all urban subjects as central to its formation and differentiation. The concept of the urban, in this framing, needs to be open to constant extension, and not restricted to only some processes or people.

The debates here resonate with a rather arcane debate which sought to determine what is only in, versus 'of', the urban (Saunders 1986; Scott and Storper 2015). The complaint that planetary urbanists leave no 'outside' to the urban is related to this – that some people and processes might be in the urban but not of it; or be only partly shaped by urbanisation processes. Certainly, "urban" studies does not exhaust analysis of social processes. And neither is the urban everywhere. Some aspects of these concerns rest on a misinterpretation of the Lefebvrian argument. Lefebvre's point was that industrial society was transforming to one where the primary determination was not industrial processes but urbanisation, which could increasingly, and *potentially*, be found anywhere. His point was not that urbanisation is already everywhere. Presumably analytically this is not an impossibility, but as Lefebvre's famously useless diagramming (just one straight line) of the 'complete urbanisation of society' from 1 to 100 indicates, 'society' globally was understood to be somewhere along that continuum. Urbanisation coexists on the planet with many other processes, some of which, like agrarian economies, could be said to be associated with 'rural' places (Krause 2013; see Balakrishnan (2019) on agrarian urbanisation), and Lefebvre explores the dynamic interactions across these processes in detail in his longer texts, such as the *Production of Space*. The advocates of planetary urbanisation might have been clearer about this in the first place, and perhaps were motivated by their aim to sketch an impressive contrast with a 'city' perspective.

Ruddick et al's (2018) concerns are crucial to the formation of any new theories of the urban – all aspects of practice and experience, in 'everyday life' in and across (and beyond) the terrains of urbanisation are relevant to how the urban might be understood. This point is central to the work of both planetary urbanists (and Lefebvre) and their feminist critics. But this needs to go along with the post-colonial insistence that whatever is in the urban is urban. Thus, any urban or urbanising context provides a foundation for theorising the urban.

If the fullness of urban life should be the basis for theorising the urban, the criticism has been levied that planetary urbanisation advocates have resorted to universalising or totalising language, reducing the rich complexity of the urban to a limited analytical focus prioritising only certain processes. This leaves a theorisation which does not attend to the rich diversity of situated and embodied experiences of urban life. Feminist, indigenous and southern perspectives are strongly at odds with such an approach (Buckley and

Strauss 2016; Leitner and Shephard 2016; Peake 2016; Ruddick et al. 2018). Goonewardena (2018) provides a response to this critique noting the closely shared agendas of the planetary urbanisation authors with feminists (both influenced by Lefebvre) eager to think through the 'everyday' and politicised urban practices. He notes that the idea of 'totality' in Lefebvre (and Marxist-feminist theorists) indicates an open analytical formation precisely seeking to think across the rich diversity of social experiences. In this spirit the ongoing project of theorisation of (planetary) urbanisation could more fully embrace the differentiated outcomes of urbanisation, and more directly support building insights from the fullness of everyday life and diverse social processes. The inexhaustible empirical reality, or 'concrete totality', which is urban space is crucial to grounding such an endeavour.

It is this rich fullness and diversity of the urban which led Brenner and Schmid (2015) to propose a broadly nominalist approach to theory building, which accommodates new terms and emergent conceptualisations. On this basis they look to find common ground with post-colonial writers:

> we endorse a nominalist approach that permits an open-ended interplay between critique (of inherited traditions of urban theory and contemporary urban ideologies), epistemological experimentation (leading to the elaboration of new concepts and methods) and concrete research (on specific contexts, struggles and transformations). It is thus in a spirit of comradely dialogue that we offer below our own set of critical reflections on the possible foundations for a new epistemology of the urban under 21st century conditions.
>
> (Brenner and Schmid 2015, p. 161)

However, postcolonial critics insist that coming to know the urban cannot rest on the insights of unspecified, unmarked and unlocated theorists. The labour of knowledge production which would yield revisable analyses of the urban is critically associated with positionality – to write as a white (northern) scholar, for example, is to produce knowledge which is inevitably marked and situated (Ruddick et al. 2018). Opening to different subjects of urban theory (Parnell and Pieterse 2016; Roy 2011b), and the broad insistence on writing the urban differently from different places and subject positions, is crucial to global urban studies. This resonates well with the intentions of Brenner and Schmid's Thesis 7, in which the 'urban as a collective project' is an open determination, shaped by a multiplicity of struggles, across different contexts and political subjects (2015, pp. 176–7). But this political instinct, their critics rightly argue, needs to stretch to the articulation of the production of knowledge too, in which authorial reach and ambition might be curtailed by acknowledging the veracity of claims, often disjunctive in relation to wider theories, made by theorists and scholars writing on different urban processes and from different contexts and positionalities (Buckley and Strauss 2016; Robinson 2014b). Who is the subject of urban theory matters, as we will explore in Chapter 7.

Those exploring the concept of planetary urbanisation, and their critics, give a strong steer on the terms on which global urban studies might be taken forward through a comparative imagination. Key elements of comparative urban practice are signposted: the urban is a conceptual determination, and revisable in relation to different urban outcomes and changing historical processes; the geographies of urbanisation which might form the starting points for comparative reflection are widely dispersed and fragmented, rather than territorially confined; and the urban is a spatial formation, a site of a rich complexity of social life and (the production of) difference. Critiques of ambitious theorisations and universalising or reductionist analyses indicate that diversifying the subjects of urban theorisation and exploring more modest, even discrepant, conceptualisations across different urban contexts is an important project for urban studies. This should set the tone for a comparative urban imagination. This last set of concerns, with the subjects of theory and the style of theorisation, is at the core of the third debate which we review next, framed through decolonial, developmental and materialities approaches in urban studies. How might the urban be conceptualised in relation to diverse and divergent urban experiences, on the terms of scholars and urban residents who live and work in different contexts? Does a focus on emergent materialities of the urban necessarily foreshorten the active role of researchers in conceptualisation? On what grounds might it be assumed that the urban can be known at all? And, do decolonial critiques entail a refusal of wider conversations about the global urban?

Decolonial, Developmental, Emergent: Different Starting Points, or Incomparability?

Ambitious theorisations of the urban contrast with positions that draw on decolonial, developmental and 'assemblage' thinking to search for different ways of approaching the urban. For some, it is in the materiality of urban life, in the many configurations of things, bodies, movements, practices and imaginations, that the multiplicity of the urban is made evident. Thinking the urban takes place in the midst of the artefacts, infrastructures, material objects and practices which are generative of the multiplicity of potential outcomes of whatever the urban might be. Rather than seeing urbanisation as broad socio-spatial 'processes' which are extended across and shape dispersed urban territories, inspired by Bruno Latour, Manuel De Landa, and the broader Science and Technology Studies these urban scholars zoom in on the discrepant and varied elements which create emergent 'assemblages' (McFarlane 2011b). These are seen as shifting, perhaps at times precarious, configurations which constitute the fabric and practice of urban life. Importantly for the concerns of comparative urbanism, materialities approaches also highlight and invite us to track the routes and trajectories by which entities and 'black box' assemblages come into being (Jacobs 2006; Latour 2007).

Urbanists working in this vein have been drawn to a perspective on the urban almost diametrically opposed to that of the political economy approaches which inform Planetary Urbanisation. Amin and Thrift pointedly resurrect the term 'city' and stress the small territorial extent of cities ('just two percent of the earth's surface'), even as they subtend so much of the global economy. For them, it is the distinctive density and heterogeneity of the materiality of infrastructure which is central for understanding urban life: '(u)ncovered, the urban infrastructure turns out to be not only as active as any community or institution, but also the medium through which much of the latter is orchestrated.' (Amin 2014, p. 156). It is the agency of 'materials themselves' which Mcfarlane wishes to bring into closer view, and the force of emergent human-non-human alignments. Through the idea of a gathering 'cosmopolitics' he sees that this 'has the potential implication of generating new urban knowledges, collectives and ontologies' (2011b, p. 221). For Amin and Thrift (2016, pp. 26–7), this leads to an 'alternative science of the city', nudging

> actors reliant on panopticon vision to concede to multiple methods, partial insights and hybrids of human and non-human intelligence, to settle for an open 'science' of urban knowing, to question canons of thought that pretend access to the hidden depths of the city. Thus, knowledge is necessarily situational, incomplete, conjectural.
> (Amin and Thrift 2016, p. 31)

The insights of these writers have been considerable in reframing approaches to urban life, and we return to them throughout the book. However, a studious absence of attention to the researcher as a subject of knowing in materialities approaches can sometimes seem to imply that the materiality of a city can be understood transparently – if only ever partially – by an observer. The city makes itself known, somehow, to observers and participants. Ignacio Farías (2010) suggests that the use of Actor Network Theory in urban studies has been somewhat empiricist and post-hoc. The question as to how new kinds of concepts of the urban emerge, from where, on whose terms, in whose voice – including, for example, the suggestion to 'see like a city' – has been less clearly articulated by advocates of this approach. This is partly a result of the efforts to approach more closely the agency of the materiality of urban life, and its emergent formations, and to put into question the value of overarching theoretical propositions (McFarlane 2011b). Within this perspective, McFarlane (2019) proposes the 'fragment' as one starting point for a more active process of recomposing understandings of the urban, in which researchers are drawn to follow certain phenomena, but with a view to a more modest scope for understanding. On this basis, he is looking for:

> An urban studies … without a consensus on what urbanism is, or on what urban politics is, or on what urban space is – an urban studies, in short, inherently open, experimental and generative around the very question of *'what is'*.
>
> (McFarlane 2019, p. 225)

The 'lure' of the fragment proposes then one way for thinking about how new knowledge of the city might be articulated by researchers in the midst of 'assemblages'. But these commentators are more discreet on the wider questions of the subjectivity of the researcher and their agency in composing and articulating concepts. On what grounds might existing concepts be mobilised, new concepts invented? Who might be proposing them, and are they only ever relevant to the specific, emergent formations in which they might be generated? If concepts are formulated in these initiatives, what might be their 'reach' (Lancione and McFarlane 2016)? More generally, the prolific circulations in which the elements of urban assemblages are entailed, suggests that understandings of the urban cannot be assumed to take the shape of a tight territoriality, as foregrounded by Amin and Thrift. Tracing the flows of policy and matter which make up urban life potentially distend the grounds and reach of conceptualisation too (Cairns and Jacobs 2014; McCann 2011).

At stake in materialities approaches and criticisms of them are two key questions for comparative urbanism. Firstly, do concepts of the urban which might be proposed have reach beyond the specific situation? And secondly, how might the subject-researcher be understood as part of the creative practices of 'learning the city' (McFarlane 2010)? Both of these issues are also raised in decolonial critiques of urban studies. Seeking to actively refuse, decentre or displace rather than simply nuance or transform inherited understandings, decolonial critiques hope to go further than post-colonial analyses in searching for active grounds for new intellectual practice. And whereas in materialities approaches the subject as researcher seems to be displaced by emergent and dissonant urban materialities, in decolonial critiques the question of who is coming to know the (global) urban is firmly in view. The subject of decolonial theorising is profoundly in question, looking beyond the critiques of researcher subjectivity implied by 'intersectionality' or postcolonial ambivalence (Hill

Collins 2019). Coming to know the urban is the undertaking of subjects whose locatedness in place and positionality within historically unjust social relations matters. Drawing on experiences of subjectivity forged in the brutalising histories of colonial, slave and violent urban histories, the call is for a thorough reversioning of the grounds of knowledge. Here black studies and indigenous studies scholars have made powerful contributions. Fred Moten (2018) looks to draw towards an 'out' of the 'outside' – grounds for thinking subjects, their ways of engaging with and coming to know the world, as well as the imagined nature and forms of worldliness which look to step aside from, to operate outside of, to refuse, inherited formulations (McKittrick 2021). All these aspects of producing knowledge need to be re-imagined, drawing on resources beyond the traditions of western philosophy. Thus, from an African perspective experiences of fracturing or doubled interiorities and openings to connected but non-integrating conceptualisations potentially inform new practices and discourses of method and philosophy (Mbembe 2017) – and ways of coming to know the urban.

The trajectories of urban scholarship, as well as its grounds and territories, after decolonial critiques, open onto dissonant and potentially divergent analyses. On what basis might discrepant urban experiences be seen as incomparable? In a considered return to the first/third world division which haunted the field of urban studies for so long (Robinson 2006), some writers suggest that developmental challenges, poverty, resource limitations and the implications for daily life significantly limit the value of extant scholarly concepts and insights (Pieterse et al. 2018). The landscape of global urban studies which developmentalism opens up, driven by the exigencies of intervention and engagement, is perhaps understandably restricted, focussing on cities with similar challenges and configurations. But seeking solutions to the challenges of poorer cities can also involve the prolific circulations entailed in 'best practice', or require the accumulation of data at a vast scale to grasp the 'global urban' in terms of its impacts at an aggregate level (Parnell and Robinson 2017). On the other hand, much engaged development practice and research takes a 'slow' form of place-based learning (Bhan 2019). Focussing on developmental agendas on a case by case basis or trying to synchronise with international development institutions' hegemonic policy agendas runs the risk of limiting learning from academic urban scholarship. For example, focussing on strengthening hierarchical forms of government as opposed to thinking across the promiscuous circulations of investment flows, design ideas, professional practice, and economic informality which compose many urban areas. Tracing these connections might bring quite different comparators into view, and open unexpected or experimental comparisons across divergent urban realities to yield surprising insights (Myers 2014; Simone 2010). Part Two of this book considers this in some detail.

Writers drawing across developmental, decolonial and materialities approaches are also at times ambitious for conceptualisations which might travel. Simone and Pieterse, in their volume, subtitled, 'Inhabiting Dissonant Times' seek to work across both developmental concerns, and the distinctive emergences of material and human capacities:

> we have attempted again to tell other stories – stories that provoke the capacity to keep on going, but knowing that providing viable homes and platforms of operation are still critical. The intricacies of everyday life can be part of the story of structural change and urban governance, just as the details of administration and finance are part of the fabric of everyday life. In this sense the book is a polemical call to abandon the disciplinary and thematic stories that weigh urban studies down, leaving it unable to contemplate the imbricated nature of emergent urbanisms.
> (Simone and Pieterse 2017, pp. 196–7)

Here, the telling of many different stories which are produced in and through urban worlds becomes method, theory and diagnosis. The urban, then, is the site where, for example, 'Lives are constantly reassociated and redistributed in shifting networks of affiliations and experiences', where 'the capacity resiliently to become many different things has become standard operating procedure' (p. 69). In concluding their book, Wirth's theorisation of the urban as density, heterogeneity and size is recast in a new register of conceptualisation:

> Divergences will have to be part of the same story, a density of stories, and, even though urbanization may no longer rely on density as its defining trope, density – of the relationships among all things – is the only urban future.
> (Simone and Pieterse 2017, p. 198)

If urban studies requires multiple, dissonant, divergent and emergent forms of conceptualisation, is a wider conversation about the urban doomed? It is worth noting that even as Simone and Pieterse's 'dissonant' narratives draw attention to the multiplicity of stories and divergent forms of the urban, this turns (in a kind of topological transformation) into a *re-conceptualisation of the urban as multiplicity, as density of stories and relationships*. The question as to on what basis such wider accounts can be proposed from particular observations remains. Particular urban contexts could be seen as the sites and stakes of political subjectification and claims without necessary reference to any overarching processes of urbanisation (Davidson and Iveson 2015b). And the analyses and insights of marginalised urban populations, hard-won in the face of dominant knowledges, might not be intended for wider dissemination (Jazeel 2019). Does this mean that understandings of located, specific urban experiences are incommensurable? If it is possible to consider distinctive, emergent and multiple urban experiences in relation to one another, how might such conversations be composed? In this vein, some writers seek to promote new kinds of ambitious theorisation from different starting points, such as 'worlding' histories of Asia to de-imperialise knowledge (Chen 2010), or recasting global connections as relations of equivalence (Glissant 1997). For some, building new insights on the urban from the specific histories of previously exceptionalised contexts is an important response (Wu 2020). For others, even though ideas may originate in one context, in the wake of their internationalisation and circulation they might subsequently be seen as already present, belonging to, and operative in, a different context (Robinson 2006). Thus, writers might be determined to name theoretical resources, whatever their 'origins', as already localised and generative of ambitious decolonial projects, such as in dependency theory or Latin American Marxisms (Vainer 2014).

Glissant insists that tracing relations between places proposes 'a form of comparison reliant on equality with and respect for the Other as different from oneself' (Myers 2020, p. 26), operating in the service of 'degeneralisation'. The theorist who looks across the related world with curiosity (perhaps in the tracks of Franz Fanon) might also be drawn by the anti-colonial comparison (the shared predicaments of the colonised), the post-colonial ambition (the connected struggles of the anti-colonial modernising nationalists), or the insistence on decolonising urban studies, where scholars from many different ex-centric contexts find shared themes and collective voice (Kipfer 2022). As openings to forge analytical connections from distinctive contexts proliferate – Worlding Africa (Simone 2001a; Mbembe 2017), Asia as method (Chen 2010), new subjects of theory (Roy 2011b; Simone and Pieterse 2017), learning networks across marginal communities (McFarlane 2011a; Patel et al. 2012), internationalist politics (Kipfer 2022) – they both puncture hegemonic universals (Lowe 2015) and generate emergent concepts. Even as the pressing challenges of urban life demand action in specific contexts, urban scholars and practitioners might often be drawn to find inspiration from experiences, struggles and responses forged elsewhere.

Decolonial, developmental and dissonant approaches to urban studies articulate and call for different grounds, practices and forms of knowing. But the place of wider conceptualisations in these initiatives remains unclear. Key questions for urban studies are posed here, and in them the potential for comparative urbanism finds both inspiration and some (dis)orientation. It is (only) on the terrain of emergent materialities and through the agency of fractured subjects that the urban can be known. And the terms on which (differently located) subjects might come to know the urban, as well as inherited Eurocentric assumptions about the nature of the knowing subject, are also very much in question. The approaches reviewed in this section also identify crucial aspects of the spatiality of the urban, notably its emergent and material form, with implications for how comparisons might be framed. Together with the other two debates reviewed above, these approaches present key contours of the nature of the urban that will inform our search for new co-ordinates of comparative urbanism, as both theory and method.

Dimensions of a Comparative Urban Imagination

Reviewing key issues involved in coming to know the urban from different theoretical perspectives has identified a number of challenges which face urban studies. How might global urban studies proceed, methodologically and conceptually, to think across a great diversity of urban contexts, and from a multiplicity of positionalities? How might a conversation about the urban be sustained when the starting points for thinking the urban, or tracing urbanisation processes might potentially be anywhere on the planet, including the expanding peripheries, edges and extended urbanisation processes? What kind of theoretical and methodological approaches would not foreclose on a deep awareness of the incapacity of theory or concepts to exhaust the fullness of the urban world, or to find their limits in dissonant urbanisms (Simone and Pieterse 2017)? How might urbanists anywhere proceed in engagement with different, often overlooked, intellectual resources from other urban contexts which might have something to contribute to understanding the urbanisation processes and urban territories they are concerned with? Might scholars work productively with existing theories while keeping conceptualisation open to inspiration from any city? What kind of theoretical practice might be commensurate with the revisability of concepts, divergent realities and different positionalities which any account of the urban entails?

With the range of approaches to global urban studies we have explored in this chapter, why consider cultivating a comparative imagination as a way forward? What can comparativism contribute to ways of knowing the global urban? This book takes inspiration from comparativism's openness to conceptual revision, and its willingness, in principle, to seek to understand and reflect on diverse experiences in different contexts – to think with elsewhere. But inspired by the spatialities of urbanisation, some of which we have explored in this chapter, it develops methodological and philosophical grounds for a new repertoire of comparative methods open to the distinctive potential which the urban presents for 'thinking with elsewhere'. Inspired by post-colonial critiques, comparative urbanism mobilises the possibility to draw insights from a wide array of contexts while acknowledging the starting point of all theoretical endeavour as always (somew)here. The inevitable locatedness of the subjects of urban theory can be viewed not so much as a constraint as an opening. New concepts might be initiated from anywhere, and inherited conversations about the nature of the urban refined or refused. In a comparative urban imagination new conceptualisations might be crafted in relation to discrepant, emergent and associational urbanisms imbricated in the materialities and the fullness of urban territories, and in the lived experiences of urban 'everyday life'. These concepts may or may not seek to reach beyond the contexts in which they are embedded, and the subjects enacting and articulating insights may or may not choose to initiate wider conversations. In this sense, positionality matters as much as location, and with feminist, postcolonial and black studies critiques comparative urbanism places the subject of theorising centre-stage.

Each of the debates we have reviewed above establishes some contours for a comparative urban imagination. Together they suggest the dimensions of a new methodological map for urban studies. Drawing on these different debates – and we will need to mobilise aspects of all the perspectives we have encountered here – a comparative imagination for global urban studies can compose new ways of coming to know the urban. And as we proceed through the book it will become evident that comparison not only offers a method for coming to know the urban, it exposes and elaborates the nature of the urban, as an emergent, (im)possible object of analysis.

In reformatting comparison as method, then, the urban also comes into (theoretical) view. Across the different perspectives discussed in this first chapter, a shared framing of the urban world has emerged, which evokes its complexity and multi-dimensionality. With the scholars reviewed here, we can see the urban as produced through the prolific interconnections and inter-relations of a globalised world, while the outcomes of these flows vary and can be strongly territorialised – the form of the urban is, then, **differentiated**, produced by circulating processes across many, even divergent, urban contexts. We are also inspired to consider the urban as **diverse**. If specifically 'urban' processes can be identified, perhaps associated with spatial arrangements, land use, the emergent and associational form of urban life, for example, these are different in different contexts, not least as they are shaped by historical trajectories of urbanisation. And the many social, economic and institutional dynamics which contribute to shaping urban outcomes are diverse and potentially divergent across the globe. Thinking about urban experiences must therefore confront but also find ways to work creatively with this diversity of both outcome and process. There are many shared features of urbanisation processes and urban outcomes which could bring diverse urban experiences into potential analytical engagement. For a comparative imagination, this opens up many creative tactics for researchers to explore the urban world. Finally, all the urban thinkers we have considered here have highlighted that the fullness and inexhaustibility of urban space forms the grounds on which they seek to craft their insights. As a complex, spatial object, with multiple determinations, emergent formations, and unforeseeable assemblages, the urban is always **distinctive**. Every urban outcome is individual. Here, we will locate the potential for thinking the urban anew, each time, launching insights from anywhere, any urban territory, in the midst of the urban world. A reformatted comparative urban imagination, then, might contribute to provoking new geographies of theorising the urban along the tracks of interconnections, across diversity and shared experiences, and in the midst of urban territories.

Theoretical innovation in understanding the urban can therefore arise through tracing the genesis of emergent urban forms, practices and imaginations in the prolific interconnections that make up whatever the urban might become. Whatever the urban might be is emergent from a multiplicity of interconnected circuits, and from the many territories in and across which distinctive forms of urbanisation unfold. The territorial (urban) outcomes of urbanisation are diverse, if often characterised by repeated elements, formed in the eddies of extensive 'social processes' and dispersed according to historic distributions of land-use, opportunities for value creation and extraction, as well as the lived realities of social and economic practices. To think the urban, then, is to be willing to trace the genesis of distinctive territorial outcomes emergent in and through an interconnected sets of socio-economic flows and relation. But it is also to be immersed in the situated, inexhaustible socio-material configurations of urban life. Forging comparative imaginations and methods adequate to this task is the challenge of this book!

By the time we reach the end of the book, then, we will have considered in detail many different ways in which urban scholars have sought to work with differentiation, diversity and distinctiveness. We will delve in some detail into different formulations for how concepts emerge across difference and in relation to the resistances and generativity of the urban world. Different approaches in urban studies grapple with the form in which the urban must necessarily come to be known. For Lefebvre (2003) the urban is quintessentially a space of assemblage, a concrete totality which realises emergent socio-spatial formations. For Massey, it is the sum of a multiplicity of trajectories which composes the open political possibilities of space. And in a Deleuzian imaginary, the very form and concept of space itself, as depth and different(c)iation, is emergent in the intertwined genesis of the material world and ideas (Dewsbury and Thrift 2005). As we saw in a 'materialities' register, inflected with the emphasis on emergent assemblages and associations, the multiplicity of possible urban outcomes are composed in the everyday articulations of materialities, things, bodies, the infrastructure of words, the composition of publics, and the arcs of connection which are traced through imagination and through the physical trajectories of the many journeys made, for example, to put together potentialities for livelihoods (Simone 2010). The multiplicity of the urban is an outcome of lived reality, of the many ways in which urban dwellers, or urban scholars, piece together the city (Ferrari 2013). Crafting an analytics of the urban therefore opens to a multiplicity of outcomes, experiences, surfaces and spatialities. Given all this, conceptualisations of the urban will themselves constitute a multiplicity. Building more globally relevant understandings of the urban will require (discrepant) conversations about urbanity amongst many different subjects of theorising across the diversity of twenty-first century cities, a multiplicity of urban experiences, and a wide range of global urban histories.

Conclusion

Sprawling, fragmented, discontinuous and globalised, as well as emergent, precarious and material, the urban requires new and multiple vocabularies; but it also requires new and agile geographies and practices of conceptualisation. Understanding urbanisation means working with the dynamic, globalising circuits which are materialising urban territories in configurations that diverge from centred norms of discrete urban form. Thinking the urban globally therefore cuts across tendencies to segment the field of urban studies on any a priori grounds. While strongly valuing insights from different urban experiences, urban studies also needs to sidestep inherited conceptual divisions and fragmentations in favour of being alert to emergent and unexpected analytical alignments across the urban world.

The central aim of this book is to contribute to a comparative imagination specifically relevant to understanding urban processes, which can be put to work to build new interpretations of the urban, in alliance with urban dwellers, through rigorous analysis and committed engagements. Starting from anywhere, a comparative approach to the problem of understanding the urban world inspires the generation of concepts in conversation with the array of related and distant analytical insights to hand and in engagement with the dynamic and emergent urban world. Generating concepts creates new insights which are in turn available for launching into wider conversations and shared practices of interrogating the urban elsewhere, where they may (or may not) find purchase.

The rest of this book presents comparativism as one possible response to questions which as we have seen in this chapter are shared across different approaches in urban studies. The book will argue that a comparative imagination is an intrinsic part of coming to know the global urban world, whatever theoretical perspective you might adopt. However, Chapters 2 and 3 explore how the inheritance of comparative method and practice in urban studies is somewhat mixed in relation to its ability to respond to the debates and demands of global urban studies. Formal methodological guidance has tended to truncate the scope for comparison of different cities. But in their vernacular practice comparative urbanists developed some helpful pragmatic ways to work across diverse urban outcomes. After considering these in turn in Chapters 2 and 3, Chapter 4 then establishes how, in the light of these traditions, comparativism might be reformatted to respond to the specific challenges of contemporary global urban studies. In the rest of this first part of the book, then, we trace the lineages of comparative urban research, and explore some resources for reframing the philosophical basis and methodological assumptions of comparative urban practice, to better fit it for global urban studies.

CHAPTER 2

The Limits of Comparative Methodologies in Urban Studies

As urbanists have grappled with the problematic of the global urban, it has become clear that 'cities' exist in a world of other 'cities'. Or, we could say that the urban only exists as a diversity of specific territories and processes. Either way, the urban is a conceptual and empirical multiplicity. This means that any attempt at a general or conceptual statement about the urban either depends upon or quickly invites comparative reflection. The budding theorist finds herself asking of the many studies she reads from different parts of the world: 'are these processes the same in the urban contexts I know? Are they perhaps similar but for different reasons? Or are the issues being considered of limited relevance to pressing issues in the contexts I am familiar with?' And yet, as this chapter will demonstrate, in the formal application of this comparative gesture at the heart of urban studies the urban world has been analytically truncated. This has meant that the experiences of many urban contexts around the world have been ignored even as the broadest conclusions about contemporary urbanity are being drawn. This chapter will argue that revitalising the comparative gesture is an important requirement if comparative methods are to be put to work for global urban studies.[1]

This chapter seeks to understand, then, why it is that in an intrinsically comparative field with an urgent contemporary need for thinking across different urban experiences, urban studies for a long time had relatively little in the way of comparative research. Moreover, it will seek to explain why, when comparisons were undertaken, they were highly circumscribed in the range of cities attended to. I suggest that restrictions built into the conventions of formal comparative urban research actively created this situation. Reviewing existing strategies for comparing cities, the chapter considers the potential for comparative methods to overcome these constraints to meet growing demands for a global and post-colonial urban studies. I draw on the spatialities of the urban, which we might think of as both **differentiated** and interconnected;

Comparative Urbanism: Tactics for Global Urban Studies, First Edition. Jennifer Robinson.
© 2022 John Wiley & Sons Ltd. Published 2022 by John Wiley & Sons Ltd.

as **diverse**, yet with shared features apparent across different urban contexts; and as **distinctive**, such that urban outcomes are always emergent, individual formations. These spatialities of the urban suggest some initial lines for recasting the methodological foundations of comparative urban studies, particularly inherited assumptions about causality and what constitutes a unit of analysis. Chapter 3 then takes this further, exploring how despite these conventions urban researchers pragmatically worked around their constraints, to some extent tracking the complex spatialities of urbanisation.

Some Analytical Limits to the 'World' of Cities: Beyond Incommensurability

The scope of urban comparative research has been profoundly limited by certain longstanding assumptions embedded in urban theory; assumptions which propose the fundamental incommensurability of different kinds of cities. Reinforced by the strict methodological propositions of comparative research, these assumptions have functioned to restrict comparisons primarily to cities which are already assumed to share certain specified commonalities. Elsewhere I have suggested that the divided nature of urban studies today can be traced back to two theoretical manoeuvres (Robinson 2006). The first, and earliest, proposed a close association between (certain) cities and the experience of modernity. In 'advanced industrial', wealthier countries cities were seen as the privileged sites for the invention, propagation and cultural experience of modernity – the celebration and privileging of newness and the contemporary. Cities were cast by theorists from Georg Simmel to Louis Wirth and many contemporary writers as places where the old (folk, tradition and primitive) was cast off in favour of modernisation (such as de-individualisation, routinisation, monetisation) and its associated cultural practices (individuation, blasé attitudes and disenchantment). In the process, though, some cities were clearly left out of this forward momentum, most notably those cities in contexts (especially Africa) where tradition was thought to be an anachronistic but present reality. The other of the modern city was not simply 'back then' in the past, it was also 'over there' in places where 'the primitive' might well have moved to the city, but in the process rendered those cities distinctly un-modern places. Certain modern cities, then, have been counterposed with those considered not modern, or troubled by tradition, for at least a century of urban theorising, placing their relative incommensurability in a field of theoretical assumptions that are very deeply embedded.

The second theoretical manoeuvre which rendered some cities incomparable with others is the much later, but perhaps more devastatingly divisive movement of developmentalism. Since some of the earlier guises of developmentalism drew on theories of modernisation, accounts of urban modernity and development have reinforced one another – markers of the not-modern came to characterise an urban in need of development. In the initial accounts of modernisation theory, the (traditional) cultural practices which had been defined as both not urban and not modern by theorists such as Park and Wirth had to disappear if development was to occur. For urbanists the markers of being less developed, under-developed or developing cohered in urban form and structure: limited urban infrastructure, informal construction methods, lack of planning, lack of economic opportunity, informal economic activities, large population growth with limited economic growth, external dependency. On the one hand an important plea came from writers from the 'urban south' demanding that the distinctive features of cities there – such as their economic duality (Santos 1979) – be accorded a different and distinctive theorisation. Moreover, theories of underdevelopment insisted that the urban experience of poorer countries was intimately tied to the organisation of wealth and power in wealthy countries. However, and on the other hand, these progressive analyses, as with the modernisation theories before them, had the unfortunate consequence of initiating decades of urban research which assumed that the experiences of wealthy and poorer cities held little of relevance for one another (Robinson 2006).

The intertwining of modernity and development in urban theory established a landscape in which assumptions about the incommensurability of wealthier and poorer cities were taken for granted, and reproduced through separate literatures which found few grounds for careful and mutual comparative reflection. One line of connection persisted, though, since accounts of wealthier cities are often generalised as claims to universal knowledge about all cities. And although those writing on wealthier contexts seldom reflect on the experiences of poorer cities, there is a substantial implicit comparativism in the writings of scholars of poorer cities who frequently choose to/need to engage with these 'theories'. For example, in working creatively to understand the situations they are working in, to secure publication in international journals, or to authorise their research findings for a wider audience.

A minor voice within the field of urban studies has consistently urged a broader comparativism and critiqued the often narrow geographical foundations for theoretical deliberations. This has regularly been expressed by scholars working on poorer contexts, who feel that the cities they study deserve wider consideration in theoretical analysis (for example, Lawson and Klak 1993; Southall 1973; Ward 1993). This claim has important resonances with contemporary calls to post-colonialise knowledge production in the western academy (for example, Chakrabarty 2000; Connell 2007). It involves recognising the locatedness of much of what passes for universal theory and substantially extending the geographical and analytical scope of theorising; in urban studies this signals the need to terminate easy claims to theorising on the basis of the experiences of a small selection of wealthier urban contexts (see Mbembe and Nuttall 2004; Robinson 2002, 2006; Roy 2005; Simone 2004). In principle such a claim is easily supported – but in practice within urban studies it falls foul of assumptions regarding the incommensurability of different urban experiences which are deeply ingrained in the discipline, most notably in its assumptions regarding comparative methods.

There have, certainly, been moments in the history of urban studies when the call for comparative research across diverse urban contexts has been more widely expressed – and the present time is one of these (see for example, Davis 2005; Harris, A. 2008; McFarlane 2006; Nijman 2007a; Roy 2005; Ward 2008). A round of comparative work flowed during the 1940s–1960s from the coincidence of extended empirical testing of the social ecology paradigm, and notably of Louis Wirth's assessment of an 'urban way of life', and the rise of anthropological research on cities in poorer contexts as urbanisation proceeded in many parts of the world (Kuper 1965; Mitchell 1968; Pahl 1968; Schwirian 1974; Wirth 1964). The strong engagement between Weberian and Marxist analysts drawing on the comparative experiences of socialist and (western) capitalist contexts saw a flourishing of reflections on comparativism in the late 1970s and 1980s (for example, Harloe 1981; Pickvance 1986), and Castells' (1983). The City and the Grassroots stands as an exception during this period, testimony to the possibility of careful international comparative research. More generally, though, as we will see in the following section, in the wake of the developmentalism of the late 1960s until the recent round of more flexible comparative work inspired by studies of globalisation, formal comparative urban research came to be largely restricted to US-European comparisons. Instructively, John Walton concludes a 1981 review of comparative urban research with the following comment:

> In the short space of the last decade urban social science has undergone a revolution. Great strides are now being made in the elaboration of a new paradigm. Most of this work, however, is not really comparative and its geographical focus has been on the advanced countries of Europe and North America. Rehearsing the experiences of earlier advances, we are once again on the threshold of developments that will depend on full use of the comparative imagination.
>
> (Walton 1981, p. 34)

Generalising and building on the comparative gesture in urban studies depends, I will argue, on countering assumptions about the incommensurability of urban experiences across different contexts and building a case for a robust comparative methodology which can cope with the diversity of global urban experiences. The following section reviews inherited conventions of comparative research in urban studies, with a view to recasting comparativism in service of global urban studies.

Conventional Strategies for Comparison in Urban Studies

Incommensurability

A range of assumptions have subtended conventions in comparative methods in urban studies; Table 2.1 offers a summary of those which are most pertinent to this discussion. The first category shown on the table reminds us, though, that underpinning the relative dearth of comparative research was the often unarticulated assumption that no comparison is possible across cities which are seen as substantially differentiated by level of development, but also by cultural or policy context, economic system or political environment. The working assumption was that in many cases urban experiences vary too much across these criteria to warrant co-investigation. In formal terms this implies that there are few aspects of urban life held in common across these different contexts, and that the causal processes shaping cities are so very different that comparative analysis is unlikely to bear any fruit.

With growing assertions of convergence and connections across urban experiences in a globalised world, ranging from globalising formal or informal economic networks to transnational networks of design, policy, culture and governance (see for example Huyssen 2008; King 2004; Marcuse and van Kempen 2000; McFarlane 2006; Sassen 2002; Smith 2001), the argument that there are few commonalities to explore across certain kinds of cities would be hard to support as a blanket claim. In the light of these trends, at least, one ought to expect the assumption that comparison is not possible to require rigorous proof rather than being assumed that is, one might expect to have to demonstrate rather than simply assert a priori that there is nothing useful to be gained by comparing different urban contexts. The working assumption might then usefully be that, given an appropriate intellectual definition and scope for a comparative research project, cities from many different contexts might well be considered alongside one another. The second argument for incommensurability is that the reasons for urban outcomes diverge significantly across different contexts. This assumes that there is nothing important to be learned when the causal processes shaping cities and the wider political–economic systems in which they are embedded vary considerably. I'll return to consider this second argument quite explicitly, to join with Pickvance (1986) to argue against it, towards the end

TABLE 2.1 Comparative Methods In Urban Studies

	Comparative strategy/ basis for selection	Causality assumptions
Can't compare	None	Plural and incommensurable
Individualising	Implicit Any city Case studies not always comparative or theory-building	Historical and specific
Universalising	Most similar or most different	Search for a general rule (universal)
Encompassing	Involvement in common systemic processes; often assumption of convergence as basis for comparison	Universal but potentially differentiated processes of incorporation into and impact of system
Variation finding	Most similar; explain systematic variations within broadly similar contexts on basis of variables held constant or changing	Universal
	Most different	Either: search for universal causality across different contexts based on similar outcomes Or: Pluralist causalities (Pickvance 1986)

of this section. Simply put, though, the assumption that variation either in outcome or process across different categories of cities (developed/underdeveloped, (post)-socialist/capitalist, Asian/South American etc.) is so substantial and thorough-going as to render these urban contexts incommensurable is, I think, fundamentally misguided. The rest of the chapter will develop a counter-argument to this position in substantial detail. More generally, although they do not explicitly outlaw such comparisons, in practice extant urban comparative methods tend to reinforce these assumptions of incommensurability and the rest of this section considers these in turn.

Individualising

Following Charles Tilly's (1984) assessment of different approaches to comparative research; Neil Brenner's (2001) careful exposition and application of this to the urban scale; and drawing as well on the contributions of Lipjhart (1971) and Pickvance (1986), Table 2.1 sets out four further conventional comparative approaches within the social sciences and for urban studies more explicitly. Brenner (2001) usefully discusses in some detail examples of these various comparative approaches within urban studies. Perhaps the most common and rich method for comparison in the field of urban studies is that of 'individualising' comparison, or the detailed case study. Here one is seeking to explain the distinctive outcomes in one city (or more than one city) through implicit or explicit (usually qualitative) comparison with other cases which might confirm hypotheses concerning causal processes and outcomes generated in the specific case study.[2] Very often in urban studies, detailed, often historical, research on one city is brought into comparative relief through careful engagement with a wider literature, either in relation to generalised statements or theories, about urban experiences or in terms of specific other individual experiences which might throw light on the case study in question. The case study strategy, Lijphart (1971) suggests, has the potential to be relatively unproductive for social-science research unless it consciously involves theory-building but when it does he insists that it is an important part of a broader suite of comparative methodologies. In relation to urban studies, bringing the experiences of different case study cities into careful conversation with one another in order to reflect critically on extant theory, to raise questions about one city through attending to related dynamics in other contexts, or to point to limitations or omissions in existing accounts has been particularly productive.

An excellent example here is de Boeck and Plissart's (2004) *Kinshasa: Tales of the Invisible City* (anthropologist Filip de Boeck with photographer M-F. Plissart). A detailed and careful anthropological study of life in contemporary Kinshasa, this book engages neatly with wider urban theory concerning space, culture, urban form and the production of urban meaning. There is much to recommend in this study, not least the opening up of analytical perspectives which bring subjectivity and the collective production of urban meaning to the fore in assessing wider urban change. His work demonstrates very clearly the potential for broader theoretical learning and innovative, critical reflection across cities which might seem outwardly different – cities dominated by informality, for example, as opposed to those dominated by formal economies, extensive regulation and more fixed built environments – but whose respective experiences speak across theoretical issues such as how imagination, rumour, duality and agency shape city life and futures. It is exemplary of an individualising comparative methodology, not simply for studying cities in poor or crisis contexts, but for offering insights into the assessment and analysis of urbanity everywhere. In some ways, taking a close look at a city which is often (inappropriately) assumed to be a limit case of contemporary urbanism (Davis 2006) might fit into Lijphart's 'deviant' or 'hypothesis-generating' case study method, which he suggests can have 'great theoretical value' (p. 692). In some ways, then, assumptions of incommensurability have prevented urban scholars from benefiting more fully from one of the potentially most theoretically generative comparative research strategies.

An individualising approach also brings into focus some of the assumptions about causality which frame other kinds of comparative research, especially formal variation finding techniques. Detailed historical analysis of urban processes in particular cities exposes specific political or economic outcomes as frequently path-dependent and/or multiply determined (see Ragin (2005) and (2006) for a discussion of the importance of combined causal conditions in comparative methodologies more generally). Seeking variation in the relationships between a limited range of well-specified individual variables, as we will explore below when discussing variation-finding strategies, might occlude the deep historical roots of processes, suggesting they are the product of more recent events than they actually are. Abu-Lughod's (1999) historically informed critique of the dual city hypothesis which comes out of global city approaches, perhaps best exemplifies this insight. And insofar as cities are routinely sites of assemblage, and hence multiplicity, urban outcomes are often best characterised as emergent from multiple overlapping and intersecting processes and events (Massey 2005; Massey et al. 1999). Contextual explanations which see outcomes as the result of the specific assemblage of diverse processes and actions are an important part of understanding the causal processes at work in urban contexts. On this basis we can identify processes and phenomena common to different urban areas, albeit variously configured; or processes which stretch across more than one city leading us to attend to the connections and circulations through which cities already inhabit one other. The final section of this chapter explores the methodological consequences of these observations in more detail. For now, I will suggest that we note the potential to build from the careful methodologies of individualising comparative analyses towards a nuanced account of causality in urban comparative research informed by the complex spatialities of the urban. Such an account would potentially draw a wide range of urban contexts into the purview of any comparative project.

Encompassing

A second strategy which has been extremely important in the field of the urban for the last two to three decades is the 'encompassing' method (Tilly 1984), in which different cases are assumed to be part of overarching, systemic processes, such as capitalism or globalisation. In this case they can be analysed as instances or units, albeit systematically differentiated, within the broader system. An excellent exposition and extension of this approach is offered by McMichael (1990), under the title 'incorporating comparison', in relation to world systems theory – clearly of substantial relevance to urban studies given the recent prominence of world and global city approaches. The one disadvantage of the encompassing approach in relation to building a comparative approach for global urban studies is that it assumes the systemic differentiation of units – in this case cities – on the basis of categories identified within the particular encompassing analysis. For urban studies, this approach therefore reinscribes a priori divisions and hierarchies into the urban world which can militate against broader comparative ambitions. For example, in underdevelopment theory, capitalism is understood to produce both development and underdevelopment jointly across different contexts, making many locations important in the investigation of world capitalist development. However, individual contexts or units of analysis are seen as substantially differentiated, with intertwined but divergent outcomes. In this approach, while urban experiences in both developed and underdeveloped contexts speak to the analysis of capitalism and urbanisation under capitalist conditions, comparisons tend to retain an assumption of incommensurability across the differentiated cases or units of analysis. For example, Lubeck and Walton (1979) offer a discussion of the ways in which cities in developed and underdeveloped contexts are enmeshed in the wider world capitalist system, but then proceed to compare two examples of urbanisation under peripheral capitalism rather than drawing any direct comparisons between these cases and cities in developed country contexts. Together, then, differently placed cities illuminate the wider system and processes, but comparison across these different experiences has been limited, and in fact actively discouraged by the a priori assumption of systemic differentiation.

McMichael (1990) develops a sophisticated account of encompassing comparison through a critical engagement with world systems theory. Like Tilly, he is drawn to the potential which, focussing on interconnections amongst cases, offers for historically grounded comparative research. But looking to move on from both Tilly and world-systems theory, he observes that both assume the existence of the system within which units of analysis are located – such as a pre-given world-economy or, the global system of slavery.

Encompassing approaches thus tend to place the comparison outside of history, either within an abstract theoretical framework, or within a historical analysis that assumes in advance the nature of the 'whole' that governs the 'parts'. There is also a tendency to assume the existence of the individual cases in advance of the study. In contrast, McMichael very helpfully proposes that we pursue a comparative strategy which he terms 'incorporating comparison' in which both the individual instances ('parts') and the 'whole' are historically, and mutually, constituted:

> Rather than using 'encompassing comparison' – a strategy that *presumes* a 'whole' that governs its 'parts' – it progressively *constructs* a whole as a methodological procedure by giving context to historical phenomena. … The whole, therefore, does not exist independent of its parts. … *neither* whole *nor* parts are permanent categories or units of analysis.
> (McMichael 1990, p. 386)

Incorporating comparison opens up a wealth of potential comparative strategies for urban studies. Focussing on connections, following Tilly, suggests strong historical grounds for doing comparative work across a wide range of different contexts. Moreover, viewing systems as themselves emergent, historically forged and therefore entirely contingent opens the way for exploring an array of different kinds of connections, not pre-determined or privileged by theory. Social, economic and cultural flows of all kinds, with varying spatial extents thus become relevant foundations for useful comparison.

This analysis maps well onto a form of spatial thinking which is commonly referred to as 'relational' (Massey 2005), and which is crucial to any comparative urban analysis. The territorial spatial entities which often form the foundations for comparative analysis (nations, places, cities, bodies etc.) are understood to exist only through wider relationships or connections, and these are, in turn, generated and transformed by the territorial entities. In McMichael's approach spatially defined units of analysis, interconnected through various historical processes, and emergent wholes mutually shape one another and do not come into existence independently of each other. In Massey's (1994) terms, we would call this an open, or global, sense of place. The units of comparison shape, as much as they are shaped by the wider connections which, for some, add up to a global (economic, social, cultural) system.

The approach needs to be pressed further than McMichael is able to, though, at least partly because the assumption that units of comparison and their connections add up to a historically and analytically meaningful 'whole' cannot necessarily be sustained. The emergent form taken by the totality of individual territorially defined phenomena and the connections amongst them might sometimes form a coherent system for analysis (as global and world cities analysis postulates in relation to the economic processes shaping 'global' cities). But the prolific and uncertain associations created by various kinds of connections or flows and their diverse territorialisations and assemblages means that we also need to hold open the possibility of more fragmentary and limited relationships amongst individual cases, however these cases are defined: a 'system' or a 'whole' might not result from these interconnections. In addition, units of analysis can properly be thought of as historically contingent, certainly, but a spatial analysis would also encourage us to move away from a focus on specifically territorial units of comparison. The final section of this chapter, as well as much of the rest of the book, will explore further the potential for a distinctive urban comparative imagination which this 'spatial thinking' opens up.

An important potential of the encompassing methodology which Tilly observes (1984, pp. 126–7) is that it directs attention to networks and connections amongst different units within the broader system being considered. For example, the historical comparative research he was considering, transatlantic slavery, connects metropolitan and colonial contexts within the same historical moment. This has certainly been important for Global and World Cities (GAWC) approaches, which has offered considerable opportunities for assessing urban experiences across a wide range of 'globalising' cities. To realise the potential of this approach, though, we would need to move beyond the relatively narrow focus of GAWC on a restricted range of economic processes to encompass the rich variety of transnational processes and connections shaping contemporary urban life (Simone 2004; Smith 2001). This would expand the range of comparable cities even further, outside of the strict focus on the global economy (Robinson 2002). In addition, I would argue that it is very important to move beyond systemic incorporation or convergence assumptions as the grounds for comparison. In this case, only cities sharing the same global economic dynamics would be seen as eligible for comparative reflection. This substantially constrains the global comparative project (cf. Dick and Rimmer 1998; Sassen 2002). And we would clearly need to question the reinscription of hierarchy, categorisation and hence incommensurability within the analysis of the encompassing systems which such approaches are prone to. Once again this analytically segments and truncates the 'world' of cities considered eligible for comparative research (Taylor 2004).

More formal comparative methods (variation finding) might offer some possibilities here since in principle they do not need to select cities based on their place within any encompassing system or relevance to overarching a priori analytical categories in order to undertake a meaningful comparison.

However, as they are currently deployed variation-finding comparisons are extremely restrictive in the cases they select for comparison. In their own way they expect a measure of convergence for effective comparison, and rely on a priori categories to select suitable cases. There are therefore some very substantial constraints to their usefulness – as currently practiced – for advancing global urban studies; but, suitably transformed, they also hold out some real possibilities for re-grounding comparative methodologies for a new generation of urban theorising.

Variation-finding

Universalising comparative strategies (Category 3 in Table 2.1) usually seek out universal laws operative across large numbers of cases, and thus are commonly quantitative and statistical exercises; I'll return to these, albeit briefly, below. Variation finding strategies, however, can be applied easily with fewer case studies, using qualitative and historical methods. In Table 2.1 I've suggested two versions of this (following Pickvance 1986): the most prominent one used in comparative urban politics at the moment involves working with most similar cases; the other, seldom used, involves comparing most different cases. In my view, both of these strategies, but perhaps more especially the latter approach, hold considerable potential for a broader comparative project despite their respective limitations in terms of formal method and actual implementation.

The fundamental methodological challenge of qualitative variation finding is, according to Lijphart (1971), the difficulty of having few cases and many variables. The response which most researchers have made to this challenge has substantially reinforced the tendency in urban studies to only think comparatively across the experiences of relatively similar cities. It is assumed that working with relatively similar contexts means that one can more easily control the likely sources of variation. Researchers are therefore advised to select cases which are 'similar in a large number of important characteristics (variables) which one wants to treat as constants, but dissimilar as far as those variables are concerned which one wants to relate to each other' (Lijphart 1971, p. 687). The difficulty of isolating sufficiently similar cases exercises him, although one suggestion appeals – to consider political units within the same region (area), such as Latin America, since, he suggests, there are more likely to be similarities than amongst randomly selected countries (p. 689). Janet Abu-Lughod (1976) has also argued persuasively for the benefits of an embedded regional approach to comparative research for this reason. For urban scholars this methodology of variation finding amongst most similar cases has been widely used to compare US and European cities, most notably in debates around regime theory and governance (for example, Harding 1994; Kantor and Savitch 2005), but also other topics such as segregation and poverty (Wacquant 1995) and city building (Fainstein 1994).

An important feature of variation finding research is that it is strongly driven by existing theory in order to identify which case studies and which variables are appropriate to consider (Denters and Mossberger 2006). From the point of view of this book's concerns encouraging a more geographically wide-ranging comparativism within urban studies, this is a major embedded disadvantage with the variation-finding method. Drawing on existing knowledge, theory and observations, the method advocates generating hypotheses with well-defined dependent and independent variables. Case studies are then selected in such a way as to control for variations in other potential explanatory variables. For example, with independent variables like national policy contexts, forms of local–central political relations, history of economic growth or decline – all of which might explain urban outcomes such as the presence, absence or specific form of urban regimes – controlling for some of these variables (most notably level of economic development and political systems) has allowed researchers to consider what specific kinds of local political and economic circumstances might produce particular kinds of urban regimes (see DiGaetano and Strom (2003) for a useful review). There are two difficulties with this methodological procedure for promoting global urban studies.

The first concerns the direct relationship between existing theory and hypothesis formation. Much urban theory is fairly parochial, with often quite locally derived conclusions circulating as universal knowledge. As Pierre (2005, p. 447) observes, 'Most dominant theories in urban politics draw on – or more correctly, are abstractions of – political, economic, and social aspects of the American city'. This convention of proceeding by deductive reasoning therefore has some very disturbing consequences. It restricts the variables or topics to be considered to those relevant to the privileged locations of theory production: perhaps other places would make one think of exploring different issues? But since research in many contexts is not seen as contributing to the generation of theoretical knowledge (Connell 2007), so many urban phenomena and experiences must remain unexplored with this methodology. Furthermore, with the expectation of controlling for variation in key independent variables, the reliance on accounts of only certain contexts for generating hypotheses has the circular and self-reinforcing effect of limiting the range of appropriate cases which can therefore usefully be drawn on to test hypotheses: places where key variables diverge would conventionally be considered unsuitable candidates for comparison.

This, then, is the source of a second and significant methodological problem with variation-finding approaches, and concerns the formal process of isolating independent variables. Since cases are pre-selected on the basis of their suitability to test hypotheses, isolating the hypothesised causal variables in complex and dynamic cities has suggested to researchers the virtue of selecting for comparison urban contexts with many background features in common (Pierre 2005). Most frequently, nationally defined levels of economic development, or forms of national political systems are kept constant as variables which are assumed to be key determinants of urban outcomes, thus exposing variations in local political structure or business politics, for example, to investigation. Thus, relatively reductionist and economistic assumptions conventionally govern the selection of case studies. This has the distinct disadvantage of reinforcing (or at least not examining) the idea that levels of economic development determine urban outcomes (such as the consolidation or form of urban regimes or the role of business in growth coalitions), when in principle much urban theory might seek to move beyond such economic determinism. Opportunities to learn about these local dynamics in a range of different cities are pre-emptively foreclosed. Furthermore, these criteria for selection persist in defining causal variables at the scale of territorial units, usually national or local. At the very least, in the light of the discussion of encompassing comparison, this diverts attention from interconnections and globalising dynamics which might arguably be equally important in explaining local outcomes (Kantor and Savitch (2005) make this point). More significantly, we also need to question the relevance of national-level criteria to making local comparisons, and to interrogate the assumption that the territorial unit of the city is the appropriate entity for comparative urban research. The final section of the chapter explores this further.

In large countries with many cities, like the USA, this methodology has encouraged an inward looking but clearly very productive form of comparative analysis. However, even selected efforts to reach across the Atlantic to the politically and economically not too dissimilar countries of Europe have provoked concerns with 'concept stretching' and a dependence on overly 'abstract theorising' because of the many apparent differences between the two contexts (Denters and Mossberger 2006, p. 565). The conventional wisdom is that stretching one's hypotheses towards more abstract analyses will undermine the ability to frame specific testable hypotheses, and introduce too many features which vary across the contexts to enable the exercise of effective control over explanatory variables. Kantor and Savitch (2005) advocate restricting the theory used to meso-level concepts to support careful and rigorous comparative procedures. But Denters and Mossberger suggest that there is a trade-off to be made between rigorous comparison and more abstract theorising which, within limits, could enable one to extend the reach of comparison – a point which the following section will return to. For example, moving to higher levels of generalisation – from regime building to questions of governance, perhaps – could possibly illuminate aspects of urban politics which might otherwise remain unattended to. This would be especially useful for engaging with pressing aspects of twenty-first century urbanism, such as the possibility for governance in urban contexts characterised by substantial informality. In the context of reviewing the potential for applying US regime analysis to UK urban development politics, Alan Harding suggested that governance could be 'a key conceptual tool for comparative research into urban development' (1994, p. 369). Drawing on a wider range of urban contexts with a diversity of forms of governance – even more so than characterise the US–UK–European nexus – might well enrich rather than undermine processes of careful theory-building.

Driven by theory, then, and drawing loosely on a scientific model of causality, formal comparative urban politics has barely considered (and then only to summarily dismiss) the possibility of comparative research across wealthier and poorer contexts. Michael Harloe, writing in the throes of the debates over comparing capitalist and socialist contexts, observed, 'most writers seem to think that direct comparisons between advanced Western nations and emergent capitalist countries at a lower level of development are of little use' (1981, p. 185). His paper reflects helpfully on some of the challenges of pursuing 'East–West' comparisons, but does not return to the possibility of making comparisons across different capitalist contexts – across cities which have, after all, shared much through the vagaries of colonialism, neo-imperialism and cultural interactions!

Kantor and Savitch (2005), in a helpful intervention on how to extend comparative studies across a wider range of contexts still found it possible to assume that it is appropriate to confine their investigations to advanced liberal democracies since they share important characteristics as well as common interests in the global economy, as evidenced by their coalition as the G7 (p. 148). Compared to their rigorous arguments concerning comparative methodology, they clearly see no need to really justify this focus on only wealthier cities – their full given reason being that 'these cities share common political and economic environments' (p. 144), a criterion which then plays no part in their broader analysis. At the core of this thoughtful treatment, then, is a far-too-easy assumption that it is appropriate to restrict comparisons to broadly similar national contexts according to their relative wealth and forms of political systems.

In contrast, a most suggestive intervention by Pickvance (1986) presents a motivation for the value in comparing 'most different' cases. His reasons for this remain absolutely current, notably the suggestion that comparative research is important 'to become aware of diversity and overcome ethnocentricism' (p. 163). As he continues, 'Awareness of diversity produces a sort of culture shock. It makes one aware of new and unsuspected connections' (p. 163). Conventionally, most different cases might be compared where similar outcomes could draw one to investigate what common feature caused these, since so much else is different and therefore unlikely to explain the common outcome: another form of methodological control (Lijphart 1971). However, Pickvance points out the more radical possibility and potential in moving away from the assumption that the same causal processes are at work in the cases being compared. Instead, he argues for closer attention to assumptions of plural causality that is, that similar outcomes might have quite different causes. For him this spoke to some deep-seated disagreements between Marxists and Weberians concerning the production of housing classes in capitalist and socialist contexts. Differentiation in the housing market may well be the result of similar processes for example, bureaucratic administration (as Ray Pahl had been arguing). However, it might equally be the outcome of two different processes, each specific to the wider system (capitalist or socialist) in which housing was being produced: income-based class differentiation in capitalist cities, and bureaucratic and technological processes in socialist contexts (as Ivan Szelenyi had been proposing).

This latter, 'relativist' model of plural causality, Pickvance points out, is seldom considered by researchers, and has remained in the shadow of comparative research focussed on assumptions of universal causality (p. 179). He observes that 'the traditional caution in urban studies towards making comparisons of very different societies reflects the … tacit recognition of the problems with methods based on universal models of causation' (p. 179). So rather than assuming that there is a problem with comparing different cities per se, he is reminding us that there are some serious flaws in the conventional assumptions concerning comparative methodology (here, specifically around the assumption of universal causality) and that there is in fact much to be learned across seemingly very different urban contexts.

Pickvance suggests some very specific ways in which to recast the comparative project, presenting three examples of cross-national comparative research across diverse contexts, none of which depend on assumptions of convergence across the different urban experiences. Assumptions of universal causality, what he calls 'linked sub-models' and plural causality can all be helpful in undertaking intelligent and carefully constructed comparative research across cities (in his examples) in wealthier and poorer countries, industrialised and more mercantile (trade-based) economies, and capitalist and socialist contexts.

In the context of most different strategies of comparison, a glance in the direction of large-N statistical studies is instructive. As Denters and Mossberger (2006) observe, samples for statistical analysis can be constructed to maximise variance in specific variables, and random samples aim to incorporate as much variation as might be anticipated in the population at large. Such approaches typically deploy a range of tools to determine the explanatory value of an array of potential variables across sometimes widely varying cases. While there are certainly important caveats to statistical analysis of this kind (and Ragin's (2000, 2006) analysis of multiple causality is relevant here), it might well be viewed as opening certain kinds of research questions to investigation across cities which are otherwise seen as incommensurable.

Overall, then, and very hopefully for any contemporary ambitions for broadening comparativism in global urban studies, Pickvance (1986) reminds us that even in cases of substantial differences in urban outcomes and processes, 'awareness of diversity through comparative studies forces one to bring theoretical assumptions into the open' (p. 163). His engagement with the foundations of comparative reasoning gives us a very useful springboard to consider what a rigorous comparative methodology for investigating the urban world today might entail.

The Potential of Comparative Research

Reviewing the current state of comparativism in urban studies has suggested some promising ways to extend and reinforce the broader comparative gesture embedded in global urban studies. While conventional practices tend to constrain comparisons to very similar urban contexts, creative intellectual engagements across a wider range of different contexts might be enhanced by exploring issues at a more abstract level (Denton and Mossberger 2006) against a broad understanding that considering diverse urban experiences would challenge scholars to revisit extant theoretical assumptions (Pickvance 1986). In pursuing this agenda, though, some significant shifts in methodology also need to follow. For example, Pickvance (1986) suggests the need to relax assumptions of universal causality in comparative research in order to consider both similar and different causal explanations for urban outcomes. And, building on an encompassing approach which places a strong emphasis on historical connections between different contexts or cases (McMichael 1990; Tilly 1984), new, non-territorial foundations for drawing comparisons across different urban contexts come into view.

Drawing on these insights, this final section of the chapter considers two specific issues which need to be addressed if we are to build a revitalised urban comparativism, more adequate to the task of thinking the urban world. Firstly, I want to suggest that we need to recast our assumptions about the appropriate units of comparative research. And, secondly, I would like to propose that the practice and understanding of urban 'theory', as well as its role in framing comparative research, needs to be reconsidered. These are two issues which establish the wider agenda for reformatting comparison for global urban studies which the rest of the book takes forward. For comparativism to be proliferated and enabled as a method for learning about and from a wide range of different urban contexts, we need to consider some thoroughgoing re-formulations of the more limiting theoretical and methodological inheritances of comparative methods. These include: procedural assumptions based on a scientific model of analysis, such as controlling for pre-determined independent variables; the relatively reductionist causal assumptions (economic, political) on which the identification of appropriate case studies is premised; a territorialised imagination of what constitutes a case for investigation, especially the privileging of the city-scale as the site of urban processes; the use of national-level criteria to determine the comparability of cities; and dependence on relatively parochial theory-driven hypotheses to generate research topics and to select case studies.

Here and throughout this book I suggest that a spatial understanding of the urban can draw us towards alternative maps of causality, differently constituted cases for comparison and new ways of bringing different urban areas together within the field of vision which is comparative research. These lines of thinking are discussed briefly here, and set the agenda for the rest of the book.

Units of Comparison

Neither the national scale nor the territory of the city can remain as the taken-for-granted units of comparison in urban studies. Of course both are relevant, and for some comparative projects these units might be the most suitable for comparison, or be the most relevant criteria for selecting case studies. For example, it might be that one would want to test the hypothesis, silently assumed in most comparative research, that urban areas in wealthier and poorer national contexts vary markedly along most dimensions of analysis. One might want to investigate, rather than assume, then, whether relative resource levels substantially affect forms of governance in large metropolitan areas, for example, or whether poorly resourced cities have less autonomy or democracy in the determination of local policies. In much comparative research there is a lazy and economistic assumption that the relative wealth of a city's national context matters to a vast array of issues – one important agenda for urban studies would be to test these assumptions and put into question conventional practices of case selection in comparative research.

More generally, for some issues, the territory of the city might well be the relevant scale for analysis. If one were investigating local government activities (policies, interventions, politics, forms of governance) it would be sensible to use more or less clearly defined local government districts as the unit of comparison. Of course across different contexts the comparability of local government entities is notoriously difficult; metropolitan fragmentation vs unification; relative levels of autonomy vis-à-vis national government; and vastly different sets of responsibilities and financing all conspire to make these kinds of comparison immensely complicated. Finding the 'functional equivalents' of urban government in different parts of the world presents a substantial challenge (Pierre 2005, p. 457). But evidence suggests that nonetheless there are many occasions when research at this scale would be very valuable (Davidson and Iveson 2015b).

Similarly complicated, but equally valuable, is comparative research which takes the functional city-region as a whole as the basis for analysis. Understanding economic regions, wider city functioning, urban spatial forms, intra-metropolitan governance structures and many other topics benefit from research at this scale (for a recent example see Scott 2001). Once again, the territory in question – the unit of comparison – would need to be carefully specified in relation to the issue being discussed. Thus comparing large, internally differentiated and multi-nucleated cities at this scale – in both wealthier and poorer contexts – might illuminate the spatial dynamics of metropolitan economies in changing economic circumstances such as structural adjustment, liberalisation, economic crisis etc. (Rogerson and Rogerson 1999; Rodriquez-Pose et al. 2001). But the choice of this scale – or territory – for the unit of analysis would need to be carefully justified in relation to the particular study rather than assumed a priori as the basis for comparative thinking.

There are, however, many urban processes for which neither formal administrative boundaries nor functional city-regions would be the relevant scale for comparison. Instead, processes which exceed both administrative and functional areas – circulations and flows – as well as phenomena which exist and operate at a smaller scale than the city should be the relevant units for comparison. Pierre (2005, p. 457), for example, proposes that when researching local economic development as an example of urban regime behaviour, relevant units of analysis might be defined as individual development projects, or specific decision-making processes (Moulaert et al. 2003 provide good examples of this).

This manoeuvre opens up a vast potential for wide-ranging international comparisons. For many phenomena in cities are tied into connections and flows which stretch beyond the city's physical or territorial extent and which entrain other urban contexts into the dynamics of that city. In a further step, these connections themselves become the units of comparisons (Söderström 2014). Similarly, there are many aspects of urban areas which are reproduced serially across the globe or influenced by the same processes and actors – governance regimes, for sure, but also phenomena such as architecture and design, detailed technologies of management, policies and political programmes, for example. Such phenomena could be considered comparable in their own right across very different urban contexts and thus be the units of comparison. See for example Moulaert et al. (2003) who compare large scale urban development projects across several cities; Jacobs (2006) on high-rise residential buildings; McNeill (2009) on global architects; Dick and Rimmer 1998 on American-influenced suburban design across Southeast Asia; Newman and Thornley 2005 on the governance of world cities, Harris, A. 2008 on gentrification.

Urban areas therefore enmesh the project of comparativism in an array of spatialities which depart significantly from the territorial forms imagined in the conventions of comparativism. Certainly, the spatiality of city connections can ground possibilities for incorporating comparisons (McMichael 1990). More generally, as cities are already interconnected, different ends of the connections might be brought into stronger analytical and not simply empirical relation. In this way cities like Liverpool and Kuala Lumpur (Bunnell 2007), Rome and Dakar (Sinatti 2009) or Kinshasa and Paris (MacGaffey and Bazenguissa-Ganga 2000), become connected sites for exploring and comparing migrant experiences, the forging of local and national identities, the impact of migration on the built environment, the place of informality in economic circuits – and in fact the myriad connections which tie the histories and fortunes of different cities together.

It is not just the two ends of a connection which come into view, though; the connections themselves might well form the focus of comparison. The connection, then, becomes the case. One might consider how the connections forged by headquarters companies in Delhi or Hong Kong and New York with their various centres of production compare. Are different forms of economic globalisation at work across different regions? Do the kinds of connections and investments developed by South African capital across Africa bear comparison with those of the Chinese?[3] The flows which connect cities, then, are an important unit for comparing urban processes, not simply as influences on the outcomes in places, but as important phenomena in their own right.

Attending to circulations would draw many different combinations of cities into the same analytical or political space and the relationships of comparison invoked would be very different from those suggested by the formal, territorialising spatial imaginations of conventional comparativism. Of course, as Sassen's (2001) iconic account of the urban impact of economic globalisation reminds us, this space of circulation is not 'smooth': it will be punctuated by nodal points (perhaps institutional disseminators of knowledge, discourse and best practice), by the infrastructures which enable or keep ideas circulating, by places which might assume some co-ordinating function in relation to particular circuits (as with the specialised nodes for the management of global economic circuits in certain cities hypothesised by Sassen). But these are urban spatialities which invite quite new, creative ways for thinking across different cities, and a different range of cities.

Drawing cities into a new array of spatial configurations through the imagination of circulations slides easily into a sense that one needs to reach for spatial imaginations beyond the topographical (Allen 2003; Amin 2002). The ways in which cities inhabit one another has often less to do with those relationships which can be mapped in physical space – as flow, dispersion or location, for example – and more to do with the experiential and imaginative ways in which places are drawn together – or kept apart. Topological spatialities, according to John Allen, are a very suggestive way to make sense of contemporary globalisations, more so perhaps than the language of connections or circuits (Allen 2008). He draws on an analysis of how different forms of power operate across and through the configuration of space to explain how people and activities in distant places can be kept close (to certain projects or points of view, for example), or proximate phenomena pushed away. These depend on achieving action or influence at a distance or stimulating imaginative affiliations (Allen 2016). The spatiality of global economic management is less one of nodes and flows than one of the seductions of ideas or the sustainability of mutual understandings generated across distances. Topological spatialities might become a comparative analytic for assessing the ways in which cities already inhabit each other. As Simone (2004), De Boeck and Plissart (2004) and Malaquais (2007) demonstrate, the livelihood strategies and imaginative worlds of city residents in places like Doula and Kinshasa are entwined with elsewheres (like New York and Brussels) both practically and imaginatively – in the sense of residents being always in the process of preparing to leave for an imagined elsewhere, of already knowing much about other cities, or living an imaginative world which is both here and there. Within a topological imagination, making one's way in a city commonly entrains a wide diversity of other places; our understandings of those places would serve us better if they were able to do the same.

When the unit of comparison is not the city as such, and the criteria for determining comparability are not restricted to national scale characteristics or stereotypical features of a city, opportunities for pursuing comparative work proliferate. Delimiting the units of comparison in a more flexible and analytically rigorous way is only one step towards opening up comparative research. A second concerns the assumptions which guide research design and analysis. Here, we bring the understandings of causality which underpin conventional methodological guidance into conversation with urban spatiality.

The Nature of (Urban) Causality

In urban studies formal comparative methodologies often enact a quasi-scientific model of causal relationships and explanation. Variables are identified – some independent (causal) and some dependent (reflecting outcomes shaped by independent variables) – and it is assumed that relationships amongst these variables can be hypothesised using existing empirical and theoretical knowledge, and that empirical referents for these variables can be identified and specified precisely in order to be tested using data which is then gathered using robust reproducible methods of enquiry. While logical and apparently rigorous, and certainly productive of interesting and generative research, these procedures and assumptions can be limiting both in terms of the kinds of processes which can be investigated and in terms of the range of forms of causality which can be explored. Nijman (2007a, p. 5) comments that comparative urbanism needs to be reconciled with 'current theoretical developments in urban geography', and to adopt an approach that 'emphasizes understanding rather than law-like explanation.' Most significantly, perhaps, quasi-scientific understandings of causality draw our attention away from possibly the most important causal agent of urban processes, the space of the city itself. One approach to space is to think of it as a simultaneity of multiplicities or trajectories and thus historically and politically radically open to future possibilities (Massey 2005). Certainly, this resonates with the function of cities as assembling in particular places multiple social processes and phenomena (Lefebvre 2003). In this light, the causality most strongly associated with cities is that where, following Charles Ragin's (2006) formulation, in a particular context a combination of causally relevant conditions contribute to a particular outcome. More nuanced approaches to explanation are needed to address this distinctive feature of urban research.

Case study research on an individualising comparison basis offers one route to more flexible possibilities for explanation, but nonetheless such studies often implicitly reproduce the formal scientific strategies of comparison e.g. in the criteria used to justify selection of case studies, background similarities used to control for/focus attention on certain specific processes and outcomes, a search for directional causal relationships or, for more Marxist-influenced studies, deeper structural or analytically identified processes. Least likely to feel the need to conform to these requirements are detailed historical studies which attempt to understand the complex processes shaping a city or cities, and to place these in relation to knowledge and understanding drawn from a wider literature (see for example, Dennis 2008). Janet Abu-Lughod's (1999) analysis of Chicago, New York and Los Angeles, is an exceptional study where this detailed historically grounded methodology is deployed to directly compare more than one city along a range of issues (including economic development, social dynamics, governance structures). A nuanced assessment of the reasons for the distinctiveness of each context – as well as shared trajectories across the three cities – is drawn out of a rich historical account.

For some this approach to explaining urban experiences is problematic. Pierre (2005) valorises comparative research as a path to more scientific and less idiographic research in urban politics: 'Urban politics seems to have embraced complexity and richness in context at the expense of parsimony' (p. 449). He urges that comparison begin with a robust causal model (p. 456). Sassen similarly complains that appeals to the complexity of the urban experience undermine the possibility for analytical insights (2002). Nuanced, complex, and contextual accounts of urban processes are not necessarily unanalytical – just differently so from a more narrowly focussed, perhaps even reductionist form of explanation. They also create important opportunities to identify the causal effects of the city-as-assemblage. Politics, experience, imagination – these are messy, nuanced, complex phenomena routinely characterised by overdetermination and multi-causality, not to mention secrecy and unknown (unknowable) motivations. If one is writing about spectrality, invisibility and provisionality – features of informality which seldom leave lasting traces in the physical environment of the city – one would hope to have an array of maps of explanation and causality at one's disposal. This would draw one, for example, to engage with psychoanalytic accounts of subjective ambivalence and fragmentation, flat emergent ontologies of Deleuze and Guattari and indigenous accounts of doubleness and deception (see for example De Boeck and Plissart 2004; Mbembe and Nuttall 2004; Simone 2004).

Understandings of theory, causality and abstraction have been transformed since the instantiation of formal variation-finding comparative methods. Working creatively with the full, inexhaustible spatiality of urban will support openings for comparative urban imaginations to explore different models of explanation and causality, and to devise creative methodological responses to the problem of understanding the global urban.

Conclusion

A revitalised and experimental comparativism could enable urban studies to stretch its resources for theory-building across the urban world. But through this chapter we have seen there are some important challenges and caveats to this project. Janet Abu-Lughod, arguably urban studies' pre-eminent comparativist, cautioned against 'throwing "into the hopper" all cities at all times from all over to see which traits and isolated characteristics appear congruent or divergent' (1976, p. 21). Targetting an audience tempted to universalising statistical comparative research, her concern directs us to consider as exemplary her own detailed and responsible scholarly practices, building comparative analyses from long term and committed accounts of specific urban processes in the regions she studied – North Africa, and the United States. In the absence of such commitment the danger is that a comparative urbanism equal to engaging with a wider range of urban contexts simply invites a new round of imperialist appropriation of international urban experiences to service western-centred theoretical projects and shore up well-resourced centres of scholarship. It is also important to pause to recall the powers and histories of comparativism in general, particularly in relation to the wider geopolitics of knowledge. As Connell (2007) notes, 'Sociology displaced imperial power over the colonised into an abstract space of difference. The comparative method and grand ethnography deleted the actual practice of colonialism from the intellectual world built on the gains of empire' (Connell 2007, p. 16). Comparative urbanism would need to avoid such scopic reductionism, and be significantly more tentative and uncertain as it initiates and engages in conversations across different urban contexts. In the difficult processes of mutual learning, it could be that the challenges of translation and the inevitability of mis-readings frame the project of 'planetary' thinking which McFarlane (2006), following Spivak, has advocated. Such a sensibility has inspired this book.

An alternative danger rides on the practice in other disciplinary fields where comparativism has at times merely signified 'area studies' or 'third world studies' or 'political science focused on other national contexts than the American case' (Pierre 2005, p. 454; also Mufti 2005). If a widened comparative project simply re-codes the differentiation of the field of the urban, or performs a new round of exclusions of certain kinds of cities, it will not have achieved its call to attend to the 'world of cities'.

As Mufti (2005, p. 486) notes, it is important that 'nonrepressive and nonmanipulative forms of knowledge … would have to be more encompassing and more comparatist, not less, than scholarship has been in the recent past'.

If comparativism is to support global urban studies, it needs reformatting – a reset, to restart on new terms. This chapter has started to outline how a reinvigorated comparative urbanism could productively draw both inspiration and method from the nature of its object of study. The prolific interconnectedness of the urban could inform and proliferate conversations across different urban contexts, and also direct us to new units of comparison. The diversity and multiplicity of urban contexts might unsettle parochially derived theoretical certainties through bringing into view different aspects of urban life, and also indicate more nuanced forms of explanation and method appropriate to the complexity of cities. Global urban studies could, then, potentially draw more urban contexts into shared fields of analysis, characterised by multiple, frequently unsettled and hopefully unsettling conversations about the urban. This style of theorising would be neither a parochial universalism nor a uniform global analytical field but a rich and fragmented array of ongoing conversations across the urban world. Inspired by the many comparative experiments under way, and informed by a detailed examination of different approaches in urban studies, the rest of this book explores what kind of comparative urbanism that might be.

Most immediately, Chapter 4 considers some of the key methodological and conceptual conundrums which a reformatted urban comparativism must confront: what is the meaning of a case in relation to wider concepts? How can we think about concepts as revisable? But first, the next chapter dives into the archives of actually existing urban comparativism. Whereas the current chapter critically interrogated the conventional methodological prescriptions concerning comparing 'cities', Chapter 3 will explore what urban comparativists did in practice. Methodological conventions were invoked to present urban comparative studies as scientific and rigorous – but how did practitioners of the 'art' of urban comparison actually proceed?

Notes

1. This chapter is drawn from 'Cities in a World of Cities' (*International Journal of Urban and Regional Research*, 2011), with some corrections to achieve a consistent vocabulary across this book and some minor cuts.
2. Tilly expresses this as 'a purely individualising comparison treats each case as unique, taking up one instance at a time, and minimizing its common properties

with other instances' (1984, p. 81). Lijphart places the case study method, central to urban studies, as closely connected to comparative studies, and his range of potential case study strategies certainly overlaps with what Tilly here calls individualising comparison.
3. Schroeder (2008) explores the distinctive interactions of post-apartheid South African investors in Tanzania.

CHAPTER 3

Comparative Urbanism in the Archives: Thinking with Variety, Thinking with Connections

Having critically reviewed some of the limits inherent in methodological norms in comparative urban studies, this chapter turns to seek inspiration and guidance for reinventing comparison from the vernacular practices of comparison as actually applied and invented by urban scholars. By exploring what comparativists in urban studies have actually done by way of comparisons, we are able to assess the pragmatic conventions which have shaped the field – as opposed to the more formal methodological statements. Science and technology studies, inspired by anthropology and actor network theory, suggest approaching scientific method and philosophy through its practice, through what scientists actually do, in the laboratory for example. This can be significantly different from the formal expectations of method. Such is the situation in relation to comparative urbanism. The chapter rifles through the archives to draw together a number of different examples of how a comparative imagination was put to work in urban studies through the late twentieth century, in search of insights for global urban studies today.[1]

The chapter identifies a contradiction between methodological conventions and the practices of urban researchers. On the one hand, establishing the grounds for comparison is often rigorously presented as narrowing the range of variables to be considered through careful selection of most similar cases. However, on the other hand, theoretical insight has often been generated through a much looser reflection on the variety of processes and outcomes assembled in the cases. Thus, I will suggest that it is 'shared features' across cases (rather than the a priori variables used to select comparators) which have often formed the practical basis for comparative insights. So, I ask, why not just start with these shared features to explore the variety of processes across diverse and even divergent urban contexts? This would allow us to consider a much wider range of urban experiences. The archive also reveals how traditional comparison across most similar cases has been stretched by tracing the processes of globalisation which shape a wider world of diverse cities.

Building on urban comparative practice, then, the grounds for composing comparisons across different urban contexts can be recast. Tracing the multiplicity of connections which link quite different cities together and produce differentiated outcomes, or exploring shared features across both similar and different urban contexts are both shown to be good grounds for comparison. This chapter also starts to bring into view a more philosophical and theoretical agenda entailed in efforts to reformat comparativism for exploring twenty-first-century urbanism. This includes questions about 'stretching' concepts across different contexts and, more generally, the grounds for treating concepts as revisable. Whereas the comparativists reviewed in this chapter have often been anxious about over-stretching concepts, and sought relatively modest revisions in inherited theorisations, Chapter 4 will consider in detail how concepts might be understood as strongly revisable. This is essential for a comparative practice committed to transforming urban studies and inventing new concepts.

Expanding the Comparative Gesture

Actually existing comparative practices within urban scholarship bequeath an ambivalent inheritance, opening up many exciting opportunities for new conceptualisations at the same time as certain spatial and analytical limits of comparative practice for a more global urban studies are revealed. On the one hand, then, urban studies has an easy familiarity with a comparative imagination – frequently writers invoke a comparative gesture to quite different contexts in order to isolate historical processes which seem most relevant to their analysis, or to signify the wide range of possibilities associated with a particular urban process. But this can have varying degrees of depth. Bagnasco and Le Galès (2000, p. 5), for example, in their rich, collaborative and in-depth comparative study of European cities also draw in a range of different contexts to establish some contours of their analysis. This includes a light-touch reach to urban India and rural Japan to set the extremes of urban density; such an important feature of their understanding of the qualities of the urban contexts they are exploring. More significantly, European cities are substantively contrasted with US cities and the analyses they have generated. Empirically, for example, this is in terms of different welfare and planning systems, the relative role of centrality in urban form, and central government in urban politics. Importantly for urban scholarship, US theories of urban 'regimes' (alliances of state and business which shape long-term growth agendas in different urban contexts) rest on an understanding of business interests and governing coalitions which are very different in the European context. In their European-centred comparative gestures, the UK serves often as an extreme (neoliberal) outlier of the European urban condition, and Eastern Europe remains a relatively unknown quantity for the analysis.

The comparative gesture in urban studies can deepen and enrich scholarship and analysis, and is likely to expand as practitioners are inspired to read more widely on urban circumstances around the world, and are able to draw in examples to support or set limits to their analysis from a much wider array of places. However, light gestures of comparison, unsupported by careful assessment of empirical evidence have their dangers – as Loïc Wacquant's (2008) important comparative analysis of 'advanced marginality' in US and French cities highlights most effectively. He argues that popular and scientific discourse in European cities developed a comparatively inspired narrative of the ghettoisation ('Americanisation') of European cities through the 1980s and 1990s, reinforcing stigmatisation of poorer areas and hardening the racialisation of political discourse. Wacquant composes an ethnographic and sociological comparison of advanced marginality in Chicago and Paris to establish the quite different functional location, spatial form and social relations associated with each. He argues that residence in French banlieues is based in the first instance on class position (and so they are heterogeneous ethnically and in terms of nationality), and residents in these areas are drawn into both social and political relations with the wider city and state. In contrast, the US hyperghettoes have developed as a result of conscious state abandonment, foundational racial discrimination and are deeply socially and spatially segregated from the wider city.

The carefully composed comparison across these two superficially similar cases allows Wacquant to identify some of the shared trends actively producing 'advanced marginality' (differently) in these and many other post-industrial economies. This has involved the disconnection of global economic cycles from low-paid employment; reconstruction of the wage relation through the growth of precarious, contract and less protected jobs; spatial stigmatisation; loss of support networks and decline of quality of living environments; and the absence of a political identity associated with the class decomposition, splintering and fragmentation of the 'precariat' (p. 244). While the 'ghettoization' thesis might support applying US policy responses such as authoritarian policing or work-fare in the European context, Wacquant energetically uses his nuanced comparative analysis to emphasise the much wider range of political choices which states have: to invest in neighbourhoods, to cultivate citizenship, to draw residents of poorer neighbourhoods into social, economic and welfare relations. He argues strongly against a US-style draconian penal response to urban marginality. Most emphatically, and in an analysis which rings true with the much larger precarious citizenry of middle- and low-income countries whose growth paths foreclose economic participation for significant proportions of the population (in South Africa, as much as one-third – Seekings and Nattrass 2006), he suggests that the fact that the 'desocialization of wage labour' means employment is no longer a route to survivability and integration convinces him that basic income grants might form the foundation for a fundamental recasting of the social and political contract of these societies (p. 279). This is also an important part of emerging welfare regimes in middle- and low-income economies (Seekings 2017).

Wacquant's study reminds us of how important sustained comparative reflection can be to dispel too-easily sedimented stereotypes, or light-touch comparative gestures, amongst scholars as much as amongst practitioners. His research practice also opens up for us some of the methodological challenges which any attempt to revisit comparative methods must address. He is very insistent that sustained '*comparative* ethnography, based on parallel fieldwork in two sites chosen to throw light upon theoretically relevant invariants and variations' remains a vital research tactic (p. 10). 'Composing' comparisons across more than one city remains, in his view, an essential component of exposing the specificity of urban experiences; in his study, the historical processes responsible for specific experiences of spatial concentration and exclusion. But such comparisons are also valuable for proposing wider conceptualisations which might be useful across different contexts. Here he is clear this is not about generating 'lively illustrations of theories elaborated outside sustained contact with the prosaic reality', but about 'enrolling ethnographic observation as a necessary instrument and moment of theoretical construction' (2008, pp. 9–10).

He is inspired to generate concepts and analytical schema through the method of Weberian 'ideal types' – 'a socio-historical abstraction from real instances of a phenomenon' (p. 233), which might be fruitful for research. At the same time he uses concepts and insights from both advanced economies and from other contexts where the production, for example, of an 'excess reserve army of labour' through mass unemployment is far more advanced (following Fernando Henrique Cardoso and Enzi Faletto writing on South America). He notes that South American writers, such as Janice Perlman, are also well placed to provide insights on the relegation of the poor to marginal neighbourhoods, and their spatial stigmatisation. He makes the argument that the specific arrangements of marginality in France are not hangovers of a colonial past (which might be another line of comparison with the racialised inequalities of South American cities), but can be seen as an effect of the transformations of the *most advanced sectors* of Western economies, 'as they bear on the lower fractions of the recomposing working class and subordinate ethnic categories' (p. 232). In drawing comparisons with South America, he excavates the future of contemporary Western capitalist economies not in the simplistic sense that these are directly following trends in other contexts (Comaroff and Comaroff 2012), nor as a result of the colonial racialised inequalities which have shaped French society (Ross 1996), but to illuminate the similar economic processes at work in the new and specific production of 'vertiginous inequalities' within US and European economies and South American economies where growth paths which permanently exclude large sections of the population from opportunities for secure wage labour have produced a predominance of precarity and informality.

For Wacquant, as with many authors turning to comparative analysis, an important goal is the ambition to develop useful concepts to be able to describe and delineate the processes at work, and more broadly to contribute to theorisation and wider debates. This is an essential feature of comparative practice, drawing writers from many different contexts to present their findings in relation to the limits or potential of existing theorisations, and to seek to build relevant concepts based on their own detailed comparative analysis of specific cases. Importantly for our thinking here, Wacquant also turns to a quite different context for suggestive insights on the processes he is exploring. In this analysis, South American analyses are treated as theoretical resources to inform his conceptualisation. Reinforcing the light-touch comparative gesture at the heart of urban studies could open up considerable scope for decolonial theoretical practices.

Thinking with Variety

If conceptual generativity is at the heart of a comparative imagination, Chapter 2 showed that variation-finding methodological conventions have, in principle, established some relatively firm procedures and limits to how concepts might be reviewed and extended based on thinking across different urban contexts. Holding certain broad variables constant, such as national GDP, national political forms, or city size, has been seen as a way to limit variation and allow focus on specific explanatory processes, such as local-level governance arrangements (see Lijphart 1971; Kantor and Savitch 2005). Nonetheless, as discussed in Chapter 2, the huge variety of features potentially held in common or varying across the selected cities and the small-n nature of these studies means that these strategies in fact barely reduce variability in the system. They also do not address significant issues of endogeneity caused by the significant interlinkages and co-causality across cities. Conventions of case selection limit the range of comparisons partly because researchers build on unexamined assumptions shaping urban studies more generally – such as, that cities with different average levels of development are categorically different and not able to be compared at all. Conventionally, then, relatively stern limits have been set to the cases admitted to comparability through the ways in which the grounds for comparison have been established which has tended to restrict the case selection. The politics of the 'third term', or the comparator, as the basis on which different cases are drawn together, as we saw in Chapter 2, is very much what is at stake in the possibility for expanding comparative practice from analysing most (or more) similar contexts towards being able to bring quite different urban contexts into analytical conversation (Jacobs 2012).

However, it is not clear from the examples I will now consider that it is these relatively restricting formal criteria for the selection of cases which have supported the conceptual generativity of actually existing variation-finding comparisons. As we will see, what supports generative insights in urban comparativism is not (entirely) given by the norms and conventions of comparative method. Thus, alternative grounds for bringing different cases together for comparison might be viable. In practice, then, the 'third term' could be formulated in a much looser and more open way. But the examples we will review here do demonstrate very clearly how thinking across several different urban outcomes can generate creative conceptualisations (theorisations) which have the potential to be put to work elsewhere. The focus of traditional types of comparison is indeed on generative conceptual work – putting different contexts into a designed analytical arrangement to allow for conceptual reflection and theoretical innovation. In fact, they seek to directly interrogate existing concepts across the different observed outcomes. This is essential work for a more global urban studies if it is to be able to extend or subvert existing theorisations and to practically open up understandings of the urban to a greater diversity of urban outcomes.

My personal favourites amongst urban comparative studies are drawn from the field of local economic development politics which has intrigued me for some time (for example, Robinson and Boldogh 1994; Parnell and Robinson 2006; Ballard et al. 2007). This has been a field which has drawn richly on comparative methods, and exemplifies something of the ambivalence of variation-finding comparative research, between conventional methodology and vernacular urban research practices. Both Susan Clarke (1995) and Hank Savitch and Paul Kantor (2004) display the potential for comparative thinking to generate significant new conceptual insights, determining the salience of new processes or proposing new concepts. Both studies also demonstrate some of the conventions and practices which have confined those innovations to a relatively narrow repertoire of urban experiences. Both seek to test concepts important in those contexts in a carefully selected range of cases. And both studies worked really hard to conform to rigorous methodological expectations of case selection (although perhaps they were also no doubt driven by knowledge and accessibility to resources and actors in the cities in question) and identification of differences and variations across cases.

Clarke sets out to determine how 'restructuring' is articulated in local urban institutions in the USA. In an effort to move beyond some of the limits of regime theory (analysis of configurations of locally dependent urban actors, shaping relatively stable local growth paths) she uses 'new institutional approaches' to bring in more complex analyses of how local political institutions respond to and are transformed by the changes brought by widespread fiscal crisis and economic restructuring, focussing on local economic development policy. Her conclusions indicate that whether more democratic or more market-centred approaches to local economic development result depends on the relative influence of local community and business organisations, as well as whether (more or less institutionally integrated) local bureaucratic procedures dominate decision-making rather than more market-oriented logics with flexible, external institutions and funding mechanisms. Her institution-focussed analysis is alert to the different ways in which local economic development policy is shaped – through interaction with federal programmes, engagement with wider circulating policy ideas, through formal bureaucratic and democratic structures, through the invention of new institutional and financing vehicles, or as a result of more informal relations with business.

She thoughtfully composes a comparison across eight smaller US cities, including some with declining manufacturing bases and some with new manufacturing growth. Her concern with achieving comparability through some measure of similarity across cases illuminates how a variation-finding research design might narrow the field of possible comparator cities in order to try to limit variability in some key aspects of the processes being considered (even though the cities would have varied significantly along many other lines):

> First, each pair is located within the same state to minimize comparability problems arising from interstate differences in state authorized spending, service responsibilities, legal municipal requirements and state policies and regulations. Second, each pair was active in federal redevelopment programmes and suffered comparable cuts in federal aid during the 1980s. Third, in varying ways, each pair of cities has

previously incorporated minority and neighbourhood interests in federal redevelopment projects.

(Clarke 1995, p. 520)

The comparative approach was important here for enabling a subtle analysis of how institutional diversity shapes outcomes in local economic development policy – an important contrast with more broad brush Marxist analyses which saw mobile capital stimulating territorial competition amongst localities and state interests articulating with that in a relatively straightforward way across localities (Cox and Mair 1988; Harvey 1989), or more descriptive analyses which focussed on the stability of governing regimes (Stone 1989; Logan and Molotch 1987). The study also brought significant insights into how particular institutional arrangements might shape the emergence of specific urban regimes, and lead to their transformation. The important lines of analysis which emerged amongst the cases across the variety of outcomes explored in the study, though, were not specifically part of the research design: the form of bureaucracy and the extent of external governance arrangements; participation or exclusion of citizens groups. But the criteria for selection established the shared relevant features which enable the analysis – that is, all cities had experienced participation and then cuts in federal programmes; all had some history of community participation in these programmes. Other criteria were less relevant. The first criterion – selecting pairs of cities from different states – only restricts slightly the variability in institutional contexts, from eight to four different state-level funding and legislative contexts. In relation to the second, broader international economic processes were also impacting the cities adversely. In fact, there was quite some variation across the cities in terms of the impacts of economic restructuring. Importantly, as a result of this selection procedure *variations* in what became the key explanatory variables (bureaucracy, participation) were distributed randomly across the study. These phenomena did not form a basis for case selection, and emerged as significant only in the course of the analysis.

In practice, it might be reasonable to suggest that the criterion for case selection which matters most analytically – the comparator, the third term, or the grounds for comparing the cases – is the *presence of the shared feature which the author wishes to explore*. In this case, these were community participation in governance and institutional responses to fiscal cuts in a context of economic decline. For Clarke, these were core to her theoretical reflections as she presented her findings. In fact, it is these concerns which were the focus of empirical investigation and defined the research question. In this case these shared features were presented as nationally circumscribed but these might be features of many different urban settings. Within the bounds of this shared feature there is significant variation across the different cities along many axes (economic growth, social divisions and inequality, social mobilisation, state-level funding and legislation, local institutional cultures and histories). There is quite some variety, then, even within the small sample considered in this study. It is this variety which turns out to be relevant and interesting to consider in relation to understanding different institutional responses to economic restructuring. Following this model, the possibility to stretch comparisons beyond the national boundary based on shared transnational processes or experiences and the variation in institutional responses across cases seems potentially feasible.

Savitch and Kantor (2004) also interrogate US-derived ideas of 'regime theory': the analysis of the politics of alliances and institutional formations ('regimes') which established the long-term contours of development and growth policies in particular US cities. In contrast to Clarke, these authors internationalise their analysis by incorporating case studies from the UK, France and Italy alongside the USA and Canada. They also attend closely to the different position of their case-study cities in relation to the international economy in addition to their relation to national policy and political institutions. Reinforcing our sense from Clarke that 'variation' is key to effective comparison, Savitch and Kantor note that

> 'our cities have been chosen because they illustrate a broad range of variation on variables that we believe are critical to urban development politics. Specifically, these cities display wide diversity in their market conditions, their intergovernmental arrangements, and the political behavior (participation and culture) of their citizens. As such, they illustrate the vicissitudes of fortune as well as common currents'
> (Savitch and Kantor 2004, pp. 23–4).

The shared characteristic that grounds this comparative study is the common experience of transformation to a post-industrial economy (see also Kantor and Savitch 2005). Their hope is that selecting a number of case studies (ten) will enable them to make generalisations about the variety of processes shaping institutional responses to this economic change. Their results include a conceptual schema exploring the variety of different kinds of governance processes shaping local economic development policy in these different contexts. Their study did much to open up 'regime theory' to a diversity of governance arrangements and national policy contexts crucial to shaping the politics of local economic development. This was in contrast to the relatively uniform US studies, and also to the rather strict critiques from British scholars, who saw in the different state forms and highly nationalised nature of business-state relations, grounds for a dismissal of this US-centred approach (although see Dowding et al. 1999 for a productive comparative application across London boroughs). An expanded comparative view in Kantor and Savitch's study opened up the potential to explore a greater diversity of institutional settings and thus identified a wider range of opportunities (and constraints) for different kinds of local governance strategies to shape development paths (Kantor et al. 1997).

These carefully designed studies created the opportunity to stretch concepts and extend understandings of different kinds of local governance responses to shared conditions across their case studies, and to explore the reasons for these variations. Clarke's insight was that local economic development initiatives remaining part of integrated local government institutions and showing a democratic responsiveness to community mobilisation formed an important contrast with more growth-oriented strategies initiated through independent bodies outside the local government, in alliance with business organisations and individuals. For Kantor and Savitch internationalising the analysis brought in a wider variety of influences, including the relative position of the city in the international economy, in relation to national political and welfare regimes, the relative democratic responsiveness of local politics, and the dynamism of individuals. In this case, identifying a shared feature (or comparator) which stretched across a diversity of national and political contexts brought into consideration a richer variety of institutional forms of local economic development to inform theoretical analysis. Both of these studies stretched the theoretically driven analyses of, say Harvey (1989) and Cox and Mair (1988), who focussed on the competitive and pro-growth initiatives of US business – local state alliances under conditions of circulating, footloose capital and growing neoliberalisation of urban governance. The comparative studies we have reviewed here drew closely on existing theoretical analyses and did not seek to overturn them. But their case studies provided grounds for new, creative insights into variations in local political regimes and political practices.

Would it be possible to extend the scope of such variation-finding studies, to include a wider diversity of cases? In her path-breaking study of three US global cities, Abu-Lughod (1999) pursued a 'more controlled comparison of the three largest global cities of the United States', rather than grapple with the complexities of different national and cultural contexts represented by global and world cities such as London, Paris, Amsterdam, Tokyo, for example. She felt that as these contexts each accreted complex and successive layers of 'vastly different patterns of development and reconstruction', they were not 'easily compared with one another, because the national and cultural contexts in which they developed are so different' (p. 3). But, reflecting perhaps some anxiety in taking a relatively narrow, national approach, she notes that 'Nevertheless, the three urbanized regions, although similar in their overarching economic, technological, social and political contexts, offer enough significant variation to make comparisons among them a fertile source for new insights into the processes of urban change in the contemporary era' (1999, p. 3). She lists eight (wide-ranging) areas in which the cities vary, which she suggests can 'shed light on the common and special qualities of global cities' (p. 4). In an aside as she concludes her analysis, she suggests that it had been helpful to her comparative exercise to consider cities within the same national context (although their differential positions and responses in relation to this nonetheless delivers great variety in outcomes). But she then goes on to suggest, rather tantalisingly, that there would be significant interest in taking a wider scope: 'A replication of this study in other non-American global cities could yield even more precise answers to the questions posed here' (p. 401) – something which studies to follow clearly demonstrated (for example, Hill and Kim 2000; Machimura 1992; McNeill et al. 2005). A more global perspective on global and world cities multiplies and intensifies her sense that there is far more to learn about 'global' and 'world' cities (Mendieta 2011; Robinson 2002).

One effect of a narrow basis for case selection in variation-finding comparisons is to reinforce a focus on relatively parochial theoretical concepts (in the cases we reviewed, regime theory, based on a largely US model of local government). A more wide-ranging approach to case selection could bring a broader range of theoretical perspectives and empirical processes into play for comparative exploration. We noted in Chapter 2 that in seeking 'fertile sources for new insights' in the comparative analysis of cities, controlling for variation in (small-n)comparisons (Lijphart 1971) eliminates only one (or a few) of an exorbitant array of different variables shaping urban outcomes. It is not clear that this is a helpful way to proceed as so much variation remains in small-n urban comparisons. Indeed, as we saw from the two comparative studies discussed here, it is the variation at the end of the day that enables interesting conceptualisation. Rather than controlling for difference, then, we might turn such restrictive formal comparative methodological advice around. Finding broadly shared processes or outcomes might form a sufficiently good basis for comparing, and analysis of the proliferation of difference across different contexts would stimulate creative thinking about the determination of that phenomenon. Fertile reflection and insight about variations in national political structures, or levels of resource for local government, for example, might emerge from the analysis rather than artificially restrict insights in advance. Formal comparative methodological conventions simply limit the variety with which to think the urban, and restrict conceptual innovation.

In the examples reviewed in this section, the range of institutional arrangements, possible policy responses, or kinds of restructuring were relatively limited in relation to the variety available to consider in a more global scope. The selection of cases was based on narrowing the focus to a clearly defined common shared phenomenon – institutional restructuring in response to fiscal and economic crises. But it was in fact the variety identified across the cases in relation to quite different variables (different forms of urban governance) which supported the generative theoretical analysis that resulted from the studies. Can comparative practices rather be developed which bring forward in the research process this potential for enriching conceptualisations of urban processes by thinking across variety, addressing a greater diversity of urban outcomes while remaining rigorous and plausible?

If the analytical interest is in the variety of institutions and the complexities of local politics, the comparative practices we have reviewed indicate there is potential for stretching comparative urban political analysis to a much wider array of cities. I would suggest that there are strong grounds in the subject matter of local economic development policy for widening the arena for both conceptual innovation and empirical investigation. On the one hand, the transnational circulation of policymaking processes (already noted in Clarke's study) and the international context shaping possibilities for urban economic development (as in Hank and Savitch) suggest that comparable cases could be selected to trace the differential effects of such transnational processes. Here, case studies of cities which are highly extraverted on both these fronts could also be illuminating to what has been a relatively parochial form of analysis focussed on the USA and the EU. Thus, in many poorer and middle-income cites, powerful external agents, such as the World Bank, international NGOs and visiting consultants are an important part of any 'urban regime'. These have been highlighted in analyses of the growth coalition associated with Mumbai First, for example (Goldman 2011; Ghertner 2015a; Harris, A. 2008a). Understanding some of the key developments in contemporary urbanisation, including significant infrastructural development and land speculation, requires attention to this wider cast of urban political actors. Internationalising regime theory would involve exploring many experiences of the transnational nature of urban governance from around the world and would also be illuminating for analyses of many western cities where international networking and prolific policy circulation also mean that a focus on locally embedded urban regimes is dated (Lauermann 2018). There are many other potential lines of theoretical learning which might run from studies of poorer/middle-income contexts. For example, the new institutional analysis which Clarke draws on so effectively highlights the importance of informal social relations in shaping institutions

(Lowndes 1996). Expanding understanding of informality is relevant both routinely in terms of how all institutions operate, but perhaps especially for the literature on urban regimes as many local development initiatives draw on informal relations amongst actors to develop non-regulatory policies and agendas which rely on institutional flexibility (Pieterse 2008). These kinds of arrangements are particularly important when responding to unprecedented crisis or ongoing economic restructuring and have significant implications for trajectories of urban development (Gordon 2003; McCann 2001). As in Kantor and Savitch's study, exploring a wider range of cases could generate richer, more varied analyses. Once the constraints of inherited assumptions of incommensurability are abandoned, it should be both appropriate and generative to stretch comparisons to include highly informalised contexts as well as developmental states (see for example Vogel et al. 2010; Weinstein 2014).

Methodological conventions surrounding the construction of a 'third term' to support comparison could be reconfigured in line with the practice of variation finding comparisons to focus on shared features which enable thinking with variety rather than trying to 'control for difference'. Flowing from this would be potential for a creative theoretical practice focussed on the revisability of inherited (and located) understandings. One of the consequences of this would be to bring together theoretical resources which are often kept apart. This raises the practical and analytical question as to whether there are some bounds to the sources of inspiration for conceptual investigation or limits to how far concepts can be stretched to interrogate different cases? The examples we have reviewed suggest that a theory-building tactic of composing comparisons across more diverse outcomes, holds out much promise for expanding the repertoire of analytical resources in urban studies and for more extensive conceptual innovation.

Stretching Comparisons: Thinking with Connections

In practice, how have urban scholars extended the range of cities drawn into comparative analysis? As we saw in Chapter 1, there has been much debate abou how analyses of urbanisation should be related to wider differentiations in the global economy, and to disjunctures across different kinds of cities in terms, for example, of forms of government, levels of resourcing, presence or absence of democracy, or quite different political orders, such as formal socialist systems. Is it possible to draw cities into shared analytical consideration across this diversity? A number of authors – and some very prominent ones – have adopted a variety of tactics for thinking across these differences.

Perhaps the most high-profile writer to have assumed the intrinsic comparability of urban processes in quite different political and economic contexts was Manuel Castells. In both *The Urban Question* (1977) and *The City and the Grassroots* (1983) he drew on substantive case studies from South America (Chile), Europe (Madrid, Spain and Paris, France) and North America (San Francisco, USA and Quebec, Canada). For Castells, urbanisation in South America and (Southern/Northern) Europe are differentiated through their differential position in global capitalism, but the theoretical analytic in both books placed all the cases within the same analytical frame, with urban planning and urban social movements shaped by similar processes, such as wider political organisations, social base (those mobilised), and political conjuncture (ruling party, nature of opposition parties).

In his careful consideration of Castells' work in terms of comparative method, Chris Pickvance (1985) explores a more macro-scale comparative project, in which the contexts of urban movements (figured nationally) might be set as variables to explain differential outcomes in mobilisation more directly. This is in contrast to Castells' bottom-up analysis comparing contexts only in terms of their direct influences on specific movement dynamics (Castells 1985). Here, as set out in his 1986 article discussed in Chapter 2, Pickvance (1985) argues for a series of linked sub-models which would be differentiated by the types of different national contexts within which urban movements are located. He observes that one should avoid 'the unjustified transfer of propositions between very diverse societies' (p. 44). The significant variable he identifies here, though, is not the level of economic development (as in 'First' or 'Third' world) but the nature of the links from social movements to wider levels of political mobilisation, or the legality of political parties, which had significant implications for the wider political significance of mass urban movements. Thus Santiago de Chile and Madrid are seen as comparable, with the authoritarian national political situations of both supporting strong levels of mass mobilisation, politically motivated organisations and transformative effects (and for this reason, the comparisons of these cases with mass urban mobilisations against apartheid in the 1980s were striking to South African scholars – McCarthy 1983; Seekings 2000). But Pickvance felt that comparisons between Madrid and Paris were less appropriate. He makes the point that a democratic context with political parties routinely organising to represent citizen interests might in fact be a priori less conducive to the transformative potential of urban movements, for the good reasons that alternative processes of engagement and participation to those presented by social movements are present. This indicates that some of the discussion flowing from Castell's work which sought to track the more general rise and fall of social movement mobilisation might have been looking in the wrong direction, for historical trends as opposed to differentiated and contextual explanations. Pickvance suggests developing 'linked sub-models' across different contexts (struggles for democracy vs democratic systems) in order to assess the important processes shaping movement formation and achievements in each category before composing a wider theoretical assessment across the sub-models.

Following Pickvance, we can conclude that attention does need to be paid to how comparability is configured across different national contexts. But in contrast to the a priori and territorialised developmental assumptions at work in methodological conventions for comparing, we see in this analysis a careful delineation of the specific processes (processes of democratisation) which might generate disjunctions in comparability and explanation for a certain research question. This does not follow conventions limiting comparisons across any a priori divide between developed and developing countries, or restricting analyses across different regions. A number of initiatives have challenged the validity of such assumptions. The importance of differentiating amongst the increasingly divergent experiences of 'peripheral capitalist countries', for example, has been discussed for some time (Lipietz 1987). And a range of analyses have sought to bring cities in 'developing countries', those subject to underdevelopment (Slater 1978), colonialism or neo-imperialism (King 1990a), part of the third world (Dick and Rimmer 1998) or the global South (Myers 2020) into comparative reflections within a wider urban world.

In one of his many contributions over the next decades drawing attention to the great potential to think with South American theorisations in relation to cities and a variety of social processes, David Slater made an early and strong intervention observing that,

> although it is certainly the case that in the last few years the theoretical analysis of capitalist urbanization has progressed considerably ... much of this progress has been rooted in the experiences of the advanced capitalist economies. This does not mean that such research is only relevant for those economies, far from it, but the general direction of these studies does tend to leave open the question of the relations between urbanization and the varying historical contexts of capitalist accumulation and socio-political structure. Also, and expressed very generally, this inevitably poses the question of why, how and in what ways are the peripheral social formations different from the central or metropolitan social formations?
> (Slater 1978, p. 27).

Slater seeks to explain the 'specificity of capitalist urbanisation in peripheral societies' (p. 43) eschewing a false dichotomy between external and internal processes. Through the case of Peru, he sees urbanisation there as shaped by investment patterns influenced by changing forms of capitalism in the West, alliances between industrial and agricultural capital, changing conditions of production in agriculture leading to rapid urbanisation, state investment, and industrial, housing and health policies. By contrast, Gugler and Flanagan (1977) draw on a more policy-inflected analysis of urbanisation in West Africa, in which excessive investment in cities and attractive wages drive urbanisation to the detriment of agriculture and rural areas. They draw on a concept of 'overurbanisation' to focus their concerns regarding the consequent 'plight of the urban masses', dependent on spontaneous housing and irregular employment. David Slater rather sees the term 'overurbanisation' as exceptionalising and mystifying the analysis of peripheral capitalism. He proposes that scholars should rather be surprised that urbanisation rates in these countries are so low compared to others. As a leading early advocate of a postcolonial perspective, he insisted on placing all these countries within the same analytical time zone rather than assuming developing countries should be considered as following a path predetermined by that already traced by developed countries.

In just this spirit, an intriguing edited collection developed a comparison of Manchester in the early-nineteenth century (1790–1850) and São Paulo in the early-twentieth century (1890 on) as rapidly growing cities experiencing unprecedented industrialisation (Wirth and Jones 1978). Although they do draw on the developmental trope of peripheral countries following (differently) earlier paths of the metropolitan centre, the lines of comparison are carefully drawn and historically specific. After rehearsing some similarities of urbanisation processes in both contexts Wirth (p. 1) notes, 'But that Manchester and São Paulo underwent broadly similar phenomena is a riskier proposition. Can we in fact compare two capitalist industrial cities at different points in time, in divergent national contexts, with different roles in the world economy?' Authors in the collection place Manchester as the atypical urbanisation experience compared to South America (Wirth and Jones 1978), and fruitfully compare the effects of the differential relations of the two urban areas to the capitalist transformation of the countryside (complete in Manchester at this time, only beginning in the hinterland of São Paulo as industrialisation kicks off). They note both their differential insertion into the global economy (São Paulo had significant competition across the globe) and their shared history of repressive labour relations.

The significant shift to Marxist analyses in urban studies from the late 1970s transformed how comparisons across divergent urban experiences were able to be considered. For example, Lubeck and Walton (1979) built on world systems analysis and the assumption that 'structural and social change must be understood in its totality and hence on a world scale' (p. 3) to explore the differential incorporation of Mexico and Nigeria into the world system. They compare class formation and urban processes (in Monterrey and Kano respectively) in each context. Moving beyond the 'controlled experiments' of variation finding across most similar (or most different) contexts, they propose a third logic, 'a more historical and systemic approach' exploring both similarities and differences in the context of a Marxist understanding of uneven development. Following Immanuel Wallerstein, they consider how the different cases are rooted in the 'historically specific totality which is the world capitalist economy' (p. 6). In effect the comparison is of two processes of incorporation of semi-peripheral nations into the world economy, at different times and with different pre-existing indigenous elite formations. However, the shared experiences of dependent industrialisation and the interventions of centralised but dependent national states can, they argue, explain the rise of worker mobilisation in each case. This is partly because of the relative inability of the states to secure localised settlements with labour movements because of the international nature of capital, and because of the presence of a growing 'lumpen-proletariat' (or reserve army of labour, undercutting wages) consequent upon agrarian transformations.

The analysis of urbanisation within the capitalist world economy opened up some opportunities for systematic comparative reflection across different urban experiences across the globe. New and relatively inclusive lines of analytical connection were forged by Friedmann and Wolff (1982) in their seminal article in which they suggested that a hierarchical system of cities (within the rubric of core, periphery and semi-periphery) played an important role in co-ordinating the world economy. They argued, provocatively, that

> What makes this typology attractive is the assumption that cities situated in any of the three world regions will tend to have significant features in common. As the movement of particular countries through the three-level hierarchy suggests, these features do not in any sense determine economic and other outcomes. They do, however, point to conditions that significantly influence city growth and the quality of urban life.
> (Friedmann and Wolff 1982, p. 311)

World cities were to be found in core and semi-peripheral parts of the world and seen to be involved in co-ordinating and controlling the economic, political and ideological functions of the capitalist world-economy, although these roles were not simply functionally determined, but subject to contestation and political action. This initial and highly prescient analysis of 'world city' economic activities and actors included the unemployed; informal activities; government;

industrial; tourism; personal, retail and property services; as well as business services. Highlighting social polarisation as an important consequence of the world city structure, and considering the 'third world' aspect to many world cities with substantial immigration from poorer countries, the social and physical restructuring of these cities (as 'urban fields' or urbanised regions) and consequences for administration and political conflict were of concern. They complained that to that date traditional urban studies had not drawn case studies of individual cities into a wider, comprehensive analysis of the processes producing human settlements, and that while Marxist analyses of the city had criticised the class relations shaping urban production under capitalism, they had not made the links with the wider processes shaping the world-economy. They turned to the world systems perspective to explore how world cities are key points of spatial articulation of the world-economy. Methodologically they encouraged a focus on the 'systemic' nature of urbanisation (as part of the world-economy) which implies placing specific urbanisation processes within this wider context:

> The critical variable in the study of particular world city regions is their *mode of integration* with the world economy.
> (Friedmann and Wolff 1982, p. 329)

Since this intervention, urban studies has not looked back: the articulation of processes of globalisation in shaping urbanisation is now essential to understanding any urban context. However, as I have argued elsewhere (Robinson 2006), at the same time that this and subsequent world cities interventions opened up the world of cities to investigation at a global scale, the global cities variant of this approach developed by Saskia Sassen (1991), systematically set bounds to comparability on the basis of the theoretical object of study, 'global' cities. Compared to Friedmann and Wolff (1982) broad ranging analysis of 'world' cities (across diverse sectors and activities, for example, and with a strong eye to the shared political and historical processes generating these urban fields), the global city was defined in a very narrow way. Economic and social processes associated with purely command and control functions of transnational economic activities as well as the dominance of international finance became the focus of theorists of the global city. This significantly limited the applicability of these analyses elsewhere and considerably narrowed the scope for urban studies to take a more global perspective on urbanisation (Robinson 2002). The opportunity Friedmann and Wolff had identified for study of a wide swath of cities across the periphery, semi-periphery and centre of the world economy on the same terms was quickly undercut by a strong focus on a very small number of 'global' cities (Sassen 1991). Divisions between 'first' and 'third world' cities were reimported into urban studies; assumptions were made about strong differences between those cities connected into the economic circuits which mattered to 'global' cities, and cities at the crossroads of a wider variety of globalising processes (Robinson 2006). The critical potential of the world cities approach also lost grounds on the backs of great policy interest in the potential for individual cities to gain entry into this special class of 'Global City' and the practical development politics associated with this term (Taylor 2004).

But even as the global cities debate set some limits, geographical (focussing attention on only a relatively small number of cities) and analytical (focussing only on certain sectors of the urban economy), on the comparative potential of urban studies, the wider focus on globalisation and the world economy signposted the possibility for thinking across quite different kinds of cities. Since these interventions, the articulation of global processes in shaping urbanisation and urban outcomes has been essential to understanding any city (Fainstein 1994; Smith 2001; Shatkin 1998).

This has generated a new mode of comparative analysis, one which works with the connections amongst cities, the globalised conditions of production of the urban. It was the changing nature of the global economy which inspired Friedmann and Wolff, whose article foreshadowed global shifts in the location of production, and the move towards financialisation and deepening inequalities, all of which are now taken for granted in analyses of the global economy, and are seen as key features shaping urbanisation. Richard Child Hill (1989), for example, compared two sets of transnational automobile production systems orchestrated through Japan and the USA (which in a later paper could be contrasted as Toyotaism and Fordism; see Fujita and Hill 1995). Michael Storper's intervention on regional industrial development in the 'Third World' reflects the broader shifts in analysis which characterised this moment. These were driven by a theoretical shift away from the Marxist analysis of neo-imperialism and Third World development and by profound empirical changes in the organisation of transnational production and the politics of development in many countries around the world. He observes that,

> The replacement of the technological-institutional model of mass production by this as yet emergent regime of production flexibility introduces a set of new realities to which policies for industrialization, urbanization and regional economic development must be addressed, in the developed countries as well as in the third world. It demands a close re-evaluation of received concepts and assumptions. It is now, to a large degree, necessary to approach problems of development in a way that is both post-Fordist and postimperialist.
>
> (Storper 1990: 441)

Susan Fainstein's (2001 [1994]) comparative study of London and New York, *The City Builders*, perhaps stretched this nascent form of comparison through connections to the limit; she presented the processes of urban property development in these two cities as effectively the same phenomenon, the production of the global city. Certainly her study investigated many aspects of urban development in the two cities which both a priori and on careful inspection repaid thinking together. Although, she insisted, there is no single model of the late-twentieth-century city:

> New York and London are special cases, but their atypicality makes them worth studying not because they present a model of all cities but because they exemplify a certain, and especially influential, class of city.
> (Fainstein 2001, p. 19)

Importantly for methodological debates and critique which often assume an infinitely mobile researcher (as Peck and Theodore 2012, note), Fainstein comments that for personal reasons it was not possible to incorporate Tokyo alongside these two cases. She astutely considers a 'mix of general and specific factors that create the London and New York of this moment in time' (p. 19). Along the way she identifies many features of urban development (in fact not unique at all to global cities, including housing programmes, redevelopment plans, community mobilisation) which demonstrate her (planner's) sensibility that there are 'areas of indeterminacy that can be seized locally within the overall capitalist economic structure': outcomes are not inevitable. Indeed, Janet Abu-Lughod's extraordinarily rich comparison of New York, Chicago and Los Angeles establishes the highly differentiated outcomes of 'global cities', where the localised histories and political economies articulating wider global processes inspire her to conclude that there is no inevitable outcome of globalisation and that the processes shaping so-called global cities are highly diverse, even within the same national system.

As the analysis of processes of globalisation and conceptualisations of the relationship between local outcomes and the wider processes associated with globalisation became more sophisticated (Massey 1994), other comparative opportunities opened up. Most notable is the possibility of using wider global networks to draw different urban experiences together analytically, or to compare the wider networks themselves. Kris Olds' pathbreaking (2001) study explored Vancouver and Shanghai together through analysing the different networks which were drawn on in the 'megaprojects' of 1 Canada Water and Pudong Island. The comparative tactic here was novel – to compare the different networks of, on the one hand, a family firm of Hong Kong-based property developers investing in Vancouver and drawing on and forging close ties to generate trust and embedding localised commitments; and on the other hand, of a group of high-profile architects (he focusses on Richard Rogers) invited to contribute to a design exercise for Shanghai's mega-project developments, whose lack of engagement with local issues saw them produce proposals with little purchase on local histories and imaginations. The two cities are treated quite equally, and both are placed within the category of 'global city', caught up in the same design and investment circuits.

Urban studies has moved far beyond the relatively functionalist approach placing cities in relation to the totality of the world-economy pioneered in early analyses of world cities. Notably, accounts of neoliberalisation of urban governance and policymaking (Peck et al. 2009) and wider analyses of policy mobilities (McCann 2011) highlight the multiplicity of links which tie cities around the world into shared processes of imagination and intervention. Similarly, the expansion of the kinds of global processes shaping the production of different cities – including, for example finance, architecture, migration, international agencies, property developers, urban forms (high-rise, urban mega-projects, satellite cities) means that the grounds for bringing cities together on the basis of the shared processes (with of course differentiated outcomes) have proliferated (Bulkely 2010; Roy and Ong 2011; Peck and Theodore 2015; Sassen [ed.] 2002; Taylor 2004).

In addition, post-colonial critics of urban studies (King 1990a, 1990b; Robinson 2006; Roy 2009b; McFarlane 2010) have argued that cities everywhere should be drawn into wider theoretical conversations about the urban. Existing theoretical statements about urbanisation have been exposed for their parochialism and locatedness (Robinson 2006), and the expectation is that urban studies would be informed by a great diversity of experiences, articulated by 'new subjects of urban theory' (Roy 2011b) and supported by a non-systemic (non-totalising) approach to the diverse processes of globalisation which shape differentiated outcomes in cities around the world (Brenner et al. 2010a; Ong 2011b; Simone 2011).

Here Anthony King's pathbreaking work in post-colonial urban studies is an appropriate platform for drawing the themes addressed in this chapter to a conclusion. His early study (1984) traced the history of the metropolitan built form, the bungalow – a one-storey sprawling house relatively common in the UK, but less conventional than the mostly two- to three-storey terraced houses which dominate the urban landscape there. He identified the origins of the bungalow in British settlement in India, and in tracing its circulation to the UK opened the history of Western cities to their colonial and imperial past, inspiring a number of analyses along these lines (see for example, Driver and Gilbert 1999). More provocatively, his books on global cities (1990b), and London in particular (1990a), cast these cities, usually placed at the centre of urban theory, as 'dependent' metropolises, insisting on interpreting them on an even analytical playing field with colonial cities. Thus, he drew world cities analysis into direct conversation with much longer histories of globalisation. He argued that cities in colonial contexts were co-produced with those like London, the metropolitan centres of Empires and trading networks.

His book on London (1990a) still stands as a research agenda for understanding the colonial inheritance of the landscape, form and socio-economic make-up of London. Certainly, London's leading position in the new financial and producer services-driven economic globalisation owes much to the network of connections and transnational relationships established during its colonial past (Massey 2007). But King makes a more expansive point, that wider colonial connections also shaped London's suburban landscapes, public architecture, corporate symbolism and, of course, its growing diverse population. He presses his comparative analysis even further when he moves from a focus on connections between colonial contexts and London, to compare London and colonial cities directly. He argues that colonial cities share with London these extraverted features of urbanisation, justifying their comparison. Pages 39–46 set out a programmatic agenda for comparison across these two different kinds of urban context.[2] Reversing the usual direction of theoretical learning from northern to southern contexts, he suggests that perhaps colonial cities can even be seen as 'forerunners of what the contemporary capitalist world city would eventually become' (p. 38). After a wide-ranging framing of London through this comparative lens, King proposes specific, and prescient, comparative insights on London's post-1980s property boom which came in the wake of the 1986 Big Bang liberalisation of the finance sector. He looks at these from the perspective of experiences of 'the old Treaty Ports of China' (p. 146) where concessions were granted to foreign investors in designated enclaves (see also Schiffer 1983). His loose framing of this comparative potential across London and colonial contexts is deliberately provocative and captures the intense class conflicts of this period of London's development (Brownill 1990):

> Another analogy is that of the colonial city, or rather, the old Treaty Ports of China. Laid bare in the international market place, the centre of the city is colonized by capital. The processes are embodied in language and represented in space; 'concessions' are granted to foreign powers; 'enclaves' are created for tax-free economic activities; and to protect themselves from the [local residents], the representatives of national and international capital retreat into 'compounds' bounded by high fences, locked gates, and patrolled by state police or the security guards of private armies. In return for its percentage, the State maintains law and order, invests in the police, and provides the [labourers] and the social and physical infrastructure.
>
> (King 1990a, p. 146)

King's deliberate mixing up and shocking use of the vocabularies and constituencies of the colonial city to discuss the global city is striking (I have chosen not to reproduce some terms in the quote above). The starkly racialised exclusions and hierarchies of colonial cities throw a light on the spatialities and social conflicts of Thatcherite Britain. The comparison across these two kinds of contexts – their empirical and analytical imbrication – can in fact be even more directly drawn than this suggestive discussion. In terms of thinking with connections, it is well known that there were direct links between investors in different parts of the world and these developments (Fainstein 1994, 2001). But there were also links between urban development practices in Hong Kong, notably Export Processing Zones and state-led mega-urban developments, and the practices of urban development in London at that time (Olds 2001). King (1990a) discusses London's developments at length, including the flagship 1980s mega-urban project, the London Docklands Development Corporation, for example, in the relatively simplistic comparison with colonial settings in the quote above. But, inspired by King, we can excavate some direct grounds for comparative analysis.

In 1977, the planner Peter Hall wrote a short article, exploring the possibility of what came to be known as 'simplified planning zones' in the UK – areas set aside for significant deregulation. The changing international division of labour had devastated employment in UK cities; by 1988 London had reached an all-time low point in both economic growth and population, 6.7 million people (Mayor of London 2016, p. 12). Hall's concern was that while industrial innovation might lead to advanced industrial economies maintaining their competitive advantage in some areas, there would still exist a structurally dislocated group of workers primarily in inner cities. He thought that corporations seeking cheap labour might relocate to these areas, 'doing in Liverpool what they already do in Singapore or in Mexican border cities' (Hall 1982, p. 418). Although likely to be zero-sum in terms of the net UK economy, he indicated that he hoped these would stimulate innovation, skills upgrades for workers trapped in declining areas, and also attract small firms, and that venture capital might play a role (as in Silicon Valley start-ups):

> ...the answer [to the inner city crisis] might be to accept the fact. It would result in a final possible answer, which I would call the Freeport solution. This is essentially an essay in non-plan. Small, selected areas of inner cities would be simply thrown open to all kinds of initiative, with minimal control. In other words, we would aim to recreate the Hong Kong of the 1950s and 1960s inside inner Liverpool or inner Glasgow.
>
> (Hall 1982, p. 417)

He continued that these would be freeports, outside UK exchange control, with 'fairly shameless free enterprise', and 'the areas would be outside the scope of United Kingdom taxes, social services, industrial and other regulations'. He was defending himself against extensive criticism (Massey 1982) and allegations that the subsequently famous Thatcherite model of loosening planning regulations, which lay behind the Docklands Development Corporation, had been something he had advocated (Thornley 1991). He insisted that he had not been recommending this, as such, but rather saw it 'as a model, and an extreme one, of a possible solution' (ibid.).

These ideas did find purchase in the establishment of enterprise zones and associated development corporations in the UK through the 1980s, the most famous of which was the London Docklands Development Corporation. Hall himself refused to accept direct responsibility for this influence, and the reviews of this initiative from left commentators and planners, including Anthony King, were scathing. They centred around the shift from state financing of social need to state spending on 'direct subsidies of capital' to enable the establishment of the enterprise zones. As in the Docklands, these often took the form of pure property development for offices rather than employment creation initiatives: £15.8 million pounds in 1981–1982 of government funding, as well as losses of local authority rates income of £7.087 m, in 1982–1983, for example (Shutt 1984, *Capital and Class*, p. 37). However, this left critique also makes clear – and here the link to Hong Kong is not coincidental – that rather than being left to the 'free market' as Hall had advocated, or read as indicators of a 'neoliberalising' state, these urban development initiatives had in fact been significantly underwritten by the state (Thornley 1991; Fainstein 2001). The trade-off involved was with alternative forms of state spending – meeting local needs in often deprived local areas, or promoting employment through industry-focussed infrastructure investment, closely linked to regional policy. Although local authorities across the country participated in these initiatives, including Labour Party areas hard hit by deindustrialisation, the lion's share of state financing went to the Docklands, where state excerption of planning control from the five boroughs who had been overseeing a programme of re-industrialisation swerved activities to a nationally strategic approach for supporting growth in commercial and financial sectors, led by private property developers constructing offices and houses (Thornley 1991).

While competition with low-wage industrialisation in Asia was not in the end successful (or not yet, as this might be one post-Brexit scenario), the format of demarcating areas for private sector property-led development became iconic in London and wider urban development practice in the UK. In terms of the activities which came to be located in London's deindustrialised Docklands, this Urban Development Corporation consolidated the financial sector-driven growth path for that city. The early UDCs, such as the LDDC, were financed by returns on sales of state-owned land for property investment, successfully leveraging in £14.3 billion of investment between 1981 and 1997 (Brownill and O'Hara 2015). We might see the Docklands, then, as a successful example of a strategic, land-value based and central-state led development which 'upgraded' London's economic base and brought forward a new development path for the country as a whole – certainly more than a shade of Hong Kong. These Asian-inspired developments established for the longue durée key elements of London's current development model. For nearly forty years a model of planning through territorial exception has formed a major part of the broad framework for large-scale urban developments across London (Raco 2005; Robinson and Attuyer 2021).

Thus, a comparative engagement tracing connections between London and Hong Kong, as King suggested and as analyses of the role of globalisation in urban development invite, explains something of the form of development in contemporary London. Focussed on fragmented segments of the city as exceptions to the planning system, many of the struggles over London's contemporary development relate to an idea with its origins and exemplars in Asian urban developments of the 1960s and 1970s. Since then, Asian connections and Asian-inspired exemplars have loomed ever larger in London, as they have in many other contexts (Roy and Ong 2011). Across and amongst different urban contexts, circuits and flows of ideas, actors, materials and practices draw urban developments into many potential conversations with elsewhere. King's prescient boundary-defying reflections across world and colonial cities, from London to Hong Kong, establish the potential for comparativism to take urban studies in some new and perhaps unanticipated directions. Quite different kinds of urban contexts are already connected through processes of globalisation and history; but more than that, in seeking to understand urbanisation processes in one context, conceptual insights from elsewhere can throw a different light on experiences. London, then, read from Asia, rather than as the pre-eminent 'global' city, or the hyper-neoliberalised outlier of a European political economy, can be seen as a racialised and fragmented 'colonial' city; and as a product of Asian models of strong state interventions to leverage a new growth path within a spatial policy of exceptions to wider modes of governing the national territory (Ong 2006). Urban studies, and urban theory, might look very different in the aftermath of comparative urbanism.

Conclusion

In this chapter we have seen that there are both cautions and inspirations for global urban studies to draw from the history of late-twentieth-century comparative urban research. We have found in the archives of urban comparativism – what comparativists actually did in their research – inspiration for expanding the opportunities for building comparisons across a wider array of contexts. We noted that a guiding motivation for comparativists has been to design research which would create opportunities to think with variety. But researchers were largely cautious in adhering to conventional methodological constraints encouraging a focus on most similar cities. The variety considered, then, was in fact very narrow. Given that controlling for difference in relation to urban complexity is somewhat futile, as Chapter 2 discussed, the vernacular interest of comparativists in thinking with variety could be expanded. We could compose comparisons based much more loosely on the shared features of even quite different cities, to bring into view a much wider variety of a phenomenon. In addition, we noted how comparativists stretched the reach of comparisons as they interrogated transnational urbanisation processes. Early political economy analyses tied urban outcomes in different parts of the world together by considering their differential incorporation into the wider world economy. This emphasis on the world economy also grounded the influential world cities approaches, locating cities as playing important economic, political and social roles articulating processes of globalisation. Thinking comparatively across different 'world' and 'global' cities has been an important aspect of urban studies since the 1980s. Some writers were inspired by these transnational approaches to look more closely at how processes of colonialism and imperialism shaped urbanisation across the globe. These also stressed the post-colonial expectation to theorise urbanity from any urban context. And, following King, this will include thinking 'global' cities from colonial urban experiences.

The 'actually existing' work of urban scholars has therefore demonstrated the potential value of the comparative imagination and comparative methods for global urban studies. However, as Chapter 1 set out, any comparative analysis for understanding twenty-first-century city urbanisation will need to be able to attend to the multiplicity of connections which exist amongst cities around the world, bring many different cities in their rich complexity into closer conceptual proximity, and also address the demand that insights from cities anywhere be launched as starting points for new theoretical conversations. Initiatives seeking to reinvent comparative urbanism would need to support theory-generation from any city, and indeed seek to confidently use a comparative imagination to stretch existing urban theories to their breaking point, rather than being concerned with theoretical over-stretch (Pierre 2005).

The following chapter builds on the potential we have identified in actually existing comparative practice – it takes forward the dual propositions of 'thinking with variety' and 'thinking with connections' as core elements of comparative urbanism. Chapter 4 also probes more fully the potential for conceptual revision which comparativism holds, but which has been muted through both methodological conventions and practical concerns about stretching concepts. Some have turned to the fall-back position of mid-range or 'meso-level' concepts to navigate these concerns. Whether concepts are of the so-called mid-range, those which emerge close to the ground or the most abstract of terms they raise questions about the relation between concepts and the urban world. Also, global urban studies requires a strongly revisable process of theorisation, attentive to the multiplicity of starting points for thinking the urban. How, then, can we imagine the relationship between concepts, which might travel and have a wider reach (or not), and the particular observations made in any given urban context ('cases')? These questions pull our discussion of comparative methods to consider the methodological and ontological assumptions subtending urban research, requiring a broader philosophical discussion, which the next chapter takes forward.

Notes

1. In places this chapter draws on an Editorial Introduction to a Virtual Issue on Comparative Urbanism (*International Journal of Urban and Regional Research*). See Robinson (2014b).
2. Amongst the 19 grounds he offers for such comparison are: their external orientation; being vehicles of political, cultural and ideological transmission; major communications and transport nodes; centres of political and administrative control; financial and international capital control functions as well as accumulation of capital; administrative and service sector employment; external sources of elite power; comprador class of internal–external cultural brokers; migration destinations; ethnic, racial and spatial stratification and polarisation, as well as confrontation and encounter, notably between indigenous and exogenous groups; strong national interest in local government affairs; ideological centres; high social costs compared to fiscal resources.

CHAPTER 4

Thinking Cities through Elsewhere: Reformatting Comparison

Both the potential and limits of urban comparativism for global urban studies have become evident through the review of formal comparative methods in Chapter 2, and the exploration of the practice of urban comparison in Chapter 3. This chapter considers, what can we take forward from a comparative urban imagination more broadly, to inform global urban studies? And what aspects of comparativism need to be radically changed to be fit for purpose? What might such a 'reformatted' comparative urban method entail?[1]

The urban world presents both conundrum and opportunity in building conceptualisations. Any attempt to theorize the urban in a world of cities immediately places insights gained in one context in relation to a multiplicity of urban experiences. While this is only a specific case of the more general problem of developing concepts through particular observations across multiple settings or instances, it gains a certain specificity in relation to the particular spatiality of the urban, notably the strongly interconnected nature of many urban phenomena. In general, the possibility to say anything more encompassing about the urban, aspects of cities, or urban processes, as opposed to discussing one 'case' or a particular experience, rests on understandings of:

- the relationship between one instance and many (perhaps repeated) instances of phenomena;
- the wider purchase of the concepts generated in relation to that instance, and the status of those concepts (how far do they stretch, how far can we trust/use/revise them?); and
- the methodological tactics and philosophical conventions which allow navigation amongst different instances in the process of building conceptual understanding.

Comparative Urbanism: Tactics for Global Urban Studies, First Edition. Jennifer Robinson.
© 2022 John Wiley & Sons Ltd. Published 2022 by John Wiley & Sons Ltd.

These are the core elements of a comparative imagination – working with concepts and questioning their applicability across a range of different cases. In this chapter, then, I set out what a reformatted comparison might entail, one which can be put to work to support global urban studies.

At a minimum, I suggest that we could reimagine comparisons as involving the broad practice of thinking the urban through elsewhere (another case, a wider context, existing theoretical imaginations derived from other contexts, connections to other places), in order to better understand outcomes and to contribute to broader conceptualisations and conversations about (aspects of) the urban. This chapter argues that in a renovated comparative method the status of the case itself needs to be reimagined. It will be helpful to establish an alternative approach to the 'case' than that of an explanatory architecture in which pre-given wider structures or concepts are drawn on to explain outcomes ('cases'). A case is often cast as a 'particular' instance of a wider universal. Thus, for example, in an 'encompassing' approach to comparison cases are linked together for comparison because they are particular cases of wider social processes, or of 'systems', such as slavery or capitalism. If comparing 'cases' is to foster conceptual innovation, do they need to be able to be seen as more open to conceptual interrogation and reformulation, rather than located in relation to existing concepts or processes? What exactly is an observation a case of? How are the multiplicity of features of any empirical phenomena to be related to wider processes or concepts?

In this chapter I draw on some more philosophically inspired debates to reframe the architecture of comparison for understanding the urban. This is the core of the book's invitation to practice global urban studies differently – comparatively. But, also, to practice comparison differently, in a way that opens urban studies to a more global repertoire of potential analytical insights. This chapter thus explicitly seeks to develop a new vocabulary and methodological grounding for doing urban comparisons. The chapter first explores these issues in a Marxist political–economy lexicon, then draws on Deleuze's philosophical project to understand how concepts emerge across both a dynamic material world and active subjects. The chapter proposes some possible new grounds for urban comparisons, which I call 'genetic' and 'generative'. The rest of the book will delve into the nitty-gritty of how to operationalise such a reformatted comparativism and how conceptual innovation might proceed through comparative methods.

Thinking with Concrete Totalities

At stake in reframing comparative methods are the conceptual challenges associated with working across specific observations to develop concepts which can communicate beyond a single case. What is the meaning and status of the single case or instance in relation to other instances, to the concepts used to discuss them, to the wider processes shaping their distinctive form? Pressing away at these issues draws urbanists into a conversation with some core philosophical questions, such as what is the relation between concepts and the world; or what is the nature of abstraction. Certainly, adjudicating amongst the many contentious debates in this area is far beyond the purview of this book. Moreover, the limited philosophical training of contemporary urbanists, myself included, restricts the possibility for sustained engagement with these issues (Goonewardena et al. 2008). But it is essential to engage with the ways in which the potential for alternative directions for comparative urbanism is limited by assumptions about how the urban world can come to be known, and what kind of shape explanations of urban outcomes might take. So, in this section I will draw on some foundational debates on these issues in a political economy tradition, as well as highlight some urban studies contributions on this terrain. And then in the following section, I will offer a reading of Deleuze's systematisation of a contemporary post-Kantian and post-representational approach to understanding how concepts are formed by subjects in the midst of a lively and dynamic material world.

There is a rich repertoire of terms to appreciate the relationship between numerous instances of empirical and observed reality and associated more general concepts. For example, we might describe our observations as particular cases of wider (common, general or universal) phenomena, for example, one human subject amongst all of humanity, or one particular instance of a conceptually identified phenomenon such as labour, or one distinctive form of a more complex widespread process such as urban agglomeration. For urban studies any given urban outcome – as a particular case – can be placed in a determinate relationship to a specified universal or general type of the phenomenon, urban. As a particular outcome, the urban is also commonly understood as profoundly shaped by a range of processes to produce distinctive, hybrid and contextually dependent forms of something found more widely.

At the limit this includes the possibility that an outcome exceeds any sense of determination by the initial specified universal. Thus particularities (specific instances of a universal) could be seen as made distinctive through hybridisation. Indeed, these distinctive outcomes could perhaps also usefully be imagined as 'singularities', specific concrete phenomena which cannot be 'deduced from the application of general categories and classifications' (Hallward 2001, p. 2). The contextualisation of an assumed wider process through a diverse range of processes and relationships potentially limits the value of interpreting that outcome through the original analytical lens (Stanek 2008, p. 64). Thinking this outcome as singularity (or 'specificity' – see Schmid 2015), rather than a particularity related to a universal, could open up the possibility to identify different processes, or to establish novel lines of conceptualisation. This could invite us to begin the process of conceptualisation from '"places" considered as natural, in their merely physical or sensory reality' (Lefebvre 1991, p. 16).

More generally, we might consider any urban outcome as 'individual' - the full reality of any phenomenon which always exceeds the universal, constantly interrupting the Hegelian dialectic of universal-particular. Lefebvre (2009 [1940]), following Marx, insists that individuals are not (statistical) '"uniques", the same everywhere, with rigid and necessary relations between them, but real beings, at a particular stage of their development, joined to each other by relationships that are complex, concrete and fluid' (p. 63). This imagination of a full, unalienated humanity was a very important manoeuvre for Lefebvre who countered the alienation of people through capitalism's production and consumption relations with the vital and sensuous, 'actual and active' process of living, with the idea of 'total man' (Lefebvre 1955). He opposed the alienation of space by 'state, capital, rationalist knowledge, and phallocentric symbolism' with the production of space as *'oeuvre'* (Kipfer 2009, pp. xxiv, xxxii).[2] This view of totality provided him with a distinctive starting point for a vital, heterodox, open and dynamic Marxist theorisation, including of space (Schmid 2022); it also brings into view some alternative approaches to abstraction and conceptualisation in the Marxist tradition. We revisit this discussion in Chapter 8.

We can draw out two different modes of abstraction which are at play in Marxist thought more generally, as well as in Lefebvre's analysis of space, and of the urban. I select Lefebvre here based on his detailed exposition of dialectical materialism as method (2009 [1940]) and because his open, heterodox Marxism has played an important role in shaping this tradition in urban studies and geography. The first mode of abstraction is deeply characteristic of Marxist thinking, and for urban studies this is very well set out by Stanek (2008) – (certain forms of) space can be seen as a concrete abstraction, mirroring Marx's theorising of the actually existing abstractions – abstractions in practice – characteristic of capitalism (money, commodities, labour). Thus private property, or abstract space is an actually existing abstraction, a one-sided form of space foundational to the operation of space under capitalism.

But for Marx, Lefebvre and Marxism in general, the problematic of 'totality' exposes other modes of abstraction which have posed important challenges for analysis throughout twentieth-century Marxist thought, and which turn out to have significant consequences for how cases are treated in urban comparison. In one version of totality, all instances of a particular phenomenon could be seen to form a part of a lateral totality (across time and space) of that phenomenon or concept (such as labour). The phenomenon is determined at a level of generality, with abstraction serving to identify the many different instances which could be thought of as part of a trans-historical totality. In Marx's view, though, such generalities, like 'production in general' (p. 88) or 'labour in general', which gather together all historical and different instances of a phenomenon, have a limited conceptual utility. They do not allow any 'real historical stage of production to be grasped' and might be inclined to confuse historical development with analytical precision. Rather than assuming that phenomena become more complex with time, for example, leaving simple forms in the past, he argues that the historical emergence of the terms themselves (like 'labour') reflects the emergence of actual historical and empirical processes of simplification (under capitalism), thus coming into being as abstractions-in-practice. Marx thus resists this move to explore 'labour in general' and rather builds towards his famous alternative approach, the 'concrete abstraction' of labour as exchange value under capitalism, which in his later work becomes a starting point rather than an end point of analysis:

> this abstraction of labour as such is not merely the mental product of a concrete totality of labours. Indifference towards specific labours corresponds to a form of society in which individuals can with ease transfer from one labour to another, and where the specific kind is a matter of chance for them, hence of indifference. Such a state of affairs is at its most developed in the most modern form of existence of bourgeois society – in the United States. Here, then, for the first time, the point of departure of modern economics, namely the abstraction of the category 'labour', 'labour as such', labour pure and simple, becomes true in practice.
> (Marx 1993 [1939], p. 104)

In the *Grundrisse* Marx thus explored the limits of starting analysis with what he saw as an 'empty' abstraction based on the supposedly self-evident empirical entirety of any one phenomenon. However, he also indicated the potential for empirical reality to be developed in thought as a rich complexity of relations, a 'concrete totality' (Marx 1993, pp. 100–101).[3] Following Hegel's critique of empty empirical abstractions (Osborne 2004), he argues against simple descriptive abstractions and for a process whereby numerous careful abstract determinations, moving 'analytically to ever more simple concepts', are then retraced to the empirical phenomenon (his example is 'population'), but 'not as the chaotic conception of the whole, but as a rich totality of many determinations and relations' (p. 100). The concrete then is always for Marx (and Lefebvre) necessarily a 'concrete-in-thought'.

Thus, the process of abstraction can also be seen to operate through the more generalised possibility of elaborating a 'concrete-in-thought' as opposed to the identification of 'abstractions-in-practice' (or concrete abstractions). Paraphrasing Marx's introduction to the notebooks which have come to be known as the 'Grundrisse', Lefebvre (2009) observes that 'the concrete is the concrete because it is the synthesis of several determinations, multiplicity made one'.[4] By contrast, abstractions are one-sided dimensions of phenomena. As a result, following Marx, Lefebvre deduces that 'this whole must be recovered by moving from the abstract to the concrete' (p. 75). This can take the form of deciphering dialectically the 'totality' formed by, for example, the two sides of a commodity (as use value and exchange value), or, for example, by the interdependent concepts of production, consumption, distribution and exchange, which mutually determine and cannot be thought without each other – 'they all form the members of a totality, distinctions within a unity' (Marx 1993, p. 99).

Here, then, Lefebvre's canny interpretation of abstraction as an 'abbreviation' of the concrete makes sense: 'Categories and concepts are elaborations of the actual content, abbreviations of the infinite mass of particularities of concrete existence' (p. 92). However, insisting that the materialist dialectic begins with content (and is not contained in the mind as in Hegel's formulations), Lefebvre ponders whether there are perhaps only ever 'concrete' abstractions (p. 76), abstractions emerging from practice in the very broadest sense. And he goes on to postulate a wide-ranging methodological programme inspired by the numerous abstractions which are produced in social practice and where critique and reflection can place this in relationship to totalities of experience or interpretation. Thus, 'the whole exists concretely' (p. 114): 'This sum-total, organised by the praxis and in which the unity of the real is recovered, no partial determinism being able to ever wholly shatter it, is the truly concrete' (p. 123).

The operative concept for me in this alternative form of abstraction is the idea of a 'concrete totality' which I want to argue remains a methodological challenge for Marxist approaches, especially in the context-dependent fields of urban studies and geography. In their restatement of a Marxist urban theory in response to McFarlane (2011b), Brenner et al. (2011) note that 'assemblage thinking opens up the prospect for thinking space as a relationally overdetermined plenitude'; they suggest that this needs to be linked to critical 'geopolitical economy' to be effective (p. 237). Indeed, such a view of space as 'overdetermined plenitude' can be deduced directly from the problematic of a concrete totality from within Marxist theory and has posed a significant interpretive challenge within this tradition. We return to consider this in more detail in Chapter 8, but I want to signpost here, from within Marxist urban studies, the idea of a concrete totality as multiple, partial and open, the concrete being infinitely complex and interesting, *'inépuisable'* (inexhaustible), characterised by a tangle of relations[5] (Lefebvre 1955, p. 64), and to embrace the important commitment to building understandings with the necessarily diverse content – the matter – of experience.

As a corollary to this, Marx and Lefebvre indicate that abstractions and conceptualisations need to be worked up in relation to specific epochs; and they (especially Lefebvre) propose a dynamic, open totality, with active human subjects shaping history, and a theorisation responsive to the specific material 'content' encountered. In a theoretical world suffused with post-colonial and post-structuralist critique, such practices can illuminate possible responses to calls for Marxism to confront its Euro-centricity (Chakrabarty 2000); and confirm the need for multiple starting points to theorisation. Peter Osborne suggests that any process of conceptualisation seeking adequate apprehension of a 'totality' will necessarily be one-sided, by virtue of the multiplicity of possible concretes-in-thought which might be proposed by 'a plurality of social subjects' (p. 27). Thus Marxism has (had) to grapple not only with the general limits of seeking to apprehend a concrete totality (which following Lefebvre must always be open, reflecting the inevitability of historical change as well as analytical failure), but also with the impossibility (and inadvisability) of seeking to grasp anything like *a* totality, in a world where multiple determinations of related outcomes must be acknowledged. Martin Jay's (1984) detailed reading of the contested adventures of the concept of 'totality', and the different Marxist and post-Marxist debates which shaped engagements with this idea offers much food for thought here. What concepts ground the possibility of comprehending the totality of capitalist society (the working class?), which elements of the totality are determinant (the economy?), and how might one conceive of an open totality? Lefebvre's dynamic open sense of historical possibility, (Adorno and) Benjamin's (1999b) fragmentation and multiplication of totality in constellations offer two contemporarily resonant possible responses. Caygill (1998) for example, describes Benjamin's conceptualisation of constellation as 'an account of experience characterised by an immanent totality' (p. 13). Martin Jay comments, 'Rather than collapsing the distance between subject and object in the manner of an expressive totality, the constellation redeemed its disparate elements by maintaining their irreducible heterogeneity' (1984, p. 251).

These concerns emerging from within Marxism can support a position that potentially one has to consider beginning again with building abstractions specific to different contexts. I also take from this the necessary openness of even concrete abstractions to the particular that is, particular labours and capitals, even under capitalism, show huge variety (as abstract labour and as lived labour), hence the 'varieties of capitalism' school of analysis. As one seeks to understand a concrete totality, the multiplicity of relationships, the infinity of the concrete, draws one towards explaining a 'singularity', indeed overdetermined by a multiplicity of historically and geographically variable processes, rather than a particular aligned with pre-given universals or concepts.

For comparative analysis this raises some useful questions. Firstly, what abstractions might one work with across different situations? Taking some of the classical concrete abstractions of Marx and Lefebvre (money, labour, abstract space), contemporary anthropological work might alert us to the way in which even a powerful 'abstraction-in-practice' can quickly lose purchase in some situations as even abstractions such as money, commodities and labour operate in a diversity of historical ways (Taussig 1997). Secondly, the plethora of processes at work in any given concrete totality, and the historically open nature of such totalities, have over time drawn Marxist theorisations increasingly towards a conjunctural, incomplete and non-determinate specification of both abstract and concrete totalities (Althusser and Balibar 2009 (1968); Jay 1984). These and a diversity of post-structuralist approaches have since set analytical agendas which sit more comfortably with this openness and plurality (Goonewardena 2018; Jay 1984).

Marxism has itself had to engage with these questions directly, including within critical post-colonial studies (Chakrabarty 2000). While Michel Foucault suggested in 1975 that 'It is impossible at the present time to write history without using a whole range of concepts directly or indirectly linked to Marx's thought' (Foucault 1980, p. 53; cited in Jay 1984, p. 520), which also rings true for urban studies and geography, even today, the decades in between have offered an array of initiatives to build non-totalising and yet still critically motivated and often politically committed theoretical and philosophical analyses. Urbanists and geographers, including Marxist geographers, have pressed the politically transformative potential of their theoretical and empirical work in the face of the plurality of the social world and the fragile uncertainties of their concepts. In many political moments and contexts, it was indeed strikingly impossible for knowledge to be political without radically embracing diversity and non-closure – and here my own South African experience is instructive where race and class jostled in a tight analytical and practical entwining with gender and urban social mobilisations to insist on complex theorisations of transformation (for example, Adler and Webster 1995).

Geography's engagement with these Marxist concerns about theorising totality and grappling with conjunctural specificity directly informed the dominant British spatial and cultural analysis of Doreen Massey and Stuart Hall (Pickles 2012). Thus, the imagination of an 'open sense of place' draws concrete contexts into a multiplicity of relationships with other contexts through tracing the extensive connections and trajectories which make up a specific place (Massey 1994, 2005). Such an analysis of space, inspired to some extent by Althusser (and for Massey, later by Deleuze and Bergson) offers then a full engagement with the concrete as distinctive 'singularity', configuring a multiplicity of wider relations and connections. It also energises a commitment to conceptual multiplicity.

We can therefore conclude by proposing the importance for Marxist theory of being critically and reflexively aware in theoretical practice of the limits of abstraction, signified by (open) concrete totalities. Both theories' starting points – the complex and specific concrete content it begins with (e.g. euroamerican capitalism) – and the concrete totalities which concepts subsequently encounter potentially destabilise received analytical categories.

In comparative urban research, a productive tension between wider concepts (universals, concrete abstractions) and particular urban outcomes has informed the vernacular practices of comparison (as opposed to the strictures of the quasi-scientific formal method). Thus the format of wider processes working out differently across different local contexts has conventionally structured the possibility of comparative enquiry. Shared processes affecting many different places (fiscal restructuring, changing international division of labour, shared policy or rule regimes) or concrete universals (like states, urban social movements) reproduced across many contexts, are seen to be present, if differently in different places; in conjunction with the specific features of each place the outcomes are different in each locality. By comparing these outcomes we of course learn something about the specificity of each locality (Tilly's (1984) individualising comparison), but we can also compare and analyse the intervening (localised) processes in each place which affect the specific outcome, as well as learn more about the wider overarching process. This variety then provides researchers with many excellent 'natural experiments' (Diamond and Robinson 2011), the basic potential of the comparative imagination in social science.

Susan Clarke's (1995) study of 'restructuring' discussed in Chapter 3 can help us to approach how the particular spatialities of the urban might impact on the operationalization of a comparative imagination. We can also draw out how assumptions regarding the relationships between concepts and phenomena have shaped vernacular comparative practice. In Clarke's study we see the postulation of a process affecting many places in the world: 'restructuring', the reorganisation of industrial production through a 'new international division of labour' made possible by changing technologies of communication, deskilling and spatial fragmentation of the labour process, and huge differentials in labour costs around the world, in the context of new trade and currency regimes. This wider process is seen to work out differently in different cities, shaped by the specific histories and combinations of economic and political activities in that place. The imagination at work, then, is of a wider process, which is somehow conceptualised as 'a' process, working out differently on the ground, in a hybridised way. A similar imagination would subtend the argument that 'neoliberalisation' shapes each locality, only instantiated differently in each case.

Peck et al. (2009) make an important move in this regard, proposing a recursive relationship between the circulation of neoliberalising policies, and their localisation and differentiation across different urban contexts. In their analysis, though, this finds a higher resolution with differentiation itself (as 'variegation') being cast as a key feature of the logic of the wider process of neoliberalisation, supporting the functional (if contradiction-ridden) search in localities for governance innovations which could resolve capitalist crisis tendencies. Nonetheless, their work presents an important opening in contemporary urban studies to establish Marxist analyses which are radically open to empirical diversity and thus conceptual revisability. We might therefore be drawn to revise understandings of the nature of neoliberalism as a result of this differentiation (Peck 2004) and, at the limit, propose that new concepts might be required to understand certain outcomes (Ferguson 2010; Robinson 2011b).

The methodological imagination that posits a duality of case/empirical observation and wider social processes which occupy some other dimension and carry great explanatory power, only hybridised in contact with localities, can be rephrased by drawing on a more nuanced spatial imagination about globalisation (Massey 1994). Moving beyond the 'global'/'local' dichotomy which retains something of the generalised process/hybrid context structure, a focus on the specific set of flows, networks, connections, influences, circulations which add up to what had been called 'globalisation', offers an alternative way to understand the empirical and conceptual connections amongst distinctive places. Specific channels can be charted (Tsing 2000); people, things and ideas can be traced; and the ways in which these come together to compose a place, a specific outcome, can be understood 'genetically' – we can trace the specific historical events and influences which explain particular urban outcomes amongst many other inter-related outcomes; we can explore the trajectories of phenomena, their 'assemblage' and co-ordination. Rather than positing a unified process, such as restructuring, or neoliberalisation, it should be possible to name and trace the production and effect, for example, of certain rule regimes for trade; the politics of the creation and circulation of ideas that shape governance practices; the techniques and regulations that generate financial practices; the bundle of geopolitical concerns that direct flows of aid, trade, arms and fighting or fleeing bodies (Larner 2009; Peck and Theodore 2012).[6]

To compose these as more general processes – capitalist restructuring, neoliberalisation – may well be helpful for some analytical purposes, such as to define and demarcate wider trends, or to interpret an effective shift in practices, or to characterise a period, for example. But postulating these as singular external processes, only hybridised in interaction with different contexts, establishes a pattern for explanation which reduces the capacity to approach the diversity of actual historical influences shaping distinctive outcomes (we already have a causal alibi in mind in the supposedly overarching process identified previously or elsewhere). This also significantly undermines the possibility that experiences in different places could shape and transform conceptualisations of these wider processes, which are often given a lot of 'weight' in analysis, thus becoming hard to dislodge.

Alternatively, a range of relevant concepts, processes or agentful historical assemblages might be identified through engagement with specific situations. This is especially important since so-called wider conceptualisations very often reflect a located view: 'capitalist restructuring' entailed significant growth and expansion of cities in many parts of the world – but the conceptualisation and analysis of restructuring in urban studies have been articulated largely through US and European cities which experienced certain forms of industrial decline and set about searching for other opportunities to renew their economic fortunes. Massively expanding and industrialising urban contexts, such as Chinese cities, Hong Kong, Singapore, Seoul and many others might also inform this analytic. Similarly, the many cities around the world whose branch plant and Import Substitution Industrialisation economies have been decimated by the more recent changing global trade regime (like many in Brazil, India, South Africa), or the many cities around the world, notably in Africa, whose systems of social support and governance were torn apart by Structural Adjustment Programmes – these all belong in the frame of these investigations too (as Peck 2004, establishes for neoliberalism). At the very least, the wider systemic processes need to be subject to interrogation and reconstitution based on empirical investigation in different contexts.

An imagination which preserves the idea that wider processes, or more strongly, structures (such as global capitalism) derived in analysis can be identified locally in a hybrid, differentiated form, generates a view of many places as residual to theorisation, marking only the hybridization of processes derived (and already conceptualised) from elsewhere. This both retains the centrality of conceptualisations informed by only some contexts, and reduces the study of different places to a form of 'defanged empiricism', unable to transform understandings of these wider processes and leaving conceptualizations relatively intact (see Chaudhury 2012; Connell 2007).

Here, then, we confront the significance of the case in the comparative imagination. Is it helpful to see the case either as:

- an example of a general concept, or wider process (here is 'restructuring' in action; here we can identify 'neoliberalism'), that is, as a particular for a specified and pre-theorised universal, or;

- as a 'context' (a concrete totality) in which circulating trajectories or processes or widely spread phenomena (concrete universals) are hybridised (but perhaps not themselves understood differently) – that is, local context adds only empirical variety but makes no analytical difference?

While both of these manoeuvres lead to a more nuanced understanding of processes and concepts, in their hybridity or their particularity in different cases, neither of these alternatives directs us to a strongly revisable theorisation, to the opportunity to initiate theoretical insights from new starting points. When, for example, is a state not a state; or neoliberalism hybridised out of existence? When does money no longer stand for the form of equivalence amongst capitalist commodities, and rather indicates a zone of magic (Taussig 1997). Would new concepts/abstractions emerge through beginning with the rich fullness of a distinctive context? Both manoeuvres identified above do little justice to the rich complexity of the urban/space.

Taking off from the post-Marxist spatial analytic of globalisation discussed above (and by extension of global urbanisation), the following section considers an alternative starting point for conceptualisation. Specifically, the following section asks, in the vocabulary of Gilles Deleuze, what if cases were approached as singularities? If cases are considered to be singularities they can be seen as distinctive outcomes on their own terms, not already interpreted as particular instances of a wider process, or of a universal category. They would be opened up for conceptualisation through a wider array of available interpretations, inter-related cases or emergent concepts. This can lead us to a focus on building understandings with and across cases through what I will call, after Deleuze and Guattari (1994), 'generative' comparative tactics, focussed on generating concepts. In addition, I suggest that in Deleuze's philosophical efforts to characterise how we come to know the world, we can also find inspiration to approach cases through their genesis within the often interconnected processes and events which produce singularities, alongside many other inter-related singularities – much as in the revised view of globalisation I outlined above. This starting point for thinking the urban, through its interconnections, specificities and repetitions, we could call 'genetic' comparative tactics. This resonates strongly with the 'encompassing' forms of comparison which have been important in shaping understandings of globalising cities (Friedmann and Wolff 1982; King 1990b; Taylor 2004).

In the following section, I explore whether reformulating comparison along these lines could offer a more sustained commitment to theoretical revisability, and provide scope for any case, any city, any urban outcome, to make a difference to existing concepts and to be a starting point for conceptualisation.

Singularities, Repeated Instances, Concepts

> *Could it be possibly here, faced with the extraordinary challenge of mapping a world-wide yet internally hierarchized and differentiated urban ensemble that the conceptual and methodological gesture facilitated through assemblage approaches becomes most productive?*
> (Brenner, Madden and Wachsmuth 2011, p. 237)

The nature of the urban world, composed of many different centres, cities, settlements and circulations, has produced a certain possibility for the comparative imagination, as discussed so far; it can also provide some direction for how we might start to reframe comparisons. Perhaps most significant are two key and related features of the urban:

(1) cities are highly interconnected with one another;
(2) across cities, urban outcomes are repetitive, even as they are at the same time distinctive.

The best example I have seen which illuminates this is Jane M. Jacobs' (2006) discussion of the serial production of the residential high rise. Here the distinctive achievement of each repetition – almost-the-same – through globalizing circulations and specific assembling of diverse elements to produce each building provides an insight into what it might mean to think with the productivity of the virtual in the sphere of the urban (Farías 2010, p. 15). The achievement of urban modernity in the repetitive architecture of international modernism emerges from the relatively unpredictable multiplicity of circulations and manifold elements able to be assembled into each construction – buildings which are both repeated and yet produced as original objects, with an equally original yet partly repeated and interconnected set of meanings crafted locally, differently each time (King 2004): 'the making of repetition – or more precisely, repeated instances in many different contexts – requires variance, different assemblages of allies in different settings' (Jacobs 2006, p. 22). For Jacobs, each instance *produces* the global *effect* of international modernism: each instance is a singularity, emergent from an array of interconnected practices, ideas and relationships, and not an example of an already given global process (Jacobs 2012). To my mind this is a significant intervention – not least directing us to reconsider how we understand the 'repeated instance', which is such a significant feature of the urban landscape – from architectural design to gated communities; from circulating brand images to low-income housing finances; from strategic visioning to market stalls; and numerous other examples.

The global/local distinction, then, is erased in favour of attending to the specific interconnected processes creating outcomes, as Jane M. Jacobs demonstrates. Thus the elements of the urban which might present themselves for (comparative) analytical reflection would be distributed across multiple 'cities', as many differentiations of inter-related urban outcomes. Thinking with both the interconnections and the differences, then, places a multiplicity of cities and urban outcomes within the same analytical frame, and provides fruitful grounds for methodological experimentation.

In my view this also offers a way to bring the spatiality of the urban into methodological imagination in new ways. Rather than starting with territorialised cases, imagined as composed of wider processes hitting the ground differently, comparative practices could engage with urban outcomes through tracing their *genesis* by means of specific connections, influences, actions, compositions, alliances, experiences, across the full array of possible elements of urban life: material-social-lived-imaginative-institutional.

An Urban Virtual?

We could arrive at an understanding of a 'virtual' urban – which could be something like all the possibilities for the production and understanding (determination) of specific urban outcomes. The 'virtual'[7] for Deleuze seeks to capture the multiplicity of conceptual-and-empirical elements which come into thought and which contribute to enabling determination of any of a perhaps infinite variety of related but specific outcomes (perhaps much as the equation describing a curve in mathematics produces an infinity of specifiable singular points; or genetic information produces any number of different but specifiable inter-related individuals). Insofar as we might imagine a virtual terrain of processes, phenomena and ideas concerned with producing the urban, this would be equivalent to placing all cities within a potentially shared analytical terrain. There is scope to benefit from some intuitive resonances with empirical forms of the urban, as in the Jane M. Jacobs example above, where a multiplicity of flows and connections, processes and practices can be traced to understand the emergence of many different, repeated instances of urban phenomena. An urban 'virtual', then, would also index the realm of 'Ideas' as the multiplicity of interconnected possibilities for bringing objects (any urban outcomes) into conceptualisation (determining outcomes). This would be imagined as developed in close association with the genetic modes of becoming of urban outcomes, in which an interconnected array of urban processes and practices might be seen as productive of 'any city whatever' (Simone 2011). Cities, though, are not only produced through the wider interconnections and assemblages that Jane M. Jacobs highlights, but the urban is also made through the active associations, practices, imaginations, experiences, alliances and heterogeneous stitching together of possibilities within and across cities (Lefebvre 1991; Simone 2011). These constitute the genesis of specific urban outcomes and experiences (see Ferrari 2013 for a fascinating operationalisation of this; also Farias 2010, who poses the question as to what an urban virtual might be). The 'urban' then might be the entire field of possibilities which are potentially instantiated in any city whatever (Simone 2011b).

The field of the urban resonates well with Deleuze's (1994) exploration of '*Difference and Repetition*' in the sense that he proposes an active process of conceptualisation in the midst of a dynamic world. We can imagine ourselves, then, as conceptualising subjects encountering an urban 'virtual'. On the basis of a multiplicity of observed phenomena (singularities)[8] we will be drawn to identify (determine) individual entities, distinctive urban outcomes. Some of these will be inter-related, repeated but different, with no sense of origin or model vs copy. To make these determinations we would be able to draw on all possible available ideas about the urban. The potential will exist to consider any urban outcomes, all cities, as part of a shared analytical field, but insist on attending to the multiplicity (difference and divergence) of empirical and conceptual possibilities.[9] If we are directed by Deleuze to rethink how to understand repeated yet differentiated outcomes, it is in the context of his much wider project of trying to re-craft philosophical interpretations of how we come to know the world in its emergence – how do phenomena come into our understanding?

Generating Concepts

In an incredibly complex formulation (and only one element of a vast philosophical contribution) in *Difference and Repetition* Deleuze sets out to recast accounts of the confrontation between a knowing subject and an impenetrable world. An important point of departure and critical engagement for his work is the Kantian imagination of how the manifold (translated in English as 'the diverse') comes into human understanding as 'diverse' pre-existent entities, known through the syntheses (apprehension, reproduction, recognition), categories (universals), and on the basis of the unchanging schema of space and time (1994, p. 356; Due 2007, pp. 24–5).[10] Deleuze famously indicates that 'Difference is not diversity. Diversity is given, but difference is that by which the given is given, that by which the given is given as diverse' (Deleuze 1994, p. 280). Deleuze draws this manifold into a much more intimate interaction with conceptualisation, in which the entities, the knowing subject, as well as space and time are emergent in processes of conceptualisation and individuation (see Flaxman 2005). Rather than seeking to conceptualise diverse pre-given entities through a representational idiom, he orchestrates a vast repertoire of philosophical endeavour to provide some alternative formulations for understanding the co-emergence of entities, and Ideas/concepts.[11]

This philosophical project does not present us with a manual for comparative urban practice, or for social science method – neither is it an effective description of the way the world is. Rather, we find in this work a contemporary rubric (full of divided subjects and shifting materialities, for example) for appreciating what might be at stake in coming to know a dynamic, emergent world. At the core of this account are the many ways in which the idea of difference can be put to work to disturb and offer some alternative imaginations for how we come to understanding, in contrast with the representational model of concepts which mirror, or fail to mirror, entities in the world.[12] The story begins with the contractions of difference as intuitions are drawn on by a fractured subject which tries (and fails) to produce understanding. In the tracks of Kant he portrays this as a series of failed syntheses based on the repetitions which this search for understanding of phenomena involves as observations are drawn towards understanding through the realms of habit (the present), memory (constituting duration and the past) and then ranging more widely across the imagination and thoughts which mobilise different available experiences and contexts. Drawing on repertoires from science, biology, mathematics, psychoanalysis as well as philosophical debates inspired by Kant, Hegel, Heidegger, Nietzche, Bergson, Leibniz and others, Deleuze postulates a process of conceptualisation which recasts Kant's subject-centred formulations to propose 'Ideas' as constellations of observations in which matter is drawn into conceptualisation. He adds a distinctive but parallel set of processes (syntheses) whereby matter is re-drawn into understanding as 'intensities'[13] (elements of matter) are explicated and individuated in relation to (a virtuality of) Ideas.

Thus he articulates a dual process of 'different/(c)iation' across two intertwined virtual series, of matter and Ideas. The determination of an entity consists of the materially inspired conceptual process of differen-t-iation, through which subjects seek to make a determination of a phenomenon within a virtual field of Ideas (themselves cast as a multiplicity of intersecting series, complexes of relations and singularities). But it also entails the explication, or dramatization, of the sensible in which the qualitative and extensive emergence of an individuated, differen-c-iated, entity is determined. This is accompanied by the production of the 'spatium', the constitution of depth, of space (on this see Dewsbury and Thrift 2005). With the subject's awareness of the intensities remaining after (ultimately failing) efforts (in habit, memory and thought) at formulating Ideas have drawn off difference through repetition (as intuition, as memory) to stimulate interpretation, a final (asymmetric) 'synthesis' is postulated which sees Ideas and sensibilities brought together to arrive at a represented object, from 'a sensibility "bubbling" with intensities and a thought "rumbling with Ideas"' (Hughes 2009, p. 168).[14]

Deleuze's philosophy offers us some new patterns for appreciating how concepts of things and the things themselves might be understood as entwined: suggesting that concepts emerge from recursive engagements with an active world, presenting itself to us, posing problems for our memory, habitual practices and finally our imagination and coming to our understanding as concepts through a series of failed efforts by a fragmented subject and a dispersed self to resolve these (extra-/intra-/inter-) subjective processes. This lengthy dynamic process arrives at an always incomplete apprehension of phenomena with residual 'intensities', and unconceptualised differences that are drawn off from emergent concepts which continue to bubble through (disturb) our concepts.

(How) Can We Use This?

This is philosophy, not method. But since much of our method has been inspired by alternative Kantian and Hegelian philosophical imaginaries, Deleuze's approach to concept formation should give us pause for thought and scope to reimagine the architecture of the active processes of conceptualisation which are at work in contributing to our understanding of the phenomena we engage with. Deleuze offers us an account of conceptualisation which draws on and works with the production and productivity of differences – actively working across related and divergent phenomena, and especially thinking with how a phenomenon is produced, with its genesis, which directs us to the multiplicity of outcomes which share this genetic field (Due 2007, p. 37). In his terms, 'difference is drawn off' through efforts to conceptualise, as we attend to repeated/differentiated phenomena and as we create our own conceptual repetitions in the quest to understand the object or problem confronted.

Concepts then can be thought of as multiplicities, constituting not overarching 'singular' solutions to understanding the generalised or simply (bare) repetitive nature of things, but opening up a set of multiple possibilities for understanding differentiated outcomes. Concepts, as Ideas, could be imagined as composed of intersecting and resonant series, and are most usually expressed by Deleuze as a multiplicity made up of 'differential elements, differential relations amongst those elements, and singularities[15] corresponding to those relations' (p. 348). These are then available for contributing to determining or dramatizing entities and individuals. The conceptual imagination Deleuze proposes roams across many possibilities for thinking a phenomenon – we are not bound to think only with genetically interconnected phenomena, but also, in line with his own practice can remain open to thinking, '*with* the thinkers of the past (not "after" or "like"), as our contemporaries and companions, and look ahead as they did' (McMahon 2011, p. 52). As Deleuze and Guattari comment, 'In any concept there are usually bits or components that come from other concepts, which correspond to other problems and presuppose other planes' (1994, p. 18).

Far from offering one isolated concept per observation or experience, then, Deleuze draws us into a proliferation of revisable Ideas (an infinite 'learning' (1994, p. 241)), already intimately connected with many other concepts and experiences but amongst which there is no origin or model, original or copy (p. 153). This is most evident in Deleuze's characterisation of the moment in which a distinctive pre-individual 'singularity' (or observation) is determined in the (virtual) Idea. He postulates this as a form of eternal return in a Nietzchean divine game of chance – signifying the Idea as a repetition without origin, an 'aleatory point at which everything becomes *ungrounded* instead of a solid ground' (p. 250). In the absence of the conventional philosophical imagination of pre-defined categories, and with no coherent subject, 'the act of thinking is a "throw of the dice"', and at each putative throw, all of chance is affirmed, every possibility is considered – the full validity of each (clothed) repetition is valorised, Ideas are thought and the potential of the virtual is apparent in this multiplicity (Hughes 2009, p.132).

Famously, and more accessibly, his approach can be characterised as provoking the generation of concepts (Deleuze and Guattari 1994). In a Deleuzian idiom we might consider then that the urban manifold in its many expressions 'makes itself known to us', as Simone (2011, p. 356) puts it; or following Deleuze, 'Something in the world forces us to think' (1994, p. 176). This generates new problems for us to reflect on, prompting processes of conceptualisation. In the case of thinking cities (in a world of cities, in the context of a wider field of 'the urban'), we are very quickly drawn to bring the experiences and conceptualisations of other cities or urban outcomes to bear on any specific problem we are confronted with. We become aware of the multiplicity of interconnected processes generating urban outcomes, acknowledging that different urban outcomes often have a shared genesis and validating the need to think them together; and we might find in the realm of conceptualisation (theoretical debate; other cases) good ideas and practices elsewhere to help to think the new context with, to different(c)iate entities, to unground concepts, to subtract from overarching singular conceptualisations.[16]

Inspired by Deleuze (1994), then, and following these two intertwined virtual series through which Ideas and matter/the manifold are seen to emerge, I suggest that urban comparisons might be thought of as 'genetic', tracing the interconnected genesis of repeated, related but distinctive, urban outcomes as the basis for comparison; or as 'generative' where variation across shared features provides a basis for generating conceptual insights supported by the multiple, sometimes interconnected, theoretical conversations which enable global urban studies. The following section explores these two starting points, or 'grounds' for comparative analysis in more detail and sets out a systematic approach to a reformatted urban comparativism.

Genetic and Generative Grounds for Urban Comparisons

Broadening the potential identified in 'variation-finding' methods Chapter 3 proposed that *composing* analytical constellations across a range of selected cases, could be grounded on *shared features* of different urban contexts. Following Deleuze this could be seen as a **generative** starting point for comparison, inspired by our own curiosity and analytical agenda, the virtuality of concepts/Ideas. Alternatively, as we saw in Chapters 2 and 3, a central opportunity for urban studies lies in describing analytical proximities through 'encompassing comparisons' which could involve *tracing connections* across diverse urban contexts. This draws on the **genetic** interconnectedness of urban phenomena as the grounds for initiating a comparative imagination. Very broadly, both such kinds of comparison would encourage *launching interpretations* from specific cases to contribute to a revisable urban theory or to generate concepts. Rather than seeking to prevent conceptual 'overstretch' (Pierre 2005), a concern of earlier urban comparativists, a revised comparative urbanism would seek to deliberately stretch concepts, perhaps to breaking point.

Taking a 'genetic' approach, starting points could be what Jacobs (2006) calls 'repeated instances', the (differently) repeated outcomes which reflect the transnational interconnectedness (globalisation) of urban processes. In this idiom, the circulations and connections which shape many different cities could constitute the basis for comparative analyses, bringing different cities into the same analytical frame, or themselves become the object of comparative enquiry. More loosely, 'generative' grounds for comparison would encourage the purposive composition of a selection of cases which suggest opportunities for enhancing conceptualisation or inventing concepts, based often on 'shared features' of different urban situations. Thus, urban experiences would be worth analysing across a very wide range of contexts, and research strategies could be developed which are adequate to the complex spatiality of urban forms.

The key comparative ambition to explain outcomes could benefit from re-framing the meaning of the 'case' in urban studies, then, as not simply an example (perhaps hybridised) of singular and analytically pre-given overarching processes (Jacobs 2012), but as so many instances, or distinctive outcomes, singularities, multiply resonant with one another, and interconnected through a shared genesis. This offers us a starting point for a quite different geography to conceptualisation – and to the comparative imagination.

We can imagine a **set of 'genetic' comparative tactics**, inspired by the core spatial form of the urban as interconnected but differentiated, as inspiration for such a mode of comparativism. The methodological practice here is genetic in the sense of tracing how a specific urban outcome emerges, and through this engagement with its production, or genesis, alongside many other interrelated phenomena, to draw it into conceptualisation.

And I suggest we can also imagine a **set of 'generative' comparative tactics**, in which a virtual field of conceptualisation can be provoked and enriched through bringing different singularities, or cases, into conversation, as inspired by the problems thrown up for/by us. With Deleuze, we can think with whatever comes to hand. Conceptualisation might be thought of as beginning anywhere, with any singularity (as outcome, case or context), but emerging through building connections with and identifying differentiations across other instances – both those which are genetically, that is, outcomes emergent from interconnected and related processes; and those which are conceptually generative, that is, helping to consolidate and delimit understandings in a field of resonant and intersecting Ideas, working with the differential elements and relations of emergent concepts (1994, p. 239).

Both sets of comparative tactics instantiate a minimalist but productive understanding of comparison as thinking through elsewhere. In practice genetic and generative approaches are not necessarily alternatives, only different methodologically robust starting points, which we might expect from the way in which cities are strongly inter-related. The tactics which flow from these different grounds for comparing might bleed into one another during the course of analysis.

Furthermore, we can gain some purchase on questions such as, *How far can concepts stretch? When should they be abandoned?* Most importantly for the project to promote a more global theoretical conversation about the urban, able to start anywhere, the conceptual repertoire of thinking with difference without origin or copy, provides a strong indication of openness to revisability. It motivates an affirmation rather than negation, externalisation (outside concepts), or disregard (in assertions of pure repetition) of difference. This, Deleuze reminds us, results from the 'multiplicity which belongs to the Idea' (Deleuze 1994, p. 336). Thus, on the one hand, following Deleuze's own terminology, we find that as unchanging concepts stretch to new cases, or are imagined as (bare) repetitions rather than 'clothed and living vertical repetition which includes difference', much difference risks becoming unconceptualised.[17] We might be left with:

- concepts without difference: they might be imagined to remain inviolate as a concept across many different instances – and the processes of generating 'lateral totalities' or 'abstraction' (both as abbreviation and as concrete abstraction) or 'universalization' would all invoke this dynamic;

- equally we would have much difference without conceptualisation, a point AbdouMaliq Simone (2016) makes in advocating a manoeuvre to trace trajectories of 'black urbanism' to initiate conceptualisation in urban situations where conceptualisation has been neglected or disavowed.

Thus, a two-fold practical strategy emerges (if my reading of these debates is productive):

- It is very reasonable to begin processes of conceptualisation anywhere, with any given singularity, or in any concrete totality, and to develop conceptualisations in relation to (any available) other concepts and also to inter-related phenomena through the empirical exploration and proliferation of connections and differences.
- Concepts emergent from specific cases will start to lose purchase, as 'difference' is drawn off. Concepts therefore are well imagined as deeply revisable, and as sites of multiplication. Whereas in conventional comparisons the 'grounds' for comparison seek to stabilise the associations amongst cases, here the postulation of concepts across cases can encounter a profound 'ungrounding', and might contribute to practices of 'subtraction' from extant conceptualisations (Jacobs 2012), extending the multiplicity of the virtual field of Ideas, or launching emergent interpretations.

Conceptualisation, then, can productively take place through attention to multiple inter-related (conceptual or empirical) urban outcomes, placing these in conversation and collaboration with elsewhere through various comparative tactics (again, both empirical and conceptual), in the interests of multiplying analyses, and revising useful concepts.

Whether through genetic or generative tactics – tracing the emergence of a phenomenon, or thinking with elsewhere – conceptualising specific contexts is placed in relation to the wider urban world. In this imagination – which is not to prejudice the specific (scientific) methodologies for exploration or questions to be explored, nor the nature of the theoretical repertoires adequate to the entities we seek to come to an understanding of – conceptualization is a dynamic and generative process, subject to rules of experimentation and revisability, embedded in wider conversations, but with the potential to start anywhere.

We are returned to a minimalist definition of comparison as 'thinking cities through elsewhere'. Such a mapping of the relationship between outcomes and conceptualisation as I have explored here calls for different tactics from those proposed in the quasi-scientific and universal-particular (or wider processes/hybridised outcomes) model of comparison.

Conclusion: From Grounds to Tactics

In this chapter I have proposed to reimagine comparison as involving the broad practice of thinking the urban through elsewhere (another case, a wider context, existing theoretical imaginations, connections to other places), in order to better understand outcomes and to contribute to strongly revisable broader conceptualisations and wider conversations about (aspects of) the urban. With Marxist traditions and Lefebvre's insistence on the urban as an 'open' and concrete totality, the urban world will always exceed our analytical determinations, characterised by an incomplete process of conceptualization. Inspired by Deleuze (1994), I suggest that urban comparisons might be thought of as 'genetic', tracing the interconnected genesis of repeated, related but distinctive, urban outcomes as the basis for comparison; or as 'generative' where other instances or other concepts inspire analytical proximity as a basis for generating conceptual insights. Both tactics are supported by and contribute to the multiple, sometimes interconnected, sometimes disjunct, theoretical conversations which enable global urban studies. This chapter thus proposed new spatialities of *theorising* which see concepts set in motion – *launched* – from anywhere, into sometimes limited, perhaps divergent, but potentially global conversations towards an ongoing reinvention of the term, urban. Part II of the book will explore in detail what kinds of comparative tactics and practices might emerge on this basis.

The field of urban studies has provoked a range of experimental comparisons which demonstrate the potential of this formulation. In fact, a few authors have quite explicitly favoured the formulation of 'genetic' and 'generative' approaches. For example, in his analysis of late entrepreneurialism, Peck proposes that 'constitutive connections and family resemblances' both offer grounds for pursuing comparative analysis across the different urban contexts he is interested in – Detroit and Atlantic City (2017a, p. 8). Similarly, Lancione and McFarlane (2016, p. 2404) suggest that their experimental comparison 'is an effort to reveal *at the same time* "interconnected trajectories" (Ward 2010) *and* differential patterns'. Others have found it helpful to specifically use these terms to justify their comparative analyses (Kanai and Schindler 2019). The rest of the book draws together a number of contributions in urban studies which help to explore further what it might mean to take forward comparative urban analysis on 'genetic' and 'generative' grounds.

The pragmatic implications of the analysis I have presented here are considerable. In my mind, we have permission to walk away from many of the strictures of the methodologies which have shaped comparative investigations of the urban these last decades. Starting anywhere, with a mind to treat urban outcomes as 'individual' or distinctive, and urban theory as multiplicity, means being open to placing under potential erasure insights which might have worked well once, somewhere. It could of course also mean openings for exciting afterlives for these theories, and enable a multiplicity of new constellations of the narratives which we inherit. For example, as Adorno is swerved to enthuse thinking in Bangkok (Korff 1986), or inspiration is found in Agamben or Lefebvre for thinking the emergent urban in some cities in Africa (Simone 2004; Mwathunga 2014). Concepts might be generated through the initiation of conversations from relatively unconceptualised urban experiences, such as black urban life (Simone 2016). Or, a comparative imagination might be used to slowly build new conceptual apparatuses to make sense of and collaborate in actions to shape the futures of the poorest urban contexts (Fourchard and Bekker 2013; Pieterse and Simone 2013). An important agenda is to expand the scope and conceptual potential for a more global urban studies by following up on unexpected comparative itineraries, for example, those which track the personal ties of researchers (Myers 2014; Roy 2003). Finally, I see an important challenge in recasting places conventionally at the centre of theorizing the urban, such as London, or Los Angeles, as destinations for theory, inspired to think their distinctive pathways through ideas launched from elsewhere (Schindler 2013b).

Thus, a reformulated comparativism can start theorising anywhere, imagine any city as a destination for thinking from elsewhere, if that seems productive, and find openings for new analyses in the certain knowledge that conceptualisation is fraught with both uncertainties and potentialities, both disjunctures and analytical proximities. We can be inspired then to proliferate opportunities for thinking the urban with elsewhere, in order to multiply and to unground analytical insights. Comparative experiments of various kinds can help to identify productive manoeuvres, initiating encounters across any urban contexts and processes whatever, along traces and leaps of connection, actual or invented. The potential is to inspire thinking both with actual connections (genetic), in which we are 'invited' to think with the spatialities of the urban, and through conceptual leaps in which we 'invent' proximities and links, drawing places together within the realm of a more topological spatiality. A reformatted urban comparativism insists on keeping open the possibility to initiate insights from any urban places, drawing experiences and events into sometimes overlapping, sometimes disjunct, but always revisable conversations about the nature and future of the urban.

The comparative imperative to think the urban 'with elsewhere' is a response to some of the core challenges of understanding global urbanisation. In Part I of the book we have seen that the discrete territoriality of the conventional comparative imagination is a poor fit with complex, networked and dispersed spatialities of interdependent urban territories, or the extended, even planetary, processes which characterise contemporary urbanisation. So, to rethink the urban it is necessary to reformat methodologies and tactics which can respond to the nature of urbanisation processes and outcomes; this is the focus of Chapters 5 to 11. The rest of the book will also explore how different theoretical perspectives on the 'shape' of the urban world matter to how comparison is configured – whether you are thinking with relations, conjunctures, assemblages, scales, connections, surfaces, differences or territories proposes different ways forward and reveals different tactics for how urban comparativism might operate. Different approaches also entrain different views as to the nature of the case, its position in relation to wider processes, contingency, or materiality, and also provide different insights about the relation between observations and conceptualisation. But the chapters to come will also delve into how any reformatted comparative urban imagination might be imagined and put to work by the subjects of urban research. How does the positionality of researchers frame and transform theoretical debates and methodologies?

This sets a formidable methodological agenda. What are some precise ways in which it might be possible to initiate or compose comparisons on genetic or generative grounds? How might we imagine the agentful researcher involved in such compositions? What is the status and revisability of concepts generated? The rest of the book explores a range of potential responses to the challenges of building comparative insights, outlining a dynamic methodological landscape of comparative tactics, on genetic and generative grounds, which resonate with the contemporary urban world.

Notes

1. This chapter is an edited version of 'Thinking Cities through Elsewhere', *Progress in Human Geography* (*PIHG*), 2016.
2. 'The true subject of the Becoming is living man. Yet around and above him the abstractions acquire a strange existence and a mysterious efficacy; Fetishes reign over him' (Lefebvre 2009, p. 85).
3. Lefebvre (2009 [1940], p. 83) starts an example with categories which are concrete abstractions (such as exchange value, abstract labour, money, capital) and proposes that 'each category has its place in the explicative whole which leads to the reconstitution of the given concrete totality'.
4. 'The concrete is concrete because it is the concentration of many determinations, hence unity of the diverse' (Marx 1993, p. 101).
5. 'le phénomène (immédiat, donné, present devant nous) est toujours plus riche, plus complexe, que toute loi et toute essence' (Lefebvre 1955, p. 60).
6. Interestingly, Deleuze sees scope for a 'genetic' account of "structure" (p. 240), including a discussion here of Marxist thought (p. 235): 'there is no more opposition between event and structure or sense and structure than between structure and genesis'; but structure as a (genetic) virtuality.

7. Joe Hughes, in his very helpful Guide to Deleuze's *Difference and Repetition* observes that we can understand 'the virtual as the field in which problems – or Ideas – are progressively determined' (2009, p. 112). This is not a virtual to come, in which the possibility of the present is to be fulfilled and is unspecifiable (Lefebvre works with such an approach to virtuality), but an emergent, genetic and historical virtuality, also constituted by our intuition or observations, and marking the potential for any number of different, related instances to emerge into our understanding.

8. Hallward (2001) offers a definition of singularity as not existing in relation to pregiven universals which is a common understanding in social science, and broadly informed the discussion above. Strictly speaking, any urban outcome is an 'individual' identified on the basis of intuitions/observations (which are the singularities in Deleuze's philosophy). The singularity for Deleuze, then, is more precise, and deeply embedded in his non-representational account of concepts. In the introduction to *Difference and Repetition*, Deleuze hinges his critique of representation on such an interpretation of the singularity as 'an immediate object of intuition without reference to any other object' (Hughes 2009, p. 30). Let us call this a 'philosophical' definition of singularity. Through the text, though, Deleuze (1994) relies a lot on mathematical metaphors, in which singularities are defined somewhat differently, and take on a variety of forms. For example, as those moments of substantial transformation in a series, in which 'repetitions' initiate a new series. These exist alongside numerous 'ordinary' repetitions (or singularities), which rather prolong a series, which could be imagined to come to an end in a neighbouring singularity, inflected as distinct (p. 251). However, the ungrounding of a sense of origin (vs repetition) (p. 252), and the generation of each (repeated) instance (concept) as an aleatory point governed by chance/metaphorical throws of the dice and constituting a constellation of a multiplicity of observations or singularities, also asserts every instance/repetition (as outcome) as a singularity. This analysis is derived from Deleuze's reading of Leibniz's calculus of infinity, as well as his more philosophical analysis of 'monads' – the 'soul' or concept 'appurtaining to' a singularity (Deleuze 2006). Chapter 11 expands on this.

9. The analytical field of the urban is indeed rich and diversified, differentiated by topic, decades of theoretical endeavour, as well as being potentially limited and truncated in its relevance to different regions or cities. I do not seek to flatten the complex terrain of social or urban theory – but I think that we can insist that the field of possibilities for understanding the urban is both analytically and empirically interconnected across the multiplicity of possible outcomes.

10. Deleuze observes the play on the invented word, '*erewhon*' (Samuel Butler), which might apply to the generic schemata as they move unchanged from place to place, but which could also be rendered 'here now' and inform the ambivalence he reads in Kant's discussion of the schema of space and time, which might 'take flight and point beyond themselves in the direction of the conception of

differential ideas', 'irreducible both to the universality of the concept and to the particularity of the now here' (p. 356; note 7).

11. In *Difference and Repetition* Deleuze counterposes representational concepts to 'Ideas' (p. 360) but later (*What Is Philosophy*) reverts to 'concepts' which are presented in the same way in which he formerly defined ideas.

12. 'An essential feature of representation is that it takes a bare and material repetition as its model, a repetition understood in terms of the Same and explained in terms of the negative' (Deleuze 1994, p. 357).

13. Intensities being the sense of matter which persists after different/ciating entities – 'Intensities pull Ideas outside of their virtuality; Ideas give form to intensity' (Hughes 2009, p. 168).

14. There is much that might be inspiring from the insistence of these intensities, the need to approach urban outcomes afresh in their distinctive, compelling, unconceptualised emergence. Pieterse (2013) mobilises some of this imagination in his quest, along with Maliq Simone, for vocabularies to understand the 'rogue urbanisms' of some aspects of cities in Africa.

15. As intuitions or immediate observations. In his dramatization of the production of concepts, singularities for Deleuze are these immediate intuitions which produce, in the recursive manner discussed below and in Chapter 11, concepts as constellations of singularities. This contrasts with the vernacular social science use of 'singularity' as one distinctive phenomenon – which would conform more precisely to the Idea/concept, or constellations of singularities, in Deleuze's vocabulary.

16. Elsewhere I suggest that we find some helpful resonances with these formulations in thinkers of the urban – Henri Lefebvre, who encourages us to consider that, 'If the urban is total, it is not total in the way a thing can be, as content that has been amassed, but in the way that thought is, which continues its activity of concentration endlessly but can never hold or maintain that state of concentration, which assembles elements continuously and discovers what it has assembled through a new and different form of concentration' (2003, p. 171). Here, the urban is an emergent, specific form which will always constitute a multiplicity (see Chapter 8). And Walter Benjamin, whose idea of thinking the present with analytical 'constellations' of the now, blasting experiences out of different historical moments (as opposed to the continuities of positivist history) can productively be mobilised to suggest an infinity of possible *urban* analytical constellations generated across time and space (Robinson 2013a, 2014a). We return to this in Chapter 11.

17. 'Repetition, by contrast, is represented *outside* the concept, as though it were a difference without concept, *but always with the presupposition of an identical concept*' (Deleuze 1994, p. 339). By contrast, 'The idea makes one and the same problem of difference and repetition. There is an excess and an exaggeration peculiar to Ideas which makes difference and repetition the combined object, the "simultaneous" of the Idea' (p. 360).

IMAGE 2.1 The City, The Fire Walker and the aftermath of copper cable theft. Queen Elizabeth bridge, Johannesburg, 29 December 2011 (Photograph by David Goldblatt)

IMAGE 2.2 'The Firewalker' by William Kentridge, in *Sculpture in the City 2016* at the junction of Bishopsgate and London Wall, London UK (Photograph by Nick Turpin)

PART II

Genetic Comparisons

Part I built on the spatialities of the urban, a review of urban comparative practices, and wider philosophies of conceptualisation to identify two broad grounds for mobilising a comparative imagination in urban studies: genetic grounds based on the prolific interconnections which produce differentiated urban outcomes, and generative grounds, in which researchers compose initiatives to explore the diversity of urban life. These broad framings guide the discussion of comparative tactics for 'global urban studies' which are presented in the rest of the book. Here in Part 2, we start with the connections. Urban settlements are intrinsically constituted through interconnections with other places. Tracing these connections opens out to an array of possible comparative tactics on genetic grounds. Tracing the flows and connections which constitute the urban brings into view processes of urbanisation, different kinds of urban territories, and repeated (or differentiated) instances which make up urban contexts. These are considered in Chapter 5. Chapter 6 then explores the genesis and interconnected nature of the urban through the prism of 'relationality'. Here, more political economy inspired perspectives open up additional comparative possibilities – interrogating the wider processes which shape many different urban outcomes; understanding how contexts, in bringing together many different social processes, generate distinctive outcomes and remake social processes; or being drawn by direct relations between urban contexts to highlight the diversity of processes and outcomes. Both sets of tactics, based on connections and relations, reveal a differentiated urban world, with scope for questioning inherited terms and opening cases to reflect on each other.

William Kentridge's sculpture, 'Firewalker', portrayed in the two photos here, makes an implicit connection between Johannesburg and London (Images 2.1 and 2.2, p. 134; colour versions of these images can be found between pages 132 and 133). All sorts of circuits tie cities together – Julie Ren (2020) has shown how art practices in which artists, venues and cultures are co-constituted across different urban settings might constitute a transnational terrain for analysis, drawing in more than one context to constitute a "theoretical" case. As the Firewalker installation moves through such a globalised art circuit, it brings together the two cities in the photographs – and raises questions for us. What can those moving through the elite financial district of London make of this sculpture, representing some of the poorest women in Johannesburg, carrying fire (in a brazier) on their heads to cook street food in the city centre? In the foreground of David Goldblatt's photo of the original sculpture in Johannesburg, part of an initiative for new public art in democratic post-apartheid South Africa, acts of vandalism have revealed some of the infrastructure of connection which makes urban life possible. This also exposes the interdependence of urbanisation in different contexts – the copper wires were being dug up and sold on as Chinese demand had pushed commodity prices so high. Traffic jams immobilised parts of Johannesburg as lights stopped working. Beijing brought Joburg to a standstill.

CHAPTER 5

Connections

Anthropologists have created considerable difficulties for themselves in their numerical vision of a world full of societies and cultures. The problem as it is perceived is both how to connect them and what to do with the connections between them.

(Marilyn Strathern 2005 [1991], p. 52)

Establishing the 'grounds' or justifications for comparison in the interconnections amongst urban contexts is only a starting point for comparative practice. To move beyond the horizon of a scientistic view of causality, isolating variables to explore explanatory factors across different cases by limiting variation (Steinmetz 2004), we need to consider exactly how the exciting, experimental, perhaps unexpected comparisons which tracing connections makes possible might be operationalised (Myers 2014, 2020).

What might be the scope and tactics for a practice of comparison through connections, which can start anywhere and build comparisons and analytical insights across a very great diversity of urban experiences? This could be disconcerting – opening up new horizons of comparative practice poses questions as to what collectively agreed sensible procedures for producing scholarly work remain relevant (Stengers 2011). How can we proceed?

This chapter and the next will explore how one of the two grounds for comparison developed in Part I of this book – the genetic interconnectedness of urban processes and outcomes – can be mobilised to critique, extend and develop new concepts in urban studies. The initial proposition is that there are good grounds for comparisons which are spatially adventurous, making use of interconnections to draw understandings of urbanisation to engage across strong differences, potentially enriching interpretations by attending to a much wider range of urban situations.

By stretching comparative analysis globally through working with connections, lively, productive and relevant insights into the nature of the urban

Comparative Urbanism: Tactics for Global Urban Studies, First Edition. Jennifer Robinson.
© 2022 John Wiley & Sons Ltd. Published 2022 by John Wiley & Sons Ltd.

can be generated. *Tracing* specific connections, such as a policy link, or a material flow, from one context to another, or across a number of different contexts will be the focus of this chapter. Tracing connections can reveal elements of the flows and interactions which make up the process of urbanisation as such, can help to identify 'repeated instances' in many different contexts, and can potentially bring into view a fuller range and variety of processes and outcomes shaping the urban world. In the highly transnationalised world of urban policy and urban development this methodological tactic could potentially link a very wide variety of diverse urban contexts. Two core research tactics flowing from this starting point will be proposed: (1) analysing and comparing connections as urbanisation processes; (2) working with cases as 'repeated instances'.

Connections as Urbanisation Processes

In the first instance, following connections directly illuminates the tracks and processes of urbanisation – infrastructure, people, ideas, practices, material flows. They trace the urban; they are cases of the urban. In so far as urbanisation is not about bounded territories, but about a complex spatiality of extension, strongly networked concentrations, dense and sprawling settlements, operational landscapes and technical, social and cultural practices which reach across different kinds of places, methodological innovations which move beyond observations in one place are essential to trace and understand these dynamics (McCann and Ward 2010; Schmid 2015). For our purposes here, this subtends two kinds of 'thinking with elsewhere' – the need to understand urbanisation processes intrinsically requires that analysis and methods stretch across many different contexts; and 'provincializing' planetary urbanisation requires that we work with the multiplicity of such processes (not simply global capitalism, for example) which opens up scope to explore differentiated connections comparatively.

This kind of 'thinking through elsewhere' has been proposed in anthropology, for example, as 'multi-sited' ethnography drawing researchers to trace the circulation of phenomena across the diverse landscapes they entrain (Marcus 1995). The 'case' then becomes the circulation itself, rather than a particular outcome. In urban studies, the recent eruption of studies of policy mobilities exemplifies this (Peck and Theodore 2015), as do analyses of operational landscapes in the framework of extended (planetary) urbanisation (Brenner 2013) – the urban infrastructures which subtend concentration even as they sprawl across the globe (pipelines, electricity pylons, shipping routes) – and the migrant circuits which tie 'township' and 'village' in one social field (Clyde Mitchell

1987; Potts 2012b), or which tie wealthier and poorer contexts together through a diasporic urbanism (Shatkin 1998; Sinatti 2009; Theodore 2007). Urbanisation is not (only) about territorialisation, and intrinsic to its analysis is the capacity to work with the many different lines of connection, spaces of extension and circuits of practice which constitute urbanisation processes.

Methodologically, Peck and Theodore (2012) discuss the 'distended case study'. Their title pays homage to Burawoy's (2009) 'extended case study', in which national and international processes are seen to play a role in the 'structuration' of cases, and thus the case study extends out to encompass processes at these scales. He also discusses 'connected comparisons', but by this he means comparisons of processes which are intrinsic to the case – such as processes of deracialisation initiated by employers on the one hand, and those initiated by the state on the other (in his case study of labour and mining in Zambia). In moving to propose the 'distended' case, Peck and Theodore isolate a sequence of interlinked processes of policy formation, stretching across numerous contexts. Along the way, policies and practices diverge from their starting positions, and what is made mobile is transformed. They articulate some of the challenges of such work as 'traveling within cosmopolitan policy networks without becoming another creature of those networks; of making sense of fast-moving "best practices" without losing sight of prosaic practice; of taking account of phenomena like policy tourism and policy tradeshows without succumbing to explanatory dilettantism, or some kind of methodological tourism, [just] tripping around from site to site' (Peck and Theodore 2012, p. 25). Of course, one has to be in a certain phase of life and institutional position to be doing such tripping – in well-resourced institutions, certainly, but other opportunities arise for those who are drawn into well-resourced developmental practices which offer connecting opportunities to ex-centrically located scholars.

Following connections cuts across territorial divisions and invites different contexts into mutual reflection: this has been very important in discussions considering how to bring the experiences of cities in contexts shaped by socialist pasts and a multiplicity of post-socialisms into a wider analytical conversation about the urban. Various commentators have sought to bring these, perhaps twice-sidelined cities (once by western-oriented urban studies, once by a post-colonial critique focused on 'global South', or the extensive interest in China) into analytical relationship. As we saw in Chapter 1, part of the difficulty has been the territorialized imagination of 'post-socialism' as a container, a demarcated regional 'other' (Tuvikene 2016). Here, tracing the many lines of connection which tie emergent dynamics of urbanisation in this region to global trends – such as those of property investment, urban design, economic flows, borrowing from valued political systems (Gentile

2017; Hirt 2012) has the effect of de-territorializing post-socialism. Offering this as a concept which might be put to work in articulating the after-lives of socialism, which emerge in continuity or opposition with socialist pasts, highly varied across this putative region, and also impactful in other contexts similarly draws attention to connections beyond the territorial container of (post-)socialism (Tuvikene 2016).

Lukasz Stanek's (2012, 2020) important study of socialist architects working across West Africa, the middle East and Asia during the early post-independence period draws a line of connection between regions which are seldom considered together. Whereas much architectural history, even that reworking histories of global south cities, has been focused on western-centric connections, Stanek argues that, 'urban histories of twentieth century Baghdad and numerous other cities in the Global South cannot be understood without accounting for the exchanges with Eastern European and socialist countries elsewhere' (2020, p. 3). But this also brings into view the substantive differences across different kinds of connections – in Africa, the colonial era architects whose racialized practices and colonial assumptions contrasted with the flatter hierarchies and engaged practices of socialist design firms and practitioners whose enterprises were more of a middling modernism kind. They opened up scope for African direction of planning and design while also promoting distinctive urban visions with an emphasis on a socialist model of modernization: 'state-centred, justice-oriented and promising fast growth' (2012, p. 300). African influence on much of the work was significant (p. 9) while Eastern European professionals met crucial skills needs in planning and design. Geopolitical and national concerns, as well as different economic conditions, shaped the sending countries choices for offering technical assistance and aid, seeking hard currency contracts or sustaining employment in large firms at home, making Africa's engagement with Eastern Europe differentiated: 'changes in the political economy under Bulgarian leader Todor Zhikov, Poland's Edward Gierek, and Romainia's Nicolae Ceauşescu modified trajectories, volumes, and composition of architectural export from these countries' (p. 15). But African leaders and decision-makers also pushed at the priorities and agendas of socialist practitioners, and were met by a different kind of architectural practice, in which collaboration and local agendas found strong representation. Stanek notes that 'What was produced was urbanisation. Individual and aggregate actors circulating in networks set up and sustained by socialist countries contributed to all dimensions of urbanization' (p. 33). He sees these movements of architectural labor and design as part of 'urbanization processes', but he looks to step back from 'globalization' as an overarching logic driven by western norms and regulations, for

Plate 1 Township-Wall by António Ole, III C 45608 – A, Ethnologisches Museum, Staatliche Museen zu Berlin. (Photograph by Martin Franken).

Plate 2 The City, The Fire Walker and the aftermath of copper cable theft. Queen Elizabeth bridge, Johannesburg, 29 December 2011 (Photograph by David Goldblatt).

Plate 3 'The Firewalker' by William Kentridge, in Sculpture in the City 2016 at the junction of Bishopsgate and London Wall, London UK (Photograph by Nick Turpin).

Plate 4 Rue Saint Antoine, Paris 1979 © Thomas Struth.

Plate 5 Pasaje de 27 Setiembre, Lima 2003 © Thomas Struth.

Plate 6 Waiting for Bus by Dilomprizulike, 2003, at Africa Remix: Contemporary Art of a Continent, Hayward Gallery, London (2005). (Photograph by Marcus Leith).

Plate 7 Detail from, Waiting for Bus by Dilomprizulike, 2003, at Africa Remix: Contemporary Art of a Continent, Hayward Gallery, London (2005). (Photograph by Marcus Leith).

Plate 8 Soweto Cooling Tower, Johannesburg, 11 July 2015. (Photo by Raphael de Kadt, flickr.com)

encompassing the connections he traces, and links instead to the fuller conceptualisations of Glissant's conceptualization of worldness (*mondialité*) and Lefebvre's 'world-forming' (*mondialisation*) which index a multiplying of relations (Glissant) and a concrete totality (Lefebvre), within which the circuits and norms of 'globalization' form only one possibility (pp. 29–30). Thus, his work supports 'differentiating urbanization processes beyond the consequences of the colonial encounter with Western Europe and the hegemony of global capitalism' (p. 306).

The multiple interconnections shaping urban places also have the potential to evoke new kinds of objects of enquiry, beyond the territorialized and discrete centralities of the conventional city form. Here global suburbanism or planetary perspectives allow us to observe emergent phenomena/territorialisations which constitute disassembled forms of urbanity, dispersed unevenly, perhaps unpredictably, across the landscape of urbanisation. So, for example, a highly varied array of suburban or peripheral urban sites, reveal and shape contemporary urbanisation processes in many contexts, but do so in a dynamic and transnational urban world which also reshapes the configuration and meaning of such sites themselves. Thinking with the variety of suburban places has enriched global urban studies, and indicates the generative potential of comparative reflections (Hamel and Keil 2016; Harris and Volm 2017). More than this, though, we also need to look to the empirical interconnections which bring suburban places across the globe into relationship with each other – and which provide an excellent example of the necessity of thinking the urban with elsewhere, in a genetic mode. Keil (2017) brings together some of the insights of a large-scale comparative project (Global Suburbanisms) in some evocative propositions around the idea of the 'global suburb', which he suggests is about a 'multifarious connectivity' (p. 47), leading to 'new assemblages of the global that surround our cities' (p. 48), replete with new centralities. He links this to emerging concepts of 'extended urbanisation' (Brenner and Schmid 2015; Monte-Mór 2014a, 2014b) and Lefebvre's (2003) famous hypothesis of the 'complete urbanisation of society'. In this context, he coins the proposition that 'it is time to bid the (conceptual) white picket fence farewell' (p. 52) and embrace the prolific interconnections which constitute global suburbanisation.

It is important, then, to look not just from the sprawling edges of the city, but from its exteriority. This draws our attention to the many power-laden processes which shape urbanisation, and which are so quickly relevant to scholars used to working in poorer country contexts – considering, for example, international agencies, donor organisations, sovereign lenders. Thus, the politics of transnational circuits requires careful attention. Here we have the models of 'policy mobilities' to draw on (McCann 2011; Wood 2014), as well as the rhythms and cadences of globalised and liberalising economies, say in the financial and information circuits which drive the classic advanced producer services clusters (Bassens and van Mieteren 2015). These circuits are by no means uniform – and tracing connections, explaining urbanisation processes, necessarily must address the diversity of circuits, including the developmental policy flows which are often interpreted and thought through the politics of aid and development (Porto D'Oliviera 2017). In all cases of circuits, differentiation – of mobile practices, investment flows or material connections – draws attention. This challenge also holds true for 'extended urbanisation' with ideas about 'operational landscapes' and questions of the ecological impact and environmental limits of 'urbanisation processes' extended, and intimately related to and punctuated with concentrations, across the globe (Angelo and Wachsmuth 2015; Brenner and Katsikis 2020; Brenner and Schmid 2015).

While seeing connections as urbanisation processes, we can bring in a directly comparative perspective by provincializing and differentiating understandings of connections and circuits. Here there is a significant opportunity for a comparative imagination. Different kinds of connections can be contrasted, or assessed, such as, the divergent trajectories of flows of specific policies (Peck and Theodore 2015), or the different kinds of networks or relations. Söderström (2014), compares contrasting sets of political and economic relations which draw two different previously isolated urban areas (Hanoi and Ougadougou) into wider articulations with global processes in quite divergent ways – one through a geopolitical articulation through city-to-city interactions, policy learning and alliances (Ouagadougou) and one through intensifying global economic connections through close relations with neighbouring Asian countries (Hanoi). Söderström initiated a comparative analysis to consider 'two cities of the South having a similar recent history of re-connection to global flows' (p. 13), which he describes as 'distant cousins', sharing 'a series of common features and family resemblances at the national level' (p. 14): both former French colonies, both with revolutionary socialist regimes in the past, both having experienced rapid deregulations in the 1990s. At a city level divergences are apparent, such as size (Hanoi over 6 million in 2010, while Ougadougou had less than 2 million), but both face considerable challenges of infrastructure, poverty and inequality, and neither has attracted much attention in wider urban studies debates, supporting efforts to stretch insights beyond the 'metrocentricity' which Bunnell and Das (2013) critiqued. These ground-clearing sensible reasons for thinking across these two cities position the analysis for what is his primary aim, 'to compare the two cities' relations with elsewhere, or, in other words, a *relational comparison*. Although in the terminology we develop in this chapter, this is more about comparing connections than tracing relations between cases. Very importantly for methodological reflections, he notes that,

> Relational thinking has been criticized for being too vague about how relations work as mechanisms of space-production and for not providing sufficient answers to the question: "What is it, exactly, that they relate?" ... It seems to me that the abundant recent literature on policy mobilities provides replies to this query by showing how relations generate policy change ... However, . I want to push this further by exploring different *generative* characters of relations and how different relations produce specific features of urban development.
> (Söderström 2014, p. 24)

Thus, especially perhaps in poorer cities, transnational relations constitute important dimensions of a city's resources and are strongly generative of urbanisation. He insists on looking across different kinds of relations – political, economic, cultural, questioning also their orientation (where do connections head to, come from) and intensity (quantity, perhaps, but also significance to the city). His main conclusions indicate that different kinds of relations have been significant in each case, that these have changed over time, and that such connections have been very important shapers of material, economic and political dynamics in each city.

While Söderström draws our attention to the diversity of circuits operating across different urban contexts, his detailed study provides an important reminder that in comparing different circuits, the complexity of what is travelling needs careful attention. This includes the materiality of what is on the move and what results in each context, as well as the different meanings attributed and political openings afforded by different connections. Furthermore, as Söderström notes, 'when we observe what it is that relations generate, we are inevitably confronted with institutional strategies and human agency that territorialize these relations in often unpredictable ways' (p. 20). His focus on material objects and issues of urban design show the intertwining of different actors and concerns in the generative effect of connections in the built environment, making circuits also a site of hybridization. As he notes, innovative design in Ougadougou certainly drew in major international design firms, but also:

> takes place 'in between' these places involving processes of mutual learning and co-produced design (what I called 'design in the wild'). I looked, in Ouagadougou in particular, at innovative design processes characterized

by a high sensitivity to social and morphological contexts. Finally, I showed that the state responds to this cosmopolitanization of architecture by promoting national narratives (through aesthetic control and architectural education) in the design of public buildings. In contrast with most existing literature in the domain, I therefore argued that transnational design in the cities considered cannot be reduced to logics of branding and capital accumulation.

(Söderström 2014, p. 152).

He insists that his relational geography and comparison 'goes beyond narratives of neo-liberalization and economic transition identifying different trajectories of globalization, different worlds of relations and ways in which they are shaping urban developments. It invites scholars in urban studies to be specific about cities' multiple relations with elsewhere and what they produce' (p. 152). Here, we can call to mind the arguments suggesting the importance of theorising with the fellow travellers of neoliberalisation (Peck et al. 2009; Collier 2005; Ferguson 2010). This brings forward the significance of a comparative imagination to work across different mobilities. Thus, tracing any particular circulating phenomenon or process necessitates close attention to what might be travelling along with it and understanding 'hybridization', for example, as not simply a consequence of localization or territorialisation but as already present in that which is mobile; as I have argued elsewhere, some ostensibly 'neoliberal' circuits might be better seen as developmental (Parnell and Robinson 2012).

A pioneer in research comparing different networks is Kris Olds' (2001) *Globalization and Urban Change: Capital, Culture and Pacific Rim Mega-Projects*. Inspired by multi-locale fieldwork emerging in anthropology in the 1990s, and a post-colonial sensibility to move beyond binary concepts of North and South (p. 7), he set about tracing two Asian-centric networks associated with mega urban projects in Shanghai (Pudong New Area) and Vancouver (One Canada Place), which involved fieldwork in those two sites but also in various nodes in the flows of finance (Hong Kong) and design (Paris), for example. Also inspired by John Law's influential (2004) article on the global as 'small' and particular, and a geographical perspective on the profoundly inter-related nature of places, he aimed to bring 'both the local and global into view simultaneously'. Although proposing a 'non-comparative comparison', perhaps as a rejection of the territorialised idea of comparison prevailing at the time. He offers careful insights on the two different kinds of connections and outcomes which emerged around the two developments, concerning different ways in which global reach was performed by key actors in the development (through close family networks and longstanding collaborations; or through formal and distanciated working relationships), different practices of localization and networking (deep local connections; technical and ephemeral interactions), and the importance of many different globalized processes running through the two localities (architecture, design, governance, money, inter-city competition), which were crucial in shaping urban development outcomes.

Olds' book proposes that 'global' cities, such as Shanghai, Vancouver, London, Paris, host many of the resources needed for mobilizing transnational networks of urban investment and design, extending 'global city' analysis to the ways in which a range of different processes interconnecting cities find sites of localization, producing centralities in various urban places. Circuits of investment (including in urban property development) have been associated with specific localizations of activities which foster and enable the intelligence and practical capacities to direct transnational investments (Bassen and van Meeteren 2015; Halbert and Rouanet 2014). Most attention has been paid to the processes of global switching, and financialisation, but it is clear that across the range of urban outcomes and processes, many different globalizing processes need to be attended to – including, for example, developmental and geopolitical circuits, as Söderström's (2014) study of the political international associations sought by Ouagadougou brings out. Attending to these interconnections and flows might also inspire different geographies or territorializations of comparison, such as Susan Fainstein's (2001) provocative suggestion to treat New York and London as one urban space, associated with and shaped in a strong way by shared phenomena and processes associated with the global city functions which she sees as having a privileged location in these cities.

An important way in which policy mobilities can inspire comparative analysis, exploring connections as urbanisation processes, is to look at direct city to city links, and networks of city governments. This provides a productive optics through which to identify the proliferation of city connections, including scope for identifying more accurately how city managers and policymakers learn from different contexts. This includes learning which moves from 'southern contexts' to the 'north' (McFarlane 2006; Campbell 2012; Peyroux 2016; Porto de Oliviera 2017) or south—south partnerships, perhaps within the context of wider transnational networked learning (Bulkeley 2010), or targeted programmes of city twinning and city to city learning (Bontenbal 2009). Here we will encounter many cautions against rushing to distinguish hard barriers between northern and southern circuits of knowledge. While it is clear there are differentiated circuits of policy and knowledge (with some segmentation of developmental interventions in the poorest cities), tracing these helps us to see that they bleed across apparently different categories of city. For example,in the case of city strategies technologies of strategic visioning from the USA (private sector led), EU (public sector policies) and international development policy (involving external agents of development) draw different urban contexts into shared circuits of policy innovation encouraging city visioning and long-term and city-wide strategic planning (Robinson 2011b, 2018a). Even as it is tempting to delineate strong north-south differences in urban policy and institutional environments (Parnell and Oldfield 2014; Parnell and Pieterse 2014; Watson 2014a), the many cross-cutting lines of policy circulation and interconnections suggest that sharp delineations might also be misguided.

The productivity of tracing the connections which shape urbanisation stands in some tension with the ways in which urban territories are not simply 'outcomes' of such circuits, but constitutive elements of them. Maliq Simone's (2010) extensive work on the 'worlding' trajectories of residents in African cities places their journeys (made or not) as responses to the exigencies of life in contexts where finding a way to piece together livelihoods and associations is an ever present concern. This speaks precisely to the entwining of cities and circuits. As he commented in an early piece, 'if you want to know where African cities are going, follow the people' (2001a).

The examples we draw on here do not all see connections as somehow adding up to pre-defined 'wider processes' which exhibit territorialized 'variegations', such as neoliberalisation. Rather, tracing particular mobilities and flows can illuminate the complex co-presence and entwinings in practice of different agents, material entities, and ideas which are the very stuff of urbanisation (Lepawsky et al. 2015). New processes of urbanisation are made; and possibly conceptualized. Nonetheless, circulations also bring territories and 'instances' into view – and different kinds of territories. These offer some different tactical propositions for comparisons on genetic grounds.

Connections Producing *Repeated Instances*

In Charles Tilly's (1984) initial formulation of encompassing comparisons which justifies drawing different places in to an analysis because they are mutually entwined in large-scale processes, such as slavery, capitalism, or perhaps for our purposes also neoliberalisation and a range of urbanisation processes, wider connections bring localities or places into view. Classically, he observes,

> It places different instances at various locations within the same system, on the way to explaining their characteristics as a function of their varying relationships to the system as a whole.
>
> (Tilly 1984, p. 83)

Philip McMichael (1990) extends these insights most helpfully, placing the 'cases' revealed through such connections into a dynamic relationship with their production through wider social (systemic) processes, that is, it is not possible to predetermine the form or nature of the particular case being considered as they are mutually produced along with the wider processes.

While we want to thicken and diversify understanding of the connections themselves, as discussed above, in this section I want to press at the nature of the 'cases' which are imagined as being entrained in the connections, as well as what they might add up to – which may not be (is unlikely to be) a 'whole'. Connections, too, may not be part of 'wider processes', or certainly not necessarily of those which we can easily identify in advance. Following the core Deleuzian insights developed in Chapter 4, I propose we can reconsider the nature of the case as such, both in terms of what constitutes a case, and what cases stand for conceptually, how they might be considered to be part of wider processes or analytical concepts. In Chapter 6, I return to the more Marxist and Weberian inheritances which shape the concerns and formulations of Tilly and McMichael. There we focus more on 'social processes', here on tracing connections.

Firstly, lets orient ourselves to the 'repeated instance' as the form of the case – here the case can be seen as initially standing only for itself, rather than as an outcome of a wider process or representative of pre-given category or 'universal'. Cases are, however, in the Deleuzian idiom, and in the context of globalized urbanisation, genetically interconnected with (produced along with) many others. The concept of 'repeated instance' refines the nature of the 'case', then, proposing to treat cases as distinctive but inter-related outcomes of a shared virtual field – in the case of the urban, all the possible urban outcomes which the interconnected processes of the production of urban spaces might entail.

How can we use this productively as 'method'? How might it be possible to both look closely at each highly specific instance, while seeking to understand some significantly 'big' or 'extensive' processes (Jacobs 2006)? How can we avoid a fascinating but limited focus on exhaustively naming and documenting (which are already theoretical and conceptual practices) the complex emergence of each instance in isolation. What might we do pragmatically with many instances of interconnected processes? What can be done with the possibility to assemble multiple, and potentially numerous, cases of repetitions in a practical empirical research project to creatively build relevant but modest concepts? Here I propose four possibly starting points.

Identify the Instance(s)

As we consider the emergence of repeated instances in the urban manifold, we need to attend to the precise nature of the territorializations which tracing connections arrives at, not just a 'place' or a 'city' or 'locality' but, perhaps: a building (Jacobs et al. 2007), a project (Pinson 2009), a distinctive policy (Baker et al. 2016). An important corollary of tracking connections to identify 'repeated instances' is that a 'case' is most unlikely to be a city (although it may be a practice or an outcome linked to an administrative or governmental unit with a certain territorial extent, of course) – so there is no a priori format for 'territory', 'place' or 'localization' of flows and connections. Indeed, 'cases' may not be spatial entities, but social formations, connections, urbanisation processes or variously mobile ideas, materialities or individuals, and their assemblages or territorialisations. In each case, inspired by the empiricist treatment of Deleuze's philosophy in ANT/STS, a socio-material approach can reveal an assemblage of actors and materials, ideas and practices, which, as allies or contestors, are involved in the realization of particular outcomes (Deville et al. 2016; Cairns and Jacobs 2014). Importantly, such cases cannot be judged in an a priori way to be an example, or a given particular, of a pre-identified wider process (Jacobs 2006; Robinson 2014a). How can we nonetheless place them in relation to other instances and wider circulations?

Empirically Additive

Following the connections across multiple instances can tell a cumulative or additive story of urbanisation processes through the vantage points of a multiplicity of outcomes. This could involve attending to the repeated instances of, for example, mass housing development (Jacobs et al. 2007; Schmid et al. 2018), satellite cities (Murray 2017), or of a certain timing and form of policy implementation, say, transit improvements (Wood 2014) or child benefit payments (Peck and Theodore 2015). Thus, through adding cases, insights would be gained of the unfolding, differentiation, or unevenness of urbanisation processes, such as infrastructure investments, and outcomes, such as large-scale peripheral urban developments (Easterling 2014; Kanai and Schindler 2019; Schindler and Kanai 2021). What comes into view as these processes are traced? Care needs to be taken though not to assume that the numerous cases can only be read through a singular set of connections, or drawn into pre-given analytical frames. Thus an alternative rubric for the 'syndrome' of neoliberalisation, for example, might be a perspective in which the 'name' or effect of the circulating practices and policies is (a) emergent and to be determined (Jacobs 2006), (b) likely to lead to a diversity of urban outcomes (not 'variegated' outcomes of a pre-determined process) and (c) might arrive at something quite different than neoliberalism, through entering other circuits, such as developmentalism, or a developmental state (Collier 2005; Ferguson 2010; Robinson 2011c) Kanai and Schindler (2019) identify, for example, another mode of globalizing urbanisation – a scramble for infrastructure, or Infrastructure-led Development.

Initiating an 'experimental comparison' across cases of large-scale developments in Dar es Salaam (Tanzania) and Manaus (Brazil), Kanai and Schindler (2019) suggest that these are examples of numerous cases of large-scale infrastructure development across many different urbanizing contexts which add up to a 'global growth coalition whose hegemony is shaping an emergent regime of infrastructure-led development. Largescale infrastructure projects underpin coordinated spatial planning initiatives reminiscent of strategies from the postwar era, and their primary objective is to 'get the territory right' (p. 307). They see this, from a 'southern' perspective as part of a 'scramble for infrastructure' which is yielding extended urbanisation processes (to follow Brenner and Schmid 2015), hoping to stimulate development through connectivity. They argue that even highly localized case studies can bring into perspective the many different actors and circuits which make up the global infrastructure scramble through numerous localized territorial reconfigurations (Schindler and Kanai 2021, p. 47). They explicitly turn from the genetic comparative analysis focussed on the connections to consider each case on its own terms as a 'generative comparison' – indicating that these two grounds for comparison might be entwined in practical analyses.

Sites or instances might be treated more substantially as part of the circuits in question, rather than simply contributing to circulations. In an innovative paper which traces electronic waste across four different sites, Lepawsky et al. (2015) bring a distinctive perspective to understanding urban concentrations of Finance, Insurance and Real Estate (FIRE) clusters as waste producers (and not as indicators of global cities). This draws them to peri-urban sites in poor city contexts where they identify highly connected clusters of economic production rather than marginalised end points for waste and recycling. They 'compose' these different moments of electronic waste production, circulation, recycling and re-production together as a 'site multiple', and on this basis raise important questions concerning 'what composes cityness' (p. 187). Drawing on Latour's propositions to move from matters of fact to matters of concern, they suggest that

> rather than subtract from reality (for example, claim the city is really merely a social construct), well-composed matters of concern are those that add to reality (for example, by leaving open the possibility that the issue of cityness may be made up of more than or something other than the urban); well-composed matters of concern open up an issue rather than close it; they stage a gathering that those who are interested can assemble to carefully dispute, debate, deal with and stitch together new ways of going on together.
>
> (Lepawsky et al. 2015, p. 187)

They draw on Mol's idea of the 'body multiple', produced through different practices – 'not plurality, but manyfoldedness'. Thus, they insist, 'the site multiple is not the same thing as multi-sited'. In this way they produce not several sites connected through some flows, but thicken and extend the spaces under consideration as both connections and territorial outcomes. Both are together 'distributed in its enactment through practices and affordances of materials patchily, unevenly and not necessarily coherently' (p. 190). They see this as an explicit contribution to 'international' comparative practice, and bring into view quite different aspects of urbanisation (and more-than-urban), as they trace the pollutants and compose the kinds of 'cityness' which this value chain reveals. They have some valuable comments on the wider implications of this approach – suggesting the 'site multiple' 'helps compose synopses, not totalities; it helps generate knowledge as partial and situated as any knowledge must be. It is a composition, not a critique' but also that it poses wider questions such as 'What is the urban made up of? What sort of urban worlds do we want? How can we coexist? What grouping(s) are we part of?' (p. 196). 'Composing' comparisons in genetic mode, then, along the tracks of production networks, for example, can build through particular sites an additive sense of what the urban might be, of how urbanisation proceeds. In a project which can be read alongside this, Armelle Choplin (2019) tracks the circulation of cement along the West African corridor, and its entraining in a multitude of individual projects of securing settlement claims, financial investments in property development, as well as large-scale urban development projects and as a marker of economic growth potential in the region. New vectors of urbanisation and new kinds of urban outcomes come into view from composing comparisons additively along connections, extending analytical frames and building insights from different urban contexts.

Analytically Subtractive

While tracing the cumulative outcomes of repeated instances for comparative analysis it is important to attend to the second (virtual) series progressing alongside the genetic emergence of multiple cases in the midst of the virtual urban (all the possible urban outcomes). This is associated with coming to an understanding of a phenomenon through drawing on the 'virtual' of ideas – all the possible ways in which we might explore and consider responding to the phenomenon presenting itself to us for interpretation. This is an important element in Deleuze's account of generating concepts. Thus, keeping open our perspective on what 'repeated instances' add up to in an analytical sense means working across the many cases – working with multiples (Jacobs 2012) – while having in mind all the possible concepts that could help us make sense of the instances in their multiplicity as they come into view. One of the beneficial effects of repeated instances is that they have the potential to draw scholars and observers across numerous academic and interpretive contexts, and therefore traditions, language communities and theoretical approaches, into conversation. This opens up the possibility for learning from ideas and practices embedded in different situations, extending and enriching potential analyses.

While it might be possible to propose repeated instances' as cases of 'wider processes' (e.g. neoliberalisation, financialisation), treating cases as distinctive starting points characterised by a rich multiplicity highlights that such wider processes are also conceptualisations (Chapter 6 explores this in detail). What does each additional instance bring to conceptualisation of wider processes? Jane M. Jacobs proposes a method of 'subtraction', to work with the multiplicity of repeated instances. The invitation of this perspective is to move beyond relatively straightforward and sometimes fairly lazy analytical habits of accumulating cases to support an extant theorisation, or to pick out yet again a familiar process or empirical dynamic which seems to be at work across many cases. She argues instead, '(t)o work with multiples (many cities, other cities, ordinary cities) not as addition (one more city case in a project of building general theory) but as subtraction (reading urban difference in the name of producing alternative futures)' (Jacobs 2012, p. 906). She insists that, 'creating the conditions to see multiplicity (through say, multiple cases), is a commitment to work against the dissimulation of singular, over-coded, explanatory frameworks' (Jacobs 2012, p. 906). In this sense, working with repeated instances is an invitation to theoretical subtraction – in some circumstances providing the resources to subtract from powerful, circulating concepts such as neoliberalisation. More generally this practice would also encourage the extension, innovation and invention of concepts.

For example, we could return here to the interrogation of global suburbanism. As Keil (2017) proposes it, starting with the places called 'suburbs' in some parts of the world brings into view a multiplicity of urban outcomes which provide starting points for insights. But into what? The suburb as a known entity? Or to stimulate insights into urbanisation processes whose reference points are not the 'cities' within which they might be embedded, but the wider, circulating processes and practices which constitute any possible peripheral urban outcome. Thus starting in peripheral, expanding parts of urban areas, we are in a position to review a series of repeated phenomena, noting their prolific interconnections to other instances. We open up the possibility for identifying quite different kinds of repeated (urban) objects, no longer seen as part of a form of urbanisation characterised as 'suburbs' but as all sorts of possibilities, each with wide-ranging and different connectivities, which might nonetheless be gathered under a new sign, that of ex-centric expansion and dynamic growth, for creative analytical reflection (see also Harris 2010). This could include satellite cities, new towns, peripheral urbanisation (Caldeira 2016), financialized low-income housing, informal settlements, displaced urbanisation, new industrial centres, "recombinant" or agrarian urbanisation (Balakrishnan, 2019); Jiehebu, or 'urban-rural juncture' (Zhao, 2020), and many others.

If we track back to the Deleuzian inspirations for Jane M. Jacob's insights here, this wide-ranging comparative exercise on the 'global suburb' might encourage some qualifications of the nature of repetitions. I would argue that we need to guard against false repetitions. Here, repeated instances which are not the result of interconnected processes but of analytical and conceptual naming are not 'repeated instances' of the kind I am proposing here. Gentrification, for example, although proposed analytically as a 'global', or even 'planetary' 'process', is not the result of necessarily interconnected transfer (cf. Lees 2012; Smith 2002): I would suggest it cannot be seen as a process at all, but as conceptualisation of a certain kind of urban outcome which is most commonly transferred as a concept (rather than as policy or purposeful practice – although it can certainly perform as a policy goal or desired outcome, and as a focus for opposition). Gentrification is an analytical term which insists on the co-presence of a certain bundle of 'shared features' of urban change to be applicable (class change; displacement; physical transformation). Comparative experiments around the concept of gentrification (or any other urbanisation process of concept) are better understood, then, within the rubric of generative comparative practices (Bernt, 2022).

In this respect Deleuze invites us to consider 'bare' and 'clothed' repetitions as markers of how repeated instances might be treated analytically. 'Bare' repetitions are emptied out of difference, difference is drawn off as each repeated instance is encountered and a concept is left unclothed, unadorned by the necessary differentiation produced through each repetition, travelling as an invariant concept (1994, p. 359). Jane M. Jacobs puts this key Deleuzian insight well: 'the making of repetition – or more precisely, repeated instances in many different contexts – requires variance, different assemblages of allies in different settings' (Jacobs 2006, p. 22). 'Clothed' repetitions emerge within the realm of ideas as always shaded and transformed with the specific features of differentiation. In the process ideas or concepts are 'clothed' as they are produced in relationship with specific outcomes. Inherited ideas are disturbed, extended, found wanting – perhaps reaching a point where their relevance is deteriorated and we are drawn to approach the 'difference' encountered as the starting points for new conceptualisations. This brings us close to the value of thinking with cases in a more Marxist idiom where the idea of the urban as contingent, or as a 'concrete totality' open to an inexhaustibility of possible analytical and empirical starting points for thinking, which we consider further in Chapter 8.

However, here it is also helpful to look more closely at the comparative potential in science and technology studies (and actor network theory) approaches, which draw inspiration from comparisons in practice which are already part of circulations and emergent outcomes. It draws us to see comparability across different cases as an achievement of complex formations of objects, practitioners and scholars – focussing on what is actually done and assembled through comparative practice – rather than a formal procedure which can be specified in advance as method (Deville et al. 2016). Particularly productive in relation to STS approaches has been the potential in taking as a starting point actually existing comparisons: comparisons that are made not by scholars in the interests of generating analytical or conceptual insights, or deepening their understanding of a situation, but 'found' comparisons, in the field (Clarke 2012a). For example, Morgan Meyer (2016), explores the comparisons made in public and specialist debates concerning the identity and social meaning of 'biohackers', and Gad and Jensen (2016) are concerned with the 'indigenous' comparisons being made on the bridge of a Danish fishery inspection vessel. Both find ways to think productively with these comparisons, drawing on them to inform their own academic analyses. And both comment on the open-ended nature of the interaction amongst their own comparative reflections and those they encountered in the field. This too is a product of the rich STS insights, which place researchers in the 'midst of things', part of emergent practices, as Gad and Jensen observe, defying any clear distinctions between description and conceptualisation, informant and researcher, human and technology. 'Tracing comparisons ethnographically', or tracing the empirically existing lateral connections being made between cases by actors in the field, opens up cases to perhaps unpredictable sources of reflection and insight (they cite the interesting work of Maurer 2005, linking Islamic banking and alternative currencies). They suggest a 'dynamic interplay between our intellectual pre-occupations *and* what we encountered on the *West Coast*'.

Personally I have found the potential to learn from the comparative imaginations and practices of policymakers I have engaged with in Johannesburg to be inspiring of the potential to build new theorisations of the urban and urban processes (Robinson 2013b). Thus, numerous comparisons in practice might draw analysts to proliferate insights, to pursue lateral connections, to explain distinctive outcomes in the midst of the prolific interconnections and possibilities of the urban, and to work with and across the rich multiple elsewheres of policy circuits to compose comparative experiments.

Every Case Matters

Along the way, as connections reveal or are part of the production of particular instances, it will be possible to shift perspective more definitively from these circulating phenomena to attend to specific urban outcomes and territorializations. Following connections can be a significant element in productively explaining distinctive territorial urban outcomes, and can be especially productive in inspiring thinking across and with the differentiation of outcomes associated with specific links, flows and connections; although this brings with it the challenge of defining and delimiting relevant territorialisations of instances. Treating each individual case or urban outcome as emergent within an interconnected multiplicity of cases, and as a distinctive starting point for analysis, leads us to ask: what perspective or insights does this case, or the next case, bring to understanding? In this last approach, we then have multiple potential starting points from which to bring interpretive enrichment to any particular instance, for each case to raise questions of the other and to contribute to enriching and thickening the analysis of each case.

The 'case' or 'instance' comes closely into view in a moment when connections stabilize into a particular form – and is especially visible perhaps when the analytical focus on replicability and wider connections falls away in the face of the production of a(n unintended) unique outcome. Jacobs et al. (2007) use the notorious/celebrated case of 'Red Road' housing estate in Glasgow, UK, to open up the 'black boxing' of the residential high rise. They observe that it might be possible to assume that 'globalization' of this form is taking place through transfer and repetition of a stable technology. But their nuanced tracing of how wider circulations of design and building elements and technologies shaped this particular development, demonstrated in fact, in the scheme's ultimate failure, the way in which very specific political and material conditions – literally the ground of the development, the land on which it was based – determined the outcome. They note how 'the plan for a high-rise design type was radically altered by the specificities of its materialisation' (p. 616). Thus, the very particular, craft production of what at first sight seem like iconically repetitive modernist towers in Glasgow is revealed. Although beginning its journey in national and local ambitions to initiate a new version of modernist replicability, the institutional context of contracting, limited technical capabilities of professional contractors, and a political desire to build to high densities on a small site, lay behind what became an innovative, but in the longer term, not very effective or reproducible set of building techniques and forms. Rather than being either a repetition of known standards, or itself setting new standards for repeating in many housing developments (which their second case of Singapore achieved with spectacular success), Jacobs et al. show how:

> Rather, Red Road had come to be a 'novel', 'unprecedented', 'experimental', 'speculative', 'singular' project and its claims to offer a housing template that was efficient and economical were deemed 'illusory' . . . . Red Road was, the Inquiry concluded, produced in an 'atmosphere of improvisation' (p. 30). The facts that the Inquiry uncovered about Red Road's production translated it from a design type (standardised, stable, mobile) to a crafted object whose final form had been (excessively) influenced by the contingencies of its making.
> (Jacobs et al. 2007, p. 620)

Thus, in its failure it is evident that rather than being a residue of globalization of modernist housing, each residential high rise, while it might look so familiar, can be seen as a repeated instance; multiple (interconnected) processes lead to repeated, but also strongly differentiated, outcomes whose emergent effect – what they add up to – is not entirely predictable, might not be what was anticipated.

A thoughtful paper by Akrich and Rabeharisoa (2016) is helpful to take forward thinking with repeated instances, as they explain how in their EU-funded project on health care users' activism they moved from the institutionally over-determined expectation that national context would both matter and explain the variations they might observe, to building a comparative analysis which traced the transnational interconnections amongst the case studies which were mutually shaped by shared circuits of knowledge. Abandoning the national framework, then, the teams worked together to generate common questions for approaching the different territorially distended cases (see Peck and Theodore 2012). 'Making comparators' (in a retrospective application of Deville et al.'s (2016) useful analytic), they also arrived at a position where each case was treated 'in its singularity'.[1] Thus most helpfully for assessing the spatialities of the comparative imagination, they explain that bringing the different cases together in their shared analytical discussions

> did not consist of extracting a few dimensions out of the singularity of each case but rather thickening its singularity in light of the other cases.
> (Akrich and Rabeharisoa 2016, p. 31)

Thus rather than seeking 'abstraction' or hoping to raise observations to 'generalisations', they imagine a quite different spatiality to the comparative imagination, one in the service of singularisation, to understand each case better. They also highlight the potential diversity of shared features of cases, seeking to think more fully about the 'common practices' of the different territorially extended patient and activist networks which they were analysing.

As a comparative practice, I found it helpful to mobilise this insight in my own research on city strategies (Robinson 2011b, 2018a). For some time I have been following three examples of city strategy, from cities not conventionally considered together: Johannesburg, London and Lilongwe. Aside from my opportunistic interest in each case,[2] I justify bringing them into comparative analysis on the grounds of their shared genesis in interconnected policy circuits: they emerge from the differentiated global circulation of a specific governmental technology (city strategy), and differentiated circuits of globalising urban policies. To be clear, the 'cases' in such an analysis are not cities as such, but the 'repeated instance' of long-term city strategies which form part of an interconnected field of urban policy, in which city strategies, as well as the policies and practices involved in their production, are circulating. Thus, while the vigorous policy circulation associated with preparing city strategies is noteworthy (Healey 2007; Robinson 2011b), each strategic vision or plan is also distinctive, representing both a close engagement with a specific context and a certain terrritorialization of urban politics (see Robinson 2011b for a wider discussion of city strategies).

Bringing these three cases of city strategy into conversation benefitted from the observation that each 'repeated instance', while interconnected with the others through the practice of preparing city strategies, is a distinctive starting point for reflection in relation to a multitude of other city strategies. Each experience of city strategy prompts analytical reflection in its own right. To draw them into comparative reflection I use this particular tactic: starting with each (repeated) instance, grounded in an interconnected and circulating urban practice, I allow them to raise questions of each other (Ward 2010), in order to 'thicken' the interpretation of each of the cases in turn (Akrich and Rabeharisoa 2016). Each case offers a different analytical starting point: London establishes the complex discursive and technical practices which subtend the territorialisation and path-dependent outcomes of circulating urban policies and divergent political interests; Johannesburg reveals the diverse ways in which local political agency recursively mobilises and contributes to transnational and international circuits; and the Lilongwe case extends the range of actors and forms of relationships involved in constituting city-wide strategies in a globalizing field of power. In a specifically post-colonial move, the experiences of both Lilongwe and Johannesburg can be returned to review understandings of the London case, throwing light on the informalised forms of power and agency there, as well as the potential for democratic outcomes in the public interest. Together these cases extend and enrich understanding (or conceptualization) of city strategies without detracting from their distinctive experiences.

Taking such a ubiquitous governmental technology as a starting point can contribute to internationalising theoretical analyses of urban development politics which have focused largely on the USA and Europe (Lauermann 2018). This can draw us to attend to a much wider range of actors, forms of constitution of urban agency, as well as different processes of globalisation. Starting from cities like Lilongwe, Malawi, hard questions are posed to the existing literature: How are urban political interests articulated in conditions of the strong trans-nationalization, even exteriorization, of economy, state and civil society; the dominant role of international agents (donors, advisors, consultants, investors, foreign governments); the significance of informalized political processes; and challenges of extreme inequality? In fact, based on the comparative analysis of the three cases of city strategies I suggest that issues of transnationalisation and informality are also important to take account of in thinking about urban politics in London, at the top of the putative international urban hierarchy, and in Johannesburg, a regional centre in a middle-income country (Robinson 2018a). Bringing these cities together for analytical reflection challenges us to explore how experiences from poorly resourced contexts can be effectively drawn into wider theoretical conversations on urban governance. This demonstrates the potential for comparisons on genetic grounds to significantly extend the theoretical range of urban political analysis through comparative research with a wider global scope, in ways that could be helpful to thinking about all cities.

A further manouevre is invited by attending to the repeated instance, which is to identify new starting points for understanding – perhaps *the difference so far unconceptualised*. Thus, potentially quite different grounds emerge for bringing cases into comparative conversations. Niranjana (2022) highlights on the potential of 'minor' theory to draw attention to the diverse processes shaping urban situations (Katz 1996). This moves the methodological approach potentially more into the realm of generative comparisons: identifying concepts or processes in one context which might draw us to compose a comparison across a selection of cases to inform conceptualization. Cindi

Katz (2001) proposes 'countertopographies' to trace, or invent, connections which could underpin oppositional possibilities for solidarity and mobilization across divergent cases – thinking about connections between New York and Howa in the Sudan articulates her sense of the need for 'equivalent, alternative abstractions' (p. 1232) as a counter to the powerful connectivities of capitalism. Focusing on the internal multiplicity and heterogeneity of any case invites new starting points for wider analysis and political imaginations. For example, while a comparative analysis might begin by following the globalizing circuits of financialisation, 'repeated instances' present researchers with a multiplicity of actors and processes assembled in emergent territorialized and transnational political formations (Fernandez and Aalbers 2016; Halbert and Rouanet 2014; Weber 2015). Thinking across this multiplicity could inspire new comparisons starting with any of the many different actors and processes shaping and contesting specific urban developments across the numerous urban contexts shaped by financialized circuits and urban policy mobilities (see Shatkin 2016, 2017, for example). Rather than seeing again and again 'neoliberalisation' or 'financialization', by tracing circuits to reveal repeated instances different actors and processes come into view. These could open onto possibilities for formulating 'generative' comparisons, composing new kinds of comparative experiments across these different instances. Chapter 8 explores further the potential for composing comparisons to reframe analyses of urban development politics across a diversity of urban outcomes.

A cautionary note on 'instances' and their repetitiveness, though, comes from Marilyn Strathern. Puzzling over the presence of certain cultural practices and objects across the interconnected cultures of Papua New Guinea Highlands, she observes the commonality of stories and repertoires associated with bamboo flutes – surely culturally connected in some way, but distinctive. She suggests 'wherever one looks, the flute is already an image. It never exists in a generic form, only in a multiplicity of specific ones' (2005, p. 73). For example, the 'scale' of analysis, she observes, is not set – either by the objects, or by the social meanings attached to them. In each case the propositions and use of objects scale differently (body, household, social group), entraining and constituting different kinds of social relations and practices (p. 75). Comparability cannot be assumed even though the (circulating) object might seem identical. For her, then, while the actualism of historical connections amongst different inter-related societies is attractive to ground the possibility of comparative analysis, this does not solve the problem of comparability:

> This being the case, the question of 'connections' between different societies ceases to be a problem. What instead becomes of interest are the

reasons for particular local adaptations, different trajectories of development in styles of leadership or types of transactions or whatever. Set into a social context like this, the cultural similarities across social boundaries become trivial.

(Strathern 2005, p. 94)

Thrown back into the realm of generating insights across different contexts, out-of-scale extensions, incompatibilities and cyborg-like partial connections come into view. Following the connections for Strathern re-forms into the problematic of what we have been calling 'generative' comparisons inspired by a researcher's creative engagement with possibly incommensurable urban worlds – tactics on the two grounds, genetic and generative, are not separable for long.

Conclusion: Thinking with Repeated Instances

This chapter addresses the question, what it is possible to do with multiple, interconnected, repeated instances within a comparative imagination? As natural experiments for destabilizing concepts, repeated instances drag researchers into tracing the connections and processes of urbanisation, and into attending to a multiplicity of differentiated empirical outcomes. I have suggested three ways to work analytically with these repeated instances: (a) *by addition*, to allow urban processes and outcomes to be approached as an empirical multiplicity, adding up to or providing starting points for insights into urbanisation processes whose reference points are not the specific 'cities' within which they might be embedded, but the diverse circulations and connections which constitute any possible urban outcome; (b) *by subtraction*, to undermine, develop or reinvent concepts which follow the traces of urban genesis; and (c) *by attending to each case*, bringing into conceptualisation the multiplicity of processes and actors allied in the production of yet another instance, treating each as a distinctive starting point for analysis.

The following chapter continues to explore how comparative insights might be inspired by connections which are producing the urban, but draws on a different theoretical repertoire. In a political economy perspective, alert to the relational constitution of the social and material world, the potential for drawing different urban experiences into analytical proximity has different grounds. Wider social processes which connect, or 'encompass', many places invite comparative analysis; different processes interweave in shaping particular 'contexts'. Both processes and contexts open up potential for further comparative tactics on genetic grounds.

Notes

1. Here they use 'singularity' in a vernacular social science sense of a 'distinctive' outcome, as opposed to the Deleuzian interpretation of singularity as an 'intuition' or empirical observation, which is the starting point of a process of conceptualisation (see Chapter 11).
2. I have followed the Johannesburg case closely since 1999, and have conducted numerous, and repeat, interviews with key city government personnel and other actors involved in the city strategy process there (Parnell and Robinson 2006; Robinson 2011b, 2013b). My comments here are drawn from these interviews, attending some public consultation meetings, and analysis of background documents as well as draft and final policies. Here the strategy represents the negotiation of a post-apartheid vision, balancing priorities of growth and redistribution. In London I have been fortunate to co-operate with the community-based network, Just Space, learning through their collective organization and engagement with the London Plan process primarily through the formal consultation process, public hearings, but also informal interactions with officials (Brown et al. 2014). Here the key issue which emerges concerns the potential for a more inclusive policy agenda to take hold in a large city with very powerful property development and business groups. My knowledge of the Lilongwe case is gained from discussions with several Johannesburg officials who were involved in a city-to-city exchange process, as well as analysis of detailed background documents, correspondence and evaluation materials. Here the question which arises concerns the implications of external actors playing a strong role in policy and urban development.

CHAPTER 6

Relations

> *"relational comparison focuses… on spatio-historical specificities as well as interconnections and mutually constitutive processes"*
> (Hart 2003, p. 3)

Relational comparisons in urban studies draw their inspiration from both spatial analysis and certain forms of social theory. The insights of geographer Doreen Massey on spatial relations have been crucial – the idea of an 'open' sense of place, in which the trajectories of people, things and ideas come together in a form of 'simultaneity' to produce a dynamic social and political formation has shaped a generation of urban scholars. Thus, places are 'relational' in the spatial sense that they involve stretched out social relations and trajectories. Marxist theory contributes a more generalised perspective focusing on the constitutive nature of space for social relations. Social phenomena are not self-standing entities, but are necessarily co-constituted through an 'ensemble of social relations' (Sotiris 2014, p. 40). For David Harvey (1996) this relationality is both social and spatial. The spatialities which shape urbanisation include uneven development, the production of scale, flows of money and credit, the fixity of the built environment.

These two theoretical propositions about space have been most influential in 'relational' approaches to urban studies. In other theoretical traditions, 'relational' can refer to an explanatory focus on the relations or social interactions amongst people, groups or networks as causes of social and historical phenomena. These might be contrasted with other explanations, such as those which focus on individuals rather than social organisations, or structural approaches (Tilly 1998, p. 24). Actor Network Theory draws attention to the constitution of agency through relations (or networks) which cut across human-non-human divisions, with 'relations' as the foundation of emergent socio-natural formations in which agency is distributed rather than attached to pre-defined individuals (Latour 2007).

Comparative Urbanism: Tactics for Global Urban Studies, First Edition. Jennifer Robinson.
© 2022 John Wiley & Sons Ltd. Published 2022 by John Wiley & Sons Ltd.

In contrast with the concept of the 'repeated instance', the spatial imagination at work in the concept of a 'relational comparison' (Hart 2003, 2018; Ward 2010) holds different possibilities for doing comparison. There are some similarities though. Both sets of comparative tactics take their cue from empirical processes linking and shaping different places (flows of various kinds and direct social relations) to draw connected cases into analytical proximity. Relational comparisons are also, then, comparisons on genetic grounds. They focus on the social relationships which link one place with others, which 'stretch' across localities. They are interested in the mutual inter-relationships between places, which bring into view differences in outcomes between cases. Comparative analysis of different cases can contribute new understandings of the nature of the connections, and the social relationships which are implicated in them. More broadly, as with direct connections, tracing these relationships can provoke reflections across cases and suggest new starting points for analysis.

But with relational comparisons some new comparative openings and problematics reveal themselves. Distinctive to urban relational comparisons is a close interest in exploring the wider or shared processes influencing different cases. This can inspire comparative analysis across cases which are not directly connected, but which are part of the same overarching (or 'encompassing') process. Comparative analysis can bring insight to understanding these wider, shared processes through exploring their different forms and ongoing (re-)constitution in specific contexts. Thinking with contexts is particularly important for relational comparisons. In this perspective contexts are conceived of as shaped by the intersection of a diversity of social processes. In any given context a social process occurs in conjunction with other processes which might be present. And each process is produced across and shaped by many diverse contexts. Relational comparative approaches therefore provide opportunities to think with the complexity of urban contexts, as well as with the pan-urban processes shaping particular urban contexts. Relational urban comparativists especially direct attention to the mutual entanglement of places in the shared social processes which are shaping many different contexts. I discuss these distinctive relational comparative practices here as: interrogating and understanding **'wider processes'**; and working comparatively with **'contexts'**. With each of these, a range of different comparative tactics become apparent.

Here we will need to interrogate what it means to consider 'wider processes' which often arrive already conceptualised within comprehensive theorisations, such as Marxist political economy, and/or have long historical durability and thus perhaps taken-for-granted meanings. This highlights one of the limitations of this approach: the weight of inherited (and often parochial) theoretical traditions may not be open to a strong revisability of conceptualisations, especially of wider processes, or leave sufficient scope for identifying emergent, new processes. This chapter therefore focusses attention on how relational comparative tactics on genetic grounds might be mobilised to promote revisable and open conceptualisations of the urban and urbanisation, starting anywhere. It considers different ways in which comparative urbanism can work creatively with cases to generate insight into 'wider processes'. This enriches analyses of these processes, but can also establish the limits of extant understandings through reference to divergent experiences.

In urban studies, numerous accounts of widespread but differentiated processes of urban neoliberalisation open up possibilities for comparative reflections, through analysis of the dynamic role which spatial differences play in shaping this wider process. This provides an example to demonstrate the potential for comparative analysis to contribute to critical interrogation of existing theorisations. Could a 'wider process' look differently if seen from an expanded range of historical and geographical settings? Might conceptualisations of urban neoliberalisation reach their limits? To go beyond this concept, the tight entangling of hybridised outcomes and the wider process of neoliberalisation which analysts have proposed (in the concept of 'variegation') needs to be loosened. Relational comparativism's enthusiasm to build understandings from 'contexts' makes an essential contribution to this. Contexts proliferate the wider processes which might be considered relevant to explaining urban outcomes. This potentially brings into focus aspects of urbanisation and urban experience which have been neglected analytically and which constitute 'unconceptualised difference'. The extensive scholarship on the multiplicity of social processes shaping urban governance alongside neoliberalisation helps to draw attention to some significant lacunae in conceptualising the global urban from this perspective. So this chapter also considers how new concepts might emerge from relational comparative analyses.

A relational comparative imagination therefore suggests a further set of comparative tactics on genetic grounds, working with 'wider processes' and 'contexts'. The final section of the chapter extends the meaning of the 'relations' which might initiate such comparisons. A wider range of spatialities can encourage more experimental comparisons, thinking with topology, partial connections and submarine relations, for example. This chapter, then, consolidates the comparative tactics which emerge when 'connections' and 'relations' offer genetic grounds for comparison.

Wider Processes

Chapter 2 considered Charles Tilly's proposed **encompassing comparisons** as a methodological fit for exploring the large historical processes and globalising forces which are essential elements in any contemporary urban analysis:

> Encompassing comparisons, however, deserve more attention than they have received. Encompassing comparisons have twin advantages: directly taking account of the interconnectedness of ostensibly separate experiences and providing a strong incentive to ground analyses explicitly in the historical contexts of the *structures and processes* they include. If we move up from the macrohistorical plane in which this book has worked to world-systemic and world-historical analyses, the importance of encompassing comparison increases, as the feasibility of universalizing and variation-finding comparison declines. For our own time, it is hard to imagine the construction of any valid analysis of long-term structural change that does not connect particular alterations, directly or indirectly, to the two interdependent master processes of the era: the creation of a system of national states and the formation of a worldwide capitalist system. We face the challenge of integrating *big structures, large processes, and huge comparisons* into history.
> (Tilly 1984, p. 147; my emphases)

There is a tendency to critique Tilly for assuming the nature of the wider entity, or system[1] – whereas Tilly in fact warns against this, presenting it as a risk of encompassing analyses. With an historian's eye, he selects his examples of encompassing comparativists, Bendix, Skocpol, Moore and Rokkan, because they 'display the value of tearing large-scale comparison away from the abstract, ahistorical stake to which social scientists have often chained it and of attaching it instead to historically specific experiences of change' (Tilly 1984, p. 86). As a historical sociologist, Tilly neither pre-determines the cases which matter, nor does he suggest that the 'large processes' with which he is concerned are formed outside of many different specific and located historical situations:

> By 'genuinely historical', I mean studies assuming that the time and place in which a structure or process appears make a difference to its character, that the sequence in which similar events occur has a substantial impact on their outcomes, and that the existing record of past structures and processes is problematic, requiring systematic investigation in its own right instead of lending itself immediately to social-scientific syntheses.
> (Tilly 1984, p. 79)

Tilly also helpfully takes us away from the geographical idiom of connections as trajectories or circulations, or the relatively thin sense of 'repetition' and 'differentiation' which attends on tracing specific empirical connections and flows of people, ideas and practices, such as in policy mobilities, or trajectories of investment and design. He traces wide-ranging historical processes which emerge, say, across regions – as in nineteenth-century European state formation which spread through competitive conflict amongst nascent states and principalities. Or which spread more extensively and in more complex ways to reconfigure many inter-related contexts through globalising processes and practices, such as markets, financialisation, trade, colonial settlement, ideologies, institutions, or the means of violence and the organisation of coercion (Mann 2012). Thus, one difference from the 'repeated instances' analytical formulations is that a relational imagination, particularly in inheritance from Marxist approaches, sees it as important to pay attention to so-called wider historical processes which are part of, produced by and shape many different contexts, say, state formation. Or the geographically extended systems within which cases might be causally located, say, capitalism, or the trade in enslaved persons. Such wider networks of interaction or interdependent historical processes draw places into comparative reflection and are themselves identified and illuminated through comparative research.

There is overlap between the methodological potential of tracing the ways in which connections reveal repeated instances, and the insights to be gained from working with the 'relational connections' between places, or cases, as well as with wider systems and extensive social formations. However, the questions which we are drawn to ask are somewhat different, concerned to illuminate and understand widespread, general and emergent systemic processes and their variation.

McMichael (1990) notes that, conventionally, cases might be assembled for comparison on two grounds. Firstly, insofar as they are considered to reflect intrinsic properties which they hold in common they can be interrogated to determine patterning across cases. This is a kind of variation finding, based on identified variables and postulated causal relations. And secondly they can be compared on that basis that they share features derived from a common global system. McMichael dismisses outright the science-influenced process of building insights through variation-finding comparisons across cases: 'Outcomes (as instances) may appear individually as self-evident units of analysis, but in reality are interconnected processes' (p. 396). In an important (albeit somewhat idiosyncratic and sometimes difficult to decipher) article, he seeks to disturb these conventions through his ideas of 'incorporated comparison', emerging from debates around world-systems theory which was dominant in some social science circles in the 1980s. The idea of 'incorporation' which he proposes concerns the ways in which different societies are drawn into relationship with wider processes, such as capitalism or state formation. Thus dependent, marginal or traditional societies might be 'incorporated' into the capitalist world system in a variety of different ways, as explored in the significant Marxist debates (in southern contexts) concerning the 'articulation of modes of production' (Wolpe 1980).

From this vantage point he is inspired to propose two alternative comparative methods. One, which he calls a 'multiple' form of incorporated comparison, can shed light on the historical emergence of wider systems through a range of case studies: 'instances are analysed as products of a continuously evolving process in and across time' (p. 389). In this way, as different places engage with the wider system, they form numerous (multiple) cases which offer different insights on these systems. He proposes an additional strategy, a 'singular' form of incorporated comparison, which takes as its focus the differentiated elements of a 'whole' which are 'competitively combined and therefore redefined, in an historical conjuncture with unpredictable outcomes' (p. 389). This focusses on 'the multi-layered character of a social configuration rather than on its replication across time' (p. 393). In an unfortunate evolutionary idiom, consigning some social orders to the past of others, he suggests that

> This is a 'cross-sectional' comparison of segments of a contradictory whole in which the segments (e.g., social units, cultures, or belief systems) 'belong' to distinct social times.
> (McMichael 1990, p. 389)

Together these two tactics respond to the relational conundrum of how to think differentiated but systemically connected outcomes. Different outcomes occur partly by the ways in which wider processes might be differently instantiated across discrete sites, and partly by how many processes are combined (articulated) in one place or context to produce distinctive outcomes. We will return to consider the methodological implications of the second contextual (singular) form of comparison in more detail in the following section.

In terms of analysing different outcomes of wider processes, world-systems analysis had proposed a 'singular' whole, in the form of an all-encompassing world economy, in the context of which multiple 'parts' or cases become units of observation of such a whole, and the basis for substantive rather than logical generalisations. McMichael draws on this, but takes issue with the dependence of this approach on a pre-figurative theoretical analysis, in which the theoretical whole and the historical totality are necessarily aligned and thus the analysis is somewhat predetermined. McMichael seeks to open this up to the idea of an 'emergent totality', in which 'totality is a conceptual *procedure*, rather than an empirical or conceptual premise' (p. 391). His intention is 'to develop historically-grounded social theory through the comparative juxtaposition of a dynamic self-forming whole' (p. 396). It is a moot point as to whether McMichael seeks to place in question the understanding of what the 'whole', such as capitalism, might be. However, even if it is historically emergent in the process of contradictory and contested incorporation of different societies and economies, for McMichael the answer to the nature of the 'whole' seems to be pre-given as 'capitalism'. Nonetheless it is certainly a strong and by now routine argument, one he shares with Tilly and many others, to see wider social processes as emergent and both produced by and producing individual instances, which cannot be delineated in advance.

McMichael's analysis has been influential in inspiring urban studies approaches to comparison (Bodnar 2019). Gill Hart explicitly aligns the idea of relational comparisons with his approach:

> relational comparison and McMichael's conception of incorporated comparison explicitly and emphatically refuse to assert any a priori general or universal process. In different although related ways outlined above, we both argue that claims about generality have to be produced through close attention to *the multiple relations and determinations at the core of Marx's method*.[2] Precisely these 'complex mediations… that make up the joints of any social problem', as Ollman puts it, are what is at stake in an open, non-teleological conception of dialectics and in a relational, non-positivist understanding of generality.
>
> (Hart 2018, p. 11; italics added)

For Hart, 'wider processes' and contexts are co-constituted in relation to one another. This deep entwining of cases, or contexts, and wider processes indicates a comparative practice which can illuminate the emergence and differentiation of historical processes encompassing different contexts and associated with a variety of outcomes. Parts and wholes, or wider processes, are seen as mutually imbricated. As Hart notes, this 'enables more general understandings of how the specific "parts" on which one has been focusing feed into and shape broader processes, rather than just reflecting or implementing them' (Hart 2018, p. 20).

Tilly commences his discussion of encompassing comparisons with Eric Wolf's *Europe and the People without History*. This influential text critiques the idea of the 'lumping together of the people far from the capitalist core in a peripheral zone of weak states and primitive peoples, sucked one by one into an orbit of dependency' (Tilly 1984, p. 128). Rather, Wolf explores different networks and the agency of actors from across the world in shaping dominant capitalist processes. Next, for Tilly, the spatial analysis of Stein Rokkan identifies a range of interactions which shaped the differentiation of European countries – urban networks, different empires and religious institutions, migrations. Tilly observes how Rokkan 'slips' into encompassing comparisons in his search for explanations of difference – including the crucial wider state-building process within the European context of inter-state competition through war (p. 130).

Following the relational production of places, or cases, therefore invites us to see and expand understanding of 'wider processes' or generalised phenomena (beyond particular places) which have been an important concern of political economy theorists: capitalist transformations, industrialisation, state formation, and any number of epochal political and ideological shifts, such as anti-colonial nationalisms or growing dominance of certain religious ideas or political mobilisations. It is certainly one of the limits of the methodological applications of actor network theory that these wider processes have been occluded in favour of accounts of emergent particularities: hence the refrain from Marxist urban scholars that such approaches neglect the 'context of contexts' (Brenner et al. 2011). But in turn critics complain that Marxist theorists are inflexible as to the characterisation of this wider context and portrayal of the processes which comprise them (Buckley and Strauss 2016; McFarlane 2011c). Following Tilly, McMichael and Hart, relational comparative analyses of urbanisation processes and urban outcomes provide an opening to draw 'wider processes' into question and diversify perspectives on their conceptualisation, provenance and substantive nature.

Questions arise, then, as to the identification of and claims made about the substantive form and nature of the 'broader processes', which are often assumed within a Marxist or political economy perspective. Perhaps most crucially, what is a 'social process'? This is such a taken-for-granted term in social analysis and is seldom defined. Tilly can once again help us here, as he elaborates his 'relational' perspective:

> Let us adopt a simple distinction among mechanisms, processes, and episodes.
>
> Mechanisms[3] form a delimited class of events that change relations among specified sets of elements in identical or closely similar ways over a variety of situations. For example, brokerage—the joining of two or more previously less connected social sites through the intervention of third parties—constitutes a political mechanism of extremely general scope.

> Processes are frequently occurring combinations or sequences of mechanisms. For example, scale shift—an alteration in the range of sites engaging in coordinated action—regularly results from a concatenation of brokerage with the mechanisms of diffusion, emulation, and attribution of similarity.
>
> Episodes are bounded streams of social life. For example, depending on our analytical purposes, we can adopt the Mexican presidential election of 2000, the 1999–2000 campaign leading to that election, or the entire period of opposition mobilisation from 1988 to 2000 as the episode under examination.
>
> (Tilly 2001, pp. 25–6)

In combination, mechanisms produce 'various outcomes' (Van Der Linden and Mitzman 2009, p. 244; see also Tilly 2010). Historical sedimentations of mechanisms and processes might be construed as 'social structures'. Sotiris notes, with the late Althusser's '*On Reproduction*', that 'structure', is immanent in social relations rather than a deep, or absent cause. Thus it might be considered as

> a social relation that exists because it lasts, and lasts because it is reproduced through the material effectivity of a system of material apparatuses that guarantees this reproduction, a system that is itself conditioned by social practices and antagonistic social relations and strategies. (Sotiris 2014, p. 29) .... Therefore social structures are not a priori social forms, but relatively and provisionally stable complexes of social relations, in their singular, multiple and conflictual/antagonistic form. There is no teleology or deeper causality that guarantees this provisional stability, their tendency to be reproduced or transformed depends upon the balance of forces in their antagonistic relations.
>
> (Sotiris 2014, p. 41)

Giddens' (1984) formulation, 'structuration', captures this by now conventional sense of 'structures' as emergent from and reciprocally transformed by social action and social processes. Such a view, though, opens social processes and structures to the vagaries of needing to be constantly reproduced, and therefore to a strong potential to be remade, differently (Butler 1990). Exploring and working with this potential for the revisability of wider processes is a key contribution of relational comparative urbanism.

Relational comparativists in urban studies are especially concerned with accounting for the relationships between 'contingent' urban places, and wider processes, or structures, especially of (global) capitalism (Peck 2017a). It is one of the perennial conundrums of social analysis to understand the nature of the relationship between contingent 'particularity' and wider processes, or systems (Cox and Evenhuis 2020; Painter and Goodwin 1995). In Marxist analyses the relationship between 'particular' capitalisms in contrast with 'capitalism' as a wider process (both as generalised condition and universal theorisation) is framed by Dipesh Chakrabarty (2000) as a dialectic, an internal relationship. For him, each particular historical outcome (a History 2) is already present in and shapes the so-called universal history, History 1. Thus, whatever History 1 is thought to be – the conceptualisation of the wider process (or system) – this is always based on analysis of someone's History 2, it is only ever known through particularity.[4] Whatever History 1 might be thought to be, History 2 is best thought of 'as a category charged with the function of constantly interrupting the totalising thrusts of History 1' (p. 66). Moreover, which we will return to consider in later chapters, 'the idea of History 2 beckons us to more affective narratives of human belonging where life forms, although porous to one another, do not seem exchangeable through a third term of equivalence such as abstract labour' (p. 71).

We are invited to consider the provisionality of the 'wider processes', systems or structures which are relevant to understanding particular outcomes. Wider processes (or systems or structures) cannot be taken as 'given' in case-based empirical and theoretical enquiries in social science. Not only are these wider processes historically changing and spatially variable – they also have a double life as empirical phenomena and concepts. Systems or wider processes are historical, and involve of course actual events and interactions, but to identify them is at root a process of conceptualisation too: 'capitalism', 'neoliberalism', 'development' are concepts which must grapple with the historical variability and diverse meaning of empirical phenomena. Some conundrums present themselves for comparative urbanists: does 'hybridisation' in contexts simply preserve intact the wider processes? To what extent can empirical observations change understandings of wider processes? What processes have been prioritised analytically, as important in shaping contexts? Have other processes been occluded or hidden from view?

Relational comparative tactics working with wider processes can:

- draw on varied experiences in different contexts to delineate the nature of a wider process;
- assess the implications of the varied expressions and forms of a wider process for conceptualisation;
- discern whether/when a wider process is transformed into something different than initially conceived, requiring new concepts.

Comparative practices which trace relationality to interrogate wider processes and social structures, the 'context of contexts', can inspire concept formation. They can open up what is often a 'black box' in social science analysis through the creative comparative interrogation of inherited concepts and 'wider processes'. In urban studies, processes of 'neoliberalisation' have provided a significant horizon of analysis for some time, and with numerous case studies, provides a rich example of putting relational comparison into practice. This work exemplifies the potential which relational comparativism offers for working with and interrogating wider processes.

Urban Neoliberalisation, Comparatively

The example of 'neoliberalisation' is especially pertinent for relational comparative urbanism, as processes of the neoliberalisation of urban policy and governance have been identified in so many different urban contexts. Closely entangled with global capitalism, neoliberalisation constitutes a prominent 'wider process' shaping contemporary urbanisation. International regulatory and policy change together with transformations in urban governance in many places mean that theoretical insights have been informed by a relatively wide variety of experiences. Circuits of neoliberal policy norms and practices have influenced a vast number of cases of privatisation, structural adjustment, reconfiguration of states, rollback of services, changing forms of service delivery and ambitious growth agendas in urban areas. These shared circuits open the possibility to understand specific urban experiences relationally. It would be quite possible to consider 'neoliberalisation' through the lens of the specific connections and flows (Ong 2007). But, much analytical effort has gone into conceptualising how different urban outcomes are both produced by and productive of a wider process of 'neoliberalisation'. This interpretation has shaped analysis of other processes, such as financialisation (Aalbers 2017) or fiscal austerity (González et al. 2018), with lasting impact on thinking the urban relationally.

Certain cases and experiences have been iconic in informing the analysis of urban neoliberalisation. David Harvey's account focusses on the initiating events of the 1975 fiscal crisis of New York's government and the overt disciplining role of major banks (creditors) in response. This pinpoints a moment when the stakes of urban government became aligned with anti-welfarist class politics in the USA (Harvey 2005). A patient international programme of ideological mobilisation after the Second World War, centred around the Austrian Mont Pèlerin organisation, sought to oppose the centralised state power which characterised fascism and the USSR (Foucault 2007). Neoliberal economic policies gained traction across international organisations and in many countries, and have sustained an ongoing and dispersed 'project' amongst a range of actors to promote these (Peck 2010). These ideas drove often highly politicised governance transformations in cities, countries, and in the international world order, notably the major regulatory institutions of the IMF, World Bank and WTO (Goldman 2005). Whereas it was initially not clear what these changes added up to – and the place holder term 'post-Fordism' was common through the 1980s and early 1990s (Amin 1994) – neoliberalisation emerged as a critical concept to describe a growing international regulatory and policy consensus. More pragmatically, long before 'urban neoliberalisation' was identified as a concept, practices of commercialisation, internal markets and outsourcing were being embedded in many local governments (Harrison 2006b). For urban governments in Western countries characterised by forms of 'managerialism' and bureaucratised post-war local government, more or less welfarist, these changes added up to a normalisation of what Harvey called 'entrepreneurial' urban governance (Harvey 1989).

The sites of invention of 'neoliberalism' were acknowledged to be quite dispersed (Peck 2004). Iconically, the radical governmental experiments in 1980s Chile made governance there to this day one of the most thoroughly privatised. Scholars of neoliberalisation have been closely attentive to these wider geographies. They have noted both national-scale varieties of neoliberalisation (Harvey 2005), as well as the ways in which neoliberalisation of the norms and practices of international financial institutions and intergovernmental developmental agencies informed the 1980s restructuring of poor countries across the world through 'Structural Adjustment Policies' and the 'Washington Consensus' (Goldman 2005). These international rule regimes stabilised more generally through the 1990s (Brenner et al. 2010; Peck 2004), only to be destabilised through crises from the late 2000s, raising the question, ultimately, as to whether the dominant formation of capitalism was 'still neoliberalism?' (Peck and Theodore 2019). Nonetheless, circuits of think tanks, policymakers, lobby groups and consultants have mobilised neoliberal ideas and policies to reshape local, national and international policy over decades (Peck 2010). As we saw in Chapter 5, tracing connections and circuits as well as interrogating many different cases can be used additively to delineate processes of urbanisation. How has thinking comparatively informed understandings of urban neoliberalisation as a social process? What comparative tactics have urban scholars used as they have developed this analysis?

In addition to the composition of generalised narratives of the global and (diverse) national histories of neoliberalisation (Harvey 2005; Peck

2010), characteristically urban studies has to confront head on the problematic of 'urban neoliberalisation' as both a wider process shaping many places and a multiplicity of specific processes and outcomes in urban contexts. This places this body of literature as a crucial resource in recrafting comparative urbanism. In contemplating this, the mutual production of wider processes and specific outcomes saw the term, 'variegation', introduced to capture this dynamic. This has implications for relational comparative tactics more generally.

The term, 'variegation' was proposed by Peck and Theodore (2007, p. 733) as a 'still inchoate but putatively alternate vision' to the 'space-blind' (p. 765) 'varieties of capitalism' analyses of the geographies of global capitalism. They suggested that thinking about 'variety' in relational terms, informed by the spatial analyses of economic geography, draws attention to the 'complex asymmetries and webs of connection that increasingly characterise the unevenly integrating global economy' (p. 766). The 'common matrix' of the contemporary capitalist system indexes the networked terrain across which varieties (or variegations) of capitalism are produced – neoliberalisation, financialisation and imperialism (p. 766). Their 'provisional' use of the term 'variegation' was firmed up considerably in the suite of papers with Neil Brenner on neoliberalisation (most fully in Brenner et al. 2010a; also Peck et al. 2009). This conceptual culmination of a long decade of work by the authors, together and separately, on policy circulations, scale and spatial differentiation, as well as neoliberalisation, has strongly influenced urban studies. Informed primarily by their knowledge of the USA and UK, but with little in the way of detailed local case studies, a broad ranging and strongly contructivist account has been developed, often in stern opposition to alternative interpretations (Peck, 2013). 'Variegation' has become an important way to conceptualise the urban as outcomes of widely circulating processes, strongly hybridised through path dependency and political contestation, but implicating and influencing systemic processes such as the rule regimes of international policy and economic regulation, as well as global capitalism more generally. Such a spatiality characterises what they have called a 'syndrome' of neoliberalisation. The term 'variegation' therefore recasts understanding of the relation between specific localised outcomes and wider systemic processes configured through connections, wider historical processes, transnational institutions and actors, but articulated in particular contexts with distinctive historical pathways.

The nuance of the analysis and its relevance to the spatiality of contemporary globalised policy and economic processes has made 'variegation' now a conventional and helpful term in urban studies, rather than a hesitant proposition. In terms of relational comparative method it indicates very explicitly how detailed case studies, understood to be part of an encompassing and interconnected set of social relations, might be able to contribute in principle to understandings of a wider process. This analysis offers practical grounds for comparisons, based on shared involvement of many different cases in such a wider process. And it suggests that different cases could be useful in tracing the contours of how a wider process is produced, transformed and diversified:

> a variegated form of regulatory restructuring: it produces geoinstitutional differentiation across places, territories and scales; but it does this systemically, as a pervasive, endemic feature of its basic operational logic …[such that] neoliberalisation represents an unevenly developed, hybrid, patterned tendency of market-disciplinary regulatory restructuring.
>
> (Brenner et al. 2010b, p. 330)

What, then, can (yet) another case contribute to conceptualising urban neoliberalisation, or wider processes in general? (How) do cases make a difference to analyses of neoliberalisation? In addressing this question, some general as well as distinctively relational comparative tactics become apparent. The rest of this section explores these in turn, from tactics which strengthen understandings of existing processes (or terms), to those which identify the fragmentation or declining relevance of an existing concept, and open up possibilities for identifying new processes.

1. More cases strengthen and enrich understanding. Within the 'variegated' model, cases have a privileged place as the motors of a dynamic wider process. All sorts of dynamics from implementation to roll out, emergent political conflicts, or failure leading to innovation have the effect of shaping, consolidating and strengthening the wider processes of neoliberalisation, staving off its demise under the weight of the inevitable contradictions of capitalist urban development (Peck et al. 2009). There have been numerous studies, then, which have been able to point out this intimate relationship between case and process, reinforcing the broad contours of existing understandings of neoliberalisation. More cases therefore strengthen and enrich understanding of the process, as well as identify emergent trends.

Here we can consider the suggestive comparison of New York and New Orleans, both US cities which faced extraordinary crises in 2001 (the twin towers attacks) and 2005 (unprecedented floods). In the aftermath of these crises, the neoliberal policy context and the growth politics of each place were substantially reconfigured, intensifying the exclusionary and elite-serving elements of neoliberalised governance (Gotham and Greenberg 2008). Forms of funding and urban development which had been in existence for some time, tied to achieving 'public benefit' or a proportion of affordable housing, were exempt from these requirements to encourage rapid recovery. However, this channelled federal contributions to private developers and the elite, in an attempt to redress damage to businesses that were affected. The poor and displaced were largely excluded from developments, with programmes for the poor in fact cut back in the wake of the fiscal impacts of the huge costs of the recovery effort. The political processes which shaped these outcomes saw new, unaccountable boards appointed, outside of usual government oversight and composed largely of those representing private sector interests. Peck (2010, Chapter 4) traces the lobbying and think-tank work that went into mobilising the responses which intensified neoliberalisation in both contexts. These moments of crisis, then, instigated experiments and innovations in market-led governance in both contexts. In a strong sense these cases demonstrate how dynamics in particular localities can remake wider processes (see also Buckley and Hanieh 2014).

Cases permit a closer look, then, at the ways in which 'contingent' place-based dynamics remake 'neoliberalisation' differently in each context. Detailed study of individual cases or comparison across cases highlights how 'neoliberalisation' is always undertaken within a specific situation. On the variegation model, through each case the wider process is also seen to be (re-)made differently, and its overall character transformed.

2. Cases illuminate contingent explanations for variable outcomes. Comparing more than one case can identify common sources and shared features of a process, as in the cases of New York and New Orleans, but can also highlight the need for explanations of variable outcomes. David Wilson (2004) made a strong case for 'contingent neoliberalism' in a comparative analysis of Chicago and Indianapolis. The growth models in these two contexts are shaped by 'different capitals in different political-cultural settings' (p. 774): in Chicago, a global city-oriented focus on physically remodeling the city for international real estate and high-tech initiatives; in Indianapolis, a more locally rooted real-estate – driven project showcasing an attractive (but highly racialised) urban environment. 'Neoliberal' policy innovations in these two contexts demonstrated 'a place-specific reflexiveness rooted in responses to situated conditions and circumstances' (p. 779), with the 'improvisational nature of urban neoliberal governance' evident, especially in the face of conflict and resistance. In each context, neoliberal innovations are woven with local concerns and understandings. In Chicago, the growth coalition responded to anxieties about economic failure and racialised poverty by encouraging developments that drew in global investors and entrenched exclusionary patterns of development; in Indianapolis a rigorous anti-state stance and an ethos of cultural whiteness sedimented middle class and elite privilege. Neoliberal-style policy innovations unfolded in both these contexts, but with varied and unpredictable outcomes. Thus, in Indianapolis unexpectedly redistributive policies resulted when 'neoliberal' urban governance initiatives collided with racialised and violent aspects of wider Indianapolis politics which had prompted significant protests in the mid-1990s. Ultimately, quite different, non-neoliberal policy outcomes resulted (p. 780). Wilson observes that '(w)ith careful looking in places like Indianapolis, we see the reality of political flux and periodic instability betraying the rhetoric of political coherence and inevitability' (p. 780). His conclusion is instructive: 'informed case studies and sensitive comparative analyses of cities are essential. Without them, our understanding of this flourishing governance will remain speculative and incomplete' (p. 781).

Wilson's cases suggest that when a process is investigated comparatively, and as cases diverge, the question might quickly become, not only 'what is [neoliberalism] like?', but also, what process is it that is evident? For Wilson, diverse growth paths, different localised cultures and histories, along with the different kinds of political coalitions point to distinctive outcomes but also to possibly different processes at work. The differentiated processes of racialisation across US cities, for example, are highly significant to both his cases and cannot be subsumed within the characterisation of neoliberalisation. Brand (2018) considers the post-Katrina reconstruction in New Orleans discussed above through the lens of W. B. Du Bois's idea of 'double consciousness' (Gilroy 1995). She names the redevelopment as a product of 'macro processes of racialization' (p. 14), and considers the potential for alternative, subaltern, visions of socially just development, emerging from communal and historic spatial practices. The 'duality of space' speaks to the importance of racialisation to any analysis of this ('neoliberal') process of reconstruction and development.

3. Cases identify alternative and/or emergent processes as explanatory. Post-socialist scholars documenting the multiple transformations of urban governance in former socialist contexts have also grappled with the relative explanatory weight of neoliberalisation. In this case, neoliberalisation has to be assessed alongside the strength of historic path-dependencies, most notably in relation to the legacy of large-scale socialist infrastructures in urban landscapes. For example, in Moscow's collective heating system selected techniques of neoliberal governance were used to sustain socialist-era collective provisioning (Collier 2005). The complexity of transitional dynamics can produce new hybrid formations which are not necessarily 'neoliberal' and which can't be easily ascribed to either the historical path dependencies of socialism or 'neoliberalisation' as such. Golubchikov et al. (2014, p. 617) argue that 'hybrid' formations might 'subsume legacy, recode its meaning, and recast the former egalitarian spaces as an uneven spatial order'.

In relation to legacy collective heating systems in Liberic, Czech Republic, for example, Bouzarovski et al. (2016, p. 628) identify how 'new path dependencies can emerge at critical junctures during such multiple transformations, when actors make contingent choices that define and consolidate a specific trajectory of development'. In this case state choices about how to govern collective legacy systems through private sector providers intersected poorly with other trends. Notable here was the unintended residualisation of collective heating systems in centrally located but poorly maintained and largely non-privatised socialist era housing, as owners of privatised properties in other parts of the city invested in individual heating systems. This radically destroyed the potential to cover the costs of the collective system through charges. The costs of heating therefore increased rapidly for the poorest residents in the city. The hybridity of the processes at work here were 'closely integrated with inherited, existing, and evolving urban landscapes' (Bouzarovski et al. 2016, p. 639). This calls for a close analysis of the specific configurations of an urbanisation process shaped by a combination of neoliberal governmental techniques, a distinctive post-socialist trajectory, inherited technical and infrastructural pathways, and local political institutions.

'Post-socialism' as a distinctive range of urban development pathways could then be treated as an alternative concept for explaining outcomes, expressing continuities and anti-continuities with historical dynamics, and reflecting hybridised and spatially relational urban formations. Tuvikene (2016, p. 144) notes of Estonia's capital, Tallinn, for example, that this 'is an ordinary, complex city composed of a multiplicity of social and material relations, some aspects of which—such as its urban fabric, its governmental practices and the valuation of property rights—may be characterised as post-socialist because they represent evidence of continuities or anti-continuities with socialist-era urban processes'.

Close examination of different cases of 'neoliberalisation' can then potentially demonstrate the attenuated demonstrate of this process in explaining outcomes, revealing alternative processes worthy of investigation. The classical comparative methodological proposition would be that the social formation under investigation could be 'cased' in an alternative way, 'as something altogether different in another interpretive project' (Walton 1992, p. 134). The growing number of very large-scale, often ex-urban, developments across Africa seem at first sight to be ambitious and speculative private (neoliberal) developments (Watson 2014a). But in their overview Van Noorloos and Kloosterboer (2018) observe that 'new city models across Africa and the governance contexts that gave rise to them can vary from clearly neoliberal, more-than-neoliberal, to not necessarily neoliberal at all' (p. 1226). They explore a range of processes and actors shaping financing of the projects as well as diverging types of governance involved in their development. Different kinds of 'connections between Africa's new cities on the one hand and investors and ideas from different parts of the world, including parts of Asia and the Middle East' (ibid.) are shaping these urban developments. Developmental as well as sovereign (geopolitical) dynamics are crucial in explaining these outcomes while governance contexts can diverge strongly from avowedly 'neoliberalised' formations, with extraction of value and benefit accruing to a range of actors, including ruling parties and incumbent politicians.

In other contexts the presence of viable non-neoliberal alternatives – such as municipal socialism, or collective political processes – can mean that the analyses need to take a different form than the variegation of one particular social processes. Contestations over forms of government across a number of South American contexts through the 1990s and 2000s saw active municipal socialism alternating with neoliberalisation, and in the end many municipalities brought together elements of both to balance concerns with both growth and redistribution (Goldfrank and Schrank 2009). This requires a different political analysis, one which focusses more closely on the diverse circuits which spread ideas about urban governance, including municipal socialism, and the many different contexts where outcomes were shaped by a range of processes.

4. Divergent cases indicate the need to start again with conceptualising a process. Before neoliberalism was coined in critical urban studies debates, Africa was already at the forefront of neoliberalisation, a 'radical testing ground for neoliberal policies' (Hilgers 2012, pp. 82–3). In the wake of the collapse of primary commodity prices, rising interest rates and a stark reversal of the terms of trade with manufactured goods, high levels of indebtedness which had been encouraged by the World Bank in developing countries across the world caused widespread economic crisis. Walton and Seddon (1994) observe that 'the role of the International Monetary Fund through the 1980s largely reflected the concern of Western governments and private banks to ensure debt repayment virtually at any cost' (p. 16). Structural Adjustment loans came to be seen as a way to impose sweeping reforms, rather than simply provide assistance for balance of payments and foreign debt difficulties. Concerted action by IMF, World Bank, private lenders and donor countries within an emerging neoliberal consensus on development left little room for manoeuvre by governments (Walton and Seddon 1994, p. 19). In this sense, these initiatives through the 1980s were one of the most important testing grounds for the wider project of neoliberalisation – but they also represented a search for new ways of promoting national economic development than that of the state-centred, primary commodity-led and import-substitution industrialisation (ISI) model of the post-independence years. In many African countries the IMF and World Bank negotiated structural adjustment programmes which devastated national economies, states and services through deregulation of foreign exchange, decimation of public employment and deregulation of the economy in both agriculture and industry. But the goal was to look for a new pathway of development in the wake of the bankrupted (literally) form of the post-independence development project, meaning that even at this intense moment, projects of economic (neo)liberalisation were paired with developmentalism (Goldman 2005). This remains a crucial horizon of interpretation of African urbanisation.

A new account of urban neoliberalisation, starting with African experiences, would require, firstly, an acknowledgement that neoliberalisation (as policy formation) is strongly scaled around national institutions.[5] The urban impacts have been considerable but have not been to do with neoliberalisation of urban governance. Neoliberalisation has entailed the informalisation of much of the urban landscape: the slummification of urban living for many, the self-provisioning of nearly all services, the precaritisation of formal employment and the destruction of the middle class. The liberalisation of the economy allowed elites, notably those with close government contacts or positions, to strengthen their grip on economic power, or to informalise distribution of state receipts to leaders and officials (Hilgers 2012, p. 84). The weakening of the state was often accompanied by expansion of peremptory, violent powers and informalised decision-making, delinked from state institutions. On the other hand, efforts in a few contexts to put in place some kind of welfare policies where state capacities have been historically weak have drawn on versions of 'neoliberal' or market forms perhaps in co-operation with communities or NGOs (Ferguson 2010; Myers 2008). This has led to some developmental outcomes. Also, extensive humanitarian and developmental ambitions, including the MDGs and SDGs, mobilise international policy which often embeds a normalised neoliberal vocabulary (Parnell 2016).

Discussions of Structural Adjustment Policies (neoliberalisation) across Africa have therefore been strongly focussed on national rather than urban processes. Generalised 'theoretical' narratives of 'urban' neoliberalisation as reflecting urban-centric policy circuits and urban governance reform therefore seldom reflect the conditions of African experiences. Many aspects of 'urban neoliberalisation' in Europe and the USA (e.g. workfare; or inter-urban competition) play little or no role in urban contexts where such welfare provisions have never been present and the institutional capabilities and priorities of local states are significantly different (Pieterse et al. 2018). A lacuna exists. As Hilgers (2012) notes, 'the analysis from Africa does not propose a vision of what true neoliberalism is, or could be, but rather shows that a change of viewpoint is necessary in order to account for its complexity' (p. 90). At the limit, after dismantling the post-independence inheritance, stealing cities and capturing states, the experience of many African contexts has evacuated neoliberalisation of its meaning while alternative wider political projects of speculative extraction and geopolitical influence have hegemonised national polities and have become dominant in the construction of new urban futures (Goodfellow 2017; Kanai and Schindler 2019).

Portes and Martinez' (2019) review of neoliberalisation and urban developments in South America suggests such an analysis would also resonate in that context. They note that, 'The adoption of neoliberal policies that did away with much of the economic and social progress achieved during the ISI period is now an episode of the past. It is defunct except in the minds of some economists of the World Bank and, especially, the International Monetary Fund who continue to prescribe the same Washington Consensus recipes that failed so thoroughly in the past' (p. 29). They acknowledge that alternative, more pragmatic policies have had some successes but note that '(w)hile poverty and indigence have declined thanks to targeted state programs, vast economic inequalities persist and, along with them, a massive informal sector that, in some countries, employs half or more of the labor force' (p. 30). Crime and forms of authority based on illegal activities are major features of urban landscapes and economies, an inheritance of neoliberalisation (Feltran 2022). They note, however, the unanticipated successes of state interventions in redressing the impacts of neoliberalisation, and indicate that to sustain this 'decisive and sustained intervention by a capable state apparatus will be necessary' (p. 31). This resonates closely with the arguments of Africanist scholars for practical state-building and developmental initiatives to be a major focus of urban studies (Parnell and Pieterse 2016).

Bluntly put, what would we say urban neoliberalisation IS if we had started to build theorisations with cases from across the African continent, in Latin American urban contexts, or perhaps in China (Wu 2010) or in India (Datta 2015)? Would neoliberalisation remain a relevant formulation for thinking about urban futures if the experiences of these contexts hegemonised urban studies?

Patrick Le Galès approaches the issue of neoliberalisation as a 'concept' directly – he takes issue with the all-encompassing definitions offered by Peck and colleagues, and poses the question, 'Does neoliberalism matter for cities?'. He notes that 'by contrast to national economic policies, urban policies and urban governments have not been so dramatically reshaped by neoliberalism' (p. 168). We noted above how in some regions (notably in Latin America and Africa) it is at the national level that neoliberalisation has been most prominent – with devastating consequences for cities, but these are not the issues that variegation theories of urban neoliberalisation tend to address. Le Galès writes from the perspective of European cities where more communal and collective dynamics are apparent. He suggests that 'these mechanisms [of neoliberalisation] need to be better specified and their limits defined: urban worlds and the urbanisation processes of cities do not change all the time, in all ways' (Le Galès 2016, p. 156). Acknowledging that neoliberalism is a political project – 'a nasty one' – he argues that the flexible conceptualisation of neoliberalisation offered by Peck, Brenner and Theodore leads to an overblown concept. He proposes a more precise and historically grounded definition, but also points to the limited effects of neoliberalisation in relation to the urban, where many different processes are at work – setting boundaries and limits to the concept, he feels is important. The hyper-constructivism of Peck and his co-authors, he argues 'has led to an overstretching of the concept and a blurring of the capacity to identify specific mechanisms' (p. 159). Along with a number of other commentators, he is looking to rein in the expansive criteria for inclusion in the 'neoliberal' family, to offer a more precise range of features which might help to determine this concept. He makes the case for a broader 'liberalism' (even a 'quiet' liberalism) in which features of social concern (climate change, inequality, development) have been closely linked to market-centric forms of economic regulation, and which is more longstanding and consensual than 'neoliberalism' (p. 160). Municipal involvement in these liberal practices is extensive through collaborative international networks (Bulkeley 2010; Parnell 2016). Western contexts, he notes, remain strongly welfarist with many non-neoliberal policies, including at the urban scale. And in other contexts, an array of different political interests, and often local solutions, shape urban development and policies (pp. 166–7; on Istanbul, see Karaman 2013). As an explanatory tool, he acknowledges, neoliberalism has weight, but its limits need to be specified, and what counts in defining the concept needs to be clarified. We might therefore conclude that the project of neoliberalisation, while significant when seen from its own perspective and agenda, is relatively tangential to many urban contexts.

5. A process might be identified as tangential, incoherent and/or fragmented. Features of neoliberalisation can be observed in many different places and configurations, but these are often delinked from the political project implied in the term, 'processes of neoliberalisation'. Michel Foucault's intervention in historical analysis focussed attention on the specific technologies and rationalities of governing rather than asserting coherent institutions or social processes as explanatory. His analyses cut across state-society divides, and emphasise how horizons of meaning and forms of governmentality are emergent, often evident in micro-tactics and new forms of subjectification. Constituted discursively, and in precise historical configurations, this calls for explanations which disperse many taken for granted entities or 'processes'.

Thus, Foucauldians concerned to understand neoliberalisation are NOT focussed on 'local' or 'specific' counters to 'wider processes' (cf. Peck 2013). Rather, they are looking for other explanations. These might be very expansive and widely influential – ways of organising institutions (prisons, schools), and individuals (new practices of self-subjectification), as Rose (2001) and Dean (1999), amongst many others detail. Governmentality analyses of neoliberalisation therefore focus on 'techniques' which circulate and are drawn into many different political projects, in different ways. This opens up the possibility for analyses of diverse formations in which elements of neoliberal governmentality might be very significant, while the political project of neoliberalisation is tangential (Wu 2010). Ong's (2006, 2007) assessments of the place of neoliberal governmental practices in the Chinese case as 'exceptions' to the generalised form of rule is a powerful application of Foucauldian analysis, as is her later contribution on the circulation of 'arts of governing' (Ong 2011b). In the case of China, then, while 'market instruments' may be crucial to governing urban development, the project in which they are enmeshed is not neoliberalisation, but using market instruments to, for example, sustain party power (Wu 2010), advance economic growth and secure urban development (Shen et al. 2020b; Wu 2018) and encourage patriotic identification (Hoffmann 2006).

With many detailed local analyses, a sophisticated understanding of how 'neoliberalisation' (or neoliberal techniques of governing) is transformed and remade in each urban context is therefore possible. There is rich potential to interrogate this process comparatively, both to enrich the concept, and possibly to move beyond it, analytically. Different regional experiences, periodicities and diverse formations of 'neoliberalisation' pose challenges for the overarching narratives which have consolidated around this process within urban studies. In terms of comparative tactics relating to wider processes more generally, a crucial question concerns how interrogating cases can make a difference to dominant understandings of a wider process. To what extent does a 'systemic' analysis of a wider process prejudge that the hybridisations which might emerge through variegation contribute to shaping that social process? Can the concept of 'neoliberalisation' be rethought and redefined? Could the term ever be exhausted, or does it establish a defined horizon of interpretation? Could this term be stretched to breaking point?

6. *New concepts might be proposed.* Peck et al. (2009) see neoliberalisation as a 'syndrome', constantly transformed and often reinforced by experimentation in variegated local situations. Peck (2017a) also proposes the image of a 'forest' rather than a syndrome: 'In principle then, the horizon

of a conjunctural analysis ought to exceed seasonal observations of the (leafier) trees, to take into account the degraded (or otherwise) state of the forest as a whole. Calling attention to such species-wide conditions, patterns and regularities is not the same as saying that these are tendentially uniform, universal or unchanging' (p. 17). Drawing directly on Stuart Hall, in more theoretical language Peck also offers the following way to conceptualise the 'unruly whole' of neoliberalisation – here, the metaphors are of an 'arc' and a horizon:

> A 'whole arc' analytical horizon necessitates more than periodisation, but empirically informed theorisation across the creative and destructive moments of what is evidently an extended and distended process, across the ebbs and flows and across cycles of resistance and slopes of normalisation. Invoking neoliberalisation at the city scale duly presupposes some kind of take on these more-than-urban dynamics.
> (Peck 2017a, p. 19)

In this perspective, in relation to how thinking across more than one case, or from (yet) another case of urban neoliberalisation might matter, the wider 'whole' to which each case contributes already has a name, neoliberalisation. As it unfolds, it entails a certain diversity, but manages to produce an arc which emerges as the (changing) horizon of a systemically dynamic set of spatially extensive processes, not confined to but incorporating urban outcomes. Or a forest with some healthy, some dying trees. In contrast, in his assessment of 'contingent neoliberalism', David Wilson (2004, p. 772) rather exposes the limits of these metaphors: 'in the world of evolving places, we see a patchwork of wildly varying neoliberal governances that often barely resemble each other'. However, that patchwork, for Peck and collaborators is 'patterned', and 'continuously remade through uneven spatial development', involving 'the patterning of contingencies across cases' (2013, p. 143). Other metaphors used are more vague – 'viral infections' and 'swarms' (2013, p. 154) – and are harder to match with the image of patterns of uneven development. In borrowing certain vocabulary from Marxist lexicons, the process of neoliberalisation is nonetheless portrayed as agentful, consequential, powerful, and associated with necessary tendencies and internally related phenomena inevitably linked to systemic processes and wider (scaled) contexts: contradictory, dialectical, unevenly developed, politically contested.

At the heart of the process-like nature of neoliberalisation in this formulation are two elements which might be helpful to disconnect. On the one hand there is a sense of *an emergent process* – many different governmental innovations, shaped by many different urban outcomes, add up to wider policy circuits, rule regimes and capitalist flows. On the other, there is *a political project* of neoliberalisation which 'fails forward', evokes resistance, embodies contradictions, and is necessarily systemically relevant as different agents seek to broadcast and operationalise the ideas. Suturing these two together imputes a political and theoretical coherence to the term, 'neoliberalisation'. This can lead to a tendency to belittle or misrepresent those who might like to step aside from this framing – as in the Foucauldians who are inaccurately presented as localists, or ethnographers who are incorrectly accused of not attending to connections, or to an 'outside-in' perspective on urban politics (Peck 2013; cf. Roy; Ong 2011b). The concern is that some seem to be not taking seriously the political (theoretical) stakes of the project of neoliberalisation. However, these two aspects of neoliberalisation-as-process might be disentangled – the emergent formation separated off from the purposeful political project, although the latter is certainly important to understand in its own right; as Le Galès (2016) observed, this can be quite 'nasty'. Then, the concept of neoliberalisation can be seen as sometimes referring to a fragmented set of governmental technologies; and sometimes a particular, strategic, political project. It may emerge as both more relevant to some places, and less significant as an explanatory process in others.

An additional term which is often used by authors to characterise the concept of neoliberalisation – 'family resemblances' – can help us to cut through this thicket and to reflect on how comparative analysis can question the analytical value of wider processes in relation to many different cases. 'Family resemblances' and the loose idea of different cases of neoliberalisation being 'relatives' features strongly in the case for the continued relevance of the term. Peck notes that 'family resemblances connect hybrid formations' (2013, p. 143), and more fully,

> 'Inside' manifestations of neoliberal logics—a privatization program in Macedonia, say, or a conditional welfare initiative in Indonesia—are locally embedded and constitutively contextual, to be sure, but they must not be shorn of their constitutive outsides, such as the actually existing and imagined 'reform families' to which they belong, as near or distant relatives to other and earlier projects, experiments, and models. This underlines the need for a continuing concern with neoliberalism's family misfortunes.
>
> (Peck 2013, p. 152)

To what extent does the term 'family resemblances' resolve the problematic relation between 'different cases' and an overarching process? 'Family resemblances' is a Wittgensteinian proposition which offers a distinctive theorisation of how a certain class of 'concepts' operates. Some concepts form in relation to a group of phenomena which do not have a consistent shared property. They have many features in common, but not always the same features. They are, then, concepts based on phenomena with 'criss-crossed and overlapping' features (the classic example is a 'game'). That a concept functions in this way does not automatically impute multiple meanings to a term, as to be a concept there is some need for consistency, for example, that a concept can be 'developed in such a direction *in the future*' (Forster 2010, pp. 70–1). Wittgenstein notes, for example, that 'we extend our concept of numbers as in spinning a thread we twist fibre on fibre' (Forster 2010, p. 71).

This approach does not preclude the possibility (indeed for Wittgenstein it is an important aspect of such concepts) that in relation to the same set of phenomena there would be 'any number of alternative family resemblance concepts which differed from our own by classifying particular cases together in subtly or not-so-subtly different ways' (Forster 2010, p. 81) – 'case-ing' them differently, to follow Ragin (2000). Differences might, for example, result from the different perspectives of observers, such as their experiences, education or classificatory systems which allow them to observe or prioritise different features. One problem might be that to the extent that 'everything resembles everything else in some way or other' this leaves the extension of family resemblance wide open. However, as Forster (2010) notes, the term refers to not just any kind of resemblance, but '*specific sorts* of resemblances between particular instances of the term' (p. 82). How to adjudicate between family resemblance concepts? He observes that 'a broad and diverse range of considerations may favour one way of casting a particular family resemblance concept over other, slightly different ways, and the relevant considerations will depend heavily on the particular concept involved and the particular context' (p. 83). Relevant responses might involve 'inter-subjectivity' – can enough people agree on the classification to ensure there is a consistent application of the term to 'the next case' (p. 84)? But it is also about judgements as to whether there is simply an 'arbitrary' application of the term, which then becomes something of a 'fig leaf' (p. 83) of a concept which could be applied without reason to an infinite and arbtitrary number of cases.[6] In the realm of social science rather than philosophy, how do we judge whether a 'family resemblance' concept is appropriately extended to cases?

An interesting aspect of family resemblance concepts is that they can always be reduced to other features – the elements of individual instances which, while not always present in every case, are the basis on which the concept can be applied. Thus, the term 'applies in virtue of features other than the feature expressed by the concept itself' (p. 85). As a social science, rather than philosophical proposition, the formulation and grounding of a 'family resemblance' concept requires more than an assertion, but rests on certain empirical observations. However, the various elements to which the concept can be reduced might be re-assembled into competing concepts; or the meaning of the concept might be reasonably considered to change as different elements become apparent; or the limits of the concept might be reached as the assembled elements in each 'next case' warrant reassessment of the original term.

We might revisit, then, the merit in casting neoliberalism as a set of more-or-less fragmented governmental practices – there are many different 'elements' on which the conceptualisation of this process relies. The overall ('family resemblance') concept is therefore potentially unstable, perhaps not holding together across different combinations of elements in particular situations. This means that being alert to conceptual revisability through comparison can identify neoliberalisation as a potentially tangential process in certain contexts: the attenuated presence of some elements, or the changing meaning of others in different configurations of action could reduce the relevance or purchase of the term. Thus, similar governmental technologies might have alternative meanings, or be more reasonably seen as configured within different processes or concepts – such as developmentalism, for example (Ferguson 2010). The idea of 'family resemblances' does not offer cover for persisting with the term neoliberalisation as the relevant process in the face of these possibilities. On the contrary, it provides an interesting invitation to identify new, emergent concepts and processes. Other terms could then emerge which configure relationships amongst elements differently, offering more persuasive explanations, different conceptualisations, and identifying alternative significant social processes and political agendas.

This section has shown how a comparative urban imagination provides scope to explore and interrogate cases which might strengthen understandings of a wider social process, such as neoliberalisation, and enrich the meaning of the term. But comparative analysis might also point to its attenuation as a relevant process shaping urban outcomes. Particularly important in opening up this possibility is the complex co-determination of outcomes by multiple processes and relations in different contexts. Thinking from 'contexts' suggests a range of additional ways of working comparatively with connections and relations, which the following section considers.

Connected Contexts

If we return to McMichael's second format of comparison, which he calls 'singular' comparison, we arrive at a form of contextual, or what he calls, 'conjunctural', analysis. Capitalism, say, only ever emerges already in relation with a diversity of other processes, and social orders – in McMichael's formulation, 'residual traditional-mercantilist' forms, or forms of non-wage labour, ante-bellum (slave) production, politically regulated colonial orders (p. 395). Thus, in his terminology, rich 'conjunctural' or contextual analyses permit insights into the differentiated or uneven 'whole' of the wider process of world capitalism, for example, but also reveal insights into a diversity of other processes (say, state formation, or nationalism), or even other economic systems (such as residual or transformed pre-capitalist formations, or emergent communal or associational economies). Gillian Hart expresses this clearly, that in contexts 'key processes are constituted in relation to one another through power-laden practices in the multiple, interconnected arenas of everyday life' (Hart 2018, pp. 4–5). Thus, different processes intersect, or are 'articulated' (in cases, conjunctures, or contexts), and produce different outcomes. This provides some insight into the transformative dynamics which produce the emergent, not pre-given wider processes that McMichael is interested in. Cases seen as connected contexts make it possible to examine the intersections amongst 'wider processes', and how these interact with other perhaps more localised or case-specific dynamics.

How can urban studies build relational comparisons from contexts? At base, the comparative insight here emerges from attending to the multiple, overlapping processes and emergent social relations at work in any given context. This exposes analysis of particular outcomes to a causal indeterminacy. Thinking comparatively with urban contexts is to attend to the inexhaustibility of such multiple relations and determinations, and to the always specific configurations of urban outcomes involving many different processes and intersecting trajectories. As Gill Hart (2018, p. 20) notes, drawing on Lefebvre (1991, p. 88), 'each fragment of space subject to analysis masks not just one social relationship but a host of them that analysis can potentially disclose'. Thus, we can conclude on the basis of the multiple determinations of contexts (or cases) that comparisons might head off from a particular context to others in many different possible directions. Researchers might be drawn to follow any of a wide variety of relations and connections which stretch beyond a given context, inspiring comparisons across many different relationally connected places.

Gillian Hart (2003) makes the case for building relational comparative analyses from 'context' in her study of transnational investments in apartheid-era South Africa. She notes that

> Rejecting any notion of pre-given 'cases' or variants of a presumed universal/general process, relational comparison focuses instead on spatio-historical specificities as well as interconnections and mutually constitutive processes.
>
> (Hart 2003, p. 3)

She continues, outlining an approach that reinforces the analysis developed in this book, explaining that

> Essentially what this conjunctural move entails is bringing key forces at play in South Africa and other regions of the world into the same frame of analysis, as connected yet distinctively different nodes in globally interconnected historical geographies – and as sites in the production of global processes in specific spatio-historical conjunctures, rather than as just recipients of them.
>
> (Hart 2003, p. 3)

In her relational comparative analysis, Gill Hart proposes 'a concrete example of how close attention to a specific set of practices, places and connections, can be used ... to shed light on how broader processes are constituted in practice' (Hart 2003, p. 15). She is drawn to understand the relationship between two otherwise unlikely comparator contexts – rural KwaZulu/Natal[7] in South Africa under apartheid, and industrialising Taiwan. Both contexts had experienced a significant land reform process but Hart demonstrates how 'sharply divergent histories of agrarian transformation have shaped the conditions of reproduction of labour, and of global competition' (p. 10). The intense and dynamic connections between globalising industrialisation (Taiwanese investors in South Africa) and land politics were revealed. In South Africa, long-term processes of dispossession from black freehold land and expulsion from white farm land had left large settlements of 'displaced urbanization' with most residents utterly dependent on migrant remittances or the very low-paid work brought by low-wage and subsidised industrialisation. A regional policy promoting industrial 'growth poles' close to these settlements was mobilised by entrepreneurial local actors to expand their population, economies and income streams. Gill Hart's study is a rich interweaving of accounts of black township mobilisations, union struggles, personal narratives of industrialists and government officials. She seeks to 'connect' processes of industrialisation and urbanisation with South Africa's fraught land politics – centuries of dispossession and exclusion was the focus of early post-apartheid initiatives at land redistribution/restitution. The dependence and destitution of the mostly female workers in these industrial areas, along with the gendered and patriarchal practices of the Taiwanese owners, shaped the sometimes dramatically oppressive labour relations of the firms which were established.

The connection with Taiwan, the initial reason for her study, lay partly in that during the 20 years in which she lived outside of South Africa, her research had been focussed on processes of land reform and industrialisation in Asia. In some ways, then, the connection she tracks here follows the form of an 'unexpected comparison' tracing links between the often disjunct personal settings of research 'site' and 'home' life for northern researchers studying or coming from global South contexts (Roy 2003; Myers 2014). Thus, on her return to South Africa, Gill Hart was intrigued by these Taiwanese industrialists concentrated in industrial areas in and near Newcastle and Ladysmith; she recognised them straight away as examples of the numerous small-scale family businesses that emerged in synergy with post–Second World War land reform processes in Taiwan, able to support low-wage industrialisation through the social wage subsidy from family farms. Facing a crisis of competition with emergent industrialisation in China, the 1980s saw dispersal of these firms to China itself, and to other low-wage nodes around the world, including a small number to northern KwaZulu-Natal.

Tracing this link and seeking to understand the relationship established between Taiwan and KwaZulu-Natal brought into view other shared features of the two interconnected cases. Notably, she identified two very different relationships between the politics of land (dispossession or redistribution) and industrialisation. It is somewhat fortuitous that such contrasting historical processes revealed themselves through following this relation. But this supported some valuable comparative insights, juxtaposing two different cases of (highly gendered) industrialisation and land reform. In this sense, then, the comparative insights are contextual, drawn through a surprising creative, (generative) comparative reflection across these two (connected) sites which emerged slowly in the course of the study. The relational approach adopted by Gill Hart attends to the wider processes of economic and social change which 'encompass' both contexts, as well as features which they share (not necessarily connected), shedding light on the uneven and divergent forms of low-wage globalised production amongst (late) industrialisers, and the highly extractive labour processes which can flow from this.

Bringing the two contexts together through tracing the relations between them, placing them analytically alongside one another, drew attention to other processes which helped to explain one place in terms of the historical dynamics of the other. Why were the industrialists from Taiwan drawn to locate in rural KZN? Hart shows how this can only be addressed by tracing the link back to the Taiwanese context and closely attending to dynamics there. The distant circumstances of the Taiwanese investors – the foundation of industrialisation in family firms dependent on land holdings, directly shaped and explain the outcomes in KwaZulu-Natal. But this also brought into view comparative insights about a different, if related process – questions of land redistribution (in Taiwan) and dispossession (in KwaZulu-Natal). This draws attention to the more generalised possibilities for relational comparisons to identify more generative grounds for comparisons. A wide range of social dynamics come into perspective across connected contexts, stimulating reflections which may (or may not) flow from tracing connections or mutual embedding in wider processes.

Bringing different contexts into comparative reflection illuminates both 'variables that remain invisible in the single case study', and the limits of the explanatory value of wider social processes (Abu-Lughod 2007). Janet Abu-Lughod's comparison of New York, Chicago and Los Angeles pointed to the need to build theorisations that exceed the encompassing processes which attract most analytical attention, or which operate across the widest scales of globalisation, and capitalism (1999). She takes issue, then, with Global and World Cities approaches which prioritise certain globalising processes as defining of different urban outcomes.

Neil Brenner strongly criticises the dualism which he reads in Abu-Lughod's approach, between globalising processes, and an 'empirical diversity of local conditions' (2001, p. 142). As the previous section discussed at length, this observation comes from the perspective of seeing local outcomes as closely tied to wider processes, or systems-wide perspectives; thus for him, globalisation is 'variegated' in and through 'global and world cities'. Abu-Lughod, though, is eager to identify what she calls the 'degrees of freedom' of local outcomes from globalising processes. What else is going on in these urban complexes, she asks? Might other processes explain some of the outcomes which are ascribed to economic globalisation? As Brenner suggests, 'Abu-Lughod's concern, in other words, is to demonstrate the degree to which sociologically significant, systemic forms of variation exist amongst world cities such as New York, Chicago and Los Angeles, which are *not* derived from their respective positions in the global division of labour' (pp. 140–1). We again reach the potential limits to an 'encompassing' analysis which rests on an assessment of the variegation of pre-determined wider processes.

Brenner argues that the detailed historical analyses Abu-Lughod offers across a wide range of social and spatial processes are 'underspecified', and that 'theoretically informed discussion of how such variations were produced and why they are sociologically significant' is needed (p. 142). However, through a rich contextual analysis, and a 'variation-finding' comparative approach Abu-Lughod compiles empirical evidence of diversity and identifies consistencies across the three cases. She attends to a range of processes constituted at local, national and global scale, which explain the distinctive 'local outcomes' she documents. Brenner summarises these as pertaining to 'politico-geographical organization, class structure, and sociospatial polarization' (p. 142). In naming these, Brenner indicates that Abu-Lughod has identified important social processes at work across all three cities, differently. Missing from his list is 'racialization' – the brutal racial orders of all three cities are starkly detailed by Abu-Lughod.

In the previous sections of this chapter, we saw how wider processes are placed in question through comparative interrogations, working across cases or contexts which are (relationally and spatially) linked. We might conclude that 'wider processes' are conceptual formations, and not simply empirical or material ties between places which can be taken for granted. Comparative analysis can enrich and flesh out understanding of a process but also, as noted in Chapter 5, potentially subtract from the term itself, as each case might deplete its resonance or reformulate its meaning. Thus 'capitalism', 'states', 'neoliberalism', 'post-socialism' and many other wider 'processes' can be seen as emergent, needing to be 'reproduced', and liable to be 'swerved' into something else (Althusser 2006; Sotiris 2014). Also, tracing one process connecting contexts brings into view a range of other processes in each context. These could be used to enrich the meaning of the original process – but can also be explored independently outside of their role in 'hybridizing'. 'Contexts', then, where multiple social relations intersect, are crucial elements of genetic relational comparisons. But, thinking with contexts brings into view a rich array of different processes and histories, opening out to the potential for composing 'generative' comparisons. As we will see, at the edges of comparative tactics on genetic grounds, the potential for creative generative comparisons is strongly indicated by the rich fullness and multiplicity of social relations which characterise contexts or places – and, more generally, the urban. Contexts, then, rather than being abstracted to their role in the formation of wider social processes, become the focus of analytical attention and theory-building in their own right and in their full complexity.

More Spatialities of the Urban: Topologies, Partial Connections, Submarine Relations

Strathern's recourse to the image of the cyborg to figure relations amongst entities, or across cases, implies an imperfect fit, where co-existing entities and formations might propose connections which follow different logics or don't come together: 'The cyborg supposes what it would be like to make connections without assumptions of comparability' (p. 38) – thus disjunct connections might imply 'compatibility without comparability'. Certainly, as

Strathern indicates, 'Partial connections require imageries other than those taxonomies or configurations that compel one to look for overarching principles or central features. Clearly such imagery is not going to take the form of a genealogy or map' (2005, p. xx). Rather, she emphasises the way in which composition of ideas and arguments are made up of 'jumps over gaps, juxtapositions, leaps – unpredictable, irregular' (2005, p. xxiii). Her description is evocative:

> The cyborg observes no scale: it is neither singular nor plural, neither one nor many, a circuit of connections that joins parts that cannot be compared insofar as they are not isomorphic with one another. It cannot be approached holistically or atomistically, as an entity or as a multiplication of entities. It replicates an interesting complexity.
> (Strathern 2005, p. 54)

On this basis then, we might consider a wide variety of forms of relation with which to think comparative possibilities. Beyond connections and contexts, the spatiality of the urban can be evoked in a range of different vocabularies: topologies, partial connections, assemblages, and fragments, for example. What can these bring to comparative urbanism? The urban world is constituted through many different kinds of relations: for example, "the encounter, – simultaneity, ... assembly"could be seen as "the specific features of urban form" (Lefebvre 2003, p. 37). It is also produced through the distributions performed by the "urban land nexus" (Scott and Storper 2015) and the effects of unpredictable juxtapositions (Amin and Thrift 2016), through presencing distant places (Allen 2016) and imagining alternative futures in the image of elsewhere (Bunnel and Das 2013). In this and the previous chapter we have worked with a relatively materialities/materialist view of connections as flows and links between places, alert to the repetitions which these generated, the relationships which they indexed and the wider processes which they were a part of. Inspired by the complex spatialities of the urban, though, the logics of comparison, of thinking with elsewhere, might build insights along less materialist lines too. Again, we are invited to some natural experiments, such as those suggested to us as we follow the logics of serial seductions by shining examples (Bunnel and Das 2013), or the folding of multiple elsewheres into the urban here ('and now') (Allen and Cochrane 2007, 2014; De Boeck and Baloji 2016). This draws us to explore how cities inhabit one another imaginatively (Malaquais 2007), or set memories on the move, and inspire ambitions (Roy and Ong 2011); or how urban practitioners arrive at urban policies in the midst of circulating and presenced ideas and insights from anywhere (Robinson 2016a).

As we explored in Chapter 5, drawing on analyses of policy mobilities means attending to the prolific ways in which cities are connected through myriad flows and appropriations, in both familiar and unpredictable directions. But circulations are not specifically about traversing physical distance or traceable connections, but might often be more convincingly understood through topological accounts of space (Allen 2016). The spatialities of the relationships involved in drawing people, ideas and activities into proximity or presence, into closer relationships, or not (Allen 2008) shape urbanisation processes which are not easily reduced to physical flows which can be traced on a map. With the concept of topological space (Allen 2016) attention turns to processes, such as off-shoring, or hedging, credit swaps and financialisation, which bring different elements of cities and economies into perhaps unexpected proximities and which require more than physical metaphors of circulation, infrastructure or operational landscapes to catch (Allen 2016). Topological spatialities, then, highlight more ephemeral processes of presencing and proximity, accounting for the interminglings of interiority and exteriority, or exploring how institutions and agents might secure influence at a distance. These are, I would suggest, crucial if we are to be able to investigate many of the spatial dynamics operative in determining urban policy outcomes, for example. Considering how 'parts of elsewhere' make up local places (Allen and Cochrane 2007, p. 1171) has the potential to stretch our analytical capabilities and vocabularies.

If we return to the example of circulations and city strategies (discussed in Chapter 5) with a topological imagination, rather than tracing the flows and connections which are arriving in a place, we would be able to consider the many different complex ways in which elsewheres are made present in urban contexts (Robinson 2013b; 2015). And also, forgotten, so mixed up they can't be traced or ascribed to any particular 'elsewhere', stubbornly aligned with national policy influences, or hanging around to haunt policy-making without being able to be named (McCann 2011). The different spatialities of how elsewheres shape urban policy deserve more attention: policies might never arrive, be ignored, be imagined, be retold a lot, be worked on with great effort, be already here, imaginative recompositions, pure repetition, involve the multiple ownership of ideas (already mine, overdetermination), be used in drawing comparisons, forgetting, losing sight of interiority and exteriority in a delirium of localism (or deferential internationalism) – these, then, are some of the topologies of transnational urban policy.

Rather than sticking to the physical routes and points of physical co-presence and alliance-building that enable flows, the topological and partial forms of interactions across here and there – as encounter, as imagination, as multiplicity – require that we attend to coexisting and possibly incommensurable differences brought together in localities. These could inspire methodological experiments, creative ways of bringing different urban contexts into conversation. Thus, the urban world again proposes to us some lines for creative composition of comparisons, this time through topological connections. But this range of (topological) comparative practices foreground different dynamics in the composition of space – the practices and experiences of 'presencing' or distancing, displacement and translation, and require attention to the cyborg, the partial, the opaque.

Relatedly, seemingly disjunct places could be seen as connected through 'submarine' relations (Myers 2020). Re-tracing urban studies through black and African urbanisms will require transformative trajectories, occluded directions, re-alignments and re-figurations along submarine, fugitive or buried connections and arcs. Eduard Glissant's powerful Caribbean and postcolonial concept of 'submarine relations' inspires attention to the kinds of interrupted, fragmentary and forgotten relations which characterise violent disruptions of ocean-borne and island globalisation – slavery, in his reckoning, but also the buried and barely recoverable circulations of indentured labourers (Shih 2013), convict settler colonies (Van Onselen 2015), and contemporary forced and refugee migrations and displacements. This could underpin a 'southern' reading of 'northern contexts', as in Myers (2020) who draws on Eduard Glissant to write together the submarine, too often erased, histories of connections across Caribbean, US and African urbanisation, naming, for example, the long occluded indigenous and slave histories of East Coast US settlements.

In this idiom Lowe and Manjapra (2019) reach for a vocabulary to catch the 'submarine and occluded' relationalities of coloniality which they argue 'call for a reckoning' (p. 33). They suggest non-Euclidean, hyperbolic relations. This has wider implications for comparative method. As Myers comments, 'Glissant's vision of comparison is "nonhierarchical and nonreductive," avoiding a "universal value system," acknowledging the "particular qualities of the community in question" and seeking "degeneralization"' (2020, p. 26). Thinking worldliness and connections, 'here and elsewhere', from the vantage point of the archipelago, Caribbean histories scarred with violence, Glissant opens distinctive vocabularies of relation, but also resets the terms and implications of thinking (with) connections. An archipelagic, transversal perspective cuts across the search to tie here and there together along tracks which somehow add up to singular processes or their concepts. He enjoins, abandon the universal! Rather, it is the 'interplay between particularities and infinite variety' (p. 75) which can underpin comparisons which celebrate 'diversity without universalist transcendence'. Colonial/Caribbean histories figure a social world where 'the most distant and heterogeneous cultural elements can be brought into relation', where 'the here and the elsewhere' are conjoined (p. 107). This illuminates so precisely the challenges of thinking cities with elsewhere. But from this place, perhaps as Fred Moten (2018) has it, from 'out of the outside', the form and implications of relationality take comparative practices in some quite different directions. Such perspectives (topologies, multiple elsewheres) figure spatialities of the urban which could inspire some innovative approaches to forging comparisons.

Conclusion

In this chapter we have focussed on the value of relations for conceptual innovation through a comparative urban imagination. Shih (2013), whose work on relational comparison in comparative literature has charted important new directions in that field, insists, as I have in this book, that anywhere is good to start theorising: 'the West Indies is as exemplary as the place from which to theorise as any other place.' I agree! But she continues to observe that, 'the point is not to elevate the specific to the universal but to deconstruct the universal altogether by way of interrelations amongst places and cultures' (p. 85). I think it is a little optimistic to assume that it is relations which can put an end to the universal. As we have seen in this chapter, interrelations are themselves as conceptually constructed as any (located) social phenomenon. Thus, while tracing connections draws one to new insights on both processes and different outcomes, and contributes emphatically to puncturing any sense of social processes as invariant, this does not dispose of concepts. *Relationality as such is not a solution to the problematic of conceptualisation or 'universals'.* Rather, the instability and promise of the revisability of concepts – 'universals' – comes from many different directions and needs to be established more generally. A spatial imagination working with connections, such as Shih mobilises here, or which we are familiar with from Massey's seminal work (2005), achieves much to decentre understandings of the urban (or any historical process), and to constitute of any context a multiplicity. Focusing on spatial relations does not of itself do away with conceptualisation, although, as this chapter has shown, both connections and contexts open to the potential to undo concepts, to revise them, or to invent new terms. The following chapter invites a wider attentiveness to the different ways in which conceptual innovation is emergent on the terrain of the urban.

Undoing inherited concepts and inventing new ones is a crucial part of a reformulated comparative practice. This raises the wider question, how might the process of conceptualisation be understood? This chapter considered how conceptualisations of wider processes are put into question through comparative analysis. More generally, at the heart of a comparative imagination is the assumption that concepts can be critically interrogated and revised through exploring difference across cases. It is in the dynamic process of conceptualisation that the potential for inventing new concepts is located. The following chapter addresses in some detail how different understandings of conceptualisation and the status of concepts might inspire different kinds of comparative practice. How are concepts understood to emerge across and speak to difference? Can concepts be of relevance to wider conversations about the urban and yet acknowledge the particular contexts in which they are generated? The tangled relationships amongst researchers, concepts and the urban world provide the setting for comparisons on generative grounds, and indicate the contours of further comparative tactics.

Part III of the book considers in detail what different tactics might be associated with purposively composed 'generative' comparisons – the invented comparison, comparative experiments escaping the logic of the spatialities of the urban to embrace the logic of the researcher. In placing the researcher at the heart of such generative comparative practice, the question of the locatedness and positionality of researchers is central. The following chapter starts from this perspective to consider how new concepts might be generated.

Notes

1. McMichael aligns Tilly's encompassing comparison with 'a systemic ideal type', that is, application of a theoretical model, rather than analysis of historically emergent processes (McMichael 1990, p. 388). This is in my view an incorrect reading of Tilly's argument.
2. McMichael does not formulate his approach in this way (the italics in the quote refer).
3. It might be helpful to make a link between this idea of 'mechanisms' and the more abstract Marxist formulations of 'contradictions' and determinations which dynamically shape historical outcomes.
4. In naming this relationship as dialectical, Chakrabarty takes us back to some classical Hegelian-Marxist concerns – any universal is always in dialectical relation with a particular realisation of that universal – but also with the specific (concrete) 'individual' which interrupts this relationship and maintains the dynamism of the dialectic. The 'universal', then, is always informed by elements of these individuals.
5. Similar arguments might be made in the Latin American context, where Portes and Martinez (2019, p. 8) discuss national processes of labour deregulation and

lifting of tariff barriers, and identify the following key urban features of neoliberalisation as 'Urban unemployment and informal employment; Urban inequality and poverty; Urban crime and victimization'.
6. 'Moreover, there is a danger that the person who does not possess a genuine concept may, as it were, attempt to cover his nakedness (from others, or indeed himself) by applying the fig-leaf of a claim to be using a family resemblance concept. Nor is this worry only theoretical, given the fondness that non-philosophers have recently shown for the model of family resemblance concepts. For example, one may encounter an art or literary critic who confidently pronounces that these objects are "art" but those not, or these texts "literature" but those not, be unable to see any rationale for his discriminations, have one's request for illumination rebuffed with an appeal to the family resemblance character of the concept involved, and be left wondering whether there is anything to this appeal or whether it is not instead merely a mask for a set of arbitrary choices or preferences' (Forster 2010, p. 83). Peck notes (2013, p. 153), '"neoliberalism did it" should never be a fig leaf for preemptive explanation'.
7. KwaZulu was the former Bantustan area which was interpenetrated with Natal, a province of apartheid South Africa. The post-apartheid region of KwaZulu-Natal amalgamated these formerly separated administrative regions. I use the contemporary name which adequately reflects the intertwining of the two apartheid jurisdictions in the narrative Gill Hart unfolds.

IMAGE 3.1   Rue Saint Antoine, Paris 1979 © Thomas Struth

IMAGE 3.2   Pasaje de 27 Setiembre, Lima 2003 © Thomas Struth

PART III

Generative Comparisons

Two photographs by Thomas Struth are staged as a more-than-one city view on the facing page (Images 3.1 and 3.2, p. 198; colour versions of these images can be found between pages 132 and 133). He did not put these two exact photos next to one another. But his collections of photos have already made this proposition (Struth 2012). Juxtaposing street scenes, the uncanny resemblances of the most basic elements of cities jump to our attention within the photographer's publications, and across years of his studied urban looking. The photographs here are from Paris, France in 1979, and Lima, Peru in 2003. The Paris street scene narrows in perspective to end with a glimpse of the characteristic monumentality of the post-Haussman urban landscape. In Lima, the streetscape terminates in the precarious hillslope developments which navigate and circumvent (and are also the result of) regulatory and mapping practices (Lambert 2021). In staging the compositional proximity of more-than-one streetscape, Struth's intervention puts one context into play with another – both the physicality of the places, and the interpretations of the images which we, as observers, produce, looking down these two streets with the photographer. In coming together, the photos disturb conceptualisations of the urban. Something as basic as a street becomes a site of proliferating difference (Zukin et al. 2016).

But the difference is not only located in the physicality of the streets, or in the most obvious impressions. Urbanists might see not only the power relations which self-evidently make the monuments and squares a focal point of attention in Paris, but also their role as gathering places for mobilisations; and one observer might find in the precarious and informalised landscapes of Lima's hillsides insights into the transversal politics of '*les pays suds*' like Peru, where many different actors, including state institutions, have produced the developments at the end of this street in Lima (Caldiera 2016). Reflecting, urbanists might find in this inspiration for other perspectives on the 'European' city, observing how the confident monumentality of Paris belies the limits of governing some parts of this city as emergent processes persistently escape governmental purview (Borraz and Le Galès 2010). An urbanist-on-the-move, a comparativist, might listen closely to voices articulating different, perhaps subterranean, insights on a place. She might be inspired in movement (for some reason) from one place to another to reflect on something quite different than scholars from that place. Struck by unexpected resonances, occluded themes might emerge. For this South African on her first visit to LA, the racialised urban form and deep inequalities formed a shocking displacement of dominant urban theories, and brought Johannesburg into immediate analytical proximity. The generativity of looser conversations as comparative experiments opens out from such surprises (Roy 2003; Myers 2014).

As we look at these photographs, then, these are not mute landscapes or sites which simply present themselves to a calculating and narrow comparative project. Urban sites of inexhaustible fullness, overlapping meaning and interconnected practices themselves proliferate openings to conceptual generativity. Together, the city, the photographer and the researcher compose reflections in response to these two urban contexts. Part 4 considers the implications of the lively generativity of the city itself for comparative practice. Here in Part 3 we focus on how repeated immersion across more than one site, in this case a looking back and forth by the urban researcher might generate insights.

There are important questions to raise about the 'will' to compare. What draws researchers to comparisons? What are the practices of engagement and solidarity, extraction or collaboration, conceptual borrowing or uneven power relations which comparison entrains? Who is the subject inspired to embark on comparison? In considering who the subject of comparative practice might be, this part of the book makes the case for researchers as both situated and (critically) open to the expansive horizons of concepts – the virtual series of ideas which we encountered in Deleuze. But, we should be alert to the deep structuring effect of the power relations of knowledge production in shaping inherited ideas and framing generative comparisons. Angled from the positions of scholars whose work is often marginalized, or 'othered', and whose situated, often committed and engaged practices inspire creative insights, the process of conceptualization has to be reimagined. What kinds of tactics might comparative urbanists bring to generating concepts?

CHAPTER 7

Generating Concepts

> *As a field of extension, the cyborg moves without travelling, as one might imagine the effect of jumping in one's thoughts from one Highlands society to another, or from one aspect of social life to another. The circuit still seems centred, however, on the perceptual tools of the anthropologist.*
> (Strathern 2005, p. 55)

> *It would be a mistake to believe that we have left behind the regime that began with the slave trade and flourished in plantation and extraction colonies.*
> (Mbembe 2017, p. 13)

> *Concepts are tools. Their values depend on whether they do the job at hand.*
> (Tilly 1998, p. 73)

Generative comparisons are creative experiments in mobility. Nimble-footed, frontier-crossing and seeking connections; but also modest, where 'conversation is privileged over conversion' and encounters open to recognition of incompleteness (Nyamnjoh 2017, p. 262). In this mode, researchers might propose slow moves or analytical leaps to draw together cases, contexts, territories, urbanisation processes or urban outcomes, to respond to the possibilities for thinking with elsewhere, thinking with more than one case. For comparison to make a difference, though, a deep sense of the precarity and revisability of concepts is essential. At the heart of comparison is the invitation to revise concepts. This is one of the features which drew me to a comparative imagination as a starting point to expand the methodological and theoretical horizons of urban studies.

Chapter 4 provided some basis for conceptual innovation in both Deleuzian and Marxist analyses. We noted how in both theoretical traditions, comparative practices can operate to significantly revise understandings, or

---

Comparative Urbanism: Tactics for Global Urban Studies, First Edition. Jennifer Robinson.
© 2022 John Wiley & Sons Ltd. Published 2022 by John Wiley & Sons Ltd.

launch new concepts, rather than simply empirically embellish inherited perspectives. This chapter explores the lively world of concepts, and the potential for generative comparisons to emerge on the terrain of conceptualisation. The focus is on different understandings of the process of conceptualisation. How might these open up tactics for comparative urban analysis?

'Generative' comparisons foreground a strong role for researchers and urban actors to create or compose comparative experiments. Strathern's (2005 [1991]) image of the cyborg comparator cautions us, though, to look more closely at the uneven terrain which shadows any comparative composition. In her text, *Partial Connections*, she counters the figure of the researcher jumping blithely across different places, motivated by her disciplinary conventions and weighty inherited concepts. With the 'partial' connection she indicates, rather, unpredictable configurations of concepts, researcher and material worlds. She focusses attention on the possibility for resemblances resonating across contexts without direct links. And the backdrop is the inevitable failure of the translations embedded in anthropological practice – what Candea (2019) calls, 'frontal comparisons'.

For Strathern, as concepts fragment in their travels, and apparent wholes emerge as fractal (parts become wholes, wholes fragment into parts), the landscape of conceptualisation is both situated and uncertain. Concepts take shape in the midst of difference and disjuncture, across connected and disconnected experiences, and insights can be generated here-and-elsewhere. The chapter reflects on four different approaches to concept formation which have shaped urban studies, and considers how they might encourage and help to frame comparative experiments.

The chapter starts with insights from feminist, postcolonial and black studies writers, considering the potential for expansive horizons of conceptualisation which are always situated and embodied. These critiques do not suggest the partiality of only some knowledges but insist on the located, racialised and historically mediated nature of all knowledge. This section probes the implications of this critique for comparative urbanism in relation to the institutions of academic knowledge; the horizons of analysis; and the grounds of conceptualising. The writers discussed here insist on the importance of both situated, embodied practice and the conceptualising energies of researchers. Even as Nyamnjoh (2017) grounds openings to rethink method through the vernacular conviviality of many African traditions, these form on the striated grounds of histories of colonisation and dehumanisation. This has important implications for the practice of urban research, and for the subjects of urban theorising. Generating concepts, then, falls (and fails, often enough) on the side of incomplete, provisional, fragmented and non-integrating insights, rather than full-blown and weighty 'theory'. Best, then, to be alert to the scarred histories of our knowing practices alongside the unruly materiality of the urban and the uncertain precarity of claims to know it. But, to follow Deleuze, concepts, somehow 'rumbling with the intensities' of the material world, also have their own dynamic which cannot be redeemed by this world. The fractured subject is immersed in this world but equally comes to know the world in the midst of prolific series of concepts/ideas. The subject is always present in processes of conceptualisation. Who, then, is the subject of comparison?

Weber's methodological propositions (and cautions), outlined in the second section, speak to these concerns from a very different kind of theoretical practice. His determinedly Eurocentric research questions highlight the pitfalls of researcher-driven comparative analyses. However, his methodological writings also demonstrate something of the potential to invent, refine and critique concepts through comparative and empirical reflection, which some urban scholars have found productive. Even as Weber's studies are immersed in historical detail and context, his concepts (as 'ideal types') are imagined as more freely floating heuristics, open to revision and purposed to address specific research questions. In contrast, Marxist methods look to concepts that port the 'concrete', as both political ambition and materialist philosophy. In this view comparative urban practices open out on the analytically saturated grounds of capitalist processes and political strategy. But within Marxist thinking and heterodox traditions, the idea of 'concrete totality', the fullness and inexhaustibility of the (urban) world, suggests a more open horizon of conceptualisation. The final section of the chapter explores the potential for concepts to emerge 'in-common' (Mbembe 2017). On what basis can concepts, or 'universals', keep conversations going? Hannah Arendt offers a view of the resolutely political nature of knowledge as grounded in the collaborative and contested constitution of concepts, emergent in situated practice. This resonates with feminist research practices, including the resistant knowledge practices and dialogical theorising advocated by Patricia Hill Collins. In Achille Mbembe's powerful decentring and reconfiguring of universals, African and black experiences open up to worldings, to the potentiality of an 'in-common' which critiques, and displaces, the racialised and dehumanising terms of western philosophy.

The shapes of conceptualisation which different writers and philosophers propose inspire different kinds of comparative exercises, and the two chapters which follow this one present a range of these – comparative tactics on generative grounds. But this book offers no solution or guide as to how best to proceed. As we explore how writers including Marilyn Strathern, Hannah Arendt, Patricia Hill Collins, Fred Moten, Achille Mbembe, as well as Max Weber, Karl Marx and Stuart Hall approach the challenges of coming to know the world across difference, we can perhaps only hope to be inspired to jump in and give it a go, to experiment in whatever theoretical register we value, alert to criticisms and concerns from other perspectives.

The Conceptualising Subject: Institutions, Horizons, Grounds

Does it matter who is undertaking comparative analysis? What draws researchers to comparisons, and what are the practices of extraction or collaboration, conceptual borrowing or uneven power relations which underpin any researcher's composition of a comparison? In considering who the theorising subject might be, and how addressing this question might shape comparative practice, this section makes the case for researchers as both situated and (critically) open to the expansive horizons of concepts. Donna Haraway's (1988) 'modest witness' is Strathern's starting point – a researcher whose own positionality, concepts, hopes and limits in the midst of and in response to the demands of a messy world shape the potential for generating insights across difference. In the opening quote for this chapter, Marilyn Strathern draws attention to the centrality of the researcher's analytical perspective in framing comparison. But in mobilising the idea of the 'cyborg' to describe this, she characterises as always 'partial' the connections which researchers necessarily make to the material and social worlds they engage with. This frames comparative initiatives as always limited, and more about 'resonance' and unpredictable compositions across cases and concepts than analytically crisp formulations of similarity/difference in search of causal explanations. For Strathern, comparisons both emerge from and construct 'cyborgs' – sometimes ill-fitting juxtapositions of unrelated things which nonetheless 'work' as an entity.

Strathern makes clear that conceptual innovation is not a smooth terrain of ideas. More than this, the 'playing field' of conceptualisation is never level, but a contested, power-laden field of embodied and located practice (Spivak 2013). As we consider the figure of the creative researcher engaged in composing comparisons, often collaboratively, it is clear that the politics of positionality, power, privilege and the challenges of (un)learning and displacing inherited assumptions are quickly relevant (Jazeel and McFarlane 2010). The deep structuring effects of the power relations of knowledge production frame the potential and limits of generative comparisons. The racialised inheritances of dominant Eurocentric modes of conceptualisation ask for a deeper questioning of the grounds and form of conceptualisation, and propose different trajectories for thinking with elsew(here). We explore in turn the institutions which underpin the power relations of comparative practice; the potential for expansive conceptualisation as situated theorists; and the grounds for dissident, or fugitive, analysis and practice which are being identified in black critical thought.

Institutions

At the broadest level, the deep institutional inequalities which represent the effects of the colonial past and present within the 'international' academy frame the kinds of comparative endeavours which are embarked on, who is involved and on what terms. In her paper on the occlusion of indigenous knowledge in climate debates and the wider 'ontological turn' (referencing Actor Network Theory and materialities approaches) in UK and US social science, Zoe Todd (2016) poses the question, *'If "material can be drawn from anywhere, anytime, and anyone", then why is this not happening?'* (Todd 2016, p. 17). She answers it with a strong assessment of the continuing role of racism, masculinity and colonialism in shaping the global academy. Sara Ahmed (2014) so resonantly names this academic institution as 'white men' – although she insists that this does not mean powerful positions in these institutions are only inhabited by white men. As Todd points out, she sees 'white men as an institution that reproduces itself in its own image' (Todd 2016, p. 13), regardless of who occupies the roles in those institutions. Todd's point is crucial. An apparatus of valuation places concepts on the side of the institution 'white men' by privileging writing by scholars from certain places and positionalities as producing theory, by privileging a certain ambitious, secure and modulated authorial voice – a 'white tone', to follow Hunter (2019). Naming certain academic work from certain places or in styles outside the mainstream academic conventions as 'not theory' (Connell 2007) authorises only certain writers to be cited, repeatedly, and to circulate and to name, to overwrite, the experiences and understandings of different contexts, thinkers and long histories of conceptualisation from different regions. The 'knowing critical subject' Walter Mignolo bitingly observes, 'is an abstract subject, a subject without gender, race, geohistorical location'. Instead he proposes that decolonial theory introduces a 'third layer' of theory, after traditional and critical theory, 'in which the knowing subject and the known object or processes are configured at the crossroads of racial and geohistorical colonial frames' (2013, p. 113).

These observations cascade conclusions – two of which are crucial for this chapter. Firstly, the knowledge that is produced in such institutional contexts can be irrelevant, misguided, focused on only certain phenomena or plainly wrong (Parnell and Pieterse 2016), or, even though it circulates widely, because it is 'unrooted' in any given context it may be impossible to translate or use in practice (Bhan 2019, p. 639). As Todd puts it, from this perspective, 'The academy is anthropology's "human error"' (Todd 2016, p.

18). A misshapen power-laden landscape of intellectual institutions (Universities, journals, language, personnel concentrated disproportionately in the north) can produce deeply inferior forms of knowledge – and as we will observe with Weber in the next section, misguided research questions. The second observation confronts the consequences of the intellectual practices nurtured in northern academic institutions. Todd notes 'The European academy's *continued*, collective reticence to address its own racist and colonial roots, and debt to Indigenous thinkers in a meaningful and structural way' (Todd 2016, p. 10). From the colonial explorers who only knew where they were thanks to indigenous porters and trackers (Fabian 2000), to the contemporary northern scholars (including those of the diaspora) who harvest the best ideas of pressured southern researchers (Rivera Cusicanqui 2012), 'white men' institutions are at risk of expropriating other knowledges. As is well known, it is these institutions that currently set the rules of the game for bringing ideas to a wider audience, rules which are often imposed on scholars of most of the world by their own institutions in the name of demonstrating international excellence.

Drawing on scholarship from 'anywhere, anytime, and anyone' remains an urgent practical challenge for the northern academy. But it is long overdue to reverse this question, and to start the problematic from the perspective of the 'anywhere, anyone'. Scholars around the world are not waiting for someone to draw on their/our work as (usually empirical) 'material' for their/our theories. Scholars of the majority urban world insist on inserting them/ourselves into conversations. Insisting on building concepts which travel (from anywhere) and are taken seriously on their own terms, not simply as embellishments on existing approaches. However, the new 'subjects' of urban theory which Roy (2011b) signals, and new conceptualisations of the urban emerge, (elsew)here, under quite different conditions of theory construction than in the northern academy. Relations of engagement and commitment, challenging for northern scholars to achieve, are more often the (at times uncomfortable) grounding expectations and exigencies of scholarly practice in a Southern context (Bhan 2019). Committed activist research, alongside consultancies and policy engagement, is also a horizon of survival for many Southern scholars, who individually carry the burdens of underfunded institutions, deeply entrenched inequalities and dangerous political conflicts. Under these conditions, to what extent might the resources of analytical and theoretical labour remain important – to counter, oppose or reframe, prospectively, alternative futures (Bhan 2019)?

Horizons

Angled from the positions of scholars whose work is often marginalised by those working in well-resourced institutions, how might conceptualisation be reimagined? This turns the question of decolonisation around. Given the dominance of the northern academy, the decolonisation of the academy is frequently written in relation to the burdens of the northern scholar moving across '(t)here and (elsew)here' – and with these tricksy brackets I want to problematise who and where, 'here' and 'elsewhere' might be. The power relations associated with travelling ideas emanating from powerful centres, or the northern scholar's engagement in a distant 'field' has for too long established the terrain of reflection on questions of the power-geometries of knowledge. It is of course crucial for northern researchers to attend to the uneasy, power-laden universe of contemporary scholarship and research practice. Decentring the 'west' or 'north' and unlearning privilege are crucial agendas (Jazeel 2019, Chapter 9; Lawhon and Truelove 2020). But so is the longstanding insistence on the powerful generativity of different "standpoints" and "intersectional" positionality as starting points for generating original analyses (Hill Collins 2019; Mama 2002). Confronting the formulation of the challenges faced by "any Western feminist" seeking to understand cultures other than her own, Zerilli (2009) suggests that even in posing that question "non-Western cultures are cast as being without the capacity to represent the universal" (p. 298). Liberal concerns with commensurability are revealed as undermining the recognition of conceptualisation as an activity which can be (is) undertaken (differently) by anyone, anywhere (Povinelli 2001).

On what grounds, then, might embodied researchers navigating specific situations (anywhere) seek to conceptualise, to compare, to launch new concepts into the wider world? Linda Tuhawi-Smith (2009) outlines the difficulties of finding a voice to write in a theoretical register. But she insists on the value of theoretical labour for indigenous politics, for her personal context, including the persistent need to engage critically with dominant theoretical ideas, noting that 'We live simultaneously within such views while needing to pose, contest and struggle for the legitimacy of oppositional or alternative histories, theories and ways of writing.' (2009, p. 39). She explores how located researchers might seek to appropriate, mistranslate and relish the ideas of her place, of other places, of her time and earlier times, including those distant situations where centuries of well-resourced institutions have generated sustained and creative intellectual production. In this view, these inherited resources can be seen as both deeply parochial (bearing the scars of their European origins), and available as a resource for anyone – to approach on a critical trajectory, certainly, and always with a view to detonating, or identifying their limit points.

Here we might recall Gayatri Spivak, certainly better seen in her early career as a located, 'southern' researcher than as a lone northern scholar heading off to the 'field'. Her interlocutors in what was a foundational postcolonial feminist intervention, *Can the Subaltern Speak* (1988), were, on the one hand, her own family traumas and colonial records which spoke to the experiences of her family. But, on the other hand, she also positioned herself as a part of French theory wars amongst a group of white, European men (Foucault and Deleuze vs Derrida). Such a researcher might produce knowledge and theory in and for her communities, to help address pressing challenges – and might equally see her insights as potentially expansive, destined to reshape the northern academy and intellectual enquiry in many places. Expansive conceptual contributions might fold out of modest, revisable and more localised concepts. In the white male French theory wars, we would have to conclude that Spivak was (a) winner. The embedded researcher, the local or indigenous, researcher, is a theorising subject.

Displacing the figure of the northern researcher, then, is to treat located knowledge, indigenous insights and analyses, as well as resistant knowledge practices **as theory**. Patricia Hill Collins (2019) forcefully articulates the potential for 'intersectionality', for example, to be seen as social theory, emerging through a process of theorising as part of resistant knowledge projects. Such theories (ideas and concepts) are not the preserve of academic institutions, where epistemic silencing and (self-)smothering sustain the dominance of elite theorisation. Instead, she argues to 'democratize the process of doing theory' – in which standpoint theory has a mobilising effect of 'bringing multiple standpoints to bear on what counts as truth' (p. 139) and recognises the 'significance of power relations in producing knowledge' (p. 140). 'Dialogical engagement' across different understandings and theoretical/methodological perspectives grounds her ideas about theory production which is not the preserve of the academy. Inspired by Sylvia Winter, Katherine McKittrick writes, 'I learned from her that sharing stories engenders creative rigorous theory. Wait. I learned from her that sharing stories *is* creative rigorous radical theory.' (2021, p. 73). Thus, feminist, queer and black urban scholars open to thinking otherwise from within the academy, and in engagement with different communities of experience (Oswin 2020), expand insights from collective and personal experience and practice, as embodied knowledge. Linda Peake, for example, insists that the often excoriating lives of women in urban contexts inform the widest analyses of the urban, powerfully noting that,

> there is a regularity with which even critical urban theorists can dismiss women, producing disembodied theory. Women who fall away from, or are not allowed for within, concepts of urban reality also fall away from conceptualizations of political possibilities, abandoned to the requirements of capital accumulation …. It is a double indignity; women can

and do fall away from sight in the urban from fear, exhaustion and violence ... while also being the objects of the epistemic violence of their dismissal from the realm of theory.

(Peake 2016, pgs. 221–22)

In an earlier collection with Martine Reiker (Peake and Reiker 2013), she ties the reclaiming of a feminist urban theory to a comparative sensibility. This flows from attending to the complex spatiality and form of the urban alongside mobilising feminism as a 'problem space'. 'The container of the city', they suggest, 'is insufficient to appreciate women's everyday experiences', and feminist analyses of the urban also need to 'account for the transnationalisation of work, consumption and reproduction, as women's lives are strung out across more than one place' (p. 12), even as immobility and containment are the experience of many women. Furthermore, they note that within urban contexts both different experiences of urban life and the situated nature of knowledge production stress the need to make space in urban theory for a variety of experiences and perspectives. They argue also for understanding the urban through tracing empirical and theoretical paths across the diversity of cities, while avoiding the pitfall of assuming a universal dimension to findings (p. 10). They do not shy from the ambition to recraft urban studies, to 'bring into being new geographical imaginaries' (p. 20).

Feminist engagements in (re-)conceptualisation can in turn be crucial resources in political practice. In their study of two theatre groups, in Minneapolis (US) and Sitapur District (India), Sofia Shank and Richa Nahar engage in the terrain encompassing embodied lived experience and conceptualisation. Through comparative analysis, they:

> attempt to learn simultaneously from ... two sites of storytelling ... by generating a dialogue on the processes of staging identity, marginalization, and activism in locations that are often not allowed to speak to one another in dominant academic frameworks. ... Our examples also suggest that our theoretical and methodological discussions on such key political questions as representation and engagement have much to lose in the absence of frameworks that highlight critical continuities between those sites and spaces that are analytically segregated from one another because of the dominant binaries of rural/urban and north/south.
>
> (Shank and Nagar 2013, p. 91, 105)

They explicitly look to interrogate how it is that representations gain power and circulate, while countering dominant binaries of experience and representation, including the urban/rural binary. In performative openings, and the variety of audience interpretations, they explore how storytelling and performance can resist the foreclosures of dominant narratives and categories. Retelling everyday experiences is also to provoke (new) representations. Retelling and performing what are emotionally wrenching narratives (collected by local political groups) of women's murder and domestic humiliation in Sitapur, challenges how these might be received or interpreted. These practices counter dominant conceptualisations with emergent, insistent accounts based on women's own stories. In this sense, even as the experiential and embodied forms the grounds for new thinking, it is (also) in the provocative reconceptualisations, in the life of concepts, that women, actors and researchers collectively propose alternative interpretations. Thinking across their two cases, experience itself, then, is destablised as a 'given empirical fact' or a reference point beyond concepts:

> by drawing attention to the political constructions of lived experiences across time and place, texts can redirect attention from the inherent meaning of "lived experience" within a given place, to the spaces where meaning is produced by writers/audiences/readers – in relation to dominant epistemologies and unequal social locations. Turning analytic attention to the interplay of the multiple locations inhabited by differentially (and unequally) positioned actors, authors, and audiences opens up necessary space to ask crucial questions of where, how, by whom, and for what purpose is experience invoked within particular texts or literatures.
>
> (Shank and Nagar 2013, p. 104)

Here, conceptualisation is evident as a practice of committed, compromised, situated retelling and performing – in contexts where the political stakes of both the production and reception of stories, and the critique and dismantling of inherited concepts shaping both places, is central. In this creative comparison, conceptualisation and the processes of reconceptualisation form the grounds for the comparison itself, as well as demonstrating and performing the very revisability of concepts.

Grounds

If conceptualisation is a practice of situated and embodied researchers, and in fact can form an important resource in political contestation, some questions (re-)present themselves for ex-centric theorists of the urban. Situated theorisation brings into the frame the problematic racialisation of urban knowledge. The constraints on presencing of black voices including black and African theorists in urban studies are in need of urgent contestation (Simone 2016), aligned with a wider consideration of the racialised grounds and practices of conceptualisation as such. The terms of this are not straightforward. Brand (2018), for example, identifies the fantasies of whiteness in the US which have underpinned both urban development and analyses of it which occlude the racialised grounds of power and urban form. However, Katherine McKittrick notes the recursive nature of critiques of racial inequality and scientific racism which reinstate/rest on biological presumptions about the difference of black bodies. She asks,

> Indeed, we must ask ourselves – and I ask myself this often – how black bodies rather than black people are informing how we understand the production of space and the production of knowledge and, as well, how these bodies that tidily uphold our academic ideas inadvertently or explicitly replicate a biocentric order.
> (McKittrick 2016, p. 4)

In her view, constantly rehearsing the effects of racist power on black bodies, while critical and exposing of power, does not move beyond the terms of scientific racism: 'I suggest, then, that the racial underpinnings of scientific knowledge, and the application of this knowledge to black bodies have, at times, foreclosed interdisciplinary conversations and a "hybridly organic" and "languaging existence"'. (p. 10). The biocentric developmentalism that places creativity beyond the 'black body' is countered by McKitttrick in a search for new grounds of analytical insight: 'a transgressive ground of understanding, a new form of life, and critical intervention are, I think, available if we shift our analytical frame away from the lone site of the suffering body and toward co-relational texts, practices, and narratives that emphasize black life' (p. 10).

Elsewhere, McKittrick places this observation explicitly within the frame of thinking the urban alongside histories of the plantation and its consequences for understandings of divided, exclusionary urban spatial forms and urban life. But this turns for her towards the manifold untold urban histories of black life:

> The plantation that anticipates the city, then, does not necessarily posit that things have gotten better as racial violence haunts, but rather that the struggles we face, intellectually, are a continuation of plantation narratives that dichotomize geographies into us/them and hide secretive histories that undo the teleological and biocentric underpinnings of spatiality.
> (McKittrick 2013, p. 12)

McKittrick's point in the quote above rests on the suggestion that the theoretical repetition of plantation logics in the present, in analytically placing 'others' in deathly places deemed 'uninhabitable' 'lands of no-one' (p. 6) might be decentred, with a 'conception of the city that is imbued with (a) version (of) black history that is neither celebratory nor dissident' (p. 12). Political initiatives and intellectual resources might locate other urban futures in the actualities of black urban life. Unfolding these histories without recouping inherited racialised binaries and segregated territories or proposing celebratory revisionist histories is one way in which new conceptualisations of the urban might be told alongside an insistent politicisation of exclusion and inequality.

This resonates very strongly with the trajectories of African urban studies – and McKittrick touches on the contribution of African scholars to post-colonial analyses of urban life. Her analysis resonates with the insistence of African scholars that, 'it is not true, as either starting point or conclusion, that Africa is an incomparable monster, a silent shadow and mute place of darkness, amounting to no more than a lacuna' (Mbembe 2001, p. 9). Thus, even as the nature of the urban can be rethought from the experiences of black urban life in the US, a central marker of decolonial analytical possibilities lies in the urgent need for conceptualisations of the urban to include African experiences (Pieterse and Simone 2013; Parnell and Pieterse 2016). But the im/possibility of knowing the actual historical content of the term 'Africa' together with the freighted historical framing of Africa within colonial discourses runs the risk of placing African experiences on the side of 'blackness' as a figure of a generalized unknowability, a site marking the inscription of doubling and darkness at the centre of language (Mbembe 2017, p. 53). Mbembe considers how on these historical grounds, Africa, the term, the place, seems unable to signify a politics of similarity, and seems to pose a difficulty for 'modern consciousness' of 'feeling links of affinity with it ... In our eyes, life down there is not just human life. It appears always as someone else's life, as others in some other place, far from us, in an elsewhere' (2017, pp. 49–50).

On the one hand, then, calls proliferate to think the urban from the many different experiences of black or African urban life. On the other, there is a need to acknowledge the powerful and disabling representations of the difference, exceptionality or incommensurability of divergent and emergent ways of urban life within dominant framings still caught in the horizons of coloniality and enslavement. In this aporia, writers search for ways to rethink the very grounds on which the urban might be thought. Fred Moten's (2018) stringent critique reads racialised histories into the most foundational European philosophical framings of the knowing subject, the researcher. In his critique of phenomenology, for example, he points to the figure of world as a kind of 'thingness' which the philosopher is imagined to confront and then represent. Moten names this posited thingness of the 'world' as (also) the enslaved and objectified human – part of the terrible confusion which arose as human beings were dissolved into 'things, objects and merchandise' (Mbembe 2017, p. 11). Moten takes the racialised formation of inherited European philosophy seriously – puts his finger directly and insistently on the uncomfortable place which is the overt expressions of racism by individual European philosophers (see also Bernasconi 2003). The very form of knowing is shaded by the colonial and racialised histories they inhabited, and the distorted subjectivities and assumptions this generated. The philosophical architecture they postulated to understand how subjects come to know the world is, in his view, irredeemably scarred by these racist histories.

Saidiya Hartman notes the pragmatic implications of the violent inheritance of racialised ways of knowing for her research on the histories of enslavement, in the 'life eradicated by the protocols of intellectual disciplines' (2008, p. 10). The archive, she suggests, 'is a death sentence' (p. 2), void of insight into the lives of those transported across the middle passage, for example. The grounds of knowing disappear, in repetition of loss and in jeopardy of re-enacting violence. Her *Wayward Lives* (2019) points urban studies away from the views of 'reformers and sociologists', or police and social workers, who have provided the dominant sources for accounts of early twentieth century urban change in the US, re-enacting in analysis their historical power. Instead, she 'elaborates, augments, transposes and breaks open archival documents' to bring to visibility the 'beautiful experiments' of young black women who 'tirelessly imagined new ways to live' in the face of dispossession, displacement and exclusion (p. xv). Moten argues more broadly for the 'undercommons' of fugitive black life as a starting point for thinking. An undercommons comes insistently into view working against the 'antiblack racism' which he identifies in philosophers including Heidegger and Arendt, as others do in, for example Kant and Locke (Bernasconi 2003) and Hegel (Mbembe 2017, p. 11–12).

Here we might turn to consider how Moten arcs this potential for different grounds of speaking/conceptualising into 'the city'. The 'undercommons' has, at times, a distinctly urban form, founded in black urban experience, making of the city a possibly privileged place for the emergence of something 'out of the outside', beyond the inherited terms of knowing:

> Generativity, our ongoing common growth in difference, is also escape in contemplative performance, reanimating the itinerant communal form of the city before as a study hall inside a dance hall. Black study is a mode of life whose initiatory figures are given as anarchic principles that are form-generating. Not just the proliferation of form, to which generativity would then submit itself, but proliferative, generative form. ... Again, this is instantiated, we might say, in the figure of the speaker, the bridge

machine, through and across whom praises (voices, forces) flow. She consents not to be a single being. 'Common alterity', he prays, 'make me your instrument'. It's the speaker's capacity to generate generative form, this fearsomeness of what the black soloist is and does, the one who, being so much more and less than one, so emphatically not but nothing other than human, discomposes for submerged choir (city), a song in flight that is sung while sunken. She moves in place, off the track he's on, for the love of the set it opens. There's an alto wind at your back, even if all you're trying to do is get out of the way of what you want to ride, so you can keep on generating these monkish dormitory chants, the archaeology of our potential, past, in the funereal birthplace, the venereal graveyard, which is a slave ship, a project, and a prison; a sound booth, a corner, and a broken window; a law school, a conservatory, and a language lab.

(Moten 2018, pp. 37–8)

The oppositional format of self and world embedded in European philosophy, centred on the singular knowing subject confronting a racialised thing-world is dispersed in Moten's assertion of the 'consent not to be a single being', the proliferating generativity of the undercommons. The speaker of this experience indicates quite different forms of articulation – as 'an instrument' of 'common alterity', perhaps. As scholar-speakers of such alterity, the absences, silences in the archives (Hartman 2008), the opacity of lives and experiences lived in the time of 'forgetting' open onto different modes of generating insights, concepts. McKittrick's *Dear Science and Other Stories* excavates methodology and knowledge as a site of rebellious, 'collaborative improvised liberations' (2021, p. 57).

Moten (2018) mobilises 'the city' (which city?) often as a pragmatic context and metaphoric potential for the undercommons – and for practicing analysis differently. The morphing lived elements of the city animate the potential for speaking (of) the undercommons. In his conclusions he pivots this argument to invoke a work by South African-born artist, William Kentridge, whose sculpture in Johannesburg ('The Fire Walker') features in the photographs opening Part II of this book. Moten hones in on scenes in one of Kentridge's animated films, where the character 'Nandi', a young black woman, mapping and documenting the deaths and devastation that have scarred the South African landscape on the cusp of freedom, escapes the (white male) artist's intentions, even as she performs his doubling in the film:

In this respect Kentridge, even if against his own grain, offers a kind of model for (what might emerge from) the philosophical realization that being tends toward escape, in a fugitive practice of animation; that the city and its practice, which finally can be reduced neither to a word nor a concept, is the continual enactment the anatopographical bearing of the trace that holds off every insistent arrival and every irreducible departure; that being's essential run toward fugitivity is the city, the ongoing history of the common underground. In that model and its models lie hope for the refusal of the perennial repetition—intended or unintended—of the philosophy of racism; in that refusal lies the mournful, joyful aesthesis of a whole other socioethical party.

(Moten 2018, p. 64)

If Nandi escapes Kentridge's directing trace, and in so doing helps Moten to express this fugitivity, the (im)mobility of one of Kentridge's sculptures reveals something about specifying the city and urban experience in question. The *Fire Walker*, was commissioned in Johannesburg as part of a post-apartheid local government initiative to remake public space – even as the statue was to stand in a place from which traders like the women it represented had been removed as part of city redevelopments. A version of the statue was re-commissioned in the city of London in 2014. A video of the statue juxtaposes the wealth of London's city and the inattention of the passers-by with this image of some of the poorest women in Johannesburg.[1] The devastating absence of response to the sculpture is also noted by researchers in Johannesburg, including one of the officials who commissioned it as part of a programme of post-apartheid public art works. Integrated into the quotidian life of the city, the statue, itself representing that everyday life, passes largely un-noticed:

> On this particular day, I saw one person lean against the Fire Walker as a wind shield while he rolled his joint, another one using it as a shade. Another two men have a cooking facility right next to the sculpture, cooking cow heads and hooves. Their clients are mostly the taxi drivers in the vicinity and other men who use the adjacent park for gambling. People seem to interact more with the black bollards surrounding the sculpture and not the sculpture itself. They sit on the bollards, two guys have placed boxes and crates on them from which they sell sweets and loose cigarettes.
>
> (Harrison and Phasha 2014, p. 28)

Simone and Pieterse's (2017, p. 70) comment is pertinent: 'This is what Harney and Moten (2013) call the act of being a fugitive, always on the run even if you are basically staying in place'. The Firewalker opens to Moten's analysis of the fugitivity of poor and migrant women's lives amid the displacements of ambitious regeneration in Johannesburg's inner city. But the politics of the Fire Walker's commissioning and creation also speaks to a moment of an inclusive political order, a project of black governmentality. Demands for inclusivity might not resonate with an 'undercommons', but in 1990s' South Africa the concept of fugitivity encounters a different history, with possibilities for an institutional urban politics; twenty years on there are still insistent claims on a compromised political order which might (yet) do something different (Brown 2015). Can South Africans afford to stand aside from engaging directly with the politics of citizenship and state-building? Meantime, the statue's appearance in the heart of the district of global financial power in London, in its pristine aestheticisation stands as something other than it ever could be in Johannesburg – meeting in silence the incomprehension of a European elite even as the brutalising exclusion of immigrants and the poor grows apace there. Mbembe names this as a '*becoming Black of the world*', in which 'capitalism sets about recolonizing its own centre' (2017, p. 179). The Firewalker haunts a connection into being which invites us to speak fugitivity across difference.

The urban researcher, then, might be *Nandi*, questioning and interrogating the inherited world. How might she frame her practice? On what grounds is she engaging with this world? McKittrick's (2021) powerful essay indicates a generous collaboration and creativity, inventing new practices, insistently refusing the terms of racialised knowledge. The undercommons grounds different ways of speaking the multiplicity and emergent form of the urban, beyond the enclave of urban theory (Ziedermann 2018). In the light of the politics of conceptualisation signalled through writing and activism on black urbanisms and African urban studies, there is much work ahead to rework, reformat and move beyond the archives of both urban theory and method. McKittrick (2021) insists that this involves 'living and resisting – psychically, physiologically, narratively – the brutal fictions of race' (p. 51). Such 'black creative work' should, in an earlier feminist idiom, demand of others equally exhausting practice to unlearn privilege and refuse to repeat inherited violence. Otherwise the burden of collective work 'against racial apartheid' (which McKittrick (2021, p. 28) portrays as a conversation amongst all/any of us, in the words of Audrey Lourde, not to 'rob ourselves of ourselves and each other') falls unevenly. Black and de-/post-/anti-colonial scholars are correct then to object to the appropriation of such extreme efforts in superficial citations.

It was as part of a critical ground-clearing exercise to expand the space for post-colonial methodological invention that I turned to interrogate the inheritances of Weber's founding statements on the theory and method of cultural sciences. Methodological pathways for urban studies are entangled in conventions of research which are in such ruins, or which my post-colonial training and anti-racist politics strongly suggests we should be in the business of detonating. Certainly, Weber's methodological experiments perform some of the effects of euro-centric positionalities which have blighted social sciences and urban studies. But, and like me, the reader might be surprised here: Weber's insights also throw some light on how new concepts might be imagined to come into being, creatively, in a world which is opaque and intransigent to representation. This following section also takes time to outline a major contribution to comparative urban studies, Weber's *Die Stadt* (The City).

A Life of Concepts: Ideal Types

> [t]he irrational reality of life, and its store of possible meanings, are inexhaustible; the concrete configuration of the value relation[2] therefore remains fluid and subject to change far into the dim future of human culture … All this should not be misinterpreted as implying that the real task of social science is a ceaseless chase after new points of view and conceptual constructions. On the contrary: in this context, nothing should be emphasized more strongly than the following proposition: helping to acquire knowledge of the cultural significance and importance of concrete historical relationships is the single, exclusive, ultimate goal, for the attainment of which the formation and critique of concepts is one of the tools.
> (Max Weber 2012 [1904], pp. 137–8)

Ideal Types

Weber's theoretical contributions have been somewhat occluded in urban studies.[3] While some quickly dismiss Weberian approaches as positivist (e.g. Hart 2018, pp. 2, 4), even though he was strongly at odds with early positivist philosophers (Bruun and Whimster 2012, p. xviii), others have drawn inspiration for 'a distinct sociological viewpoint resistant to sweeping blueprints and receptive to historically situated investigation, causally delimited explanations, and the surprising complexity of human interaction' (Portes 2017, p. 33). There are problems with turning to Weber for insight on global urban studies, of course. He stands fully centred in the flow of European enlightenment, his writing shot through with racist and colonial assumptions. We can learn from this to interrogate our own power-laden practices and struggle collectively against those. But Weber's methodological work also grapples with the philosophical and practical aspects of research in a way that is still recognisable and of potential interest to scholars today, and which is particularly pertinent to the problematic of comparative urbanism. His concerns include the creative role of the researcher in framing comparative analysis and the status of the relationship between empirical observations and concepts.

For Weber the driving force for intellectual enquiry is the researcher, and his focus is firmly on concepts. He accepts the necessary role of the 'value relation', or alignment between the researcher's motivations (analytical concepts and cultural values) and the subjects of research, in shaping understanding. It is in this sense that he argues that 'a new standpoint and a new conceptual apparatus' is inevitable in the course of scientific work (2012 [1904], p. 138). But the empirical world is present too. It is the direct motivation for research as an effort to understand and explain the social world. The quote at the beginning of this section indicates Weber's abiding sense that the world is always going to exceed the concepts researchers propose, with the result being 'the perpetual reconstruction of those concepts through which we seek to comprehend reality' (Weber 1949, p. 105). There is therefore in his work a 'radical degree of underdetermination between empirical reality and intelligible abstractions from it' (Turner 2018, p. 581). As Spencer notes, this is undertaken 'in the spirit of nominalism, as analytical constructs that are not to be confused with (i.e. reified into) social reality' (1977, p. 522). In this regard, detailed historical analysis remains a crucial part of Weberian method, as we will see below in exploring his comparative text, *The City*. In his discussion of this work, Spencer evokes that the researcher, having constructed more general concepts, 'must turn and plunge again into the concrete historical moment' and surrender the idea of imposing categories on 'an unsystematic and unsystematizable historical reality' (p. 522).

Weber wanted to move beyond the neo-Kantian philosophy prevalent at the time he was writing, which focused critical attention on the 'pre-conditions' of knowledge, seeking to ensure that knowledge might be considered objective. Rather, he sought to build an understanding of the empirical world on the premise that the researcher was inevitably enmeshed in contemporary cultural values (Turner 2018, p. 578). Concepts would therefore always be both subjective and subject to contestation and change. Weber was aware that social analysis had to communicate ideas to contemporaries, and that 'cultural science' had to take place within the social world of the researcher. In addition, he observed that commonly available terms and ideas about social phenomena have real 'causal significance for the manner in which the action of real persons occurs' (Weber 2019, p. 90). People act in certain ways because they have certain ideas and understanding of 'the state', for example. Thus, scholars had little choice but to use the terminology available in their cultural worlds to describe phenomena, and to empathetically seek to understand the reasons given for, and the meaning of, social action expressed in these terms.

Contrary to Marx's 'genetic' or other developmental concepts which sought to derive or map concepts and explanations in direct relationship to historical processes, Weber did not see his causal accounts as equivalent to inexorable historical laws, but rather as the basis for probabilistic explanations of historical outcomes of individuals' actions, and the individual and social processes shaping associations and institutions (Turner 2018). The aim of the formulation of ideal types, for example, was explanation of social action. They were not seen as ends in themselves or concepts which seek to approximate the social world, but as 'heuristics' to identify 'rational' actions shaping historical events. Weber noted that, 'concepts become *ideal*-Typical – that is to say: (empirically,) they cannot or can only rarely be found in (their) completely *pure* conceptual form.' (Weber 2012, p. 127). As Turner notes, 'it was a fatal error to confuse these idealizations with reality' (2018, p. 580); their value came from their clarity, and whether they 'were in fact useful to the historian', depending on their 'intellectual purposes or "interests"' (p. 582). These explanations are fallible and exist alongside other accounts and other causal processes (Turner 2018, pp. 581–2). This supports a relatively open analytical project. He proposed concepts, then, to explain historical events, and as the necessary vocabulary for developing an answer to questions which researchers might be interested in. When used 'genetically' – to explain outcomes – certain partial characteristics of phenomena might be emphasised (2012, p. 127).

Ideal Types can help to identify processes and choices relevant to understanding a situation, but are highly unlikely to apply fully or directly to any particular context as such (Weber 2019, Chapter 1, pp. 85–6). For example, explanation can be complicated by a lack of access to the reasons for outcomes, or there being a multiplicity of possible causes of events. An individual might not understand why they did something (unconscious motivations), very different reasons might underpin the same evident actions by different individuals, or an individual might have contradictory motivations for an action. In these cases, an Ideal Type explaining outcomes based on certain evident reasons for individual action would have only limited relevance. This is also the case for analyses of social orders, such as associations and institutions, where a range of different potential reasons for initiating social formations, grounds for legitimising them, or forms of organisation could be identified, significantly complicating any overarching Ideal Types, such as 'communalization' or 'sociation', or states (Weber 2019, p.123). The social processes and outcomes which concepts are trying to characterise and explain, he repeatedly insists, are 'extremely fluid' (e.g. p. 109).

But while Ideal Types might not apply in any particular situation fully, this is not to suggest that Ideal Types are necessarily far removed from historical experience. In general, Ideal Types emerge from synthesis of historical evidence. Swedberg (2018) cites Weber's description of how he arrived at an Ideal Type (which is an instructive contrast with the discussion of Marxist method):

> A specifically historical formation like [the spirit of capitalism] can only be raised to conceptual clarity ... through the synthesis of its individual

components, as historical reality presents them to us. We do this in such a way that from the reality of the historically given we select in their sharpest, most consistent form those individual features which we find exerting their effect there in a variously arranged, fractured, more or less consistent and complete way, more or less mixed with other heterogeneous features, and combine them according to how they belong together, so producing an 'ideal-typical' concept.

(Swedberg 2018, p. 185; citing Weber 2001)

Ideal Types can vary widely in scope, from very specific terms, to 'universal' or 'pure' types at a very abstract level which can enable broad comparisons, in our terminology, potentially bringing a range of different contexts, outcomes, cases or processes within a shared analytical framing (Kalberg 1994, p. 89). In addition, in any given context a range of different historical processes and phenomena might coexist. Ideal Types can then form a vocabulary with some consistency across different contexts to clarify the meaning of phenomena, but, given historical variability 'this degree of conceptual consistency will probably never assume this absolutely ideal **pure** form in reality, just as little as a physical reaction is calculated assuming absolutely empty space' (Weber 2019, p. 97). In tandem with the importance of using culturally embedded concepts, this potentially supports the generation of a vast array of diversified and distinctive 'Ideal Types' in different contexts.

Ideal Types constructed based on syntheses of empirical observations illuminate the search for adequate (by which he means having a high probability or chance of being relevant) causal explanations for historical events (Turner 2018; Tribe 2019, Introduction). As Tribe notes,

> Contingency plays a major role, visible in his relentless use of Chance to denote opportunities, probabilities, and risks, doubled by the figure of "orientation"—agents are always (more or less) "oriented" to particular actions, so that any judgement of actual outcomes is relatively indeterminate and context dependent.
>
> (Tribe 2019, p. 65)

Turner (2018, p. 579) outlines the distinctive probabilistic approach to explanation which Weber adopted, influenced by his colleague, Johannes von Kries. Identifying the probability of a historical event occurring with one set of potential influences, and then eliminating from that set one particular cause and again assessing the probability of the outcome could yield a view on the 'adequacy' of that cause as an explanation. Subtracting the two probabilities, with a result above a certain threshold, would determine whether this was an 'adequate cause'. This, Turner notes, was a consistent technical language used by Weber who posed the question of causality succinctly in his 1906 essay on 'Objective Possibility':

> [w]ithin the totality of those infinitely numerous 'factors' which had to be just like that and no different for just *this* result to come about, what causal *importance* should really be attributed to this individual decision?
>
> (Turner 2012 [1906], p. 169)

Here, very low probability causes (classically, an unexpected individual decision of a ruler) might in fact be decisive in historical outcomes. Keith Tribe notes the concept of 'chance' as one of the key elements of Weber's approach, previously occluded for English readers by the available translations (2019, Introduction). A corollary of this idiosyncratic approach is that context matters greatly in explaining outcomes, and that there are many different possible explanations for outcomes. Within contexts, certain forms of social action might 'pervade' or be dominant across a range of domains or social orders, and distinctive relationships amongst different domains could lead to Types specific to that context, for example, religious practices might shape law and the state. Both diachronic (historical continuities, for example) and synchronic (interactions within a certain context) dynamics are important in accounting for these interactions (Kalberg 1994). Weber's analysis, then, speaks of multiple causes of historical outcomes (e.g. law, religion, language, trading), and the inexhaustibility and distinctiveness of empirical outcomes.

These practices of generating Ideal Types inspire contextually based concept formation. On the one hand, taking seriously the contextual terms and concepts through which people understand their actions and social and cultural worlds in creating scientific terms and concepts. And on the other, being attentive to the complexities and diversity of possible explanations for different empirical phenomena. This means that any explanation of outcomes would be non-exhaustive. Given this, comparative method was central to the kind of explanatory social and historical enquiry envisaged by Weber, working with Ideal Types. He sought to identify the distinctive causal processes at work in particular contexts when set in contrast to others. For this, 'idealizations' needed to work across diverse historical contexts – 'made to look comparable for the purpose of constructing a class of "same" causes' (Turner 2018, p. 580). Let's see how this worked in relation to his comparative analysis of *The City*.

"The City"

Weber's (1958) essay on *The City* was sub-titled, 'non-legitimate domination', reflecting the analytical focus of his discussion. He interrogated the historical development of political and economic institutions in the Occidental Medieval City compared to cities of antiquity, as well as compared to Medieval cities in other contexts, notably Asia, India and the 'Near East'. He documents how in medieval Occidental cities 'the governed delegitimize the autocratic ruler of the city and replace his authority with a new authority they create themselves as they find new ways to come together' (Sunar 2018, p. 209). This is an interesting essay for a (this) contemporary urbanist to read, as Weber ranges widely in his assessment of different cities, considering how the economic foundations and political development of cities in antiquity differed from those of the middle ages; and how forms of political rule and economic association in the 'Occident' varied from other contexts such as West Africa and central America, but considering in more detail India, China and the Middle East. Weber's classical historical training and longstanding interest in the history of cities (Sunar 2018, p. 209) is evident, and he draws on a vast array of sources: his scope and capaciousness remains impressive. Michael Mann (2012, p. 9) comments, 'the highest praise I ever received was that I am "our generation's Max Weber"'. In some ways this work is an inspiration for an urban comparativist, interested in a global approach to cities. But this study also has some deep flaws. They signpost to the contemporary reader the central importance of a reflexive and critical approach to the role of researchers and their positionality in framing comparative analyses on generative grounds. It also distinctly raises the question of the terms of comparison across different contexts.

On what basis does Weber 'compose' his comparative imagination? How he framed this exposes some methodological pitfalls. One logical assumption he offered was in the frame of J. S. Mills' logic – also influential for Theda Skocpol (Hewitson 2014, pp. 168–9). He was interested in 'concrete effects' of 'concrete causes' (Weber 2012, p. 172) of events in their 'individuality' (p. 173). But in line with his probabilistic analysis, sought to explain the causal adequacy (relative significance, effective impact on outcomes) of certain components of historical situations. One logical way of operationalising this was to show the absence of certain causal features in some cases and their distinctive presence in others; could this explain differential outcomes through comparative analysis? Certain features might 'block' the emergence of certain outcomes in certain situations or undermine the effectivity of certain causal interconnections (in the sense of their causal adequacy – Weber 2019, pg. 183). Linked to his Eurocentric perspective, though, this way of operationalising a 'comparative' method, had some fatal consequences for his comparative analysis of institutional and associational developments associated with cities in history.

We can note how the comparative analysis is driven by his research question. As Saunders notes (1986, p. 36), 'his concern throughout is not to develop a theory of urbanism, but to generate an historical understanding of the roots of capitalism'. Nonetheless, immediately we are in the midst of what is a significant problem with Weber's work for contemporary readers. As with his wider writings, the question he is seeking to answer concerns the role of the city in the emergence of capitalism in the Occident. This is clearly a Eurocentric question. It points to the distinctiveness of cities in Europe, certainly a valid comparative perspective. But his comparative analysis brings other cases into view on a 'negative' basis (Sunar 2018, p. 216), as opposed to the 'reciprocal comparison' of more recent scholars (e.g. Pomeranz 2000).[4] Weber asked, why did the kinds of urban developments in China, India, Africa, *not* lead to the emergence of a city-based rule of law, certain individual freedoms and political representation at the urban scale as in the 'Occident'? As Hamilton (1985, p. 66) notes of this, 'what makes China China cannot be learned from a theory about Europe'. He argues that 'China should be treated as the positive case (not the negative), and, accordingly, the concepts and theories of analysis should take their meaning from China's historical experience' (Hamilton 1985, p. 207). More generally, in assimilating the Chinese experience to Ideal Types derived from European cases, Weber drew wrong conclusions (Derman 2018, p. 528). And, as Sunar (2018) argues in relation to the Turkish case, in reading the politics of medieval Turkish cities from their then present circumstances, Weber misallocated the forms of political and redistributive power relations at work in medieval times with an overemphasis on the institutions of rulers. At that time, non-governmental institutions cross-cut state and society and played an important part in forms of rule and provisioning. The concentration of activities in the state from the early nineteenth century, Sunar argues, obscured Weber's analysis which consequently both misrepresents 'classical Ottoman social structures' and also has 'hampered the development of an understanding of the oriental modernization process' (p. 220).

In using European-derived questions to interrogate processes in other contexts Weber misrecognises the nature of urban based developments outside the 'Occident'. Economic associations usually based on home villages and regions fostered an expansion of trade and production in China, for example. But this is occluded in Weber's analysis because they were not organised at an urban scale and did not give rise to the political institutions in cities which Weber saw as crucial to the West's development: 'In China and India the guilds and other professional associations had competencies with which the officials had to reckon … However, … there was ordinarily no joint association representing a community of city burghers *per se* … Citizenship as a specific status quality of the urbanite is missing' (Weber 1958, p. 83). He points to the 'blockage' of the emergence of political associations at a city scale in contexts where strong status and religious affiliations and organisations prevented this, such as in India. The 'lack' of emergence at the city scale of an Occidental-style association of guilds and forms of representation for traders in China is ascribed to the overriding role of the state and seen as an explanation for the absence of capitalism. In fact, though, as Hamilton (2012) shows very clearly, the Chinese state permitted these regulating functions to be undertaken by home and region-based traders' associations, emergent in urban contexts, which very effectively enabled economic trade and production.

An alternative conclusion to Weber could be that cities had important functions in incubating elements of contemporary economic formations, including in contexts where Occidental-type urban 'communities' and political institutions were 'absent'. The role of informal networks in the contemporary economic development of China may well speak to the relevance of quite different processes than those identified by Weber, which might have equally inspired capitalist development (Derman 2018, p. 528). Across many situations urban-based innovations contributed to historical change in interaction with processes of innovation in technologies of rule, military conflict and state formation which involved a wide array of actors in different settings. Weber's analysis of the city was written before the more systematic elements in what English readers know as *Economy and Society* (likely 1911–13), so how the city-based social and historical processes he identifies in *Die Stadt* might precisely interact with his more comprehensive historical analysis is not entirely clear (Tribe 2019). But such a wider historical analysis could benefit from an analysis of the varied dynamics of urbanisation in different contexts, as Mann's sweeping historical sociology confirms (Mann 2012, Chapters 16 and 17).[5]

Generating an Ideal Type: Die Stadtgemeinde

Weber's research question concerning the role of the city in historical development of the Occident leads to his coining an overarching ideal type, the city community (die Stadtgemeinde). Exploring this will give some indication of how Weber thought concepts might be treated comparatively. On p. 81 of the 1958 English translation of Weber's *Die Stadt*, a theoretically saturated 'ideal type' of an 'urban community' is presented. In the first chapter, the contours of the historical argument are outlined, and the concept of an 'urban community' is proposed on the basis of a wide-ranging historical discussion of cities across the world. The historical sweep of this chapter is therefore 'global' in scope and ranges from antiquity to modern times. In the rest of the book, Weber's attention focuses on the variety of cities across

Europe (especially contrasting Italian, German and English cities) and offers a detailed comparison of 'Occidental' cities in Antiquity with those of Medieval times. This comparison is undertaken with a view to informing his overall argument, which focuses on the processes involved in creating, in some places, urban communities. By community Weber refers to a sociological formation which is not thought of organically, or as a self-evident or persistent 'whole'. Weber suggests that 'most significant empirical sociological work always begins with the question: Which motives **determined,** and do **determine**, the individual functionaries and members of this "community" to behave in such a way that this community was first **created** and **continues to exist?**' (Weber 2019, p. 95).

In this sense, and in language we and not he would use, Weber is considering how at certain times and in certain places, an emergent, distinctive and dynamic territorialisation of political and economic institutions and processes can be identified in some cities. What is of interest to him analytically (his research question), is the urban invention of regulations and institutions to govern markets, and the emergence of a collective form of urban political representation which was not associated with pre-existing forms of legitimate authority (feudal, manorial, religious). In his view, this contributed to the historical development of the forms of state and economic regulation, as well as the appropriation of individual political rights, which supported the emergence of capitalism in the Occident (Saunders 1986, pp. 28–38, provides a summary). To explain this process, he offers an 'ideal type' term, 'urban community'. It is a mistake to read this text as offering a definition of 'the city' (which Saunders does, p. 35), or 'a systematic theory of urbanism' (Martindale 1958, p. 56). Similarly, it cannot support the conclusion that therefore there can be no theoretical or sociological interest in 'the city' as such when there is no strong city-based 'communalization', political formation or distinctive contributions to system-wide social developments (Saunders 1986, p. 38). It can't be concluded from Weber's analysis that as the nation-state formed the key focus of post-Second World War institutions in the West, there was no future for a sociologically relevant account of the city (at the least, Castells (1977) demonstrated otherwise).

Rather, *Die Stadt* offers a politico-administrative concept as an outline of the processes relevant to explaining the emergence of an 'urban community' [eine Stadtgemeinde] at a particular place and historical time. With this term, Weber identifies politically and socially relevant institutions which were created in certain cities. And in response to his wider research question, he sees this as the basis of a distinctive contribution by emergent processes of 'sociation' (open and non-ascriptive organisations) in urban settings to wider social transformation in these contexts. Famously, in his key essays on sociological categories

(Weber 2012, pp. 273–301), and concepts (Weber 2019, Chapter 1), the process[6] of 'communalisation' is introduced in tandem with that of 'sociation' to describe the different foundations of 'social relationships' leading to 'communities' or 'societies'. Both of these forms of social action can have varied characteristics (open-closed, more or less regulated), giving rise to organisations with different forms of rule and enforcement, and many different grounds for legitimacy. Some will be territorially based, and involve political corporate bodies. Guilds and democratic cities (of ancient and medieval times) are only mentioned specifically in *Economy and Society* in relation to the different incentives for groups to open membership (to enhance power), or to restrict it (in the interests of monopoly) (p. 125).

Weber (1958) identifies, then, in some urban situations, 'a partially autonomous association, a "community" with special political and administrative arrangements' (1958, p. 74). It is in this sense that a special *area* (or locale) might 'belong to the city', even if economically it was primarily an agricultural settlement. More generally, Weber posits a fluid relationship between consensus based 'associative groupings' and political communities which are characterised by ascribed belonging (e.g. on the basis of territory) and institutions with rational orders and an apparatus for implementation and coercion to comply (2019, p. 296). It is in relation to the great diversity of possible forms of association, that Weber identified the apparently distinctive formation of an 'urban community' (Stadtgemeinde) in some Occidental cities. He suggests, though, that even in Occidental cities these processes are only partially evident, while, 'as far as is known today, with possible isolated exceptions, and even though they had markets and fortresses, [Stadtgemeinde] were not evident or only in rudimentary form in the cities of Asia'.[7]

The summary statement and the analytical discussion of Chapter 1 of *Die Stadt* foreshadows the detailed historical analysis which follows in the rest of the book which presents a rich array of historical forms of rule, legitimacy, power and institutions relevant to the analysis of the features of 'Stadtgemeinde'. The absence of such communities in many different European cities is clearly documented in great detail (for example, in Italy). In the historical analysis which follows, numerous contextual dynamics are recounted to explain in detail the specific outcomes in each case. While rich in historical depth, the analysis is related closely to the research question Weber has posed, concerning the antecedents of capitalism in the Occident. This can lead to no conclusions about 'cities' as such, or undermine the possibility that quite different urban dynamics (i.e. some social formation that is not a 'Stadtgemeinde') might be qualitatively central to historical developments in other times and places. But the research question strongly skews the way in which different contexts are interpreted, with a severe narrowing of attention driven by his interest in documenting the presence/absence of certain features, and the relatively parochial assumptions behind his analysis.

In sum, what seems like a static definition (a 'rule' to define a 'city' for many English readers of Weber) is rather a dynamic and process-driven analysis which is deeply sensitive to the wide variety of historical outcomes, not all conforming to the overall interpretation offered. The 'ideal type' of the urban community offers a broad and nuanced synthesis of the overall historical detail, signposting the key elements of the analysis to come, and seeking to provide an account of the 'chances' of such a historical outcome ('eine Stadtgemeinde') emerging in relation to a variety of possible social processes. The discussion is also strongly mindful that this term is only partially adequate to explain historical developments – the 'ideal type' only indicates 'possible' or 'likely' outcomes, even if all the various historical processes he identified were present.

So, what can we glean from this text on the purpose and nature of Weberian concepts?

Concept Formation

On the one hand, Weber develops Ideal Types in order to be able to engage with historical evidence to answer his research questions. He claims he is seeking 'theoretical means for the purpose of intellectual mastery of the empirically given' (Weber 2012, pp. 134–5). This is a strong phrase which belies Weber's broader view of the fragility of the status of explanations developed in historical and cultural sciences. Open to and emergent from (synthesising) historical evidence, Weber's Ideal Types have a specified and relatively narrow purpose as 'tool(s) for understanding' (Turner 2018, p. 581) with potential to communicate. While they have definite limitations, then, as purely heuristic constructs dependent on the framing of the research question, as the example of *Die Stadt* indicates, they are nonetheless closely informed by empirical evidence. In his methodological statements, still thought-provoking to read today, these heuristics are always open to 'new knowledge which we can and *desire* to wrest from reality' (Swedberg 2018, p. 184).[8] We see in his delineation of key sociological concepts, how these types fragment and complexify in response to the 'fluidity' of the social world.

Swedberg (2018, p. 184) notes that one valuable feature of the Ideal Type is that 'It allows the social scientist to take a first step in the analysis of a topic that is little known or explored'. Or in Weber's phrase, the ideal type may function as 'emergency safe havens until one has learned to find one's bearings while navigating the immense sea of empirical facts' (Weber 2012, p. 133). These then provide a kind of working scaffolding for seeking to identify wider ranging models which can explain particular outcomes in different contexts (Kalberg 1994). Ideal Types are not static, but informed by historical and empirical evidence, in a 'back and forth' relationship and 'are designed to aid sociologists engaged in comparative historical work' (Kalberg 1994, p. 204). Ragin (1981, p. 114) indicated the potential of this formulation for comparative analysis, able to draw together 'commonalities' across societies, at the same time as highlighting theoretically relevant differences between them.

Overall the 'ideal type' (or 'types') proposes a certain style of formulating concepts, with flexibility, alert to their direct relationship with empirical evidence and potential variability with respect to difference cases. I wonder if this might inspire in scholars today a stronger experimentation with terminology and engagement with a wider range of processes shaping historical outcomes? The potential equivalence of any context in supporting the development of concepts ('types') uniquely related to that place, drawn into the construction of wider types based on detailed attention to research and evidence, and possibly articulated across a wide sweep of global history, has even been seen by some as inspiring to those in search of a post-colonial methodology. Kalberg (1994, p. 205) suggests that this might be of relevance for theorists eager to build theorisations anew across a wide range of contexts, rather than drawing on existing Western centric analyses.

Weberian method is not so easily dismissed as purely 'positivist', then, and it is not clear that the method of composing 'ideal types' is in itself, or insofar as it invokes a comparative imagination, intrinsically the locus of a 'colonial' approach. Rather, the colonial presumptions at work in his comparative exercises are located in the way in which he mobilised Eurocentric concepts, and posed his questions from his own Eurocentric perspective, for example, why did rational Ideal Types of behaviour predominate in the West, or why did certain types of 'urban community' emerge, and can they explain the early appearance there of capitalism. Bringing the subject of theorising closely into view, a critical reading of a Weberian approach strongly endorses those concerned with identifying and critiquing the implications of the researcher's personal perspectives for method and theory. Weber's loosening of the relationship between concepts and cases, as well as the nuanced way in which 'context' is treated, offers some continuing insights for contemporary comparative practice. As Turner (2018) observes, 'We, from our present point of view, can construct concepts systematically, but they are no better than ideal-types. They can make no claim to unique validity and therefore no claim to necessity' (p. 458). In critically engaging with this inheritance, then, we find more motivation to more clearly locate and take responsibility for the role of researchers in the conceptual generativity of analysis. Who the subject of comparative analysis is, matters.

A recent example of Weberian method in urban studies can be found in Wacquant's (2008) comparative analysis of Chicago and Paris, including engagements with concepts emerging from South America to compose his key analytical term, 'advanced marginality'. He is inspired to generate concepts and analytical schema through the Weberian method of 'ideal types' – 'a socio-historical abstraction from real instances of a phenomenon' (p. 233), which seeks to constitute potentially useful comparative concepts in dynamic relationship with empirical observations. On this view of the entwining of concepts and empirical phenomena, the weightiness of theorisation is radically undermined and the potential to synthesise and draw on insights from a range of different contexts is exemplified. Le Galès, writing on European cities, is drawn, partly through a Weberian influence, to the analytical identification of 'the city as collective actor' (Le Galès 2002, p. 7) – raising issues of 'integration and redistribution', crucial to understanding the politics of cities in Europe, but which he claims have been 'wiped off the map' of urban theory (p. 184). Le Galès continues to explain how insights from Weber's analysis of medieval European cities might be taken forward:

> looking at the development of cities does not, in terms of methods, involve abandoning the idea of local societies or the collective actor city, even though the context differs strongly and even though local society is not viewed as established. This analysis suggests we look at the interplay and conflicts of social groups, interests and institutions, and the way in which, to some extent, regulations have been put in place through conflicts and the logics of integration.
>
> (Le Galès 2002, p. 7)

Key to the more recent history of the collective agency of cities in Europe has been the strong role of the nation-state in framing this. And, as Le Galès explores at length, cities might be framed more precisely as 'incomplete societies' in a Weberian sense, as a result of the contestations and variable 'autonomy' in relation to the national and global orientations of economic processes, and interdependence across different scales (levels) of governance. Oosterlynck et al. (2018) pose this question of the constitution of 'city' political agency in relation to global processes – which transnationalises the Weberian processes of 'communalisation' or 'sociation', bringing into consideration the processes framing transnational inter-municipal collective action (see pp. 206–8). Attentiveness to a range of causal processes and diverse kinds of social collectivities remains a long term inheritance of a more Weberian perspective in urban studies.

A Weberian mode of forming concepts is not necessarily weighty, nor authoritarian, nor positivist, and outlines some contours for empirically grounded heuristics. This might support concept generation from diverse contexts and historical experiences, in a phase of experimental comparison, especially where inherited theorisations might be unhelpful, wrong or limited in relevance. The methodological conundrums with which Weber grappled remain relevant, and his ambition to counter 'essentialisms and ontologizations' (Turner 2018, p. 592; Barnett, 2017) can encourage de-centring of dominant approaches. His willingness to loosen concepts from historical outcomes in the interests of clarity of causal explanation makes visible researcher agency in defining research questions within the context of subjective value choices and context. The feminist and decolonial critiques of positionality are important cautions here. Moreover, the mobilisation of specific or currently intelligible terms for analysis and communication and the probabilistic approach to explanation which downplayed 'necessity' in favour of 'Chancen' both sit poorly with Marxist critiques. Marxist theorists see concepts as laden with capitalist assumptions and draw attention to the necessary dynamics which are associated with capitalist historical processes. The ambitions of Marxist theory to ground analysis in the 'concrete' contrast strongly with Weber's nominalist and empirical sensibilities. Whereas Weber's 'adequacy' was in relation to explaining the causes and probability, or 'chance', of empirical outcomes, Marxist writers have sought to find alternative grounds for judging adequate explanations: resting in political efficacy and seeking to closely align concepts with historical process and the substantive content of concrete reality. Weber's equivocal observation that 'any concept that goes beyond *mere* classification leads away from reality' (2012, p. 127) poses in turn some difficulty for Marxist analysis.

Thinking the 'Concrete'

To understand the grounds and potential for conceptual innovation in Marxist approaches it is necessary to interrogate philosophical claims regarding the relationship between the 'concrete', and concepts. A number of writers have imputed insights on this from some brief methodological comments of Marx's in the Grundrisse. The question of the 'concrete' relates to the fullness of the empirical world, and is directly relevant to how 'the urban' in its rich complexity and multidimensionality might be conceptualised and drawn into comparative analysis.

Stuart Hall's (2003) close reading of the Introduction to the *Grundrisse* expands on Marx's methodology and approach which we discussed in Chapter 4. He draws us closer to the concerns which animated Marx to build understandings of real historical relations, as opposed to thin abstractions or superficial concepts which might simply reflect the objective interests of capital. This concern with 'real historical relations' is to do partly with the need to distinguish his approach from the Hegelian dialectic in which, he observed, 'the act of abstraction revolves within its own circle' (p. 121). As Stuart Hall comments on Marx's essay on The Poverty of Philosophy, working only with logical abstractions *ad absurdium* everything can be logically incorporated in the most abstract formulations '…if the whole world can be drowned thus in a world of abstractions, in the world of logical categories – who need be astonished at it?' (Marx, in Hall 2003, p. 119). As a critique of Hegel this is crucial to Marx's argument. In Chapter 4 we noted the argument Marx made against 'empty' or lateral abstractions which ranged trans-historically to constitute a general concept of labour, for example, evident in any mode of production. This was counterposed to the historically specific identification of 'labour-in-general', produced as a 'concrete in practice' in capitalism in which all kinds of labour are rendered interchangeable: the idea of labour as such becomes true in practice; this abstract category is a product of real historical relations (Marx 1993, p. 105).

The example Marx offers in outlining his approach to the concrete is that of 'population'. He argues that if one was to simply seek to describe the entirety of a population, one would arrive at a chaotic conception of 'the whole' (Hall 2003, p. 128). This would involve moving to 'ever thinner abstractions' as opposed to bringing forward understanding of the relationships involved in shaping that population. The aim, then, is to construct a 'complex concrete' through accounting for all the 'determinations and relations' which have produced it. In Marx's method, 'Thought accomplishes such a clarification by decomposing simple, unified categories into the real, contradictory, antagonistic relations which compose them.' (Hall 2003, p. 129). This contrasts the simply 'empirically given' with 'the concrete in thought'. Here Hall (2003) makes the important observation that this analysis speaks to the 'determinateness of thought within the present historic organization of social formations' (p. 136) that is, we think from when/where we are. This approach insists on thinking from the present, to counter simplistic historicism, and to trace the conditions of emergence of phenomena as they have been framed within the capitalist order. This again sidesteps any overly simplistic intellectually derived 'categories' which might only reflect the power relations and objective interests of capital.[9] Classically, and Hall uses this example, money emerges as a measure of historical processes of abstracting exchange value from use value (p. 138). The entwining of concepts with historical process and concrete reality, then, is seen as a crucial element of Marxist analysis. But this is also a foundational concern for many approaches in social science and philosophy; different ways to take this forward have been developed in the meantime. It is not clear that Marxist approaches either uniquely pursue or realise this ambition.

To what extent does the vision of 'working up to the concrete' to realise the 'adequacy' of concepts, leave scope for an open and emergent relationship between conceptualisation and the concrete? Might it not limit generativity in conceptual formation, if existing analyses or concepts are mobilised to map out all the relations and determinations which give rise to any given concrete formation? Concerns with the relation between 'concepts' and the 'concrete' haunt Marxist materialism, seeking to ground dialectics in a materialist starting point (in praxis) as opposed to Hegel's idealist version of the dialectic (starting and ending with concepts). This requires some closer attention for our purposes.

Helpful here is Stuart Hall's (2003) analysis of method, in which he plunges into not only the *Grundrisse* but also other philosophical texts and letters of Marx, as well as subsequent Marxist debates, including debate around Althusser's contributions which were deeply influential to him (Hall 2016). He notes, with what feels from this moment in time something of a sleight of hand, that

> Both the specificities and the connections – the complex unities of structures – have to be demonstrated by the concrete analysis of concrete relations and conjunctions… The method thus retains the concrete empirical reference as a privileged and undissolved 'moment' within a theoretical analysis without thereby making it 'empiricist': the concrete analysis of concrete situations.
>
> (Hall 2003, p. 128)

But once a 'concrete in thought' has been assembled out of the myriad 'relations and determinations' identified in analysis of the concrete, one does only have concepts, with the familiar messy relationship with 'reality' to contend with.[10] Detailed and at times obscure debates have circled around this question. Hall wonders about this relationship, in close association with Althusser and considers a Marxist criterion of 'adequacy':

> But, how then to think the relations of identity, similarity, mediateness and difference which could produce, at the conceptual level, in thought, a 'thought concrete' adequate in its complexity to the complexity of the 'real relations' which is its object?
>
> (Hall 2003, p. 122)

The solution for Hall rests on Marx's ambition that the truth of concepts will be revealed in political practice, as a test for whether the concepts are *adequate to the political challenges of the moment*. A distance between the concrete and concepts is acknowledged. Similarly, in retaining Marx's formulation that the concrete remains an 'undissolved' moment in theoretical analysis, the resolution of this question is postponed, in a suitably dialectical rhetoric.[11] Hall remarks on Althusser's suggestion that there is an impassable threshold between thought and its object – and thereby explains his later emphasis on 'theoretical practice' (p. 130). However, in *Reading Capital*, Althusser makes the opposite manoeuvre, resolving this tension in the realm of the concrete. This is framed in relation to the progression of Marx's argument through Capital Volumes 1–3. Althusser argues that this does not cross the frontier between concept and concrete, that Marx does not move from the 'abstract-in-thought to the real-concrete' (p. 210). He insists that there is no common space between concrete and real to justify the use of the term 'frontier'; and that it is in the concrete that the phenomena of structure and fetishism exist. That is, in this case it is not that fetishism or structure are purely conceptual, but that they exist in the concrete and *the apparent relation between concept and phenomena is in the concrete* (Althusser and Balibar 2009 (1968), pp. 210–11). This is implied in the formulation of a 'concrete abstraction', but famously this argument also provided a legitimation for claiming a certain scientific foundation to Marxist analysis.

Hall suggests that, in some cases, the conceptual process of moving from abstract insights to a concrete-in-thought (layering in many relations) could mirror the sequence of the historical emergence of phenomena through multiple relations. This seems likely to be rather unusual (p. 131), although it does speak to the regressive-progressive method popularised in urban studies by Lefebvre, which traces the historical emergence of phenomena as a guide to the lines of explanation of contemporary processes. This gives a different dynamic from that implied in working from 'abstract' relations and determinations 'up' to the concrete-in-thought (Hart 2018). Working with 'concrete abstractions', and the contradictions which they embody (like contradictions between exchange and use value in commodities or property), might inspire a certain confidence concerning the relevance of concepts to historical dynamics. Insofar as the concrete is already present in conceptual labour, either as an 'undissolved' moment in a 'concrete-in-thought', or as 'concrete abstractions', Marxism's relational ontology hopes to expand the scope of conceptualisation beyond categorisation and empiricism, and to refuse to treat concepts as pure 'heuristics' (to follow Weber). As Stuart Hall (2003) notes, 'Thought always has built into it the concrete substratum of the manner in which the category has been realized historically within the specific mode of production being examined.' (p. 131). Concepts, then, are more generally part of the dynamic historical concrete world and even as concepts are brought into question at the very moment of their engagement with the specific and complex material world, the ongoing process of theorising is 'always grounded in a historical conjuncture, "thought presupposes society"' (Macgregor Wise 2003, p. 107).

As we reflect on these debates, it is apparent that in the entwining of the concrete and concepts in Marxist thought and method, Marxist concepts can in the end have no privileged relation to the material world, only ever approaching the concrete, in Engel's phrase, asymptotically: never arriving, then, at the actual concrete (Hall 2003). Alternative Marxist-inspired comparative methods which treat the 'concrete', after Lefebvre, as inexhaustible, requiring that any concepts remain open to practice, history and becoming (Lefebvre 2009; Schmid 2005, 2022, Chapter 3), might foster a different mode of conceptualisation. Concepts might then be considered more as open-ended formulations generated in the midst of the inexhaustible 'concrete', always with an excess or remainder, rather than involving the construction of a correct or politically adequate 'concrete-in-thought'. In urban studies, Henri Lefevbre's reading of Marx's method in his *Dialectical Materialism* (Lefebvre 2009) offers a succinct and engaging analysis and foreshadows his later approaches to space, everyday life and the urban. He broadly agrees with Hall's reading of Marx's *Grundrisse* (although proposing this more than half a century earlier!). Dialectics, he argues, in his early commentary on this text, is a 'method of exposition' which, for Marx, is:

> nothing less than the complete reconstitution of the concrete in its inner movement, not a mere juxtapositioning or external organization of the results of the analysis. We must start from the content. ... The whole must be recovered by moving from the abstract to the concrete. The concrete totality is thus the conceptual elaboration of the content grasped in perception and representation: it is not, as Hegel thought, the product of the concept begetting itself above perception and representation. The whole, such as it appears in our brain as a mental whole, is a product of this thinking brain, which takes possession of the world in the only way open to it, *that is by scientific study*. The actual datum can therefore remain always present as content and presupposition.
>
> (Lefebvre, 2009 [1940], pp. 74–5; my italics)

By demystifying Marist method as a mode of scientific study, concepts are rendered uncertain and open to empirical observation. More fundamentally, in his original reading of the idea of totality, with his characteristic focus on action (2009, p. 93) and the idea of 'total man', Lefebvre posits the idea of an 'open totality' which through history and action is 'perpetually in the process of being transcended, precisely insofar as they will be expressing the solutions to the problems facing concrete man' (2009, p. 99). Any 'concrete totality' is characterised by the permanent excess or inexhaustibility of the material world and of experience and life itself. This constituted an important aspect of Lefebvre's distinctive processes of conceptualisation as a three-dimensional dialectics driven by processes of becoming which were grounded in such excesses and residuals (Schmid 2008, 2022). Marxist insights can then be thought of as grounded in an agentful and incomplete analysis (praxis) of dynamic, inexhaustible 'concrete totalities'. Additionally, insofar as the 'abstractions' and 'relations' which need to be drawn on to produce a 'concrete in thought' are both multiple and revisable, Marxism opens to conceptual revision through comparative analysis. If accounts of 'concrete' phenomena entail analysis of contingent formations in particular situations (for Hall, a 'conjuncture' rather than a context), such analyses cannot aspire to universalising or overly ambitious conceptualisations (Hart 2018). Chapter 8 explores further some ways in which Marxist concepts might be rendered revisable through comparative urban studies – notably in the openings offered by thinking the urban as contingency and 'conjuncture'. The final section of this chapter considers some further approaches to navigating the relationship between concepts and the world, which remain attentive to the political stakes of conceptualisation.

Negotiated Universals: Concepts 'In-common'

This section explores with feminist writer Linda Zerrilli and philosopher Hannah Arendt the potential for seeing concepts, or 'universals', as a horizon of contested, collective practice. This chimes with comparative urbanism, in which 'the urban' is an open horizon, urban theory is emergent and provisional, and, following Lefebvre, the future of the urban is a collective historical project. There are challenges and risks to such hopes of collective, if contested, concepts. Not least that for those forms of knowledge which claim to speak in a universal voice it is 'the relations of power at the heart of these traditions' which necessarily frame those very possibilities (Mbembe 2017, p. 8). Achille Mbembe, in an often devastating critique, looks for alternatives to the forms of conceptualisation proposed in an inherited Western philosophy scarred by racist and colonial histories. Is it possible to imagine a practice of emergent universals, on new grounds, from different subjects? Mbembe asks, for example, can there be a practice of conceptualisation committed to 'the articulation, from Africa, of a *thinking of circulation and crossings*' (p. 8).

So far this chapter, and book, across a range of perspectives and theoretical traditions, has suggestd that a reformatted urban comparativism requires a way of understanding and working with (revisable) concepts. In the first section we considered the critical grounds of the subjects of theorisation; the second section opened to the possibilities of revisable concepts, as heuristics, in a critical reading of Weber; and in the third section through Marxist concerns with the concrete and abstraction we noted the unruly and potentially disruptive presence of the full urban world in destabilising inherited concepts. Here these diverse concerns come together as we explore approaches which posit an open horizon of concepts, forged in the midst of political contestation and practical engagements. Generalisation and power are risks attached to all concepts, or 'universals'.

The shorthand social science critique, 'universalising', refers to the generalising and encompassing ambition with which otherwise relatively modest, hard won and generally insecure 'universals' might be put to use. But without universals (concepts), and the ability to talk consistently about phenomena and characteristics (e.g. 'red' or 'hot'), it would be truly challenging to sustain collective social life, or communicate across a distance, or engage in conversation. Certainly, it is often the case that the terms we use in the world hold us hostage to conceptualisations from positions of power, and to ambitious attempts to scope and contain divergent points of view (universalising). An important question, and opportunity, for generative comparative urban practice therefore concerns the tension between embeddedness of concepts in contexts and the pragmatic need for their use in a wider geographical scope ('generalisation'). While much of the discussion in this chapter has been written from the point of view of a 'researcher', 'scientist' or 'scholar', in the field of urban studies concepts are often emergent from and strongly implicated in governance and practice, and politics (Madden 2018). Terms such as 'urban age', but also 'region', 'metropolitan area', 'neighbourhood' or 'public space' are emergent terms, with often strong stakes attached to them in terms of their definition, delimitation (who is included or excluded from an area? what are the implications of limiting or extending governance?) and their imputed qualities – which areas might be valued highly and which stigmatised? How might renaming or requalifying areas lead to displacement, for example?

Important here is the pragmatists' assumption about 'the continuity between the patterns of inquiry that go on in everyday practices and in more specialized fields of thought' (Barnett and Bridge 2016, p. 1194), contesting the 'vocation of critique' by scholars (p. 1201). This resonates with Weber's sensibilities about the embeddedness of scientific concepts in the contemporary cultural world of researchers and their interlocutors. For example, from an analytical point of view what is named as 'urban' in pragmatic interventions, problematics, or '*dispositifs*', or in territories designated as urban (local governments), may not be about the 'urban' as such: 'Models of city-level intervention developed to address challenges, for example, of climate change, or regional innovation, or health issues, might be better understood as strategic responses to difficulties in specific fields of action for which certain aspects of urban practice become effective sites for engagement, experimentation and refinement.' (p. 1190). Wider concepts of the urban, Barnett and Bridge (2016) argue, can be mobilised strategically by all sorts of actors to solve many different problems. They suggest that 'we might want to be a little more charitable towards the uses of urban concepts found in these other fields' (p. 1201). Thus, 'thinking problematically recasts critical analysis as a less singularly academic vocation than is often supposed in current debates about the futures of urban theory. It does so by helping to open up self-consciously critical traditions of urban studies to a broader range of sites and sources for theoretical reflection and insight' (p. 1201).

Barnett and Bridge offer the example of the creation of an urban Goal in the 2015 UN SDGs. Certain formulations of the concept of 'city' as cause (concentrating problems), potential (to solve problems through their dynamism) and action (which city scale institutions can take effectively), facilitated the successful inclusion of urban development as a priority (Barnett and Parnell 2016). More strongly, Pieterse et al. (2018), suggest that 'Over the next decade, academic thinking on urban life and infrastructure is likely to flow from and/or critique the sustainable development goals' (SDG) aspirations for cities in general, and the African city in particular' (p. 2). This might tie scholarly critique closely to the instrumental concerns and power relations of developmental institutions and activities, circumscribing the beneficial use of creative scholarly resources. Although he was eager to develop concepts which had purchase in everyday and public communication, Max Weber also expressed some misgivings about simply adopting 'found' terms, which those of us raised within the horizon of a hermeneutics of suspicion, and Marxist critical theory might share:

> The use of the undifferentiated, collective concepts belonging to everyday language is always a cover for woolly thinking or unclear aims of action; quite often it is a tool that leads to questionable half-truths; and it invariably serves to inhibit the correct formulation of the problem.
>
> (Weber 2012, p.137)

He advocated submitting such terms to interrogation by developing 'clear and distinct' (ideal type) concepts, with which to confront the empirical material. But in the pragmatist and Arendt-ian propositions which I discuss here, concepts are part of a practical and contested world, not the prerogative of the isolated self-reflecting theorist – although of course 'scientific' inquiry and scholarly contributions are recursively part of these practices, as academic ideas are grabbed and remobilised in practical circuits of knowledge production. The idea of 'global city' is one such formulation, for example, both drawn from policy circuits initially, and later strongly shaping them (Taylor 2004). More generally, though, in starting with the pragmatic life of urban concepts, and their deep politicisation, an opening can be found for thinking 'universals' or concepts differently.

In his valuable contribution to geographical theorising on Justice and philosophy, *The Priority of Injustice*, Clive Barnett opens up an important set of debates drawn from his close engagement with Iris Marion Young, as well as feminist theory and Hannah Arendt's work, to consider the construction of 'universals'. As a contested, political practice, he proposes understandings which are founded not in seeking to define a pure conceptualisation of 'justice' but in the practical, contextual and contested search to find some collective agreement on when injustice takes place. In this view, constituting shared understandings and concepts which might travel across more than one instance or case, takes place in communities of interpretation both contextualised in place and stretched out along the lines of globalised social processes. Emergent concepts might operate as a collectively-defined horizon of meaning, one which we might reach for and contest in the process of forging collectives of action and responsibility. It is important to note here that this constitutes 'locatedness' or 'positionality' in a clearly 'connected' rather than territorially bounded way. As Martha Nussbaum notes, reaching for judgement takes place in a context 'where every culture turns up inside every other' (in Zerilli 2009, p. 300) making any ideas of bounded particularism unfeasible. Thus, rather than abandoning the search for concepts as being necessarily associated with power, or being narrowly defined in ethnocentric ways, inspired by Hannah Arendt, Linda Zerilli seeks to 'foreground the power of judgment as a central feature of critical feminist political practice' (2009, p. 298). As she observes,

> Universalism's entanglement with colonialism and imperialism gives it a deeply fraught legacy for contemporary feminist politics. And yet it is hard to imagine feminist politics without some appeal to universality, for politics involves forms of collective action, action in concert.
>
> (Zerilli 2009, p. 298)

She powerfully asks, 'What would it mean to take the contexts of local particularity as a starting point for a critical political encounter in which the universal criteria for cross-cultural judgments could be articulated rather than assumed?' (2009, p. 303). This, she notes, 'is to treat the local or particular as a potential source of ever new iterations of universality, where the very idea of the universal will not be decided once and for all but will always remain open to further political interrogation.' (2009, p. 304). With Haraway she notes that the alternative to both objectivism and relativism 'is partial, locatable, critical knowledges sustaining the possibility of webs of solidarity in politics and shared conversations in epistemology' (p. 306). As a political project, producing new insights, new universals or concepts is important: 'pure particularism in politics is self-defeating; individuals and groups must issue judgments and claims in a language that resonates with others who do not necessarily share the same social location' (p. 299).

Zerilli (2016) turns to a close analysis of Hannah Arendt's mature theoretical work on knowing – Mind, Will and the unfinished work on Judgement – to develop these arguments. I have drawn much inspiration from Arendt's articulation in *The Life of the Mind* of the complex and productive spaces of coming to and criticising knowledge of the world – including her fascinating engagement with Socrates' formulation of thought as a conversation with the fellow at home (oneself), resonating with Deleuze's (contemporaneous) depiction of the fragmented knowing subject. In tandem, the late 1960s and 1970s disruption of strong universals in both science and politics (post-structuralism, post-modernism etc.), meant for Arendt an important opening to recast assumptions about knowledge and concepts. As Zerilli notes of Arendt, 'it is the very idea that criteria must be given as universal rules governing from above the application of concepts to the particulars of political life that has, in her view, led partly to the breakdown of the capacity to judge critically in the first place. And it is only with the breakdown of such criteria, she argues, that the power of critical judgment can come into its own. Thus, where others see relativism and a crisis of judgment, Arendt sees the chance to practice judgment critically anew' (2009, p. 308): 'Understood in a political rather than philosophical idiom, universality is an achievement that is deeply dependent on practical context and thus fragile.' (p. 315).

Povinelli (2001) offers an important rejoinder to the liberal and pragmatist ambitions for a horizon of intelligibility across radical alterity, which she renames as a 'horizon of good intentions' (p. 328). This rehearses the concerns of McKittrick (2016) concerning the reprisals of biological-determinist and racist forms power involved in radical critiques of racial inequality, and Moten's devastating critical analysis of the relevance or existence of (even a contested) shared arena of public debate such as Arendt imagines. Povinelli notes that

'Listening to the articulated cry of a pained minority subject is the only means by which liberals can know when they are inflicting harm, pain, and torture on others, and why this pain is unjustified' (p. 329; see Rose-Redwood et al. 2018). Might theoretical endeavours be allied with such a liberal imagination of political commensurability, when 'the stakes of forcing liberal subjects to experience the intractable impasse of reason as the borders of the repugnant – actual legal, economic and social repression' (p. 329), exposes how 'the late liberal diaspora shifts the burden for social commensuration from the place it is generated (liberalism) to the place it operates on' (p. 329–30). In Povinelli's critique, circulations as grounds for producing 'we-horizons' (p. 326) are equally embroiled in problematic initiatives to ground new kinds of democratic polities across difference which carry the intentions of the powerful. The questions she poses direct radical scholars to interrogate their implicatedness in the institutional and wider power relations of the horizons of both meaning and solidarity: 'the delicate and dramatic ways in which institutionalised conventions of risk and pleasure commensurate social worlds – make radical worlds unremarkable' (p. 325). It is here that other starting points beyond the horizons of collectively agreed and contested meaning – of refusal, or fugitivity – are indicated.

Achille Mbembe (2017) draws on a wider history of race and 'blackness' to place in question the terms of commensuration, universalism and conceptualisation. He writes, 'As objects of discourse and objects of knowledge, Africa and Blackness have, since the beginning of the modern age, plunged the theory of the name as well as the status and function of the sign and of representation into deep crisis' (p. 12). This crisis, he suggests, means that 'as soon as the subject of Blacks and Africa is raised, words do not represent things; the true and the false become inextricable; the signification of the sign is not always adequate to what is being signified. It is not only that the sign is substituted for the thing. Word and image often have little to say about the objective world.' (p. 13). In this economy, race is one of the raw materials, he suggests 'from which difference and *surplus* – a kind of life that can be wasted and spent without limit – are produced' (p. 34). 'Race is an instrumentality that makes it possible both to name the surplus and to commit it to waste and unlimited spending. It is what makes it acceptable to categorise abstractly in order to stigmatise, disqualify morally, and eventually imprison or expel' (p. 34–5). The logic of enclosure – plantation, apartheid, colony – marks the calculations of 'circulation and capture' which form historical and contemporary technologies productive of a 'multilated humanity' (p. 36). Mbembe is scathing of the 'massive coating of nonsense, lies and fantasies' (p. 39) which stands in place of Black life and language – both in the forms of racism and its inverted opposition in a longing for community in place of loss.

As he works through historical, cultural and philosophical resources of black and African experience/representation, he shows how creative theorisation might emerge in conversation or in solidarity with other places, through diverse and often transnational intellectual trajectories. Mbembe insists, writing from Johannesburg, that European traditions 'are not at all foreign to us' (2017, p. 8). But as he notes, and demonstrates in *Critique of Black Reason*, 'When it comes to speaking the world in a language for everyone, however, there exist relations of power at the heart of these traditions' (p. 8). His ambition, then, is not to 'deepen the distance between Africa and the world' but to 'make possible the emergence, relatively lucidly, of the new demands of a possible universalism' (p. 8). His book turns on the key point that the enlightenment thinking which forms the basis for contemporary (northern/universal) theory, philosophy and method emerged on the same terrain and grounds as racialised violence and dehumanisation. New terms of 'human', new moments of world making, require a critique of the violent inheritances of slavery, colonialism and race, as well as the 'racism without races' which sees these technologies now reframing the brutal exploitation of the poor and excluded across the world (p. 7).

In recasting the possibilities of 'universals' on the grounds of a critique of black reason, Mbembe articulates that 'The universalism of the name "Black" depends not on repetition but on the *radical difference without which the disenclosure of the world is impossible*' (p. 160). His analysis casts across novels speaking of doubleness, nocturnality and spirit worlds; fractured, precarious African historical experiences give shape to his argument that the search for new grounds of reason 'must bring us back to Africa, or at least take a detour through Africa, the double of the world whose time we know will come' (p. 160). Different potentialities of humanity, of life, of ways of being across self, others and world come into view. The contrast with 'black reason' forged on (or in opposition to) the deathly grounds of 'race' is evident:

> Life is henceforth but a series of instants and trajectories that are almost parallel, with no overarching unity. There are constant jumps back and forth from one experience to another, from one horizon to another. The entire structure of existence is such that, in order to live, one must constantly escape permanence, which is the bearer of precariousness and vulnerability. Instability, interruption, and mobility, on the other hand, offer possibilities of flight and escape. But flight and escape are also bearers of danger.
> (Mbembe 2017, p. 147)

In the context of the 'distribution of violence on a planetary scale' (p. 179), which worlds both blackness and Africanness as generalised forms of brutality, Mbembe searches nonetheless for ways in which (thinking) the world (as a project of the in-common – p. 183) might be imagined as necessarily shared. If 'the Other is at once difference and similarity united', a politics of humanity must rest, paradoxically he suggests, on 'the difference we share' (p. 178), along with the 'proximity of the distant' (p 182). Even as the cuts and scars of history demand reparations and a relaunching of the search for reciprocity (p. 181). The possibility of figuring insights 'in-common' is evident in Maliq Simone's (2016) discussion of how an idea of 'generic blackness' might take shape across different histories to destabilise accounts of the urban:

> Black people have struggled in cities for a long time. For blackness has made many instances of urbanization possible and is also a result of certain urbanizations. These functions are difficult to sort out clearly. Still, there is something of enormous potential within the experiences of actual black bodies and the various notions of blackness that shroud, mark, reveal and define these bodies. This potential is hard to come to words. It seems immediately qualified by histories of all kinds. But there is something left over that can potentially be called upon, put to work, that is both connected to black urban experiences but detached as well. Something that moves across territories and situations as a manoeuvre to gather, cull and distribute knowledge that cannot be pinned down. A resource to go with the 'curse', and that belongs to no one in particular.
>
> (Simone 2016, p. 184)

For Simone, in the urban context, this generic potential of blackness is also a reservoir of actual potential – which he names as being 'about the persistence of potentiality within any format of urbanization – its black side' (p. 185). In other contexts he has proposed 'blackness' as the 'unsettling' of the territorial hallucinations of whiteness, its segregations and settled formations. Passing through borders, dissimulating, unsettling, extending. Other urban futures, as Simone's work makes clear, are being made and written, in many black cities – and not only the ones which are conventionally seen as black. He argues that 'blackness' is also at stake in many cities which may not seem black. For example, the future of urban life made through the reductive inter-operability of different systems of data and surveillance in which 'the capacity resiliently to become many different things has become standard operating procedure' (p. 69). Mbembe (2017, p. 7), too, draws attention to the phenomenon of 'racism without races' subtends a generalisation of forms of dehumanisation in the contemporary era. The spatialities of the urban which are indexed for Simone by 'blackness' and for McKittrick (2013) by black life, open out to emergent, and different understandings of the urban. In reaching for an 'outside' of the grounds or territories of urban theory, which might be located to some extent in 'black lives' or 'generic blackness', there also comes into view, as we have seen, emergent possibilities for the practice of conceptualisation.

Conclusion

This chapter has suggested that seeing researchers as active agents composing comparisons, as part of conversations which rest on revisable concepts, opens up the potential to interrogate the conceptualisation of urbanisation processes and 'the urban'. Whatever the urban is, it emerges at the horizons of collective practice, in lives lived 'out of the outside', in a myriad processes of creative conceptualisation, in revisable assessments of the relations and determinations which underpin the 'concrete-in-thought', in the inexhaustible totalities of the urban. Many different resources to think conceptual generativity can be found. With these in mind, how might comparisons proceed?

In researcher-led comparisons, on generative grounds, it is the potential for revising concepts which draws our attention – critical vigilance in relation to the power relations embedded in inherited traditions of thought is crucial, but also an openness to the productive potential of new concepts. A comparative imagination, and more importantly, comparative practice, opens the opportunity to make or repurpose the 'universals' or concepts which sustain conversation across more than one case. How to achieve this without relying on 'universalisms', or performing any more of a god-trick than anyone else who uses words?

Chapters 8 and 9 look in detail at comparative tactics which emerge on the grounds of generative comparisons. Some of these flow from ways in which the 'shape' of the urban might be configured in different theoretical perspectives – as 'conjunctures', as specific outcomes, or as diverse. These offer different starting points for composing comparisons, and have different implications for the potential to generate or revise concepts. But comparative tactics also flow from researchers' experiments, as comparative objects emerge, conversations unfold across cases, or concepts are put on the move. The next two chapters engage further with dominant theoretical traditions in urban studies, but also find inspiration in the comparative experiments which urban scholars have initiated as they have sought innovative ways to compose generative comparisons across the diversity and distinctiveness of the urban world.

Notes

1. https://youtu.be/tlTdNjtkptk.
2. This refers to the analytical perspective of the researcher, and the reasons for their empirical engagement.
3. And yet so many people commented as I was preparing the book that I should 'take a look' at Weber's ideal types!! Peter Saunders' (1986) *Social Theory and the Urban Question* offers a rare commentary from within urban studies, but does not engage closely with the issues I raise here, notably Ideal Types as concept formation and comparative method. The fate of Weber in urban studies is matched perhaps by that in sociology and social science more generally, in which his post-War translators and interpreters in English language scholarship misrepresented his ideas and mistranslated is terms. A number of new translations are now available which inform a new wave of Weber-inspired analyses.
4. Mann (2013, p. 378) describes it as an incautious, superficial comparative sociology which seeks to place societies above or below each other on a developmental trajectory – 'More frequently, societies *differ* in their achievements'.
5. Mann (2012) places the European 'leap' forward much earlier than Weber and, in contrast to Pomeranz, does not rest this on either of the two later historical 'accidents' of Europe's violent extraction from the rest of the world through colonial conquest and settlement, or the proximity of coal discoveries to England's existing industrial activities. Rather, while significant, he sees these as deep-rooted, complex and long historical processes (such as the intensification of agricultural production). Late-medieval transition from feudalism to capitalism institutionalised a leap that had already occurred by the time of Weber's medieval cities; his account is focussed on the expanding and extensive fiscal capacities of the state, trade and military. But cities in some parts of Europe played an important role in this, he agrees with Weber. He outlines the important institutional innovations (p. 437), role of wars across Europe in increasing the demands on the state to raise money, the taxation of merchants and new settlers (p. 423), and the costs of expanding the military capacities of towns (p. 426).
6. Influenced by the terminology of Tönnies, but rejecting the descriptive and binary nature of his analysis in favour of a focus on process.
7. The extant English translation (1958, pp. 80–1) imports a certain rigidity to the analysis, and inaccurately transfers the focus of the analysis to 'the city' rather than the 'urban community', which neither reflects Weber's methodological ambition nor the meaning of the German text. 'Measured by this rule ["benchmark"] the "cities" of the Occidental Middle Ages only qualify in part as true cities [following the German, this should read that they are only to a

certain extent "urban communities"]; even the cities of the eighteenth century were genuine urban communities only in minor degree. Finally measured by this rule, with possible isolated exceptions, the cities of Asia were not urban communities at all even though they all had markets and were fortresses.' (Weber 1958, pp. 80–1). The German text reads, 'An diesem Maßstab [rule, benchmark, gauge, standard] in seinem vollen Umfang [extent, scale] gemessen [to measure, to benchmark, to gauge] waren freilich auch die Städte des okzidentalen Mittelalters nur teilweise und diejenigen des 18. Jahrhunderts sogar nur zum ganz geringen Teil wirklich »Stadtgemeinden«. Aber diejenigen Asiens waren es, vereinzelte mögliche Ausnahmen abgerechnet, soviel heute bekannt, überhaupt nicht oder nur in Ansätzen. Zwar Märkte hatten sie alle und Festungen waren sie ebenfalls'.

8. My favourite comment from this paper: 'You should not force empirical reality into a concept as into a procrustean bed.' (p. 184; Weber 2012, p. 127). The online free dictionary translates this as, 'Procrustean bed. A situation or place that someone is forced into, often violently. In Greek mythology, the giant Procrustes would capture people and then stretch or cut off their limbs to make them fit into his bed.' So clearly not a good way to treat our research 'subjects'!

9. Hall: 'History, we may say, realizes itself progressively. Theory, however, appropriates history "regressively". Theory, then, starts from history as a developed result, post festum. This is its presupposition, in the head. History, but only in its realization as a "complexly structured totality", articulates itself as the epistemological premise, the starting point, of theoretical labour.' (p. 136–7). 'Marx's "historical epistemology", then, maps the mutual articulation of historical movement and theoretical reflection, not as a simple identity but as differentiations within a unity.' (p. 137).

10. What Hart (2018, p. 17) describes as 'advancing from the abstract to the concrete' – but following Marx and Hall, one does not have the concrete actually in thought, one has a 'concrete-in-thought'.

11. Not so dissimilar perhaps to Deleuze's reaching for the 'rumbling intensities' which remain present in – with the potential to disrupt – concepts?

CHAPTER 8

Composing Comparisons

> *The city's transformations are not the passive outcomes of changes in the social whole.*
>
> (Henri Lefebvre 1996, p. 100)

This chapter dives into how comparative experiments might be composed on generative grounds to support conceptual innovation in urban studies. Chapter 7 considered different ways of understanding dynamic processes of conceptualisation. We noted how a comparative imagination is emergent in practices of conceptualisation, entangled (in different ways) with dynamic materialities and empirical observations. The unsettled nature of the urban world inspires researchers to work creatively with concepts, in dialogue with others, through empirical and comparative experimentation. The messy materiality and diversity of urban life disturbs tendencies to solipsistic reverie on the part of the researcher–composer.

A 'generative' comparison, then, emerges on the terrain of conceptualisation, through the active role of the researcher in the context of the double virtual series of matter and ideas/concepts. Teasing these apart would run counter to Deleuze's entire analysis, as we saw in Chapter 4: concepts and entities are co-emergent in an uneven and complex synthesis, as conceptualising subjects encounter a material(ising) world. But I suggest we use these as organising devices to identify a range of generative comparative tactics which rely more on researcher agency. These might start with the ways in which the urban is conceptualised, as considered in this chapter and the next. Or they might start with the urban world pressing at researcher imaginations as discussed in Chapter 10.

All these tactics, discussed in the rest of Part 3 and in Part 4, involve always the inextricable intertwining of the two virtual series of Ideas and a dynamic urban world – which Chapter 11 explores more fully, drawing on the insights of both Gilles Deleuze and Walter Benjamin.

In the rest of the book, Parts 3 and 4, the focus is on generative, researcher-led tactics to compose comparisons which support the potential for new con-

Comparative Urbanism: Tactics for Global Urban Studies, First Edition. Jennifer Robinson.
© 2022 John Wiley & Sons Ltd. Published 2022 by John Wiley & Sons Ltd.

cepts of the urban to emerge. The tactics explored in this chapter are specifically linked to different conceptualisations of the urban which each support different ways to frame comparisons. We leave aside the genetic interconnections which establish good grounds for thinking across 'differentiation' (emergent from interconnections) and 'variegation' (tied to wider processes). The tactics explored here compose comparisons with and across the diversity of the urban, rather than tracing connections or focussing on relations. In the absence of connections or relations, what criteria can replace conventional assumptions of similarity, difference and causality, discussed in Chapters 2 and 3, to guide the crafting of compelling comparisons? This chapter argues that the way in which the nature of the urban is conceived – as a context, a socio-political conjuncture, a spatial form, as an inexhaustible and distinctive reality, or as a diversity of processes and outcomes – can inspire different kinds of generative urban comparisons. These are strongly inflected by the theoretical traditions and practices adopted by researchers. So, for example, in this chapter we encounter researchers thinking with regulation theory and Althusserian theoretical Marxism; we find a Gramscian-inspired interest in the political 'conjuncture' in conversation with Lefebvre's heterodox Marxist theorisation of the urban. In addition, a more eclectic theoretical repertoire informs free-ranging experiments in search of emergent concepts across the diversity and divergence of global urban experiences. Even as new concepts emerge through comparative experiments which bring different urban experiences into a shared analytical framing, how this 'difference' is conceptualised shapes the kinds of tactics adopted and the potential for revising concepts.

Each perspective on the urban world makes possible certain kinds of comparative experiments, but places limits on others. For example, the idea of 'conjuncture' is suggestive for thinking the social world in its rich complexity, a key concern for any analysis of the urban. 'Conjunctural' analysis highlights the significance of contingency, and yet also insists on the importance of structures and wider social processes, all seen from a critical and politically attuned perspective at a precise historical (and implicitly geographical) moment. Certainly, this is an appealing mix. It is important to note, however, that 'conjuncture' does not map onto 'context', and has an awkward relationship with the urban. It is also far from being the only way in which to approach questions of historical contingency and explanatory multiplicity. So, what exactly can this term bring to interrogating the nature of the urban? This chapter explores how generative comparative tactics might emerge in relation to 'conjuncture', but also in relation to contingency, specificity and diversity. Overall, the chapter moves in the direction of theorising from urban distinctiveness – from theoretically saturated 'conjunctures', to contingent formations and 'concrete totalities', and then to specificities or distinctive urban outcomes which open the fullness of urban life to all kinds of comparative experiments. I draw towards the end of the chapter on some of my own collaborative research which engages with urban development politics and large-scale urban developments. We ask how generative comparative tactics might work to build theoretical analyses across the diversity of urban outcomes, treating contexts as rich starting points for conceptualisation.

Working with 'Conjuncture'

> *Stuart Hall's premise, as I have already said, was relationality, and everything—so much—followed from this. Recognizing that relations were the basic elements of reality entailed a commitment, above all, to complexity, contingency, and change. Complexity was central for him: it is, we might say, complexity everywhere, and "all the way down." (Hybridity, which is commonly slotted into that phrase, is just one instantiation of the complexity).*
>
> (Grossberg 2015, p. 6)

In his moving tribute to Stuart Hall, Grossberg signals a major intellectual influence in British Marxism and cultural studies, and highlights his major contribution as what he calls the 'discipline of the conjuncture' – 'to think with the contradictory and complex realities that shape people's everyday lives' (p. 2015, p. 6). Hall's (2016) 1983 lectures exquisitely outline the intellectual journey of his approach, from critical encounters with E.P. Thompson, Raymond Williams, Durkheim and Levi-Strauss via an extended engagement with Marxist analyses, especially with Althusser and Gramsci, to arrive at his understanding of conjunctural analysis. As we noted in Chapter 7, for Hall, the idea of seeing 'the concrete as the unity of many determinations and relations' – a differentiated unity – is a 'methodological and theoretical key' (Hall 2003, p. 127) to Marx's analysis. Hall is inspired by Althusser to account for the 'complex relationships of overdetermination between the different social practices in any social formation' (Hall 2016, p. 159) in a 'non-reductionist' way. For example, this would involve seeing the independent dynamics of emergent cultural and class formations, 'without pulling them so apart they fall into totally autonomous positions' (p. 194). He was cautious, though, not to see this as a 'necessary' non-determination, as opposed to a not necessarily deterministic analysis (Hall 1985, p. 95). For him, conjunctural analysis as political practice, after Gramsci, required this: his interest was in how the cultural practices of subjects opened up new political possibilities through creatively articulating different elements of social formations.

This approach has been so significant for urban studies. This is not directly via Hall, although he has been crucial to some contributions (Hart 2003; Ziedermann 2018), but instead via Doreen Massey, whose *For Space* (2005) articulates the 'simultaneity' of space as part of the problematic of thinking the contingent formation of social relations in place (Callard 2004). Clarke (2018) observes that Massey effects an analysis of how different dynamics are 'articulated' in place, knowingly using a key Althusserian term. However, in his influential essay from the late 1970s, Hall (2003) notes, that 'Marx insists that the superiority of the dialectical method lies in its ability to trace out the "inner connection" between the different elements in a mode of production, as against their haphazard, and extrinsic "mere juxtaposition"' (p.120). But 'space' and 'the urban' are precisely such haphazard and fortuitous arrangements of diverse phenomena; it is the possible outcomes amongst unrelated but spatially proximate phenomena which makes the urban effective, as 'agglomeration', for example. If there is a logic or determination to space, or the urban, it is, to follow Lefebvre, emergent and self-organising (2003, p. 171). Thinking the urban conjuncturally, then, might be a little difficult.

Somewhat contradictorily, though, Hall also suggested that the articulation of different cultural, class and political practices was the result of juxtapositions and surprising alignments. He saw here the 'possibility of new subjectivities' emerging (p. 197). In these articulations, while emergent forms (of social movements, of cultural practices, or subjectivity) 'do not contain their own guarantees, they do contain real possibilities' (p. 206). Both with and *contra* Hall, then, we can read the urban, following Massey (and space more generally), as a site of the contingent 'articulation' of diverse processes and practices (Hart 2018; Roy 2011b), and also as a site of emergence and possibility.

The term conjuncture indexes a field of Marxist analysis which mobilises a repertoire of theoretical terms which have potential to guide the composition of urban comparisons by offering explanations for diverse and divergent outcomes as shaped by multiple and varying 'determinations and relations', or in Althusserian terms, 'levels' and 'overdetermination'. Those urban scholars who have been inspired by this analysis frame a conceptual task focussed on identifying the multiple 'relations and determinations' which work together to shape specific conjunctural moments (Hart 2018; Peck 2017a). This broadly takes forward Marx's brief methodological comments in the introduction to the *Grundrisse*, which we discussed in Chapters 2 and 7, and is strongly inspired by Gramsci. Conjuncture then comes to be about the (co-constitutive) relations amongst the many different elements which can be used to build an understanding of a particular historical moment. On the one hand, this goes strongly in the direction of suggesting that urban outcomes are 'contingent' (Hart 2018). On the other hand, for some the term 'conjuncture' is appealing as it invites an analytical perspective on how particular outcomes are always embedded in more general processes and structural formations. Practically, this is less about tracing wider social processes (as we discussed in Chapter 6), but being alert to extensive political, economic and ideological formations (Leitner et al. 2019).

For a Marxist-inspired comparative urban imagination, 'conjunctures' are a productive starting point, and define a careful and distinctive range of interpretive comparative tactics, beyond concerns with similarity-difference. Comparisons which work closely with conjunctural analysis are inspired to generate creative, emergent understandings, responsive to the dynamic and situated nature of social formations. There is scope as well to consider variations across different conjunctural formations. 'Revisable theory claims' (Peck 2017a, p. 25) are anticipated by proponents of 'conjunctural urbanism', using comparative tactics which are influenced by the spatial imaginations they layer into conjunctural analysis. Thus, although thinking spatially is a weak point of conjunctural analyses more generally, a spatial perspective on Marxist analyses of the 'conjuncture' provides significant openings to frame comparative urban research. A 'conjunctural analysis', focussed on context, relationality and nested scalarity, offers a range of opportunities for comparative urban experiments.

Scalar Conjuncturalism

There is often an implicit national methodologism to conjunctural analysis and little explicit consideration of spatiality (Grossberg 2019). But a complexity of spatial dynamics can be inferred from key thinkers. Writing of Engels' comments on the relation between economic determination and contingent historical determinations, Althusser comments that 'History "asserts itself" through the multiform world of the superstructures, from local tradition to international circumstance' (For Marx, p. 218)). And also from Gramsci, as Hart writes,

> My own understanding draws most fully on Gramsci (1971, p. 175–85; Q13§17), for whom conjunctural analysis incorporated what he called 'relations of force at various levels' – an analysis that is also profoundly spatial: 'international relations intertwine with these internal relations of nation-states, creating new, unique and historically concrete combinations', and 'this relation between international forces and national forces is further complicated by the existence within every State

of several structurally diverse territorial sectors, with diverse relations of force at all levels' (1971: 182). This formulation makes clear the anti-teleological and anti-reductionist character of a conjunctural framework.

(Hart 2018, p. 18)

In his effort to define the idea of 'conjuncture' Grossberg (2019) noted, 'I realised that I did not have, and I could not find anywhere in the literature of cultural studies, a well-theorised understanding of how conjunctural analysis is to be done, and how a conjuncture is to be defined or constituted' (Grossberg 2019, p. 40). Ascribing some key initial use to Lenin, Gramsci and Althusser, and noting that the use of the term was very vague, he builds his insights from Gramsci and Stuart Hall. In his search for some kind of definition of conjuncture, Grossberg disconnects 'conjuncture' from 'context'. He notes that 'conjuncture' is 'too often treated as a context defined by some boundary, often but not necessarily a given space and a period of time' (p. 40). Rather, he suggests that conjunctural analysis may not be 'a goal but a practice, a process, a critical analytic' (Grossberg 2019, p. 42). Grossberg sees conjunctural analysis as a characteristically Marxist (politically inflected) commitment to work 'at a particular level of abstraction' and 'at the level of the social formation as some sort of totality, however fragile and temporary' (p. 42) which is articulated conjuncturally, in a determining 'moment'.

Conjunctural analysis is rarely aligned with a defined space, then– although space is used in metaphorical ways to delineate (analytical) 'maps', or unspecific 'times and spaces' (Grossberg 2019, p. 45) or 'radical contextuality' (p. 46), or 'domains and planes' (p. 48), or as a convenient and poor shorthand to explain 'articulation' through the metaphor of urban–rural interaction (p. 53), or as a 'cartography' to metaphorically 'map' the three levels of analysis Grossberg proposes (p. 63). Nonetheless, as a largely analytical and political project (committed to thinking with totalities) it operates often on an assumed or unexamined terrain of nation-states, albeit in process of reconfiguration through globalisation and embedded within wider horizons of shared political and economic processes (p. 58). A brief statement from Grossberg seems to imply attention to spatiality in 'efforts to map the conjuncture as a number of different forms of interrelated and overlapping contexts, each with its own spatial and temporal scales' (p. 59). But this remains unexplored in favour of a focus on the three aspatial 'levels' of analysis he proposes, which bring forward the unity of analysis for any conjuncture. These are a Gramscian 'war of positions', the 'problem space' generated through 'multiple problematics' cutting across these positions, and a sense of unity defined in terms of a Gramscian 'organic crisis' (p. 43).

More helpful for urban scholars, perhaps, is Grossberg's suggestion that one might apply this analytic to provide insight into 'the energetics and densities of everyday life', including his own substantive research in cultural studies (p. 64). This seems to resonate with Hart's comparative imagination based on 'place', but again here the assumed space of the conjunctural analysis rests on the assumption that national and globalising terrains shape the experiences of everyday life: 'the organic crisis of modernity is being reconstituted around or recentred on the very nature of individuation and the locus of sovereignty' (p. 66). He speculates that in this moment of crisis and transformation (for whom?, where?), 'it may be that the conjunctural and the epochal have become so intersected, so inter-determining, that they appear as expressions of one another (e.g. an epochal crisis of the political nomos is expressed as a crisis of governance and a resurgence of nationalism)' (p. 67). His reflections are profoundly US–EU centric, for sure. For our purposes, at no stage is there a sense that the 'conjuncture' has any alignment with the urban. Given the definitions Grossberg has culled, we have to observe that there is no necessity that the political-strategic concerns motivating conjunctural analysis will line up with an urban 'scale'. Of course, the urban may become conjuncturally significant, as Castells (1977) famously argued in relation to collective consumption, or as Peck's (2017a, 2017b) analysis of new forms of local government fiscal discipline in the US implies. However, any given urban context cannot be construed as a 'conjuncture' as such. Those interested in thinking conjuncturally about the urban work around this by repurposing the vocabulary. For example Peck suggests we might consider 'cities as conjunctural alloys or socio-political moments in wider, structurally patterned systems' (Peck 2015, p. 9).

The theorisation and problematic of conjuncture has drawn interest from some comparative urbanists precisely because it indicates a broader, cross-scalar and politically resonant analysis. 'Spatializing' conjunctural analysis supports building a comparative perspective on 'pan-urban processes' (Peck 2015), and provides some important ideas about 'composing an urban "case"'. Conjunctural analysis inspires comparisons to be composed across spatial extents, through connections, or by reviewing multiple urban situations which are part of shared social formations, or from other 'conjunctures' which might bear some resemblance or resonance with concerns emerging in those contexts to inform political judgement. Determining the 'case' of the study is delinked from the territory of the 'city'.

Peck (2017a) draws on Michael Burawoy (2009) whose idea of the 'extended case' focuses attention on the wider settings of case study research. Working from the immediate context of a case out and up involves tracing issues from their immediate starting point (say, in a mine, or urban setting) across institutional hierarchies and levels of the state. For Burawoy, 'relational' comparison is intrinsic to the case itself, as one case reveals differentiation across 'scales' and also across different periods, in which, say, different approaches taken at different moments by the same actors or institutions can be understood and contrasted.

Here, a key opportunity for comparative analysis is afforded by the way in which the 'conjuncture' highlights 'multiple relations and determinations', any of which might be drawn on to initiate interesting and potentially valuable comparative experiments. With possibility for thinking about a range of different processes on the basis of any specific case, and given the extent and reach of many of the 'relations' or wider processes which influence urbanisation, this could encourage composing comparisons across diverse contexts.

These writers also propose that a social formation be imagined as shaped by scalar arrangements (Peck 2017) – albeit scales that are socially produced and changing (Brenner 2005). This suggests a certain nested and extended set of social processes which give some possible shape and opportunity for 'thinking with elsewhere', or through and beyond a delimited case. It implies a direction and dimensionality to comparative analysis (Leitner et al. 2019). The complex spatiality of scales therefore encourages thinking analytically across and within different scalar dimensions, for example, across different emergent local formations, across diverse national contexts; or to consider the active processes of scaling and re-scaling associated with regulatory and institutional transformation (Leitner and Sheppard 2020). This contrasts with a relational analysis which might track connections or relations between 'cases' or their interaction within contexts.

On the basis of this spatial analysis, 'conjunctural' perspectives propose ways of bringing cases into wider reflection across different experiences of a 'phenomenon' entrained within the same 'conjuncture', which can then be interrogated. One drawback, though, is that while 'revisable theory claims' (Peck 2017a, p. 25) are anticipated by proponents, there is a really high bar to overcome to dislodge the imputed concepts of Marxist political theory and an analytics of scale, both of which are highly valued in these perspectives (Peck 2013).

Comparative possibilities are thus revealed as internal to (multi-scalar) cases. Leitner and Sheppard (2020) insist on both a 'horizontal' (connections) and a 'vertical' (scales) dimension to the spatiality of 'conjuncture'. They insist that 'cities are … related "vertically", through their embeddedness in processes operating at supra-urban scales: national regulatory systems, globalisation, global heating and the like.' (p. 496). Peck (2017a) suggests this implies an 'orthogonal' manoeuvre, 'spiralling up and down through cases and contexts as a different (but arguably complementary) strategy to that of working laterally, "between" cases' (p. 9). This can inspire a distinctive set of comparative practices. For example, for Leitner and Sheppard (2020), considering 'how conjunctures vary across space as well as time' (p. 496) is one tactic. This involves exploring the complex articulations of forces behind 'shared general tendencies and particularities' (p. 497), including larger scale processes and ideologies or longer term and larger scale geohistorical trajectories. Methodologically, then, the task is to identify shared tendencies across space and time from detailed analysis of spatially and temporally specific particularities (p. 498). In this perspective, this implies a multiscalar research design, from individuals and neighbourhoods to local and national governments, and global processes.

Leitner and Sheppard (2020, p. 498) stress the importance of leaving scope for relevant 'spatiotemporalities' to emerge during the course of research. In designing a comparative research project they explain how were inspired to explore dispossession and land grabs (because of their concerns with social justice) in 'southern' contexts (because they were concerned to contribute to postcolonialising urban studies). Starting in two selected urban regions revealed the various connections which shape each place, with 'the trajectories of some cities subsequently shaping those of others' (p. 496): 'as we traced flows of capital and people, important relations with other places became visible: connecting Jakarta with Singapore, Tokyo and Beijing, and Bangalore with New York City. Horizontal connectivities, then, cannot be identified a priori but must emerge through empirical investigation.' (p. 498). Their conjunctural comparison across the two contexts considered through a multi-scalar and extended analysis gave rise to an emergent concept, which they label as 'mid-range', 'Interscalar Chains of Rentiership' (ICR): 'ICR provides insight into both the drivers of land transformations and the emergence of a rental economy—characterized by the ways in which urban residents from all walks of life, not just developers and financial institutions, turn to rent extraction in order to accumulate wealth or support their livelihood practices.' (p. 505).

Such a spatialised conjunctural analysis was also developed in Peck's extended case study of Atlantic City (2017a, 2017b). He brought into his analysis the transformation of both municipal finances and the dominant local economic development model in that context, which had been dependent on certain place-based political alliances. He also explored the crosscutting influences of national policies, and circuits of municipal financialisation reshaping local governments across the US (and to some extent beyond). Thus, 'neoliberalism' finds itself transformed in the connected and cross-scalar configurations that came together in this context. The interactions amongst municipal speculative financing mechanisms, and the decline of a formerly dynamic local development model based on tourism and gambling, coincide with new national strategies for governing municipalities. He proposes a wider theorisation of late entrepreneurialism which entails state-level top-down, often punitive, control of local governments in response to the devastating fiscal effects of financial exposure to bond markets on the capabilities of the local state.

On the basis of his conjunctural analysis, Peck (2017b) defers occasionally to the comparative analysis of Detroit (although his discussion focusses almost entirely on Atlantic City). His informants, though, speak of some other comparators that might have been drawn on to inform his theoretical and empirical analysis. They complain of being treated like 'a third world country' or having the disciplining authorities come in with a 'plantation mentality' (p. 353). These evoke the lines of political analysis and insistent dissonant interpretations that theorists working on and with different 'cases' across the world have urged on those thinking about urban neoliberalisation. Some close comparators to the Atlantic City case could be those urban contexts subject to disciplining structural adjustment policies over the last half century, those where national government has long usurped any local democratic decision-making capacity, and those where resource bases have been entirely exanguinated through a mix of colonial, corporate and corrupt extractivisms. These were not brought into view in developing this analysis – suggesting perhaps some of the limits to 'conjunctural' scalar imagination.

Some Caveats on Scalar Conjuncturalism
Working out and up from a case might confine one to assumed tracks of direct influence and institutional contiguity. Despite Peck's suggestion in passing that 'family resemblances' 'near and far' are relevant to analysis, with a scalar conjunctural analysis these do not automatically make an appearance. It is also not clear how this proposition to explore distant cases could be grounded within a substantivist political economy approach which treats 'conjunctures' as distinctive socio-spatial formations. If conjunctures are politically resonant moments which articulate a certain configuration of social processes and historical developments, which open through extensivity and connection to specified different places, this invites comparison only with a defined array of 'elsewheres'. Insofar as these are not world-wide formations, cases and their comparators are necessarily restricted (although see Wu (2022) for engagement with the 'global conjuncture' from a China-centric perspective). Grounds for comparison other than 'conjuncture' would need to be found to bring these contexts into view.

So, for example, the observations about the emergence of peremptory and authoritarian intra-state and external power relations could perhaps work as a different starting point and indicate alternative directions for comparative practice. But this would require a different basis for drawing comparative insights, opening up the US case to other contexts where such authoritarian and peremptory urban political dynamics of bankruptcy and limited resources are very well understood. The lines of conceptual emergence, then, would have nothing to do with wider wholes, resonant political conjunctures, or being enmeshed in a shared inter-scalar verticality. Rather, the shared features of forms of authoritarian governance in urban politics across divergent settings might repay comparative attention. We consider this in the last section of this Chapter. Being open to composing comparisons across shared features in otherwise unconnected contexts, or those which are not brought into view through conjunctural analysis, requires additional, agile ways to bring diverse urban contexts into conversation. As discussed in Chapter 6, the open nature of concepts formulated in a 'family resemblances' mode, in which different features of cases can be variously assembled to generate (a multiplicity of) concepts (Forster 2010) indicates scope for a much wider range of cases to inform an emergent conceptualisation.

One major problem for urban comparisons composed through the concept of 'conjuncture' is that this is a largely epochal term, spatial only to the extent that it imports unexamined and loosely assumed territorial delimitations such as states or wider regions (e.g. Europe, China). In adding a spatial analysis to conjuncture, urbanists have tended to conflate 'conjuncture' with 'context' (all the way up and down across scales – Peck 2017a) or 'territory'. Although conjuncture can be thought spatially (Hart 2018), an interpretation of conjuncture as (a) space is not borne out in the wider definitions of conjuncture which have been proposed. And as we noted earlier it is not clear that the 'urban' can, except in certain specific situations, be seen as in itself 'conjunctural', that is, relevant to analysis of a conjuncture as historical moment. A rare example is found in Castells' (1983) conjunctural analysis of the urban as central to a moment when 'collective consumption' centred on cities had become the key political stakes of the advanced welfare state, as well as a core site of contestation in the revolutionary transitions of late industrialisers (in Chile, but this analysis also resonated well in Brazil and South Africa). But this does not justify treating all urban contexts, or urbanisation processes, *as a conjuncture*.

In terms of developing a spatial reading of conjuncture, Hart (2003, 2018) draws on Gramsci to confirm a spatial analytic which is largely influenced by Doreen Massey – Gramsci notes the role of transnational connections in shaping conjunctures, for example. But even insofar as the problematic of the Althusserian 'conjuncture' with its complexity of 'levels' and spaces (nations, international, regions, thick mutual determinations in contexts) initiated Massey's theory of space, she arrived at a somewhat one-dimensional analysis of 'space' as the intersection of 'trajectories' and a philosophical sense of 'space as simultaneity' (2005). The fullness of space as a lived experience, or the many diverse spatialities of urbanisation and urban outcomes, were very far from her radar and are also arguably absent from conjunctural analyses which focus on 'context', 'connections' and 'scale'. While this presents some limitations for analyses of the urban, other aspects of conjunctural analysis – a focus on totality and contingency – offer openings to comparative analyses which are more explicitly grounded on space or the urban.

Contingent Conjunctures

As we noted in discussing Stuart Hall's approach to conjuncture, he understood this as somehow tying fragments and elements of social relations to each other in a 'totality' imagined as comprised of so many relations and determinations. This provides opportunities for opening out analysis of any place to many different contexts, comparing with and across these multiple determinations. Gill Hart's close ethnographic sensibilities as well as her theoretical emphasis on a broad dialectical analysis and an open sense of totality see her interpretation of 'conjuncture' focus on these multiple determinations and on the unpredictable outcomes of specific (located) social formations. As we saw in Chapter 6, her comparative analyses build from a nuanced theorisation of place and draw attention to the formation (rather than simply hybridisation) of wider social processes in particular contexts. Places are not only sites of interconnection of different trajectories and processes (which she takes from Massey), but also produced through practice and political mobilisation, working across many different aspects of the social formation in that place. Thus, for her, 'the focus of relational comparison is on how key processes are constituted in relation to one another through power-laden practices in the multiple, interconnected arenas of everyday life; and that "clarifying these connections and mutual processes of constitution – as well as slippages, openings, and contradictions – helps to generate new understandings of the possibilities for social change"' (Hart 2018, pp. 4–5).

Hart's (2018) perspective develops out of an 'open, non-teleological conception of dialectics' (p. 19), together with a strongly political and spatialised sense of the conjunctural, inspired by Gramsci. She invites us to think across contexts from specific elements of a social formation – 'fragments of space'. Inspired by Lefebvre (1991, p. 88) she suggests that 'the hyper-complexity of social space "means that each fragment of space subject to analysis masks not just one social relationship but a host of them that analysis can potentially disclose". Analyzing different fragments in relation to one another through their specificities as well as their interconnections provides powerful additional leverage – especially when linked to a broader conjunctural analysis' (Hart 2018, p. 20).

The possibility to start with any element or relation of a contingent socio-spatial formation radically expands the scope for composing generative comparisons. These can be quite open, to reflect one case on another, to understand more broadly, across some variety, the specific nature and effectivity of certain processes or embedded practices, or to explore the entanglement of processes and practices across cases. Hart turns to explain her evolving interest in comparing two places (in this case, countries) through a somewhat fortuitous analytical, as opposed to empirical, opening. In the quote here she explains how she arrived at the possibility of pursuing a productive comparison between the South African and Indian contexts, inspired within the creative and lively intellectual environment at the University of the Witwatersrand where she is now located some of the time:

> My interest in thinking about the intertwining of intensifying nationalisms and neoliberal forms of capitalism in South Africa in relation to those in India was sparked by Sumit Sarkar's 'Inclusive Democracy and its Enemies' (2006), originally delivered as a lecture in Johannesburg. As I delved more deeply into Indian analyses and debates, I came to see how they were the products of interconnected spatio-historical processes that bore remarkable parallels and convergences – as well as divergences – with those in South Africa. These simultaneously conceptual and empirical provocations gave me new angles of understanding and, as mentioned earlier, several of the major arguments in my book Rethinking the South African Crisis (2014), developed in conversation (both explicit and implicit) with these Indian engagements.
>
> (Hart 2018, p. 16)

An intellectual spark, then, alerted her to 'convergences – as well as divergences' between the two cases. Certainly there do exist numerous precise historical interconnections across India and South Africa; such as, large population movements, notably indentured labour flows to the East Coast of South Africa from South India; to a small extent shared anti-colonial nationalist struggles; some intellectual parallels, not often acknowledged, especially in terms of 'subaltern' studies in India and the social history movement in South Africa; and a few high profile political links, like Mahatma Gandhi who is much celebrated for his short stay in South Africa. However, what Hart notices here, in the midst of these prolific interconnections which provide some broad scope for thinking the two contexts together, is the potential for a resonance with Indian academic analysis and the questions that drive wider historical and political studies. This entices her to delve more deeply, to look to generate a comparative perspective across the entwining of neoliberalism and nationalism in both contexts. She introduces a concept she feels might be useful to use and work with across the two contexts – passive revolution. This seems like a comparative experiment that will be great to think with. It highlights the sometimes speculative 'spark' of connection which drives many comparative experiments. And it informed a wider "global conjunctural" analysis considering resonant and divergent ways in which exclusionary nationalisms and rightwing populism have risen to prominence in a number of contexts in recent decades (Hart, 2020). Her conjunctural analysis identifies the close inter-relations at a global scale amongst long histories of racist and colonial orders, and contemporary neoliberal forms of capitalism, to explain the different temporalities and forms of populist nationalisms in India, the US and South Africa. Here we see how a comparative analysis can evolve over time, as a thick practice, replete with serendipity, rather than a one-off research design, to build conceptual insight from and across conjunctures.

The situated and culturally inflected analyses which thinkers like Hall took from Althusser's concept of overdetermination (his relatively anti-humanist analyses notwithstanding), has been strengthened by more recent analyses which re-read Althusser's analysis of 'structure' and conjuncture in a more contingent way. In principle a conjunctural approach focusses on the interactions amongst different processes (or more properly, 'levels' of analysis i.e. political, economic, ideological) to identify some as conjuncturally less or more important than others (the Althusserian inheritance) and also to see the potential for transformation in wider processes resulting from their co-constitution in the midst of historical and contextual entanglements (a Gramscian political inspiration). Ideas of contingency and overdetermination inspired some important earlier debates in urban studies – such as regulation theory's interest in modes of production, regimes of accumulation and relatively autonomous social structures of Accumulation (Benko and Lipietz 1998; Painter and Goodwin 1995), or questions about the relationship between class-based contradictions and their articulation with other political subjectivities (Hart 2008).

Attention to historical contingency is a feature of much of Althusser's writing but was strengthened in his final works, notably his 2006 [1978–1987] *Philosophy of the Encounter* (Sotiris 2014). Montag (1998) notes, for example, that his analysis of the 'concrete expressions' of general contradictions articulated a growing sense of the emergent nature of structure: 'There are only exceptions, only singular cases each of which must be explained without reference to the universal principle that would supply the generality into which their specificity might be resolved' (p. 69). Montag observes previous shifts in Althusser's position (including edits to later editions of *Reading Capital*) consistent with a strengthening of a view of 'structure' as emergent from, although not exhausted by, its effects and constituent elements. A 'structure present only in its effects … becomes the principle of the diverse – that is, the principle that makes the diverse intelligible without reduction or unification' (p. 72). Here the diverse refers to the manifold, as we saw in Deleuze – the fullness of what is.

Althusser's programme of a *Philosophy for Marxism* evolved into an account of an 'aleatory' materialism – a random, or contingent materialism. A radical conjuncturalism, then, in which 'structure' or generality is entirely contingent and emergent informs attempts to 'devise new concepts, new theoretical vocabularies, new theoretical metaphors' (Sotiris 2014, p. 48). This is also a dynamic vision of Marxism as a theoretical and political project which must evolve historically and conjuncturally – a point Stuart Hall was eager to make, and which inspired many *post*-Marxists who remain politically and analytically tethered to a post-*Marxism*, although inspired to attend to contingency and multiplicity. Sotiris (2014) summarises Althusser's evolving analysis, as

> an unfinished project, one of the most fruitful confrontations with the question of the complex and necessarily contradictory relation between structural and conjunctural determinations. In the Althusserian endeavour, historical materialism emerges as a radically new way to think social reality, without resorting to law-like certainties, but as an open process, full of conflicting tendencies, with only relatively and provisionally stable points of reference, a process full of singular relations, collective non-subjects, antagonistic contradictions, of which we form part and which determine the ability to see events erupt, either as subtle changes or as abrupt ruptures, but also explain them in the necessity of their contingency, the contingency of their necessity and even the contingency of their contingency. In this view we can find the theoretical potential and dynamics of historical materialism, but also the contradictions that necessarily traverse it as open questions and theoretical tensions that sometimes seem to remain unresolved.
> (Sotiris 2014, p. 47)

Trying to account for the aleatory (or contingent) in Marxism was a persistent concern of Althusser's work. In his revisions of Reading Capital (and in conversation with Deleuze) he concluded against an 'absent' structure or depth explanation (Montag 1998), and for social formations to seen as 'singularities' – the 'specific', he could conclude, is 'universal' (Althusser 2006; Sotiris 2014). Here is an insistence that structures, contradictions and determinations can only ever exist as contingent historical formations:

> This overdetermination is inevitable and thinkable as soon as the real existence of the forms of the superstructure and of the national and international conjuncture has been recognized – an existence largely specific and autonomous, and therefore irreducible to a pure phenomenon. We must carry this through to its conclusion and say that this overdetermination does not just refer to apparently unique and aberrant historical situations (Germany, for example), but is universal; the economic dialectic is never active in the pure state; in History, these instances, the superstructures, etc. – are never seen to step respectfully

aside when their work is done or, when the Time comes, as his pure phenomena, to scatter before His Majesty the Economy as he strides along the royal road of the Dialectic. From the first moment to the last, the lonely hour of the 'last instance' never comes.

(Althusser 2005, p. 113)

It is perhaps in the 'under-determination' of contingent outcomes (Sotiris 2014, p. 30) – the necessity of contingency – that we find some ideas for the possibility of a turn to theorising the urban. Partly at stake here, then, are some issues we have already discussed in this book: in Chapter 6, the relationship between wider processes and their always hybridised or contingent form; and in Chapter 7, the relationship between concepts and the concrete (for example, abstractions such as 'contradictions' and relations, while identified theoretically, only exist as contingent and historical): 'the idea of a "pure and simple" non-overdetermined contradiction is, as Engels said of the economist turn of phrase "meaningless, abstract, senseless"' (Althusser 2005, p. 113).

Any Caveats?

Once again, though, locating 'the urban' analytically in contingency is not straightforward. On the one hand, given the generality of the contingent in shaping all aspects of social life, analyses of the urban ought not to be seen as any exception. But, on the other, 'contingency' implies some kind of relationship to general or wider processes (or universal analyses, say of contradictions) and suggests that the urban is made up (contingently) of these processes. Lefebvre's comment at the beginning of this chapter is pertinent here – the urban is not just a (passive) outcome of wider processes. We noted in Chapter 6 how comparative analysis of specific urban outcomes might revise understandings of wider social processes and a contingent conjuncturalism makes a strong contribution to how that might be done. But this still leaves as a void any account of the urban as such.

Conjunctural analysis comes with a complex concern for the lines of determination amongst different intersecting or co-constituting processes or co-existing levels, constituting some kind of 'whole' or totality. It matters, though, how different processes are to be considered alongside each other within a contingent 'context' or conjuncture. Strathern, following Haraway (1987), notes that, with a cyborg perspective, 'the relationships for forming totalities from parts are questioned' (2005, p. 37). Also, as discussed in Chapter 7, the search for an 'adequate' concept, composed of multiple determinations and relations able to capture the fullness of a concrete totality, is perhaps misguided (Hart 2018, p. 20). Differences, divergent processes, provisional suturings (de Boeck and Baloji 2016) and partial connections (Strathern 2005 [1991]) lead away from such an achievement. More importantly, the idea of (partial) or open totalities captures a key feature of the urban or place. To follow Massey rather than Hall, this can be seen as being more about juxtaposition than about 'necessary' inter-relationships. A looser form of a 'totality' is arguably a better fit with the nature of the urban, in which the delineation of cases, meaning, practice and outcomes are unpredictable, and relations and wider processes are emergent, indeterminate and changing as well as at times characterised by disconnection and divergence. An 'open' totality provides scope for the 'excess' to any analysis of rich social (and urban) worlds to 'generate new questions that make the old ones uninteresting. Indeed, we may not even bother to fill in the answers, the new questions seem so much more enticing' (Strathern 2005, p. xxii). This is especially relevant to thinking (with) the urban, where its spatial form (of assemblage, juxtaposition, mediation) means that such an excess (or inexhaustibility) of the urban world is inevitable.

An important question would be, then, what kinds of comparative practices might emerge on the basis of the urban, as a spatial form? Not as part of variegated territorialisations of social processes, or scalar conjunctures of intersecting processes and wider social formations – but as a three-dimensional and lived spatiality. In the next section we explore Lefebvre's imagination of the urban as an emergent totality in which 'relations and determinations' are embedded in/emergent from the urban itself, and from social and spatial praxis.

Conceptualising from Specificity

Complex, open totalities, can be seen as emerging and changing historically, thus 'totalizing' in the sense of making the social world (becoming) rather than completed. Goonewardena (2018) argues that to think with 'totality' has potential for taking forward conversations across different critical and political starting points:

> For the recognition that the concept of totality in . . . Marxist, anti-colonial and socialist-feminist strands of critical theory includes by definition dialectical notions of contradiction, difference, mediation, and articulation is most helpful to theorize how capitalism, patriarchy, and colonialism co-determine the complex whole of society—which it is the task of revolutionary politics to interpret and change.
>
> (Goonewardena 2018, p. 467)

This analysis aligns with the conventional approach to thinking totality, discussed in the previous section, in which different 'levels' of analysis or a range of different social processes are articulated in a contingent but determinable way.

He outlines an idea of 'totality' which he ascribes to Lefebvre, who proposes an alternative set of 'levels' to those associated with Althusser – usually political, economic and ideological. Rather, Lefebvre invents cross-scalar 'levels' of the Global, Urban (as a space of Mediation of the other two) and Private, each understood as open totalities, each with complex spatialities, and articulated to produce a totality, the social world (Schmid, 2022). This draws on one aspect of how Lefebvre considered the urban might be understood, as mediation (Schmid 2005). But, from the perspective of theorising the urban more substantially, it is the quite different approach to theorising 'totality' which Lefebvre developed over many decades that offers a way to start with the urban, as opposed to treating the urban as just any other kind of contingent social outcome.

More generally, Lefebvre criticised the concept of totality for its ability to frame a desire for 'power', asking 'How can we conceive of totality if we do not share its point of view? Once it becomes dominant, the most general category tends to absorb particularities and specificities, and therefore to neglect differences and types' (2014, p. 479). He was also insistent that totality no longer remained a distinctly Marxist category as it had been adopted by many non-Marxist analysts (writing in 1961). He indicates quite forcefully that 'we are abandoning the category of totality. At the same time we are adopting it again, in a dynamic sense' (2014, p. 481). He writes in *The Urban Revolution* (2003), published in 1970 'What about totality? Dialectically speaking, it is present, here and now. It is absent as well' – meaning it is both a lived immediacy but also only ever a horizon of action/interpretation (p. 144). This approach had been set already in his *Dialectical Materialism*, published in 1940. The lived immediacy for Lefebvre is the fullness of social life and, as with the human subject ('total man'), indicates a totality, but in concrete terms. As a horizon of action/interpretation, Lefebvre mobilised a distinctive way to open up understanding of the urban as 'concrete totality' (2003, p. 133). That is, rather than an analytical totality of a 'concrete-in-thought' made of multiple relations and determinations seeking to approximate the concrete, the 'totality' only ever exists as a historical concrete: 'the given content is always a concrete totality' (Lefebvre 2009, p. 75).

This kind of 'totality' – the totality of all there is in a concrete situation – comes into conceptualisation as always partial, open and revisable, only ever knowable in an incomplete way. On the one hand, 'reality thus overflows the mind' (p. 97); and on the other, historically, 'an open totality, (is) perpetually in the process of being transcended' (p.99). Rather than approaching the concrete from the abstract (Hart 2018), the concrete comes into view (only ever partially) from concrete (real-world) abstractions embedded in practice (and Lefebvre felt that there would be many of these, emergent, historical, real abstractions). In a dialectical analysis, contradictions unfold to expose (but never completely) the fullness of a concrete situation. But the fullness of human experience and the inexhaustible content of social life (or space) are always in tension with concrete abstractions, instigating the dynamism of any conceptualisation. This is a dialectical materialism which prioritises the process of 'becoming', which looks for dynamism and movement, and where analysis is driven by the contradictions between concrete abstractions and the fullness of experience, indicated by ideas of 'total man' or a 'total content' (Schmid 2022).

Acknowledging the 'will for totality' as a feature of critical practice eager to engage across the fullness of social life (the political motivations we identified in Hart, Hall, Grossberg and Peck), Lefebvre (2014) suggested conceiving of 'totalization' 'not ontologically, but strategically i.e. programmatically'. He asked in terms of knowledge production, 'How do we avoid being trapped in dilemmas? Where do we start from, from the whole or from the parts? From the general or from particularities?' (p. 482). He opened up an analytical – dialectical and materialist – route to appreciating the totality of, for example, everyday life. He started with what he called then, a 'total phenomenon' (a 'formant'), determined from praxis, 'which would reveal a totality without granting it any theoretical or practical power, without allowing it to be defined and controlled' (p. 482). Whatever the totality might be, for him it would need to be seen as open, to both analytical interpretation and historical practice. The starting points for analysis, or formants, were conceived as dialectically inter-related terms (usually three so they conformed to his distinctive dialectical imagination), emergent in praxis, but without any ontological claims to define the essence or substance of the 'concrete totality' they were implicated in. His thinking here was inspired by the Marxist starting points of the commodity form, or money as a concrete abstraction, in which different dimensions of these formed a dialectical analytical unity around the fullness of the phenomenon in tension with the abstracted form under capitalism. Thus, commodity as use value, exchange value and fully historical physical object. And, perhaps most vividly, the tensions between labour power, the act of labouring, and the full lives of the individuals labouring; or in property as delimited territory, traded commodity and a full, replete space of conception, experience and inhabitation (Stanek 2008; Schmid 2022). In his view, there were many forms of concrete abstractions abbreviating social life, generating contradictions (e.g. between individualism, individualisation and the individual) and these formed starting points for dialectical analyses that grappled with inexhaustibility across a number of different terrains (Lefebvre 2009, p. 155).

Lefebvre's understanding of totality rested on his unique formulation of dialectical reasoning (Schmid 2008). The formants which he portrays as mutually implicated in each other describe a 'partial or open totality, so nothing can be determined in isolation' (p. 483). Starting from praxis, he reaches, then, for aspects of a total human phenomenon – of space, or everyday life, of the urban – which insofar as they are driving its 'Becoming', will reveal this emergent, open and concrete totality. The 'totality' comes into (partial) view through the dialectical, conflictual and dynamic interaction across 'triplicities' (p. 486). For example, of need, labour, pleasure (as mutually interacting and conditioning starting points to frame the totality of everyday life); of perceived, conceived and lived [aspects of] space (Schmid, 2022); and, in Schmid's (2005) formulation, of difference, centrality and mediation in relation to the urban. The urban, then, comes into view as an open totality, fully open to history, practice and interpretation across the dynamic nature of space, and the intertwined terms of centrality-difference-mediation:

> It [the urban] is form itself, as generator of a virtual object, the urban, the encounter and assembly of all objects and subjects, existing or possible, that must be explored.
> (Lefebvre 2003 [1974], p. 122)

This analysis scopes an opening to understanding aspects of the dynamics and contradictions of urbanisation and urban life, in the same (limited) way as the contradictory dimensions of the commodity, and especially labour as both commodity and lived lives initiated a wide-ranging analysis of a partial totality, the economy (which, as Lefebvre observes, is not the whole of social life). And, whatever the 'concrete totality' of the urban might be in Lefebvre's terms, it is fundamentally unknowable – so there is no 'adequacy' of concepts to approach a complete account of this, no accumulation of a range of social processes to serve as lenses through which we might exhaust the reality, building from our concepts to the fullness of a concrete-in-thought. 'But then, this makes any conceptualisation of the urban uncertain, empirically determined (also in "praxis"), historically located, changing, diverse (specific) – and therefore contestable.' In this account any given urban outcome can only ever be a specificity – there is no 'universal' urban to propose, no full or adequate account to be given of a social formation, no analytical 'totality' ('concrete-in-thought') to construct out of abstract relations and determinations. The concrete totality itself articulates these relations (Lefebvre 2003, p. 171) and concepts emerge (and find their limits) in praxis, beginning with an active immersion in the concrete.

This opens up a potentially fertile empirical-theoretical agenda. It may well be time to query his starting points for the dialectical contradictions he drew out ('formants'). Perhaps there would be alternative ways to think the urban, differently, from its rich and varied totality. Indeed, he makes such an invitation: 'tertiary or *triadic* analysis grasps becoming (or at least comes nearer to it than the rest) which in no way rules out the possibility of further extensions, multidimensional analysis or the introduction of new parameters' (in Elden et al. 2017, p. 73). His reasons for formulating the partial totalities or formants in the way he did are deeply enmeshed in debates within European Marxism (Jay 1984 offers a valuable overview), and occasional engagements beyond (Kipfer and Goonewardena 2013; Schmid 2008). Other starting points might be sought for unfolding the dynamic becoming of different cities, in different contexts, inspired by alternative conceptual repertoires (see Bhan 2019, for example).

The three co-ordinates which we might take from Lefebvre's imagination of a 'concrete totality' are:

- Rather than seeing the urban as a contingent outcome of wider social processes, we could be encouraged to hone in on distinctive elements of the dynamic becoming of the urban as such.
- To think (from) the urban it is necessary to think of the urban as a space.
- Whatever the urban is, it is an open horizon, a concrete fullness which will never be approximated in thought.

Lefebvrian analysis invites us to see the urban as specific. Not simply as unique places, amenable only to description, but specificity as an outcome of the way in which the urban is produced (Schmid 2015, p. 288); specificity results from considering the urban as a spatial formation. This reinforces the need for a distinctive 'urban' starting point for analysis without necessarily resorting to the variegation of pre-ordained social processes, scales or conjunctural determinations by extensive social formations as a stand-in for thinking the urban. This provides rich potential for thinking across a range of urban outcomes, to explore conceptual resources emergent across different urban contexts and to propose innovative conceptualisations.

Having identified the Lefebvrian 'formants' of the urban as centrality, difference and mediation, Schmid (2015) makes a more general case for approaching the urban as specific. While there might be wider circuits (repeated formulae, circulating rules and norms, utopian visions of the ideal city, or investments driven by financialised circuits) and extensive social formations at play in shaping the urban, he insists that 'all these ultimately break down, in the current of generic operations, into specific situations and configurations' (p. 289). With a broad view of urbanisation as both the 'comprehensive transformation of a certain territory' (p. 290) and 'a comprehensive transformation of society', he follows Lefebvre in seeing this as a 'total phenomenon' (p. 289). But why should this very general and relatively indeterminate process result in specific *urban* outcomes? This has a lot to do with the spatial form of the urban, including spatial fixity: 'previous urbanisation traces mean that urbanization is never like footprints in the sand, the direct expression of a general, social development. The land, the territory is never empty or primal; it is always already occupied, in one way or another; it bears the marks of earlier processes and is embedded in wider contexts and dispositives' (p. 290). Thus, 'every urban area has its own features and follows a particular path of development' (p. 290). The spatial organisation of the urban is a key element of specificity: each urban context will have different spatial dynamics shaping urbanisation. The specificity of urban contexts rests additionally on the ways in which particular (social) differences are negotiated in each place, generating 'a multiplicity of possibilities and potentials' (p. 290). Finally, Schmid indicates that distinctive regulatory formations evolve in urban territories. In sum, then:

> The confrontation of general tendencies with local conditions leads to the formation of the most diverse urban situations. And, in the process, it becomes clear that the urban is always both geographically and historically specific. The urban is not a universal category; it is a specific category that is always dependent on concrete conditions and historical developments.
>
> (Schmid 2015, p. 305)

This is not about treating each place as simply a 'unique' composition of wider processes. Rather, Schmid (2015) states that his 'focus is on embedding the question of specificity in the wider context and on exploring its constitutive meaning for urbanization; we want to identify how specificity is produced and reproduced, what role it plays in the production of urban spaces, and how it influences the planetary trajectory of urbanization' (p. 288). This goes along with a theorisation of the urban as a concrete totality which provides the justification for exploring distinctively urban dynamics. On this basis, different 'urbanisation processes' can be identified. These are associated with the production of space, as well as being linked to 'more general social processes', but 'follow a logic of their own and accordingly display a different kind of dynamic' (Schmid 2014, p. 211).

As proposed by Schmid et al.[1] (2018) thick socio-spatial configurations of 'urbanisation processes' might be identified as shaping specific urban outcomes in one context, but might also be relevant to explaining other urban situations, especially given the emergence of shared spatial configurations, as well as wider tendencies and influences on urban life. Some such urbanisation processes have been analytically dominant in the field – and we look at gentrification in the next chapter. Often, though, conceptualisation of urbanisation processes emerges on the basis of one case or a restricted category of cities. These authors argue that there is value in identifying and building concepts of urbanisation processes through an experimental form of comparativism, grounded in deep empirical research, developing insights across different urban territorial outcomes. Leveraging the open totality which a Levebrian analysis postulates, and alert to the post-colonial critique of a narrow base for urban theorising, this team of researchers drew on empirical research in eight urban contexts. Their comparisons were developed on the understanding that 'Urbanisation is always a concrete process shaped by specific local conditions, structures, and constellations' (p. 71). Based on their shared engagements with Lefebvre, and an understanding of the complex spatialities of contemporary urbanisation, they identified a range of urbanisation processes which were present in some (not all) of their case study contexts. These processes are styled as dynamic and changing:

> Urbanisation processes do not simply unfold within fixed or stable urban 'containers', but actively produce, unsettle and rework urban territories, and thus constantly engender new urban configurations.
> (Schmid et al. 2018, p. 23)

Their project identified a number of candidate processes emergent across a diversity of urban contexts. One they call plotting urbanism, when urbanisation proceeds plot by plot, iconically evident in African contexts such as Lagos (see also Huchzermeyer 2011). Another, drawing on South American conceptualisation, they name as 'popular urbanisation', when communal and collective resources are mobilised in contexts of auto-construction (see also Caldeira 2016). And another is defined as 'bypass urbanism' as the configurations of dispersed urban settlements comprising large scale urban developments, private sector investment and shaped by a 'scramble for infrastructure' (Kanai and Schindler 2019) drawing urbanisation to abandon, or bypass, old centralities with decaying infrastructure and highly informalised networks (see also Shatkin 2008).

Diversity subsequently becomes the idiom in which these processes might be identified as emergent across different urban situations. Certain consistent characteristics or shared features, as well as variations across contexts support and elaborate insights into different urbanisation processes, bringing the rich distinctiveness of specific urban contexts into wider conversation and analysis.

Probing further, these comparative tactics which arise on the grounds of specificity must also attend to other potentialities of the urban. That similar urbanisation processes might be identified in different contexts is of course also down to the prolific circulations of ideas, practices and investments which produce an often untraceable connectivity amongst familiar-looking urban outcomes. And on the other hand, similar outcomes – a sprawling and haphazard periphery, assembling a great diversity of functions – might result from quite different dynamics. The piecemeal development of peripheral land in traditional ownership (Gough and Yankson 2000; Lambert 2021; Mercer 2017; Sawyer 2014); the fragmented developments of a post-hacienda landscape (Varley and Salazar 2021); or the intensification of land use in collectively owned 'rural villages' in China might yield a shared urbanisation process – such as 'plotting', a plot-by-plot development which characterises the format of urban expansion in much of the world:

> Plotting offers a pragmatic and viable solution to the concrete problem of urban development in specific contexts, where affordable housing is missing, access to land is restricted, and territorial regulations are unclear, ambivalent and/or contested. Even if *highly specific circumstances* and factors have led to plotting in our case studies, the cumulative effects of the individual plot-by-plot strategy have demonstrated astonishing transformative capacities in relatively short periods of time: plotting was the main urbanisation process at a given time in each of the cities we analysed, and it allowed the rapid and massive urban growth in a crucial moment of urban development.
> (Karaman et al. 2020, p. 1144; emphasis added)

Also at work in framing these particular examples of urbanisation processes are theoretical 'formants' of the urban, drawn from Lefebvre's analysis, notably, ideas of 'difference' and 'centrality'.

The conceptualisation of 'urbanisation processes' is modest – they were identified in only a few selected cases, are not imagined to apply everywhere, and, for Karaman et al. (2020) they were already varied across the cases in which they were identified. They note that, 'As a result of our comparative analysis we finally arrived at "plotting urbanism" as a concept that we think might enrich the vocabulary of urbanisation. We believe this concept could be fruitfully applied to other places and could thus help to conceptualise hitherto unrecognised urbanisation processes.' (p. 1144). The practice of building comparisons across specificity, to identify shared urbanisation processes, opens to the possibility of theorising the urban from anywhere – including from the dynamic peripheries of urbanisation across most of the world (Ghertner 2015b). Some conceptualisations of urbanisation processes might remain as limited generalisations attached to specific contexts. But emergent concepts might also inspire insights which point to similar dimensions of urbanisation in many different contexts – new terms might be launched into much wider conversations about the urban – we consider this second possibility in Chapter 9, as 'mobile concepts'.

Initiating insights on the basis of seeing the urban as specificity does not need to be mediated by Lefebvre, of course. McFarlane and his co-authors have also emphasised the value of conceptualising urbanisation processes from specificity. McFarlane et al. (2014), explore 'informal sanitation processes' as part of a complex and changing 'everyday'. Their study considered two different settlements within the city of Mumbai, Rafinagar and Khotwadi, in order to more fully explore 'spatial variation' in the nature of sanitation, and also to be alert to its networked nature (p. 1007). They comment on how having two cases expanded their insights:

> We could not have made the case for the four [sanitation] strategies we discussed here without conducting comparative work. A focus on Khotwadi alone would have foregrounded patronage and political parties, whereas a focus on Rafinagar alone would have emphasized self-managed processes. It is not that elements of these processes do not exist in the other neighborhood—they do—but that the key features of how sanitation is produced and contested on a day-to-day basis are significantly different in both sites. This allows us to present a broader canvas of sanitation poverty than one case alone would have done, and it has demonstrated the importance of a geographical approach that foregrounds social and spatial variation. The purpose of comparison here is explicitly to seek out apples and oranges as an analytical tool, to use difference as a route to a more plural understanding of a key dimension of urban poverty and marginalization.
>
> (McFarlane et al. 2014, p. 1008).

'Informal sanitation processes' is a conceptualisation which emerges close to the empirical domain and lived experiences of urban life, and is built up from different cases and diverse experiences. Here, an intra-city comparison yields a valuable set of insights, able to inform understanding and action in relation to urbanisation processes which are important in many poorer (southern) urban contexts – in this case, sanitation. In this way a conceptualisation might emerge bottom-up, from engagement across different cases, with only restricted relevance. Or it might potentially travel widely if others find these insights helpful, perhaps on the basis of identifying shared features with the originating cases.

Thinking across Diversity

Understanding the urban as 'a specific category that is always dependent on concrete conditions and historical developments' (Schmid 2015, p. 305) inspires a comparative practice which brings into view the diversity of urbanisation processes and urban outcomes. Charles Tilly notes that variation finding, attention to detailed analysis of diversity across different cases, 'promises to help us make sense of social structures and processes that never recur in the same form, yet express common principles of causality' (Tilly, p. 143). Certain shared features of urban processes, say, 'urban land nexus' or 'agglomeration economies' (Scott and Storper 2015), are a function of the spatial form of urbanisation. We might follow Tilly, then, in exploring 'causal mechanisms that operate in an enormous variety of times, places, and social settings' (1998, p. 39). Across the urban world the causal mechanisms and urban processes at work in allocating land uses are much more diverse than the capitalist land markets which Storper and Scott (2015) indicate, though. Urban land nexus must stretch to include attention to diverse forms of governmental reason, informality and violence, for example.

Thinking with diversity moves us definitively away from designing comparisons in the tracks of interconnected processes or relations, or with the dimensions of 'conjunctures'. Certainly, any urban processes are likely closely entwined with many changing and extensive, circulating forms of investment, design, or governance practices. But land use management and planning are key sites in which strong path dependencies of regulation emerge and shape the spatial form and dynamism of cities; they are also the grounds of specific and distinctive urban outcomes. Starting with issues and topics which affect or are present in a wide range of cities but are not approached as repeated instances or parts of putative wholes[2] could ground interesting comparative openings across diverse and even divergent urban contexts.

Urban development politics brings together two important loci of urban specificity and diversity I have just mentioned – land use, and territorial regulation. These are shared features of urban areas which vary considerably across different contexts. Perhaps for this reason, this topic has also been the focus of a long tradition of urban comparativism – as Chapter 3 discussed. There we observed that even though urban scholars had sought out relatively similar urban contexts to compare, they in fact developed their insights based on the variety reflected across their cases. We speculated as to whether it would be possible to deliberately seek out cases which bring into view a wide variety of the processes we might be interested in understanding better to deepen and enhance our thinking and analysis? In this way it would also be possible to build explanations of specific outcomes in relation to a more diverse array of urban experiences (see for example, Nijman 2007b). Theorisation of the politics of urban development might then be able to bring into the analytical frame a wider cast of actors and diversity of processes that are shaping urban politics across different urban contexts. Not only would this mean that urban theory might be more relevant to more places, but it might be possible to think anew about familiar cases as we look from situations (perhaps previously seen as exceptional) back to iconic or more well-known (to some …) cases.

Continuing in the vein of the examples we explored in Chapter 3, let's say we are interested in institutional and political responses to the challenges of urban development (Clarke 1995; Kantor et al. 1997). How might comparative tactics on generative grounds be used to extend understandings of this? The observation which emerged in Chapter 3 was that conventional comparisons unfolded towards thinking across the variety of a shared feature which came into view during the comparison. The specified grounds for comparison which had been studiously composed to meet methodological strictures somehow faded into the background. Perhaps, we asked, it would be valid to compose a comparison starting with such shared features in the first place? So, what might be such a feature and how might conceptual innovation emerge from such comparative practice?

One feature of urbanisation which has attracted both scholarly and political interest are large-scale urban developments. 'Mega-urban projects', satellite cities, major transit-oriented development initiatives and 'cities within cities' have drawn attention from urban scholars in many different contexts. Could these be a generative shared feature to start exploring urban development politics, comparatively? There are many cases of large-scale urban developments in which, for example, the role and nature of the state is exposed, or certain configurations of land value extraction emerge. Looking across multiple cases of large-scale development projects, we could perhaps build new understandings of urban politics. These projects lend themselves to a 'diversity' model of comparison. Vast circuits of investment, visions, experts and materials certainly shape large-scale urban developments, and so in some ways they could operate as a terrain of 'genetic' comparative tactics. But in practice it is difficult to find a priori connections amongst different developments, for example, a single firm operating across different settings; or a range of examples of engagement with a certain 'model'. In the collaborative project[3] I was involved in, which compared large-scale developments in Shanghai, London and Johannesburg, the actual connections amongst our cases were very weak or not apparent (even though we looked for them specifically). But we found significant potential to ground a comparison of different large-scale developments on the basis of their shared features.

Our justification for comparing these three cases from quite different contexts (China, South Africa, UK) rested on the shared characteristics of large-scale developments. These kinds of developments bring forward significant institutional and financial challenges, associated with the multi-jurisdictional and extended temporal nature of large-scale urban development projects. In each case, undertaking the planned development has required marshalling diverse existing sources of income as well as securing exceptional financial investment and managing the phasing of development to maximise different income streams. It has also required co-ordinating a multiplicity of institutional actors and finding ways to sustain development in the face of changing political, policy and economic conditions. In all three cases, the strategic value of the development to wider political and planning agendas is evident, but so are the challenges of innovation and co-ordination involved in realising them. Consequently, and as is characteristic of large-scale, or mega-urban, developments (Flyvberg 2014; Gualini and Majoor 2007), none of the three developments has come to fruition as initially expected. However, significant progress has been made in each, and we were able to document and observe the detailed institutional and financial arrangements associated with initiating and advancing each development.

Specifically, one aspect of the developments that came into view were the different business models which enable large-scale urban developments to come to fruition (see Robinson et al. 2020). Taking a view from three rich and complex – specific – urban contexts, we were able to move beyond a focus on wider, globalised processes (neoliberalisation, financialisation) or extensive social formations to attend to the diverse mechanisms and sources of financing which support large-scale urban developments. These business models are strongly shaped by specific territorialised regulatory formations (Allen and Cochrane 2007; Schmid 2015), including historically embedded ways of taxing urban activities, the distinctive forms of land value capture in each context, and the range of financial instruments available to actors. In all three of our cases the opening for development was crafted through complex and path dependent state strategies, reflective of extant institutional forms and particular territorial configurations of political interests. All three projects depend (at least in the long term) on realising financial value through the development and directing this in some way to covering the costs of the development. In all three projects we identify that assembling the finances for large-scale, cross-jurisdictional and long-term projects has required innovations in the institutional architecture and the political room to manoeuvre to build a (usually transcalar) constituency in support of the development and to establish the basis on which it is made possible.

We also found inspiration in the comparison to learn more about each case through the others. Notably, we changed our analysis of the London case by thinking with the experiences of urban politics we identified from the Chinese context. Here state agency is the overriding feature of urban development, and analyses of the complexity and territoriality of state interests and the ways in which urbanisation has shaped these interests predominate (Hsing 2010; Shatkin 2017; Shen et al. 2020b; Wu 2003; Wu and Phelps 2011). We drew on these 'as theoretical insights' to inform our analyses of London. Here state interests and power are playing a significant role in remaking that city, but the local analysis has focussed on the overpowering extractive interests of global developers in shaping urban development. Little insight was on offer to think about the role of the state. We were able to think London from elsewhere – learning from analyses of Asian politics (Robinson and Attuyer 2021).

The recent work of Gavin Shatkin (2016, 2017) establishes a strong basis for turning to Asian insights on urban politics. His comparative analysis of three large-scale developments in Jakarta (Indonesia), Chongqing (China) and Delhi (India) convenes a range of forms of state and varieties of modes and territories of governing within an explanatory analysis which starts with the issues so prominent in many 'southern' and 'Asian' contexts, and yet absent from much of the theoretical repertoires of urban politics. Thus he explored: strong or peremptory state intervention; state control over land or state willingness to displace communities from land entitlements; and a range of both authoritarian and informal states. Far too often, accounts of urban development in such contexts are treated merely as case studies with features distinctive to their contexts which fit poorly with the existing conceptual categories, and which have had little capacity to penetrate wider urban theorising (Wu 2020). However, Shatkin demonstrates how these cases can be treated as starting points for new analyses, appropriate to contemporary global urbanisation. This encompass 'state capitalism', the land grabs characteristic of peremptory states, as well as the often exuberant and informalised political contestation associated with democratic but poorly capacitated states.

An important aspect of taking the shared feature of large-scale developments as a starting point for comparative analysis is that they significantly help to decentre 'northern' theoretical perspectives on urban development politics, potentially helping to reach escape velocity from the theoretical perspectives which have hegemonised US and to some extent European experiences. Here a 'shared feature', the emergent and distinctive formations of political institutions which coalesce in response to the complexities of delivering large-scale urban developments, helps to decentre northern/western analyses. Numerous cutting-edge large-scale developments are found all over the world – and in fact are a much more characteristic feature of urbanisation processes in Asia and prominent in the often analytically sidelined African context. Building comparisons with such a shared feature therefore offers the realistic opportunity of starting to build theoretical insights from the Asian context (Robinson et al. 2020; Wu 2020), and to navigate conversations in new directions (e.g. South–South; Africa–China). In addition, places like London can become *destinations for theory from elsewhere*, learning from analyses of state interests in land development in Asia, for example. At the same time, in a world where all cities might be thought of as 'ordinary' cities, we might as well learn from London as elsewhere. In our study the London case and the Johannesburg case both drew attention to residents' mobilisation and engagement (beyond narrower ideas of 'participation') in large-scale Chinese developments (Wang 2020; Wang and Wu 2019). Such comparative experiments initiate what will likely be an ongoing conversation about the diverse ways in which urban politics is configured.

Conclusion

I have taken the time to offer a detailed worked example here from my own research, but there have been numerous experiments with composing comparisons on the basis of shared features across urban diversity, and divergence. These lively and proliferating experiments show great potential to stretch urban conceptualisations. In these comparisons, 'context' is the starting point rather than the incidental difference of theorising, and the relevant theoretical register is not predetermined (for example, Boudreau et al. 2016; Fourchard 2021; Kern and Mullings 2013; Nijman 2007b).

Composing comparisons across the variety of urban experiences in relation to certain shared features of urban life reconstructs the conventions of variation-finding methodologies, inventing new grounds for building theoretical insights across diversity. The potential for emergent conceptualisations is evident. Chapter 9 takes this further, to consider more exploratory 'conversations' across diverse and divergent urban situations, and starts to bring into view the potential for comparisons which emerge in relation to the urban seen as distinctive.

Notes

1. The team of authors includes: Christian Schmid, Ozan Karaman, Naomi Hanakata, Pascal Kallenberger, Anne Kockelkorn, Lindsay Sawyer, Monika Streule and Kit (Tammy) Wong.
2. It is worth recalling that tracing connections (as genetic comparative practice) brings different cases into conversation, and may in the process reveal interesting and productive opportunities for (generative) comparative reflection. The resulting comparative insights might have been entirely unpredictable (as in the case of Gill Hart's (2003) study discussed in Chapter 6). But they might also have been a purposive part of the research design – precisely why a particular connection was traced to bring into view diverse or differentiated cases, for example, tracing a connection consisting of investment in property development including both wealthier and poorer cities might be designed to consider whether or

how very different capacities for land use regulation affect outcomes of large-scale urban developments.
3. This research project, with Fulong Wu, Jie Shen, Allan Cochrane, Phil Harrison and Alison Todes as well as Katia Attuyer, Zheng Wang and Romain Dittgen, was funded by an ESRC Urban Transformations grant ES/N006070/1, Governing the Future City: A comparative analysis of governance innovations in large scale urban developments in Shanghai, London, Johannesburg.

CHAPTER 9

Conversations

Method, in the reincarnation that I am proposing, will often be slow and uncertain. A risky and troubling process, it will take time and effort to make realities and hold them steady for a moment against a background of flux and indeterminacy.'

(Law 2004, p. 10)

Comparative questions that appear interesting at a distance, on closer inspection may well fragment into a host of subsidiary (and probably more interesting) questions.

(Strathern 2005 [1991], p. xiii)

Positioned as an open questioning, method and methodology are unhinged from the stasis of noun and thrown into the less predictable work of verb.

(McKittrick 2021, p. 44)

Chapter 8 explored some of the comparative possibilities which emerge depending on how the urban is conceived by researchers: as conjuncture, specificity and diversity. The argument of this chapter is that to expand our capacity to think the urban with elsewhere, openings to comparative experimentation and inventiveness can move beyond the confines of tracing connections, 'relations' or 'conjunctures', or even carefully composing comparisons across 'shared features' of specific urban contexts.

This chapter seeks to further expand the tactics for mobilising an urban comparative imagination. The urban world, in its diversity, inspires researchers to craft experimental conversations across difference. We explore some of these here – creative experiments and sometimes dissident comparative practices have seen researchers place even quite divergent places alongside one another for reflection.

Comparative Urbanism: Tactics for Global Urban Studies, First Edition. Jennifer Robinson.
© 2022 John Wiley & Sons Ltd. Published 2022 by John Wiley & Sons Ltd.

Part of this creative working across and with difference involves researchers setting concepts on the move, in an effort to make sense of urban experiences across the globe. Once generated, mobile concepts which have purchase, or not, in different contexts can be a crucial resource for framing comparative practice. But at times they can crowd out and diminish other insights – power relations matter. Putting concepts on the move across contexts might enhance comparative thinking, then, but comes along with some associated pitfalls and cautions.

As researchers set a concept in train and it is drawn into wider circulation, the power relations of intellectual practice are exposed. Here the example of gentrification will help us think this through. We find resources in the prolific work on 'global gentrification' to bring forward our discussion of the figure of the creative researcher–composer. But we must also consider how inherited concepts as well as locational and institutional privilege reinforce certain kinds of comparative imagination and tactics, but perhaps restrict others. Nonetheless, as a creative comparative practice, mobilising concepts can take place from anywhere – for example, the mobilities of the concept of 'informality' whose journeys begin in the African and South American contexts. We discuss this in Chapter 11, as a process of inventing and 'launching' concepts from anywhere. With this in mind, and as an alternative formulation less beholden to the power relations associated with the originating sites of concepts (too often familiar places and figures), I revisit the idea of 'arriving at' concepts in relation to multiple elsewheres (after a model of thinking about policy mobilities).

For Marilyn Strathern, comparisons both emerge from and construct 'cyborgs' – sometimes ill-fitting juxtapositions of unrelated things which nonetheless 'work' as an entity. This observation warns us that the practice of comparison on generative grounds, seeking to 'unsettle' concepts, is potentially discomforting as well as productive! Certainly, researchers report the challenges of conceiving and carrying out experimental comparisons. Long, dynamic and sometimes tortuous efforts to configure comparability can make insights from bringing cases into conversation hard-won. The chapter starts, then, with some reflections on the 'thick' practice of comparisons (Scheffer and Niewöhner 2010).

Shifting Grounds: Comparison as Practice

Comparisons can take a meandering route. Bringing even just two complex, rich, multidimensional contexts into conversation to generate new analytical insights about both or either, is a long, drawn-out process with many twists and turns. Insofar as phenomena and concepts are emergent in the engagement with contexts, or with a material world, and not given a priori, the process of research design is necessarily stretched throughout the process and practice of enquiry and analysis. Like all research, comparison involves unintended outcomes and unexpected pathways. In working beyond the single case, the objects of comparison and the terms of comparability – the very grounds of the comparison – might shift, or might only come clearly into view through the course of the research. How we write up research and how we train students often doesn't take sufficient account of this fundamental uncertainty introduced by comparison; who has not seen a research focus change significantly between proposal and empirical research, for example? This section explores the implications for comparative practice when identifying the 'grounds' for comparison transgresses the conventional timetables of research; when the shifting grounds and emergent terms of comparison make it a 'thick' and 'slow' process, rather than a methodological convention confined to the moment of 'scientific' research design. The process of identifying the grounds for comparison stretches out in front of such starting points, and the terms of comparison are remade as the practice of research recasts objects, sites – and the researcher herself.

The progress of research defines and recasts the terms of comparison as well as the object of study. Thus, at the same time as providing reasonable grounds for comparison at the start of a research project it is also important to appreciate that these grounds might – almost certainly will – shift in the course of research. Conceptualisation and practice, are, at times at least, the same thing; as a comparison unfolds some measure of shape-shifting is probably inevitable. In fact, here we bring the practice of comparison and the processes of conceptualisation close together. John Law (2004) indicates that method is an intrinsic part of theory building, as it produces the possible object of study.

This is partly because grappling with the potential for emergent insights across difference brings the complexity and inexhaustibility of the urban world fully into view. Seeking to draw a dynamic world in flux, in its fullness, diversity and indefiniteness, into an even temporarily stable narrative is challenging, if not impossible, as it always exceeds our interpretations, escapes our terms and concepts, our practices and imaginations. As a result, the analytical and methodological imperatives of experimental comparative practice slow us down, making of method a slow process, even a 'stop'. John Law writes, 'This is a book about method – and reality – that is also about the stop. *The stop slows us up*. It takes longer to do things. It takes longer to understand, to make sense of things. It dissolves the idea, the hope, the belief, that we can see to the horizon, that we can see long distances. It erodes the idea that by taking in the distance at a glance we can get an overview of a single reality' (Law 2004, p. 10; my emphasis). He sees this as a general condition of the social sciences, in face of the complexity of the world. The practice of comparison highlights this dimension of social analysis.

Classically, comparison invites a research design which attempts to identify in advance shared variables across 'cases' and to use these to assess the relative importance of different processes or phenomena in explaining differentiated outcomes. By contrast, in experimental comparisons, thinking with elsewhere is not constituted through an a priori 'research design', or the fictive presentation of reporting findings in the sliver of time that holds the relatively stabilised insights which (hopefully) flash into perspective at a certain moment in the research process – perhaps even near the end! The 'stop' which Law invokes is not a geometric 'point', but an expansive territory. Comparative practice is often a long, slow, bringing-into-conversation of complex and differentiated situations. All elements of a comparison – the cases, the comparator, the third term, the insights – emerge throughout the research process. Comparison, then, is a practice. Or, as Deville et al. (2016) formulate it, the comparator is 'assembled' across numerous entities and over quite some time, in all phases of the research. This is one reason why comparative practice indexes a strong potential for creative insights, hard won, and not prefigured in method – why each comparison is in its own way an experiment.

One way to take forward an interrogation of the practices of comparative method, then, is to consider what scientists actually do (in an STS framing, perhaps) in the name of comparison. So rather than relying on the quaint scientific narratives which are retold in the interests of securing methodological certainty, or complicity, we might ask how meaning or method is part of the extended 'event' of producing commensurability. How in practice do comparativists authorise the narratives and findings which circulate in the name of that event? We explored this in relation to urban comparativism in Chapters 2 and 3, where we concluded based on actual practice (rather than restrictive conventions about controlling for difference) that urbanists drew insights from across a variety of different cases based on loosely defined, and often emergent, 'shared features' rather than the criteria embedded in their original research design. Reaching into a different idiom of comparative practice, Monika Krause (2016) focusses in on the 'case' as defined within the framework of clinical trials. In these studies, researchers set different groups into a competition to ascertain which 'works', or wins. Comparative method, she suggests, becomes like the 'race track', the conditions which are set in place to be able to draw some analytical conclusions. Clarifying those conditions which make comparative insight possible is an important element of analysis.

This emphasis on the ways in which scientists or observers create the conditions for the 'event' of the comparative experiment, emerges out of the Science and Technology studies tradition. For example, Isabelle Stengers (2011) insists that the achievement of 'rapport', some kind of relation across different entities which supports comparison, is singular, and 'has the character of an event rather than of a methodological enterprise' (pp. 49–50). Staging the 'race' and inventing the 'race-track' in the clinical trial, then, would be exemplary of this. However, she warns that we cannot rush too quickly to dispense with conventions in method, or with what the 'scientist' might consider to be a fair or good practice. As Stengers continues, there might be a desire to ascribe objectivity to 'experiments' which are thought to be produced naturally. For example, social comparativists are often reliant on the emergence in the world of variation which they can think with: experiments prepared by the ubiquity of differentiation in social outcomes. However, Stengers is also stringent in bringing the figure of the scientist back in to the production and use of these events. As she reminds readers, it is the 'possibility of a collective game to bind colleagues' (p. 54), or a common concern, which establishes the analytical potential of the methodological event, and its scientific meaning.

The practices of making comparability are strongly brought into view by Deville et al. (2016). For them the comparator, the agency creating the 'event' of comparison is 'an assemblage that undertakes comparative work' (p. 2), including the individuals, technologies, institutions, settings, and comparative practices of others. An open, often asymmetric and exploratory process of assembling the comparator emerges, as the authors 'bounce around' their cases, 'feeding the comparator' (p. 21). Thus, what comparativists and their socio-technical allies actually do matters – they make the comparator, they produce (in)commensurability, they compose the events to think with. Thus the dimensions of comparison – the definitions of the entities compared, the grounds for comparison, the potential for emergent conceptualisations – are not able to be defined a priori, but are generated in the practices of working across different cases. Their essay sits as a core contribution in a path breaking book bringing a number of STS-style comparative experiments together. Through these several essays, different elements of this comparator are exposed and interrogated – science-fiction-like in its rumbling multiplicity, ubiquitous presence, its often ill-formation, unpredictability and attendant emergent disturbances. The power relations and historicities of a number of the elements and events contributing to the monstrous 'rapport' (Stengers 2011) being generated across entities and observations, across time and space, are teased out through reflections on a range of comparative experiments. This is a helpful response to Jane M. Jacobs' (2012) call to reconsider the nature and role of the 'third term', the comparator which operates to enable comparisons and whose limits in conventional urban comparative methods we considered in Chapter 2.

It is in this thick practice of comparison, the long periods of back and forth across different cases, or tracking their rapport, relations, interconnections and mutual embeddings, that comparative 'method' is produced, distinctively each time, in a very wide range of theoretical and methodological idioms. The possibilities for conversations or commensurability identified early in a research project might morph and change, to stimulate quite different lines of emergent analysis across new entities, new objects of concern, on new bases. The 'grounds' and 'tactics' for comparative research are then only so many starting points for building conceptual insights 'with elsewhere'. Along the path of experimental comparisons, there is rich potential but there are also significant challenges involved in bringing into focus both the objects and terms of comparison.

Comparison as Conversations

> *Perhaps the greatest lesson cities in Africa may have for a city like Hartford or for cities in China is to never lose sight of the fluid, flexible, undetermined, non-linear, everchanging, unpredictable and surprising things that await us around any corner in a city.*
>
> (Myers 2014, pp. 114–15)

A few years after she moved to New York, Janet Abu-Lughod put pen to paper to reflect on how what she called her 'urban apperception mass' (the taken-for-granted constellation of information against which an individual might evaluate new information) helped her make a certain kind of sense of this new city, based on her much longer experiences and research in Chicago, where she lived for two decades, and Cairo, where her long-term research had been located. She comments, 'I have been trying to figure out why my Cairo experience is so much more relevant to living in New York than my Chicago experience' (1990, p. 307). Her thoughts dwell firstly on 'passing perceptions' (p. 310), and go to the spatial segregation which scars the postcolonial city of Cairo and the racially divided city of Chicago; to the fine-grained street patterns and density and diversity of land uses which make the experience of streets and public spaces in New York and Cairo more alike as do enthusiasms for distinctive dress codes which indicate group belonging. And although she sees a commonality in the small-scale and family-owned 'sweat-shops' in New York and Cairo, once she delves more deeply into the 'underlying processes' (of demography, economy, law and social institutions) she sees beyond common elements (rent-controlled housing which asserts rights and access for established urban dwellers) to differences (illegal construction and state-led developments in Cairo) to assert that 'The resemblances between New York and a Third World City like Cairo, then and in the last analysis, turn out to exist only at the most superficial level.' (p. 315). She describes New York's economy with the common epithet at the time – 'Switz-Kong' – a combination of Swiss financial services and Hong Kong's small scale industrial enterprise – which no longer resonates at all in this way, as Hong Kong is now a major world financial centre and New York far surpasses anything Switzerland offers on that front too. However, this economic difference allows Abu-Lughod to frame divergence across these two cities (New York and Cairo) on the basis of 'their significantly different roles in the international or global economy' and consigns the resemblances she has considered to the 'superficial level', characterising these as inevitable differences between US cities and a 'Third World City like Cairo' (p. 315). But she then proceeds to sketch Cairo's impressive role as a regional and global centre – once in cotton production, in the international aid networks that support what she calls a heavily indebted pauper nation, and the continuing 'symbolic, cultural and economic' role as a capital city in the Arab region. And she observes that the small-scale sweatshops in New York at the time, partly an in-situ restructuring to respond to the New International Division of Labour, with their reliance on 'imported' low-cost labour are suggestive of how global cities acquire some 'superficial resemblance' to 'Third-World centres' (p. 317).

This is a rare moment in which Abu-Lughod placed her abiding research interests in both Cairo and US cities alongside each other. Her trained eye alights on a range of elements which open up conversations to probe her intuitive sense that New York is much more like Cairo than Chicago. In her notes she refers to others who made close links between the feel of New York and that of Buenos Aires, or Bombay. In a footnote she writes, revealingly for our purposes, 'To my mind only one definition of a city holds up operationally, regardless of scale, time period and culture area: a city is a place where unexpected happenings are to be expected – where, when you turn the corner, you don't know what you will find. In this sense, Cairo and New York are both more urbane than Chicago.' (p. 318). Although she turns, then, to the 'fundamental' global economic differences here to resolve something incommensurable about the two cities – a move she abjures in her comparative analysis of New York, Chicago and Los Angeles (Brenner 2001) – her internal conversation about these like and unlike places yields so many potential lines of reflection.

Urban contexts, imagined as the fullness and inexhaustibility of space, present a rich diversity of potential grounds for thinking different cases together, which may not always be the most obvious starting point for comparative reflection. Abu-Lughod demonstrates so clearly the proliferation of possible lines of connection across even conventionally quite distanced cases. But is there a way forward analytically for such 'conversations' to become effective experimental comparisons, which don't have to run aground, as they did for her, on the rocks of apparently fundamental (economic) differences? Lancione and MacFarlane put this potential well, in the context of their work on sanitation infrastructure across Mumbai, India, and Turin, Italy: 'Experimental comparison is one methodological attempt to generate questions, stretch and challenge understandings, and inform contextual futures: difference-making as a tool to produce critical forms of knowledge in a heterogeneous urban world.' (2016, p. 2418).

This potential for experimentation also speaks to opportunities to fracture regional and geopolitical categories (North Africa, North America, 'Third World'). Abu-Lughod's formal comparative contributions (1976, 1999) were focussed within regions, preventing her from bringing her different cases together for more sustained analysis. Some of the differences she notes in her reflections on New York and Cairo – the shared experience of housing crises and rent controls, as opposed to the distinctive features of illegality, corruption and state-led housing development in Cairo – have led some to feel comparative insights might be unproductive (Pieterse et al. 2018). However, following Abu-Lughod's reflective lead, cities of the 'global south', for example, might open themselves to many different experimental reflections with cities in quite different situations. For example, in her discussion of housing crises across the urban world, Deborah Potts (2020) indicates that European contexts might have something to contribute to thinking about meeting housing need in the poorest contexts, and vice versa. Like Abu-Lughod, Potts brings together two kinds of contexts not often thought comparatively, but which are directly linked by her personal trajectory. This opens up some distinctive perspectives.

Talking of the segmented nature of housing markets, which both excludes the poor from 'most types of housing' and opens up access to the city in some contexts, she notes that 'This is true in poor and rich countries – the same processes play out whether you are in Harare, Zimbabwe, or Haringey, London, places with which I am deeply familiar' (p. 8). Taking apart the terms which often distinguish analysis of housing problems in each place – like informality, or slums – she looks to the shared dynamics to bring forward insights which travel in both directions. It is norms, regulations and standards which regularised housing in the North in twentieth century, and these same standards which make housing unaffordable to most in the global South. The so-called informal sector is woven into the generalised dynamics of processes of housing affordability and delivery across north and south, rather than seen as a separate starting point for addressing problems of only poorer cities. As she writes, 'The geographical variability of the scale of really chronic housing issues across the world and the obvious differences in the outcomes, particularly in terms of highly visible, large expanses of what are often labelled "slums" in many cities of the so-called Global South, can easily divert attention away from the underlying processes at work', and 'lead to an almost binary approach' (p. 12). 'the presence of widespread "informality" in the cities of the Global South is usually felt to hinder comparisons with planned and regulated cities elsewhere' (p. 15). She insists that comparing contemporary informality with the processes which led to nineteenth century slums in the global North suggests that wider comparative analysis of contemporary housing processes in both contexts is needed, not least to understand why such housing is no longer prevalent in places like London. The answers are well known but revealing – state intervention in housing and welfare provision, charity, and rising income levels. Her conclusion is that 'it is only a segment of non-market-priced housing in global North cities that prevents mass recourse (again) to the sort of insecure and inadequate housing that is now sometimes assumed to be uniquely characteristic of the global South. In other words, the underlying conditions that can lead to urban people living in such housing are universal.' (p. 17). Market processes of supply and demand, relative income levels and the terms of access to land become dimensions of analysis which bring housing affordability crises in the global north and south together.[1] It also suggests a different perspective on 'informal' housing. Rather than needing to be eradicated, Potts argues that this form of housing should be seen as a 'solution' arrived at by urban dwellers to resolve the difficult-to-square circle of housing affordability, need and delivery.

In this vein, some intriguing comparative analyses and potentially generative insights across quite different contexts come to light. The significant Co-operative housing movement in a few European contexts has important lessons: how to take land out of circulation for collective housing provision. This is a hugely challenging achievement in some of the most expensive cities in the world (cf. Chatterton 2015), but is possibly an important alternative model to the land value capture developmental imagination currently being considered in African urban development planning (Berrisford et al. 2018; Turok 2016). As Potts notes, land is perhaps one of the most exceptionalist elements of African urban experiences. But, she suggests it is communal and traditional institutions and popular (informal) housing initiatives which have sustained access to land and housing for some of the poorest (Potts 2020, pp. 93–8). Demarketised land is a major asset for housing the poor in the richest contexts, too. In Zurich, for example, housing co-operatives work with financing arrangements which do not require paying off the capital value of a mortgage. This permits a very long-term horizon and low costs, while land removed from the market preserves accessibility in perpetuity. This makes available to residents housing which does not factor in speculative land values – about a quarter of all housing stock in the city is not for profit (Bernt et al. 2017; Jones and Shelley 2016). But as with so many forms of accessible housing provision, it also locks in access to a certain generation, whose good fortunes (and scope for continuous self-gentrification and improvement of their housing stock) contrast badly with newcomers and younger generations who are thrown into the speculative and expensive private sector housing market (on China, see Wang and Murie 2011).

In using the term 'conversation' to figure analytical engagements across diverse or divergent cases (Robinson 2011a; see also Heslop et al. 2020; Teo 2021; Ward 2010 call this a 'dialogue'), I seek to propose looser openings to learning in a field which has historically significantly divided analysis between northern and southern contexts, and still faces the prospects of being carved up against the grain of the connectedness and potential for mutual learning about the nature of the urban. The ubiquitous light 'comparative gesture' (Chapter 2), seemed to me to be evidence that scholars have long been reaching for insights across differences which seemed to evade rigorous analytical reflection. In this space I would place the creative, unexpected comparisons which are forged on the trajectory of, for example, personal connections or the accidents of personal geographies (Myers 2014). Researchers find themselves reflecting across the sites of their research and those places where they are living – temporarily as a student, or longer term working. Their deep knowledge of another place throws their current, perhaps more familiar, context into relief and effects in some cases a reversal of the colonial gaze (see Katz 2001; Ren 2020; Roy 2003). Or, classically, after a long period of researching a particular place, life changes limit travel and researchers might turn to delve more deeply into the context where they are currently living and teaching (my own experience, Robinson and Attuyer 2021; see also Myers 2020, turning his long research experience and personal connections to Zanzibar to inform his analysis of Hartford, Connecticut). This can provoke a sustained engagement across diverse urban experiences and divergent literatures and analyses. Both Abu-Lughod and Potts demonstrate that the personal trajectories of some scholars have opened up substantial and potentially robust comparative conversations – and firm analytical insights – across quite divergent urban experiences.

Such juxtapositions can also emerge more purposively, through determined initiatives to do the hard work of opening up conversations that have been rendered all but impossible by the itineraries and strictures of our inherited rubrics, conventional analyses and institutional norms. Myers (2018, 2020) offers a strong effort to think with urban villages in China to provide insights for informal settlements in Africa, and back; as well as pursuing buried and subterranean connections across different contexts which, once exposed, can make us think quite differently about certain contexts. The slave history and indigenous dispossessions which ought to be a central part of the analysis of the towns and cities of the US Eastern seaboard, for example; or a detailed analysis of the presencing of Caribbean histories and migrations in these places both expose significantly occluded dynamics of US cities. More generally, experimental comparisons offer scope to craft theoretical propositions from contexts which are not usually treated as sources of wider analytical insights and apply these elsewhere – as Austin proposes, to see world history 'in an African mirror' (Austin 2007).

'Conversation' is also a way to refer to the complex and long process of bringing two cases (or more) into a productive engagement, perhaps entailing a significant change in focus or object of study. In his classical analysis of 'comparative political corruption' James C. Scott (1972, p. 2) considered together turn of the twentieth-century US where political machines orchestrated vote buying, seventeenth-century England where aristocratic titles were sold, or twentieth-century sale of import licenses by Indonesian political leaders. Refocussing attention from violence and corruption as 'pathological', the three cases together illuminated rather a diversity of ways which institutions have found over time to accommodate new political demands and need for representation for emergent groups in societies in transition where existing 'formal' procedures become inadequate, as rules serve only some groups' interests. This he felt offered a new perspective on the normative critique of corruption in contemporary 'developing nations' which in his view 'betray both western prejudice and historical naiveté' (p. 10):

> Since no state, old or new, is entirely free of corruption, the question is not its presence or absence. The relevant analytical problem is rather to determine how different political systems foster diverse levels and varieties of corruption and to assess the effects of corruption in that political system.
> (Scott 1972, p. 10)

Rather than focussing on 'corruption', then, the analysis opens to compare similar political practices across quite different contexts in terms of their role in regime change and maintenance. As no perfect 'experimental' combination of highly comparable cases is possible, he grasped at the potential for thinking across quite diverse contexts, with the opportunity to de-exceptionalise western critiques of 'third world' corruption.

In his 'conversational' comparative analysis, Shaun Teo (2022) began with two 'progressive' projects in Shenzhen and London (urban development projects which sought to demonstrate scope to positively change existing practices), but over time his back and forth across the two contexts yielded insights rather on the 'symbiotic state'. This is a term he coined for the positive collaborations across civil society and state actors which sustained both the projects he was studying. Sometimes conversations can be quite literal – as one group of researchers discovered in thinking about theorising state agency in three very different situations, Báfatá, Guinea Bissau; Tallin, Estonia; and Berlin, Germany. Here the insight emerged that unpacking what was meant by the term 'informality', more usually associated with poor and deeply informalised state actors in Báfatá (Neves Alves 2021), might yield significant insights across all three cases. On this basis the authors also propose a new way of thinking about the processes which were bundled into the term, 'informality' in relation to the state, such as the productive idea of legal voids, or the ways in which selective enforcement or active state agents might shape or negotiate governance outcomes in many different contexts (Hilbrandt, Neves and Hibrandt 2021; Tuvikene 2016). The potential, then, for 'conversations to open up new analytical insights' (Teo 2022), either in a serendipitous or bespoke way, speaks to the value of an open and exploratory approach to thinking the urban across difference. A good 'hunch' about possible learning across difference might be a most creative starting point, and the slow crafting of a 'tertium' as well as an emergent object of comparison could be a pragmatic way to produce innovative concepts.

Comparative conversations might proceed in different ways on the journey to conceptual insight. Ren (2020) follows the same path as Teo, seeking to develop conceptual insights through a sustained conversation across two contexts, defining a shared feature which emerged as the research progressed. She offers a rich example of how working across Berlin and Beijing (a 'methodologically oriented critique' focussed on 'how cities are compared') opened up scope to frame an emergent, 'mid-level' concept, 'art spaces'. Detailed tracing of connections between the contexts, drawing on informants' own interpretive insights across art settings and practices in the two places, and a combined thematic to draw out shared (if varied) experiences structured a back-and-forth conversation which supported this emergent concept. In the broadest sense, she insists that rather than inspiring a rush to study 'non-European sites', a post-colonial and comparative urban studies proposes 'a way to reflect on the lens with which we look at all cities' (Ren 2020, p. 24). It is in this context that she argues for a comparative method based on identifying the "theoretical case", following Walton (1990), rather than starting with different urban contexts as cases. Schilling et al. (2019) take a more conceptually driven approach, developing terms which can open up the possibility to bring aspects of youth experiences of precarious work in three urban contexts into conversation. Although very different in terms of resourcing, institutional and economic opportunities, the experiences of young people in Abidjan, Berlin and Jakarta provide insights into different aspects of the 'instability' which is core to precarious livelihoods. Detaching from pre-given paths or expectations while gathering up new connections and possibilities highlights the significance of fleeting social relations, the 'unpredictability of intersecting practices in a given moment' (p. 1344) for these young workers. While working differently in the three contexts, conceptual repertoires are developed across the three cases which shed light on them all. The close interweaving of empirical insights and emerging innovative conceptual terms is often a significant feature of such comparative experiments. In an even looser example of bringing different cities into conversation, Gandy's (2014) *Fabric of Space* explores shared themes of water and modernity across quite different cities and over long time periods in each case (Paris, London, Los Angeles and Mumbai, amongst others, are brought into conversation). His approach, driven by a close historical analysis and detailed attention to socio-natures and political dynamics, leads Ponder and Webber (2019, p. 195) to observe that in the careful weaving of overlapping themes, Gandy's text achieves more of a 'suggestive juxtaposition than exacting comparison'. In a very general sense his study reinforces the value of treating cities as 'ordinary', not least insofar as the different histories he carefully explores, as well as different political and technological formations, are quite straightforwardly understood as leading to 'different expressions of, and elaborations on, the experience of modernity' (ibid., p. 191).

In a more conventional formulation, Paige (1999) contrasts the quasi-statistical approach adopted by Ragin (2000) and Skocpol and Somers (1980), looking systematically for variations in variables, outcomes and causal patterns across a set of cases, with 'historically conditional' analyses which bring rich historically specific cases together to test and develop theoretical insights and analyses across the two cases, learning both from their similarities (e.g. in terms of outcomes) and differences. Seidman's (1994) instructive analysis of the rise of social movement unionism in Brazil and South Africa during the 1970s and 1980s tested theorisations of militant unionism and social transformation across these two exceptions to the failure of working-class movements to achieve revolution within capitalism (Adler and Webster 1995). This is of great interest to South African urban scholars, and I assume Brazilian too, as close relations between urban-based social movements and union organising framed the potential for national-democratic revolutions in both. Aside from the encouragement to bring interesting cases together for 'testing' and enhancing wider understandings of social processes (such as the political dynamics and transformation of 'late-industrialisers'), Paige comments that 'much of the power of Seidman's analysis depends on just how unexpectedly similar her two union movements are' (p. 793). Bringing two cases into conversation may seem, at first sight, a challenge. But the hard work of building comparators across complex specific cases, can produce compelling and ultimately even intuitively sensible comparisons (see Sanchez Jiminez 2017) out of the 'natural experiments' (Bloch 2015; cited in Paige 1999, p. 793) which the prolific historical-geographical diversity of the urban presents.

As Simone (2010, p. 279) observes, keeping open the possibility to understand the articulation of urban life across quite different urban settings brings into view aspects of urban life 'that otherwise would have no readily available means of conceptualisation'. And, in their retrospective, or found, 'experimental' comparison on sanitation and marginalisation in Turin and Mumbai, Lancione and McFarlane (2016) insist that 'differences matter, they expand and push how we think about what sanitation is and signifies, and how the urban world is lived' (p. 2415). The creativity of experimental comparisons as conversation, and their orientation to generating innovative concepts, is a strong recommendation.

Theoretical Reflections

Openings to conversations which allow researchers to 'think with elsewhere' can also be explored in a more theoretical register. Rather than detailed empirical case study research, it could be just as helpful to bring disparate literatures from different contexts into conversation. Often literatures from different regions or national contexts address similar themes but are seldom considered together. Personally, I found a potential conversation across the European debates on 'Post-democracy' and the Brazilian founded insights on 'insurgent citizenship' highly instructive for my research in London. At the same time as post-political analyses of London's urban politics have suggested mobilisation is futile (Swyngedouw 2005; Raco 2014), the city is brim full of mobilisation, contestation, protests, and lobbying (Lipietz, Lee and Hayward 2014; Lees 2014b; Minton 2017; https://justspace.org.uk). Each regeneration initiative, or large-scale development (more than 40 'Opportunity Areas' have been identified for intensive development across the city) calls forward its resident's organisations, its protest groups, its opposition. Thus, a relatively gloomy academic prognosis co-exists with ongoing and extensive, time-consuming community efforts at engagement from groups of a wide variety of different demographics, neighbourhoods and political persuasions.

The 'relentless pessimism' (Larner 2014, p. 190) of some of the academic accounts of urban politics has been strongly influenced by a form of analysis known variously as 'post-democracy', or 'post-politics' (see a helpful summary by Wilson and Swyngedouw 2014). The post-political analysis of UK urban politics has its foundation in Eric Swyngedouw's (2011) incisive contributions, drawing on French political theorist, Jacques Rancière. On this basis Swyngedouw sees little scope for the properly political to emerge within UK urban politics, commenting that,

> The act of resistance ('I have to resist the process of, say, neo-liberalisation, globalisation or capitalism, or otherwise the city, the world, the environment, the poor will suffer') just answers the call of power in its postdemocratic guise. Resistant acting is actually what is invited, but leaves the police order intact.
> (Swyngedouw 2011, p.377)

This analysis partly reflects an epochal account of the UK political system, presented by Colin Crouch (2004) which describes a disaffected electorate, lack of feedback mechanisms, disconnect between citizens and the state, rule by focus group rather than electorate, and technocratic solutions portrayed as necessary/determined by experts/good for everyone. Nonetheless, the UK is a country with a long history of democracy, a functioning electoral system, parliament and a sizeable, if residual, welfare state.

In contrast, in many places where politics is considerably more formally restricted, with democratic institutions substantially diverted to personal gain and very little state investment in society, analysts of urban politics pay close attention to the nuanced possibilities which informal governance settings offer for reframing political discourses and potentially securing political gains for the poor or reinforcing state redistributive capacities (Benjamin 2008; Bénit-Gbaffou and Katsaura 2014; Holston 2007; Roy 2003; Lee and Zhang 2013). Claire Benit-Gbaffou and Obvious Katsaura (2014) call attention to the 'micro-politics of the local', for example, bringing out the 'double dealing' of community representatives in the post-apartheid context, engaging down to build legitimacy with local communities, and engaging up to build standing with governments and other official representatives. Mamadou Diouf and Rosalind Fredericks (2014) highlight the 'arts of citizenship' in which highly informalised public performances of music, fashion, production of urban services and practices, reconstitute civic relationships, identities and expectations, and have achieved significant material gains in some contexts. These micropolitics of urban citizenship have been exposed most fully in highly informalised urban contexts, places where the terms and terrains of urban politics are emergent and potentially in dynamic relationship to institutions which themselves may be open to reinvention or change. This might be societies in transition, for example, or those shaped by highly personalised actions and appropriations, or by peremptory interventions ('weak states'), or characterised by high degrees of informality or permeability across state and society. These kinds of politics are not necessarily spectacular or even intuitively oppositional, although they might be as Claire Benit-Gbaffou and Sophie Oldfield (2014) argue in their essay in *Handbook for Cities of the Global South*.

The potential and actual achievements of associational dynamics and emergent micro-politics are acknowledged, often in very tough and frequently opaque political contexts (Diouf and Fredericks 2014). This includes the patient engagements built up over long periods of time, for example, in the practices of the world famous SDI (Patel et al. 2012; Levy 2015), and the insurgent citizenship of Brazilian Favelas (Holston 2007). These patient practices recognise the need for engagement to achieve real improvements in the lives of poor urban dwellers as soon as possible, given the crushing need in many poorer urban contexts. While often based in everyday and patient organising, these movements can amount to a significant shifting of power relations and decision-making practices. This echoes Ferguson's re-assessment of the politics of neoliberal forms of government in light of the question, what if politics is 'about getting what you want?' (2007, p. 167).

With these kinds of analyses in mind, although inspired by the same writer, Jacques Rancière, Julian Brown draws on the South African experience to argue almost exactly the opposite from Swyngedouw. Instead of a transformative politics being impossible, or at least possible only in distant situations of extreme political contestation, Brown suggested that

> One of the key insights of Rancière's approach is that there is no exclusive site of politics – neither parliament nor protest – and that therefore any site can provide the context within which a political act can be made and responded to.
>
> (Brown 2015, p. 31)

Brown proceeds to explore the emergence of new political subjects on the terrain of post-apartheid, in a narrative which will be familiar and resonant to South African scholars, through lawcourts, or in contested accounts of police violence, squatter or service delivery movements, in the right to protest. South Africa constitutes a situation in which delivery of urban based services is closely tied to citizenship entitlements, and is central to political mobilisation. Thus, it is not hard to link the multiplicity of contestations on the ground in urban situations to a wider political narrative of national transformation – even if this is unmatched (yet) by empirical connections amongst diverse political actions or the clear emergence of a national political subject of transformation. He concludes, though, in a positive tone drawing heavily on Holston's Brazilian analysis, that 'a society of equals can be forged in the present moment, by South Africa's already-insurgent citizens' (p. 161). Important for this historical moment of political malaise and state capture, he concludes that in South Africa, 'we have not reached the end of politics, and that change is possible' (p. 162).

I do not wish to speculate on whether the potential for political change in London is as/more/less possible than in South Africa, but rather to take analytical inspiration from the close attention writers from contexts such as Brazil and South Africa pay to the micro-politics and the fine arts of affiliation, mobilisation, engagement and emergent political voice. Those dynamics which characterise political analysis in the majority urban world are often determinedly focussed on making specific gains in the present, to respond to intensely challenging urban contexts (Diouf and Fredericks 2014). For our assessment of urban politics in London, this has drawn us to a much more generous assessment of the potential for mobilisation and engagement to both build organisational capacity for the long term in relation to community engagement in the politics of urban development, but also to consider the possibilities for openings to influence and shape these processes in different settings (Robinson and Attuyer 2020).

As the loosest of comparative methods, opening the potential for a 'conversation' across scholarly writing which is often deeply embedded in and specific to divergent contexts may feel like the least rigorous of comparative methods. But the examples here indicate the rich potential to build insights in this way. There is much to learn, especially from scholarship which has largely been occluded from wider analytical view by institutional practices which narrow the conceptual range and exclude different scholars, and thus different urban experiences, from being part of the eminent domain of urban 'theory'.

Mobile Concepts, or 'Arriving at' Concepts

Extending further the creative potential of conceptualisation as a starting point for comparison, we consider in this section, rather than a mobile researcher, how concepts emergent in one context might be put to work across other contexts to support comparative experiments and extend comparative imaginations. *Mobile concepts* as a comparative tactic highlights examples where the active agency of researchers is most identifiable, pressing concepts to (and beyond) their limits of relevance in different contexts – or drawing them in to inform specific analyses. From the first perspective – putting concepts into circulation – we see many examples of researchers purposively putting concepts emergent in one location to work in many others (Korff 1986; Morange and Spire 2019; Mwathunga 2014). 'Gentrification' has been one of the most successful and widely circulated concepts in the repertoire of especially northern urban studies, so I will take that as an example. It is helpful as it does not describe a circulating process – 'gentrification' is not a policy on the move, but a circulating concept, a definition which rests on a certain set of features initially characteristic of one case of urban change. Ruth Glass's initial observation in London made a powerful and long-lasting intervention on the basis of that context:

> One by one, many of the working-class quarters of London have been invaded by the middle classes—upper and lower … Once this process of 'gentrification' starts in a district it goes on rapidly until all or most of the original working class occupiers are displaced and the whole social character of the district is changed
>
> (Glass 1964, p. xviii)

Even the term, 'gentry', which she selected is a very Anglo-centric term, indicating an aristocracy. Over time more and places and periods have been drawn into the orbit of this concept, increasingly hyphenated, culminating in 'global' and 'planetary' formulations which seek to expand its relevance to many different contexts (Lees, López-Morales and Shin (eds.) 2015; Lees, López-Morales and Shin 2016). Many authors deeply familiar with different contexts have found this a useful analysis of urban change, and especially value the political meaning which the term connotes. Gentrification is associated with displacement (Slater 2017), revanchism of middle classes (Smith 1987, 2002) and valued as a potential political slogan to oppose regeneration (see Bernt, 2022). A slimmed down definition has much buy-in:

> Gentrification is a process involving a change in the population of land users such that the new users are of a higher socio-economic status than the previous users, together with an associated change in the built environment through a reinvestment in fixed capital… Any process of change fitting this description is, to my understanding, Gentrification.
>
> (Clarke 1995, p.x)

Huge (and often acrimonious) debates have circled around the concept of 'gentrification', as well as what it expresses. Some of these reflect different experiences in different contexts, such as whether gentrification was caused by demand or supply (say, larger developer-led processes more common in the US at the time of this debate); cultural (such as gay or dual income no-kids lifestyles) or economic dynamics (like rent gaps). It was also questioned what these urban changes reflected – whether class displacement or the French *embourgeoisement* indicating more generalised improvements in income and class status initially identified in Paris (on this see Préteceille 2007 on Paris; Hamnett 2003 on London; see Crankshaw 2017 and Crankshaw and Borel-Saladin 2014 for a recent engagement in relation to Cape Town).

A vast archive of implicit 'comparative' analysis has emerged on the basis of this concept. Much of this involves case studies which are placed in wider conversations in relation to a shared theoretical debate (see Butler 2007, for an accessible review). There are a few bespoke comparative analyses, such as Carpenter and Lees (1995) who explicitly consider three cases which had been instrumental in grounding the concept – New York, London and Paris. They reflect systematically across the processes shaping the production of gentrification, and consumption-related landscapes which result, noting the similar processes and outcomes, with recognisably similar consumption landscapes resulting, but with some contextual differentiation. A more determinedly global comparative initiative has flowed from the rise of comparative urbanism as such (Lees 2012). Lees (2012) called for comparative gentrification studies which might attend to the different gentrification experiences in the global south, following what she saw as the 'fast policy' circuits which spread 'gentrification ideology'. This suggested a somewhat Eurocentric imperative to explore how 'Gentrification began to take off in the Global South at the turn of the 21st century' (p. 156) somewhat ignoring the vast array of (comparable) transformations across the urban global south which had shaped cities for many decades. In the more recent analysis, *Planetary Gentrification* (Lees et al. 2016), the three co-authors drew on their varied regional expertise (across East Asia, Europe–US and South America) to bring together concerns which not only address the different forms of gentrification but also interrogate whether similar outcomes might have 'different processes and logics, thus challenging the "western-convergence" thesis' (p. 21). A stronger emphasis on the role of the state, and the question of displacement, together with insights from a wide range of scholarship from the different contexts considered, all reflect clear efforts to bring a more global perspective to this concept.

More generally, though, gentrification has been an approach which is quite strongly committed to preservation of the original term in the face of difference: hyphenated (e.g. state-led-gentrification), the concept proposes its relevance to anywhere, complete with its original baggage, namely, a very specific bundle of features defining the term = class change, physical change, private appropriation of a rent gap, and displacement. Maloutas (2012) argues that in such wide circulation the term has become 'detrimental to analysis' (p. 44), noting that 'eventually, this conceptualization of urban regeneration – whose context/dependence becomes increasingly invisible due to its dominance – may not be adequate to travel around the world as it actually does' (p. 34). On this view, the attempt to assert the pertinence of this concept to different contexts sees its purchase, although repeatedly asserted and demonstrated, become thinner and thinner in its capacity to really explore the variety of urban experiences encountered (Maloutas 2012; Mosselson, 2016; Tang 2017). Much is left out, and instead of being used to stretch, enrich and potentially replace the concept, key elements of the context being considered risk falling from view, or are assimilated into a pre-existing conceptualisation. Deleuze would find us staring at a 'bare' concept, one with little purchase any longer on the intensities and singularities we are confronting, leaving us with much still to conceptualise (much experience without conceptualisation), at the limit with nothing at all to grasp with the term.[2] In her contribution on 'Gentrification in China?', Julie Ren (2015) identifies a potential conceptual over-stretch in the use of the term, with a focus on 'variation-finding' within the conceptual frame rather than looking for theoretical innovation which might be expected to emerge when applying the concept across different situations. She draws on Chinese-centric literature to indicate the range of different causes and consequences of urban inequality and displacement there (including some potential positive attitudes to displacement inspired by strong compensation packages – see Wang and Wu 2019). She notes the relative absence of specific strategies for experimental comparisons at that time (at least partly redressed through her own, see Ren 2020), and that research on gentrification has obscured attending to processes more relevant in Chinese cities. Nonetheless, although objecting to imposing externally derived concepts, such as gentrification, she is clear that she is not advocating a kind of 'Chinese exceptionalism', but rather asks: 'how can research on urban China inform an understanding of not only "Chinese urbanism", but "Urbanism with a capital "U"'' (Ren 2015, p. 342).

Mathias Bernt poses the question of this mobile concept well: 'Put differently, is gentrification a very particular experience without much face value and action guidance for "much of the world" (Ghertner 2015b), or have rent gaps gone "planetary" (see Slater 2017) and has the struggle against gentrification become global?' (Bernt 2016b, p. 638). Strong contestations of the term have been made by those, such as Ghertner (2015b), who explore how the experiences of displacement and redevelopment in many poorer cities bear no resemblance to the features identified with 'gentrification'. And by others who explore how the outcomes associated with the core dynamics of gentrification might be very different – representing even beneficial vernacular processes and not leading to the kinds of class change generally considered relevant to gentrification (Maloutas 2012; Mosselson 2016). One option for diversifying analysis has been put forward by Schmid and collaborators (Schmid et al. 2018), considering how gentrification might be identifying one possible kind of 'urbanisation process' associated with class change, physical renewal and displacement. As we have explored in the rest of this part of the book, many other processes could be identified through comparative analyses on the grounds of contingency, specificity, diversity and open conversations across contexts. Scholars are alert, then, to the limits of a term such as gentrification – when finally, its utility is exhausted as the 'difference' of the context we hope to understand is drawn off, even occluded, by the concept. The Hong Kong based urban scholar, Wing-Shing Tang seeks to 'critique its generalization on the grounds that the processes of land development and property development are basically distinguishable in any city. Why should we conflate them through the would-be universal concept of gentrification?' (2017, p. 487; cf Ley and Teo 2014).

A rejoinder from Ley and Teo (2020) recounts various elements of the concept gentrification which they argue nonetheless applies to Hong Kong. They especially refer to the hyphenated term 'state-led' gentrification as good grounds to continue using the term in that context. But as Tang makes very clear, the diverse empirical features drawn into the concept, gentrification, might as well be assembled into a more focussed analytical attention to the motivations, politics and outcomes which actually inform the differential agency and interests of the state in urban development in specific contexts. States may: play a small role in redevelopment, pursue extractive market-led property development, seek budgetary resources from such developments, or mobilise large-scale development to meet housing and welfare needs through tight control of land use and land values (Haila 2015; Robinson and Attuyer 2021; Shin 2016). Clearly many find the concept useful, and are able to nuance the analysis to draw insights in different contexts – as López Morales (2011) suggests, for example, that although class-based displacement was not occurring in the redevelopment of Santiago de Chile, the imbalance of power relations and uneven regulatory expectations between small-scale homeowners and property developers led to homeowners being dispossessed of increases in property value. In his view, despite the nuance and complexities of this case of urban development, this 'may suffice for gentrification to exist' (p. 353). Shin (2016) considers the process of 'displacement' a crucial state-led precursor to creating the possibility for gentrification as a market-led process in Asia (albeit often undertaken by state-owned enterprises). The complexities of collective rights to land by often 'rural' village entities, as well as the significant compensation received by many, nuance the story of displacement as some benefit greatly (Shin 2016; Wang and Wu 2019). A stronger focus on the process of displacement, then, in its own right, has become warranted (Moreno and Shin 2018). The moment to declare the exhaustion of a concept is a judgement for scholars, and scholarly communities; the fertility of comparative insights and the strength of local and regional scholarly efforts to invent new concepts might also simply displace such dominant circulating concepts. Bernt's (2022) elegant comparative analysis of the always contextual and institutional processes which make gentrification possible yields the term, "commodification gap" to replace the more abstract generalisation, "rent gap". What are the processes which allow land and property to be commodified, and therefore to contribute to gentrification? He advocates conceptualisations which arise directly from the specificity of different urban experiences, in his case, London, St Petersburg and Berlin.

In the spirit of theorizing from diversity, and treating 'context' as the starting point for conceptualisation, as opposed to simple 'variety' – it is possible to further divert analysis from the concept of gentrification towards a theoretical interrogation of contextual difference. Gavin Shatkin's book, *Cities for Profit* (2017), takes up this challenge. He narrows the concept of gentrification sufficiently that it can bring many different contexts into view on their own terms, targeting the difference across contexts as the starting point for conceptualisation. He returns to Neil Smith's insights on the 'rent gap' – only one, tightly analytical, element of the bundle that conventionally makes up 'gentrification'. He puts this term to work to bring quite different cases into alignment (Indonesia, India, China) and identifies the different outcomes and diverse operations of power producing and benefitting from extreme rent gaps. In turn this reconfigures political and capitalist interests which coalesce around massive urbanisation schemes across Asia (and of course elsewhere). Here is a starting point, then, for thinking about the nature of urban change across a wide range of contexts, which does not pre-empt what we will identify as analytically interesting, or impose a certain concept, model or political meaning on urban outcomes. Indeed, it opens itself to the necessary difference of the cases selected, to propose new grounds for thinking the nature of urban politics, framing new theoretical challenges – inciting the possibility of thinking with diversity (as discussed in Chapter 8).

An alternative perspective on mobile concepts which I want to propose here draws inspiration from the prolific learning experiences of urban policy makers. In any context, an array of transnational processes shape distinctive policy outcomes and development paths. The relevant analytical concern then is to explore how 'elsewhere' is folded in to localised growth paths through these prolific circulations – how policies are arrived at, rather than arrive in places via circuits and connections (we discussed this in Chapter 5). In some ways this maps onto the virtuality of ideas, following Deleuze. As we seek to make sense of a phenomenon, we might explore the potential in all the available ways of conceptualising a phenomenon and draw on these selectively to 'arrive at' understanding. Of course, both policy circuits and scholarly ideas are unevenly structured and all possible ideas are not infinitely or seamlessly available. But the possibility of composing distinctive, innovative and unique ways of understanding urban processes through actively drawing in potentially productive insights from anywhere/elsewhere strikes me as a creative comparative imagination, fit for thinking with ideas drawn from across the urban world.

These two approaches to building comparative insights through mobilising concepts across different contexts are quite different – radiating concepts from a centre of intellectual authority and applying the term in many different places; or 'arriving at' insights drawn from a wide range of possible sources of conceptual inspirations. While both highlight the parochial and deeply specific grounds on which conceptualisations of the urban emerge, and both engage with wider processes of conceptualisation, they go in quite different directions. The former seeks to bring anywhere within its purview; the latter reinforces the assessment that theorisation might begin anywhere, significantly decentring the production of urban concepts. Of course, these two might meet – active subjects of located theorisation might well draw on 'gentrification' as a powerful concept for making sense of changes they are concerned to understand (He 2019; López-Morales 2011), or find analyses from contexts experiencing resonant political processes highly relevant, such as with urban social movements (Reintges 1990). Initiatives might mobilise concepts which have already become part of the urban political discourse more generally, such as the 'right to the city' (Brown 2013; Kuymulu 2013; Morange and Spire 2019; Parnell and Pieterse 2010). And emergent concepts may be put on the move from anywhere – perhaps within a more modest project. For example, Ortega (2020, p. 679), develops a revised Desakota 2.0 concept and proposes 'worlding it as a conceptual vector, one that will not asphyxiate contexts where it travels but instead activate a deep accounting of the site's histories and relationalities while facilitating conceptual formulation and theoretical conversations.'

Conclusion

'Arriving at concepts' brings us back to the agent of theorisation as located anywhere, thinking with elsewhere, in a myriad of inventive ways, for many different reasons. Here, then, we can locate the potential for here and there to be brought together in creative and perhaps surprising ways. Anderse et al. (2015) invoke Anderson's (1998) metaphor of the 'inverted telescope' in which situated and far-seeing magnifications are simultaneously present. They consider the range of possible ways in which 'Inverting the telescope across time and space recognizes both zooming and generalising as performances in which versions of reality are enacted' (p. 15). The grounds for their concerns are that European 'borders' are not only situated and lived in Europe but made and performed at a distance, as a result of both colonial histories and contemporary migration politics. These can be tracked, for example, in the realm of literary and personal imaginations to explore the ways in which here and there fold topologically into one another in the course of mobile lives and trajectories of cultural and political influences. These foldings form part of imaginative reflections and interpretations across different contexts, and are important potential analytical resources (Lowe 2015; Kramsch, 2022). Through experiences and memories imaginative configurations of relations amongst places might stretch to reformulate the way so-called particular-general arrangements might be figured. The global or distant might be very close and intimate. Thus, the terms of mimesis, allegory and the twists and turns of memory speak also to broader repertoires for constructing meaning across difference (Chaudhury 2012). As Cheah (2013) notes, though, being drawn to such 'spectral' comparisons (Anderson 1998) in colonial and post-colonial contexts remains deeply entwined with the power relations of colonialism and globalisation. Comparative reflections and tracings along 'submarine relations' open up the possibility for critique and recovery of sometimes buried pasts (Myers 2020).

Imagined proximities and creative connections across contexts can therefore potentially emerge in so many unexpected ways – resonant with Strathern's (2005 [1991]) view that nothing is intrinsically comparable (or incomparable?). Topological or imaginative comparisons are not only evident within the colliding worlds of actors and literary imaginations, but might also legitimately drive the comparative interests of researchers. We could be inspired towards more experimental configurations, and strange conjunctures. We might attempt imaginative leaps which question, as (elsew)here comes into view, whether the different experiences have to fit together at all ('In allegory, the realities made manifest do not necessarily have to fit together' (Law 2004, p. 90)). One context may simply illuminate unspoken, unseen elements of another reality, another context, to great analytical effect.

Chapter 10 takes forward more openings for thinking the urban in the midst of the urban world, across and from different urban territories, to explore a further set of comparative tactics on generative grounds. Part IV, then, turns attention to comparative experiments which begin with the urban world, insistently pressing its demands on us, offering sometimes disorienting juxtapositions for reflection as we work towards understanding.

Notes

1. A different but also compelling global approach to housing crisis can be found in Rolnik (2019), working with financialisation as a primary process shaping housing outcomes across the global north and south. See also Fernandez and Aalbers (2020).
2. 'One is bare repetition which can be masked only afterwards and in addition; the other is a clothed repetition of which the masks, the displacements and the disguises are the first, the last and only elements' (Deleuze 1994, DR, p. 359).

IMAGE 4.1 Detail from Waiting for Bus by Dilomprizulike, 2003, at Africa Remix: Contemporary Art of a Continent, Hayward Gallery, London (2005). (Photograph by Marcus Leith)

IMAGE 4.2 Soweto Cooling Tower, Johannesburg, 11 July 2015. (Photograph by Raphael de Kadt, flickr.com)

PART IV

Thinking from the Urban as Distinctive

Part IV of this book brings to the fore perhaps the most generative of comparative tactics. Starting with urban territories expands the potential to subtract from extant conceptualisations, inviting us to engage with the fullness and complexity of distinctive urban outcomes. A significant feature of the comparative experiments discussed in Chapters 10 and 11, then, is that they encourage a strong orientation to identifying dynamics and processes which might have been ignored by extant theoretical perspectives. Bringing these observations into encounters with other urban territories and conversations with other urban scholars potentially expands the scope of insights. Also, as territories assemble matter, practices and meanings, they highlight aspects of urban life elsewhere. Comparative tactics which are responsive to the dynamic materiality of the urban world are essential for conceptual innovation. Chapter 10 establishes that attending closely to the urban world in its distinctiveness and fullness is far from a still or mute point – rather, this is the very moment when the intensities of the urban world might incite conceptualisation. And Chapter 11 suggests that it is those contexts which have historically been treated as exceptions to concepts of the urban, where the opacity and density of urban dwellers' efforts to forge livelihoods perhaps turn away from conceptualisation, that potentially destabilise inherited terms, and insist on new approaches.

Zooming in on part of the Nigerian artist Dilomprizulike's sculpture *Waiting for Bus* draws us to a closer focus on the matter of urban life, assembled here into defined figures conveying the experience of immobility in many challenging urban contexts (Image 4.1, p. 304; a colour version of this image can be found between pages 132 and 133). In this moment of standstill, though, meaning is assembled, subjectivity is constituted, and potentiality condensed in anticipation of movement. What are the people planning, where are they heading, what are they taking with them? Constellations of matter, here the assembled figures, prefigure a futurity. For Walter Benjamin the moment of analytical standstill, when times and places are assembled in a constellation, 'now', is tightly wound with insight, and with possibility. Such a moment could stand at a crossroads of intense danger. A historical crisis framed his text, *On the Concept of History*, which, as Löwy (2005) observes, drew on a sense of imminent danger – sounding the alarm as the Second World War loomed, also provoking a personal crisis for him.

What is at stake in such an analytical standstill, when pasts and elsewheres erupt into the moment of reflection and interpretation? An entry in *One Way Street*, 'Underground Works', highlights a troubling of Benjamin's unconscious by colonial history. He reports a dream, which erupts in laughter as a joke ('Witz') sits in the middle of the name he ascribes to the 'Mexican' church erupting into the Weimar market-place. It resonates with Benjamin's call to 'wake up', through the shock effect of suddenly recognising what is happening 'now'. Or as a waking moment before a dream fades, in which to uncover the meaning of a dream constellation. Historically, for Benjamin the momentum of the shock is felt in the urgent constellation of disparate pasts to account for and force recognition of what is 'now', and to open the present to possible futures. What is seldom discussed, though, is that this now-famous formulation of 'now-time' ('*Jetztzeit*') emerged out of Benjamin's longstanding approach to history and to method. He developed the slow (comparative) practice of building concepts across patiently assembled observations, which led to understandings of the nature of an artwork, a genre, or a historical object, such as the modern city.

Reading Benjamin with Deleuze, Chapter 11 considers the form of concepts of the urban. If the urban is a theoretical object (Brenner and Schmid, 2014), what kind of concepts might match up to this phenomenon? If Benjamin portrays concepts as constellations, in historical terms configured as a multi-temporal analytic of 'now-time', could we imagine concepts as configured across the space-times of an 'urban now'? How could Deleuze's philosophical drama of conceptualisation be imagined in the context of generating insights about the urban world? The final image of this book, a photograph of one of two disused Cooling Towers from a power station in Soweto, Johannesburg, dramatises how the urban might present itself, now, as changing constellations of multi-temporal urban experiences, always in the midst of elsewheres (Image 4.2, p. 304; a colour version of this image can be found between pages 132 and 133). These vast concrete constructions were long symbols of the ambitious but fractured modernity of apartheid Johannesburg: like many noxious land uses, they were placed close to black townships. Now disused yet still prominent features of the landscape, they were redecorated as part of the 2010 FIFA World Cup preparations. The images on the towers condense many aspects of Johannesburg's urban life - long journeys in taxis, street fires in braziers in the cold winters, ubiquitous adverts for informal hairdressers, churches and neighbourhoods. At the same time, they draw us to consider how the production of the football world cup generated new constellations of the future city: globalising ambitions for tourism and economic growth, transnational policy learning for a new bus rapid transit system, as well as displacements of traders and some residents for building the new stadiums. A decade later they form a part of the mundane, slow unravelling of the concrete inheritance of the city in the midst of the wider crises of state capture and political division. This chapter considers how, starting with such materialities of urban territories, the 'urban now' might reveal itself. The final chapter, then, explores the potential for conceptualisation of the urban to be energised through constellations of insights across here and (elsew)here, starting in the midst of urban territories, often in a close-up view.

CHAPTER 10

Territories

Incomparability is the life of comparison.
(Osborne 2004, p. 15)

A further series of experimental comparative tactics come into view on the unsteady ground of urban territories. We attend to the many ways in which the urban world presses on the conceptualising practices of researchers, posing 'problems' (and comparative opportunities) for us. It is helpful to return to Deleuzian understandings of virtuality. Here it is the virtual series of the material world, all the possibilities of the emergent urban world, which demands our attention. Being open to whatever the (urban) territory presents involves thinking with the unruly proximities of the heterogeneous elements which make up the urban, focussing in on fragments of urban life, or following 'lures' in unpredictable directions. Urban territories present multiple starting points for conceptual practice, from the diversity of extensive and fragmented urban territories, or along the dispersed 'operational landscapes' of urbanisation. This chapter explores possibilities for investigative experiments which emerge from another distinctive spatiality of urbanisation – territorialisations. We will ask the question as to 'what territories' might form the basis for comparative analysis. The emergent territorialisations of the urban offer intriguing potential for thinking comparatively across a wide range of different urban outcomes.

The experimental comparative tactics identified in this chapter direct us to processes of conceptualisation without the figures of 'universal', 'specific', 'conjuncture' or 'general'. Here and in Chapter 11 we approach **the urban as distinctive, each outcome an 'individual'**. This chapter therefore expands the ways of analytically treating urban outcomes and generating concepts and considers new possibilities for comparative method which flow from those. We have seen the consequences for comparative method of treating urban outcomes as differentiated or as 'repeated instances', as variegated or 'contingent' on wider processes, as a 'conjuncture', as specific or as 'diverse'. Here we

Comparative Urbanism: Tactics for Global Urban Studies, First Edition. Jennifer Robinson.
© 2022 John Wiley & Sons Ltd. Published 2022 by John Wiley & Sons Ltd.

explore further the implications of seeing the urban as distinctive – perhaps as 'assemblages', events or singularities. The grounds for comparison, then, might be cast as 'any urban territory'.

Starting with territories, with the urban world, also helps to move away from comparative conventions of starting with 'cities' or the former centres of urbanisation (which many studies still index, e.g. 'Mumbai' or 'Atlantic City'). It is crucial for global urban studies to establish grounds for building understandings which start from the dispersed, fragmented outcomes of contemporary urbanisation processes. These present to us challenges but also new opportunities. Challenges, because the fundamental terms of urban studies are in question: what are 'urban spaces'? What constitutes an 'urban' territory? How can urbanised areas be identified, for example, when they are embedded in agrarian economies and 'rural' governmentalities, and thoroughly porous to all kinds of circulations (Balakrishnan 2019; Roy 2016)? Beginning comparative analyses from 'any urban territory' definitively establishes the potential for urban studies to truly begin anywhere. This chapter will, however, leave us with some significant open questions – not least how we assess whatever might be urban about territories, what territories might be urban, and how to get along with the urban as a multiplicity of possibilities.

Thinking from Territories

In the context of the multiplicity of transnational circuits and the extensive (or multi-scalar) social formations shaping global urbanisation, what benefit is there in starting to think the urban from territories? This seems to imply taking a more classical comparative perspective across 'places', or returning us to the imagination of the urban as an intersection of trajectories or processes making 'contingent' outcomes. Rather, the proposition here is to theorise from whatever an urban territory entails. This implies moving away from a city-centric view to explore how comparative urban analyses can work with the diverse territorialisations emergent from multiple circuits, urbanisation processes and situated practices. Can we get beyond treating these as 'contexts', contingent outcomes of wider processes, as residuals of or variegated contributions to wider circuits? On what basis can we treat the complex territorialisations of urbanisation, urban territories, as the grounds from which the field of the urban might come into view?

A most revealing exercise in thinking from urban territories has been the critical engagement with the term, 'suburbanisation'. Shifting attention from the 'inside-out' theorisations of urbanisation as spreading from a putative centre has definitively changed the perspective of urban studies (Brenner and

Schmid 2014, 2015). This represents an essential dislocation of urban studies to the 'peripheries' – to the diverse territories where the impacts of the coming urban transitions in different parts of the world will be strongly felt. These are the territories where millions of men, women and children will be finding places to settle and to seek livelihoods or where enterprises will seek to establish. Such sites, even in the poorest of urban contexts, are also often venues of value creation for global capital. Starting from 'the suburb', from the outside in, has been an essential manoeuvre for developing the analytical resources to understand and address the future shape and challenges of urbanisation. As Keil observes, 'it is time to argue for an intervention into urban theory on the basis of the suburban explosion' (2017, p. 42).

It is clear that if non-central, expanding urban formations ('suburbs') are to be drawn into analytical focus, taking a global approach is essential – from beyond the (city) centre, but also from beyond the usual northern reference points, starting anywhere.[1] Whatever 'suburbs' are or might become, this ex-centric reference point embraces a very wide variety of urban forms across the globe. There is a great diversity of processes of (sub-)urbanisation evident across different regions and urban settlements. At the same time, ex-centric urbanisms in different places are also closely interconnected through a range of transnational processes, and thus they are also part of repeated-but-differentiated formations within wider circulations and circuits of urbanisation and globalisation. In search of insights into 'suburbs', their afterlives and future trajectories, then, it is helpful to think from and with both diversity (outcomes are specific in different places perhaps because of long historical trajectories of development) and differentiation (interconnected processes associated with repetition and differentiation of urban form). But perhaps most generative has been to assess whether the basis for comparative analysis could be any (sub)urban territory. A global suburbanisms research project co-ordinated by Roger Keil from York University, Canada, with over 50 collaborating researchers from across the world, has inspired and enacted significant methodological and conceptual innovation in order to grapple with this problematic of diverse, interconnected and distinctive ex-centric urbanisms.

The immediate challenge in thinking from 'Zwischenstädte', as Keil (2017) suggested, drawing on the contributions of Thomas Sieverts, is that it requires thinking across so many very different meanings and experiences of 'suburb'; there is a world of suburbs, which Richard Harris (2010) very quickly began to explore in the context of the 'global suburbanisms' initiative. As Keil puts it, they encountered 'the Babylonian plurality in naming settlement away from the core' (2017, p. 46). It was not just the names that were diverse, though, as the collection of Harris and Vorms (eds) (2017) demonstrates, 'suburb' and the myriad lexical terms used for urban peripherality index a wide range of urban experiences. Thus, any concept beginning with the US model, with features such as low density, peripherality and exclusiveness, quickly breaks down in the face of the diversity of suburban forms, such as French *banlieue* and South African townships, both of which are peripheral, dense and poor. After numerous such examples, only a remnant of the suburban remains: peripherality. In this way a new and minimalist definition of the suburban emerged: *a combination of non-central population and economic growth with urban spatial expansion.* (Ekers et al. 2012, p. 407). Richard Harris suggested a focus on 'the ordinary urban periphery within a worldwide frame of reference' (2010, p. 16), bringing together literatures across the global North and South, which at that time he could say, 'had hardly communicated' (p. 20). The *Global Suburbanisms* project has fundamentally changed that, bringing these diverse ex-centric urban contexts into conversation.

In the ensuing critical reflections, it has become clear that divergences from the putative 'origin' model of the suburb abound. This origin has often been located, as Keil (2017, p. 45) describes it, in the 'marked term' indexing the 'classic' US model of the suburb. Certainly, the historical origins of the term 'suburb' are more complex and much older than this and can be seen, for example, in the 'beyond the city walls' meaning developed within the historical experience of European urbanisation (Phelps et al. 2017, and see Christian Topalov's (2017) fascinating account of the emergence and circulation of urban terminology). The distinctiveness of the US case of car-dependent private home-ownership by the middle classes is quickly apparent when bringing other contexts into consideration. For example, relocating to the periphery was often forced on residents and was not the classic individual consumer choice of the US suburb – the cruel displacement of South African black people to distant townships from often vibrant central locations is foremost in my mind. And that many on the periphery are not escaping the city but arriving in it. Thus, the central city remains the focus of many sub/urban dwellers expending significant investments of mobility and daily effort to find livelihoods and to sustain life, often in modes of informality. For many, suburbs represent a base from which to secure 'an approach to the city rather than an escape from it' (Phelps 2017, p. 7).

Keil's (2017) overview text, '*Suburban Planet*' succinctly proposes a wider conversation across a range of expanding, peripheral urbanities. France's banlieues, for example, join many other contexts in dispossessing the periphery of privilege and low density. So, we can reflect on the high rises at the edge of Istanbul which signal dispossession by a peremptory regime, loss of livelihoods, and financial ruin. Or, as Teresa Caldeira (2016) has reminded us in her paper comparing peripheral urbanisations, the similarly financed and cognate developments in South Africa which there stand for a revolution won, a developmental state until recently committed to redistribution and a better life, if not for all then for many. Or the Indonesian low-income high rises which signal both dispossession from dense, diverse inner-city neighbourhoods and a site for new associational projects (Simone 2019). The hyper-privatised and gated suburbs of post-socialist Sofia, protecting personal freedoms longed for in the socialist era (as Sonia Hirt 2012, has explored) need to be thought alongside the modest peripheral socialist era housing estates which keep intact an accessible and socially mixed urbanity in Prague (to follow Ouředníček 2016).

The 'periphery', then, is a multiplicity of urban forms and experiences. The diversity of ex-centric urban settlements across Africa highlight the multiplicity of kinds of peripheral urbanisation processes: piecemeal developments by small-scale private developers (such as in Lagos – Sawyer 2014; Karaman et al. 2020); intensifying and modernising, while also linked to traditional authorities (Beall et al. 2015); extractive while at the same time aspirational (Nairobi – Murray 2017; Van Den Broeck 2017); emergent in the tracks of countervailing historical processes, such as the post-apartheid townships dependent on apartheid era land holdings (Johannesburg – Butcher 2020); ambitious and internationally oriented while enmeshed in precarious forms of governance (Kigali – Tom Goodfellow 2014, 2017); a multitude of settlements throughout the continent which are at once precarious but also very longstanding (Lusaka – Myers 2011); juxtapositions of traditional settlement histories and elite developments (Durban – Alison Todes 2014); shaped by concerns of rural settlements and extended, spatially dispersed families (Dar es Salaam – Claire Mercer 2017). These diverse (sub)-urbanisms can be detected from across a continent which remains so neglected in urban studies, and urban theory (Myers 2011; Simone and Pieterse 2017). Telling these as accounts of peripheral urbanisation/suburbanisation places these experiences both conceptually and methodologically within the frame of the wider conversations of urban studies beyond the developmentalism that conventionally frames analyses of 'African cities' (Bloch 2015; Mabin et al. 2013).

A starting point for comparative analysis in exploring suburbanisation has therefore been a certain kind of territory, in its multiple forms across the globe, with the shared features of being relationally positioned in urban peripheries and a site of urban expansion. This comparative tactic has opened up the term 'suburb' to a form of concept formation responsive to whatever the urban world is: thinking the 'suburban' from whatever is found in these kinds of territories. Thus, in terms of what this project contributes to a comparative imagination and method, on the one hand the effect of researching 'global suburbanisms' has been to continue to deploy (rather than jettison) the terms 'sub-urb/s-urbanisation-urbanism' as a referent of urban processes.[2] But, unlike the way in which the term gentrification has been sustained around a core definition, this project has insisted on opening to whatever the suburb might be to generate new meanings and to enable its widest relevance. Using the concept in this way proposes to embrace variety and difference, constantly questioning and transfiguring the term in unanticipated ways. This has the effect of displacing extant analyses and redefining the urban from its peripheries – both the physical peripheries of urbanisation and the peripheries of urban theory. If you like, a concept initially seeking to universalise itself by naming a phenomenon across different cases has been assumed (taken on), but also cut down to size and opened up to radical revision through collaborative research. A multiplicity of concepts of suburb have resulted. On the basis of thinking from a certain kind of urban territory across many cases, a conversation has been enabled which is inclusive of any peripheral urban context. In the process, the initial concept has been significantly mediated, transformed, thickened, 'clothed' (to follow Deleuze) in the variety of the cases, perhaps till it looks like something else altogether. In this sense, the framing concept, 'suburb', has been lightened sufficiently as needless parochial detail has been drawn off, or rendered non-determinate as more of an organising frame for conceptual innovation. The term has transformed in its travels, accumulated difference to multiply meanings and emerged as variable and complex, with potential to play a part in shaping understandings of distinctive urban outcomes by stimulating thinking across contexts.

A form of comparative analysis based in a certain kind of ubiquitous urban territory – urbanising peripheral areas – has flourished out of the initially very parochial concept of the 'suburb'. Here we see the potential for opening up conceptualisation of the urban to the rich diversity of urban territories. But how might the spatial formation which is an urban territory be delimited? We have piggy-backed here on an inherited term, the suburb, which invited us to take peripheral urbanising territories as starting points for analysis. More generally, though, in a world where urbanisation does not necessarily take place in or produce 'cities', what kinds of urban territories might it be good, or necessary, to think with? The next section explores this.

Which Territorialisations?

Which urban territories might be the focus of attention, might form the grounds for comparative experiments? Not only Planetary Urbanisation theorists (Monte-Mòr 2014a, 2014b; Brenner and Schmid 2014) but also scholars in different regions who seek to understand the sprawling and complex forms of urbanisation have grappled with this. In coming to terms with the urbanisation of India, for example, Zérah (2020, pp. 23–6) insists that urban India does not stop with the metropolitan regions. About 30% of urban dwellers live in increasingly interconnected secondary cities, participating in globalising economic circuits which are often much less studied. For some regional centres, the regional and globalising economic connections which they generate or form part of may bypass the globalising processes and circuits which characterise India's largest urban regions, meaning they are in some ways functionally disconnected from these 'urban' economies. She brings into view what she and her colleagues call 'Subaltern urbanisation' (Denis et al. 2012; Denis and Zérah 2017) – emergent forms of urbanisation embedded in regional and small towns, including urbanised villages and so-called census towns (those enumerated as large urban settlements but at times governed through rural administration). Almost 40% of urban dwellers (120 million people in 2011) can be found in fast-growing small settlements, often not counted as urban. Some might be tied into larger urban conurbations. But, significantly, the smallest settlements are not transitioning to more familiar forms of urbanisation. They are a sustained response to agricultural decline and structural unemployment with a distinctive economy (Zérah 2020).

These kinds of disjunctures and fragmentations of the urban characterise urbanisation across many regions – and are not necessarily new. How might comparative analytics be forged around fragmented, dispersed and emergent territorialisations of the urban? In the context of such diverse forms of urbanisation, Zérah insists, the 'net of comparison needs to be cast quite wide', to think far beyond the idiom of comparing 'cities' or metropolitan regions: 'La voix spécifique de l'urbanisation indienne permet justement d'aller au-delà et nous enjoin à lancer plus loin le filet de la comparaison' (Zérah 2020, p.289).

In this light, the conundrum as to what territories might form starting points for urban studies is reflected well in one of the core topics of comparative urbanism – urban politics. With such a range of territorial forms, how might urban politics be understood? Zérah's study *Quand L'Inde s'urbanise* exemplifies these challenges. Across all the urban settings she explores, a bricolage of types of government, management and financing of services can be identified; neoliberalisation is at best partial, with many private initiatives especially in secondary cities taking different forms, adapted to the norms and socio-economic conditions of users (p. 279). Technocratic solutions requiring access to transnational finance and initiatives to promote global competitiveness coexist with political clientelism, and all manner of enterprises delivering urban services, such as small family firms, coexist with efforts to bring in corporate private sector actors to contribute to urban government.

For the smallest settlements, rural government status brings financial gains (p. 70), a diversity of forms of service delivery, and political formations which align with highly localised privileges and affiliations. Settlements could have very different qualities and fates depending on the governance arrangements (to be governed as a village or an urban area matters). Furthermore, in some contexts urban politics might be driven more by traditional forms of land ownership, locally based economic interests and religious and ethnic politics, with implications for the nature of service delivery and access to state resources for infrastructure.

More generally, there is a pressing need to rethink extant 'theorisations' of urban politics in response to empirical trends in urbanisation as well as the great diversity of urban forms across the planet. The vast expansion and fragmentation of urban settlements, their dispersal over extended urban regions or corridors, and the expanded role of globalised circuits shaping urbanisation (such as policy circuits, networks of urban actors, and investment flows) create a complex landscape of urban politics. Particularly, if those contexts which have historically not informed urban 'theory' are starting points for conceptualisation, different concerns emerge in seeking to understand urban politics: the provision of essential services is crucial, the politics of access to and titling of land, the diverse interests of state actors (as opposed to 'the state') and varied forms of political authority, alongside informal regulation of urban processes, the co-ordination of everyday life and mobilisation of popular concerns through many kinds of associational practices.

This sits against an inheritance of theories of urban politics which rest on an earlier era and on certain parochial political contexts, notably the United States (see John Lauermann 2018, for an excellent summary of this literature and its limits). As we discussed in Chapter 3, the classic Cox-Harvey approach to understanding the urban politics of local economic development was focused on municipalities competing for footloose capital, and a range of analyses of urban regime politics also flowed from the US context. In this view, locally dependent municipalities and firms configured political formations whose interests were assumed to be aligned with a competitive growth agenda. Regime theory extended these insights to a more nuanced assessment of how actors with different local interests might assemble a coalition, often informal, establishing a stable and consistent growth path with different political complexions (Stone 1989). Savitch and Kantor (2004) expanded the range of concerns to include European experiences, which meant considering municipalities more broadly in relation to their national political context, local political mobilisations, and also the place of cities in a wider understanding of international economic relationships. However, even these more nuanced approaches struggle for explanatory purchase in contexts where business and other actors are nationally focused rather than locally dependent (Cox 2017; Gordon 1995), where local governance and fiscal systems are strongly centralised (Ward 1996), and where the institutional basis and scope for operation of local government is weak or highly informalised, or interwoven with traditional/communal forms of land ownership and governance (Beall et al. 2015). Strong transnational actors, such as resource extraction companies (oil, minerals), sovereign development organisations, International NGOs and actors such as the World Bank also bring a very different configuration to urban politics (Robinson 2018a).

Certainly, understandings of urban politics for the twenty-first century need some new starting points. Connections themselves are sites of the urban political, as observed in Chapter 5 and in relation to the discussion of neoliberalisation in Chapter 6. Thus, urban politics is constituted not only in (urban) territories, but also through international arenas, transnational agencies and global actors. Urban politics happens in these circuits, then, as much as in the territories (Roy and Ong 2011b; Acuto 2013; Robinson 2021). More concretely, circuits constitute new 'territories' of urban politics including, for example: networks and associations of municipalities inserting their interests into global policy agendas such as the SDGs (Parnell 2016); processes of disseminating the urban agendas of global agencies (such as 'rolling out the SDGs' – Kanuri et al. 2016); forming inter-municipal networks to share experiences on many different topics from climate change to resilience (Bulkeley 2010); or more collaborative advocacy-based initiatives such as the Cities Alliance, or grassroots international organisations such as the Slum Dwellers International (McFarlane 2011a; Patel et al. 2012). Thus, the power relations and dynamics of globalised circuits and networks are 'urban' politics, and necessarily involve actors from a wide range of urban contexts and transnational institutions.

Reconfiguring analyses of urban politics also needs to take account of the diverse territorialisations which result from the multiple circuits shaping urbanisation. The territorial formations of the urban under planetary urbanisation as extended, fragmented, sprawling, operational (Brenner and Schmid 2015), and the transnational politics of a 'scramble for infrastructure' currently shaping territorial reconfigurations of global urbanisation (Kanai and Schindler 2019) both need to be considered. What is needed is an approach that can potentially speak to a wide range of emergent territorialised urban formations in the midst of globalised and interconnected but also often dispersed and fragmented urban outcomes. Ludovic Halbert suggests the term, 'Transcalar Territorial Networks' (Halbert and Rouanet 2014). In my view, this analysis offers a way forward to revisit the territories of urban politics beyond municipal-based global competition, or the entrepreneurial state.

Multiple globalising circuits shape the future trajectories of urban settlements and more generally the extended and fragmented territories which are the outcomes of urbanisation processes (Keil 2017; Schmid et al. 2018). Globalised processes of investment, such as financialisation or sovereign investors, produce repeated, seemingly identical urban forms – the serially reproduced satellite or smart city, the repetition of 'iconic' architecture, the endlessly borrowed concept or design. However, during our research on the politics of large scale urban developments in London we became aware that each of the apparently identical buildings being developed there required two to three years of meetings between planners and developers to negotiate the financing, planning gain, social and hard infrastructure provision, and the detailed design of buildings (Robinson and Attuyer 2021). Actors with varying global reach and different capacities were drawn together around each development, along with conventions and calculative devices (Christophers 2014) and a vast array of legislation and policy. All were at stake in each negotiated outcome. More generally, new cities or infrastructure are the result of numerous globalising or translocal circuits and many different actors from national governments to local residents. Thus, any urban development likely brings into perspective many different circuits of policy, planning visions, national political ambitions, globally competitive economic development strategies, financial investment decisions, or local populations positioning themselves to benefit in some way from planned developments, perhaps long in advance of anything ever being built (Kanai and Schindler 2019; Van Den Broeck 2017).

In the settings of new urban developments, then, a range of transcalar actors and networks are territorialised in the cooperation, contestation, and creative production of new urban territories. Halbert and Rouanet's concept of transcalar territorial networks takes seriously this complexity of circulations and territorialisations:

> The concept of transcalar territorial networks (TTN) is suggested to explain how resources from multiple horizons are pulled together in a given business property development, from a fixed plot of land to capital allocated in distant investment committee boardrooms.
>
> (Halbert and Rouanet 2014, p. 472)

Allen and Cochrane's (2007) conceptualisation of 'regional assemblages' is also helpful here – different 'scales' are flattened into a patchwork of overlapping territorialisations of different institutional agency. This opens up new lines of investigation for thinking about urban politics.

Thus, across a range of territories – extended and city-regional configurations, corridors, dispersed territorial fragments of the urban – political formations are assembled out of diverse actors operating with varied reach, capacity and transcalar competencies. It is important to also layer in the specific regulatory pathways that emerge in urban contexts, perhaps around jurisdictions or governance structures, such as municipalities, metropolitan areas, countries, regions. We can take a cue here from a regulationist idea of a 'rapport territorial' – territorial relations of regulation emergent in different metropolitan contexts: 'The territorial relationship generates a contradictory and complex system of dependencies, jurisdictions and rules […] it consists not only of laws, bylaws and prescriptions, but also of diverse unwritten, implicit rules; as a result it is often barely comprehensible to outsiders – and even so to insiders' (Schmid 2015, 297). Often, large-scale developments accumulate bespoke institutional and regulatory arrangements to enable the many challenges to be navigated (Robinson et al. 2020).

Thus, the territorial grounds for urban politics could be conceived as emergent territorialisations, constructed through transcalar territorial networks that constellate around designated urban projects and programmes, as well as the complex formations associated with territorialised regulatory assemblages. Rather than competing municipalities and footloose capital, we can acknowledge the emergence of (new) territories on which urban politics is constituted, such as large-scale development projects, satellite cities, extensive infrastructural developments, or the transcalar regulatory contexts that establish pathways of development. In these settings, a diverse cast of actors with differently configured interests and concerns emerge, varying from context to context (even within the same city, region or country).

In this light, the interests and practices of actors may be surprising: 'global' developers and architects whose local reputations and relationship inspire more modest goals for developments may be at odds with states whose commitment is to intensify extraction to support their own ambitions. Or developmental state interests in securing an adequate housing supply might be aligned with new processes of globalised investment—financialisation or 'build to rent'. Thus, we need to take seriously the ways in which processes of territorialisation simultaneously produce and localise both (global) developers and states (Brill, 2018; Robinson and Attuyer 2021; Todes and Robinson 2020). As a corollary, within the scope of these territorialised formations openings for effective state agency might not depend on building strong institution-wide agency in municipalities or national governments but could involve having some capacity to shape decision-making and negotiations in relation to specific developments. This potentially opens up a significant perspective on questions of African urban governance, for example, where analysts and development organisations have been perplexed by, and highly critical of, the extensive investments in large-scale urban developments across the continent (Murray 2017; Van Noorloos and Kloosterboer 2018; Watson 2014a). Here, a determinedly scalar developmental imagination of government/governance could be enriched by a view of transcalar governance and the overlapping circuits (private, developmental, sovereign) shaping new urban territories in Africa. Rather than a good governance agenda focused on improving hierarchical interjurisdictional arrangements (Pieterse et al. 2018), close attention to the transcalar territories of urban development might indicate targeted opportunities to improve outcomes (planning gain, application of international law). Improved understanding of the territorialisation of actors, their emergent interests, and scope for intervention in these developments could possibly yield stronger public benefit from investments (Goodfellow 2020; Turok 2016).

With so many cases of large-scale developments and urban extensions globally (see Kanai and Schindler 2019; Murray 2017), in theorising urban politics we can immediately pay attention to the diversity of issues, actors, interests, circuits, relationalities which matter in a majority urban world: land, law, associational mobilisations, complex and competing authority structures, peremptory states; bargained authoritarianism (Lee and Zhang 2013) rather than entrepreneurialism. My orientation and interest here is to excavate a way of thinking urban politics which resonates with and builds on insights from urbanisation processes in the majority urban world, which attend as much to the urgent challenges of services and housing, as to the worlding and worlded nature of highly globalised circuits of investment pressing on some of the poorest urban contexts.

Like processes of urbanisation themselves, the politics of urban development needs to be thought along the 'extensions' of urban form, urban livelihoods and urban lives (Brenner and Schmid 2015; Simone 2020). The 'scramble for infrastructure' (Kanai and Schindler 2019) has emerged as a crucial setting for urban politics in the context of an urban development model dominated by the concerns of geopolitical actors (sovereign states, state-mandated and state-owned enterprises, national aid agencies). These developments are often explicitly scaled beyond municipal territories or extant urban forms and particularly involve national governments. Large-scale infrastructural projects form territories of urbanisation across regional, national and international jurisdictions. Thus, just as the processes of the neoliberalisation of urban life and governance in many parts of the world were scaled nationally, the politics of contemporary urban development is often more properly a 'geopolitics' in which national and sovereign actors are central. At the same time, the extension and territorialisation of urban life proceeds through actions of myriad actors, and many different kinds of urbanisation processes. These might entail extended urbanised landscapes of mineral development, dispersed industrial production, or the disjunct juxtapositions of diverse activities in urban peripheries (Arboleda 2016; Monte-Mòr 2014a, 2014b; Ortega 2020). But urban territories might also be shaped by 'spaces of circulation', such as the flows of goods, traders and construction materials extending urbanisation along the emergent West African corridor (Choplin and Hertzog 2020), or the shifting associations and temporary initiatives which draw urban actors 'to extend' activities into peripheries, along familiar routes of labouring, in search of transformative 'lateral' connections across disparate landscapes and activities (Simone 2020).

The multiple processes of speculation, investment and extraction which frame the vast extensions and urbanised landscapes of the contemporary urban world (Brenner and Schmid 2014, 2015) are therefore initiated and shaped by actors ranging from foreign sovereign states and inter-governmental organisations, to the precarious efforts of residents and sojourners across dispersed territories. They involve a wide variety of interests, actors, practices and imaginations. These constitute not only the frontiers of urbanisation in many places, but also the sites and predicaments in need of critical attention in urban studies. Comparative tactics engaging with the diverse territories of urbanisation might helpfully start with documenting the variety of actors and outcomes, processes and configurations which extend urban life, form and processes. How these remake older centralities would also be important to document (Sawyer et al. 2021). The processes at work in what seems like a new phase of urbanisation across the world's surface call for practices of emergent conceptualisation. Such analyses will need to remain open to the diverse outcomes and processes which coalesce in different territories and initiate analytical insights across distinctive urban formations. But they could also work with actors and circulating formats of development common to many different contexts – the interconnected processes making such territories include investments from sovereign or development actors or circulating planning ideas, for example, opening once more to genetic comparative tactics.

Urban studies is embracing a research agenda driven by the unfamiliar, emergent formations of twenty-first century urbanisation, with many of these presenting themselves outside the heartlands of earlier rounds of urban theorisation. New urban territories are strongly emergent in *les pays suds*, and often driven by new Asian, Middle Eastern and other southern hegemons of urban development – private and sovereign interests from Brazil, Turkey and India, for example, are active across many African contexts. Building repertoires for conceptualising from (any) urban territories will be an essential component of a comparative urban imagination for the twenty-first century. The next section, as well as Chapter 11 consider some methodological propositions for how this might proceed.

Assembling Territories: 'Lures' for Comparative Imaginations

In his presentation of experimental comparative tactics inspired by a materialities perspective as well as the Indian 'subaltern studies', McFarlane (2019) proposes to treat 'fragments' of urban space, politics and the historical archive as starting points to rethink the urban and urban studies:

> the fragment as a marker of the edges of how cities and the urban are understood and represented – ways of living and being and imagining and making the city that have been at the margins or even invisible to much of urban studies, and which may point to new kinds of knowledge. The fragment, in this analysis, acts as a kind of lure, an invitation to pause and stay with difference.
> (McFarlane 2019, p. 219)

More generally, in thinking the urban from territories, 'assemblage' or materialities approaches provide crucial resources. Within this repertoire of theoretical analysis, the territory proposes distinctive propositions for a comparative imagination. A replete spatiality comes into view on the terrain of the territory – what Amin and Thrift (2016) index as 'seeing like a city'. This is somewhat different from the Lefebvrian perspective we considered in Chapter 9, in the sense that the fullness of subjective experience and lived realities is somewhat sidelined in favour of attempts to presence the materiality of 'city' life as the effective jumbled proximities of heterogeneous elements in which resides the potential for emergent socio-natural configurations, assemblages, or entities. These proximities also indicate an open potentiality for researchers to forge or follow emergent associations across diverse entities within territories, rather than assume dialectical articulations of wider processes or prejudge relations between 'fragments' and 'wholes' (McFarlane 2018; see also Strathern 2005).

For urban scholars, it is worth thinking about this juxtapositional logic beyond the materialities emphasis of these writers. Layoun (2013) explores this in relation to the rise of 'modern' experiences (in the early twentieth century) in which movements and dislocations brought quite different people together in cities. She astutely observes that 'juxtaposed differences, however stark, are not in themselves a comparative act. Yet the *recognition* of difference is both predicated upon and calls out for a concept of comparison' (p. 212; my emphasis).[3] The juxtapositions wrought by territories might inspire the urban researcher, in her 'recognition' of opportunities for thinking differently across the surprising juxtaposition of different elements of urban life, which need not be considered only as matter, or 'socio-natures'. Within her textual analysis, Layoun is inspired to explore a 'comparison-in-practice called out by … juxtapositions' across historical time and cultural-linguistic difference (p. 216). She places this comparative potential 'not only across differences but amongst them' which would rely on the more 'tenuous and fragile *creation of connection* in the comparative effort itself' (p. 228; my emphasis). In the same collection, Susan Stanford Friedman (2013) suggests the imagination of 'collage' as a juxtapositional comparative methodology (inspired, she notes, by Dadaism and modernist poetics – drawn into close conversation with urban studies by both Benjamin and Lefebvre). Within the framework of literature, she sees this as a way of composing insights which inspire generalities based on shared aspects of texts, while maintaining the particularity of each, refusing hierarchy and instrumentalism. Ambitiously, she suggests on this basis that 'Comparison through cultural collage enables the production of new theories' (p. 42). Such a juxtaposition of different 'fragments', unexplained 'residues' or the disruptive conceptual assemblages inspired by urban proximity, can inspire comparative reflection.

A materialities perspective particularly draws attention to the multiplicity of elements making up any urban territory, and highlights innumerable possible starting points for comparative reflection. The dynamic 'becoming' of territories might be figured as a product of the juxtapositions of difference, the genetic dynamism of the material world, or the emergent agency of socio-natures. But the potentiality of territory is also forged through connections – the openness of any territory is evident (Massey 2005). Thus, tracking how heterogeneous elements might be configured into emergent formations both within and across territories is an important orientation for comparative tactics. There might be grounds to bring into analytical juxtaposition the elements of emergent 'assemblages' across different territories. This might be fully on the side of similarities which are identified through a researcher's curiosity, or inspired by material resonances, emergent or found connections (Lancione and McFarlane 2016). The prolific interconnections shaping the urban which underpinned the materialities-oriented genetic comparative tactics explored in Chapter 5 are joined here by a more directive, agentful researcher. Fragments might certainly suggest themselves to the researcher, but the practice of actively tracking and tracing perhaps occluded connections, or pursuing the implications of juxtapositions, is as much a product of researcher interest as of material agency or mobility.

Colin McFarlane (2018, 2019) has proposed and exemplified ways to take this forward. He engages critically with the potentiality which others find in fragments (or parts) to tie them in to a wider whole – capitalist urbanisation, for example.[4] The 'fragment' is helpfully not seen by McFarlane as a 'particular' – it is not imagined as already interpreted within some conceptual frame or an imagined 'whole'. It is precisely the open potential of elements of the urban taken as 'fragments' which he is interested in, notably 'subaltern' fragments which index marginality and exclusion from history, and so have the potential to displace pre-existing interpretations. The special case of the 'fragment' within a 'subaltern imagination' indicates 'the fragment (as) an uncertain, searching and challenging provocation that may form new abstractions and ways of seeing' (p. 223). As a 'lure', fragments open opportunities to displace conventional imaginations of 'abstraction', as in their formation they often point to the power relations associated with excluded subjects, knowledges or practices; they invite speculative thought rather than incorporation into a 'whole'. The fragment could also offer critical insight into how any wider 'whole' in which it might be implicated, might be re-interpreted.

In a practical example, McFarlane (2018) explores the relationship between political mobilisations in Cape Town and Mumbai. He adopts three tactics – 'attending to fragments', 'generative translation with fragments', 'surveying the whole' (p. 1008) – to invite a creative engagement with found elements of urban territories. His empirical study identifies fragments of examples of a popular politics of sanitation in both urban contexts, which he sees as disruptive of political orders in both places. But, he also is drawn by the political practices he observes to address how activists themselves place these fragments into conversation with the wider institutions of each context (in relation to the 'whole'). The enumeration of pavement dwellers in Mumbai, for example, makes pragmatic immediate claims on authorities there. And in bringing sanitation politics to the centre of political authority in Cape Town in dramatic ways (depositing 'poo' on the steps of the city hall), activists there instantiate a wider political frame of reference. In both places, political mobilisation and urban transformation draw 'fragments' into emergent wider movements, institutions and conceptualisations. In the case of South Africa, especially, the anti-apartheid movement which yielded a revolution in power at a national scale was fundamentally based on urban social movements. Subaltern studies in this context, known as the social history movement, followed the traces of African political mobilisation over decades to reveal a full, rich and ambitious series of class, race and gender movements which coalesced to overturn apartheid. In this context the search for 'fragments' in the archive, inspired by E.P. Thompson and the subaltern studies movement alike, was a practical project of political analysis and movement building (Bozzoli 1990). 'Fragments' in the archive, then, were a 'lure' inspiring understanding of the historical formation of political subjects whose concerns were rather more consequentially holistic than McFarlane suggests, in the service of national revolution.

In an 'experimental comparison' together with Michele Lancione, McFarlane clarifies how wider conceptualisations might emerge through comparisons within this materialities perspective. Although broadly eschewing generalisation, they bring their separate case studies together – everyday sanitation experiences in Turin and Mumbai – to explore how urban dwellers in 'radically different contexts that have seemingly little in common' (2016, p. 2402) cope with the lack of sanitation. They consider homeless people in Turin, and shack dwellers in Mumbai. With a focus on what they call 'Infra-making' – 'the interstitial labour of human and non-human agencies and atmospheres that takes place in the production of forms of sanitation' – they develop a shared analysis across the two cases but emphasise the heterogeneity and differences across the cases and insist that

> heterogeneity is worth sticking with rather than passing over to the end point of 'generalisation'. We do not argue against generalisation, but reposition it. Heterogeneity stretches and unsettles the categories we use ... We seek out resonances across our cases, but we emphasise uniqueness and contextuality.
> (Lancione and McFarlane 2016, p. 2403)

They seek to position generalisation (as opposed to specificity) 'as an informant ... to enlighten understanding and intervention in specific contexts'. Before they initiate the practice of conceptual emergence which such a comparison proposes, they pull together a rich conceptualisation of 'infra-making' across a range of theoretical resources that index both materiality and the subjective experiences of marginalised urban life:

> Infra-making does not only speak – as the accounts of infrastructure and assemblage ... do – of the more-than-human mingling making up life at the margins, but also highlights how these processes are a matter of constant, laborious and tiresome junctions and disjunctions between one's own wishes, capacities, opportunities, and the vast arrays of agencies and powers at play in the city.
> (Lancione and McFarlane 2016, p. 2407)

With this they are actively drawing in to their 'experimental comparison' a range of pre-existing conceptualisations which help them to both identify and interpret their 'case' and to specify a new, emergent, concept. As a found, retrospective comparison, this experiment has an effective 'third term' in a shared conceptual repertoire. This is informed by UK Geography's interest in materialities, a distinctive conceptualisation of atmospheres and emotionality which comes out of that tradition, and a wide-ranging literature on 'informality'. Considerable conceptual labour is needed in this paper to identify what the experiences they document are. This involves bringing into comparability two sets of observations through construction of a theoretically laden third term: 'infra-making'. I imagine that the effort required to bring the two cases into conversation was much assisted by their shared conceptual starting points which mean that each case was already interpreted within the shared perspective. In this case, then, the potentiality of comparative tactics on generative grounds is working actively across both inextricable Deleuzian series, the virtuality of Ideas, and of matter.

Reflecting on their findings after working with both cases, they think through the achievements of the analysis in terms of both 'specification' and 'generalisation'. They identify that the politics and configurations of infra-making they identified are shared across many urban contexts, but are 'first and foremost contextual endeavours' (p. 2415). They identify 'resonances' or shared grounds across their cases which underpin some 'generalisations' which they draw out from bodily experiences identified in both places: continuous displacement, forceful negotiation, unavoidable exposure, which they link to 'ordinary affects of exhaustion, stress and shame' (p. 2417). They propose their 'generalisation' as not detached from the specificities generating them, but propose that 'generalisation is less an end-point and more an informant to specific contexts', and seek to hold 'specificities and generalisation at the same level' (p. 2417) and to provide 'generalisations that orient critical thinking in relation to context' (p. 2418). This is an important marker of what makes for a useful conceptualisation – and refers to the arguments of those inspired by developmental or more broadly global south commitments to yield research which is relevant to the context. These are hard-won generalisations across divergent processes, achieved on the side of both empirical and theoretical resonance, through inventing concepts with a limited reach, respectful of heterogeneity.

Holding on to difference and heterogeneity while proposing conceptualisations as only slightly extended generalities (generalisations across more than one case), they highlight different practices of conceptualisation. For them the difference is evident between 'universalisations', ambitious concepts that mobilise a claim on all possible instances of something, often theoretically saturated or seeking to establish an abstract conceptualisation, and 'generalisations', empirically driven and open conceptualisations which might frame interpretations close to difference, across a certain empirical extent. For Lancione and McFarlane, insisting that the concepts they develop remain closely allied to the challenges and politics of the contexts they emerge from is a valuable example of how conceptualisation may proceed outside of a search for 'universals' or ambitious abstractions. Inspired by the materialities sensibilities of the De Landa and Latourian perspectives, this indicates one way in which different urban territories might be brought together imaginatively to inspire conceptual innovation. Thinking with the urban territory as such, in all its heterogeneity, is an effort to move away from both the 'monomania of the imagination' which brings a pre-given conceptualisation to bear, and the 'dream of the whole' which integrates observations into a relational unity (Chakrabarty (2000), cited by McFarlane 2019, pp. 214–15). However, in this case, it is a third term saturated with very abstract conceptualisations which provides a broader systemic framing of the cases. These then port a more universalising ambition even as the authors insist on the prioritisation of difference and heterogeneity.[5] Occluding the (theoretical) grounds on which the comparison was effected leaves uninterrogated the more complex dynamics and potentiality of conceptualisation in favour of an assertion of an alleged materiality. What this suggests is that attending to the dynamics of conceptual generativity, as much as heterogeneous materiality, could be important for generative comparisons grounded in urban territories. In their thoughtful essay on 'Deleuze and Space', Dewsbury and Thrift (2005, p. 105) observe: 'Territories are not made up of land but still empirical territories nonetheless for they emerge out of apprehension-thoughts created out of nature's affirmative flux.' Chapter 11 will probe this close entwining of dynamic matter and conceptual vitality.

Conclusion

Thinking from urban territories as the site of jumbled proximities and emergent assemblages, new conceptualisations can sidestep extant theorisations and draw researchers to think with both heterogeneity and elsewhere. This chapter drew attention to two dimensions of comparative practice which the problematic of thinking the urban from territories provokes. The first is the treatment of urban outcomes as distinctive, unique, specific and particular, characterised by heterogeneity both within any urban territory and across different urban outcomes. On this basis concepts and insights reflect the rich diversity of urban life (as in rethinking the meaning of the term, suburbs, for example) or emerge along with the territorialisations of the urban (as in large scale or Infrastructure-led developments), open to the heterogeneity and specificity of these formations. The second dimension of comparative practices starting with territories concerns how conceptualisations might be imagined to emerge on this basis. Diving even further into the territory as a starting point for thinking the urban, the perplexity of the relation between the observation, or 'fragment', and the 'whole', or wider concept, is revealed (McFarlane 2019). We have seen a few different ways of thinking of the 'whole' – the structured totalities of Gramsci and Althusser; the urban as concrete totality proposed by Lefebvre with an open horizon of dynamic conceptualisation. And McFarlane (2018) proposed to weave fragments of political action into a more empirically defined totality – an emergent politics of the 'whole' city, in which the urban is constituted and contested politically. The problematic of the territory returns us, then, to the question of generating concepts, in the midst of an unruly material urban world, in the midst of urban territories.

In his reflections on area studies and comparison, Peter Osborne (2004) engages in conversation with Deleuze about the relationship between observations and concepts. As we saw in Chapter 4, Deleuze developed his understanding of the multi-temporality of processes of conceptualisation, across habit, memory and imagination in response to a dynamic and generative material world. In this process, subjects draw the manifold (all there is) into differenc/tiation as objects, within the horizon of the 'absolute totality in the synthesis of possible appearances' (p. 13) – each determination opens to the possibility of the whole world, all of time, all of concepts. It is in the process of generating concepts of the world that Osborne places the centrality of noncomparability for a comparative imagination, casting the incomparable as signposting 'epistemologically privileged moments motivating new conceptual constructions to try to restore consistency within ideas (such as "humanity") between the totality of their instances. In this respect, incomparabilty is the life of comparison' (p. 16). Singularities, then, are potentially privileged sites of conceptualisation. These moments of dissonance are prolifically present in 'relational encounters': even though heavily power laden as, say in colonial contexts, 'the generality of anthropological and social concepts is necessarily *translational or transcultural* in character'. He continues,

> *Incomparability* is thus a relative term designating that degree of non-identity, within the relevant field, that marks the limit of the intelligibility of a particular comparison. Strictly speaking the incomparable is unthinkable. This is the insurmountable critical difficulty for all notions of singularity as the nonconceptual/unthinkable element in experience (pure aesthesis, ontological difference, and the rest), but one cannot *experience it cognitively* qua singularity. As such, it cannot form the basis for either a knowledge or a politics, except mystically.
>
> (Osborne 2004, p. 17)

Osborne sees the grounds for comparability especially sustained in Deleuzian and Benjaminian responses to the problematic of concept formation. On the one hand, the 'unity in distribution' of concepts (that they are brought together in some way) is necessary for some imagination of comparability. But on the other, difference, and thus comparison, is not treated as an unthinkable limit, a point at which representation is doomed to fail. Instead, for both these thinkers difference and comparison are figured pragmatically: both the 'manifold' (the world) and concepts are seen as 'virtual', encompassing all possibilities in Deleuze, and Benjamin's 'constructions of juxtapositional differences, within the speculative horizon of a [weak] messianic conception of the historical whole' (pp. 21–2) presents this in a similar way, as we will explore in the following chapter. The problematic of generating concepts with and across the ostensibly incomparable, or that which is at the limits of thought (matter), can be understood from within propositions about the complex dynamics by which subjects come to experience and know the (urban) world. It is this problematic that frames the next chapter: how both incomparability and matter do not lead to the abandonment of conceptualisation, but generate a multiplicity of emergent conceptualisations. These approaches offer a way forward for comparative urban practice, rather than different urban experiences being cast as simply the unthinkable difference (outside) of dominant theories; or running ashore on the chimera of expressing the material world without conceptualisation.

Taking cues from Deleuze and Benjamin, then, Chapter 11 considers the generation of concepts, emergent from the urban world and practice, close up to the phenomena that make up the urban. The discussion follows some urban scholars to the limit points of the urban territory in terms of its knowability – its opacity and objectality. But with both Deleuze and Benjamin we find ways to think about understandings of the urban as composed as much through the unruly materialities of the urban world, as through the generative, creative virtuality of concepts. Ironically, it could be here, in the very moment when we must acknowledge the maximum occlusion and divergence of the urban world, that the generativity of concepts too is maximised. The agency of the researcher (and urban subjects) in generating concepts is closely aligned with the generativity of emergent urban formations.

Notes

1. Some aspects of the rest of this section are reversioned from Robinson, J. 2022. The after-lives of 'suburbs': Methodological and conceptual innovations in urban studies. In Keil, R. and Wu, F. (eds). *After Suburbia: Urbanisation in the Twenty-First Century*, Toronto: University of Toronto Press.

2. Zhao (2020) nonetheless expresses concern that the term 'suburb' represents a hegemonisation of a certain contextual experience. His response is to start with other terms for peripheries, which are emergent in different contexts and which bundle elements of the expanding urban periphery differently according to specific planning histories and urban dynamics. This opens up new kinds of conversations across different peripheralities. I agree this is a really creative 'comparative conversation' which potentially enriches the vocabulary of urban studies.
3. Stanford Friedman comments that 'Sometimes juxtaposition is just juxtaposition, not comparison' (2013, p. 41).
4. Although his reading of Lefebvre's sense of 'totality' or 'whole' underestimates the openness and concrete nature of this approach to totality.
5. This reverses the tension between defining very narrow grounds for comparison while thinking productively with variety which characterised conventional comparative methods (Chapter 3). In this inspiring paper by Lancione and McFarlane (2016), the stated commitment to thinking with variety (as both empirical reality and analytical commitment) is somewhat at odds with the strongly articulated shared theoretical grounds. Opening these theoretical grounds up to interrogation (and difference) could indicate new opportunities for conceptual generativity.

CHAPTER 11

Into the Territory, or, the Urban as Idea

> *Baudelaire mingles his voice with the roar of the city as one might mingle one's voice with the breakers on the shore.*
> (Walter Benjamin 2003a [1939], *Central Park*, p. 177)

> *Die Ideen verhalten sich zu den Dingen wie die Sternbilder zu den Sternen.*
> *Ideas are to things as constellations are to stars.*
> (Walter Benjamin 2016 [1928], *Ursprung des deutschen Trauerspiels*, p. 10)/2019, *Origin of the German Trauerspiel*, p. 10)

Some urbanists have called for the idea of 'city' to be kept in play, as one way of seeing the urban – in its often jumbled up heterogeneity (Amin and Thrift 2016). Seeing like a city, in this way, brings us up close with the myriad elements and activities which compose urban life, jostling together in territories. It is certainly not the case, though, that as one gets closer to the ground, in the midst of objects or events, or alongside urban dwellers, it becomes any easier to know what is going on in the city, or what the urban might be. And approaching the up-close, or small scale, or a brute materiality does not make conceptualisation any less relevant, or the problematic of elsewhere in the constitution and thinking of the urban disappear. But myopic vision, looking close up, minimising the distance or finding ways for physicality and objects to reveal themselves and present their agency can bring forward ways to see the city 'awry' (Cairns and Jacobs 2014). Close-up, the city cannot be easily apprehended through the light and ordering arrangements of an enlightenment perspective, which relies on a certain distancing stance; we might rather see it piled up, Baroque style, filled with unrelated elements and ruins, waste and excess,

Comparative Urbanism: Tactics for Global Urban Studies, First Edition. Jennifer Robinson.
© 2022 John Wiley & Sons Ltd. Published 2022 by John Wiley & Sons Ltd.

even as we search for (or stitch together) dimly perceivable shapes or forms (ibid, p. 51; p. 61; Benjamin 1998). The figure of the researcher might be closer here to the 'rag-picker'[1] than the flâneur, Stephen Cairns and Jane M. Jacobs indicate, as they seek to develop a 'feeling for the inert' (p. 7) in their analysis of the death of buildings.

It is tempting, from this positioning, in the midst of ruins or unpredictable juxtapositions and emergent associations in the close-up territory of the urban, to embrace the shadows of unknowability in all concepts. Seeking insight along with the resistant ensembles resulting from the 'strange' alliances and improvisations through which many urban dwellers compose the urban, the urbanist might find their voice as part of the general 'roar' of the city (Benjamin, 2003a [1939], p. 177). As part of the crowd, 'detached from the interpretive gaze' (Simone 2019, p. 49) rather than trying to capture meaning or truth from afar, how might the urban present itself? It is in the torsions, the poor fit, of concepts with 'individuals', the always uneasy arrangements of thought and things, or the tensions between associational connections and distanciating refusals, that urbanists and urban dwellers find their bearings. From this perspective, it is clear that conceptualisation of the urban is hard won. But, I will suggest, it is here that it is also perhaps at its most generative.

In this chapter, the urban is considered as distinctive, each outcome 'individual' rather than a 'universal', 'specific' or 'diverse', for example. Treating each urban outcome as distinctive initiates a highly generative mode of concept formation. In this chapter, then, we draw together an account of a core feature of comparison: it's fundamental orientation to generating and revising concepts. Concepts of the urban, to follow Deleuze, are not genres infinitely divided (or hyphenated) and patched together to fit the particular case, or infinitely extended universals which are able to work themselves out across many cases. Rather, whatever the urban might be (and it could be a growth machine, or a generator of inequality, a certain regulatory pathway or a platform for reproduction), it can be seen as emergent – 'as the actualisation of preindividual singularities' (1993, p. 73). Here, for Deleuze, singularities are direct intuitions or observations, which together can form/be formed as 'constellations', generating ideas/concepts. Singularities are the multiplicity of starting points in determining (what) a phenomenon (is).[2] We come back, then, to a different imagination of concept formation from that in which concepts are opposed to reality, constantly fail to represent it, or are asserted to adequately convey that reality. With Deleuze, and as we will see also with Walter Benjamin, we can place conceptualisations of the urban as a multiplicity, emergent in close association with (the formation of) each urban outcome/observation, but implicated in the virtuality of all the possible ways we can think (about) the urban. Concept formation is intrinsically connected to wider conversations. In some ways, this chapter continues the discussion in Chapters 4 and 7 about generating concepts. So, running through this chapter is a double meaning of the urban as individuality. On the one hand, in our social science vernacular, as discussed in a simple Hegelian sense, the 'individual', as the fullness of reality (distinctive, unique), persistently interrupts processes of conceptualisation, with inevitable residuality, driving dialectical reasoning. But 'individual' in a Deleuzian sense implies an emergent 'existent', which is not pre-determined, but known in relation to an active process of determination. Extended across singularities/observations, then, a comparative imagination which starts in the midst of urban territories is mixed up in the materialities and experiences which compose/are urban life, but is also tethered to the virtuality of ideas about the urban.

The distinctiveness and opacity of urban life, deflecting and turning away from concepts, could also be seen as opening to moments of maximum creativity, initiating new, relevant and embedded insights on the urban in all its diversity. Here, comparative urbanism – as strongly open to revisability, as starting to think the urban from (anyw)here – incites attentiveness to insights which might emerge in situated engagements, or charts filaments of connection across divergent experiences. We have seen throughout this book how the historical object, urban, is empirically and conceptually composed across here and (elsew)here. This chapter develops the most general statement about how insights about urban experiences are emergent from and across distinctive urban contexts, including those which have too often been excluded from analytical repertoires in urban studies. We return to the metaphor of 'launching' concepts we discussed in Chapter 4. Launching concepts, from whatever urban territories, draws distinctive urban experiences into ongoing conversations about the nature of the urban. In the last section of this chapter, we consider this by tracing the emergence, proliferation and fragmentation of the term, 'informality'.

Detachment

The dense heterogeneity of urban life energises observations about emergent 'assemblages' of many different associational activities of the urban poor (Simone 2001b; McFarlane 2011b). But in Simone's *Improvised Lives*, the practices which are the 'grounds of urban sociality' are seen as resting also on ways of rendering urban life opaque, illegible to and detached from other urban actors. The 'uninhabitable', largely peripheral places in urban contexts are produced as such, often as the result of interventions – of speculation, development, displacement, exclusion (p. 11, p. 23). But while these are sites of injustice, Simone wishes to see these 'districts of the poor and working class across the South where I have worked' (p. 15) as more than simply areas of concern in relation to development need or a resistant politics of freedom/autonomy or potential. He draws out practices of 'care' which emerge out of necessity, in situations of extreme difficulty. Across dissonances and detachments, as well as affinities, where people have forged some kinds of collective ways to be in and beyond those places, he sees 'rhythms' of endurance, reliant on extending connections and forging compositions, but also on occluding or refusing relations. This is a detachment, for Simone, also from the 'imperative to compare' (p. 9), making of the uninhabitable also a methodological proposition.

As with many urbanists, Simone is motivated to draw on the experiences he has observed, 'improvised' urban lives, to prepare a way of thinking the urban. It is a response, too, to how ways of thinking about the urban are already implicated in making places uninhabitable. So, forging endurance comes to rely on detachment from development practices flowing from various ways of knowing the urban. Thus, a refusal to relate (p. 9) to the external imperative of 'comparison' which looks to aggregate (harms), to mobilise (displacements) or to assess (for developmental investments). It is not an unrealistic dystopic assessment that the insidious elite politics of speculation and investment in urbanisation as value production prefigures a kind of jettisoning of the poor (from the earth). In this context, then, he considers that detachment, and 'a peripheral politics is vital for the way it doesn't show its cards, becomes nearly impossible to pin down' (p. 33). Even as 'God' seems to have forgotten these places, residents improvise rhythms of endurance and sociabilities of rogue care. Simone identifies a conceptual and methodological potential in this refusal of implicated and inadequate ways of knowing (the urban), in favour of the 'uninhabitable as a method to think about these *rhythms of endurance*' (p. 10) and, more broadly, as a conceptualisation of the urban. Thus, he notes, 'In terms of its role as method I want to look at the uninhabitable as a lure, how it draws one into a place and situation in a way that does not describe or account for it?' (pp. 10–11). He cautions, though, that the uninhabitable could be a 'lure that draws us into particular kinds of observations' which reconstitute peripheral places as problems to be solved, or within the critiques of freedom and autonomy. He wants to look closer than those given perspectives permit, since 'under the veneer of these observations and the kinds of realities they constitute runs another surface "besides" them' (p. 27).

These analytical and methodological propositions, emergent from the lived experiences of urban dwellers, are thoroughgoing in their sustained opposition to many of the ways in which understandings of the urban might conventionally emerge, across heterogeneity and across difference. Not translateable into overarching terms, not proposing analogies, the spectre of an inclusive 'we' is repudiated (pp.26–7). Radical detachment is posed analytically as non-relationality, in opposition to processes of conceptualisation 'where differences turn to each other'. He asks, 'what would happen if such analogies were cut?' (p. 26). It is not simply that such conceptual connections might somehow do violence to the experiences and lives he is recounting, but 'detachment also indicates that by the time a certain life at the margins comes to be represented, it has already moved on somewhere else' (p. 27). For Simone's own text, then, and any we might choose to compose, inscriptions of urban experience, incorporations of the practices and ideas in/as scholarship necessarily betray an urban life composed of disparate actors and entities, utterly contingent, refusing relationality, open to 'the being of anything whatsoever' and evading composition. What does it mean to turn this empirical account of the detachments and refusals of associational life in peripheral urban contexts into a propositional research method and a mode of conceptualisation?

Simone's analysis of resistance to conceptualisation rests also on 'blackness', and practices of black life, cultural resonances and music inform his interpretations. Blackness is seen in a number of ways as a decomposing the possibility of knowing: as a 'supplement on the run from a fundamental relationship of the social, a relationship between self and other that wavers between denigration and indifferent detachment', or, after Fanon, as 'something always misrecognised'. Crucial to this are the challenges of writing history as 'genealogy' framed in the wake of the loss and devastation of slavery, in which 'Nothing has to be what it seems to be' (p. 92, p. 91). The impossibility of producing knowledge in/of the 'middle passage' and the aftermaths of slavery's displacements and death (Hartmann 2008) weigh heavily on any project of thinking the urban in some contexts (McKittrick 2011). Thus forms a conceptualisation of the urban as a relative darkness, opaque and unknowable.

It is an important observation that in the intensity of overlapping practices, the opacity of dense urban life potentially renders a (comparative) trajectory of interpretation (to or from) elsewhere impossible. In this sense, the urban is best seen as 'somewhere'. Simone develops the notion of 'compression', which has a few different implications. This can stand 'as a mode of visibility (invisibility) for how seemingly divergent components of something – a collective or a housing development, for example – might operate in conjunction with each other without necessarily showing that any such mutuality might exist' (p. 39). Differences, then, are not 'turned' to one another. Compression also calls forward a digital metaphor, in which elements are 'withdrawn from distinction', made generic and not needing to be related to be made inter-operable. Finally, this is a somewhat metallurgic metaphor. Acquiring a certain density, rendered opaque through non-relationality, experiences seem utterly closed to the potential of comparability. In this sense he looks to 'convey a sense of the urban as uninhabitable ... where the vectors of here and there, now and then are largely undistinguishable'; in this context urban life – and the conceptualisation of this – comes to be about 'rhythms of endurance' (Simone 2019, p. 93), and 'ensembles' of practice and interpretation. The example he returns to regularly concerns high rise residential developments in Jakarta, where he observes that

> It is difficult to work out how they all impact on each other, compressed as they are into a space where so many distinct things seem to be happening. As such, the integrity of any of these elements, their distinctiveness as objects for comparison or integration, becomes inoperable. This is not about the assemblage of hybrid urbanizations but rather a continuous proliferation of non-subsumable details incapable of being made interoperable.
> (Simone 2019, p. 76).

So many different processes and practices are assembled in a specific context, often needing to operate away from the gaze of surveillant authorities, or hidden from alternative projects and practices. These are nonetheless generative situations: 'Everything is packed into a density of contact, of the discrepant rubbing up against each other as multiple frictions, sparks that ignite chain reactions, the webs of many crammed causations looking out for any possible vehicle of release' (p. 11).

The metaphor of 'compression' indicates something about the urban, not only a descriptive account of heterogeneous urban life, close to actors and activities, but also a series of propositions about 'conceptualising the urban, and method' (p. 45)[3]. To some extent, opacity or compression is an ever present reality for urban researchers, for activists – in some ways it is the fundamental condition of the urban which in its multiplicity and extension always hides something from us. But for Simone this resonates specifically with a perspective on 'blackness' as an analytic of the urban – as unrecognisability (pp. 92–3). 'Blackness' performs one pivot of conceptualisation across different contexts for Simone – and the global south another. Despite detachment and refusal, a concept – the (un)inhabitable – has emerged which has a very wide reach, based on Simone's engagement, as he states, with the 'scores of working class districts in which I have worked and lived over the past decades' (p. 14). On what grounds does this conceptual extension (as opposed to cutting or turning away from relations) emerge? 'In circumstances of intense volatility and uncertainty – circumstances that characterize many urban districts across the South' (p. 16). Across the many south/s, a shared conceptualisation is proposed. This rests on an idea of the south not as a political third way or developmental proposition, but as a form of 'passage', of residents (and scholars?) 'trying to reach each other even if they may have only vague ideas about each other' (p. 12). This South is 'made up as it goes along, like science fiction' (p. 12), of which Simone has the afrofuturists in mind, motivated to 'write themselves into a future foreclosed to them' – 'to imagine non-human futures devoid of racial tropes' (p. 12). These explorations of wider analytical perspectives go in a somewhat different direction but are not unrelated to his suggestions in 2010 that cities in the global north and south are 'neighbours in metropolitan space', and that the trajectories of urban actors 'both willingly and unwillingly have acted to make discrepant, often widely diverse cities close to each other' (p. 263; p. 268). 'Black urbanism' becomes, then, an 'inventive method' for tying together the 'situations and tactics' associated with the 'long history of African people moving into and around a larger world' (p. 268). What are the grounds for thinking the urban somewhere, in the midst of such circuits and the occlusions of compression?

In proposing a method which follows the refusal of peripheral actors to relate to elite accumulation and developmental projects, and takes its cues from the protective framing of ensembles of fugitive care as detached from urban knowledge, an insistence on the possibilities of non-relationality and opacity offers an important (cautionary) stopping point for comparative ambitions analytically. But 'fugitive graces' escaping the dominant gaze also quite self-consciously offer new starting points for method and theoretical practice inspired by urban life and motivated by thinking from 'blackness', black urban experiences and racialised histories. As Simone notes, he explores

> how ensembles constitute a tissue of conceptualisation, a quilting of notions, and how this quilting is a rhythm, a text read rhythmically across and in the midst of a crisscross of patterns and fragments that retain their capacity to be composed of various elsewheres.
> (Simone 2019, p. 29)

In the person and practice of Maliq Simone, a motivated conceptualisation in the form of an 'ensemble' of terms and insights, an enduring entwining of improvisation and opacity arrives at something more than singular, unrelatable experience. A 'they', perhaps, of childhood recollections, which points to open and generous receptivity to constituting and redefining the collective while performing a protective occlusion of its activities, in equal measure (p. 44). The uninhabitable emerges as both concept and experience. There remain, though, quite some aporias – impossibilities – in the project of operationalising the uninhabitable as a method, or a practice of conceptualisation, which relies on connection and communication. In the pragmatic world of conceptualisation, of coming to know about anything, like 'the uninhabitable', the question arises, even in the midst of a social world of detachment, how might concepts emerge alongside and in the midst of practices, associations, occlusions; and what are concepts for? In the midst of opacity and refusal, how might the connections and 'elsewheres' that nonetheless proliferate in both peripheral and elite urbanisation be relevant?

Suturing

If the mountains surrounding Kinshasa, and the skyscrapers within, formed creative metaphors for thinking that city and its futures for all manner of actors in pre-colonial, colonial and post-independence times, Filip de Boeck and Sammy Baloji's (2016) contribution on the difficult urban context of Kinshasa exposes how the 'dismal, dreary' quality of contemporary urban life there has led residents to turn to new figures to make sense of the city (p. 14). In contrast to the ambitious dreams of former times, the ubiquitous 'holes' – potholes, soil erosion, mining, graves – have made of this term a 'mastertrope' in local discussions of urban life (2016, pp. 13–14). Surely one of the places on earth which conforms to Simone's uninhabitable, de Boeck follows Kinois (residents of Kinshasa) who confront the 'dark matter of urban praxis' (p. 15), invoking an emergent vocabulary 'to overcome chaos' (p. 88). Darkness is, as in the opacity fostered by the urban residents Simone discusses, more than simply depletive; here it also metaphorically elides 'how life continues through, and despite, decline' (p. 16). In the 'zero' of an impossible life, as he cites Mbembe, 'the end is deferred and the question of finiteness remains unanswered' (p. 16) as residents 'read potential, promise and prospect into the blackness of the hole' (p. 17). Simone (2019) offers at least some scope for this within his observations: 'to navigate relationships with those whose "surfaces" are always partial, always partly withdrawn, always proceeding in different directions simultaneously', residents may have some need for inscription as maps. But this would be maps as ways of going on rather than determined knowledge or clear mappings of the way forward. Nonetheless he notes, 'residents may operate in the dark ... But even within this darkness, there is more than impulsive wandering' (Simone 2019, p. 31).

Any resources for forging shared meanings and collective life in Kinshasa are not easily located in northern analytics, though. For example, Derrida's hospitality runs aground in the 'uninhabitable' that undermines co-habitation, or the lacerating suspicions and accusations that fracture traditional practices of hospitality in the wake of extreme poverty (de Boeck and Plissant 2004). Although de Boeck (and Simone) both keep open conversations with analyses from many different contexts, the main conceptualisations de Boeck turns to are those of the Kinois. The shadows are reframed as the very site of the production of the urban, whether as the doubled nocturnal 'second' world of local conventions and imaginaries (De Boeck and Plissart 2004), or the matter through which technologies of fixing, repairing and reusing, and surviving the degradations of the city are crafted. Simone (2019), again, treads on this terrain observing in relation to the forms of emergent sociality, 'a care that makes it possible for residents to navigate the need to submit and exceed, submerge themselves into a darkness in which they are submerged but to read its textures, its tissues, to see something that cannot be seen' (cited in De Boeck and Baloji 2016, p. 20).

Attending to the shadows is relevant to the production of urban theory too. The 'shadow', de Boeck insists, is produced through and alongside speculative and extractive forms of the urban. The Kinois cultural imaginary itself embeds a doubling, in which the nocturnal-invisible-spiritual coexists with day-visible-physical. But urban theory is implicated in placing these everyday urban practices of Kinshasa on the side of its own shadow. He notes that

> the ordinariness of many of the lines and connections we make analytically is often responsible for creating the black hole itself. By contrast, the lines and connections drawn out by people in the context of the everyday movements of their lives often defy such closure and exclusion, and call into question established notions of flexibility and fixture.
>
> (de Boeck and Baloji 2016, p. 69)

Rather than an opacity which should (or can)not be revealed, in order to survive, the city cannot be taken for granted. Insofar as it exists as mystery, it 'needs constant elucidation' (p. 296). Emergent on this terrain are lines of desire, possibilities of collective action and dreams of some kind of shared future (p. 60). De Boeck ties this to an urgent demand for 'visibility and presence', expressed through the infrastructure of bodies, and speech (in Lingala): '*Tozali (we are here); Eza, (it is …)*' (de Boeck and Baloji 2016, p. 297).

Like Simone, de Boeck proposes a methodology and a theory in addition to (and along the tracks of) rich ethnographic, close-up, description. Acupuncture (a term he takes from the weak architecture movement) invites an interrogation of specific settings (such as a funeral) or elements of the built environment (graveyards, buildings). As residents compose the city around them, he joins their efforts to 'connect the dots' between events/sites, to activate the desire lines which are emergent in social imaginations. He invites theorists to reflect on the place of Kinois in a global world (as digital, connected, mobile) rather than dropped from theorisation or seen as irrelevant to understandings of global urban life. Erroneously placed in the shadows of urban theory, the contributions of Kinshasa and its residents to remaking of urban life, globalisation, of states, identity and kinship, for example, are prolific and reshape many other urban contexts besides (pp. 63–5).

De Boeck's research practice is one found in many urban contexts. It exemplifies a long commitment to detailed analysis of an individual city. The embedded urban researcher, whose energies are mobilised by the specific urban context, often in engaged political practice and inspired by regionally specific scholarship, has long shaped a central genre of urban studies – the detailed case study of one city with ambitions to inspire insights closely dependent on and responsive to that city's history and politics. With his/her starting point for conceptualisation framed within this context, this practice holds the potential for theorising from anywhere – launching ideas into wider conversations about the urban. As has long been the case, this is one of the most valuable formats of comparative urban enquiry and theorisation. It also establishes the potential for a multiplicity of starting points for globalising urban studies, and firmly establishes that conceptual innovation can begin (anyw)here in the urban world – wherever 'here' is. This methodology carries with it the figure of the dedicated urban scholar – the scholar whose city and life are interwoven, whose intellectual work and practice are inextricable. As critical thinking exposes power relations and disturbs the obfuscations of space, Sophie Oldfield (2022) argues that, equally, engaged and committed political practice reveals the dynamics of urban processes in a place, makes urban theory.[4] This informs the extraordinary contributions which have emerged in some dynamic centres of urban studies – the African Centre for Cities and the Indian Institute for Human Settlements,[5] for example. A 'translational' praxis values the potential of state intervention in specific urban settings, calling for effective long term transformation but also insisting on the room to convince the powerful to take immediate action (Pieterse, 2008; Patel et al. 2012). Gautam Bhan seeks to generalise this practice in the mode of 'Southern' scholarship, in which

> The choice to speak specifically from and about Indian cities is deliberate. I believe that speaking of practice requires rooting oneself in an empirical specificity. It is open to debate whether a set of cities

within a nation-state is the correct scale or form of this specificity. For example, I could look collectively at megacities across the South. For now, I choose to rely – as we often do in polemical and exploratory writing – on contexts where my knowledge is more intimate and reliable. I do not believe that vocabularies of practice can be created other than incrementally from multiple locations, so that they may then begin to speak to each other to see if shared theoretical frames can emerge across these locations. Such work then holds the possibilities to generate and imagine both localized forms of practice and more generalized forms of theory.

(Bhan 2019, p. 641)

'Scaling' this approach as sub-continental (more than a billion people) or the hundreds of millions who live in megacities, Bhan nonetheless indexes the highly localised and engaged practices which he proposes as new starting points for planning theory – **squat, repair, consolidate**. These vocabularies could well do service as replacement 'formants' for a Lefbvrean open totality, especially as they are certainly closely embedded in 'praxis'. In proposing these terms, though, Bhan is also insistent that conceptualisation and action in situations of immediate need and challenge does not always rest on accuracy, or cannot afford to wait for the facts (Simone and Pieterse 2017). With Gibson-Graham (1996) he suggests that theory buildings is 'as much a discursive intervention as a task of accurate representation.' (p. 640). More broadly, developmental practice in close engagement with the messy politics of poorly resourced cities, might generate new terms of thinking the urban (Pieterse et al. 2018). Such practices then are starting points for the kinds of concepts which could well do service across wider regions ('India', or 'the global South'). In the process, as with any concepts, inherited or newly emergent, they would open themselves to the necessary differences of urban territories.

The enmeshment of the conceptual biographies of Simone, De Boeck and Bhan across cities like Jakarta, Kinshasa and Delhi might suggest that the approaches to the openings and closures, the detachments and the suturing of the city in conceptualisation which they discuss might be a feature of the relative inscrutability of urban life in such places. However, these impulses have something to say to other urban experiences, and to thinking the urban across many different outcomes. To reflect on this, we can turn back almost a century, to consider an analysis of experiences of city life in nineteenth century Paris. Here, too, the apparent opacity of urban life and the materiality of the city figure strongly. Walter Benjamin (1892–1940), a cultural critic and philologist, committed himself over several years to thinking the city close-up, preparing a historical analysis of modernity in Paris. He, too, charts a moment in urban experience when representation seems to fail.

Standstill

Walter Benjamin's method, as cultural and literary critic,[6] and in relation to the city he was studying (Paris), involved slowing thought down to look closely, at objects, at texts, at experiences. His critical analyses of art, literature and history were far-reaching in their implications for politics, history and thought, but a significant part of his later work started with something quite specific, concrete, and distinct – the city. In his twenty-year (unfinished) *Arcades Project* (AP) he explored the nature of city life and the remaking of the built environment in nineteenth-century Paris through the lens of his distinctive approach to materialist dialectics, a kind of 'materialist physiognomy': 'Physiognomics infers the interior from the exterior, it decodes the whole from the detail; it represents the general in the particular' (Tiedermann 1999, p. 940). He explored directly how conceptualisation and the experiences and materiality of city life could be brought together, and how they might be severed.

His early work on German Baroque tragic drama *(Trauerspiel)* (Benjamin 2019) gave him an abiding interest in allegory as a distinctive form of expression/conceptualisation, aligning materiality and meaning in unexpected ways. Also from this study came his attention to the generative potential of 'reception' in determining the meaning of performances which laid out a vast multiplicity of figures, symbols and physical features for audiences to 'see' and 'read'. The value of the performances was only realised in this audience interpretation, resulting in a multiplicity of meanings. Together with the variety of historical forms of this genre, this work influenced his famous piece on art in the age of technological reproduction (1999b [1955]) as well as his broader critical method. He critiqued the high cultural investment in the 'aura' of original paintings whose value and meanings were assigned in the systems of power and wealth – in favour of attending to the multiplicity of origins and afterlives framing meaning, inspired by the different form of reproducible photographic art works (Benjamin 1979b). From his early work on *Trauerspiel* he also took an ongoing interest in the Baroque mathematician and philosopher, Leibniz, whose formulation of singular conceptual entities, 'monads',[7] and a mathematically informed metaphysics of 'infinity/infinitesimal', shaped Benjamin's method and his understanding of conceptualisation. Benjamin even named his analysis 'monadology'. Monads, a metaphysical entity, the invisible, smallest component of reality[8] – the 'soul' of a singularity[9] – were thought to reflect, in abbreviation and from their perspective, with more or less clarity, the whole of the world (Deleuze 1993, *The Fold*, TF). The object, conceived by Benjamin as a Leibnizian 'monad', 'expresses' the world – 'expressing' this, as active entities, rather than purely being seen as a result of the 'mediations' of political economy.[10] Upending the Marxist perspectives, of then and now, which find relations and determinations coalescing in an (historical) object (1999a, AP, N1a,6), something else goes on when starting with the object.

In weaving together allegory and ideas, infinity, experience and time, his insights resonate with a number of the philosophical interventions of Deleuze (Flanagan 2009), whose 'speculative realism' (the term 'speculative' suggesting the continued relevance of conceptualisation) drew on many of the same resources that inspired Benjamin's 'concrete but nonetheless speculative analysis of modern experience' (Caygill 1998, p. 29).[11] There is nothing straightforward about coming to knowledge for either thinker, and their close emphasis on materiality drew them to formulate distinctive ways of knowing – of producing concepts, or 'Ideas' in encounters with the material world, or in Benjamin's case, the experiences of the 'big city'.

Thinking with 'the physiognomy of the big city' (*Some Motifs in Baudelaire* (SMB), 1973 [1939], p. 131) draws attention to how the 'experience' of the city emerges in the context of its prolific materiality and fleeting encounters – the trace and force of matter instigates experiences, reflections and conceptualisation. Benjamin explored the often brutal reduction of the experience of 'big city' life in the 'age of high capitalism' to exchange value. He dwelt on how the impact of the insistent 'shocks' of city life, in jostling crowds devoid of recognition for the individual, could result in loss of a sense of meaning. A close textual analysis of the lyric poetry of Charles Baudelaire is the one fully worked element of his planned 'Arcades' book (but also envisaged as part of a proposed book on Baudelaire), as the various 'exposés' he prepared, and his notes, clarify (1999a, AP, pp. 1–28; 914–15). Baudelaire records the traces of the modern city through an allegorical poetry which sought new ways to express the experience of the city, finding meaning directly in the material elements and experiences of city life; in the end this enterprise found itself (and the poet) exhausted. The nineteenth century city, it seems, presented an onerous experience to the impoverished and ill-recognised poet, alienated in the 'brutal indifference' of the crowd (Engels, cited in *The Paris of the Second Empire in Baudelaire* (PSEB), 1973, [1955 (published), 1938 (written)], p. 58) in which he had sought recognition, or empathy. His fascination with the phantasmagoria of the urban spectacle saw him entranced, like many, with the big city crowd. But he also faced up to the disquieting, threatening and uncanny nature of the city (1973, PSEB, p. 40), its 'infirmity and decrepitude' (*Central Park* (CP) 2003a [1939], p 176). The crowd dragooned individuals into certain behaviours, even as a repetitive and degrading labour process might (1973, SMB, p. 134). And the devastation of Haussman's remodelling made Paris 'uninhabitable' with construction (1973, PSEB, p. 86).

Baudelaire is portrayed by Benjamin as staging 'the breakdown of modern man' (SMB 1973, p. 139). We might reflect on how coming to terms with the challenges of city life has evoked many different contemporary forms of literature – self-help texts, the detective novel, novels of extreme personal effort and psychic fragmentation in the face of the immense hardship of city life in many contexts across Africa, for example (Primorac 2010). In these, perhaps, the interpretations of Simone and De Boeck can be placed alongside Benjamin's analysis of the nineteenth century.

Baudelaire's poetry seeks a direct, allegorical apprehension of the materiality and banal experiences of the city.[12] Words and terms spring from city life itself – famously Baudelaire writes of 'stumbling against words as against cobblestones' (1973, PSEB, p. 68). Associations proliferate in dynamic and unanticipated alignment with elements of the rapidly changing city. He incites words to express whatever this city might seem to be, its experiences, subjects, things, in sometimes unfamiliar configurations. He brings into focus the intrinsic allegorical form of the commodity presenting itself to the buyer as (advertising) image or 'price', distinct from its material form and process of production (1999a, AP, p. 909). To Benjamin, Baudelaire's allegorical poetry presented the experiences and materiality of the city in direct, unpredictable associations, with the potential to work across an 'abyss' of difference between its terms and experiences/objects (1973, PSEB, p. 42). Formulating these representations, searching for meaning in the city in the face of its cruel disregard and opacity, is implicated in Baudelaire's increasingly burdened and fractured subjectivity.

Benjamin's close reading explores how Baudelaire worked psychically to keep his encounters on the side of *Erlebnis* (pure time/duration), storing the shocks of city life as direct impressions on the psyche, away from the dulling, protective effect of the unconscious (a form of detachment?). Simmel (1971 [1903]) had identified this defensive detachment as a coping mechanism of city dwellers. The allegorical poet instead searched the city for images and words to directly propose these experiences. Baudelaire's openness to 'empathy with inorganic things', his search for recognition in the crowds ('Empathy is the nature of the intoxication to which the poet abandons himself in the crowd' – 1973, PSEB, p. 55), the proliferating phantasmagorical representations which populate city life, including the 'aura' of the explosion of commodities he encountered, reflected for him the intoxicating experience of the new (1973, PSEB, p. 55). But in this city of 'high capitalism' the fascination of the crowds recedes in non-recognition, the 'newness' of commodities, often symbolised in archaic mythical fantasies, simply masked their fundamental nature as the eversame. Benjamin noted in his correspondence with Theodore Adorno on this work: 'The price makes the commodity identical to all other commodities that can be purchased for the same amount. The commodity empathizes (and this is the key correction to last summer's text) not only and not so much with the buyers as with its price'; ultimately, the commodity's aura and identification was purely with exchange value and offered no consolation to the poet (Eiland and Jennings 2003, *Selected Writings Vol.4* (SW4), Letter to Theodore Adorno (TA) 23 February 1939, p. 208).

The poet, and the poetry he produced, was also a commodity, in search of a market ('he takes the abstract concept of "For Sale"-ness on a stroll through the streets' (ibid), broken in rejection and poverty (1973, PSEB, p. 29, p. 70). Baudelaire's critique erupts and eviscerates the mythical nature of modernity: 'The Baudelarian allegory – unlike the Baroque allegory – bears traces of the rage needed to break into this world, to lay waste its harmonious structures' (2003a, CP, p. 174; a rage which was not apolitical – 1973, PSEB, p. 15). The roar of the poet emerges in and joins with the city: 'Baudelaire mingles his voice with the roar of the city as one might mingle one's voice with the breakers on the shore' (2003a, CP, p. 177). The poet's efforts at representation are defeated by the city. In Baudelaire's poetry, the night sky is devoid of stars.[13] Benjamin turns to a Nietzchean metaphor of the concept in which the star (the poet, the commodity, the city) is 'without atmosphere' – it has no 'aura', no relationality, no interpretation' – no meaning (1973, *Paris, Capital of the Nineteenth Century* (PCN), p. 154). The poet faces an abyss.[14] Matter, and the experience of the city, are figured as unable to be drawn into conceptualisation. 'To his horror, the melancholy man sees the earth revert to a mere state of nature. No breath of pre-history surrounds it; there is no aura' (1973, SMB, p. 145) – as in Bergson's notion of time as pure durée,[15] isolated from both private and collective meaning, from historical interpretation (1973, SMB, p. 111). Observing that Bergson's philosophy arose in the 'inhospitable, blinding age of big-scale industrialism. … His philosophy thus indirectly furnishes a clue to the experience which presented itself to Baudelaire's eyes in its undistorted version in the figure of his reader' (1973, SMB, p. 111).

However, this account of the collapse of meaning in the city of high capitalism also carries a theory of coming to know the urban, as object. Benjamin's unique 'allegorical materialism' (Eiland and Jennings 2014, p. 623) focussed attention on how concepts or meaning might emerge in relation to matter, objects, experience. The energy of the prolific, limitless potential for the production of allegorical concepts in Baudelaire's poetry, across the abyss of difference, imagined as directly recording sensations, is suggestive. But even in the hands of the allegorist the object is not redeemed as such – 'in his hands the object becomes something different' (1998, *The Origin of German Tragic Drama* (OGTD), p. 184). In Baudelaire's defeat, the city seems to emerge as a mute object of unrepresentability. But neither of these options – direct representation or failing interpretations – were Benjamin's intention for a conceptualisation of the historical experiences of city life. Rather, these 'failures' establish the very terms and possibilities of conceptualisation. Here we can return to consider the poet's failed attempt at 'empathy' with matter, with commodities, and crowds. The 'aura' – the sensation that something inert or unfathomable is looking back at us, presenting itself to us – provides a focus for how meaning is produced in encounters with urban life, in the search for recognition in the eyes of passersby, in the fascination with commodities.

In his longer essay on Baudelaire ('The Paris of the Second Empire in Baudelaire'), a range of different ways in which the inhabitants of the big city try to make sense of their (new) experiences are explored. For example, he counters the 'aura' with the 'trace' – the Lyric poet with the detective novel. The 'menacing aspects' of the big city crowd, and its ability to shield asocial elements, to obliterate the 'trace' of the individual (1973, PSEB, p. 43) gave rise to a genre of fiction in which a detective, acting on the side of the 'citizen' and police order, looked for traces of what is no longer there, the criminal or evidence. The detective's search provides reassurance in the face of the impenetrability of the meaning of city life. Benjamin observes that 'The concept of the trace finds its philosophical determination in opposition to the concept of the aura' (Eiland and Jennings 2003, SW4, Benjamin to Adorno, 9 December 1938, p. 106; 1973, SMB, pp. 147–8). It is the 'disintegration of the aura' which Baudelaire experiences in the vacant stares of passersby: 'What is involved here is that the expectation roused by the look of the human eye is not fulfilled. Baudelaire describes eyes of which one is inclined to say they have lost their ability to look.' (1973, SMB, p. 149). Benjamin observes, though, with some psychoanalytic insight, that the deeper the remoteness, the stronger the spell emanating from the gaze, reflecting the unsatisfied desire of the subject. In the city, the unrecognising, unseeing gaze dominates. As Simmel observed: 'That the eye of the city-dweller is overburdened with protective functions is obvious' (Simmel, in 1973, OSM, p. 151). In the eye of the passerby, we see only defence and evasion (detachment). Baudelaire lost himself to the spell of things and eyes that did not return his gaze – 'your eyes, lit up like a shop window' (p. 150), like the deceptive aura of a commodity. But commodities, in the end, reflected only their price; the eyes of passersby offered no recognition.

We might think, then, that in being drawn to the trace, in following it through the city, and pouncing on it, the truth of the city might be found, whereas all is lost in the 'aura'. But Benjamin observes:

> Trace and aura. The trace is appearance of a nearness, however far removed the thing that left it behind might be. The aura is appearance of a distance, however close the thing that calls it forth. In the trace we gain possession of the thing; in the aura, it takes possession of us.
> (Benjamin, 1999a, AP, p. 447, M16a,4)

The trace, apparently so close in its pure materiality despite its absence, is simply what the detective wants/desires. For Benjamin, it is rather in taking account of the distancing effects of the aura, the apparent remoteness of the object although it is right here, that we have a chance of finding out something about it.[16] More generally, he observes that:

> The point of departure of materialist method is the object riddled with error, with δοξα [conjecture]. The distinctions with which the materialist method, discriminative from the outset, starts are distinctions within this highly mixed object, and it cannot present this object as mixed or uncritical enough. If it claimed to approach this object the way it is 'in truth', it would only greatly reduce its chances… it does not pursue the 'matter itself' behind men's backs.
> (Benjamin, 1973, PCN, p. 104, Addendum).

The aura indexes the multiplicity of meanings which surround the object – in 'error and conjecture'. In the many different ways in which an object is represented, or experienced, we might locate it. Ironically, in the trace, we find only ourselves – the detective's desire on behalf of the social order.

In coming to terms with the object, then, Benjamin indicates we might turn from the abyss and reconsider the constitution of ideas. In his extensive notes for the Arcades Project, which he left in the care of Georges Bataille, hidden in the Bibliothèque Nationale in Paris for the war, some plans for his book about Paris remain. Benjamin declared the proposed conceptual arc of the analysis: 'What is the historical object? – Answer: dialectics at a standstill/dialectical image' (1999a, AP, p. 916).

The 'dialectical image', is the answer Benjamin planned to offer to the question he intended to pose in Part 1 of the book, 'What is the historical object' (1999a, AP, p. 916)? How did he imagine that the idea of the city, the 'historical object' of Paris in the nineteenth century, might emerge as a 'dialectical image'? He also made this suggestion in relation to his analysis of Baudelaire (2003a, p. 183). We will explore this in the following section. However, it is clear from the many approaches we have reviewed in this book that any conceptualisation of the urban entails more than close attention to a discrete physical object, text, or singular experience. Any city convenes itself through both juxtaposition and connection, across differences/diversity and in relation to elsewheres. The following two sections, then, take one final perspective on the possibility of conceptualising the urban, this time, the generation of 'Idea' from in the midst of any urban territory, but one inevitably immersed in 'elsewhere'.

Ideas

Key to approaching the object for Benjamin, now it is in view, is his idea of 'dialectics at a standstill', a practice and perspective which he developed from some of his earliest work to the last. His close textual reading saw him advocate slowing (dialectical) analysis to a standstill. This was the textual practice of 'philology'. To seek to escape overarching perspectives, to cultivate a sceptical attitude, he advocated a 'pause for breath':

> Such scepticism may be compared to the deep breath taken by thinking before it can lose itself at its leisure, and without ever feeling winded, in the smallest detail. Indeed, the smallest things will always be the focus of attention when observation is immersed in the work and form of art in order to take the measure of its content. The *routinier* tends to snatch at things hastily, as though stealing a purse – and for no better reason than to foster bonhomie amongst philistines. In the case of true contemplation, on the other hand, the rejection of deductive procedures is associated with an ever more wide-ranging, ever more intense reaching back [zurückgreifen] to the phenomena.
> (Benjamin, 2019, *Origin of the German Trauerspiel* (OGT), p. 23)[17]

This was not simply about constituting 'objects of vague wonder',[18] or what Adorno, cruelly and fatefully called 'pragmatic pointing'. Benjamin counters Adorno with the insistence that 'When you speak of a "wide-eyed presentation of facticity" you are in fact describing the proper philological attitude' (Eiland and Jennings 2003, SW4, p. 107).[19] In his final text, written as he was making plans to flee Paris as the Nazi army approached, he confirmed the vitality of this method (2003b [written, 1940], *On the Concept of History* (OCH) p. 396). Drawn partly from his voluminous notes for the Arcades Project, he explained this central idea, with some implication of Hegel:[20] 'To thinking belongs the movement as well as the arrest of thoughts. Where thinking comes to a standstill in a constellation saturated with tensions – there the dialectical image appears. It is the caesura in the movement of thought' (1999a, AP, N10a,3, p. 475). The tensions indicate the constellation as a moment of intense dynamic energy. In historical analysis this is released by blasting objects from the continuum of history and analytically assembling the different pasts which are implicated in the 'now'. More generally, following Hegel, a perpetual movement of contradiction and synthesis in thought achieved increasing clarity of a phenomenon. Benjamin imagined the movement of thought halted at a moment in time, in mid-stream, supposedly bringing the dynamic of the dialectical analysis to a standstill. The object can be thought, then, in the 'crashing together' of the different elements implicated in the dialectical movement. This standstill is an internally dynamic moment: 'The movement of a work, of an era and of the course of history are arrested not in order to present them as a dead thing to sad contemplation, but in order to expose time and make it intrinsically productive' (Hamacher 2005, p. 55), as a kind of 'petrified unrest' (p. 59). The moment of the 'now of recognition' is full of energy, opening to new possibilities of history and interpretation.

Benjamin's distinctive methodological practices of 'dialectics at a standstill' and 'monadology' recast processes of conceptualisation in relation to the the materiality of urban life and the opacity of experience. Helpfully for us they frame this in ways which open to 'thinking with elsewhere'. This is at least partly because dialectics at a standstill as historical analysis has its resonance, and perhaps its origins, in the city. Just as Baudelaire's poetry gives expression to an experience which is 'specific to the metropolis' (Steiner 2010, p. 163), it is the juxtaposition and coexistence within the city of different times (and I will suggest of a multiplicity of elsewheres) which provides a starting point for an analysis of the urban in Benjamin, and specifically his focus on the Arcades (covered shopping streets). In nineteenth century Paris, the simultaneous existence of archaic ruins, the destruction of an earlier era's fashionable buildings, and the reconstructions of Haussman composed a multi-temporality of experience: at once, past, present and future was evident. More generally, in the city, as Cairns and Jacobs (2014) suggest, 'buildings are often out of time, in place' (p. x). This produces a sense that 'time freezes into space forming what Benjamin variously described as an allegorical or dialectical image' (Caygill 1998 p. 141). Caygill (p. 69) notes that one of the earliest drafts of text for the Arcades project begins with an account of an opening of a new 'Parisian *passage*' which depicts 'a past which has become space [*raumgewordene Vergangenheit*]':

> For its inaugural ceremony, a monster orchestra in uniform performed in front of flower beds and flowing fountains. The crowd broke, groaning, over sandstone thresholds and movedalong before panes of plate glass, saw artificial rain fall on the copper entrails of late-model autos as a demonstration of the quality of the materials, saw wheels turning around in oil, read on small black plaques, in paste-jewel figures, the process of leather goods and gramophone records and embroidered kimonos. In the diffuse light from above one skimmed over flagstones. While here a new thoroughfare was being prepared for the most fashionable Paris, one of the oldest arcades in the city

had disappeared – the Passage de l'Opéra, swallowed up by the opening of the Boulevard Haussmann. Just as that remarkable covered walkway had done for an earlier generation, so today a few arcades still preserve, in dazzling light and shadowy corners, a past become space.

(Benjamin 1999a, AP, p. 871)

As in world exhibitions, popular at the time, the Arcades trained and produced the consumer, as much as they displayed the phantasmagoria of the commodity.[21] In the dual presence of the fashionability of new arcades, and the decay of earlier ones, thinking about the nature of the arcades at this time placed past alongside present and future. They also placed the wider world within the intense juxtapositions of city life. Whatever the 'historical object' city might be, it certainly involved 'elsewheres'.

Adorno challenged Benjamin to consider the self-evidently international context of capitalism and imperialism in shaping the phenomena he was exploring (Kraniauskas 2000, pp. 140–1). This he sidelined – although it might be said to have weighed on his unconscious. A dream image of a Mexican church steeple pushing through the market place at Weimar, made him awake with laughter – something was going on there. The eruptive presence of the Mexican church in Europe – perhaps it was already there, both obvious but not graspable within his perspective (1979, *One Way Street* (OWS), p. 60; Kraniauskas 2000). His notes for content of the projected Arcades book document instances of the presence of people, commodities and ideas from across world, with potential sub-headings being, 'America and Asia in Paris' (1999a, AP, p. 920), 'The dream of empire' (p. 905), including possible English influences. The discussion of England was prominent through his published and unpublished material – Dickens, Poe on London, Marx and Engels, and Crystal Palace in the context of the iron construction of the Arcade. He noted occasionally the presence of people from different parts of the world as documented in novels and commentary. Some of his notes reflect more generally on the array of phenomena gathered in the city, extracting from a Balzac novel the experience of a young man in a four-storey antique shop, whose initial sense of these relics of 'civilisations and religions, deities, royalties, masterpieces of art, the products of debauchery, reason and unreason, each one representing a whole world' ended up with his 'senses numbed at the sight of so many national and individual existences ... For him this ocean of furnishings, inventions, fashions, works of art, and relics made up an endless poem' (1999a, AP, p. 487, N19,3). The problematic of 'milieu' was on his mind – as an explanatory dynamic opposed to 'forces of production', for example (1999a, AP, p. 487, N19a,1). An insight drawn from the Surrealists on Paris considered that in the city 'inconceivable analogies and connections between events are the order of the day' (1979, OWS, p. 231; Beck 2019, p. 127).

Any Idea of an urban object, an object-urban, abbreviating and expressing the world from its own perspective (as a monad) would be clarifying and enfolding the wider world, as 'elsewhere' and exteriority constitute it from afar. For the flâneur at least, 'far off times and places interpenetrate the landscape and the present moment' (1999a, AP, p. 419, M2,4). In this perspective, how might the Idea of the city, the historical object of Paris in the nineteenth century, emerge? For Benjamin, the historical 'object' – here, Paris in the nineteenth century – comes to be known as 'dialectical image', resonant with his more general framing of coming to know something, which he developed in his much earlier work on the history of the German Baroque Tragic Drama (*Trauerspiel*). Benjamin's plans for his Arcades Project book noted that in his conclusions he would draw on his earlier study on the 'origins' of the obscure theatrical form of *Trauerspiel*. He proposes a historical perspective, but taking a very different approach from simply tracing the immediately preceding versions or antecedents of a phenomenon. Casting across (comparing) the multiple historical versions and determinations of an object generates an Idea (concept) of that object – in the same way as with Benjamin's insight into how multi-temporalities converge in the 'now' time at the heart of the 'dialectic at a standstill'. This relies once again on his Leibnizian monadology:

> If the object of history is to be blasted out of the continuum of historical succession, that is because its monadological structure demands it. This structure first comes to light in the extracted object itself. And it does so in the form of the historical confrontation that makes up the interior (and as it were the bowels) of the historical object, and into which all the forces and interests of history enter on a reduced scale. It is owing to this monadological structure that the historical object finds represented in its interior its own fore-history and after-history. (Thus, for example, the fore-history of Baudelaire ... resides in allegory; his after-history in Jugendstil).
> (Benjamin 1999a, AP, p. 475, N10,3)

Thus, 'Actualized in the dialectical image, together with the thing itself, are its origin and its decline' (AP, p. 917). Such an historical object exists only from the perspective of 'now' – to be 'recognised' from this standpoint entails 'an engagement with history original to every new present' (Benjamin 1979 [1937], *Eduard Fuchs, Collector and Historian* (EF), p. 352). In his later, and last, works this perspective informs an analysis of historical time in general (Benjamin, 2003b). The dialectical image also holds the potential of the future, wresting a (weak) revolutionary impulse from the unique configuration of elements of past experience in relation to 'now'. It is 'now-time' which stages a 'leap' across differential historical time, pregnant with both the potentiality of our own critical concerns and the dissonances/differences of past times. The dialectical image stages the multiplicity of time. But it also forms the basis for the multiplicity of the historical object.[22]

As he approached the task of analysing the *Trauerspiel*, Benjamin proposed that Ideas of a historical object 'take shape immanently' (1998, OGTD, p. 44) and 'exist in irreducible multiplicity' (p. 43).[23] Stretched across numerous instances, extremes and excesses, he insisted on a conceptual interpretation of empirical observations: the 'general is the Idea' and not the 'average' (p. 35). But the form of Ideas which he proposes is distinctive and provided the foundations for 'dialectics at a standstill' and 'now-time'. He comments, Ideas 'do not make the similar identical, but they effect a synthesis between extremes' (p. 41).[24] An Idea of something is composed out of all the possible cases which reveal elements in tension with the idea. The methodology associated with 'Ideas' rests on exploring, initially foregoing any sense of the whole (p. 56), the 'remotest extremes and apparent excesses of the process of development, reveals the configuration of the Idea – the sum total of all possible meaningful juxtapositions of such opposites' (p. 47). Thus, 'phenomena do not enter into realm of Ideas whole' but as aspects or elements which are held together in the Idea (p. 34):

> The Idea takes in the series of signature historical formations – but not for the sake of constructing unity out of them, still less of extracting a common denominator from them. Between the relation of the particular to the Idea and its relation to the concept there is no analogy: here it falls under the concept and remains what it was – particularity; there it stands in the Idea and becomes what it was not – totality. That is its Platonic 'salvation'.
>
> (Benjamin 2019, OGT, p. 25)[25]

In this monadological perspective,[26] the 'particular' (the specific aspect or example of the *Trauerspiel* identified) is preserved in the Idea as the totality of all possible elements and cases of the genre, its existent variety and potentiality (Chaudhury 2012). Ideas, then, are not pre-determined philosophical systems, or overarching universals, they are not averages or summation of what is in common. But 'Ideas are to objects as constellations are to stars' (1998, OGTD, p. 34). Here, the apparently most incomparable of phenomena might be the most enlivening: 'Ideas come to life only when extremes are assembled around them' (p. 35).[27] Elements of phenomena are arranged in relation to one another, configured by the 'Idea' – the Idea determines their relationship to each other. Ideas 'do not make the similar identical, but effect a synthesis between extremes' (p. 41).

As Benjamin notes, 'just here begins the task of the researcher' (2019, OGT, p. 25), who has to determine whether a fact 'is so essential as to reveal it as an origin' (1998, OGTD, p. 46). The active, contemplative return to the object ('an object of discovery'), a 'continual breathing in and out' punctuates the intentionality of the researcher': 'Just as the majesty of mosaics remain intact when they are disassembled into capricious bits, so philosophical observation fears no dissipation of momentum' (2019, OGT, p. 3). The 'essence' or Idea of a phenomenon is then completed in its totality – its historical becoming – all that it could possibly have been (past) and will become (future):

> The construction of the Idea, as stamped by totality in contrast to its own inalienable isolation is monadological. ... The Idea is a monad – this means, in nuce: each Idea contains the image of the world. For the task of its presentation nothing less is required than to inscribe, in its abbreviation, this image of the world.
> (Benjamin 2019, OGT, p. 27)[28]

There are many similarities between Benjamin's articulation of 'philosophical historical' method, and Deleuze's dramatisation of how subjects come to knowledge, and objects to determination. This is most helpful for this book, and arrives through their shared inspiration from Leibniz (Flanagan 2009) and other common philosophical reference points. From our point of view, that Benjamin's focus was historical and cultural analysis can help to ground Deleuze's highly abstracted philosophical formulations. Reading Benjamin together with Deleuze reveals resonances which opens up to a rich and dynamic account of the process of conceptualisation in relation to the urban.[29]

Benjamin's interest in allegory indicates something about how the relationship between particular observations and ideas might be considered. It is to Benjamin that Deleuze (1993, *The Fold*, TF) turns to consider the allegorical form of the Baroque imagination in his discussion of Leibniz. Deleuze writes that in the two-storey Baroque imagination the relation between the 'upper' and 'lower' floors – monads as souls (concepts) and singularities as bodies (matter) – is imagined as distinct but inseparable. The relationship is one of appurtenance (belonging)[30] (1993, TF, p. 136) – which is also the nature of the relationship he proposes amongst monads which together make up complex monads, or ultimately constitute individuals (pp. 123–4). Appertaining, belonging to, is key to allegory which is a quite different way of conceptualising from the symbol (p. 143). Leibnizian philosophy, then, 'must be conceived as the allegory of the world, no longer as symbol of the cosmos in the former manner' (TF, p. 145). Hence at times Benjamin's approach is seen as an 'allegorical' materialism (Caygill 1998).

In Baudelaire we noted the poet whose 'star' of representation finally had no atmosphere, whose poetry included no representations of stars, indicating the poet facing the abyss between meaning and things in the city. This Nietszchian image of the star with no atmosphere as a sign of the failure of representation finds a new opening in Deleuze's reading of *Thus Spake Zarathrustra*[31] (1994, *Difference and Repetition* (DR), p. 251). The stars return as a metaphor for the infinity of possible observations which are drawn on by subjects in thinking 'Ideas' – and as in Benjamin, for Deleuze these are configured as 'constellations'. Important here is Nietzsche's concept of 'eternal return' which frames not the return of the 'eversame' as in a dialectic, negative, analogy or the similar (Deleuze 1994, DR, p. 370), all failures of representation. But it marks the infinite return of concepts as multiplicities of constellations forged in difference, associated with a metaphor of chance – as each throw of the dice, each attempt to reach understanding, invokes all of chance, all the possibilities for thinking. In the sky (of virtuality), Ideas (concepts) 'shine like differential flashes which leap and metamorphose' (Deleuze 1994, DR, p. 183).

The spectacular throw of the dice against the sky of chance, opens up all of chance with each throw (each attempt at the determination of Ideas/entities). Constellations of stars signify the dynamic, open site of the constitution of concepts. The search for concepts is not a search to represent the world, but a creative response to seek to determine the world presented before the subject (Deleuze 1994, DR, pp. 354–5; Hughes 2009, pp. 47–50). In some relation to Benjamin's analysis of Baudelaire, the drama of Deleuze's account of conceptualisation (as we discussed in Chapter 4) follows the failure of the (fractured) subject to synthesise (passively) the singularities/observations (of intensities) which have been experienced. This follows Benjamin's outline of Bergson, as phenomena are initally apprehended in the realm of habit, then reflected on as memory, before entering a realm of conceptualisation as imagination (Benjamin 1973, SMB, p. 111)). Even at the end of these complex and recursive engagements, perhaps we are left still staring, uncomprehending, what is this? The subject is then imagined to initiate new rounds of active syntheses across the apprehended singularities in their relations to one another. In close engagement between the virtualities of Ideas and the persistent intervention of intensities (phenomena, matter), dynamic processes of 'differenc/t/iation' across both Ideas and matter finally bring into view, determine, an object. The object, in turn, 'expresses' the Idea which has emerged. Perhaps here, it is hard to tell 'where the sensible ends and the intelligible begins' (Deleuze 1993, TF, p. 137). For Benjamin, too, the monadological approach sees the object as expressing the Idea.

This returns us to the issue which has concerned us throughout this book: how to think the urban across so many observations, so many instances, so many cases, and such a superfluity of elements of urban life.

In the conceptualisation of the Idea in both Deleuze and Benjamin, we find a different way of navigating this: the formation of the Idea as 'totality', as an empirical gathering of all elements of a phenomenon (in active determination) across (and as) multiplicity. The subject, the researcher, associates 'particulars' or 'singularities' within an Idea as (one of many possible) 'constellations' emergent from a subject's active processes of thinking; and of the ongoing 'rumbling' presence of intensities (the material) which indicates the active 'expression' or belonging (appurtenance) of the determined existent phenomenon (individual) in the Idea.[32] And although Benjamin uses the term 'dialectical', and at times explores contradictory dynamics in his 'dialectics at a standstill', both he and Deleuze insist on moving beyond contradiction as the form of thinking. Benjamin was exploring filmic ideas of 'dissolve', and repetition, and an infinity of possible constellations replaced a dialectical determination of objects and history (Eiland and Jennings 2014, p. 618). Deleuze developed a fully 'affirmative' Nietzchean analytic, as opposed to the 'Dialectic (which) thrives on opposition because it is unaware of far more subtle and subterranean differential mechanisms: topological displacements, typological variations' (Deleuze 2006, *Nietzsche and Philosophy* (NP), p. 149). Ideas of the urban, then, might be composed as topologies (Allen 2016) or along subterranean, barely discernable, or historically occluded relations (Glissant 1997; Myers 2020). What might it mean to compose concepts, or Ideas, of the urban 'now' as constellations. And with only some hesitant ideas from Benjamin and Deleuze, what are the possibilities for doing this in relation to 'elsewhere'?

An Urban 'Now'

Benjamin famously suggested in his last essay, the need 'to brush history against the grain' (2003b, OCH, p. 392); it is at the moment of standstill that this happens. In the arrest, the teleological unfolding (of concept, of history) is subject to a 'displacement of the angle of vision' (1999a, AP,3, p. 459, N1a,3) such that the shaded 'negative' of the dialectic as well as the array of processes at work are brought into view in new emergent conceptualisations. This has the potential to displace historical tradition, wresting history from narration by its victors (2003b, OCH). (Lefebvre (2009), too, wanted to treat all dimensions of the dialectic as full, equal, and social, processes). At the moment of standstill, concepts are emergent as constellations, the historical object flashes into existence, convening the world at an angle to inherited terms – whether this is the Marxist 'mediations' of pre-given terms of economy-culture, or the continuous historical time of conventional historians, or the analyses which have been able to be written of the past from the perspectives (of the victor) which have somehow won out and thereby persisted to narrate the past on their own terms. In this emergent constellation, in the tightly sprung energy accomplished in the coming together of different times, or different instantiations of a phenomenon, crystallised in the moment of inner dynamism, is released the possibility of something new (Hamacher 2005; Löwy 2005). The generativity of the Idea, then, lies in its accumulation and constellation of 'singularities' and the configuration of relations amongst them. In this resides the (or a) potential to recognise the world differently, in each 'now', and in each 'here', and to be inspired towards new concepts.

Exploring the relationship between Benjamin's work on cities and this 'dialectics at a standstill', Howard Caygill presents a reading of Benjamin's early writing on colour and philosophy. This places his later work on cities and modernity in the context of his philosophy of knowledge. Benjamin's search for a speculative method (conceptualisation informed by an immanent reality rather than purely transcendent or subjectively pre-given categories and judgements) is drawn out of a very early fragment on colour which includes discussion of 'a double infinity' at play in producing meaning: 'the transcendental infinity of possible marks on a given surface (or perceptions within a given framework of possible experience) and the speculative infinity of possible bounded but infinite surfaces or frameworks of experience' (Caygill 1998, p. 4). The resonance with Deleuze's virtualities of both materialities and concepts is evident. Caygill tracks this speculative method through Benjamin's writing on language, as well as his analysis of the '*Trauerspiel*'. In literary criticism – and urban analysis – Benjamin's methodology of tracing the many fore- and after-lives of objects and phenomena (in their transformation and constant reworking in critique, in practice, decay and reuse) reveals the multiplicity of possible interpretations of objects/texts, and grounds the 'Idea' as totality, as multiplicity. Specifically, in relation to the conceptualisation of 'now-time', Benjamin observes that 'The multiplicity of "histories" is closely related, if not identical, to the multiplicity of languages' (Eiland and Jennings 2003, SW4, p. 404) – indicating the infinity of possible constellations of 'now-time'. Caygill (1998, p. 22) suggests that 'Following the pattern of thought established in his philosophy of colour, he regards particular languages as infinite surfaces produced by a capacity for configuring linguistic surfaces which exceeds all discrete languages'. However, Benjamin himself observes that any attempt to reduce this multiplicity (of languages) to a universal would be the philosophical equivalent of Esperanto.

Helpfully for the current discussion, Caygill suggests further that 'Benjamin's city writings exemplify his speculative method: the city in question, whether Naples, Moscow, Berlin or Paris, can only become an object of knowledge indirectly, obliquely reflected through the experience of other cities, each of which is its own infinite surface ... this reflexive experience of the city is not only geographical, but also temporal' (1998, p. 119). The speculative method of 'setting a particular surface (such as the experience of Paris in 2016) within a set of possible surfaces defined spatially and temporally (the experience of other cities or the same city at other times)' (p. 119) hints at an imagination attuned to thinking across a diversity of urban experiences. Of course, the terms and scope of thinking across difference matter and amongst his comparative reference points Benjamin did entrain tropes embedded in colonial habits of the time, which need further interrogation (Kraniauskas 2000; Robinson 2006). Caygill expands on this speculative method through a reading of Benjamin's short pieces on cities other than Paris (Berlin, Naples, Moscow) and suggests that it might be reinforced by the observation that 'The experience of a city is shot through with allusions to other cities' (p. 119) – offering the kernel of thinking with elsewhere.

What sort of an analytic of the present might we expect, then, from an *urban* 'now'? Thinking of Ideas as constellations re-aligning disparate historical events from the perspective of now, together with Caygill's extension of Benjamin's speculative method to think across different cities, can inspire us to consider the space-time constellations an urban 'now'. Thus, any conceptualisation of an urban, 'now', would involve potentially blasting elements and observations from individual urban contexts either proximate or distant in both time and space. Relying on patient tracing, careful alignments, or leaps of explanation and connection reaching back in time as well as across to other observations and/or other places (elsewhere) could constitute an immanent multiplicity of interpretive space-times of a global urban. A multiplicity of Ideas of the global urban could be imagined. In such Ideas, interpretations of different urban contexts might be intimately interconnected – not least as they emerge through specific material encounters or analytical engagements with other contexts and urbanisation processes. Any concept of the urban thus stands in relation to the infinity of (possible concepts of) different urban outcomes, which are multiply interconnected through many shared circulations and mutual inhabitations.

Treating concepts of the urban as 'constellations' resonates with the insights of a number of urban scholars. For Lefebvre the form of urban space is quintessentially that of "assembly, encounter and simultaneity", and in that form accumulates vast archives of past urban experiences

(1991, p. 149). In a 'materialities' register, as well as in analyses of informality and emergent associations, the multiplicity of the urban is produced in the everyday articulations of materialities, things, bodies, the infrastructure of words, the composition of publics (De Boeck and Baloji 2016), as well as the arcs of connection through which efforts to generate livelihoods are traced across the city and beyond (Simone 2010). The multiplicity of the urban is therefore a lived reality; urban life could be seen as the totality produced from the many different ways in which urban dwellers piece together the city in their practices and imaginations (Ferrari 2013). So, too, Ideas of the urban are generated in the midst of the urban world, in the practices and engagements of residents, practitioners, researchers.

But the generative production of conceptualisations of the urban, from any urban territory, often up-close, in encounter with specific objects, activities and experiences must figure a way to deal with difference/diversity and with elsewhere. The vital dynamism and virtuality of Ideas, able to draw on all of 'chance', on all possibilities, all available concepts – charts a manifesto for thinking the urban in its full multiplicity, across and with ungrounding difference (which is the difference Deleuze intends). Singularities, (always pre-individual (Deleuze 1994, DR, p. 223, p.252), sub-organism, elements/observations) might be configured/configure expressions of the urban world as Ideas. These might be inspired from any urban context, as they add to the potentiality of an Idea. They are necessarily part of all kinds of subject-ive and inter-subjective practices. Subjects seek understanding of the world for so many reasons, and in often power-laden conditions and histories. With Deleuze, the subject concerned is not the knowing, integral subject of European philosophical lore – for him Ideas do not belong to or emerge from a singular knowing subject. Subjects are intrinsically fractured, uncertain, ungrounded, unable to directly access their own observations, and find themselves on deeply unstable ground, rumbling with the necessarily unexpressed intensities of the world (1994, p. 244). The process of determination of this world is always unfinished. For sure, the challenge of building new insights needs new accounts of subjectivity, a new politics of knowledge (Mbembe 2019; McKittrick 2021; Moten 2018) with the potential for new meanings of the object 'urban', or to initiate new kinds of constellations altogether.

As we explored in this Chapter, there are good reasons to sometimes withdraw, to regionalise, to protect located insights and understandings, or to "detach" from the interpretive gaze altogether (Jazeel 2019a; Simone 2019). But insights grounded in particular places would also have to be generated, relying on a multiplicity of observations as well as a virtuality of Ideas, borrowed or longstanding, from (elsew)here or here. With Deleuze, though singularities are not places (place is a necessary multiplicity). They are also neither stopping points nor isolates – they are the observations that initiate conceptualisation.[33] But also, within a Deleuzian (and Leibnizian) perspective singularities are in close association with other singularities – they extend (up to the next singularity) along branches. Thus, as the smallest elements of existence, one could say that singularities/monads illuminate certain regions with clarity, up to the obscure/indistinct zones which other monads encroach on.[34] With Deleuze and Benjamin we find the singularity, the observation/intensity which sparks thought, at the starting point of the journey of any concept, any Idea. And we find that as concepts flash up in the specific conditions of their creation ('now' 'here'), they too exist as multiplicities, in close association with many other possible constellations of observations. Any concept, then, is a multiplicity, resting on a multiplicity of observations (singularities). And concepts exist as multiplicities – alongside the many other possible constellations of observations. Crafting an analytics of the urban which opens to a multiplicity of observations, and a multiplicity of alternative interpretations, reinforces the potential for building more globally relevant understandings of the urban which will inspire conversations about urbanity amongst many different subjects of theorising across the diversity of twenty-first century cities and their multiple histories.

The next section explores how the repositioning of the concept of informality, invented as a marker of exception and, at the limit, non-urbanity, has been repositioned as a core conceptualisation of the urban. This reflects the successes of scholars crafting new narratives and analyses of the urban from beyond the powerful centres of scholarship. I take this to exemplify how 'Ideas' might emerge and be transformed across diverse urban experiences. And, more specifically, move 'beyond the Africa problem of global urban theory' (Myers 2018).

Informality, as Idea

African urbanism for long stood as the exception to urban theory, partly because it (theory) was often irrelevant to (our) concerns (Parnell and Pieterse 2016; Robinson 2002). But also because African urban contexts were marked as exceptions to the urban, notably in some (western) narratives of informal economies. In now familiar accounts, African urbanisation was portrayed as associated with irrationally burgeoning urban centres, urbanisation without economic growth and the formation of extensive 'irregular' settlements with self-built housing (Drakakis-Smith 2000 provides a summary perspective). But as urban studies has globalised, more of it's practitioners have attended much more closely to the many writers, theorists and practitioners of African (and other global south) urban worlds, for whom informality is the majority reality of urban economies and urban life. Debates on this term have been wide-ranging and intensive and I characterise them here not to be comprehensive but to make a point about the openness, emergence and vitality of Ideas – what has happened with the concept of 'informality' in urban studies?

The history of the idea of the 'informal economy' has been recounted very often within urban studies. Considering Accra in the 1970s, Keith Hart (1973) observed that a significant proportion of the urban economy could be characterised as autonomous, unregulated, unregistered, illegal, uncounted, untaxed, small-scale and involving low technology activities. This saw him invent the term, 'informal economy'. Much debate ensued in development studies (less so in urban studies) about what this might be, and how to define it. The elements and their valuation varied as did the hypothesised relation with the 'formal' economy. It was not straightforward to seek to document 'informal' economic activities as these have historically not been included in national accounting systems and are deeply opaque to data gathering, although some approximations are possible (Chen 2012). In urban studies the term, 'informal' merged into a broader sign of the informalisation of many aspects of social life, settlements, governance and planning in poorer cities (Lindell 2008; Roy 2005; Watson 2009). For those more external to these contexts, informality emerged as something of a marker of a future devastation of the city, or stood for that which could not be defined as properly 'urban', an indicator of an analytical abyss between Western cities of concrete, and those urban places whose peripheries were marked by auto-construction (Koolhaas et al. 2000; Davis 2006).

In their comparative reflections on the 'informal economy' across case studies from Latin America, the US and Europe (with one case from Malaysia), Castells and Portes (1989) sought to distance their analysis from those concerned with its role in survivalist economies or as continuous with long standing or traditional practices (although for the Malaysian example both of these were important). Effectively pressing a divide between their cases and Africa and India, they suggest that 'the informal economy is not a marginal phenomenon for charitable social research, but a fundamental politico-economic process at the core of many societies' (p. 15). It is fundamental, for example, for regulation theory analysis because it emerges in and is defined in relation to, wider economic dynamics and state institutions. The informal economy is incorporated within restructured enterprises following economic crisis, or comprises activities which fall outside of state regulation. Restructuring of US, European and Latin American economies through the long post-1973 economic crisis saw a growth in contracting out, competitive decline of regulatory standards in the face of Low Wage Industrialisation in Asia, retreat from worker's rights, and the deep casualisation of labour in the collapse of the Import Substitution Industrialisation model in South America (Portes and Martinez 2019). Tellingly, what draws attention in the Malaysian case is the globally linked and opposite trend of the rise of formal employment in a Newly Industrialising Country, even as employees relied on extensive social networks to gain access to these jobs and sustain life in low paid work. The persistence of longstanding (informal) Chinese-ethnic businesses is also noted in this context. In the African context, the thorough-going nature of the informalisation of the economy made regulationist analyses focussed on the subsumption of informal activities in formal economic and institutional relations redundant (except to some extent in South Africa – see Wellings and Sutcliffe 1984).

The definition of 'informality' which evolved to predominate in urban studies expansively concerned itself with a very wide range of 'informal' practices making both cities and economies – the associational interactions which produced and shaped economic activities and urban life (Simone 2001b). At the same time, 'formal' institutions and economic processes were seen to have a thorough-going element of informality – as illegality and 'corruption' but also as ways of making the state 'work' (Bayart 1994; Chabal and Daloz 1999). In an Indian context the extensive flexibility, personal patronage and informality of governance drew urbanists to comment on the way in which 'informality' itself came to be a strategic resource of governance – arguably permitting certain plainly illegal or unplanned activities in order to secure state objectives (Roy 2005) or, more brutally in Israel–Palestine, to secure permanent termporariness and non-belonging (Yiftachel 2009). Informality, from these contexts, appeared as more of a 'mode' of urbanism, a way in which the city is produced and governed, than categories of economy or associational activities beyond the state. In many contexts, the state itself was understood as a highly informalised entity (Neves Alves 2021) – and more generally, institutions everywhere can be seen as entwining formal rules with informal cultures and practices (Altrock 2016; Hilbrandt 2021).

The understanding of informality has stretched far beyond either the 'informal settlement', or unregulated or precarious labour, as McFarlane and Waibel (2016, p. 9) observe: 'informality-formality variously emerges as a governing tool, a way of life, a means of knowing the city, a set of dispositions, and a continuum'. They present the case studies in their book as contributing to 'the possibility of an enlarged and more comprehensive understanding of urban informality.' They consider the core of current analyses to be the twin perspectives of informality as a 'mode of urbanism' (governance, planning) and as a way of negotiating urban life (associational, emergent). Both of these indicate that substantial aspects of economic, social and urban life are relevant to the concept of informality, and have been the focus of prolific analyses in the countries and contexts which have informed the concept – largely across Asia, Africa and South America. The concluding chapter in their book arrives at 'hybridity' of formal and informal as a way forward. However, the contributions of Simone and De Boeck which I considered earlier, as well as the broader arguments of Roy (2009b), press these insights further. Their work suggests that the processes which have come together under the term, 'informality' pertain to the very core features of the urban. Thus, it is the urban itself which is characterised analytically and produced materially by the very dynamics which the term 'informality' points towards. In a move from 'exception' to core theoretical proposition, the unpredictable emergence of associations, practices or concepts, or the improvisations which sustain getting by in the city, are identified as the form and nature of the urban as such. It is in this sense that Simone and Pieterse reappropriate the foundational concept of urban 'density' as a rubric to characterise the emergent nature of urban worlds (Simone and Pieterse 2017), or de Boeck suggests that the emergent meanings of the urban are constituted in everyday life, as 'rumours', for example (De Boeck and Plissart 2004).

This opens up to the inclusion of many different contexts and activities in exploring the term, 'informality' (Harris 2017); at the very same time, the term itself seems to have found its limits. Thus, drawn to learn from the analyses of African urbanists, questions of informality can be explored in Berlin concerning the peremptory inconsistencies of state policing and negotiated implementation of rules (Haid 2017; Hilbrandt 2021). Or, considering the strategic approach to informality by the state, together with the limitations in state reach and capacity which characterise many poor contexts, Le Galès (2011) poses the question of a context like Paris, as to 'what is governed'? If new subjects are emergent in urban contexts, and new kinds of associations formed, as per the conceptualisation of informality, limits to state capacity are inevitable. In a fruitful comparative reflection, Tuvikene et al. (2016) place Berlin, Tallin (Estonia) and Bafatà (Guinea Buissau) alongside one another to navigate the transition from 'informality' to alternative analytical terms which can characterise the complex interactions of state and society. They seek to replace the encompassing and in the end exceedingly vague term, 'informality'. They focus on the 'voids' in legislation which permit activities to emerge and persist in all three contexts; and on the variations in the practices of state agents, and the relations between extant norms and regulations, which make of 'the state' a negotiated achievement and only a more or less predictable institution, everywhere.

The very marker of the former untheorisability of global South cities, informality, in the end speaks to the very core of what(ever) the urban might be: 'informality' indexes the emergent, associational, provisional (Devlin 2018). The social life of cities which emerges in rumours, in everyday practices and movements. The governance capacities which arrive at the interstices of institutional reach, where improvisations and duality are what makes things happen, or which, in being evaded or negotiated, make living in the city possible. 'Informality' has highlighted some of the core features of urban life: emergence, proximities, transience, the social worlds and words which produce whatever space or the urban might be(come). It might be that prominent theorisations invoke the potential planetarity of urbanisation under conditions of global capitalism (Brenner and Schmid 2015), or systematic analysis of common elements of all urban form (Scott and Storper 2015). But it is from patient research attending to the immediate, the given, the emergent in some of the poorest cities in the world that a core feature of the nature(s) of the urban has come to be known, and that which makes urban living possible has been identified. The concept of informality, launched from so many urban contexts which have lived under the sign of theoretical erasure as (not) urban, now circulates widely, finding purchase to address many different urban contexts. Many writers on Northern and other contexts have come to find the generative conceptualisation of informality good to think (the urban) with more generally (Le Galès 2011; Schilling et al. 2019; Schindler 2013b).

The life cycle of the concept, 'informality' traced from 1973 to now, articulates a pragmatic approach to the process of conceptualisation and connects us back to the philosophically inflected methodological reflections of Benjamin (in conversation with Deleuze). An Idea of the urban economy as informal emerged in a specific context, defined in a narrow way, and establishing somewhat fierce borders with an apparently opposite term, the "formal" economy. It gained in richness with mobility across continents and cities, as well as finding resonance with different constituent elements. It has confounded attempts to define it, while at the same time opening up repeatedly to the potentiality it offers in relation to observations and experiences in many different urban contexts. The deep 'informality' across all elements of urban life in many African contexts, as well as the forms of associational governance in Indian cities (Benjamin 2008; Bhan 2016; Ghertner 2015a; Sundaresan 2019) have driven the expansion of the term, as have the diverse experiences and meanings of the '(I)n(f)ormal' across these regions. But in its successful circulation, the constellation/concept has perhaps reached its limits: 'We might need new terms', Garth Myers notes, 'for the apparently fading dichotomy of formal and informal given how interwoven they are' (Myers 2011, p. 103). And given how very core 'informal' processes are to whatever the urban might be.

The term, informality, has migrated in terms of the contexts considered, been reconfigured in terms of the constituent elements, and completely relocated in terms of its analytical centrality. It now draws attention to core aspects of urban life. In its generalisation, moving from exception to the urban to key formulation of what the urban is, 'informality' is now fragmenting as a term. Other 'stars' will dazzle us in their illumination as they realign the 'singularities' of observation and experience in new formulations. These emerge now on the field of a global urban, rather than one of 'Third World' or 'African' cities, and so have the potential to de-exceptionalise these experiences, placing them at the centre of understandings of urban life, globally.

Conclusion

This chapter has outlined a different perspective on the drama of conceptualisation, starting from the challenges of coming to know the urban world from in the midst of urban territories and how this might contribute to understandings of the urban, globally. For Deleuze, different temporalities (habit, memory, imagination) in the process of coming to Ideas drive an open process of determination/knowing across dynamic matter and fractured subjects. As in Benjamin, conceptualisation is also a moment of making the future. In the constitution of the 'Idea', 'something forces us to think' (Hughes 2009). Habit, memory and imagination rework intuitions (observations, singularities) in an order of differentiation and 'chance' (all of possibility). Ideas bring both subject and object into view. The thinker emerges in the midst of constellating singularities and their relations into entities, along with quantity and quality, extension and depth; space is constituted at the same time, not pre-given (Dewsbury and Thrift 2005). Dramatisation of intensities (matter) takes place as both actualising and individuating – as intensities can also be understood as actualising entities and expressing the content of Ideas. Differenc/t/iation is this entire complex process – a (very long) detective story of how the subject, object and Ideas come to be.

For Benjamin it is also a differential form of time (a multiplicity of pasts) which holds the energy with potential to blast open the past and explode new ideas and (weak) hope into the future. In the dialectic at a standstill it is the coming together of different times in the 'now of recognition' that provokes the energy evident in a 'Tiger's Leap' across different times: 'now is the time differential' (Hamacher 2005, p. 61). Prefiguring Deleuze, for Benjamin this links to insights into conceptualisation in general – the way in which singularity and repetition are conditioned by each other in the Idea, and exist beyond origin and copy (1999a, AP, p. 867, Q° 21); any origin is always a becoming, any Idea a multiplicity. As we have explored in this chapter, Benjamin's famous analysis of historical time as 'now-time' (*Jetztzeit*) is closely tied to his reflections on method as set out in the *Trauerspiel* book (2019): 'Both the ability of the thing to be known and the ability of the historian to know it have a share in the recognizability as well as in the Now' (Hamacher 2005, p. 60). Dialectics at a standstill as method is the process of coming to know an historical object (including, for Benjamin, Paris). Arriving at Ideas (as constellations) requires working across many different, perhaps obscure and tangential, instances, cases and times. Benjamin's descriptions of this method reflect a patient, careful practice of generating concepts, assembling difference and thinking cautiously about extremes.

The urgencies of the historical moment which shaped the Theses *On the Concept of History* find an energy in the 'leap' of differential time (Benjamin 2003b (OCH), XIV). The historian of Baroque drama, however, worked in great detail through the remnant records of an extinct theatrical form. The energy in the constellations of careful observations ('singularities') across different (urban) experiences which might flash into arrangement in the sky of possible concepts, is perhaps modest. Certainly, though, the clock of human experience might be again, as Benjamin sensed it in 1939, at 'a moment of danger' (2003b, OCH, VI). The catastrophes of urban life certainly pile up in our lifetime (2003b, OCH, IX), compounded by the disintegration of political orders and challenges to life itself, whether climate, viral, or violence. Opening up conceptualisations of the urban to all its possibilities across space-time through the crafting of collaborative engagements and wider conversations might crystallise insights which disturb ('shock') what has been taken for granted, and find scope to speak, perhaps with some urgency for the future, in the midst of the urban world.

Notes

1. A motif which Benjamin (1973, p. 79) identified in Baudelaire: 'Everything that the big city threw away, everything it lost, everything it despised, everything it crushed underfoot, he catalogues and collects'.
2. There is a slight confusion looming here, as in Chapter 4. The social science vernacular tends to use singularity to imply a single case or phenomenon of anything, standing only for itself. In Deleuze's philosophical account of conceptualisation the singularity is rather one observation/intuition, which exists in a prolific series with many other observations, together constellating into a concept, and contributing to the determination of an object/phenomenon. Such a constellation, such a concept, will by definition always define a singularity in the social science vernacular sense. But a singularity that is one of a series, with potentially many neighbouring concepts/objects, and perhaps a role in determining (as an inflection point) the nature

of those neighbours (Deleuze 1994, e,g. pp. 348–9). In this perspective, singularities are composed of multiplicities and are themselves part of multiplicities – not isolates (for a summary of different forms of singularities see Deleuze, 1993, p. 104). We might say, then, in the totality associated with an Idea, 'everything is ordinary, everything is unique' (*ibid*, p. 104). Instead of reducing 'representation' to one thing per concept, Deleuze's analysis opens (in both virtual series, the material and Ideas) to the prolific generation of Ideas, across many observations or singularities which are always one of a kind, and always multiple.
3. This text includes a quite personal discussion of how he comes to 'a particular methodology of an urban researcher, specializing in the conjunctions of the disconsonant, working in spaces not habitable in any clear terms' (p. 45).
4. My personal training reflects this tradition, with the inspiration of South African scholar Jeff McCarthy, for whom this entwining was central to a political practice at the most dangerous of times; and then in London, the example of Michael Edwards has been outstanding for me and many others in this context. Practice has its price, though, and the understated commitment of some of the best minds in urban studies whose thinking and insight comes from praxis and spreads through generosity, deserves more recognition.
5. See https://www.africancentreforcities.net and https://iihs.co.in/about.
6. He interrogated genres (Baroque Drama; photography), poets, novelists and playwrights (Baudelaire, Proust, Brecht), built form (iron construction), a certain urban space (arcades, streets, interiors).
7. A 'monad' is the equivalent in metaphysics of the 'singularity' in mathematics – for Leibnez, monads ('souls') are indissociable elements of every 'body' or entity of existence (pre-individual). Duffy (2010) comments, 'Leibniz determines the singularity in the domain of mathematics as a philosophical concept' (p. 105); 'the continuity characteristic of infinitesimal calculus is isomorphic to the series of predicates contained in the concept of a subject' (p. 105). For Leibniz, the subject of any predicate is a monad, 'a simple, invisible, dimensionless metaphysical point' (p. 106). In his schema, they 'express' the whole world – although 'distinctly' only a region of it. Deleuze's (1993) account of Leibniz's philosophy, *The Fold* is helpful. McDonnell (2010) notes that expression involves the monad 'reading the world folded into itself in the passage of its internal states', constituting a 'point of view defined through the principle of activity and change' (p. 75). It is as active 'predication' that the monad exists.
8. For Leibniz, a monad is 'a simple, invisible, dimensionless metaphysical point' (Duffy 2010, p. 106).
9. In Leibniz, 'We witness the honeymoon of singularity and the concept' (Deleuze 1993, p. 77).
10. Benjamin described his project as one of 'monadology' in his 1938 defence to Adorno. This monadism became a source of contention in his discussions with

Theodore Adorno, who noted that, 'It fails to do justice to Marxism because it omits the mediation by the total societal process and because, almost superstitiously, it attributes to materialist enumeration powers of illumination which are reserved solely to theoretical interpretation and never to pragmatic pointing' (Adorno to Benjamin, 10 November 1938, in Eiland and Jennings (2003), SW 4, p. 102). Benjamin was in turn challenged by the Marxist analyses which framed reality through the mediations of economy, and which explored complex ways to map infrastructure and superstructure, economy and culture. As a philologist, reduction was not an option – the work had to be considered on its own terms. Challenged by Adorno that he did not bring in the mediations of political economy, he wrote, 'On est philologue, ou on n'est pas' (one is either a philologist or one is not) and drawing deep from his dignity and resources, existential and philosophical, he insisted that his project was one of 'monadology'. (ibid., p. 460): 'Marx lays bare the causal connection between economy and culture. For us, what matters is the thread of expression. It is not the economic origins of culture that will be presented, but the expression of the economy in its culture'. (1999, AP, N1a,6). A rather loosely written statement on the commodity clarifies (1973, pp. 103–7). And a statement in the AP alongside numerous quotes from Karl Krauss on base-superstructure etc, saw him comment that commodities or objects 'express' economic relations. This Leibnizian term instills an agency for the object, a sense of generativity in shaping the world. 'The essence of capitalist production would be comprehended vis-à-vis the concrete historical forms in which the economy finds its cultural expression'. (Tiedermann 1999, p. 940). Cruelly blocking publication of his Baudelaire essay (PSEB) on the basis of these criticisms, and wasting precious time we know now he did not have, Adorno's correspondence cast Benjamin into a deep depression (Eiland and Jennings 2014, p. 624).

11. This was 'speculative' in that it 'exceeds given experience' (Caygill 1998, p. 57) rather than transcendental, in which certain elements are separated and proposed as the 'conditions of the possibility of experience' (p. 57); Benjamin's was a 'non-Hegelian speculative philosophy of experience' (Caygill 1998, p. 34).
12. 'He is on the lookout for banal incidents in order to approximate them to poetic events' (1973, PSEB, p. 99; 1973, SMB, pp. 119–20).
13. 'That the stars are absent from Baudelaire's poetry is the most conclusive sign of its tendency to eradicate semblance' (2003a, CP, p. 186).
14. Benjamin (1973) notes that 'The sense of 'the abyssal' is to be defined as 'meaning' – produced across the abyss of two terms brought into direct allegorical relation (PSEB, p. 42) – 'Such a sense is always allegorical' (1999a, p. 271, J24, 1). 'It is a secularised space: the abyss of knowledge and meanings' (p. 271, J24, 2). Allegory establishes a different relation between concepts and things than the symbol – Deleuze (1993) discusses this in *Le Pli* (The

Fold), from Benjamin – p. 145: 'appertaining – belonging to – is the key to allegory'.

15. Benjamin's reflections here speak directly to one aspect of Deleuze's (1994) analysis of conceptualisation. Following vocabulary from Bergson, Proust and Freud, Benjamin suggests that 'the structure of memory is decisive for the philosophical pattern of experience. Experience is indeed a matter of tradition, in collective existence as well as in private life … it is less a product of facts firmly anchored in memory than a convergence in memory of accumulated and frequently unconscious data' (1973, SMB, p. 111).

16. Didi-Huberman (2003, p. 6) notes this dynamic process as a dialectic of desire which 'supposes alterity, lost object, split subject, a non-objectifiable relationship'. It points to the difficulties of working across objects and concepts: 'The difficulty of our problem lies in this: in opposition to a discourse of specificity that pronounces and carries out its dogmatic death-sentences (the aura is dead, so much the better), and to a discourse of non-specificity that invents eternal and ahistorical entities (let us seek transcendence …), we must in each instance formulate something like a 'specificity of the non-specific. Let me explain, we must seek in each work of art the articulation between *formal singularities* and *anthropological paradigms*'.

17. John Osborne's translation offers: the 'pause for breath … after which thought can be totally and unhurriedly concentrated even on the very minutest object without the slightest inhibition' (Benjamin 1998, pp. 44–5). Also, 'zurückgreifen' perhaps carries the notion of 'grabbing', grasping, and suggests a link to *der Begriff*, concepts.

18. Osborne's (2004) translation; Eiland's (Benjamin 2019) renders this as 'objects of dull astonishment', and in the original German Benjamin (2016, p. 21) writes, 'eines trüben Staunens'.

19. His (sometime) friend/rival, Ernst Bloch noted, 'he had an extraordinary eye . . for the unusual and unschematic, the disruptive, individual being (Einzelsein) which doesn't fit into the mo(u)ld' (Buck-Morss 1977, p. 75). Adorno noted: 'almost the entire effort of his philosophy can be defined as an attempt to rescue the particular' (Buck-Morss 1977, p. 189).

20. In fact at several moments in the outlines he prepared for the possible contents of the Arcades Project book, he notes to himself to go back to Hegel on the Dialectic at a standstill. He allocates a section to this in some of his plans for the Arcades book. His few notes on Hegel, though, are rather removed from these concerns, focussed on Hegel as a historical and political figure.

21. (1999a, AP, p. 894): 'World Exhibitions propagate the universe of commodities'. Also; 'world exhibitions were training schools in which the masses, barred from consuming, learnt empathy with the commodity' (AP, p. 805).

22. The multiplicity of Ideas and times is a theme Benjamin pursues in the Leibnizian terms of 'differentials' and 'Infinity'. In seeking to work out what Trauerspiel was, he suggests that 'origin is an eddy in the stream of becoming' (Benjamin, 1998, p. 45). And, 'The guidelines of philosophical contemplation are inscribed in the dialectic intrinsic to origin. It is by virtue of this dialectic that, in everything essential, singularity and repetition prove to be reciprocally determined' (2019, OGT, p. 25).
23. Benjamin, 2019, OGT, p. 43: 'Whereas induction reduces ideas to concepts by failing to arrange and order them, deduction does the same by projecting them into a pseudological continuum'.
24. 'The value of fragments of thought is all the greater the less direct their relation to the underlying idea' – provoking brilliance, as in a mosaic. (2019, OGT, p. 29).
25. 'When the Idea absorbs a sequence of historical formulations, it does not do so in order to construct a unity out of them, let alone to abstract something common to them all. There is no analogy between the relationship of the individual to the Idea, and its relationship to the concept; in the latter case it falls under the aegis of the concept and remains what it was: an individuality; in the former it stands in the Idea, and becomes something different: a totality. That is its Platonic redemption.' (Benjamin 1998, p. 46).
26. The Idea is a monad (Caygill 1998, p. 58): 'Benjamin sees "every Idea" as a monad' (p. 129). In the dialectics at a standstill, 'thinking is crystallised as a monad': 'He takes cognizance of it in order to blast a specific era out of the homogenous course of history; thus he blasts a specific life out of the era, a specific work out of the lifework' (2003b, OCH, p. 396). Eiland and Jennings (2014, p. 625): 'Benjamin's highly compressed mode of construction aimed at constituting the historical object, in the eyes of the present, as a monad: 'The base lines of this construction converge in our own historical experience. In this way the object constitutes itself as a monad. And as in the monad everything that formerly lay mythically petrified within the given text comes alive'.
27. The importance of extremes to thought and method is a point Deleuze notes in Nietzsche (2006, NP, pp. 102–3).
28. The German is more resonant with the Leibnizian formulations: 'Ihre Darstellung ist zur Aufgabe nichts Geringes gesetzt, als dieses Bild der Welt in seiner Verkürzung zu zeichnen' (Benjamin, 2016 [1928], p. 23).
29. For example, Benjamin writes, 'The principles of philosophical contemplation are recorded in the dialectic which is inherent in origin. This dialectic shows singularity and repetition to be conditioned by one another in all essentials' (2019, OGT p. 46).

30. Perhaps this would be a better translation of Benjamin's use of 'Verhältnis' as an alternative to 'relation'. Eiland translates it as 'comportment' (2019 (2026), p. 12, note 15).
31. And this turns on Deleuze's reading of the unfinished third element of *Thus Spake Zarathrustra*, where the failure of representation Benjamin identifies turns to a new potentiality (Deleuze 1994, DR, p.115, p. 248; Deleuze 2006).
32. 'We teach that, in the stratification of the dream, reality never simply is, but rather that it strikes the dreamer. And I treat of the arcades precisely as though, at bottom, they were something that happened to me' [1999a, AP, p. 908 materials for expose 1935].
33. Rather than being singular, as opposed to universal (or the particular in relation to general), in the mathematical imaginary underpinning Deleuze the singular can be thought as referring to being 'distinct from or opposed to "regular". The singular is what is outside the rule' (Flanagan 2009, p. 120). But Deleuze offers his own definitions of different kinds of singularities – and Flanagan notes that the invention of a calculus of divergence opened up the singularity to be more distinctive and divergent from other possible series.
34. The resonances with Benjamin's reflections on method are significant.

Conclusion
Starting Anywhere, Thinking with (Elsew)here

Through the course of this book, we have left behind the former object of comparative urban methods, 'the city' as a territorially bounded entity from which flows the kind of restricted research practices where 'cases' are isolated, researchers leap across the 'interstellar void' between them and, guided by a rigid imagined architecture of 'comparability', find themselves reflecting on a relatively narrow range of urban contexts and processes. Instead we have opened up to the prolific interconnections and embedded practices which frame, on the grounds of each urban territory, all the possibilities of what the urban might be. In the process we have reimagined the urbanist as a scholar, practitioner, a resident who is eager to understand her context, but is keenly aware of the connections, flows and imaginations that link her settlement to multiple elsewheres, whether this is through the climate change activists, the donor evaluators, the housing specialists in the community, communications with distant friends and family, the traders who arrive to set up store, or the consultants working for the developer planning a nearby satellite city. In search of understanding, starting from (somew)here, with a committed determination to shape that context, opening up to the possibility of thinking with elsewhere arrives quickly.

Thinking the urban, with its differentiation, across its diversity, and through its distinctiveness can only ever yield a partial perspective offered by someone, starting somewhere, in what is always a distinctive urban situation. But, also, any attempt to think that specific urban entrains a multiplicity of elsewheres, of other urban experiences, in the tracks of the many interconnections which shape every urban territory and produce many repeated/differentiated outcomes. Whoever the someone is, from wherever they are thinking, a comparative gesture quickly follows. Thinking the urban in a 'world of cities' incites the potential for insights to emerge from the diversity of the urban world, across interconnected processes of spatial formation and shared histories, or in relation to divergent outcomes.

All these, as we have seen, inspire comparative experiments. On this basis the book has explored how thinking the urban from (somew)here, in relation to

Comparative Urbanism: Tactics for Global Urban Studies, First Edition. Jennifer Robinson.
© 2022 John Wiley & Sons Ltd. Published 2022 by John Wiley & Sons Ltd.

elsewheres, can help to displace inherited knowledge, revise concepts and disperse weighty, over-ambitious theorisations circulating parochial insights as universal claims. The wide array of practices which emerge from this ambition, I have called 'comparative urbanism'.

Comparative experiments establish a site of conceptualisation of the urban as 'virtuality': a multiplicity of possible concepts of the urban and urbanisation processes, and openings to possible urban futures. With a reformatted comparative imagination we can anticipate concepts and insights which are emergent from and creatively engage with the challenges of particular urban contexts. At the same time, there is scope for concepts to be part of wider conversations about whatever 'the urban' might be. There could be good ideas and insights which gain traction, inspire and motivate researchers across many different contexts; or which coalesce into robust and wide-ranging formulations, perhaps even 'theories'. But if concepts of the urban are to be operative within diverse urban contexts, to grow out of and inform mobilisations of urban dwellers, to contribute to contesting and remaking cities, then it is the argument of this book that configurations of insights need to be responsive to the diverse urban world, open to being inspired and transformed by any urban experience.

A Reformatted Urban Comparison

This book has put in place the different elements for a new range of comparative urban practices: starting anywhere, thinking with elsewhere, to revise insights and generate new concepts about the urban world. In the wake of postcolonial critiques, it has proposed an agenda towards a decolonised urban studies.

Part I of the book established the need for global urban studies to explore new methodologies which would be pragmatic ways forward to build a decolonised field of knowledge and respond to the extensive, fragmented forms of urbanisation emerging through the twenty-first century. With these aims in mind, the first four chapters considered the potential for building on key elements of the comparative imagination, such as the interest in revising concepts, displacing ethnocentrism and thinking with elsewhere. It drew on these to articulate new grounds for composing comparisons, and a range of new tactics for thinking across different urban contexts. An important insight is that through the slow process of bringing more than one urban context or experience into conversation, both the object and the terms of comparison often emerge and change in the course of the comparative practice. As starting points for comparative experiments, though, the spatiality of the urban inspired numerous possibilities. The two core sections of the book deal with, in turn, Genetic (inspired by the urban world) and Generative (researcher-led) grounds for comparison. We identified these approaches as latent in the practices of urban comparativists, whose creative comparative analyses emerged from working pragmatically with the shared features of urban contexts, rather than from dogmatically following the formal methodological strictures, and who had been inspired by globalising processes to think with connections.

Genetic grounds for comparison, then, inspire comparative practices which trace the prolific interconnections amongst urban territories and work with the wider processes shaping urbanisation and urban outcomes. In Part II of the book, two broad theoretical perspectives informed each chapter and suggested different kinds of tactics. From the more materialities perspective, in Chapter 5 we considered how attending closely to connections and flows can build up insights about urbanisation processes. And how working across differentiated outcomes can perhaps subtract from existing analytical framings, or initiate looser processes of learning across interconnected cases. These tactics might also help to identify cases for 'comparative conversations', or offer inspiration for composing comparisons for more structured insights on the variety of urban processes associated with diverse urban outcomes. From the more political economy perspective we explored in Chapter 6 how interrogating wider social processes through different cases might expand, enrich or undermine existing analyses. Especially where numerous processes converge in 'contexts', there is potential to identify alternative explanatory dimensions through comparative reflection. Rather than simply strengthening existing analyses or assuming cases feed back into shaping already identified processes (as in the extensive research on 'variegated neoliberalisation'), comparative practice can help to assess claims to 'family resemblance' across cases. The multiple (and diverse) elements entailed in each case might open out to define different social processes altogether than those which originally inspired the comparison.

The shifting shape and focus of comparison during the course of research emerges most clearly in Part III of the book, where 'generative' grounds for comparison are the focus of attention. The comparative tactics developed here are inspired by researcher curiosity and seek to generate new concepts, and interrogate inherited terms. Who the researcher is matters. This opens to interrogation of how taking account of positionality inspires and shapes comparative practices and methodological innovations. Rather than starting from the perspective of the researcher as a northern scholar, facing up to the challenges of their privileged relational position and global travels, a de/post-colonial methodology begins from the position of researchers anywhere. Critiques of racialised intellectual inheritances, new starting points for thinking and creative practices initiated by those historically excluded from or sidelined within the academy, as well as the potential for collaborative methods within and across contexts, support new modes and horizons of conceptualisation. Starting anywhere, the question nonetheless arises, how might urban researchers generate new concepts? A range of different ways of imagining concept formation, in the midst of an urban world, were considered, placing Weberian Ideal Types, Marxist accounts of a 'concrete-in-thought' alongside Arendt's view of universals as collective 'horizons' of meaning and Mbembe's speculations on new grounds for an 'in-common'. In the midst of the urban world, concepts inevitably emerge. And in each of the different approaches considered, concepts are understood to port somehow the material world, even as each offers different openings for comparative practice. In Weber, a looser view of concepts as heuristics for expanding understanding of the world is potentially helpful for experimenting with new terms and specifying their scope in different contexts. The Marxist assessment of the embeddedness of concepts in the power relations of urban political economy is a crucial corrective to seeing concepts as purely free-floating; this opens to comparative analyses which closely track the contours of the 'concrete abstractions' and geographies of capitalism. Hannah Arendt and feminist scholars bring into sharper perspective the political stakes and contestation of terms within and across different contexts as well as amongst (distributed, often conflictual) collectives. Here, comparative practices might think with and through the pragmatic formulations of insights in the midst of the spatially extended political fray. Valuing committed and engaged formulation of concepts and insights in collaboration with urban actors flows easily from this perspective. Nonetheless, even as framing comparisons and thinking with and across difference holds scope for the generation of new concepts, it takes place in a field of striated histories, fractured subjectivities and contested power relations.

Delving more specifically into the generation of concepts of the urban, possible tactics for comparison on generative grounds depend on how the shape of the urban is imagined. Thinking conjuncturally, focussing on contingent urban outcomes, or seeing the urban as 'specific' or 'diverse' frame different opportunities for comparative experiments. These terms delimit which contexts are drawn into comparative reflection, on what basis, and set some limits to the potential for productive comparisons within that perspective. For example, while certain contexts might be considered as part of a certain political 'conjuncture' or moment, even if expansively defined others could be hidden from view and excluded from consideration. Ideas of the radical contingency of social processes move towards a view of the urban as distinctive – always an 'individual', interrupting efforts at universal conceptualisations. One additional aspect of the urban is crucial for developing this insight further. This is that the urban is not a two-dimensional context on which wider social processes are played out, but a rich, inexhaustible and three-dimensional space which produces social relations and (urbanisation) processes. This assessment grounds the possibility of building concepts of the urban from specificity. As specificity, the urban is also diverse. Insights developed in specific urban contexts might speak also to other urban contexts; they might not. Insights across diverse urban territories might build on shared features, such as urbanisation processes or certain mechanisms, such as those associated with distinctively urban dynamics of land use, agglomeration or territorial governance/regulation. New concepts of the urban and urbanisation emerge, then, through comparative experiments devised in response to urban diversity, including across divergent urban contexts.

Opportunities for comparative experiments proliferate on generative grounds. For example, placing different urban contexts within the same putative 'conjuncture' alongside one another to interrogate the shared processes and dynamics which characterise that moment (e.g. fiscal retreat, localised imaginations of aspiration, or displacement of poor residents); considering different contexts as starting points for building analyses to shed light on the multiple processes shaping complex historical events (e.g. comparing different post-colonial transformations, or assessing the possibilities for securing traditional land rights within land reform initiatives); identifying emergent urbanisation processes in one specific urban context, and exploring other contexts where that process can be identified but might work out differently (such as 'plotting urbanisation', or 'gentrification'). Composing comparisons on the basis of widespread shared features (such as large-scale urban developments) to bring into view the diversity (variety) of urban processes for direct reflection is an important way of expanding analyses. For example, comparative reflection on urban development might draw attention to different forms of state agency in relation to land, and offer the potential to extend accounts of urban politics to speak to the wide range of actors involved in urban development across different contexts. For many aspects of urban life, composing comparative reflections across diversity is a key tactic for expanding the conceptual horizons of global urban studies, including more exploratory ways of initiating conversations across different contexts. However, such conversations are often theory-laden, and the power relations of mobile concepts can limit innovation. A more reflexive and decentred approach to the mobility of concepts might focus on the (ex-centric) situated researcher, engaged in a critical 'drawing in' of useful ideas, as opposed to focussing on the (often ambitious) process of putting ideas into circulation from a position of power and authority. Critical reading practices and interrogation of the locatedness of 'theory' can bring divergent theoretical traditions into conversation, inspiring comparative insights.

The final part of the book considers how urban territories might form the basis for framing comparisons, and explores which urban territories might be productive to think with. This leaves us, though, with a question which is unresolved in this book – what are urban territories?! A number of suggestions for comparative tactics grounded on territories (say, 'suburbs' as a certain relational configuration of urban territory) are offered. Crucially this needs to extend to include any urban territory emergent within the contemporary context of fragmented and dispersed urbanisation. So, the diverse processes of territorialisation, producing urban territories, become an important focus for comparative analysis. Starting from territories elaborates new kinds of openings and challenges for urban comparativism. The 'territory' focusses attention on the materiality of urban form, on the complex juxtapositions characteristic of urban space, and on the practices of urban dwellers. Together these processes forge distinctive outcomes in each urban territory. Territories also bring to the fore the opacity and unpredictability of urban experience. With a focus on urban scholarship from often exceptionalised contexts, the potential for particularly innovative comparative practices, at precisely those moments when the urban seems perhaps most occluded, is apparent. Insights emerge in association with the generativity of urban residents, or in the insistent failures to determine exactly what this object urban is. Here the perspective afforded by Deleuze's philosophy helps. The virtuality of both the urban world (as emergent) and all possible concepts of the urban provides a setting for conceptual innovation. With Walter Benjamin's consideration of the historical object of the city, and Deleuze's dramatisation of the generation of concepts, an account is offered of concepts of the urban as revisable, and as a multiplicity. The final chapter embraces concepts of the urban forged in the midst of territories, close up to the materialities and experiences of the urban, still in the shadow of elsewhere. An account of conceptualisation, generated from any urban territory, and in which all emergent conceptualisations across distinctive, diverse and divergent urban experiences matter, is a crucial element of reformatted comparative urban methodologies. Part IV presents some resources which go in this direction, and which can replace representational imaginaries of comparison based on similarity and difference, on distinct (spatial) entities, and reliant on interrogating the success or failure of singular, hegemonic 'theories'.

I have not skirted around the concern that there are moments when incomparability is more than a celebration of the unique qualities and potential of each urban context, of thinking from (somew)here, but a break on learning from other situations. I have, however, resisted incentives to cut urban experiences off from one another on *a priori* grounds, particularly the insistence that levels of 'development', histories of colonialism or current resourcing and governance challenges demarcate a zone of either necessary incomparability or obvious commonality. All of these differences matter, terribly. But they are not necessarily reasons to seek to build segmented theorisations of the urban. I have shown through numerous examples how, while in relation to some questions, certainly, the scope for insight across deep divides may be limited, grounds for accepting the geopolitical categories of 'South' or 'global South' as foundational for reinventing urban studies as fundamentally divided are slim. At the very least, the term, 'South' as a marker of analytical and political exclusion needs to be treated as itself a multiplicity – many Souths, *les pays Suds*. The multiplicity and complexity of urban life, and the profound interconnectedness of urbanisation processes across different contexts asks for a different perspective. Both historically and perhaps especially under contemporary conditions of intensifying international developmental intervention, extractive private capital and ambitious geopolitical stakes, the urban needs to be thought in its exteriority, through and along the myriad tracks that entrain multiple elsewheres. There is perhaps no surprise as to where some of these tracks lead – to sites of power and decision-making, to illicit and shocking profit taking from the poorest cities, to stolid barely comprehensible or secret meetings of supposedly accountable political bodies. To valorise disconnection is to draw attention away from some of the most disconcerting aspects of globalised urbanisation and the power relations which seek to shape, confine and discard urban life. It diverts conceptual energies from the many surprising ways in which the connections which make the urban cross-cut any singular divisions we may invent. Insights into urban life and urbanisation might emerge just as much along the interconnections, filaments and capillaries that cross-cut urban territories, and that make urban worlds.

There is no inevitable productivity to 'thinking with elsewhere', but this book has demonstrated that this is a crucial element in global urban studies. The comparative imagination we have explored here, along with many scholars and along different theoretical lines, relies on the creative generativity of the researcher but also necessarily works with the emergences, trajectories and genetic connections of the urban worlds they are part of, trace and encounter. Where these worlds stop, or signpost incommensurabilities, so be it. We encountered this perhaps most compellingly in the alchemy of 'compression' and the orientation to detachment (Simone 2019), where what the researcher and the urban dweller might be experiencing is other than what the connections shaping places or ostensible intensity of social interactions might imply, and where grounds for comparability are occluded. Together with opacity comes an unknowability – the urban is not necessarily presented for the researcher's engagement, urban dwellers do not need to be known to one another, or to seek connections beyond their immediate experience. Violent and erasing histories hide both the past and elsewhere, leaving histories and geographies profoundy unredeemable. This is a reminder that the urban world is not pressing on the researcher with any particular desire to be known;

in fact, the urban hides much from those who live there (especially about the power relations that shape cities), or those who seek understanding about urbanisation. The urban world, on the contrary, often becomes known only incrementally, in alliance with the agency of subjects engaging in particular contexts. It is in the creative exploration of urban settings, the generation of new insights from the torsions evident as urban worlds are brought into disjunctive relation with available concepts by active urban researchers, that specific urban outcomes connect to wider conversations.

Rather than stopping points for thinking the urban, this book has argued, distinctive urban contexts 'in their individuality' operate (also) as conceptual inflection points, starting and turning points, which intervene in understandings of urban life with perhaps new and different experiences. The 'diversity' of the urban world, and the many places, territories and trajectories which make up urbanisation incite new kinds of reflections. And it is in diversity as well as in difference (repeated instances), in the prolific interconnections from which both opacity and distinctiveness are necessarily made, that 'the urban' emerges. But as we have seen, only ever in multiplicity, openness and indeterminacy. This is not to underestimate the value of ideas that can be put to work (for a while at least) somewhere, or in a certain range of contexts, or the potential to forge strong and coherent analyses with critical purchase and intent. But to insist that in the global urban world, whatever the urban/urbanisation might be, it surely always has to remain open to the possibility of being different, elsewhere. Strongly revisable concepts are key to the practice of global urban studies, and to comparative urbanism.

Conceptualisation

Throughout this book I have insisted that the problematic of the urban cannot escape the challenges of conceptualisation. Indeed, running through this book is an extended account of the process of conceptualisation, crafted in relation to the specific challenges of coming to know the urban. Comparative method directs us to this. Its active engagement across more than one context necessarily dislocates concepts, and problematises insights based on the experiences of any particular case. As a method, even in its traditional guise, comparison invokes an insistent interrogation of received ideas. I have strongly acknowledged that much more remains to be done in urban studies to confront the foundational devastations of racialisation which emerged alongside and inhabit the enlightenment tropes of dialectics and democracy (Mbembe 2017) or operatively underpin the ways in which 'subjects' and 'objects' might be framed (Moten 2018), or which imparted racist restrictions on understandings of urbanity (Robinson 2006). The intellectual future is being made, in so many experiments, and, importantly, in collaborative and collective ways within the growing practices of black, feminist and anti-racist studies (McKittrick 2021). In this regard, alongside the propositional content of this book about reformatting urban comparisons, it also contributes a ground-clearing exercise, seeking to identify the blockages to any urban scholar 'starting (anyw)here' to think the urban. What are the conventions which impede both the production and the acknowledgement of inventive concepts from certain scholars or places, or which occlude creative openings to different urban futures? The narrow conventions framing urban comparative methods, inequalities in the institutions of scholarship, and rigid adherence to (and power-laded imposition of) weighty theoretical concepts, singular processes and parochial terms have all been interrogated through the book. Equally, this book has also sought to explore in an open but critical way resources which are close at hand for destabilising inherited concepts and approaches.

For many urban scholars – those thinking with both Marxism and materialities, those driven by post-structuralist analytics and decolonial politics, those seeking to think from '*le pays suds*', global south(s), the rich, diverse, inexhaustible urban world is our inspiration. This world incites our analysis, leaving always residuals and resistances, 'rumbling intensities', exceeding whatever we think. In this sense I have tracked the concerns of Marx, dominant in urban studies and the horizon of my personal academic biography, to begin with the material world, interpreting this with Lefevbre as the rich inexhaustibility of the 'concrete'. But I have resisted the insistence by some Marxists that certain concepts have a privileged relation to the 'concrete'. I have also expressed my concerns about the new version of a god-trick which has followed in the wake of the strong materialities turn. In disavowing generalisation and simplification (McCormack 2012), at times this approach has inadvertently presented the researching subject as a transparent being able to somehow instantiate the material world in academic writing. Concepts are in these two cases either far too weighty (assumed to port the concrete), or have simply 'disappeared' such that the material world has no apparent mediation in the activities and thoughts of subjects (although see Dewsbury 2003 for a nuanced analysis inspired by Deleuze). I have instead been rigorous and explicit in naming the concepts and active thinkers which underpin urban analyses, and pointing out the inevitable distance, and yet intimate proximity, between concept and the concrete, between Ideas and the urban/material world.

Concepts are a presence in any analysis, any coming to know the (urban) world. As conceptualisation is core to comparativism, to thinking the urban across diversity and difference, much more needs to be done to interrogate and reframe how processes of conceptualisation might be imagined. This book has addressed this question in some detail. I have presented concept formation as a generative, potentially collaborative practice grounded in different experiences (Hill Collins 2019; McKittrick 2021; Oldfield 2022). Concepts (universals) might be understood as forming a horizon for action, and for collective and political deliberation (Zerilli 2016). In these perspectives, then, concept formation is a distributed practice. Rather than the preserve of scholars, conceptualisation is the outcome of concerted agency and critical, political subjects (Barnett 2017). Thinking along with writers from Mbembe to Weber and Stuart Hall, and drawing on Deleuze and Benjamin's accounts of generating concepts, I have presented a number of different ways in which to imagine a highly generative process of conceptualisation by active subjects, and to recognise the different ways in which the material world inserts itself into conceptualisation. In Weber's carefully empirically grounded Ideal Types, as well as Marx's 'concrete-in-thought', the material world is an active presence in conceptualisation. Specifically, through this book we have explored how the urban world draws us to track flows and processes across different settings, and to respond to its genesis in interconnections, juxtapositions, and embedded practices.

Whatever the urban might be is determined in alliance with (our) observations and experiences. We explored how the urban world incites a multiplicity of Ideas (concepts) as constellations made up of so many singularities (observations), ungrounded always by the (as yet unconceptualised) intensities of the material world, and the differences which destabilise any conceptualisation. We might see the urban after Deleuze and Benjamin partly as an 'expressing' concept but, since it can only ever be apprehended from a particular context, offering a necessarily abbreviated distinctness, in the midst of indistinction and obscurity, and alongside a multiplicity of such expressions/concepts. So, unlike a 'representational' approach, in which 'resemblance remains fixed in the concept … and applicable by right to a multiplicity of things', this book has probed how the rumbling intensities of the material (urban) world constantly present/ce themselves to 'challenge and unsettle any concepts we might arrive at' (Deleuze 1994, p. 13). On this basis a dynamic form of conceptualisation is proposed:

> it is a question of producing within the work a movement capable of affecting the mind outside of all representation; it is a question of making movement itself work, without interposition; of substituting direct signs for mediate representations; of inventing vibrations, rotations, whirlings, gravitations, dances or leaps which directly touch the mind.
> (Deleuze 1994 [1968], p. 9)

For Lefebvre, too, the recasting of the dialectic as three dimensional was a move to escape the self-referential circuits of both Hegelian and Marxist dialectics, and to focus on the movement, the open becoming of social worlds (2009). Concepts embedded in and emergent in human praxis, and an open sense of 'totality', held for him the promise of political action for making alternative futures (Schmid 2022, Chapter 2). One of the crucial (political) moments of becoming, of excess to the social orders of capitalism, for him, was the urban, whose proper form is 'space'. In this regard, we noted the inadequacy of formulations which seek to reconstitute the urban as a collation of (already well known) wider processes, as a two-dimensional context. Approaching the urban as 'space' invites attention to the emergent urbanisation processes and forms. For sure, then, as we seek for ways to come to know and think the urban, its dynamic and fundamental inexhaustibility and incompleteness should press us towards emergent, modest, revisable conceptualisations, open to new futures and different starting points.

With and against the different approaches considered in this book, therefore, I have explored ways in which we might work with the resistance of the urban world to attempts to draw off from its diversity, materialities and differentiations singular, static or bare concepts. As Deleuze writes, 'multiplicity must not designate a combination of the many and the one, but rather an organisation belonging to the many as such, which has no need whatsoever of unity in order to form a system' (1994 [1968], p. 230). The urban is never 'one' thing or process. For some critics, the effort has been to reduce the 'many' side of this equation – seeking 'generalities' which have only a limited reach, or considering only the most modest conceptualisations (the 'one') as a strong and sufficient response to these concerns (Lancione and McFarlane 2016). But with Deleuze, cautions remain. While he notes that 'the essence is nothing, an empty generality, when separated from *this* measure, *this* manner and *this* study of cases' (Deleuze 1994 [1968], p. 230; *my emphasis*), he also observes that 'there is a significant difference between generality, which always designates a logical power of concepts, and repetition, which testifies to their powerlessness or real limits' (p. 14). In this he reveals the precarity of seeking to ground insights in the powerful ambitions of 'generality', even if that is modest (say, two cases rather than world-wide). 'Multiplicity', he notes, 'replaces the one no less than the multiple' (p. 230). As we have seen, it is precisely the powerlessness, the limits of concepts, the repetition which is never the same, which inspires conceptualisation. It is prolific difference which ungrounds concepts, and generates them. Benjamin presciently considered that we need not have recourse to universals such as 'colour' or 'language' but only an infinite multiplicity of colours and languages (Osborne 2004). Following Benjamin's methodological reflections, we considered how observations (particulars for him) might constellate into more or less firm Ideas, energised by extremes and diversity rather than generalisations.

Moreover, while a certain Idea/constellation might emerge on the basis of certain elements of entities, this would not preclude alternative ideas from coming into view in relation to the same empirical content. A 'family resemblance' view, where only some entities in a category share common elements, and a range of different features are distributed across the entities, indicates strongly the potential for other constellations to be proposed on the basis of different elements of the same entities.

Would it be beneficial to urban studies to consider Ideas/concepts as multiplicities? If terms might be multiplied, would scholars feel more able to mobilise and expand concepts, set them on the move/draw them in while also identifying a differentiated version or a new term? Would this allow a proliferation of insights able to deal with the specificity, diversity and individuality of urban contexts, while keeping open the possibilities for conversations across the urban world? And, indeed, in the face of the explosion and dispersion of 'urban' settlements would this sustain meaning for the very term, urban, itself?

On the one hand, we could consider that any concepts rest on 'multiplicities' of observations (singularities). We have considered how these might operate/coalesce through 'appurtenance' (Deleuze) or 'comportment' (Benjamin) – forms of allegorical belonging – to make up, to determine what is an entity or a phenomenon. This places thinking across more than one observation at the core of conceptualisation. Potentially, it incites a comparative imagination in response to, in engagement with, the global urban world. How to think with a multiplicity of observations, perhaps stretching across different urban contexts? How to remain open to the possibilities that observations in another urban context, elsewhere, or emerging in the rich diversity of the specific context, might expand, exceed or strengthen any concept-constellaton-Idea?

On the other hand, concepts can also be thought of as themselves a multiplicity (many different possible constellations of observations). New observations or cases can reform Ideas, extend and distort concepts, reframing them. Singularities (observations) could form new inflection points, constellating with (different) neighbouring singularities and initiating a new concept. As we noted in the case of gentrification, the term has stretched and evolved across new cases and examples, but scholars have sought to preserve/protect it. If we were more alert to the possibility that a concept might be a multiplicity, rather than a 'one' concept seeking to hegemonise 'many' cases (and if the academy did not reward bare repetition of terms), a more creative and generative assembling of observations into a proliferation of terms might drive towards a conceptual break (see for example Bernt, 2022). With neoliberalism, we noted how the term rested on identifying only certain elements of cases, while other aspects were disregarded. We discussed, for example, developmentalism and racialisation. Characteristic of any Benjaminian or Deleuzian Idea, as distinctive arrangements of observations in 'constellations', would be the potential to inspire different configurations, attentive to different elements, with extremes and excesses forging the vitality of conceptual innovation, rather than being seen as exceptions to be disregarded. Ideas as multiplicities could provide inspiration to thinking differently across and with differences (and repetitions-as-differences). This could indeed, for example, provoke a swarm of, perhaps increasingly divergent, conceptualisations of neoliberalisms (Peck 2013). But these would be concepts whose allegiance is uncertain, open to being interpreted as part of different associations, different constellations, and new Ideas. Additional cases might provoke a multiplicity of terms whose conceptual fulcrum was located somewhere else than the features of neoliberalism. Say, observations about urban development politics might constellate across developmentalism and socialist planning, with emergent terms such as 'land value capture', or varied forms of state agency (Robinson et al. 2020; Shatkin 2017). In such an imagination of conceptualisation, the energy to suppose something else might be going on - that some other Idea than those one has inherited might be relevant - would be palpable. We saw this in the case of 'suburbs', where attending to a multiplicity of experiences drove a new constellation to emerge giving a quite different meaning to the term. And also in relation to the term, informality, which has arguably exhausted its pertinence because of the vagueness of its purchase on the multiple features and processes it indicates, and its dependence on exceptionalising the experiences of much of the urban world. This term now fragments into multiple concepts and insights which had previously been configured into this analytical 'constellation' and which now reveal themselves to be core features of the urban world.

As a caution to critics, it is essential to insist that opening concepts to multiplicity and difference is not to narrow their analytical purchase. The suggestion that some might be advocating one concept per observation is surely countered by a comparative imagination. Nor does the approach adopted in this book cede concern with major political stakes or world-wide concerns, or the 'context of contexts'. In an era when, after more than a century and a half, revolutionary ideas about capitalism still rely on Marx's theory, while whatever capitalism is has transformed radically, and is so deeply varied, concepts as constellations could be one way to re-energise and revitalise the capacity for critical political economy concepts to have agency in the world (Vandenberghe 2008). Abstract propositions of philosophy are only interesting to critical social scientists if they can support us in generating new ideas, new approaches, new insights with relevance and transformative potential in the world. In this book I have reviewed debates about the dynamic lives of concepts to build support for the outlines of methodologies for understanding, engaging with, and transforming, the twenty-first century urban world.

In relation to situated and partial conceptualisations of the urban, or insights which might emerge from modest generalisations, or in the generative explosion of urban concepts as multiplicities, some important questions remain. Marilyn Strathern's pithy and condensed insights on feminist comparisons have kept me company throughout the preparation of this book. Here, we might note with her that 'Partiality is the position of being heard and making claims, the view from a body rather than the view from above' (2005, p. 32). For her, in the fractal imagination that inspired her in the late 1980s, a feminist is 'Never one person; never a complete person' (p. 34). The modesty of the concepts which the urban as multiplicity proposes is matched by a multiplicity of 'modest witnesses', especially in the face of the incompatibilities and lack of 'wholeness' which characterises conceptualisations of the 'urban'. Fred Moten's (2018) insistence on the 'consent not to be a single being' which underpins his determination to track the grounds for an 'out of the outside' in practice and thought is resonant. In relation to the practice of comparison, Strathern observes, it is in 'the tension of holding incompatible things together because both or all are necessary and true' that 'Cyborgs set different thoughts in train' (Strathern 2005, p. 35; emphasis in original; citing Haraway 1987, p. 65). For her it is in making 'connections without assumptions of comparability', through exploring intellectual, perhaps magical, perhaps 'therapeutic' resemblances, that gaps show up. And it is in extending into those gaps, reaching out across difference and diversity from in the midst of each distinctive urban, that 'excess and insufficiency' might instigate something new, and might reach towards the horizons of conceptualisation which, after Arendt, constitute themselves on the terrain of political contestation and collective action (Zerilli 2016). And with Glissant, reconstituting worlding (thinking comparatively) after the cuts of colonialism is to cultivate relations of equality, modes of reaching out, which respect rather than obliterate difference (Myers 2020).

Thus, any conceptualisation of the 'urban' finds its limits as a comparative imagination opens up to the horizons of that term. This is not to reinstate a familiar 'whole' (the urban) or to articulate a particular (an urban) we already more or less know the shape of by reference to the universal it appears to refer to. But rather, as we seek to make sense of aspects of the urban, comparatively, extending into the gaps of what can be thought and attentive to a diversity of experiences, we are likely to find that the concept we have started to formulate has moved out of focus. It might reappear as differentiated variants, or contribute to formulating other terms entirely. The imaginative mobilities across difference which comparison implies are often creatively re-configured as research unfolds, or literally composed 'on the move', as extending insights on the urban will need to track wherever it might be going – either as moving urban dwellers, as circulating practices, or in explorations at the literal edges of urbanisation which may not be fully redeemable in existing terminology (Simone 2020). In these times, urbanisation is perhaps especially confounding inherited terms. The extended and dispersed nature of urbanisation sets a challenging terrain for methodological experiments: the grounds for comparison become 'any urban territory'. The provocations of planetary urbanisation have drawn attention to this (Brenner and Schmid 2015), even as much longer standing urban studies concerns point in the same direction: indigenous worlds and agrarian processes craft new trajectories; mobilities generate translocal social worlds or, as African urbanists from several decades ago noted, describe a single social field at once urban and rural; and the splayed trajectories and stalling of travel (along a West African coastal road, for example) betray the grand spatial metaphor of 'corridor' (Choplin 2019). The future of urbanisation is drawing us to question the residual demarcations which splice fragmented territories into planning and governance fictions, and to find ways to challenge the powerful terraforming urbanisation processes driving speculation and constituting the vectors of gargantuan and dispersed urban territories (Friedman 2019, 2020; Kanai and Schindler 2019).

I hope very much that this book will encourage more comparative experiments for thinking the urban 'through elsewhere', generating conceptual insights, and opening up new trajectories for engaging with and transforming the complex emergent formations and territorialisations of global urbanisation.

An Explosion of Urban Studies

Finding ways to respond to the explosive exteriority (extraversion) of the contemporary urban condition is closely aligned with a broader post-colonial critique of the foundational influence of the experiences of wealthier and western cities in shaping urban theory. The expectation of such a critique is that the experiences of all urban territories around the world are relevant to understanding the nature of the urban. The call for a more global urban studies is based on the simple but generative assumption that all cities are cities; thus the formulation of 'ordinary cities' which insisted that all cities properly belong to the realm of theoretical reflection on the nature of the urban (Robinson 2006). The term 'ordinary' is of course not to detract from what might at times seem like the extraordinary and impressive nature of some aspects of cities or to argue against their differentiation in respect of many features. Rather, the ordinary cities manoeuvre sought to carve an analytical pathway across the divisive categorisations which had plagued twentieth-century urban theory (developmental, regional, continental) and to insist that there is no privileged starting point for constructing theorisations of the urban. As part of a number of different projects to recast urban studies, this manoeuvre established grounds for the proliferation of many new practices of theoretical reflection and experimentation which contribute to building understandings across the great diversity of urban outcomes around the world. This book has therefore been able to mobilise insights from a range of perspectives and debates to propose a practice of research and theorisation which we might sum up as, *'starting anywhere, thinking with elsewhere'*, within a reformatted comparative practice committed to strongly revisable concepts. Conceptualisations of the urban today therefore need to be able to open to different subject positions and to support urban scholars from many different contexts to draw all kinds of cities or urban territories into the practice of theorising the urban. Amongst the range of responses which have been made to the demands of conceptualising the urban as diverse and differentiated across the globe I have argued that a comparative imagination might form a positive and generative mode of coming to know and build concepts in the midst of the 'urban now': thinking urbanisation across different times and contexts, in emergent interpretations of past trajectories, current experiences and possible futures.

There is much work underway which is experimenting with, proposing and putting into practice new tactics for global urban studies. The world of scholarly production on cities is also changing rapidly. The growing output from Asian scholars, for example, documenting and thinking through the extraordinary growth of cities there has already created a new centre for urban theoretical reflection; the potential for comparative reflection starting from Asian contexts is increasingly demonstrated (Wu 2020). However, while editors of urban studies journals report a growing proportion of submissions from scholars based in or writing about this region, rejection rates are by a long way highest for papers submitted by scholars based outside of northern and western institutional contexts, and especially for scholars based in African contexts (Boudreau and Kaika 2013). One important reason for this lies in the expectations generated by the 'theory culture' of critical urban studies. It is a disappointing outcome indeed if the terms of widening the scope of debates in urban studies are that scholars are forced to engage with ambitious, universalising and often not very relevant western analytical concepts in order to find international publication outlets. For all that this book has taken time for an extended engagement with philosophy and inherited theory in the interests of clearing the ground for new kinds of trajectories in urban studies, the conclusion of this book is fairly straightforward: it is from those places previously excluded from theorisation, and those voices and scholars least presenced in the field, that the most innovative insights are anticipated. On this basis analysis of global urbanisation can be multiplied, can become a multiplicity. I hope that Chapter 11 has emphatically established that case through the example of 'informality'. Sue Parnell and Edgar Pieterse (2016) discuss the importance of new subjects and centres of writing on cities in Africa. They consider the opportunities and need for emergent theorisation as well as foundational empirical research across the continent. There is an urgent agenda in urban studies to build cultures of theorising and institutions for publishing which appreciate and foster a diversity of theoretical starting points. If urban studies is to address the uneven presence of different urban situations and different scholars in conceptualisation, it needs a renewal and transformation of institutional cultures able to treat in a scholarly and clear fashion the insights of writers from a very wide range of languages, theoretical traditions, geographical contexts and, not least, the extreme inequalities in institutional and personal resources amongst scholars (Ferenčuhová 2016).

Certainly, much work is needed to transform the institutional supports which generate certain knowledge as 'theoretical' and others as empirical and which privileges only certain concepts as international and worth reproducing (Connell, 2007). In this regard, international institutional commitments to resourcing and training in urban studies in poorer contexts, collaborative research and publishing, and a massive shake up of the criteria of what passes for international or excellent research and knowledge are all urgently needed (Watson, 2014b). Critiquing the parochial state of urban studies in the 2000s (and earlier), initial manoeuvres for a global urban studies involved locating and then dislocating the conceptual foundations of what appeared as 'Western' urban studies. Now, almost two decades later, while much has changed in the field theoretically, institutional transformation remains weak. The risk is that it is Northern scholars who once again are the ones undertaking research across the urban world, and defining anew the terms of a now global urban studies. The call to the northern urban scholar, then, is to decentre yourself!

Given that well-resourced largely Anglo-American scholars still dominate the key journals, including radical and critical publishing venues, not to mention the concentration of institutional resources dedicated to international urban research, those concerned for a more global perspective, or who live in, work on and think through different kinds of urban contexts will need to self-reflexively review, critique and change institutional practices which sustain research privilege. The challenge here is that ideas generated within the idiom of Northern intellectual practice, even if named as parochial, or emerging from research in less well-explored contexts, continue to be styled as universal and 'theoretical' arguments and thus gain traction and set themselves on the move, becoming hard to avoid when scholars from less well-resourced contexts seek to publish their work. In fact these claims are self-defining: what counts as excellent is embedded within the norms and definitions of northern and well-resourced academies. And claims to universalisation are associated with a certain authorial voice (confident, dominating, authorising, unmarked, vigorously clearing aside competitors) and enabled through the practicalities of unevenly resourced circuits of knowledge and publishing. These urgently need to be dissipated through embedding expectations of quite different practices of excellence and rigour, originality and value – not only a critical personal reflexivity on the part of writers, but valorising different forms of knowledge (such as detailed empirical research and reports on practice – Parnell and Pieterse 2016), and privileging scholars whose embedded knowledge and long engagement with contexts offers rich insight. Essential is the presentation and propagation of arguments as actively open to being revised, much more modest in their voice, collaborative in their endeavours, and precise about locational co-ordinates (both physical and social). In fact, as I finish writing this book, I feel that some of us need to write much less, and dedicate our energies to the infrastructural and institutional transformations which are the necessary and sufficient conditions for opening urban studies to the future of the urban, and to its differences, its diversity, its divergences.

References

Aalbers, M. (2015). 'The potential for financialization'. *Dialogues in Human Geography*, *5* (2), 214–219.
Aalbers, M. (2016). *The Financialization of Housing: A Political Economy Approach*. London, Routledge.
Aalbers, M. (2017). 'The variegated financialization of housing'. *International Journal of Urban and Regional Research*, *41* (4), 542–554.
Aalbers, M., Van Loon, J., and Fernandez, R. (2017). 'The financialization of a social housing provider'. *International Journal of Urban and Regional Research*, *41* (4), 572–587.
Abu-Lughod, J. (1976). 'The legitimacy of comparisons in comparative urban studies: A theoretical position and application to north African cities'. In: The City in Comparative Perspective: Cross-National Research and New Directions in Theory (eds. J. Walton and L.H. Masotti), 17–40. New York, Sage.
Abu-Lughod, J. (1990). 'New York and Cairo: A view from street level'. *International Social Science Journal*, *125*, 307–318.
Abu-Lughod, J.L. (1999). New York, Chicago, Los Angeles: America's Global Cities. Minneapolis and London, University of Minnesota Press.
Abu-Lughod, J. (2007). 'The challenge of comparative case studies'. *City*, *11* (3), 399–404.
Abubakar, I.R. and Doan, P.L. (2017). 'Building new capital cities in Africa: Lessons for new satellite towns in developing countries'. *African Studies*. doi: 10.1080/00020184.2017.1376850.
Acuto, M. (2010). 'High- rise Dubai urban entrepreneurialism and the technology of symbolic power'. *Cities*, *27* (4), 272–284.
Acuto, M. (2013). 'The new climate leaders?'. *Review of International Studies*, *39* (4), 835–857.
Adler, G. and Webster, E. (1995). 'Challenging transition theory: The labour movement, radical reform, and transition to democracy in South Africa'. *Politics & Society*, *23* (1), 75–106.
Agyemang, F., Kekeli Amedzro, K., and Silva, E. (2017). 'The emergence of city-regions and their implications for contemporary spatial governance: Evidence from Ghana'. *Cities*, *71*, 70–79.
Ahmed, S. 2014. White Men. Feminist Killjoys Blog. http://feministkilljoys.com.
Akrich, M. and Rabeharisoa, V. (2016). 'Pulling oneself out of the traps of comparison: An auto-ethnography of a European project'. In: Practising Comparison: Logics,

Relations, Collaborations (eds. J. Deville, M. Guggenheim and S. Hrdličková), 130–165. Manchester, Mattering Press.
Alden, C. and Jiang, L. (2019). 'Brave new world: Debt, industrialization and security in China-Africa relations'. *International Affairs*, 95 (3), 641–657.
Alexander, P. and Chan, A. (2004). 'Does china have an apartheid pass system?' *Journal of Ethnic and Migration Studies*, 30 (4), 609–629.
Allen, J. (2003). Lost Geographies of Power. Oxford, Blackwell.
Allen, J. (2008). 'Powerful geographies: Spatial shifts in the architecture of globalization'. In: The Handbook of Power (eds. S. Clegg and C. Haugaard), 157–173. Los Angeles, London, Delhi, Singapore, Sage.
Allen, J. (2016). Topologies of Power: Beyond Territory and Networks. London, Routledge.
Allen, J. and Cochrane, A. (2007). 'Beyond the territorial fix: Regional assemblages, politics and power'. *Regional Studies*, 41 (9), 1161–1175.
Allen, J. and Cochrane, A. (2014). 'The urban unbound: London's politics and the 2012 Olympic games'. *International Journal of Urban and Regional Research*, 38 (5), 1609–1624.
Allen, J. and Pryke, M. (2013). 'Financializing household water: Thames water, MEIF, and "ring-fenced" politics'. *Cambridge Journal of Regions, Economy and Society*, 6 (3), 419–439.
Althusser, L. (2005 [1969]). For Marx. London, Verso.
Althusser, L. (2006). Philosophy of the Encounter: Later Writings, 1978-1987. London, Verso.
Althusser, L. and Balibar, E. (2009 [1968]). Reading Capital. London, Verso.
Altrock, U. (2016). 'Conceptualising informality: Some notes towards generalisation'. In: Urban Informalities: Reflections on the Formal and Informal (eds. C. McFarlane and M. Waibel), 172–193. London, Ashgate.
Amelang, J. (2007). 'Comparing cities: A Barcelona model?'. *Urban History*, 34 (2), 173–189.
Amen, M.M., Archer, K., and Bosman, M.M. (2006). Relocating Global Cities: From the Centre to the Margins. Lanham, Maryland, Rowman and Littlefield.
Amin, N. (1994). Post-Fordism: A Reader. Oxford, Wiley-Blackwell.
Amin, N. (2002). 'Spatialities of globalisation'. *Environment and Planning A*, 34, 385–399.
Amin, A. (2014). 'Lively Infrastructure'. *Theory, Culture and Society*, 31 (7/8), 137–161.
Amin, N. and Thrift, N. (2002). Cities: Reimagining the Urban. Cambridge, Polity.
Amin, A. and Thrift, N. (2016). Seeing like a City. Oxford, Wiley-Blackwell.
Andersen, D.J., Kramsch, O.T., and Sandberg, M. (2015). 'Inverting the telescope on borders that matter: Conversations in Café Europa'. *Journal of Contemporary European Studies*, 23 (4), 459–476.
Anderson, B. (1998). The Spectre of Comparisons: Nationalism, Southeast Asia and the World. London, Verso.
Andreotti, A., Le Galès, P., and Fuentes, F.J.M. (2013). 'Controlling the urban fabric: The complex game of distance and proximity in European

upper-middle-class residential strategies'. *International Journal of Urban and Regional Research*, 37, 576–597.
Angelo, H. and Goh, K. (2020). 'Out in space: Difference and abstraction in planetary urbanization'. *International Journal of Urban and Regional Research*, 45, 732–744
Angelo, H. and Wachsmuth, D. (2015). 'Urbanizing urban political ecology: A critique of methodological cityism'. *International Journal of Urban and Regional Research*, 39, 16–27.
Arabindoo, P. (2011). '"City of sand": Stately re-imagination of marina beach in Chennai'. *International Journal of Urban and Regional Research*, 35, 379–401.
Arboleda, M. (2016). 'Spaces of extraction, metropolitan explosions: Planetary urbanization and the commodity boom in Latin America'. *International Journal of Urban and Regional Research*, 40 (1), 96–112.
Austin, G. (2007). 'Reciprocal comparison and African history: Tackling conceptual euro-centrism in the study of Africa's economic past". *African Studies Review*, 50 (3), 1–28.
Auyero, J. (1999). '"This is a lot like the Bronx, isn't it?" Lived experiences of marginality in an Argentine slum'. *International Journal of Urban and Regional Research*, 23, 45–69.
Bagnasco, A. and Le Galès, P. (eds.) (2000). Cities in Contemporary Europe. Cambridge, Cambridge University Press.
Baker, T., Cook, I. R., McCann, E., Temenos, C., & Ward, K. (2016). 'Policies on the Move: The Transatlantic Travels of Tax Increment Financing'. Annals of the American Association of Geographers, 106 (2), 459–469.
Balakrishnan, S. (2019). 'Recombinant Urbanization: Agrarian–urban Landed Property and Uneven Development in India'. International Journal of Urban and Regional Research, 43 (4), 617–632.
Ballard, R., Bonnin, D., Robinson, J. and Xaba, T. (2007). 'Development and new forms of democracy in Durban'. *Urban Forum*, 18, 265–228.
Ballard, R., Dittgen, R., Harrison, P., and Todes, A. (2017). '"Megaprojects and urban visions: Johannesburg's corridors of freedom and modderfontein", Transformation'. *Critical Perspectives on Southern Africa*, 95, 111–139.
Barnett, C. (2017). The Priority of Injustice: Locating Democracy in Critical Theory. Athens, University of Georgia Press.
Barnett, C. and Bridge, G. (2016). 'The Situations of Urban Inquiry: Thinking Problematically about the City'. *International Journal of Urban and Regional Research*, 40 (6), 1186–1204.
Barnett, C. and Parnell, S. (2016). 'Ideas, implementation and indicators: Epistemologies of the post-2015 urban agenda'. *Environment and Urbanization*, 28 (1), 87–98.
Barnett, C., Robinson, J., and Rose, G. (eds) (2008). Geographies of Globalisation: A Demanding World. London, Sage.
Bassens, D. and Van Meeteren, M. (2015). 'World cities under conditions of financialized globalization: Towards an augmented world city hypothesis'. *Progress in Human Geography*, 39 (6), 752–775.
Batty, M. (2013). The New Science of Cities. Cambridge MA, MIT Press.
Bayart, J.-F. (1994). The State in Africa: The Politics of the Belly. London, Longman.

Beal, V. and Pinson, G. (2014). 'When mayors go global: International strategies, urban governance and leadership'. *International Journal of Urban and Regional Research*, 38, 302–317.

Beall, J., Crankshaw, O., and Parnell, S. (2002). Uniting a Divided City: Governance and Social Exclusion in Johannesburg. London, Earthscan.

Beall, J., Parnell, S., and Albertyn, C. (2015). 'Elite compacts in Africa: The role of area-based management in the new governmentality of the Durban city-region'. *International Journal of Urban and Regional Research*, 39 (2), 390–406.

Beauregard, R.A. (2012). 'What theorists do'. *Urban Geography*, 33 (4), 474–487.

Beaverstock, J., Smith, R., and Taylor, P. (1999). 'A roster of world cities'. *Cities*, 16 (6), 445–458.

Beaverstock, J., Smith, R., and Taylor, P. (2000). 'A new metageography in world cities research'. *Annals of the Association of American Geographers*, 90 (1), 123–134.

Beck, H. (2019). 'Chapter 5. Walter Benjamin and the Now-Time of History'. In: The Moment of Rupture, 124–153. Philadelphia, University of Pennsylvania Press.

Becker, J., Klingan, K., Lanz, S., and Wildner, K. (Eds.) (2013). Global Prayers: Contemporary Manifestations of the Religious in the City. Zurich, Lars Mueller Publishers.

Bekker, S. and Fourchard, L. (Eds.) (2013). Politics and Policies: Governing Cities in Africa. Pretoria, HSRC Press.

Bénit-Gbaffou, C., Didier, S., and Peyroux, E. (2012). 'Circulation of security models in southern African cities: Between neoliberal encroachment and local power dynamics'. *International Journal of Urban and Regional Research*, 36, 877–889.

Bénit-Gbaffou, C. and Katsaura, O. (2014). '"Community leaders and the construction of political legitimacy. Unpacking Bourdieu's political capital in post-apartheid Johannesburg'. *International Journal of Urban and Regional Research*, 38 (5), 1807–1832.

Benjamin, S. (2008). 'Occupancy urbanism: Radicalizing politics and economy beyond policy and programs'. *International Journal of Urban and Regional Research*, 32, 719–729.

Benjamin, W. (1973). Charles Baudelaire: A Lyric Poet in the Era of High Capitalism. London, Verso.

Benjamin, W. (1979a [1937]). 'Eduard Fuchs, collector and historian (EF)'. In: One Way Street (W. Benjamin). London, Verso, 349–386.

Benjamin, W. (1979b). One Way Street. London, Verso.

Benjamin, W. (1998 [1963]). The Origin of German Tragic Drama [OGT] (translated by John Osborne). London, Verso.

Benjamin, W. (1999a). The Arcades Project [AP]. Cambridge, Mass., Harvard University Press.

Benjamin, W. (1999b [1955]). Illuminations. London, Pimlico.

Benjamin, W. (2003a [1939]). 'Central park'. In: Walter Benjamin. Selected Writings Vol. 4 (eds. H. Eiland and M.W. Jennings), 161–199. Cambridge, MA, Harvard University Press.

Benjamin, W. (2003b [1940]). 'On the concept of history'. In: Walter Benjamin. Selected Writings Vol. 4 (eds. H. Eiland and M.W. Jennings), 389–400. Cambridge, MA, Harvard University Press.

Benjamin, W. (2016 [1928]). Ursprung des deutschen Trauerspiels. Edition Holzinger (Printed by CreateSpace Independent Publishing Platform).
Benjamin, W. (2019). Origin of the German Trauerspiel, (Translated Howard Eiland). Cambridge, Mass., Harvard University Press.
Benko, G. and Lipietz, A. (1998). 'From the regulation of space to the space of regulation'. *GeoJournal, 44* (4), 275–281.
Bernasconi, R. (2003). 'Will the real Kant please stand up: The challenge of Enlightenment racism to the study of the history of philosophy'. *Radical Philosophy, 117*, 13–22.
Bernt, M. (2016a). 'Very particular, or rather universal? Gentrification through the lenses of Ghertner and López-Morales'. *City, 20* (4), 637–644.
Bernt, M. (2016b). 'How post-socialist is gentrification?: Observations in East Berlin and Saint Petersburg'. *Eurasian Geography and Economics, 57* (4–5), 565–587.
Bernt, M. (2022). The Commodification Gap: Gentrification and Public Policy in London, Berlin and St. Petersburg. Oxford: Wiley-Blackwell.
Bernt, M., Colini, L., and Förste, D. (2017). 'Privatization, financialization and state restructuring in Eastern Germany'. *International Journal of Urban and Regional Research, 41* (4), 555–571.
Berrisford, S., Cirolia, L., and Palmer, I. (2018). 'Land-based financing in sub-Saharan cities'. *Environment and Urbanization, 30* (1), 35–52.
Beswick, J., Alexandri, G., Byrne, M., Vives-Miró, S., Fields, D., Hodkinson, S., and Janoschka, M. (2016). 'Speculating on London's housing future'. *City, 20* (2), 321–341.
Beswick, J. and Penny, J. (2018). 'Demolishing the present to sell off the future? The emergence of "financialized municipal entrepreneurialism" in London'. *International Journal of Urban and Regional Research, 42*, 612–632.
Bhan, G. (2016). In the Public's Interest: Evictions, Citizenship and Inequality in Contemporary Delhi. Delhi, Orient Blackswan and Athens: University of Georgia Press.
Bhan, G. (2019). 'Notes on a southern urban practice'. *Environment and Urbanization, 31* (2), 639–654.
Bloch, R. (2015). 'Africa's new suburbs'. In: Suburban Governance: A Global View (eds. P. Hamel and R. Keil), 253–277. Toronto, University of Toronto Press.
Bodnár, J. (2019). 'Comparing in global times: Between extension and incorporation'. *Critical Historical Studies, 6* (1), 1–32.
Bontenbal, M.C. 2009. Strengthening urban governance in the South through city-to-city
Borraz, O. and Le Galès, P. (2010). 'Urban governance in Europe: The governance of what?'. *Pôle Sud, 32*, 137–151.
Boudreau, J.-A., Gilbert, L., and Labbé, D. (2016). 'Uneven state formalization and periurban housing production in Hanoi and Mexico City: Comparative reflections from the global South'. *Environment and Planning A: Economy and Space, 48* (12), 2383–2401.
Boudreau, J.-A. and Kaika, M. (2013). 'Reflections on the academic and economic environment'. *International Journal of Urban and Regional Research, 37*, i–v.
Boudreau, J.-A., Hamel, P., Jouve, B., and Keil, E.R. (2006). 'Comparing metropolitan governance: The cases of Montreal and Toronto'. *Progress in Planning, 66* (1), 7–59.

Bourdieu, P. and Wacquant, L.D. (1992). An Invitation to Reflexive Sociology. Chicago, University of Chicago Press.

Bouzarovski, S., Sýkora, L., and Matoušek, R. (2016). 'Locked-in postsocialism: Rolling path dependencies in Liberec's district heating system'. *Eurasian Geography and Economics*, *57* (4–5), 624–642.

Bozzoli, B. (1990). 'Intellectuals, audiences and histories: South African experiences, 1978–88'. *Radical History Review*, *1* (46–47), 237–263.

Brand, A.L. (2018). 'The duality of space: The built world of Du Bois' double-consciousness'. *Environment and Planning D: Society and Space*, *36* (1), 3–22.

Brandt Commission. (1980). North-South: A Programme for Survival: Independent Commission on International Development Issues Report. University of California, Pan Books.

Brenner, N. (2001). 'World city theory, globalization and the comparative-historical method: Reflections on Janet Abu-Lughod's interpretation of contemporary urban restructuring'. *Urban Affairs Review*, 124–147. September.

Brenner, N. (2003). 'Stereotypes, archetypes, and prototypes: Three uses of superlatives in contemporary urban studies'. *City and Community*, *2* (3), 205–215.

Brenner, N. (2005). New State Spaces: Urban Governance and the Rescaling of Statehood. Oxford, OUP.

Brenner, N. (ed) (2013). Implosion/Explosion. Jarvis.

Brenner, N. and Katsikis, N. (2020). 'Operational landscapes: Hinterlands of the capitalocene'. *Architectural Design*, *90*, 22–31.

Brenner, N., Madden, D., and Wachsmuth, D. (2011). 'Assemblage urbanism and the challenges of critical urban theory'. *City*, *15* (2), 225–240.

Brenner, N., Peck, J., and Theodore, N. (2010a). 'Variegated neoliberalization: Geographies, modalities, pathways'. *Global Networks*, *10* (2), 182–222.

Brenner, N., Peck, J., and Theodore, N. (2010b). '2010b'. *After Neoliberalization, Globalizations* September 2010, *7* (3), 327–345.

Brenner, N. and Schmid, C. (2011). 'Planetary urbanisation". In: Urban Constellations (ed. M. Gandy). Berlin, Jovis.

Brenner, N. and Schmid, C. (2014). 'The "urban age" in question'. *International Journal of Urban and Regional Research*, *38* (3), 731–755.

Brenner, N. and Schmid, C. (2015). 'Towards a new epistemology of the urban?'. *City*, *19* (2–3), 151–182.

Brenner, N. and Theodore, N. (eds.) (2002). Spaces of Neoliberalism. Oxford, Blackwell.

Brill, F. (2018). Playing the game: A comparison of international actors in real estate development in Modderfontein, Johannesburg and London's Royal Docks. *Geoforum*, online early view, https://doi.org/10.1016/j.geoforum.2018.05.015.

Brown, A. (2013). 'The right to the city: Road to Rio 2010'. *International Journal of Urban and Regional Research*, *37*, 957–971.

Brown, J. (2015). South Africa's Insurgent Citizens: On Dissent and the Possibility of Politics. Johannesburg, Jacana Press.

Brown, R., Edwards, M., and Lee, R. (2014). 'Just space: Towards a just, sustainable London'. In: Sustainable London: The future of a global City (eds. R. Imrie and L. Lees), 43–66. Bristol, Policy Press.

Brownill, S. (1990). Developing London's Docklands. London, Paul Chapman.

Brownill, S. and O'Hara, G. (2015). 'From planning to opportunism? Re-examining the creation of the London docklands development corporation'. *Planning Perspectives, 30* (4), 537–570.

Bruun, H.H. and Whimster, S. (2012). 'Introduction'. In: Max Weber, Collected Methodological Writings (eds. H.H. Bruun and S. Whimster translated, H. H. Bruun), xi – xxxii. London, Routledge.

Buck, N., Gordon, I., Hall, P., Harloe, M., and Kleinman, M. (2002). Working Capital. Life and Labour in Contemporary London. London, Routledge.

Buck-Morss, S. (1977). The Origin of Negative Dialectics: Theodore W. Adorno, Walter Benjamin, and the Frankfurt Institute. New York, The Free Press.

Bryceson, D.F. (2006). 'African urban economies: Searching for sources of sustainability'. In: African Urban Economies (eds. D.F. Bryceson and D. Potts). London, Palgrave Macmillan.

Buckley, M. and Hanieh, A. (2014). '"Diversification by urbanization: Tracing the property-finance nexus in Dubai and the Gulf'. *International Journal of Urban and Regional Research, 38* (1), 155–175.

Buckley, M. and Strauss, K. (2016). 'With, against and beyond Lefebvre: Planetary urbanization and epistemic plurality'. *Society and Space, 34* (4), 617–636.

Buire, C. (2014). 'The Dream and the ordinary: An ethnographic investigation of suburbanisation in Luanda'. *African Studies, 73* (2), 290–312.

Bulkeley, H. (2010). 'Cities and the governing of climate change'. *Annual Review of Environment and Resources, 35,* 229–253.

Bunnell, T. (2007). 'Post-maritime transnationalization: Malay seafarers in Liverpool'. *Global Networks, 7* (4), 412–429.

Bunnell, T. (2013). 'City networks as alternative geographies of Southeast Asia'. *TRaNS: Trans-Regional and -national Studies,1,* 1, 27–43.

Bunnell, T. (2016). From World City to the World in One City: Liverpool through Malay Lives. Chichester, UK, John Wiley & Sons.

Bunnell, T. and Das, D. (2013). 'Urban pulse—a geography of serial seduction: Urban policy transfer from Kuala Lumpur to Hyderabad'. *Urban Geography, 31* (3), 277–284.

Bunnell, T. and Maringanti, A. (2010). 'Practising urban and regional research beyond metrocentricity'. *International Journal of Urban and Regional Research, 34,* 415–420.

Burawoy, M. (2009). The Extended Case Method: Four Countries, Four Decades, Four Great Transformations, and One Theoretical Tradition. Berkeley, University of California Press.

Butcher, S.C. (2020). 'Appropriating rent from greenfield affordable housing: developer practices in Johannesburg'. *Environment and Planning A, 52* (2), 337–361.

Butler, J. (1990). Gender Trouble: Feminism and the Subversion of Identity. London, Routledge.

Butler, T. (2007). 'For Gentrification?'. *Environment and Planning A: Economy and Space, 39* (1), 162–181.

Cain, A. (2017). 'Alternatives to African commodity-backed urbanization: The case of China in Angola'. *Oxford Review of Economic Policy, 33* (3), 478–495.

Cain, A. (2014). 'African urban fantasies: Past lessons and emerging realities'. *Environment and Urbanization*, *26* (2), 561–567.
Cairns, S. and Jacobs, J. (2014). Buildings Must Die: A Perverse View of Architecture. Cambridge, MA, MIT Press.
Caldeira, T. (2016). 'Peripheral urbanization: Autoconstruction, transversal logics, and politics in cities of the global south'. *Environment and Planning C, Society and Space*, *35* (1), 3–20.
Callard, F. (2004). 'Doreen Massey'. In: Key Thinkers on Space and Place (eds. P. Hubbard, R. Kitchin, and G. Valentine), 219–225. London, Sage.
Campbell, T. (2012). Beyond Smart Cities: How Cities Network, Learn and Innovate. London.
Candea, M. (2019). Comparison in Anthropology: The Impossible Method. Cambridge, Cambridge University Press.
Carmody, P. and Owusu, F. (2016). 'Neoliberalism, urbanization and change in Africa: The political economy of heterotopias'. *Journal of African Development*, *18*, 61–73.
Carpenter, J. and Lees, L. (1995). 'Gentrification in New York, London and Paris: An International Comparison'. *International Journal of Urban and Regional Research*, *19*, 286–303.
Castells, M. (1977). The Urban Question - A Marxist Approach. Cambridge, MIT Press.
Castells, M. (1983). The City and the Grassroots. London, Edward Arnold.
Castells, M. (1985). 'Commentary on G C Pickvance's "The rise and fall of urban movements…"'. *Environment and Planning C: Society and Space*, *3*, 56–61.
Castells, M. and Portes, A. (1989). 'World underneath: The origins, dynamics and effects of the informal economy'. In: The Informal Economy: Studies in Advanced and Less Developed Countries (eds. A. Portes, M. Castells and L. Benton), 11–37. London and Baltimore, The Johns Hopkins University Press.
Castriota, R. and Tonucci, J. (2018). 'Extended urbanization in and from Brazil'. *Environment and Planning D: Society and Space*, *36* (3), 512–528.
Caygill, H. (1998). Walter Benjamin: The Colour of Experience. London, Routledge.
Chabal, P. and Daloz, J.-P. (1999). Africa Works: Disorder as Political Instrument. Bloomington, Indiana University Press.
Chakrabarty, D. (2000). Provincialising Europe. London, Routledge.
Chant, S. (1996). 'Women's roles in recession and economic restructuring in Mexico and the Philippines'. *Geoforum*, *27* (3), 297–327.
Chari, S. and Verdery, K. (2009). 'Thinking between the Posts: Postcolonialism, postsocialism, and ethnography after the cold war'. *Comparative Studies in Society and History*, *51* (1), 6–34.
Chatterjee, P. (2004). The Politics of the Governed: Reflections on Popular Politics in Most of the World. New York, Columbia University Press.
Chatterton, P. (2015). Low Impact Living A field guide to ecological affordable community building. London, Routledge.
Chaudhury, Z.R. (2012). 'Subjects in difference: Walter Benjamin, Frantz Fanon, and postcolonial theory'. *Differences*, *23* (1), 151–183.

Cheah, P. (2013). 'The material world of comparison'. In: Comparison: Theories, Approaches, Uses (eds. R. Felski and S. Stanford Friedman), 168-190. Baltimore: Johns Hopkins University Press.

Chen, K.H. (2010). Asia as Method: Toward Deimperialization. Durham, Duke University Press.

Chen, M.A. (2012). *The Informal Economy: Definitions, Theories and Policies.* WIEGO Working Paper No. 1. WIEGO.

Chen, X. and Kanna, A. (2012). Rethinking Global Urbanism: Comparative Insights from Secondary Cities. London, Routledge.

Cheshire, P.C. and Gordon, I.R. (1996). 'Territorial competition and the predictability of collective (in)action'. *International Journal of Urban and Regional Research*, 20, 383–399.

Chome, J. and McCall, M.K. (2005). 'Neo-customary title registration in informal settlements: The case of Blantyre, Malawi'. *International Development Planning Review, 27* (4), 451.

Choplin, A. (2019). 'Cementing Africa: Cement flows and city-making along the West African corridor (Accra, Lomé, Cotonou, Lagos)'. *Urban Studies, 57* (9), 1977–1993.

Choplin, A. and Hertzog, A. (2020). 'The West African corridor from Accra to Lagos: A megacity-region under construction'. In: Handbook of Megacities and Megacity-Regions (eds. D. Labbé and A. Sorensen), 205–221. London, Edward Elgar.

Christophers, B. (2014). 'Wild dragons in the city: Urban political economy, affordable housing development and the performative world-making of economic models'. *International Journal of Urban and Regional Research, 38* (1), 79–97.

Chung, H. (2010). 'Building an image of Villages-in-the-City: A clarification of China's distinct urban spaces'. *International Journal of Urban and Regional Research, 34*, 421–437.

Cities Alliance. (2006). Guide to City Development Strategies: Improving Urban Performance. Washington, The Cities Alliance.

Cities Alliance. (2010). Cities Alliance in Action: Johannesburg-Lilongwe Partnership Leads to a Robust City Development Strategy. https://www.citiesalliance.org/resources/knowledge/cities-alliance-knowledge/cities-alliance-action-johannesburg-lilongwe

City of Johannesburg. (2011). City of Johannesburg: Growth and Development Strategy 2040. City of Johannesburg.

Clarke, J. (2014). *Conjunctures, Crises, and Cultures, Focaal, 70*: 113–122.

Clarke, J. (2018). 'Finding place in the conjuncture: A dialogue with Doreen'. In: Doreen Massey: Critical Dialogues (eds. M. Werner, J. Peck, R. Lave and B. Christophers). Newcastle, Agenda Publishing. Chapter 15. https://www.agendapub.com/books/31/doreen-massey

Clarke, N. (2012a). 'Actually existing comparative urbanism: Imitation and cosmopolitanism in North- South interurban partnerships'. *Urban Geography, 33* (6), 796–815.

Clarke, N. (2012b). 'Urban policy mobility, anti-politics, and histories of the transnational municipal movement'. *Progress in Human Geography, 31* (1), 25–43.

Clarke, S.E. (1995). 'Institutional logics and local economic development: A comparative analysis of eight American Cities'. *International Journal of Urban and Regional Research*, *19*, 513–533.
Clyde Mitchell, J. (1987). Cities, Society, and Social Perception: A Central African Perspective. Oxford, Clarendon Press.
Cochrane, A. (2006). Understanding Urban Policy: A Critical Approach. Oxford, Blackwell.
Cochrane, A. (2011). 'Making up global urban policies'. In: The New Blackwell Companion to the City (eds. G. Bridge and S. Watson), 738–746. Chichester, UK, Wiley-Blackwell.
Cohen, M.A. (2015). 'From Habitat II to Pachamama: A growing agenda and diminishing expectations for Habitat III'. In: Environment and Urbanization, 0956247815620978.
Collier, S. (2005). 'Budgets and biopolitics'. In: Global Assemblages: Technology, Politics, and Ethics as Anthropological Problems (eds. A. Ong and S.J. Collier), 373–390. Oxford, Blackwell.
Comaroff, J. and Comaroff, J. (2012). Theory from the South: Or How Euro-America Is Evolving Towards Africa. Paradigm Publishers.
Connell, R. (2007). Southern Theory: The Global Dynamics of Knowledge in Social Science. Cambridge, Polity Press.
Cox, K. (2017). The Politics of Urban and Regional Development and the American Exception. Syracuse, Syracuse University Press.
Cox, K. and Mair, A. (1988). 'Locality and Community in the politics of local economic development'. *Annals, Association of American Geographers*, *78*, 307–325.
Cox, K. and Evenhuis, E. (2020). 'Theorising in urban and regional studies: Negotiating generalisation and particularity'. *Cambridge Journal of Regions, Economy and Society*, *13* (3), 425–442.
Crankshaw, O. (2017). 'Social polarization in global cities: Measuring changes in earnings and occupational inequality'. *Regional Studies*, *51* (11), 1612–1621.
Crankshaw, O. and Borel-Saladin, J. (2014). 'Does deindustrialisation cause social polarisation in global cities?' *Environment and Planning A: Economy and Space*, *46* (8), 1852–1872.
Croese, S. (2018). 'Global urban policymaking in Africa: A view from Angola through the redevelopment of the Bay of Luanda'. *International Journal of Urban and Regional Research*, *42*, 198–209.
Crot, L. (2010). 'Transnational urban policies: "relocating" Spanish and Brazilian models of urban planning in Buenos Aires'. *Urban Research & Practice*, *3* (2), 119–137.
Crouch, C. (2004). Post-Democracy. Cambridge, Polity Press.
Danso-Wiredu, E.Y. (2018). Housing strategies in low income urban communities in Accra Ghana, Geojournal, *83*, 663–677.
Datta, A. (2015). 'New urban utopias of postcolonial India: 'Entrepreneurial urbanization' in Dholera smart city, Gujarat'. *Dialogues in Human Geography*, *5* (1), 3–22.
David, L. and Halbert, L. (2014). 'Finance capital, actor-network theory and the struggle over calculative agencies in the business property markets of Mexico City metropolitan region'. *Regional Studies*, *48* (3), 516–529.

Davidson, M. and Iveson, K. (2015a). 'Beyond city limits'. *City, 19* (5), 646–664.
Davidson, M. and Iveson, K. (2015b). 'Recovering the politics of the city: From the 'post-political city' to a 'method of equality' for critical urban geography'. *Progress in Human Geography, 39* (5), 543–559.
Davis, D. (2005). 'Cities in global context: A brief intellectual history'. *International Journal of Urban and Regional Research, 29* (1), 92–109.
Davis, M. (2006). Planet of Slums. London, Verso.
De Boeck, F. (2011). 'Inhabiting ocular ground: Kinshasa's future in the light of Congo's spectral urban politics'. *Cultural Anthropology, 26* (2), 263–286.
De Boeck, F. and Baloji, S. (2016). Suturing the City; Living Together in Congo's Urban Worlds. London, Autograph ABP.
De Boeck, F. and Plissart, M.-F. (2004). Kinshasa: Tales of the Invisible City. Ludion Press.
Dean, M. (1999). Governmentality: Power and Rule in Modern Society. London, Sage.
Deleuze, G. (1993 [1988]). The Fold [TF]. London, Continuum.
Deleuze, G. (1994 [1968]). Difference and Repetition. New York, Columbia University Press.
Deleuze, G. (2006 [1962]). Nietzsche and Philosophy. London, Bloomsbury.
Deleuze, G. and Guattari, F. (1994 [1991]). What Is Philosophy? London, Verso.
Denis, E., Mukhopadhyay, P., and Zérah, M-H. (2012). 'Subaltern urbanisation in India'. *Economic and Political Weekly, 47* (30), 52–62.
Denis, E. and Zérah, M-H. (Eds.) (2017). Subaltern Urbanisation in India: An Introduction to the Dynamics of Ordinary Towns. Berlin, Springer.
Dennis, R. (2008). Cities in Modernity: Representations and Productions of Metropolitan Space, 1840 – 1930. Cambridge, Cambridge University Press.
Denters, B. and Mossberger, K. (2006). 'Building blocks for a methodology for comparative urban political research'. *Urban Affairs Review, 41* (4), 550–571.
Derickson, K. (2018). *Environment and Planning D: Society and Space, 36* (3), 556–562.
Derman, J. (2018). 'Max Weber and the idea of the occident'. In: The Oxford Handbook of Max Weber (eds. E. Hanke, L. Scaff and S. Whimster), 519–536. Oxford, Oxford University Press.
Desai, R. and Sanyal, R. (2012). Urbanising Citizenship: Contested Spaces in Indian Cities. London, Sage.
DeVerteuil, G. and Manley, D. (2017). 'Overseas investment into London: Imprint, impact and pied-à-terre urbanism'. *Environment and Planning A, 49* (6), 1308–1323.
Deville, J., Guggenheim, M., and Hrdličková, Z. (2016). 'Same, Same but different: Provoking relations, Assembling the comparator'. In: Practising Comparison: Logics, Relations, Collaborations (eds. J. Deville, M. Guggenheim, and Z. Hrdličková), 99–129. Manchester, Mattering Press.
Deville, J., Guggenheim, M., and Hrdličková, Z. (eds) (2016). Practising Comparison: Logics, Relations, Collaborations. Manchester, Mattering Press.
Devlin, R. (2018). 'Asking "Third World questions" of First World informality: Using Southern theory to parse needs from desires in an analysis of informal urbanism of the global North'. *Planning Theory, 17* (4), 568–587.

Dewsbury, J.D. (2003). 'Witnessing space: "Knowledge without contemplation"'. *Environment and Planning A, 35,* 1907–1932.

Dewsbury, J.D. and Thrift, N. (2005). '"Genesis Eternal!": After Paul Klee'. In: Deleuze and Space (eds. I. Buchanan and G. Lambert), 89–108. Edinburgh, Edinburgh University Press.

Diamond, J. and Robinson, J. (2011). Natural Experiments of History. Boston, Harvard University Press.

Dick, H.W. and Rimmer, P.J. (1998). 'Beyond the third world city: The new urban geography of Southeast Asia'. *Urban Studies, 35,* 2303–2321.

Didi-Huberman, G. (2003). 'The Supposition of the Aura: The now, the then, and modernity'. In: Walter Benjamin and History (ed. A. Benjamin), 3–18. London, Continuum.

Didier, S., Peyroux, E., and Morange, M. (2012). 'The spreading of the city improvement district model in Johannesburg and cape town: Urban regeneration and the neoliberal agenda in South Africa'. *International Journal of Urban and Regional Research, 36,* 915–935.

DiGaetano, A. and Strom, E. (2003). 'Comparative urban governance: An integrated approach'. *Urban Affairs Review, 38* (3), 356–395.

Diouf, M. and Fredericks, R. (2014). The Arts of Citizenship in African Cities: Infrastructures and Spaces of Belonging. London, Palgrave MacMillan.

Dobbin, F., Simmons, B., and Garrett, G. (2007). 'The global diffusion of public policies: Social construction, coercion, competition, or learning? *Annual Review of Sociology, 33,* 449–472.

Doel, M. (1996). 'A hundred thousand lines of flight: A machinic introduction to the nomad thought and scrumpled geography of Gilles Deleuze and Félix Guattari'. *Environment and Planning D: Society and Space, 14,* 421–439.

Dolowitz, D. and Marsh, D. (2000). 'Learning from abroad: The role of policy transfer in contemporary policy-making'. *Governance, 13* (1), 5–24.

Douglas, R. (2010). 'Postsocialisms unbound: Connections, critiques, comparisons'. *Slavic Review, 69,* 1–1.

Dowding, K. et al. (1999). 'Regime politics in London local government'. *Urban Affairs Review, 34* (4), 515–545.

Drakakis-Smith, D. (2000). Third World Cities. London, Routledge.

Driver, F. and Gilbert, D. (1999). Imperial Cities: Landscape, Display and Identity. Manchester, Manchester University Press.

Due, R. (2007). Deleuze. Cambridge, Polity Press.

Duffy, S. (2010). 'Leibniz, mathematics and the monad'. In: Deleuze and the Fold: A Critical Reader (eds. S. Van Tuinen and N. McDonnell), 89–111. Berlin, Springer.

Easterling, K. (2014). Extra-statecraft: The Power of Infrastructure Space. London, Verso.

Edensor, T. and Jayne, M. (eds) (2012). Urban Theory beyond the West: A World of Cities. London, Routledge.

Eiland, H. and Jennings, M.W. (eds.) (2003). Walter Benjamin. Selected Writings Vol. 4. Cambridge, MA, Harvard University Press.

Eiland, H. and Jennings, M.W. (2014). Walter Benjamin: A Critical Life. Cambridge, MA, Harvard University Press.

Ekers, M., Hamel, P., and Keil, R. (2012). 'Governing suburbia: Modalities and mechanisms of suburban governance'. *Regional Studies*, *46* (3), 405–422.

Elden, S., Lebas, E., and Kofman, E. (2017). Henri Lefebvre: Key Writings. London, Bloomsbury.

Elmqvist, T., Bai, X., Frantzeskaki, N., Griffith, C., Maddox, D., McPhearson, T. et al. (2017). The Urban Planet: Patterns and Pathways to the Cities We Want. Cambridge, Cambridge University Press.

Englund, H. (2002). 'The village in the city, the city in the village: Migrants in Lilongwe'. *Journal of Southern African Studies*, *28* (1), 137–154.

Enright, T. (2020). 'Beyond comparison in urban politics and policy analysis'. *PS: Political Science & Politics*, *53* (1), 29–32.

Eriksen, S. (2017). 'State effects and the effects of state building: Institution building and the formation of state-centred societies'. *Third World Quarterly*, *38* (4), 771–786.

Fabian, J. (2000). Out of our minds: Reason and madness in the exploration of central Africa. Berkeley, University of California Press.

Fainstein, S. (1994). The City-Builders: Property, Politics and Planning in London and New York. Oxford, Blackwell.

Fainstein, S. (2001). The City Builders: Property Development in New York and London, 1980-2000. Lawrence, University of Kansas Press.

Fainstein, S.S. (2008). 'Mega-projects in New York, London and Amsterdam'. *International Journal of Urban and Regional Research*, *32*, 768–785.

Farías, I. (2010). 'Introduction'. In: Urban Assemblages: How Actor-Network Theory Changes Urban Studies (eds. I. Farías and T. Bender), 1–24. London, Routledge.

Farouk, B.R. and Owusu, M. (2012). '"If in doubt, count": The role of community-driven enumeration in blocking eviction in Old Fadama, Accra'. *Environment and Urbanisation*, *24* (1), 47–57.

Fawcett, C.B. (1932). 'Distribution of the urban population in Great Britain, 1931'. *The Geographical Journal*, *79* (2), 100–113.

Felski, R. and Stanford Friedman, S. (2013). Comparison: Theories, Approaches, Uses. Baltimore, Johns Hopkins University Press.

Feltran, G. (ed.) (2022). Stolen Cars: A journey through São Paulo's urban conflict. Oxford, Wiley-Blackwell.

Ferenčuhová, S. (2016). 'Accounts from behind the curtain: History and geography in the critical analysis of urban theory'. *International Journal of Urban and Regional Research*, *40* (1), 113–131.

Ferguson, J. (1990). 'Mobile workers, modernist narratives: A critique of the historiography of transition on the Zambian copperbelt [Part Two]'. *Journal of Southern African Studies*, *16* (4), 603–621.

Ferguson, J. (2006). Global Shadows: Africa in the Neoliberal World Order. Durham, Duke University Press.

Ferguson, J. (2007). 'Formalities of poverty: Thinking about social assistance in neoliberal South Africa'. *African Studies Review*, *50*, 71–86.

Ferguson, J. (2010). 'The uses of neoliberalism'. *Antipode*, *41*, 166–184.

Fernandez, R., Hofman, A., and Aalbers, M.B. (2016). 'London and New York as a safe deposit box for the transnational wealth elite'. *Environment and Planning A*, 48 (12), 2443–2461.

Fernandez, R. and Aalbers, M. (2016). 'Financialization and housing: Between globalization and Varieties of Capitalism'. *Competition and Change*, 20 (2), 71–88.

Fernandez, F. and Aalbers, M.B. (2020). 'Housing financialization in the global south: In search of a comparative framework'. *Housing Policy Debate*, 30 (4), 680–701.

Ferrari, B. (2013). Living in Interesting Times: An Urban View from Beijing Innovators. Lausanne, PhD thesis, Laboratoire Chôros, Institut de l'urbain et des territoires, Ecole Polytechnique Fédérale de Lausanne.

Fields, D. and Uffer, S. (2016). 'The financialisation of rental housing: A comparative analysis of New York City and Berlin'. *Urban Studies*, 53 (7), 1486–1502.

Firman, T. (1998). 'The restructuring of Jakarta metropolitan area: A "global city" in Asia'. *Cities*, 15 (4), 229–243.

Flanagan, T. (2009). 'The thought of history in Benjamin and Deleuze'. In: Deleuze and History (eds. J.A. Bell and C. Colebrook). Edinburgh, Edinburgh University Press.

Flaxman, G. (2005). 'Transcendental aesthetics: Deleuze's philosophy of space'. In: Deleuze and Space (eds. I. Buchanan and G. Lambert), 176–188. Edinburgh, Edinburgh University Press.

Flyvberg, B. (2014). 'What you should know about megaprojects and why: An overview'. *Project Management Journal*, 45 (2), 6–19.

Forster, M. (2010). 'Wittgenstein on family resemblance concepts'. In: Wittgenstein's Philosophical Investigations: A Critical Guide (ed. A. Ahmed), 66–87. Cambridge, Cambridge University Press.

Foucault, M. (1980). Power/Knowledge: Selected Interviews and other writings 1972-1977. USA, Random House.

Foucault, M. (2007). Security, Territory, Population: Lectures at the College De France, 1977 – 78. London, Palgrave Macmillan.

Fourchard, L. and Bekker, S. (eds) (2013). Governing Cities in Africa: Politics and Policies. Pretoria, HSRC Press.

Fourchard, L. (2011). 'Lagos, koolhaas and partisan politics in Nigeria'. *International Journal of Urban and Regional Research*, 35 (1), 40–56.

Fourchard, L. (2021). Classify, Exclude, Police: Urban Lives in South Africa and Nigeria. Oxford, Wiley-Blackwell.

Fox, S., Bloch, R., and Monroy, J. (2017). 'Understanding the dynamics of Nigeria's urban transition: A refutation of the "stalled urbanisation" hypothesis'. *Urban Studies*, 55 (5), 947–964.

Franzese, R. (2007). 'Multi-causality, context-conditionality, and endogeneity'. In: Oxford Handbook of Comparative Politics (eds. C. Boix and S. Stokes), 27–72. Oxford University Press.

Friedland, R., Fox Piven, F., and Alford, R.R. (1977). 'Political conflict, urban structure, and the fiscal crisis'. *International Journal of Urban and Regional Research*, 1 (4), 447–471.

Friedman, S.S. (2013). 'Why not compare?'. In: Comparison: Theories, Approaches, Uses (eds. R. Felski and S. Stanford Friedman), 34–45. Baltimore, Johns Hopkins University Press.
Friedmann, J. (2019). 'Thinking about complexity and planning'. *International Planning Studies*, 24 (1), 13–22.
Friedmann, J. (2020). 'Thinking about mega-conurbations and planning'. In: Handbook of Megacities and Megacity-Regions (eds. D. Labbé and A. Sorensen), 21–32. Cheltenham, Edward Elgar.
Friedmann, J. and Wolff, G. (1982). 'World city formation: An agenda for research and action'. *International Journal of Urban and Regional Research*, 6, 309–344.
Fujita, K. and Hill, R.C. (1995). 'Global Toyotaism and local development'. *International Journal of Urban and Regional Research*, 19 (1), 7–22.
Gad, C. and Casper Bruun Jensen, C.B. (2016). 'Lateral comparisons'. In: Practising Comparison: Logics, Relations, Collaborations (eds. J. Deville, M. Guggenheim and S. Hrdličková), 189–219. Manchester, Mattering Press.
Gandy, M. (2014). The Fabric of Space. MIT Press.
Gädeke, D. (2018). 'How to think the world? Achille Mbembe on race, democracy and the African role in global thought'. *Constellations*, 25, 497–506.
Geddes, M. (2005). 'Neoliberalism and local governance – Cross-national perspectives and speculations'. *Policy Studies*, 26 (3–4), 360–377.
Geenen, K. (2012). 'How the People of Butembo (RDC) were Chosen to Embody "the New Congo": Or What the appearance of a poster in a city's public places can teach about its social tissue'. *International Journal of Urban and Regional Research*, 36 (3), 448–461.
Gentile, M. (2018). 'Three metals and the "Post-Socialist City": Reclaiming the peripheries of urban knowledge'. *International Journal of Urban and Regional Research*, 42 (6), 1140–1151.
Ghertner, A.D. (2014). 'India's urban revolution: Geographies of displacement beyond gentrification'. *Environment and Planning A*, 46 (7), 1554–1571.
Ghertner, D.A. (2015a). Rule by Aesthetics: World-Class City Making in Delhi. Oxford, Oxford University Press.
Ghertner, A.D. (2015b). 'Why gentrification theory fails in "much of the world"'. *City*, 19 (4), 552–563.
Gibson-Graham, J.-K. (1996). The End of Capitalism (As We Knew It): A Feminist Critique of Political Economy. Oxford, Blackwell.
Giddens, A. (1984). The Constitution of Society: Outline of the Theory of Structuration. Cambridge, Polity Press.
Gidwani, V. and Sivaramakrishnan, K. (2003). 'Circular migration and rural cosmopolitanism in India'. *Contributions to Indian Sociology*, 37 (1–2), 339–367.
Gilroy, P. (1995). The Black Atlantic: Modernity and Double-Consciousness. Boston, Harvard University Press.
Gintrac, C. and Giroud, M. (2014). Villes Contestées: Pour Une Géographie Critique De L'urbain. Paris, Les Prairies Ordinaire.
Glass, R. (1964). London: Aspects of Change. London, MacGibbon and Kee.
Glissant, E. (1997). Poetics of Relation. Minnesota, University of Michigan Press.

Glock, H. (2010). 'Wittgenstein on concepts'. In: Wittgenstein's Philosophical Investigations: A Critical Guide (ed. A. Ahmed), 88–108. Cambridge, Cambridge University Press.

Gluckman, M. (1961). 'Anthropological problems arising from the African industrial revolution'. In: Social Change in Modern Africa (ed. A. Southall), 67–82. London, NY, Toronto, Oxford University Press, for International African Institute, Kampala.

Goldfrank, B. and Schrank, A. (2009). 'Municipal neoliberalism and municipal socialism: Urban political economy in Latin America'. *International Journal of Urban and Regional Research*, 33 (2), 443–462.

Goldman, M. (2005). Imperial Nature: The World Bank and Struggles for Social Justice in the Age of Globalization. London, Verso.

Goldman, M. (2011). 'Speculative urbanism and the making of the next world city'. *International Journal of Urban and Regional Research*, 35 (3), 555–581.

Golubchikov, O., Badyina, A., and Makhrova, A. (2014). 'The hybrid spatialities of transition: Capitalism, legacy and uneven urban economic restructuring'. *Urban Studies*, 51 (4), 617–633.

González, S. (2011). 'Bilbao and Barcelona "in motion". How urban regeneration "Models" travel and mutate in the global flows of policy tourism'. *Urban Studies*, 48 (7), 1397–1418.

González, S., Oosterlynck, S., Ribera-Fumaz, R., and Rossi, U. (2018). 'Locating the global financial crisis: Variegated neoliberalization in four European cities'. *Territory, Politics, Governance*, 6 (4), 468–488.

Goodfellow, T. (2014). 'Rwanda's political settlement and the urban transition: Expropriation, construction and taxation in Kigali'. *Journal of Eastern African Studies*, 8 (2), 311–329.

Goodfellow, T. (2017). 'Urban fortunes and skeleton cityscapes: Real estate and late urbanization in Kigali and Addis Ababa'. *International Journal of Urban and Regional Research*, 41 (5), 786–803.

Goodfellow, T. (2020). 'Finance, infrastructure and urban capital: The political economy of African "gap-filling"'. *Review of African Political Economy*, 47 (164), 256–274.

Goonewardena, K. (2018). 'Planetary urbanization and totality'. *Environment and Planning D: Society and Space*, 36 (3), 456–473.

Goonewardena, K., Kipfer, S., Milgrom, R., and Schmid, C. (eds) (2008). Space, Difference, Everyday Life: Reading Henri Lefebvre. London, Routledge.

Gordon, I. (1995). 'London: World City: Political and organizational constraints on territorial competition'. In: Territorial Competition in an Integrating Europe (eds. P. Cheshire and I.R. Gordon), 295–311. Aldershot, Avebury.

Gordon, I. (2003). Capital Needs, Capital Growth and Global City Rhetoric in Mayor Livingstone's London Plan, paper presented at the Annual Conference of American Geographers, New Orleans, March 2003.

Gotham, K.F. and Greenberg, M. (2008). 'From 9/11 to 8/29: Post-disaster response and recovery in New York and New Orleans'. *Social Forces*, 87 (2), 1–24. December 2008.

Gottmann, J. (1961). Megalopolis. The Urbanized Northeastern Seaboard of the United States. New York, The Twentieth Century Fund.

Gough, K. and Yankson, P.W.K. (2000). 'Land markets in African cities: The case of Peri-urban Accra, Ghana'. *Urban Studies*, *37* (13), 2485–2500.

Grant, R. (2008). Globalizing City: The Urban and Economic Transformation of Accra, Ghana. Syracuse, Syracuse University Press.

Grossberg, L. (2014). 'Cultural studies and Deleuze-Guattari, Part 1'. *Cultural Studies*, *28* (1), 1–28.

Grossberg, L. (2015). 'Learning from Stuart Hall, following the path with heart'. *Cultural Studies*, *29* (1), 3–11.

Grossberg, L. (2019). 'Cultural Studies in search of a method, or looking for conjunctural analysis'. *New Formations*, *96*, 38–68.

Guarneros-Meza, V. and Geddes, M. (2010). 'Local governance and participation under neoliberalism: Comparative perspectives'. *International Journal of Urban and Regional Research*, *34* (1), 115–129.

Guggenheim, M. and Söderström, O. (eds) (2010). Re-Shaping Cities. How Mobility Transforms Architecture and Urban Forms. London, Routledge.

Gugler, J. and Flanagan, W.G. (1977). 'On the political economy of urbanization in the Third World'. *International Journal of Urban and Regional Research*, *1* (1–3), 272–292.

Gualini, E. and Majoor, S. (2007). 'Innovative practices in large urban development projects: Conflicting frames in the quest for "new urbanity"'. *Planning Theory & Practice*, *8* (3), 297–318.

Guironnet, A., Attuyer, K., and Halbert, L. (2016). 'Building cities on financial assets: The financialisation of property markets and its implications for city governments in the Paris city-region'. *Urban Studies*, *53* (7), 1442–1464.

Haesbaert, R. (2013). 'A global sense of place and multi-territoriality: Notes for dialogue from a "peripheral" point of view'. In: Spatial politics: Essays for Doreen Massey (eds. D. Featherstone and J. Painter), 146–157. Malden, Wiley-Blackwell, 2012.

Haid, C.G. (2017). 'The Janus face of urban governance: State, informality and ambiguity in Berlin'. *Current Sociology*, *65* (2), 289–301.

Haila, A. (2015). Urban Land Rent: Singapore as a Property State. John Wiley & Sons.

Halbert, L. and Attuyer, K. (2016). 'Introduction: The financialization of urban production: Conditions, mediations and transformations'. *Urban Studies*, *53* (7), 1347–1361.

Halbert, L., Attuyer, K., and Sanfelici, D. (2016). 'Financial markets, developers and the geographies of housing in Brazil: A supply-side account'. *Urban Studies*, *53* (7), 1465–1485.

Halbert, L. and Rouanet, H. (2014). 'Filtering risk away: Global finance capital, transcalar territorial networks and the (un)making of city-regions: An analysis of business property development in Bangalore, India'. *Regional Studies*, *48* (3), 471–484.

Hall, P. (1966). The World Cities. London, Weidenfeld and Nicholson.

Hall, P. (1982). 'Enterprise zones: A justification'. *International Journal of Urban and Regional Research*, *6* (4), 16–421.

Hall, S. (1985). Signification, Representation, Ideology: Althusser and the poststructuralist debates. *Critical Studies in Mass Communication*, *2* (2), 91–114.

Hall, S. (2003). 'Marx's Notes on Method: A "Reading" of the 1857 Introduction'. *Cultural Studies*, *17* (2), 113–149.
Hall, S. (2016). Cultural Studies 1983: A Theoretical History. London and Durham, Duke University Press.
Hallward, P. (2006). Out of This World: Deleuze and the Philosophy of Creation. London, Verso.
Hallward, P. (2001). Absolutely Postcolonial: Writing between the Singular and the Specific. Manchester, Manchester University Press.
Hamacher, W. (2005). '"Now": Walter Benjamin on historical time'. In: Walter Benjamin and History (ed. A. Benjamin), 38–68. London, Continuum.
Hamel, P. and Keil, R. (eds.) (2016). Suburban Governance: A Global View. Toronto, University of Toronto Press.
Hamilton, G. (1985). 'Why no capitalism in China? Negative questions in Historical Comparative Research'. *Journal of Developing Societies*, *1* (2), 187–211.
Hamnett, C. (1991). 'The blind men and the elephant: The explanation of gentrification'. *Transactions of the Institute of British Geographers*, *17*, 173–189.
Hamnett, C. (2003). Unequal city: London in the global arena. London: Routledge.
Hancock, M. and Srinivas, S. (2008). 'Spaces of modernity: Religion and the Urban in Asia and Africa'. *International Journal of Urban and Regional Research*, *32*, 617–630.
Hannerz, U. (1980). Exploring the City. Inquiries Towards an Urban Anthropology. New York, Columbia University Press.
Haraway, D. (1987). 'A manifesto for Cyborgs: Science, technology, and socialist feminism in the 1980s'. *Australian Feminist Studies*, *2* (4), 1–42.
Haraway, D. (1988). 'Situated knowledges: The science question in feminism and the privilege of partial perspective'. *Feminist Studies*, *14* (3), 575–599.
Harding, A. (1994). 'Urban regimes and growth machines: Towards a cross-national research agenda'. *Urban Affairs Quarterly*, *29* (3), 356–382.
Harloe, M. (1981). 'Notes on comparative urban research'. In: Urbanisation and Urban Planning in Capitalist Society (eds. M. Dear and A. Scott). London, Methuen.
Harney, S. and Moten, F. (2013). The Undercommons: Fugitive Planning & Black Study. New York, Minor Compositions.
Harris, N. (1995). 'Bombay in a global economy: Structural adjustment and the role of cities'. *Cities*, *12*, 175–184.
Harris, A. (2008). 'From London to Mumbai and back again: Gentrification and public policy in comparative perspective'. *Urban Studies*, *45* (12), 2407–2428.
Harris, R. (2008). 'Development and hybridity made concrete in the colonies'. *Environment and Planning A*, *40* (1), 15–36.
Harris, R. (2010). 'Meaningful types in a world of suburbs'. In: Suburbanization in Global Society (eds. M. Clapson and R. Hutchinson), 15–50. Bingley, UK, Emerald. Research in Urban Sociology No.10.
Harris, R. (2017). 'Modes of informal urban development: A global phenomenon'. *Journal of Planning Literature*, 1–20.

Harris, R. and Vorms, C. (eds) (2017). What's in a Name? Talking about 'Suburbs'. Toronto, University of Toronto Press.

Harrison, K. and Phasha, P. 2014. Public Art: Aesthetic, Evocative and Invisible? Johannesburg: Johannesburg Development Agency and University of the Witwatersrand. (accessed 12 April 2020). http://wiredspace.wits.ac.za/bitstream/handle/10539/17150/Report7_Harrison_1006LR.pdf?sequence=1&isAllowed=y

Harrison, P. (2006a). 'On the edge of reason: Planning and urban futures in Africa'. *Urban Studies, 43* (2), 319–335.

Harrison, P. (2006b). 'Integrated development plans and third way politics'. In: Democracy and Delivery: Urban Policy in South Africa (eds. U. Pillay, R. Tomlinson and J. Du Toit), 186–207. Cape Town, HSRC Press.

Harrison, P. (2015). 'South-south relationships and the transfer of 'best practice': The case of Johannesburg, South Africa'. *International Development Planning Review, 37* (2), 205–223.

Harrison, P. and Todes, A. (2015). 'Spatial Transformations in a "Loosening State": South Africa in a comparative perspective'. *Geoforum, 61*, 148–162.

Hart, G. (2003). Disabling Globalisation: Places of Power in Post-apartheid South Africa. Berkeley, University of California Press.

Hart, G. (2008). 'The provocations of neoliberalism: Contesting the nation and liberation after apartheid'. *Antipode, 40* (4), 678–705.

Hart, G. (2018). 'Relational comparison revisited: Marxist postcolonial geographies in practice'. *Progress in Human Geography, 42* (3), 371–394.

Hart, G. (2020). Why did it take so long? Trump-Bannonism in a global conjunctural frame. Geografiska Annaler: Series B, *Human Geography, 102* (3), 239–266.

Hart, K. (1973). 'Informal income opportunities and urban employment in Ghana'. *The Journal of Modern African Studies, 11* (1), 61–89.

Hartman, S. (2008). 'Venus in two acts'. *Small Axe, 12* (2), 1–14.

Hartman, S. (2019). Wayward Lives, Beautiful Experiments. London, Serpent's Tail.

Harvey, D. (1978). 'The urban process under capitalism: A framework for analysis'. *International Journal of Urban and Regional Research, 2* (1–3), 1468–2427.

Harvey, D. (1989). 'From managerialism to entrepreneurialism: The transformation in urban governance in late capitalism'. *Geografiska Annaler B, 71*, 3–17.

Harvey, D. (1996). Justice, Nature and the Geography of Difference. Oxford, Wiley-Blackwell.

Harvey, D. (2005). A Brief History of Neoliberalism. Oxford, Oxford U.P.

Harvey, D. (2010). The Enigma of Capital and the Crises of Capitalism. London, Profile.

Harvey, D. (2013). Rebel Cities: From the Right to the City to the Urban Revolution. London.

Hawthorne, C. (2019). 'Black matters are spatial matters: Black geographies for the twenty-first century'. *Geography Compass*, doi: https://doi.org/10.1111/gec3.12468.

He, C. and Zhu, S. (2018). 'China's foreign direct investment into Africa'. In: The State of African Cities 2018: The Geography of African Investment (eds. R.S. Wall, J. Maseland, K. Rochell and M. Spaliviero), 106–127. Nairobi, UN Habitat.

He, S. (2019). 'Three waves of state-led gentrification in China'. *Tijdschrift Voor Economische En Sociale Geografie, 110,* 26–34.

Healey, P., Khakee, A., Motte, A., and Needham, B. (eds) (1997). Making Strategic Plans: Innovation in Europe. London, UCL Press.

Healey, P. (2007). Urban Complexity and Spatial Strategies: Towards a Relational Planning for Our Times. London, Routledge.

Healey, P. (2009). 'In search of the "Strategic" in spatial strategy making'. *Planning Theory and Practice, 10* (4), 439–457.

Hei, C. and Zhu, S. (2018). 'China's Foreign investment into Africa'. In: The State of African Cities, 106–127. Nairobi, UN-Habitat.

Henneberry, J. and Parris, S. (2013). 'The embedded developer: Using project ecologies to analyse local property development networks'. *The Town Planning Review, 84* (2), 227–249.

Hentschel, C. (2015). 'Postcolonializing Berlin and the fabrication of the urban'. *International Journal of Urban and Regional Research, 39* (1), 79–91.

Herbert, C. and Murray, M. (2015). 'Building from scratch: New cities, privatized urbanism and the spatial restructuring of Johannesburg after apartheid'. *International Journal of Urban and Regional Research, 39,* 471–494.

Heslop, J., McFarlane, C., and Ormerod, E. (2020). 'Relational housing across the North–South divide: Learning between Albania, Uganda, and the UK'. *Housing Studies, 35* (9), 1607–1627.

Hewitson, M. (2014). History and Causality. London, Palgrave Macmillan.

Hilbrandt, H. (2021). Housing in the Margins: Negotiating Urban Formalities in Berlin's Allotment Gardens. Oxford, Wiley-Blackwell.

Hilgers, M. (2012). 'The historicity of the neoliberal state'. *Social Anthropology/Anthropologie Sociale, 20* (1), 80–94.

Hill, R.C. (1989). 'Comparing transnational production systems: the automobile industry in the USA and Japan'. *International Journal of Urban and Regional Research, 13* (3), 462–480.

Hill, R.C. and Kim, J.W. (2000). 'Global cities and developmental states: New York, Tokyo and Seoul'. *Urban Studies, 37* (12), 2167–2195.

Hill Collins, P. (2019). Intersectionality as Critical Social Theory. Duke University Press.

Hillier, J. (2000). 'Going round the back? Complex networks and informal action in local planning processes'. *Environment and Planning A, 32* (1), 33–54.

Hirt, S. (2012). Iron Curtains: Gates, Suburbs and Privatization of Space in the Post-Socialist City. Oxford, Wiley-Blackwell.

Hoffman, L. (2006). 'Autonomous choices and patriotic professionalism: On governmentality in late-socialist China'. *Economy and Society, 35* (4), 550–570.

Holston, J. (2007). Insurgent Citizenship: Disjunctions of Democracy and Modernity in Brazil. Princeton, Princeton University Press.

Home, R. (2014). 'Shaping cities of the global south. Legal histories of planning and colonialism'. In: The Routledge Handbook on Cities of the Global South (eds. S. Parnell and S. Oldfield), 75–85. London, Routledge.

Hsing, Y. (2010). The Great Urban Transformation: Politics of Land and Property in China. Oxford, Oxford University Press.

Huat, C.B. (1991). 'Not depoliticized but ideologically successful: The public housing programme in Singapore'. *International Journal of Urban and Regional Research*, *15* (1), 24–41.

Huat, C.B. (2011). 'Singapore as model: Planning innovations, knowledge experts'. In: Worlding Cities: Asian Experiments and the Art of being Global (eds. A. Roy and A. Ong), 27–54. Oxford: Wiley-Blackwell.

Huchzermeyer, M. (2011). Tenement Cities: From 19th Century Berlin to 21st Century Nairobi. Trenton, NJ, Africa World Press.

Hughes, J. (2009). Deleuze's Difference and Repetition. London, Continuum.

Hunter, M. (2019). Race for Education: Gender, White Tone, and Schooling in South Africa. Cambridge, Cambridge University Press.

Huyssen, A. (Ed.) (2008). Other Cities, Other Worlds: Urban Imaginaries in a Globalizing Age. Durham and London, Duke University Press.

IJURR Editors. (1977). 'Editorial statement'. *International Journal of Urban and Regional Research*, *1* (1), 1–3.

Jacobs, J.M. (1996). Edge of Empire: Postcolonialism and the City. London, Routledge.

Jacobs, J.M. (2006). 'A geography of big things'. *Cultural Geographies*, *13* (1), 1–27.

Jacobs, J.M. (2012). 'Commentary: Comparing comparative urbanisms'. *Urban Geography*, *33* (6), 904–914.

Jacobs, J.M., Cairns, S., and Strebel, I. (2007). '"A tall storey ... but, a fact just the same": The red road high-rise as a black box'. *Urban Studies*, *44* (3), 609–629.

Janoschka, M., Sequera, J., and Salinas, L. (2013). 'Gentrification in Spain and Latin America — A Critical Dialogue'. *International Journal of Urban and Regional Research*. doi: 10.1111/1468-2427.12030.

Jones, E.L. and Shelley, P. (2016). How Housing Co-operatives Built a City. Architectural Review, October, https://www.architectural-review.com/archive/how-housing-co-operatives-built-a-city.

Jay, M. (1984). Marxism and Totality: The Adventures of a Concept from Lukács to Habermas. Berkeley, University of California Press.

Jazeel, T. (2012). 'Spatializing difference beyond cosmopolitanism: Rethinking planetary futures'. *Theory, Culture and Society*, *28* (5), 75–97.

Jazeel, T. (2014). 'Subaltern geographies: Geographical knowledge and postcolonial strategy'. *Singapore Journal of Tropical Geography*, *35*, 88–103.

Jazeel, T. (2019a). 'Singularity. A manifesto for incomparable geographies'. *Singapore Journal of Tropical Geography*, *40*, 5–21.

Jazeel, T. (2019b). Postcolonialism. London, Routledge.

Jazeel, T., and McFarlane, C. (2010). 'The limits of responsibility: a postcolonial politics of academic knowledge production'. *Transactions of the Institute of British Geographers*, *35* (1), 109–124.

Jessop, B. (2002). 'Liberalism, neoliberalism and urban governance: A state-theoretical perspective'. *Antipode*, *34* (3), 452–472.

Jones, G.A. and Varley, A. (1999). 'The reconquest of the historic centre: Urban conservation and gentrification in Puebla, Mexico'. *Environment and Planning A, 31*, 1547–1566.

Kaika, M. and Ruggiero, L. (2016). 'Land financialization as a "lived" process: The transformation of Milan's Bicocca by Pirelli'. *European Urban and Regional Studies, 23* (1), 3–22.

Kalberg, S. (1994). Max Weber's Comparative Historical Sociology. Cambridge, Polity Press.

Kanai, J.M. and Schindler, S. (2019). 'Peri-urban promises of connectivity: Linking project-led polycentrism to the infrastructure scramble'. *Environment and Planning A: Economy and Space, 51* (2), 302–322.

Kantor, P. and Savitch, H.V. (2005). 'How to study comparative urban development politics: A research note'. *International Journal of Urban and Regional Research, 29* (1), 135–151.

Kantor, P., Savitch, H., and Vicari, S. (1997). 'The political economy of urban regimes: A comparative perspective'. *Urban Affairs Review, 32* (3), 348–377.

Kanuri, C., Revi, A., Espey, J., and Kuhle, H. (2016). Getting Started with the SDGs in Cities Report, Sustainable Development Solutions Network. (Accessed 12 December 2019) http://unsdsn.org/wp-content/uploads/2016/07/9.1.8.-Cities-SDG-Guide.pdf

Kaplinsky, R., Mccormick, D., and Morris, M. (2007). The Impact of China on sub-Saharan Africa. Institute of Development Studies, University of Sussex.

Karaman, O. (2013). 'Urban neoliberalism with Islamic characteristics'. *Urban Studies, 50* (16), 3412–3427.

Karaman, O., Sawyer, L., Schmid, C., and Wong, K.P. (2020). 'Plot by plot: Plotting urbanism as an ordinary process of urbanisation'. *Antipode, 52* (4), 1122–1151.

Katz, C. (1996). 'Towards minor theory'. *Environment and Planning D: Society and Space, 14* (4), 487–499.

Katz, C. (2001). 'On the grounds of globalization: A topography for feminist political engagement'. *Signs, 26* (4), 1213–1234.

Keil, R. (2017). Suburban Planet: Making the World Urban from the outside In. Cambridge, Polity.

Keil, R. and Wu, F. (2022). After Suburbia: Urbanisation in the Twenty-First Century. Toronto: Univ of Toronto Press.

Kern, L. and Mullings, B. (2013). 'Urban neoliberalism, urban insecurity and urban violence: Exploring the gender dimensions'. In: Rethinking Feminist Interventions in the Urban (eds. L. Peake and M. Reiker), 23–40. London, Routledge.

King, A.D. (1984). The Bungalow: The Production of a Global Culture. London, Routledge and Kegan Paul.

King, A.D. (1990a). Global Cities: Post-Imperialism and the Internationalization of London. London, Routledge.

King, A.D. (1990b). Urbanism, Colonialism and the World-Economy. London, Routledge.

King, A.D. (2004). Spaces of Global Cultures: Architecture, Urbanism, Identity. London, Routledge.

Kipfer, S. (2009). Introduction to Dialectical Materialism (H. Lefebvre). Minneapolis, University of Minnesota Press.

Kipfer, S. (2022). 'Comparison and political strategy: Internationalism, colonial rule and urban research after Fanon'. *Urban Studies*. October 2021. doi: 10.1177/00420980211049346.

Kipfer, S. and Goonewardena, K. (2013). 'Urban Marxism and the post-colonial question: Henri Lefebvre and "Colonisation"'. *Historical Materialism, 21* (2), 76–116.

Kipfer, S., Saberi, P., and Wieditz, T. (2012). 'Henri Lefebvre: Debates and controversies'. In: Progress in Human Geography.

Klink, J. (2013). 'Scalar and spatial restructuring in Rio de Janeiro'. *International Journal of Urban and Regional Research, 37*, 1168–1187.

Knox, P. and Taylor, P. (eds.) (1995). World Cities in a World-system. Cambridge & New York, Cambridge University Press.

Kombe, W.J. (2010). 'Land acquisition for public use, emerging conflicts and their socio-political implications'. *International Journal of Urban Sustainable Development, 2* (1-2), 45–63.

Koolhaas, R. (Harvard Project on the City), Boeri, S. (Multiplicity), Kwinter, S., Tazi, N. and Obrist, H.U. (2000). Mutations. Barcelona: Bordeaux, France: ACTAR; Arc en rêve centre d'architecture.

Korff, R. (1986). 'Who has power in Bangkok?'. *International Journal of Urban and Regional Research, 10* (3), 330–350.

Kramwch, O. (2022). 'Comparative Urbanism as Spectral Critique: "Hiddenness" at the Antipodes of the Chinese Belt and Road Initiative' in Routledge Handbook of Comparative Urbanism (eds. P. Le Galès and J. Robinson). London and New York: Routledge.

Kraniauskas, J. (2000). 'Beware Mexican Ruins! "one-way street" and the colonial unconscious'. In: Walter Benjamin's Philosophy: Destruction and Experience (eds. A. Benjamin and P. Osborne). Manchester, Clinamen Press.

Krause, M. (2013). 'The ruralization of the world'. *Public Culture, 25* (2), 233–248.

Krause, M. (2016). 'Comparative research: Beyond linear-causal explanation'. In: Practising Comparison: Logics, Relations, Collaborations (eds. J. Deville, M. Guggenheim and S. Hrdličková), 45–67. Manchester, Mattering Press.

Kuper, H. (ed.) (1965). Urbanization and Migration in West Africa. Berkeley, University of California Press.

Kusno, A. (2000). Behind the Postcolonial: Architecture, Urban Space and Political Cultures in Indonesia. Routledge.

Kuymulu, M.B. (2013). 'The vortex of rights: "right to the city" at a crossroads'. *International Journal of Urban and Regional Research, 37* (3), 923–940.

Lambert, R. (2021). 'Land trafficking and the fertile spaces of legality'. *International Journal of Urban and Regional Research, 45* (10), 21–38.

Lancione, M. and McFarlane, C. (2016). 'Life at the urban margins: Sanitation infra-making and the potential of experimental comparison'. *Environment and Planning A, 48* (12), 2402–2421.

Larner, W. (2000). 'Neo-liberalism: Policy, ideology, governmentality'. *Studies in Political Economy, 63*, 5–26.

Larner, W. (2009). 'Neoliberalism, Mike Moore and the WTO'. *Environment and Planning A*, *41*, 1576–1593.

Larner, W. (2014). 'The post-political and its discontents: Spaces of depoliticisation, spectres of radical politics'. In: The Post-Political and Its Discontents: Spaces of Depoliticisation, Spectres of Radical Politics (eds. J. Wilson and E. Swyngedouw), 189–207. Edinburgh, Edinburgh University Press.

Larner, W. and Laurie, N. (2010). 'Travelling technocrats, embodied knowledges: Globalising privatisation in telecoms and water'. *Geoforum*, *41* (2), 218–226.

Larner, W. and Le Heron, R. (2004). 'Global benchmarking: Participating "at a distance" in the globalizing economy'. In: Global Governmentality. Governing International Spaces (eds. W. Larner and W. Walters), 212–232. London, Routledge.

Larner, W. and Walters, W. (Eds.) (2004). Global Governmentality: Governing International Spaces. London, Routledge.

Latour, B. (2007). Reassembling the Social: An Introduction to Actor-Network Theory. Oxford, Oxford University Press.

Lauermann, J. (2018). 'Municipal statecraft: Revisiting the geographies of the entrepreneurial city'. *Progress in Human Geography*, *42* (2), 205–224.

Law, J. (2004). After Method: Mess in Social Science Research. London, Routledge.

Lawhon, M. and Truelove, Y. (2020). 'Disambiguating the southern urban critique: Propositions, pathways and possibilities for a more global urban studies'. *Urban Studies*, *57* (1), 3–20.

Lawson, V. and Klak, T. (1993). 'An argument for critical and comparative research on the urban economic geography of the Americas'. *Environment and Planning A*, *25*, 1071–1084.

Lawton, P. (2019). 'Unbounding gentrification theory: Multidimensional space, networks and relational approaches'. *Regional Studies 52* (2), 268–279.

Layoun, M.N. (2013). 'Endings and beginnings: Reimagining the tasks and spaces of comparison'. In: Comparison: Theories, Approaches, Uses (eds. R. Felski and S. Stanford Friedman), 210–235. Baltimore, Johns Hopkins University Press.

Lee, C.K. and Zhang, Y. (2013). 'The power of instability: Unraveling the microfoundations of bargained authoritarianism in China'. *American Journal of Sociology*, *118* (6), 1475–1508.

Lees, L. (2000). 'A reappraisal of gentrification: Towards a 'geography of gentrification''. *Progress in Human Geography*, *24* (3), 389–408.

Lees, L. (2012). 'The geography of gentrification: Thinking through comparative urbanism'. *Progress in Human Geography*, *36* (2), 155–171.

Lees, L. (2014a). 'The urban injustices of New Labour's "new urban renewal": The case of the Aylesbury Estate in London'. *Antipode*, *46* (4), 921–947.

Lees, L. (2014b). 'Gentrification in the global South?'. In: Handbook for Cities of the Global South (eds. S. Parnell and S. Oldfield), 506–521. London, Routledge.

Lees, L., Shin, H., and López-Morales, E. (eds.) (2015). Global Gentrifications: Uneven Development and Displacement. Bristol, Policy Press.

Lees, L., Shin, H., and López-Morales, E. (2016). Planetary Gentrification. Cambridge, Polity Press.

Lefebvre, H. (1955). 'La notion de totalité dans les sciences sociales'. *Cahiers Internationaux De Sociologie, Nouvelle Série*, *18*, 55–77.

Lefebvre, H. (1991 [1974]). The Production of Space. Oxford, Blackwells.

Lefebvre, H. (1996). Writings on Cities (eds. and trans E. Lebas and E. Kofman). Oxford, Blackwells.

Lefebvre, H. (2003 [1974]). The Urban Revolution. Minneapolis, University of Minnesota Press.

Lefebvre, H. (2009 [1940]). Dialectical Materialism. Minneapolis, University of Minnesota Press.

Lefebvre, H. (2014). Critique of Everyday Life. The One-Volume Edition [1947, 1961, 1981]. London, Verso.

Le Galès, P. (2002). European Cities: Social Conflicts and Governance. Oxford, Oxford University Press.

Le Galès, P. (2011). 'Urban governance in Europe: What is governed?'. In: The New Blackwell Companion to the City (eds. G. Bridge and S. Watson). Oxford, Wiley-Blackwell.

Le Galès, P. (2016). 'Neoliberalism and urban change: Stretching a good idea too far?'. *Territory, Politics, Governance*, *4* (2), 154–172.

Lehrer, U. (1994). 'The Image of the periphery: The architecture of flexspace'. *Environment and Planning D: Society and Space*, *12* (2), 187–205.

Leitner, H. (1990). 'Cities in pursuit of economic growth: The local state as entrepreneur'. *Political Geography Quarterly*, *9* (2), 146–170.

Leitner, H., Peck, J., and Sheppard, E. (eds) (2019). Urban Studies Inside/Out: Theory, Practice and Method. London and New York, Sage.

Leitner, H. and Sheppard, E. (2016). 'Provincializing critical urban theory: Extending the ecosystem of possibilities'. *International Journal of Urban and Regional Research*, *40* (1), 228–235.

Leitner, H. and Sheppard, E. (2020). 'Towards an epistemology for conjunctural inter-urban comparison'. *Cambridge Journal of Regions, Economy and Society*, *13* (3), 491–508.

Leitner, H., Sheppard, E., Sziarto, K., and Maringanti, A. (2007). 'Contesting urban futures: Decentering neoliberalism'. In: Contesting Neoliberalism (eds. H. Leitner, J. Peck and E. Sheppard), 1–25. Guilford, New York.

Lemanski, C. (2014). 'Hybrid gentrification in South Africa: Theorising across southern and northern cities'. *Urban Studies*, *51* (14), 2943–2960.

Lepawsky, J., Akese, G., Billah, M., Conolly, C., and McNabb, C. (2015). 'Composing urban orders from rubbish electronics: Cityness and the site multiple'. *International Journal of Urban and Regional Research*, *39* (2), 185–199.

Levy, C. (2015). 'Expanding the "Room for Manoeuvre": Community-Led Finance in Mumbai, India.' In: The City in Urban Poverty (eds. C. Lemanski and C. Marx), 158–182. London: Palgrave Macmillan.

Ley, D. and Teo, S.Y. (2014). 'Gentrification in Hong Kong? Epistemology vs. Ontology'. *International Journal of Urban and Regional Research*, *38* (4), 1286–1303.

Ley, D. and Teo, S.Y. (2020). 'Is comparative gentrification possible? Sceptical voices from Hong Kong'. *International. Journal of Urban and Regional Research*, *44* (1), 166–172.

Li, Z., Ma, L., and Xue, D. (2009). 'An African enclave in China: The making of a new transnational urban space'. *Eurasian Geography and Economics*, *50* (6), 699–719.

Lijphart, A. (1971). 'Comparative politics and the comparative method'. *The American Political Science Review*, *LXV*, 682–693.

Lindell, I. (2008). 'The multiple sites of urban governance: Insights from an African City'. *Urban Studies*, *45* (9), 1879–1901.

Lipietz, A. (1987). Mirages and Miracles: The Crises of Global Fordism. London, Verso.

Lipietz, B. (2008). 'Building a vision for the post-apartheid city: What role for participation in Johannesburg's City development strategy'. *International Journal of Urban and Regional Research*, *32*, 135–163.

Lipietz, B., Lee, R., and Hayward, S. (2014). 'Just Space: Building a community-based voice for London planning'. *City*, *18* (2), 214–225.

Liu, C.Y. (2012). 'From Los Angeles to Shanghai: Testing the applicability of five urban paradigms'. *International Journal of Urban and Regional Research*, *36*, 1127–1145.

Liu, W. and Dunford, M. (2016). 'Inclusive globalization: Unpacking China's belt and road initiative'. *Area Development and Policy*, *1* (3), 323–340.

Logan, J. and Molotch, H. (1987). Urban Fortunes: The Political Economy of Place. Berkeley, University of California Press.

Van Loon, J. and Aalbers, M. (2017). 'How real estate became "just another asset class": The financialization of the investment strategies of Dutch institutional investors'. *European Planning Studies*, *25* (2), 221–240.

Lopes De Souza, M. (2019). 'Decolonising postcolonial thinking'. *ACME: An International Journal for Critical Geographies*, *18* (1), 1–24. Retrieved from: https://acme-journal.org/index.php/acme/article/view/1647.

López-Morales, E. (2011). 'Gentrification by ground rent dispossession: The shadows cast by large-scale urban renewal in Santiago de Chile'. *International Journal of Urban and Regional Research*, *35*, 330–357.

Lowe, L. (2015). The Intimacies of Four Continents. Durham, Duke University Press.

Lowe, L. and Manjapra, K. (2019). 'Comparative global humanities after man: Alternatives to the coloniality of knowledge'. *Theory, Culture and Society*, *36* (5), 23–48.

Lowndes, V. (1996). 'Varieties of New Institutionalism: A critical appraisal'. *Public Administration*, *74*, 181–197.

Lowry, G. and McCann, E. (2011). 'Asia in the mix: Urban form and global mobilities – Hong Kong, Vancouver, Dubai'. In: Worlding Cities: Asian Experiments and the Art of Being Global (eds. A. Ong and A. Roy). Oxford, Blackwell.

Löwy, M. (2005). Fire Alarm. Reading Walter Benjamin's 'On the Concept of History'. London, Verso.

LSE and UCLG. (2016). Habitat Policy Unit 4: Urban Governance, Capacity and Inc.

Lubeck, P. and Walton, J. (1979). 'Urban class conflict in Africa and Latin America: Comparative analyses from a world systems perspective'. *International Journal of Urban and Regional Research*, *3* (1), 3–28.

Mabin, A. (2014). 'Grounding southern theory in time and place'. In: The Routledge Handbook on Cities of the Global South (eds. S. Parnell and S. Oldfield), 21–36. London, Routledge.

Mabin, A., Butcher, S., and Bloch, R. (2013). 'Peripheries, suburbanisms and change in sub-Saharan African cities'. *Social Dynamics*, *39* (2), 167–190.

Mabogunje, A.L. (1990). 'Urban planning and the post-colonial state in Africa: A research overview'. *African Studies Review*, *33* (2), 121–203.

McCann, E. (2001). 'Collaborative visioning or urban planning as therapy: The politics of public-private urban policy making'. *Professional Geographer*, *53* (2), 207–218.

McCann, E. (2011). 'Urban policy mobilities and global circuits of knowledge: Towards a research agenda'. *Annals of the Association of American Geographers*, *101* (1), 107–130.

McCann, E. and Ward, K. (2010). 'Relationality/territoriality: Toward a conceptualization of cities in the world'. *Geoforum*, *41*, 175–184.

McCann, E. and Ward, K. (eds.) (2011). Mobile Urbanism: Cities and Policy Making in a Global Age. Minneapolis, Minnesota University Press.

McCarthy, J.J. (1983). 'The political economy of urban land use: Towards a revised theoretical framework'. *South African Geographical Journal*, *65* (1), 25–48.

McCormack, D. (2012). 'Geography and abstraction: Towards an affirmative critique'. *Progress in Human Geography*, *36* (6), 715–734.

McDonald, D. (2007). World City Syndrome: Neoliberalism and Inequality in Cape Town. New York, Routledge.

McDonnell, N. (2010). 'Leibniz's combinatorial art of synthesis and the temporal interval of the fold'. In: Deleuze and the Fold: A Critical Reader (eds. S. Van Tuinen and N. McDonnell), 65–88. Berlin, Springer.

McFarlane, C. (2006). 'Crossing borders: Development, learning and the North-South divide'. *Third World Quarterly*, *27* (8), 1413–1437.

McFarlane, C. (2010). 'The comparative city: Knowledge, learning, urbanism'. *International Journal of Urban and Regional Research*, *34* (4), 725–742.

McFarlane, C. (2011a). Learning the City: Knowledge and Translocal Assemblages. Oxford, Wiley-Blackwell.

McFarlane, C. (2011b). 'Assemblage and critical urbanism'. *City*, *15* (2), 204–224.

McFarlane, C. (2011c). 'On context: Assemblage, political economy and structure'. *City*, *15*, 375–388.

McFarlane, C. (2012). 'Rethinking informality: Politics, crisis, and the city'. *Planning Theory & Practice*, *13* (1), 89–108.

McFarlane, C. (2018). 'Fragment urbanism: Politics at the margins of the city'. *Society and Space*, *36* (6), 1007–1025.

McFarlane, C. (2019). 'Urban fragments: A subaltern studies imagination'. In: Subaltern Geographies (eds. T. Jazeel and S. Legg), 210–230. Athens, University of Georgia Press.

McFarlane, C., Desai, R., and Graham, S. (2014). 'Informal urban sanitation: Everyday life, poverty, and comparison'. *Annals of the Association of American Geographers, 104* (5), 989–1011.

McFarlane, C. and Waibel, M. (eds) (2016). Urban Informalities: Reflections on the Formal and Informal. London, Ashgate.

MacGaffey, J. and Bazenguissa-Ganga, R. (2000). Congo-Paris: Transnational Traders on the Margins of the Law. James Currey.

McGee, T.G. (1991a). 'Presidential address: Eurocentrism in geography - The case of Asian urbanization'. *The Canadian Geographer, 35* (4), 332–344.

McGee, T. (1991b). 'The emergence of "Desakota" Regions in Asia: Expanding a hypothesis'. In: The Extended Metropolis: Settlement Transition in Asia (ed. N. Ginsberg), 3–26. Honolulu, University of Hawaii Press.

McGee, T. (1995). 'Eurocentrism and geography: Reflections on Asian urbanisation'. In: Power of Development (ed. J. Crush). London, Routledge.

McGee, T. (2015). 'Deconstructing the decentralized urban spaces of the mega-urban regions in the global south'. In: Suburban Governance: A Global View (eds. P. Hamel and R. Keil), 325–336. Toronto, University of Toronto Press.

McGranahan, G. and Satterthwaite, D. 2014. *Urbanisation concepts and trends.* IIED Working Paper. IIED, London. http://pubs.iied.org/10709IIED.

Macgregor Wise, J. (2003). 'Reading Hall Reading Marx'. *Cultural Studies, 17* (2), 105–112.

Machimura, T. (1992). 'The Urban restructuring process in Tokyo in the 1980s: Transforming Tokyo into a world city'. *International Journal of Urban and Regional Research, 16*, 114–128.

MacKenzie, D. (2008). An Engine, Not a Camera: How Financial Models Shape Markets. Boston, MIT Press.

McKittrick, K. (2011). 'On plantations, prisons, and a black sense of place'. *Journal of Social and Cultural Geography, 12* (8), 947–963.

McKittrick, K. (2013). '"Plantation Futures," *Small Axe:'. A Caribbean Platform for Criticism, 17 42* (3), 1–15.

McKittrick, K. (2016). 'Diachronic loops/deadweight tonnage/bad made measure'. *Cultural Geographies, 23* (1), 3–18.

McKittrick, K. (2021). Dear Science and Other Stories. Duke University Press.

McMahon, M. (2011). 'Difference, repetition'. In: Deleuze: Key Concepts (ed. C. J. Stivale), 44–54. London, Routledge.

McMichael, P. (1990). 'Incorporating comparison within a world-historical perspective: An alternative comparative method'. *American Sociological Review, 55* (3), 385–397.

McNeill, D. (2002). 'The mayor and the world city skyline: London's tall buildings debate'. *International Planning Studies, 7* (4), 325–334.

McNeill, D. (2009). The Global Architect: Firms, Fame and Urban Form. London, Routledge.

McNeill, D., Dowling, R., and Fagan, B. (2005). 'Sydney/Global/City: An Exploration'. *International Journal of Urban and Regional Research, 29* (4), 935–944.

Madden, D. (2018). 'Pushed off the map: toponymy and the politics of place in New York City'. *Urban Studies, 55* (8), 1599–1614.

Mains, D. (2007). 'Neoliberal times: Progress, boredom, and shame among Young Men in Urban Ethiopia'. *American Ethnologist*, *34* (4), 659–673.

Malaquais, D. (2007). 'Douala/Johannesburg/New York: Cityscapes Imagined'. In: Cities in Contemporary Africa (eds. M.J. Murray and G.A. Myers), 31–52 London, Palgrave Macmillan.

Mama, A. (2002). Beyond the Masks: Race, Gender and Subjectivity. London, Routledge.

Manda, M.Z. (2014). 'Where there is no local government: Addressing disaster risk reduction in a small town in Malawi'. *Environment and Urbanization*, *26* (2), 586–599.

Mann, M. (2012). The Sources of Social Power: Volume 2, the Rise of Classes and Nation-States, 1760–1914. Cambridge, Cambridge University Press.

Marcus, G. (1995). 'Ethnography in/of the world system: The emergence of multi-sited ethnography'. *Annual Review of Anthropology*, *24* (1), 95–117.

Marcuse, P. and Van Kempen, R. (Eds.) (2000). Globalising Cities: A New Spatial Order? Oxford, Blackwell.

Marques, E. (Ed) (2020). The Politics and Policies of the Urban in São Paulo. Oxford, Wiley-Blackwell.

Marx, K. (1993 [1939]). Grundrisse: Foundations of the Critique of Political Economy (Rough Draft). London, Penguin Books.

Massey, D. (1982). 'Enterprise Zones: A Political Issue'. *International Journal of Urban and Regional Research*, *6* (4), 429–434.

Massey, D. (1994). Space, Place, and Gender. Minneapolis, University of Minnesota Press.

Massey, D. (2005). For Space. London, Sage.

Massey, D. (2007). World City. Cambridge, Polity.

Massey, D., Allen, J., and Pile, S. (1999). City Worlds. London, Routledge.

Maurer, B. (2005). Mutual Life, Limited: Islamic Banking, Alternative Currencies, Lateral Reason. Princeton, NJ, Princeton University Press.

Mawdsley, E. (2015). 'DFID, the private sector and the re-centring of an economic growth agenda in international development'. *Global Society*, *29*, 339–358. doi:1 0.1080/13600826.2015.1031092.

Mawdsley, E. (2013). From Recipients to Donors: The Emerging Powers and the Changing Development Landscape, Zed.

Mayor of London. (2016). The London Plan: The Spatial Strategy for London, consolidated with alterations since 2011. Greater London Authority, City Hall, The Queen's Walk, London (Accessed 17 December 2021). https://www.london.gov.uk/sites/default/files/the_london_plan_2016_jan_2017_fix.pdf.

Mbembe, A. (2001). On the Postcolony. University of California Press.

Mbembe, A. (2017). Critique of Black Reason, trans. Laurent DuBois. Durham, Duke University Press.

Mbembe, A. and Nuttall, S. (2004). 'Writing the world from an African metropolis'. *Public Culture*, *16* (3), 347–372.

Maloutas, T. (2012). 'Contextual diversity in gentrification research'. *Critical Sociology*, *38* (1), 33–48.

Mann, M. (2013). The Sources of Social Power, 2e. Vol. *1*. Cambridge, Cambridge University Press.

Martindale, D. (1958 [1921]). 'Prefatory remarks: The theory of the city'. In: The City (M. Weber, trans. D. Martindale and G. Neuwirth), 9–62. New York, The Free Press.

Mawdsley, E. (2018). '"From billions to trillions": Financing the SDGs in a world "beyond aid"'. *Dialogues in Human Geography*, *8*, 191–195.

Mendieta, E. (2011). 'Medellin and Bogotá: The global cities of the other globalization'. *City*, *15* (2), 167–180.

Mercer, C. (2017). 'Landscapes of extended ruralisation: Postcolonial suburbs of Dar Es Salaam in Tanzania'. *Transactions of the Institute of British Geographers*, *42* (1), 72–83.

Merrifield, A. (2013). 'The urban question under planetary urbanization'. *International Journal of Urban and Regional Research*, *37*, 909–922.

Meyer, M. (2016). 'Steve jobs, terrorists, gentlemen, and punks: Tracing strange comparisons of Biohackers'. In: Practising Comparison: Logics, Relations, Collaborations (eds. J. Deville, M. Guggenheim and S. Hrdličková), 281–305. Manchester, Mattering Press.

Mignolo, W. (2013). 'On comparison: Who is comparing what and why?'. In: Comparison: Theories, Approaches, Uses (eds. R. Felski and S. Stanford Friedman), 99–119. Baltimore, Johns Hopkins University Press.

Mignolo, W. and Walsh, C. (2018). On Decoloniality: Concepts, Analytics, Praxis. Durham, NC, Duke University Press.

Minton, A. (2017). Big Capital: Who's London For? London, Penguin.

Minton, A. and Watt, P. (2016). 'London's housing crisis and its activisms'. *City*, *20* (2), 204–221.

Miraftab, F. (2009). 'Insurgent planning: situating radical planning in the Global South'. *Planning Theory*, *8* (1), 32–50.

Mitchell, J.C. (1968). 'Theoretical orientations in African Urban Studies'. In: The Social Anthropology of Complex Societies (ed. M. Banton), 37–68. London, Tavistock Publications.

Mitchell, J.C. (1987). Cities, Society, and Social Perception. A Central African Perspective. Oxford, Clarendon Press.

Mitlin, D. and Satterthwaite, D. (eds.) (2013). Urban Poverty in the Global South: Scale and Nature. London, Routledge.

Molotch, H. (1976). 'The city as a growth machine: Toward a political economy of place'. *American Journal of Sociology*, *82* (2), 309–332. Sep., 1976.

Molotch, H. and Vicari, S. (1988). 'Three ways to build: The development process in the United States, Japan, and Italy'. *Urban Affairs Quarterly*, *24* (2), 188–214.

Montag, W. (1998). 'Althusser's nominalism: Structure and singularity'. *Rethinking Marxism*, *10* (3), 64–73.

Monte-Mòr, R.L. (2014a). 'Extended urbanization and settlement patterns in Brazil: An environmental approach'. In: Implosions/Explosions (ed. N. Brenner), 109–120. Berlin, Jovis.

Monte-Mòr, R.L. (2014b). 'What is the urban in the contemporary world?'. In: Implosions/Explosions (ed. N. Brenner), 260–267. Berlin, Jovis.

Moodley, S. (2019). 'Defining city-to-city learning in southern Africa: Exploring practitioner sensitivities in the knowledge transfer process'. *Habitat International*, *85*, 34–40.

Morange, M., Folio, F., Peuroux, E., and Vivet, J. (2012). 'The spread of a transnational model: "Gated Communities" in Three Southern African Cities (Cape Town, Maputo and Windhoek)'. *International Journal of Urban and Regional Research*, *36*, 890–914.

Morange, M. and Spire, A. (2019). 'The right to the city in the Global South. Perspectives from Africa'. *Cybergeo: European Journal of Geography [En Ligne]*. Espace, Société, Territoire, document 895, consulted 15 mai 2021. http://journals.openedition.org/cybergeo/32217.

Moreno, L. and Shin, H.B. (2018). 'Introduction: The urban process under planetary accumulation by dispossession'. *City*, *22* (1), 78–87.

Mosselson, A. (2016). '"Joburg has its own momentum": Towards a vernacular theorisation of urban change'. *Urban Studies*, *54* (5), 1280–1296.

Moten, F. (2018). The Universal Machine. Duke University Press.

Moulaert, F., Rodriguez, A., and Swyngedouw, E. (2003). The Globalized City: Economic Restructuring and Social Polarization in European Cities. Oxford, Oxford University Press.

Mufti, A.R. (2005). 'Global comparativism'. *Critical Inquiry*, *31* (Winter), 472–489.

Müller, M. (2020). 'In search of the global east: Thinking between North and South'. *Geopolitics*, *25* (3), 734–755.

Müller, M. and Trubina, E. (2020). 'The Global Easts in global urbanism: views from beyond North and South.' *Eurasian Geography and Economics*, *61* (6), 627–635.

Murray, M.J. (2015). 'Waterfall city (Johannesburg): Privatized urbanism in extremis'. *Environment and Planning A*, *47* (3), 503–520.

Murray, M. (2017). The Urbanism of Exception: The Dynamics of Global City Building in the Twenty-First Century. Cambridge, Cambridge University Press.

Murray, P. and Szelenyi, I. (1984). 'The city in the transition to socialism'. *International Journal of Urban and Regional Research*, *8*, 90–107.

Mwathunga, E. (2012). 'Informal settlements: A product of deficient formal land management policies'. In: Small Town Geographies in Africa: Experiences from South Africa and Elsewhere (eds. R. Donaldson and L. Marais), 433–450. New York, Nova Science Publishers.

Mwathunga, E., 2014. Contesting space in urban Malawi: A Lefebvrian analysis. Dissertation presented for the degree of Doctor of Philosophy in the Faculty of Arts and Social Sciences at Stellenbosch University, South Africa.

Mwathunga, E. (forthcoming) Perceived spaces and spatial practices in the production of urban space in Lilongwe city, Malawi. Manuscript available from the author.

Mwathunga, E. and Donaldson, R. (2018). 'Urban land contestations, challenges and planning strategies in Malawi's main urban centres'. *Land Use Policy*, *77*, 1–8.

Myers, G. (2003). Verandahs of Power: Colonialism and Space in Urban Africa. Syracuse, Syracuse University Press.

Myers, G. (2005). Disposable Cities: Garbage, Governance and Sustainable Development in Urban Africa. Aldershot, Ashgate.

Myers, G. (2008). 'Peri-urban land reform, political-economic reform, and urban political ecology in Zanzibar'. *Urban Geography*, *29* (3), 264–288.

Myers, G. (2011). African Cities: Alternative Visions of Urban Theory and Practice. London, Zed Books.

Myers, G. (2014). 'From expected to unexpected comparison: Changing the flows of ideas about cities in a post-colonial urban world". *Singapore Journal of Tropical Geography*, *35* (1), 104–118.

Myers, G. (2018). 'The African problem of global urban theory: Re-conceptualising planetary urbanisation'. *International Development Policy (Revue Internationale De Politique De Developpement)*, *10*, 231–253.

Myers, G. (2020). Rethinking Urbanism: Lessons from Postcolonialism and the Global South. Bristol, Policy Press.

Ndjio, B. (2009). '"Shanghai Beauties" and African Desires: Migration, trade and Chinese prostitution in Cameroon'. *European Journal of Development Research*, *21* (4), 606–621.

Ndjio, B. (2017). 'Sex and the transnational city: Chinese sex workers in the West African city of Douala'. *Urban Studies*, *54* (4), 999–1015.

Neves Alves, S. (2021). 'Everyday states and water infrastructure: Insights from a small secondary city in Africa, Bafatá in Guinea-Bissau'. *Environment and Planning C: Politics and Space*, *39* (2), 247–264.

Newman, P. and Thornley, A. (2005). Planning World Cities: Globalization and Urban Politics. Basingstoke and New York, Palgrave MacMillan.

Nhuân, N. (1984). 'Do the urban and regional management policies of socialist Vietnam reflect the patterns of the ancient Mandarin bureaucracy?'. *International Journal of Urban and Regional Research*, *8*, 73–89.

Nielsen, M. (2011). 'Inverse governmentality. The paradoxical production of peri-urban planning in Maputo, Mozambique'. *Critique of Anthropology*, *31*, 329–358.

Nijman, J. (2007a). 'Introduction: Comparative Urbanism'. *Urban Geography*, *28*, 1–6.

Nijman, J. (2007b). 'Place-particularity and "deep analogies": A comparative essay on Miami's rise as a world city'. *Urban Geography*, *28* (1), 92–107.

Niranjana, R. (2022). 'An experiment with the minor geographies of major cities: infrastructural relations among the fragments'. *Urban Studies* (in press).

Nyamnjoh, F.B. (2017). 'Incompleteness: Frontier Africa and the currency of conviviality'. *Journal of Asian and African Studies*, *52* (3), 253–270.

Ogata, S. (2007). Africa Remix at the Mori Art Museum, in Eastern Art Report, No. 53, pgs 21–25. (Accessed 10 December 2020). http://easternartreport.net/wp-content/uploads/2014/01/EAR53_AfricaRemix.pdf.

Oldfield, S. (2014). 'Between activism and the academy: The urban as a political terrain'. *Urban Studies*, *52* (11), 2872–2086.

Oldfield, S. (2022). High Stakes and High Hopes. Forthcoming, Georgia University Press.

Olds, K. (2001). Globalization and Urban Change: Capital, Labour and Pacific Rim Mega-Projects. Oxford, Oxford University Press.

Olds, K. and Yeung, H.W. (2004). 'Pathways to global city formation: A view from the developmental city-state of Singapore'. *Review of International Political Economy*, *11* (3), 489–521.

Ong, A. (2006). Neoliberalism as Exception: Mutations in Citizenship and Sovereignty. Durham, Duke University Press.

Ong, A. (2007). 'Neoliberalism as a mobile technology'. *Transactions of the Institute of British Geographers*, *32* (1), 3–8.

Ong, A. (2011a). 'Hyperbuilding: Spectacle, speculation, and the hyperspace of sovereignty'. In: Worlding Cities: Asian Experiments and the Art of Being Global (eds. A. Roy and A. Ong). Oxford, UK, Wiley-Blackwell.

Ong, A. (2011b). 'Worlding cities, or the art of being global'. In: Worlding Cities: Asian Experiments and the Arts of Being Global (eds. A. Roy and A. Ong), 1–26. Chichester, Wiley-Blackwell.

Ong, A. and Roy, A. (2011). Worlding Cities. Oxford, Wiley-Blackwell.

Oosterlynck, S., Bassens, D., Beeckmans, L., DeRudder, B., Braeckmans, L., and Segaert, B. (eds The City as a Global Actor. London, Routledge.

Ó Riain, S. (2009). 'Extending the ethnographic case study'. In: Handbook of Case-Based Methods (D. Byrne and C. Ragin). London, Sage.

Ortega, A.A.C. (2020). 'Desakota 2.0: Worlding hybrid spaces in the global urban'. *Urban Geography*, *41* (5), 668–681.

Osborne, P. (2004). 'The reproach of abstraction'. *Radical Philosophy*, 21–28.

Oswin, N. (2020). 'An other geography.' *Dialogues in Human Geography*, *10* (1), 9–18.

Ouředníček, M. (2016). 'The relevance of "Western" theoretical concepts for investigations of the margins of post-socialist cities: The case of Prague'. *Eurasian Geography and Economics*, *57* (4-5), 545–564.

Owusu, G. (2010). 'The operation of traditional landholding institutions in Sub-Saharan Africa: A case study of Ghana'. *Journal of International Real Estate and Construction Studies*, *1* (2), 201–203.

Owusu, G. and Oteng-Ababio, M. (2015). 'Moving unruly contemporary urbanism toward sustainable urban development in Ghana by 2030'. *American Behavioural Scientists*, *59* (3), 311–327.

Pahl, R. (1968). Readings in Urban Sociology. London, Pergamon Press.

Paige, J. (1999). 'Conjuncture, comparison, and conditional theory in macrosocial inquiry'. *American Journal of Sociology*, *105* (3), 781–800.

Painter, J. and Goodwin, M. (1995). 'Local governance and concrete research: Investigating the uneven development of regulation'. *Economy and Society*, *24* (3), 334–356.

Palmer, I., Moodley, N., and Parnell, S. (2018). Building a Capable State: Service Delivery in Post-apartheid South Africa. London, Zed Press.

Park, B., Hill, R.C., and Saito, A. (2011). Locating Neoliberalism in East Asia. Oxford, Blackwells.

Park, R.E. (1952 [1914]). Human Communities: The City and Human Ecology. New York, The Free Press.

Parnell, S. (1997). 'South African cities: Perspectives from the ivory towers of urban studies'. *Urban Studies*, *34*, 891–906.

Parnell, S. (2007). 'Urban governance in the South: The politics of rights and development'". In: A Handbook of Political Geography (eds. K. Cox, M. Low and J. Robinson), 595–608. London, Sage.

Parnell, S. (2016). 'Defining a global urban development agenda'. *World Development*, 78, 529–554.

Parnell, S., Crankshaw, O., and Acuto, M. (2017). '2030 endorsements by the United Nations of a sustainable urban future: Implications for research'. *Urban Studies*, in press.

Parnell, S. and Oldfield, S. (eds) (2014). Handbook for Cities of the Global South. London, Routledge.

Parnell, S. and Pieterse, E. (2010). 'The "Right to the City": Institutional imperatives and the developmental state'. *International Journal of Urban and Regional Research*, 34 (1), 146–12.

Parnell, S. and Pieterse, E. (eds) (2014). Africa's Urban Revolution. London and New York, Zed Books.

Parnell, S. and Pieterse, E. (2016). 'Translational global praxis: Rethinking methods and modes of African urban research'. *International Journal of Urban and Regional Research*, 40 (1), 236–246.

Parnell, S., Pieterse, E., and Watson, V. (2009). 'Planning for cities in the global South: An African research agenda for sustainable human settlements'. *Progress in Planning*, 72, 233–240.

Parnell, S. and Robinson, J. (2006). 'Development and urban policy: Johannesburg's city development strategy'. *Urban Studies*, 43 (2), 337–355.

Parnell, S. and Robinson, J. (2012). '(Re)theorising cities from the global south: Looking beyond neoliberalism'. *Urban Geography*, 33 (4), 593–617.

Parnell, S. and Robinson, J. (2017). 'The global urban: Difference and complexity in urban studies and the science of cities'. In: Sage Handbook of the 21st Century City (eds. S. Hall and R. Burdett), 13–31. London, Routledge.

Patel, S., Baptist, C., and D'Cruz, C. (2012). 'Knowledge is power – Informal communities assert their right to the city through SDI and community-led enumerations'. *Environment and Urbanization*, 24 (1), 13–26.

Peake, L. (2016). 'The twenty-first century quest for feminism and the global urban'. *International Journal of Urban and Regional Research*, 40 (1), 219–227.

Peake, L. and Reiker, M. (eds) (2013). Rethinking Feminist Interventions into the Urban. London, Routledge.

Peake, L., Koleth, E., Tanyildiz, G.S., Reddy, R.N., and Patrick, D. (2021). A Feminist Urban Theory for Our Time: Rethinking Social Reproduction and the Urban. Blackwell, Oxford.

Peck, J. (2004). 'Geography and public policy: Constructions of neoliberalism'. *Progress in Human Geography*, 28 (3), 392–405.

Peck, J. (2010). Constructions of Neoliberal Reason. Oxford, Oxford University Press.

Peck, J. (2013). Explaining (with) Neoliberalism, Territory, Politics, Governance, 1 (2), 132–157.

Peck, J. (2015). 'Cities beyond compare?'. *Regional Studies*, 49 (1), 183–186.

Peck, J. (2017a). 'Transatlantic city, part 1: Conjunctural urbanism'. *Urban Studies*, 54 (1), 4–30.
Peck, J. (2017b). 'Transatlantic city, part 2: Late entrepreneurialism'. *Urban Studies*, 54 (2), 327–363.
Peck, J. and Theodore, N. (2007). 'Variegated capitalism'. *Progress in Human Geography*, 31 (6), 731–772.
Peck, J. and Theodore, N. (2010a). 'Recombinant workfare, across the Americas: Transnationalizing fast social policy'. *Geoforum*, 41, 195–208.
Peck, J. and Theodore, N. (2010b). 'Mobilizing policy: Models, methods, and mutations'. *Geoforum*, 41, 169–174.
Peck, J. and Theodore, N. (2012). 'Follow the policy: A distended case approach'. *Environment and Planning A*, 44 (1), 21–30.
Peck, J. and Theodore, N. (2015). Fast Policy: Experimental Statecraft at the Thresholds of Neoliberalism. Minneapolis; London, University of Minnesota Press.
Peck, J. and Theodore, N. (2019). 'Still neoliberalism?'. *South Atlantic Quarterly*, 118 (2), 245–264.
Peck, J., Theodore, N., and Brenner, N. (2009). 'Neoliberal urbanism: Models, moments, mutations'. *SAIS Review*, XXIX (1), 49–66.
Peck, J., Theodore, N., and Brenner, N. (2010a). 'Postneoliberalism and its malcontents'. *Antipode*, 41s, 94–116.
Percival, T. and Waley, T. (2012). 'Articulating intra-Asian urbanism: The production of satellite cities in Phnom Penh'. *Urban Studies*, 49 (13), 2873–2888.
Peyroux, E. (2016). 'Circulation des politiques urbaines et internationalization des villes: La stratégie des relations internationales de Johannesburg'. *EchoGéo*, 36. URL: http://echogeo.revues.org/14642.
Peyroux, E. (2018). 'Building city political agency across scales: The Johannesburg international relations strategy'. In: The City as Global Political Actor (eds. S. Oosterlynck, L. Beeckmans, D. Bassens, B. Derudder, B. Segaert and L. Braeckmans). London, Routledge.
Phelps, N. (ed.) (2017). Old Europe, New Suburbanization? Governance, Land and Infrastructure in European Suburbanization. Toronto, University of Toronto Press.
Phelps, N., Mace, A., and Rodieri, R. (2017). 'City of villages? Stasis and change in London's suburbs'. In: Old Europe, New Suburbanization? Governance, Land and Infrastructure in European Suburbanization (ed. N.A. Phelps), 183–206. Toronto, University of Toronto Press.
Phelps, N. and Wu, F. (2011). International Perspectives on Suburbanization: A Post-Suburban World? London, Palgrave-Macmillan.
Pickles, J. (2012). 'The cultural turn and the conjunctural economy: Economic geography, anthropology, and cultural studies'. In: The Wiley-Blackwell Companion to Economic Geography (eds. T. Barnes, J. Peck and E. Sheppard), 537–551. Oxford, Wiley-Blackwell.
Pickvance, C. (1985). 'The rise and fall of urban movements and the role of comparative analysis'. *Environment and Planning D: Society and Space*, 3, 31–63.
Pickvance, C. (1986). 'Comparative urban analysis and assumptions about causality'. *International Journal of Urban and Regional Research*, 10 (2), 162–184.

Pierre, J. (1999). 'Models of urban governance: The institutional dimension of urban politics'. *Urban Affairs Review*, *34* (3), 372–396.

Pierre, J. (2005). 'Comparative urban governance: Uncovering complex causalities'. *Urban Affairs Review*, *40* (4), 446–462.

Pieterse, E. (2008). City Futures: Confronting the Crisis of Urban Development. London, Zed Books.

Pieterse, E. 2013. *Epistemic practices of Southern Urbanism* International Journal of Urban and Regional Research lecture, Annual Conference of the Association of American Geographers, April 2013. Webcast at. (last accessed 23 June 2013) http://www.ijurr.org/details/lecture/4803221/2013-IJURR-Lecture-Epistemic-Practices-of-Southern-Urbanism.html

Pieterse, E., Parnell, S., and Haysom., G. (2018). 'African dreams: Locating urban infrastructure in the 2030 sustainable developmental agenda'. *Area Development and Policy*, *3* (2), 149–169.

Pieterse, E. and Simone, M. (2013). Rogue Urbanism: Emergent African Cities. Johannesburg, Jacana Press.

Pinson, G. (2009). Gouverner La Ville Par Projet: Urbanisme Et Gouvernance Des Villes Européenes. Paris, Presses de la foundation national des sciences politiques.

Pomeranz, K. (2000). The Great Divergence: China, Europe, and the Making of the Modern World Economy. Princeton, Princeton University Press.

Ponder, C.S. and Webber, S. (2019). 'Visualizing liquid cities: on Matthew Gandy's Fabric of Space: Water'. In: Urban studies Inside/Out: Theory, Practice and Method (eds. H. Leitner, J. Peck, and E. Sheppard), 186–195. London and New York: Sage.

Porter, L. and Yiftachel, O. (2018). 'Urbanizing settler-colonial studies: Introduction to the special issue'. *Settler Colonial Studies*, *9* (2), 177–186.

Portes, A. (2017). 'Reflections on a common theme: Establishing the phenomenon, adumbration, and ideal types'. In: Merton: Sociology of Science and Sociology as Science (ed. K. Robert), 32–53. New York, Columbia University.

Portes, A. and Martinez, B. (2019). Latin American Cities: Their Evolution under Neoliberalism and Beyond. Typescript, University of Miami.

Porto D'Oliviera, O. (2017). International Policy Diffusion and Participatory Budgeting: Ambassadors of Participation, International Institutions and Transnational Networks. London, Palgrave Macmillan.

Potts, D. (2010). Circular Migration in Zimbabwe and Contemporary sub-Saharan Africa. Oxford, James Currey.

Potts, D. (2012a). 'Whatever happened to Africa's rapid urbanization?'. *World Economics*, *13* (2), 17–29.

Potts, D. (2012b). 'Challenging the myths of urban dynamics in sub-Saharan Africa: The evidence from Nigeria'. *World Development*, *40* (7), 1382–1393.

Potts, D. (2020). Broken Cities: Inside the Global Housing Crisis. London, Zed Books.

Poulantzas, N. (1978). State, Power, Socialism. London, Verso.

Povinelli, E. (2001). 'Radical worlds: The anthropology of incommensurability and inconceivability'. *Annual Review of Anthropology*, *30*, 319–334.

Pow, C.-P. (2012). 'China exceptionalism? Unbounding narratives on urban China'. In: Urban Theory beyond the West: A World of Cities (eds. T. Edensor and M. Jayne), 47–64. Abingdon and New York, Routledge.

Préteceille, E. (2007). 'Is Gentrification a Useful Paradigm to Analyse Social Changes in the Paris Metropolis?' *Environment and Planning A: Economy and Space, 39* (1), 10-31.

Primorac, R. (ed.) (2010). African City Textualities. Routledge.

Prince, R. (2012). 'Policy transfer, consultants and the geographies of governance'. *Progress in Human Geography, 36,* 188–203.

Quayson, A. (2014). Oxford Street, Accra: City Life and the Itineraries of the Transnational. Durham and London, Duke University Press.

Raco, M. (2005). 'A step change or a step back? The Thames gateway and the re-birth of the urban development corporations'. *Local Economy, 20* (2), 141–153.

Raco, M. (2014). 'The post-politics of sustainability planning: Privatisation and the demise of democratic government'. In: The Post-Political and Its Discontents: Spaces of Depoliticisation, Spectres of Radical Politics (eds. J. Wilson and E. Swyngedouw), 25–47. Edinburgh, Edinburgh University Press.

Raco, M., Parker, G., and Doak, J. (2006). 'Reshaping spaces of local governance? Community strategies and the modernisation of local government in England'. *Environment and Planning C: Government and Policy, 24,* 475–496.

Ragin, C. (1981). 'Comparative sociology and the comparative method'. *International Journal of Comparative Sociology, 22* (1–2), 102–120.

Ragin, C. (2000). Fuzzy-Set Social Science. Chicago, Chicago University Press.

Ragin, C. (2005). 'Core versus tangential assumptions in comparative research'. *Studies in Comparative International Development, 40* (1), 33–38.

Ragin, C. (2006). 'How to lure analytical social science out of the doldrums: Some lessons from comparative research'. *International Sociology, 21* (5), 633–646.

Rancière, J. (1999). Disagreement: Politics and Philosophy. Minneapolis, University of Minnesota Press.

Rapoport, E. (2014). 'Utopian visions and real estate dreams: The eco- city past, present and future'. *Geography Compass, 8* (2), 137–149.

Rapoport, E. and Hult, A. (2017). 'The travelling business of sustainable urbanism: International consultants as norm-setters'. *Environment and Planning A, 49* (8), 1779–1796.

Reintges, C.M. (1990). 'Urban movements in South African black townships: A case study'. *International Journal of Urban and Regional Research, 14,* 109–134.

Ren, J. (2015). 'Gentrification in China?'. In: Global Gentrifications: Uneven Development and Displacement (eds. L. Lees, H. Shin and E. López-Morales), 329–348. Bristol, Policy Press.

Ren, J. (2020). Engaging Comparative Urbanism: Art Spaces in Beijing and Berlin. Bristol, Bristol University Press.

Revi, A., Jana, A., Malladi, T., Anand, G., Anand, S., Bazaz, A. et al. (2015). Urban India 2015: Evidence. Bangalore, Indian Institute for Human Settlements.

Rivera Cusicanqui, S. (2012). '*Ch'ixinakax utxiwa*: A reflection on the practices and discourses of decolonization'. *South Atlantic Quarterly, 111* (1), 95–109.

Robinson, J. (2002). 'Global and world cities: A view from off the map'. *International Journal of Urban and Regional Research, 26* (3), 531–554.

Robinson, J. (2006). Ordinary Cities: Between Modernity and Development. London, Routledge.

Robinson, J. (2007). 'Development and new forms of democracy in Durban'. *Urban Forum, 18*, 265–287.

Robinson, J. (2008). 'Developing ordinary cities: City visioning processes in Durban and Johannesburg'. *Environment and Planning A, 40*, 74–87.

Robinson, J. (2011a). 'Cities in a world of cities: The comparative gesture'. *International Journal of Urban and Regional Research, 35* (1), 1–23.

Robinson, J. (2011b). 'The spaces of circulating knowledge: City strategies and global urban governmentality'. In: Mobile Urbanism: Cities and Policymaking in the Global Age (eds. E. McCann and K. Ward), 15–40. Minneapolis, University of Minnesota Press.

Robinson, J. (2011c). 'The travels of urban neoliberalism: Taking stock of the internationalization of urban theory'. *Urban Geography, 32* (8), 1087–1109.

Robinson, J. (2011d). 'Comparisons: Colonial or cosmopolitan?'. *Singapore Journal of Tropical Geography, 32* (2), 125–140.

Robinson, J. (2013a). 'The urban now: Theorising cities beyond the new'. *European Journal of Cultural Studies, 16* (6), 659–677.

Robinson, J. (2013b). '"Arriving at" urban policies/the urban: Traces of elsewhere in making city futures'. In: Critical Mobilities (ed. O. Söderström et al.). Lausanne and London, EPFL and Routledge.

Robinson, J. (2014a). 'New geographies of theorising the urban: Putting comparison to work for global urban studies'. In: Handbook for Cities of the Global South (eds. S. Parnell and S. Oldfield). London, Routledge.

Robinson, J. (2014b). 'Introduction: Comparative urbanism. Virtual issue on comparative urbanism'. *International Journal of Urban and Regional Research.* https://www.ijurr.org/wp-content/uploads/2016/04/Comparative-Urbanism-JR-Intro.pdf

Robinson, J. (2016a). 'Thinking cities through elsewhere: Comparative tactics for a more global urban studies'. *Progress in Human Geography, 40* (1), 3–29.

Robinson, J. (2016b). 'Comparative Urbanism: New Geographies and cultures of theorising the urban'. In: Global Urbanisms and the Nature of Urban Theory (eds. J. Robinson and A. Roy). *International Journal of Urban and Regional Research* Debates and Developments Symposium, 41, 1: 187–199.

Robinson, J. (2016c). 'Comparison'. In: Urban Theory (eds. M. Jayne and K. Ward), 84–98. London, Routledge.

Robinson, J. (2016d). '"Arriving at" urban policies: The topological spaces of urban policy mobility'. *International Journal of Urban and Regional Research, 39* (4), 831–834.

Robinson, J. (2016e). 'Starting from anywhere, making connections: Globalizing urban theory'. *Eurasian Geography and Economics, 57* (4–5), 643–657.

Robinson, J. (2016f). 'Theorizing the global urban with "global and world cities research": Beyond cities and synechdoche'. *Dialogues in Human Geography, 6* (3), 268–272.

Robinson, J. (2018a). 'The politics of the (global) urban: City strategies as repeated instances'. In: The City as a Global Actor (eds. S. Oosterlynck, D. Bassens, L. Beeckmans, B. DeRudder, L. Braeckmans and B. Segaert), 100–131. London, Routledge.

Robinson, J. (2018b). 'Policy mobilities as comparison: Urbanization processes, repeated instances, topologies'. *Revista De Administração Pública*, *52* (2), 221–243. doi: 10.1590/0034-761220180126.

Robinson, J. (2021). 'New territories of urban politics'. In: Spatial Transformations (eds. A. Million, C. Haid, I. Castillo Ulloa, and N. Baur), 269–284. London, Routledge.

Robinson, J. and Attuyer, K. (2020). 'Contesting density: beyond nimby-ism and usual suspects in governing the future city'. *Urban Geography*, *41* (10), 1294–1301.

Robinson, J. and Attuyer, K. (2021). 'Extracting value, London style: Revisiting the role of the state in urban development'. *International Journal of Urban and Regional Research*, *45* (2), 303–331.

Robinson, J. and Boldogh, C. (1994). 'Operation Jumpstart: an urban growth initiative in the Durban functional region'. In: Urban Development Planning: Lessons for the Economic Reconstruction of South Africa's Cities (ed. R. Tomlinson), 191–214. London, Routledge.

Robinson, J., Harrison, P., Shen, J., and Wu, F. (2020). 'Financing urban development, three business models: Johannesburg, Shanghai and London'. *Progress in Planning*, *154*. doi: 10.1016/j.progress.2020.100513.

Robinson, J. and Parnell, S. (2010). 'Travelling theory: Embracing post-neoliberalism through Southern Cities'. In: New Blackwell Companion to The City (eds. G. Bridge and S. Watson), 521–531. Oxford, Blackwell.

Robinson, J. and Roy, A. (2016). 'Introduction: Debate on Global urbanisms and the nature of urban theory'. In: International Journal of Urban and Regional Research Debates and Developments Symposium (eds. J. Robinson and A. Roy), *40* (1), 181–186.

Robinson, J., Scott, A., and Taylor, P. (2016). Working/Housing//Urbanising. Berlin, Springer Press. Invited publication for International Year of Global Understanding (International Geographical Union) series.

Rodriguez-Posé, A., Tomaney, J., and Klink, J. (2001). 'Local empowerment through economic restructuring in Brazil: The case of the greater ABC region'. *Geoforum*, *32*, 459–469.

Rogers, D. (2010). 'Postsocialisms unbound: Connections, critiques, comparisons'. *Slavic Review*, *69*, 1–15.

Rogerson, C.M. and Rogerson, J.M. (1999). 'Industrial change in a developing metropolis: The Witwatersrand 1980-1994'. *Geoforum*, *30*, 85–99.

Rolnik, R. (2019). Urban Warfare: Housing under the Empire of Finance. London: Verso.

Rose, N. (2001). The Politics of Life Itself: Biomedicine, Power, and Subjectivity in the Twenty-First Century. Princeton University Press.

Rose-Redwood, R., Kitchin, R., Rickards, L., Rossi, U., Datta, A., and Crampton, J. (2018). 'The possibilities and limits to dialogue'. *Dialogues in Human Geography*, *8* (2), 109–123.

Ross, K. (1996). Fast Cars, Clean Bodies: Decolonization and the Reordering of French Culture. Boston, MIT Press.

Rouanet, H. and Halbert, L. (2016). 'Leveraging finance capital: Urban change and self-empowerment of real estate developers in India'. *Urban Studies*, *53* (7), 1401–1423.

Roy, A. (2003). 'Paradigms of propertied citizenship: Transnational techniques of analysis'. *Urban Affairs Review, 38,* 463–490.
Roy, A. (2005). 'Urban informality: Toward an epistemology of planning'. *Journal of the American Planning Association, 71* (2), 147–158.
Roy, A. (2009a). 'The 21st century metropolis: New geographies of theory'. *Regional Studies, 43* (6), 819–830.
Roy, A. (2009b). 'Why India cannot plan its cities: Informality, insurgence and the idiom of urbanization'. *Planning Theory, 8* (1), 76–87.
Roy, A. (2011a). 'Conclusion: Postcolonial urbanism: Speed, hysteria, mass dreams'. In: Worlding Cities (A. Roy and A. Ong). Oxford, Wiley-Blackwell.
Roy, A. (2011b). 'Slumdog cities: Rethinking subaltern urbanism'. *International Journal of Urban and Regional Research, 35,* 223–238.
Roy, A. and AlSayyad, N. (Eds.) (2004). Urban Informality: Transnational Perspectives from the Middle East, Latin America and South Asia. Maryland USA, Lexington Books.
Roy, A. (2016). 'What is urban about critical urban theory?'. *Urban Geography, 37* (6), 810–823.
Roy, A. and Ong, A. (eds) (2011). Worlding Cities: Asian Experiments and the Art of Being Global. Oxford, Wiley-Blackwell.
Ruddick, S., Peake, L., Tanyildiz, G.S., and Patrick, D. (2018). 'Planetary urbanization: An urban theory for our time?'. *Environment and Planning D: Society and Space, 36* (3), 387–404.
Rusca, M. and Schwartz, K. (2012). 'Divergent sources of legitimacy: A case study of international NGOs in the water services sector in Lilongwe and Maputo'. *Journal of Southern African Studies, 38* (3), 681–697.
Salskov-Iversen, D., Hansen, H.K., and Bislev, S. (2000). 'Governmentality, globalization and local practice: Transformations of a hegemonic discourse'. *Alternatives: Global, Local, Political, 25* (2), 183–223.
Sanchez Jimenez, A.A. (2017). *Urban crises across the North-South divide: A comparative study of institutional transformations and urban policy responses in Valencia and Mar del Plata.* Doctoral thesis (Ph.D.), UCL (University College London).
Santos, M. (1979). The Shared Space: The Two Circuits of the Urban Economy in Underdeveloped Countries. London, Methuen.
Santos, M. (2021). The Nature of Space. Durham: Duke University Press.
Saunders, P. (1986). Social Theory and the Urban Question, 2e. London, Hutchinson.
Savini, F., Majoor, S.J.H., and Salet, W.G.M. (2015). 'Urban peripheries, reflecting on politics and projects in Amsterdam, Milan and Paris'. *Environment and Planning C: Government and Policy, 33* (3), 457–474.
Sassen, S. (1991). The Global City: New York, London, Tokyo. Princeton, N.J, Princeton University Press.
Sassen, S. (1994). Cities in a World Economy. Thousand Oaks, Calif, Pine Forge Press.
Sassen, S. (2001). 'Global cities and global city-regions: A comparison'. In: Global City-Regions: Trends, Theory, Policy (ed. A. Scott), 78–95. Oxford, OUP.

Sassen, S. (ed.) (2002). Global Networks, Linked Cities. London, Routledge.
Satterthwaite, D. (2007). The Transition to a Predominantly Urban World and Its Underpinnings, Human Settlements Discussion Paper Series, Urban Change - 4. London, IIED.
Satterthwaite, D. (2016). 'A new urban agenda?'. *Environment and Urbanization*, 28 (1), 3–12.
Saunier, P.-Y. (2002). 'Taking up the bet on connections: A municipal contribution'. *Contemporary European History*, 11 (4), 507–527.
Savitch, H. and Kantor, P. (2004). Cities in the International Marketplace: The Political Economy of Urban Development in North America and Western Europe. Princeton, Princeton University Press.
Sawyer, L. (2014). 'Piecemeal urbanisation at the peripheries of Lagos'. *African Studies Quarterly*, 73 (2), 271–289.
Sawyer, L., Schmid, C., Streule, M., and Kallenberger, P. (2021). 'Bypass urbanism: Re-ordering center-periphery relations in Kolkata, Lagos and Mexico City'. *Environment and Planning A: Economy and Space*, 53 (4), 675–703.
Sayın, Ö., Hoyler, M., and Harrison, J. (2020). 'Doing comparative urbanism differently: Conjunctural cities and the stress-testing of urban theory'. *Urban Studies*, 59 (2), 263–280.
Scheffer, T. and Niewöhner, J. (2010). Thick Comparison: Reviving the Ethnographic Aspiration. Leiden, Brill Academic Publishers.
Schiffer, J. (1983). 'Urban enterprise zones: A comment on the Hong Kong Model'. *International Journal of Urban and Regional Research*, 7, 429–438.
Schindler, S. (2013). 'Understanding urban processes in Flint, Michigan: Approaching "subaltern urbanism" inductively'. *International Journal of Urban and Regional Research*, 38 (3), 791–804.
Schindler, S. (2017). 'Towards a paradigm of Southern urbanism'. *City*, 21, 47–64.
Schindler, S. and Kanai, M.J. (2021). 'Getting the territory right: Infrastructure-led development and the re-emergence of spatial planning strategies'. *Regional Studies*, 55 (1), 40–51.
Schmid, C. (2005). 'Theory'. In: Switzerland: An Urban Portrait (R. Diener, J. Herzog, M. Meili, P. De Meuron and C. Schmid), 163–223. Basel, Birkhauser.
Schmid, C. (2008). 'Henri Lefebvre's theory of the production of space: Towards a three-dimensional dialectic'. In: Space, Difference, Everyday Life: Reading Henri Lefebvre (eds. K. Goonewardena, S. Kipfer, R. Milgrom and C. Schmid), 27–45. London, Routledge.
Schmid, C. (2011). 'Henri Lefebvre, the right to the city and the new metropolitan mainstream'. In: Cities for People, Not for Profit (eds. N. Brenner, P. Marcuse and M. Mayer), 42–62. London, Routledge.
Schmid, C. (2014a). 'Patterns and pathways of global urbanization: Towards comparative analysis'. In: Implosions/Explosions (ed. Brenner), 203–217. Berlin, Jovis.
Schmid, C. (2014b). 'A typology of urban Switzerland'. In: Implosions/Explosions (ed. N. Brenner), 398–427. Berlin, Jovis.

Schmid, C. (2015). 'Specificity and urbanization: A theoretical outlook'. In: The Inevitable Specificity of Cities (eds. C. Diener, J. Herzog, M. Meili, P. De Meuron, M. Herz, C. Schmid and M. Topalovic), 287–307. Zurich, Lars Müller Publishers.

Schmid, C. (2022 [2005]). Henri Lefebvre and the Theory of the Production of Space [translation of Stadt, Raum, und Gesellschaft]. London, Verso.

Schmid, C., Karaman, O., Hanakata, N., Kallenberger, P., Kockelkorn, A., Sawyer, L., Streule, M., and Wong, K.P. (2018). 'Towards New Vocabularies of Urbanization Processes: A comparative approach'. *Urban Studies*, *55* (1), 19–52.

Schilling, H., Blokland, T., and Simone, A. (2019). 'Working precarity: Urban youth tactics to make livelihoods in instable conditions in Abidjan, Athens, Berlin and Jakarta'. *The Sociological Review*, *67* (6), 1333–1349.

Schindler, S. (2013b). 'Understanding urban processes in Flint, Michigan: Approaching "Subaltern Urbanism" inductively'. *International Journal of Urban and Regional Research*. doi: 10.1111/1468-2427.12082.

Schindler, S. (2017). 'Towards a paradigm of Southern urbanism'. *City*, *21* (1), 47–64.

Schroeder, R. (2008). 'South African capital in the land of Ujamaa: Contested terrain in Tanzania'. *African Sociological Review*, *12* (1), 20–34.

Schwirian, K.P. (ed.) (1974). Comparative Urban Structure. New York: D.C. Heath.

Scott, A.J. (ed.) (2001). Global City-Regions: Trends, Theory, Policy. Oxford, Oxford University Press.

Scott, A. and Storper, M. (2015). 'The nature of cities: The scope and limits of urban theory'. *International Journal of Urban and Regional Research*, *39* (1), 1–16.

Scott, J.C. (1972). Comparative Political Corruption. New Jersey, Prentice-Hall.

Seekings, J. (2000). A History of the United Democratic Front in South Africa 1983-1991. Cape Town, David Philip. Oxford, James Currey.

Seekings, J. (2017). 'State capacity and the construction of pro-poor welfare states in the "developing" world.' In: States in the Developing World (eds. M. Centeno, A. Kohli and D. Yashar, with D. Mistree), 363–379. Cambridge, Cambridge University Press.

Seekings, J. and Keil, R. (2009). '*The International Journal of Urban and Regional Research*: An Editorial Statement'. *International Journal of Urban and Regional Research*, *33* (1), i–x.

Seekings, J. and Nattrass, N. (2006). Class, Race and Inequality in South Africa. Pietermaritzburg: University of KwaZulu-Natal Press.

Seidman, G. (1994). Manufacturing Militance: Workers' Movements in Brazil and South Africa, 1970-1985. Berkeley, University of California Press.

Shank, S. and Nagar, R. (2013). 'Retelling stories, resisting dichotomies: Staging identity, marginalisation and activism in Minneapolis and Sitapur'. In: Rethinking Feminist Interventions into the Urban (eds. L. Peake and M. Reiker). London, Routledge.

Shatkin, G. (1998). '"Fourth world" cities in the global economy: The case of Phnom Penh'. *International Journal of Urban and Regional Research*, *22*, 378–393.

Shatkin, G. (2008). 'The city and the bottom line: Urban megaprojects and the privatization of planning in Southeast Asia'. *Environment and Planning A*, *40* (2), 383–401.

Shatkin, G. (2013). Contesting the Indian City: Global Visions and the Politics of the Local. Oxford, Wiley-Blackwell.

Shatkin, G. (2016). 'The real estate turn in policy and planning: Land monetization and the political economy of peri-urbanization in Asia'. *Cities*, *53*, 141–149.

Shatkin, G. (2017). Cities for Profit: The Real Estate Turn in Asia's Urban Politics. Ithaca, Cornell.

Shen, J., Luo, X., and Wu, F. (2020a). 'Assembling mega-urban projects through state-guided governance innovation: The development of Lingang in Shanghai'. *Regional Studies*. doi: 10.1080/00343404.2020.1762853.

Shen, J., Luo, X., and Wu, F. (2020b). 'Assembling mega-urban projects through state-guided governance innovation: The development of Lingang in Shanghai'. *Regional Studies*. doi: 10.1080/00343404.2020.1762853.

Shen, J. and Wu, F. (2017). 'The suburb as a space of capital accumulation: The development of new towns in Shanghai, China'. *Antipode*, *49* (3), 761–780.

Sheppard, E., Leitner, H., and Maringanti, A. (2013). 'Provincializing global urbanism: A manifesto'. *Urban Geography*, *34*, 893–900.

Shih, S-M. (2013). 'Comparison as relation'. In: Comparison: Theories, Approaches, Uses (eds. R. Felski and S.S. Friedman), 79–98. Baltimore, Johns Hopkins University Press.

Shin, H.B. (2016). 'Economic transition and speculative urbanisation in China: Gentrification versus dispossession'. *Urban Studies*, *53* (3), 471–489.

Shutt, J. (1984). 'Tory enterprise zones and the labour movement'. *Capital & Class*, *8* (2), 19–44.

Sidaway, J.D., Woon, C.Y., and Jacobs, J.M. (2014). 'Planetary postcolonialism'. *Singapore Journal of Tropical Geography*, *35*, 4–21.

Sieverts, T. (2015). 'On the relations of culture and suburbia: How to give meaning to the suburban landscape?'. In: Suburban Governance: A Global View (eds. P. Hamel and R. Keil), 239–250. Toronto, University of Toronto Press.

Silverman, M., Zack, T., Charlton, S., and Harrison, P. (2005). Review of Johannesburg's City Strategy: Summary of Key Innovations in Existing City Strategies and Learning from Their Implementation. Johannesburg, Central Strategy Unit. July 2005.

Simmel, G. (1971 [1903]). 'The metropolis and mental life'. In: Georg Simmel: On Individuality and Social Forms (ed. D. Levine), 324–339. Chicago, Ill., University of Chicago Press.

Simon, D., Arfvidsson, H., Anand, G., Bazaz, A., Fenna, G., Foster, K. et al. (2015). 'Developing and testing the Urban Sustainable Development Goal's targets and indicators – A five-city study'. *Environment and Urbanization*, *28*, 49–63.

Simone, A. (2001a). 'On the Worlding of African Cities'. *African Studies Review*, *44* (2), 15–41.

Simone, A. (2001b). 'Straddling the divides: Remaking associational life in the informal African City'. *International Journal of Urban and Regional Research*, *25*, 102–117.

Simone, A. (2004). For the City yet to Come: Changing African Life in Four Cities. Durham and London, Duke University Press.

Simone, A. (2010). City Life, from Dakar to Jakarta: Movements at the Crossroads. London, Routledge.
Simone, A. (2011). 'The surfacing of urban life'. *City*, *15* (3–4), 355–364.
Simone, A. (2013). 'Religiously urban and faith in the city: Reflections on the movements of the youth in central Africa and Southeast Asia'. In: Global Prayers: Contemporary Manifestations of the Religious in the City (eds. J. Becker, K. Klingan, S. Lanz and K. Wildner), 156–163. Zurich, Lars Mueller Publishers.
Simone, A. (2016). 'It's just the city after all!'. *International Journal of Urban and Regional Research*, *40* (1), 210–218.
Simone, A. (2019). Improvised Lives: Rhythms of Endurance in an Urban South. Cambridge, Polity.
Simone, A. (2020). 'To extend. Temporariness in a world of itineraries'. *Urban Studies*, *57* (6), 1127–1142.
Simone, A. and Pieterse, E. (2017). New Urban Worlds: Inhabiting Dissonant Times. Cambridge, Polity.
Sinatti, G. (2009). 'Home is where the heart abides. Migration, return and housing in Dakar, Senegal. *Open House International*, *34* (3), 49–56. special issue 'Home, Migration, and The City: Spatial Forms and Practices in a Globalising World'.
Sintomer, Y., Herzberg, C., and Röcke, A. (2008). *International Journal of Urban and Regional Research*, *32* (1), 164–178.
Sjöberg, Ö. (2014). 'Cases onto Themselves? Theory and Research on Ex-socialist Urban Environments.' *Geografie*, *119*, 299–319.
Skocpol, T. and Somers, M. (1980). 'The Uses of Comparative History in Macrosocial Inquiry'. *Comparative Studies in Society and History*, *22* (2), 174–197.
Slater, D. (1978). 'Towards a political economy of urbanization in peripheral capitalist societies: Problems of theory and method with illustrations from Latin America'. *International Journal of Urban and Regional Research*, *2* (1), 26–52.
Slater, D. (1992). 'On the borders of social theory: Learning from other regions'. *Environment and Planning D: Society and Space*, *10*, 307–327.
Slater, D. (2004). Geopolitics and the Postcolonial: Re-thinking North-South Relations. Malden, MA, Blackwell.
Slater, T. (2017). 'Planetary rent gaps'. *Antipode*, *49* (1), 114–137.
Smart, A. and Smart, J. (2017). 'Ain't Talkin Bout Gentrification: The erasure of alternative idioms of displacement resulting from Anglo-American academic hegemony'. *International Journal of Urban and Regional Research*, *41*, 518–525.
Smith. A. (2009). 'Informal work in the diverse economies of "Post-Socialist" Europe'. In: *Informal Work in Developed Nations* (eds. E. Marcelli, C.C. Williams, and P. Joassart). London: Routledge, Chapter 4.
Smith, M.P. (2001). Transnational Urbanism. Oxford, Blackwell.
Smith, N. (1987). 'Gentrification and the rent gap'. *Annals of the Association of American Geographers*, *77* (3), 462–465.

Smith, N. (2002). 'New globalism, new urbanism: Gentrification as global urban strategy'. *Antipode, 34* (3), 427–450.

Söderström, O. (2014). Cities in Relations: Trajectories of Urban Development in Hanoi and Ougadougou. Oxford, Wiley-Blackwell.

Soja, E. and Kanai, M. (2007). 'The urbanization of the world'. In: The Endless City (eds. R. Burdett and D. Sudjic), 54–69. New York and London, Phaidon.

Sotiris, P. (2014). 'Rethinking Structure and Conjuncture in Althusser'. *Historical Materialism, 22* (3–4), 5–51.

Southall, A. (1973). 'Introduction'. In: Urban Anthropology: Cross-Cultural Studies of Urbanization (ed. A. Southall), 3–14. New York, Oxford University Press.

Spencer, M. (1977). 'History and sociology: An analysis of weber's "the city"'. *Sociology, 11* (3), 507–525.

Spivak, G. (1988). 'Can the subaltern speak?'. In: Marxism and the Interpretation of Culture (eds. C. Nelson and L. Grossberg), 271–313. Chicago, University of Illinois Press.

Spivak, G. (2013). 'Rethinking Comparison'. In: Comparison: Theories, Approaches, Uses (eds. R. Felski and S.S. Friedman), 253–270. Baltimore, Johns Hopkins University Press.

Stacey, P. and Lund, C. (2016). 'In a state of slum: Governance in an informal settlement in Ghana'. *Journal of Modern African Studies, 54* (4), 591–615.

Stanek, L. (2008). 'Space as concrete abstraction: Hegel, Marx, and modern urbanism in Henri Lefebvre'. In: Space, Difference, Everyday Life: Reading Henri Lefebvre (eds. K. Goonewardena, S. Kipfer, R. Milgrom and C. Schmid), 62–79. London, Routledge.

Stanek, L. (2011). Henri Lefebvre on Space: Architecture, Urban Research and the Production of Theory. Minneapolis, University of Minnesota Press.

Stanek, L. (2015). 'Architects from socialist countries in Ghana (1957–67): Modern architecture and *mondialisation*'. *Journal of the Society of Architectural Historians, 74* (4), 416–442.

Stanek, L. (2012). 'Introduction: The "Second World's" architecture and planning in the "Third World"'. *The Journal of Architecture, 17* (3), 299–307.

Stanek, L. (2020). Architecture in Global Socialism: Eastern Europe, West Africa, and the Middle East in the Cold War. Princeton, Princeton University Press.

Steiner, U. (2010). Walter Benjamin: An Introduction to His Work and Thought. Chicago, University of Chicago Press.

Steinmetz, G. (2004). 'Odious comparison. Incommensurability, the case study and small Ns in sociology'. *Sociological Theory, 22* (3), 371–400.

Stengers, I. (2011). 'Comparison as a matter of concern'. *Common Knowledge, 17* (1), 48–63.

Stenning, A. and Hörschelmann, K. (2008). 'History, geography and difference in the post-socialist World: Or, do we still need post-socialism?'. *Antipode, 40,* 312–335.

Stone, C. (1989). Regime Politics: Governing Atlanta, 1946-1988. Lawrence, Kansas University Press.

Stone, D. (2004). 'Transfer agents and global networks in the "transnationalization" of policy'. *Journal of European Public Policy, 11* (3), 545–566.

Storper, M. (1990). 'Industrialization and the regional question in the third world: Lessons of postimperialism; prospects of post-Fordism'. *International Journal of Urban and Regional Research, 14*, 423–444.

Storper, M. (2010). 'Why does a city grow? Specialisation, human capital or institutions?'. *Urban Studies, 47* (10), 2027–2050.

Storper, M. and Scott, A.J. (2016). 'Current debates in urban theory: A critical assessment'. *Urban Studies, 53* (6), 1114–1136.

Strathern, M. (2005 [1991]). Partial Connections. Lanham, MD., Rowman and Littlefields.

Stren, R. (2001). 'Local governance and social diversity in the developing world: New challenges for globalising City-Regions'. In: Global City-Regions: Trends, Theory, Policy (ed. A.J. Scott), 193–213. Oxford, Oxford University Press.

Struth, T. (2012). Unconscious Places. Schirmer/Mosel.

Sunar, L. (2018). 'The Weberian city, civil society, and Turkish social thought'. In: The Oxford Handbook of Max Weber (eds. E. Hanke, L. Scaff and S. Whimster). Oxford, Oxford University Press. doi: 10.1093/oxfordhb/9780190679545.013.12.

Sundaresan, J. (2019). 'Urban planning in vernacular governance: Land use planning and violations in Bangalore, India'. *Progress in Planning, 127*, 1–23.

Swedberg, R. (2018). 'How to use Max Weber's ideal type in sociological analysis'. *Journal of Classical Sociology, 18* (3), 181–196.

Swyngedouw, E. (2005). 'Governance innovation and the citizen: The Janus face of governance-beyond-the-state'. *Urban Studies, 42* (11), 1991–2006.

Swyngedouw, E. (2011). 'Interrogating post-democratization: Reclaiming egalitarian political spaces'. *Political Geography, 30* (7), 370–380.

Swyngedouw, E., Moulaert, F., and Rodriguez, A. (2002). 'Neoliberal urbanization in Europe: Large-scale urban development projects and the new urban policy'. *Antipode, 34* (3), 542–577.

Sykora, L. and Stanilov, K. (2014). 'The challenge of postsocialist suburbanization'. In: Confronting Suburbanization: Urban Decentralization in Postsocialist Central and Eastern Europe (eds. K. Stanilov and L. Sykora), 1–32. Oxford, Wiley Blackwell.

Tang, W.S. (2017). 'Beyond gentrification: Hegemonic redevelopment in Hong Kong'. *International Journal of Urban and Regional Research, 41* (3), 487–499.

Tang, W.S. (2021). 'Reframing urban China research: A critical introduction'. In: Urban China Reframed: A critical introduction (eds. W.-S Tang and K.W. Chan), 1–16. London, Routledge.

Taussig, M. (1997). The Magic of the State. London, Routledge.

Taylor, P. (1997). 'Hierarchical tendencies amongst world cities: A research proposal'. *Cities, 14*, 323–332.

Taylor, P. (2004). World City Network: A Global Urban Analysis. London, Routledge.

Taylor, P.J. (2012). 'Extraordinary cities: Early "City-ness" and the origins of agriculture and states'. *International Journal of Urban and Regional Research, 36*, 415–447.
Teo, S.S. (2022). 'Shared projects and symbiotic collaborations: Shenzhen and London in comparative conversation'. *Urban Studies.* online early. doi: 10.1177/00420980211048675.
Theodore, N. (2007). 'Closed borders, open markets: Day laborers' Struggle for Economic Rights'. In: Contesting Neoliberalism: Urban Frontiers (eds. H. Leitner, J. Peck and E. Sheppard), 250–265. New York, Guilford.
Theurillat, T. and Crevoisier, O. (2012). 'The sustainability of a financialized urban megaproject: The case of Sihlcity in Zurich'. *International Journal of Urban and Regional Research, 37* (6), 2052–2073.
Theurillat, T. and Crevoisier, O. (2014). 'Sustainability and the anchoring of capital: Negotiations surrounding two major urban projects in Switzerland'. *Regional Studies, 48* (3), 501–515.
Thornley, A. (1991). Urban Planning Under Thatcherism: The Challenge of the Market. London, Routledge, Chapman and Hall.
Tiedermann, R. (1999). 'Dialectics at a standstill: Approaches to the *Passagen-Werk*'. In: The Arcades Project (ed. W. Benjamin and Translated, H. Eiland and K. McLaughlin), 929–945. Cambridge, Mass, Harvard University Press.
Tilly, C. (1984). Big Structures, Large Processes, Huge Comparisons. New York, Russell Sage Foundation.
Tilly, C. (1998). Durable Inequality. Berkeley, University of California Press.
Tilly, C. (2001). 'Mechanisms in political processes'. *Annual Review of Political Science, 4* (1), 21–41.
Tilly, C. (2010). 'Mechanisms of the middle range'. In: Robert K. Merton: Sociology of Science and Sociology as Science (ed. C. Calhoun), 54–62. New York, Columbia University Press.
Todd, Z. (2016). 'An indigenous feminist's take on the ontological turn: "Ontology" is just another word for colonialism'. *Journal of Historical Sociology, 29* (1), 4–22.
Todes, A. (2012). 'Urban growth and strategic spatial planning in Johannesburg'. *Cities, 29*, 158–165.
Todes, A. (2014). 'New African suburbanisation? Exploring the growth of the Northern Corridor of eThekwini/KwaDakuza'. *African Studies, 73* (2), 245–270.
Todes, A. and Robinson, J. (2020). 'Re-directing developers: New models of rental housing development to re-shape the post-apartheid city?'. *Environment and Planning A: Economy and Space, 52* (2), 297–317.
Tomas, A. (2022). In the Skin of the City: Spatial Transformation in Luanda. Durham, N.C.: Duke University Press.
Tomlinson, R. and Harrison, P. (2018). 'Knowledge of metropolitan governance in the South'. *International Journal of Urban and Regional Research, 42*, 1127–1139.
Topalov, C. (2017). 'The naming process'. In: What's in a Name? Talking about 'Suburbs' (eds. R. Harris and C. Vorms), 36–67. Toronto, University of Toronto Press.

Travers, T. (2004). The Politics of London: Governing an Ungovernable City. Basingstoke, Palgrave Macmillan.
Tribe, K. (2019). 'Introduction to Max Weber's *Economy and Society*'. In: Economy and Society. A New Translation (ed. and trans. By K. Tribe), 2–73. Cambridge, Mass., Harvard University Press.
Tsing, A. (2000). 'The global situation'. *Cultural Anthropology*, *15* (3), 327–360.
Tuhawi-Smith, L. (2009). Decolonizing Methodologies: Research and Indigenous Peoples. London, Zed Books.
Turner, S. (2018). 'Causation, value judgements, *Verstehen*'. In: Oxford Handbook of Max Weber, 575–593. Oxford, Oxford University Press.
Turok, I. (2014a). 'Linking urbanisation and development in Africa's economic revival'. In: Africa's Urban Revolution (eds. S. Parnell and E. Pieterse), 60–81. London, Zed Books.
Turok, I. (2014b). 'The urbanization-development nexus in the BRICS'. In: Handbook for Cities of the Global South (eds. S. Parnell and S. Oldfield), 122–138. London, Routledge.
Turok, I. (2016). 'Getting urbanization to work in Africa: The role of the urban land-infrastructure-finance nexus'. *Area Development and Policy*, *1* (1), 30–47.
Tuvikene, T. (2016). 'Strategies for comparative urbanism: Post-socialism as a de-territorialized concept'. *International Journal of Urban and Regional Research*, *40* (1), 132–146.
Tuvikene, T., Neves Alves, S., and Hilbrandt, H. (2016). 'Strategies for relating diverse cities: A multi-sited individualising comparison of informality in Bafatá, Berlin and Tallinn'. *Current Sociology*, *65* (2), 276–288.
UN-Habitat. (2014). The State of African Cities 2014 Re-imagining Sustainable Urban Transitions. Nairobi, UN-Habitat.
UN-Habitat. (2015). Towards an Africa Urban Agenda. Nairobi, UNHCS.
UN-Habitat. (2018). The State of African Cities 2018. The Geography of African Investment. Nairobi, UN-Habitat.
Vainer, C. (2014). 'Disseminating "best practice"? The coloniality of urban knowledge and city models'. In: The Routledge Handbook on Cities of the Global South (eds. S. Parnell and S. Oldfield). New York, Routledge.
Vaiou, D. (2004). 'The contested and negotiated dominance of Anglophone geography in Greece'. *Geoforum*, *35* (5), 529–531.
Valencia, S., Simon, D., Croese, S., Nordqvist, J., Sharma, T., Taylor Buck, N., and Versace, I. (2019). 'Adapting the sustainable development goals and the new urban agenda to the city level: Initial reflections from a comparative research project'. *International Journal of Urban Sustainable Development*, *11* (1), 4–23.
Vandenberghe, F. (2008). 'Deleuzian capitalism'. *Philosophy & Social Criticism*, *34* (8), 877–903.
Van Den Broeck, J. (2017). '"We are analogue in a digital world": An anthropological exploration of ontologies and uncertainties around the proposed Konza Techno City near Nairobi, Kenya'. *Critical African Studies*, *9* (2), 210–225.
Van Der Linden, M. and Mitzman, L. (2009). 'Charles Tilly's historical sociology'. *International Review of Social History*, *54* (2), 237–274.

Van Gils, M., Van Haaren, J., and Wall, R. (2018). 'The attraction of direct greenfield foreign real estate investments into Sub-Saharan Africa'. In: The State of African Cities 2018. The Geography of African Investment, 182–191. Nairobi, UN-Habitat.

Van Horen, B. (2000). 'Informal settlement upgrading: Bridging the gap between the De Facto and the De Jure'. *Journal of Planning Education and Research, 19* (4), 389–400.

Van Loon, J., Oosterlynck, S., and Aalbers, M. (2019). 'Governing urban development in the Low Countries: From managerialism to entrepreneurialism and financialization'. *European Urban and Regional Studies, 26* (4), 400–418.

Van Mieteren, M., Derudder, B., and Bassens, D. (2016). 'Can the straw man speak? An engagement with postcolonial critiques of "global cities research"'. *Dialogues in Human Geography, 6* (3), 247–267.

Van Noorloos, F. and Kloosterboer, M. (2018). 'Africa's new cities: The contested future of urbanisation.'. *Urban Studies, 55* (6), 1223–1241.

Van Onselen, C. (2015). Showdown at the Red Lion (The Life and Times of Jack MacLoughlin, 1859-1910). Cape Town, Jonathan Ball Publishers.

Varley, A. (2013). 'Postcolonialising informality?'. *Environment and Planning D: Society and Space, 31* (1), 4–22.

Varley, A. and Salazar, C. (2021). 'The Impact of Mexico's Land Reform on Periurban Housing Production: Neoliberal or Neocorporatist?' *International Journal of Urban and Regional Research, 45* (6), 964–984.

Vicari, S. and Molotch, H. (1990). 'Building Milan: Alternative machines of growth'. *International Journal of Urban and Regional Research, 14*, 602–624.

Vogel, R.K., Savitch, H.V., Xu, J., Yeh, A.G.O., Wu, W., Sancton, A., Kantor, P., and Newman, P. (2010). 'Governing global city regions in China and the West'. *Progress in Planning, 73*, 1–75.

Von Schnitzler, A. (2008). 'Citizenship Prepaid: Water, calculability, and technopolitics in South Africa'. *Journal of Southern African Studies, 34* (4), 899–917.

Von Schnitzler, A. (2016). Democracy's Infrastructure" Techno-Politics and Protest after Apartheid. Princeton, Princeton University Press.

Wachsmuth, D. (2014). 'City as ideology: Reconciling the explosion of the city form with the tenacity of the city concept'. *Environment and Planning D: Society and Space, 32* (1), 75–90.

Wacquant, L. (1995). 'The comparative structure and experience of urban exclusion: "Race", class, and space in Chicago and Paris'. In: Poverty, Inequality and the Future of Social Policy: Western States in the New World Order (eds. K. McFate, R. Lawson and W.J. Wilson), 543–570. New York, Russell Sage Foundation.

Wacquant, L. (2008). Urban Outcasts: A Comparative Sociology of Advanced Marginality. Cambridge, Polity.

Waley, P. (2012). 'Japanese cities in Chinese perspective: Towards a contextual, regional approach to comparative urbanism'. *Urban Geography, 33*, 6.

Walton, J. (1981). 'Comparative urban studies'. *International Journal of Comparative Sociology, 22* (1–2), 22–39.

Walton, J. (1990). 'Theoretical methods in comparative urban politics'. In: Beyond the City Limits: Urban Policy and Economic Restructuring in Comparative Perspective (eds. J.R. Logan and T. Swanstrom), 242–257. Philadelphia, Temple University Press.

Walton, J. (1992). 'Making the theoretical case'. In: What Is a Case? Exploring the Foundations of Social Inquiry (eds. H.S. Becker and C. Ragin), 121–137. Cambridge, Cambridge University Press.

Walton, J. (2018 [1977]). 'Accumulation and comparative urban systems'. In: The Globalizing Cities Reader (eds. X. Ren and R. Keil), 41–46. London, Routledge.

Walton, J. and Seddon, D. (1994). Free Markets & Food Riots: The Politics of Global Adjustment. Oxford, Wiley-Blackwell.

Wang, Y. P. and Murie, A. (2011). 'The new affordable and social housing provision system in China: Implications for comparative housing studies'. *International Journal of Housing Policy*, 11 (3), 237–254.

Wang, Y.P., Wang, Y., and Wu, J. (2009). 'Urbanization and informal development in China: Urban villages in Shenzhen'. *International Journal of Urban and Regional Research*, 33 (4), 957–973.

Wang, Z. (2020). 'Beyond displacement – Exploring the variegated social impacts of urban redevelopment'. *Urban Geography*, Online First Publication. doi: 10.1080/02723638.2020.1734373.

Wang, Z. and Wu, F. (2019). 'In-situ marginalisation: Social impact of Chinese mega-projects'. *Antipode*, 51, 1640–1663.

Ward, K. (1996). 'Rereading urban regime theory: A sympathetic critique'. *Geoforum*, 27 (4), 427–438.

Ward, K. (2006). '"Policies in motion"', urban management and state restructuring: The trans-local expansion of Business Improvement Districts'. *International Journal of Urban and Regional Research*, 30 (1), 54–75.

Ward, K. (2008). 'Commentary: Toward a comparative (re)turn in urban studies? Some reflections'. *Urban Geography*, 29 (4), 1–6.

Ward, K. (2010). 'Towards a relational comparative approach to the study of cities'. *Progress in Human Geography*, 34 (4), 471–487.

Ward, K. (2017). 'Financialization and urban politics: Expanding the optic'. *Urban Geography*, 38 (1), 1–4.

Ward, P. (1993). 'The Latin American inner city: Differences of degree or of kind?'. *Environment and Planning A*, 25, 1131–1160.

Watson, V. (2009). 'Seeing from the south: Refocusing urban planning on the globe's central urban issues'. *Urban Studies*, 46 (11), 2259–2275.

Watson, V. (2014a). 'African urban fantasies: Dreams or nightmares?'. *Environment and Urbanization*, 26 (1), 215–231.

Watson, V. (2014b). 'The case for a southern perspective in planning theory'. *International Journal of E-Planning Research*, 3 (1), 23–37.

Watt, P. and Minton, A. (2016). 'London's housing crisis and its activisms'. *City*, 20 (2), 204–222.

Weber, (1949 [1904]). '"Objectivity" in social science and social policy'. In The Methodology of the Social Sciences (Trans. And Ed. M. Weber, E.A. Shils and H.A. Finch), 50–112. New York, The Free Press. (see also Weber (2012) 100-138).

Weber, M. (1958 [1921]). The City, (trans. Martindale, D. and Neuwirth, G.). New York, The Free Press.

Weber, M. (1979 [1949]). The Methodology of the Social Sciences. London, Routledge.

Weber, M. (2001). The Protestant Ethic Debate: Max Weber's Replies to His Critics, 1907-1910 (eds D. Chalcraft and A. Harrington). Liverpool, Liverpool University Press.

Weber, M. (2012). Max Weber. Collected Methodological Writings (eds. H.H. Bruun and S. Whimster Translated, H. H. Bruun). London, Routledge.

Weber, M. (2019). Economy and Society. A New Translation (Edited trans. By K. Tribe). Cambridge, Mass., Harvard University Press.

Weber, R. (2010). 'Selling city futures: The financialization of urban redevelopment policy'. *Economic Geography*, *86* (3), 251–274.

Weber, R. (2015). From Boom to Bubble: How Finance Built the New Chicago. University of Chicago Press.

Weinstein, L. (2008). 'Mumbai's development mafias: Globalization, organised crime and land development'. *International Journal of Urban and Regional Research*, *32* (1), 22–39.

Weinstein, L. (2014). '"One- Man Handled": Fragmented power and political entrepreneurship in globalizing Mumbai'. *International Journal of Urban and Regional Research*, *38* (1), 14–35.

Weinstein, L. (2017). 'Insecurity as confinement: The entrenched politics of staying put in Delhi and Mumbai'. *International Sociology*, *32* (4), 512–531.

Wellings, P. and Sutcliffe, M. (1984). '"Developing" the urban informal sector in South Africa: The reformist paradigm and its fallacies'. *Development and Change*, *15* (4), 517–550.

Werlen, B. (1992). Society, Action and Space: An Alternative Human Geography. London, Routledge.

Wilson, D. (2004). 'Toward A contingent urban neoliberalism'. *Urban Geography*, *25* (8), 771–783.

Wilson, J. and Swyngedouw, E. (2014). 'Seeds of dystopia: Post-politics and the return of the political'. In: The Post-Political and Its Discontents: Spaces of Depoliticisation, Spectres of Radical Politics (eds. J. Wilson and E. Swyngedouw), 1–24. Edinburgh, Edinburgh University Press.

Wirth, J.D. and Jones, R.L. (eds) (1978). Manchester and São Paulo: Problems of Rapid Urban Growth. Stanford, Stanford University Press.

Wirth, L. (1938). 'Urbanism as a way of life'. *American Journal of Sociology*, *44* (1), 1–24.

Wirth, L. (1964). Louis Wirth: On Cities and Social Life. Chicago, University of Chicago Press.

Wolf, E. (1982). Europe and the People without History. Berkeley, University of California Press.

Wolpe, H. (ed.) (1980). The Articulation of Modes of Production. London, Routledge and Kegan Paul.
Wood, A. (2014). 'Moving policy: Global and local characters circulating bus rapid transit through South African cities'. *Urban Geography*, 35 (8), 1238–1254.
Wu, F. (2003). 'The (Post-) socialist entrepreneurial city as a state project: Shanghai's reglobalization in question'. *Urban Studies*, 40 (9), 1673–1698.
Wu, F. (2010). 'How neoliberal is China's reform? The origins of change during transition'. *Eurasian Geography and Economics*, 51 (5), 619–631.
Wu, F. (2015). Planning for Growth: Urban and Regional Planning in China. London, Routledge.
Wu, F. (2016). 'Emerging Chinese cities: Implications for global urban studies'. *The Professional Geographer*, 68 (2), 338–348.
Wu, F. (2018). 'Planning centrality, market instruments: Governing Chinese urban transformation under state entrepreneurialism'. *Urban Studies*, 55 (7), 1383–1399.
Wu, F. (2020). 'Adding new narratives to the urban imagination: An introduction to 'New directions of urban studies in China''. *Urban Studies*, 57 (3), 459–472.
Wu, F. (2022). Handbook of Comparative Urban Studies (eds. P.L. Galès and J. Robinson). London, Routledge.
Wu, F. and Phelps, N.A. (2011). '(Post)Suburban Development and State Entrepreneurialism in Beijing's Outer Suburbs'. *Environment and Planning A: Economy and Space*, 43 (2), 410–430.
Wu, F. and Shen, J. (2015). 'Suburban development and governance in China'. In: Suburban Governance: A Global View (eds. P. Hamel and R. Keil), 303–324. Toronto, University of Toronto Press.
Yiftachel, O. (2000). 'Social control, urban planning and ethno-class relations: Mizrahim in Israel's development towns''. *International Journal of Urban and Regional Research*, 24 (2), 417–434.
Yiftachel, O. (2001). 'From "Peace" to creeping apartheid: The emerging political geography of Israel/Palestine'. *Arena*, 16 (3), 13–24.
Yiftachel, O. (2006). 'Re-Engaging Planning Theory? Towards 'South-Eastern' Perspectives'. *Planning Theory*, 5, 211–222.
Yiftachel, O. (2009). 'Theorizing "Gray Space": The coming of urban apartheid?'. *Planning Theory*, 8 (1), 88–100.
Yiftachel, O. (2020). 'From displacement to displaceability: A southeastern perspective on the new metropolis'. *City*, 24 (1–2), 151–165.
Zérah, M.-H. (2020). Quand L'Inde S'urbanise: Services Essentiels Et Paradoxes D'un Urbanisme Bricolé. Avignon, Editions de l'aube.
Zerilli, L. (2009). 'Towards a feminist theory of judgement'. *Signs*, 34 (2), 295–317.
Zerilli, L. (2016). A Democratic Theory of Judgement. Chicago, University of Chicago Press.

Zhao, Y. (2020). '*Jiehebu* or suburb? Towards a translational turn in urban studies'. *Cambridge Journal of Regions, Economy and Society*, *13* (3), 527–542.

Ziederman, A. (2018). 'Beyond the enclave of urban theory'. *International Journal of Urban and Regional Research*, *42* (6), 1114–1126.

Zukin, S., Kasinitz, P., and Chen, X. (eds) (2016). Global Cities, Local Streets: Everyday Diversity from New York to Shanghai. London, Routledge.

Index

Note: Page numbers followed by "t" refers to tables and "n" refers to notes.

abstraction, 75, 82, 108–9, 110–115, 156, 230–3, 235, 252, 372
    as abbreviation, 112
    concrete, 111–2, 233, 264–5, 372
    and totality, 112–5, 130n3
Abu-Lughod, Janet, 60, 64, 75, 76, 88–9, 190–191, 284–7, 288
actor network theory, 42, 79, 148–150, 153, 161, 168
acupuncture and weak architecture, 337–8
'advanced marginality', 81, 229
Africa, 7, 240–2, 257, 269, 275, 284–7, 291
    and Brazil, 291–5
    China, 289
    and neoliberalisation, 177–180
    and philosophy, 212, 241–2
    suburbs, 311
    urban development planning, 287
    urban governance, 318
    urbanism, 357, 383
    urban scholarship, 29–31, 179, 212, 356
African Centre for Cities, 338
'aleatory' materialism, 260–2
'allegorical materialism,' 343, 351
allegory, 342–3, 351–2
Allen, John, 73, 193–4
Althusser, 232–3, 249, 260
    and 'conjuncture,' 257
'antiblack racism,' 213
anti-colonial comparison, 46
anti-racist politics, 216
Apartheid, 187–190, 214–6, 291–2, 306
Arcades project, 340, 341, 345–347, 349, 366, 366n20
Arendt, Hannah, 16, 203, 213, 235–240, 372

Asia
    in knowledge production, 46, 275
    inspiring developments, 103
assemblage approach, 42–3, 112, 119, 150, 283, 307–8, 320–1, 423
Austrian Mont Pèlerin organisation, 171

'Bare' repetitions, see repetitions
Barnett, Clive, 236–8
Baudelaire, Charles, 341–348
Benjamin, Walter, 19–20, 113, 239–230, 305–6, 326–7, 340–357, 362–3, 379–80
    speculative method, 354–5
Bhan, Gautam, 33, 206, 338–9
Black studies, 7, 37, 44, 205, 208, 210, 212–216, 376
Black urbanism, 126, 216, 242, 335
Brazil, 29, 117, 149, 257, 291–5, 319
Brenner, Neil, 59, 112, 119, 168, 173–4, 190–1, 254, 308, 312, 315, 318–9
    and Schmid, 35–6, 308, 312, 315, 318–9
'bypass urbanism,' 269

Cairo (and New York), 284–7
Can the Subaltern Speak (Spivak), 208
capitalism, 173, 186
    state, 275
    welfare state, 36
'capitalist restructuring,' 116
Cases, 117–8
    and caseing, 154, 177, 185
    connections as, 138–146
    in comparisons, 107, 174–186
    distended, 139
    and selection, 66, 70–71, 89

Comparative Urbanism: Tactics for Global Urban Studies, First Edition. Jennifer Robinson.
© 2022 John Wiley & Sons Ltd. Published 2022 by John Wiley & Sons Ltd.

theoretical case, 135
and wider processes, 146–7
Castells, Manuel, 36, 225, 257, 358–9
Causality, 74–6
  contextual, 60
  relative/plural, 68
  scientific, 67
  variables, 66
Caygill, Howard, 347–8, 354–6
China and urban studies, 30, 117, 139, 182, 273–5, 298
  exceptionalism, 298
  Weber on, 223–4
circular migration, 37
Cities for Profit (Shatkin), 300
City, use of term, 34–6,
'*The City*' (Weber), 221–224
city strategies, 156–7, 193
Clarke, Susan, 85–7, 88, 115–6
'clothed' repetitions, see repetitions
collaborative knowledge production, 6, 11, 15, 211–6, 315, 338, 377–8
collective heating systems, 176, 177
colonial city, 100–1
colonial histories, 194–195
colonialism and knowledge, 76
comparative imagination, 2–4, 6, 9, 13, 14, 26, 41, 47–50, 51, 75, 84, 104, 128, 144, 153, 186, 195–6, 222, 253, 320–325, 370, 375
comparative method, 53–4, 57, 58t, 191, 282, 374
  comparative gesture, 53, 80–83
  conventional strategies, 51, 56–69, 75, 77, 89, 129, 291
  conversations, 284–92, 290, 328n3
  encompassing, 58t, 61–4, 108, 118, 125, 146–7, 162, 164–8, 174, 190
  ethnography, 82
  individualising, 59–60
  potential, 47, 68, 69–76, 201, 254
  practice, 79–80, 280–4
  reformatted, 47–50, 108, 370–376
  shared features, 79, 86–7, 156, 257, 272–6
  stretching comparisons, 91–103
  thinking with variety, 83–91
  unit of comparison, 70–4

and urban theory, 4–6, 48, 65–6
variation-finding, 64–69, 75, 190
in Walter Benjamin, 350–1
comparative tactics, 13, 126, 182, 203, 302, 305, 319, 374
comparator (third term), 9, 66–68, 70–72, 84, 155, 282–4, 290–2
compression, 333–4
concepts, 124
  adequacy, 232–4
  and heterogeneity, 323–6
  and the 'in-common', 235–242
  launching, 20, 49–50, 125, 127, 331, 338
  mobile, 295–301
  as multiplicities, 123, 356–7
  generating, 201–243, 325
conceptualisation, 15, 121–3, 352–3, 376–383
  Deleuzian theory of, 121–4, 362, 352–3, 378–9
conceptual labour, 324
concrete abstractions, 110–6, 126 130n, 231–233
concrete-in-thought, 111–2, 231, 233, 235, 245n10
concrete totalities, 38, 40, 112–3, 203, 235, 266, 267
  in comparison, 114, 117–8, 127
  emergent, 167
  in *Grundrisse*, 111, 232–3
  in Lefebvre, 128, 264–7
  Marxism, 109–114
  and neoliberalisation, 115–6
  open, 112
  post-colonial idiom, 117
  'total man/content', 110, 264–5
conjunctural urbanism, 251–258
conjuncture, 19, 166, 187–8, 248, 249, 251, 252, 256–258, 262, 374
  Althusser, 260–2
  and context, 235, 252
  contingent, 169, 258–263
  and comparison, 251, 253–6, 257, 258–60
  definition, 252–3
  Stuart Hall, 249–251
  Hart, Gill, 258–9

scalar, 254–6
  and space, 257–8
  spatiotemporalities, 255
connections, 91–103, 137
  as cases, 153–158
  comparing, 72–3, 97, 119–121, 137–8, 142–4
  limits in comparison, 158–9
  and Repeated Instances, 119–121, 146–153
  tracing, 137–138
  and urban politics, 315–6
  as urbanization processes, 138–146
concrete totality, 112–4,
constellations, 19, 269, 306, 329–30, 346, 350–357, 363, 379–81
context, 60, 162, 166–168, 186–191
'Context of contexts', 168, 171
conversations
  as method, 279
  comparison as, 280–292
  mobile concepts or 'arriving at' concepts, 295–301
  researcher trajectories, 288
  theoretical reflections, 292–295
co-operative housing movement, 287
corruption and comparative method, 289–90
'countertopographies,' 158
Cox, Kevin, 88, 170, 314–5
Critique of Black Reason (Mbembe), 241
cross-national comparative research, 68
cyborgs, 191–2, 201, 262, 280

Dear Science and Other Stories (McKittrick), 214
De Boeck, Filip, 49, 59, 73, 75, 336–339, 342, 360, 336–339
decolonial theory, 21, 41–6, 205, 207, 371
'defanged empiricism,' 117
Deleuze, Gilles, 10, 13, 19–20, 49–50, 120–4, 126, 203, 306, 326–7, 329–31, 351–3, 356–7, 362
  conceptualisation, theory of, 121–4, 352–3, 362, 378–9
  space in, 122, 325
detachment, 330–336, 342, 344,
deterritorialise post-socialism, 28
developmentalism, 41, 44, 55, 146, 172, 178–179, 237

Dialectical Materialism (Lefebvre), 264
dialectics, 250, 258, 265
  in Lefebvre, 264–6
Die Stadt (Weber), 217, 224–227
Difference and Repetition (Deleuze), 10, 121–3, 131n8, 131n11
differentiated, urban as, 4, 14, 48, 138, 145, 155–6, 159, 309, 376
different/(c)iation, 121–3, 352
Dilomprizulike, 22–24, 304–5
'displaced urbanization,' 188
distended case, 139
distinctive, urban as, 5, 17–20, 49, 307–8, 325, 330–1, 369, 372, 376
divergent, urban as, 25, 179, 250, 257, 260–2, 272, 276, 288, 295, 324, 331–3, 368m33, 369, 373–4, 381
diverse, urban as, 5, 16–17, 31, 48, 266, 269, 271–6, 288, 309, 312, 314, 331, 345, 356, 370–1, 373–4, 376–7, 381
  and large-scale developments, 273–275
  in comparison, 87–91, 271–6
  and urban politics, 271–6, 312–20
'double consciousness,' 176
dual city hypothesis, 60

Economy and Society (Weber), 226
'encompassing' method, 61–64
'entrepreneurial' urban governance, 128, 172, 316–8
Euro-American scholarship, 30
Eurocentrism, in knowledge production, 33, 37, 47, 81, 113, 204, 212–3, 216, 356, 385
Europe and the People without History (Wolf), 167–8
European political economy, 103
European urbanisation, 310
experimental comparative tactics, 243, 286, 307, 323
'extended urbanisation,' 141–2, 318–9
  and politics, 318–9

Fainstein, Susan, 98
'family resemblances', 184–186, 197n6, 257, 371
Feminism, 16, 37–40, 202–3, 208–210, 230, 239–40, 372, 382

Fire Walker (Kentridge), 134–6, 214–6
The Fold (Deleuze), 351
For Space (Massey), 250
Foucauldian analysis, 114, 181–2
fragment, 320–1, 322–4
Friedmann, John, 95–6
'frontal comparisons,' 202

generative comparative tactics, 15, 118, 149, 199–203, 247, 249, 258–9, 371–3, 378, 384
  and conceptualising subject, 204–217
  and 'concrete,' 230–235
  and ideal types, 217–230
  and 'in-common,' 235–243
generality, 19, 323–6
'generic blackness,' 242–3
genetic, definition, 276n2
'genetic' comparative tactics, 11–13, 118, 120, 124–6, 128, 135–6, 137–160, 161–3, 191, 371, 375
'genres of urbanism,' 8
gentrification, 152, 280, 296–300, 301, 380
geopolitics, 112, 145
  and global South, 31
  non-aligned movement, 32
  and urban development, 318–9
German Tragic Drama, see *On German Tragic Drama* (Benjamin)
Glissant, Edouard, 34, 46, 141, 194–5, 382
Global and World Cities (GAWC), 63, 88–89, 95–6, 98, 190–1
'globalisation,' 116, 316, 375
Globalization and Urban Change: Capital, Culture and Pacific Rim Mega-Projects (Olds), 144
'global'/'local' dichotomy, 116, 119
global South, 26, 31, 375–7
  global souths (*les pays suds*), 199, 319, 375, 377
  and non-aligned movement, 32
'global suburbanisms,' 309, 311
Grundrisse (Marx), 111, 230, 232, 234, 250

Halbert, Ludovic, 315–7
Hall, Stuart, 114, 230–4, 249–251
  and Doreen Massey, 250, 257, 263
Handbook for Cities of the Global South (Parnell and Oldfield), 33, 294

Hart, Gill, 167, 187–90, 233, 251–2, 257–260
Harvey, David, 86, 88, 161, 171–2, 314
Haussmann, 199, 347
Hegel, Georg Wilhelm, 5, 110, 111, 123, 196n4, 331, 346, 366n20
heterogeneity, and concepts, 323–6
Hill Collins, Patricia, 203, 208
History 1 and History 2, 170
housing, 285–8, 290
  demarketised land, 288

'Idea', 19, 132n11, 132n17, 349–360, 379–80
  informality, as Idea, 357–62,
  and method, 350–1
Ideal Types, 82, 217–228, 229–30
  Die Stadtgemeinde as, 224–7
  in urban studies, 229–230
Import Substitution Industrialisation model, 117, 359
Improvised Lives (Simone), 326–331
incommensurability (incomparability), 54–58, 307, 326–7
'incorporated comparison,' , 61, 62, 165
India, 29, 80, 99, 117, 180, 209–10, 269–60, 275, 286, 300, 313, 319, 338–9, 358–9, 361
Indian Institute for Human Settlements, 338
Indigenous studies, 3, 37, 44, 153, 206
Individual (in philosophy), 3, 5, 37, 110, 121, 124, 131n8, 167, 219, 221, 265, 331, 353, 355–6, 366n19, 367n25, 372
  urban outcomes as, 4, 18–19, 110, 128, 196n4, 307, 331, 372, 376
informality, 12, 45, 75, 156–7, 287, 290, 358–9, 360
  and housing, 285–8, 290
  and sanitation processes, 270, 271
infrastructure, 149, 269, 318
Institutional change in urban studies, 2, 21, 30, 384–6
institutional inequalities, 205
'insurgent citizenship,' 12, 292
intellectual traditions, diversity of, 33
intensities, 120, 123, 132n13, 132n14, 203, 245n11, 305, 352–3, 356, 362, 377, 378

Interscalar Chains of Rentiership (ICR), 255
Jacobs, Jane M., 119–20, 150–2, 154–5, 283–4
Johannesburg, 214–6, 273–6, 306
   and China, 134, 273–6
   and London, 273–6

Kantian syntheses, 121
Kantor, Paul (and Savitch, Hank), 66, 67, 84–5, 87,-88, 91, 314–5
Kentridge, William, 135, 214–6
King, Anthony, 99–103
Kinshasa, 59, 73, 336–8
Kinshasa: Tales of the Invisible City (de Boeck and Plissart), 59

labour movements, 95, 102, 291
land use management, 29
language and urban studies, 30
large-scale development, 177–8, 273–5, 317
   and infrastructure, 149, 318
late-medieval urban transition, 244n5
Law, John, 279, 281–2, 302
LDDC, see London
Lefebvre, Henri, 16, 35, 49, 110, 141, 233–5, 250, 258, 263–9, 339, 355–6, 377–9
Le Galès, Patrick, 80–1, 180–1, 229–30
Leibniz, Gottfried Wilhelm, 340–1 (see also monad)
The Life of the Mind (Arendt), 239
Lilongwe, 156–60
London, 98–103, 147–8, 292–5
   Docklands Development Corporation, 102
   and Hong Kong, 103
   and Johannesburg, 156–7, 215–6, 273–6
   and Lilongwe, 156–7
   and New York, 98
   and Shanghai, 273–4
   and Shenzhen, 290
   and South Africa, 292–5
   as theory destination, 275
low-wage industrialisation, 102, 358–359

McFarlane, Colin, 43, 128, 270–1, 286, 320–5, 359–60
   and Michele Lancione, 323–6, 379

McKittrick, Katherine, 208, 211–216, 239, 242
McMichael, Philip, 61–2, 165–7, 186–7
macro-scale comparison, 92
Marxism, 16–17, 108–13, 118, 161–2, 230–2, 237, 254, 261, 377
   and comparative methods, 234, 251
Massey, Doreen, 4, 49, 62, 114, 161, 250, 257
   and Stuart Hall, 250, 257, 263
'materialist physiognomy,' 340
materialities and urban theory, 42, 50, 320–1, 356, 371
Mbembe, Achille, 16, 203, 212, 216, 240–2
'mechanisms,' 168, 271–2
'mega-urban projects,' see large-scale development
'middle-range' theory, 15, 255
'minor theory,' 157–8
modernisation theory, 55
modernism, 119, 155
monad, 131n8, 340–1, 340, 350–1, 364n7, 364, n8, 367n26
monadology, 340, 347, 349, 364n10
Moten, Fred, 16, 195, 212–6, 382
'multiple elsewheres,' 192
multiplicities, 6, 45, 50, 123, 352, 357, 363–4n2, 370, 378–9, 380–1
   concepts as, 123, 357, 379–1
   urban as, 382
   singularity and, 363–4n2, 380
'multi-sited' ethnography, 138
Mumbai, 90, 271, 286, 292, 322–4
   and Cape Town, 322–3
   and Turin, 286, 292, 323–4
municipal socialism, 178
Myers, Garth, 31, 34, 46, 129, 189, 194, 288, 302, 353, 357, 361

national-democratic revolutions, 291
national state, 66
   in economic development, 178, 180
neoliberalisation, 115, 116, 171–186, 255, 380
   and Africa, 179–80
   contingent, 175–6, 183
   economic policies, 172
   governance, 176

governmentality, 177, 182
origins, 171–2
policies, 174–6, 180
and post-socialism, 176–7
and South America, 180
and Structural Adjustment Policies, 178–80
urban, 14, 163, 171–186
New International Division of Labour, 97, 285
New Orleans, 174–6
and New York, 174–5
Nietszche and Philosophy (Deleuze), 353
nominalism, 40–1
'non-comparative comparison,' 144
non-integrating conceptualisations, 44
'non-legitimate domination,' 221
non-market housing, 287
non-neoliberal alternatives, 178
non-neoliberal policies, 181

'Objective Possibility,' 221
occidental-style association, 224
occidental-type urban 'communities,' 224
Oldfield, Sophie, 32–4, 294, 338
Olds, Kris, 98–9, 144–5
Ole, Antonio, cover, 22–24
On German Tragic Drama (Trauerspiel) (Benjamin), 340, 349–350, 354, 362
On the Concept of History (Löwy), 305, 363
One Way Street (Benjamin), 306
'opacity', 332–7, 339, 375
Ordinary Cities (Robinson), preface, 383–4
Ottoman social structures, 223
'overdetermined plenitude,' 112
'overurbanisation,' 94

'pan-urban processes,' 253
Park, Robert, 10, 55
Parnell, Susan, 29–30, 32–4, 146, 160, 179, 212, 237, 294, 315, 357, 385–6
and Edgar Pieterse, 29–30, 205, 212, 357, 385–6
and Sophie Oldfield, 32–4, 294
Partial Connections (Strathern), 202
particular, 109, 115, 170, 196n4, 251–2, 258, 302, 330, 340, 350–1, 354–6, 366n19, 368n33,
Peake, Linda, 208–10

Peck, Jamie, 116–7, 139, 173–5, 180–4, 197n, 253–4, 255–7
peripheral urbanisation processes, 311
Philosophy for Marxism (Althusser), 260
Philosophy of the Encounter (Althusser), 260
Pickvance, Chris, 56–8, 67–9, 92–3
Pieterse, Edgar, 29–30, 205, 212, 338–9, 357, 360, 385–6
Planetary Gentrification (Lees, López-Morales and Shin), 297
planetary urbanisation, 1, 18, 26, 35–41, 76, 138, 142, 312, 315, 319–20, 383
plural causality, 68
policy mobilities, 141, 142, 145–6, 153, 156, 192–3, 300
and topological space, 193, 382
post-colonial critiques, 46, 48, 55, 99, 117
'post-democracy,' 292–5
post-independence urban development, 179
post-industrial economy, 87
post-Marxism, 118
'post-politics,' 12, 292–5
post-socialism, 28, 29, 139, 176–7
and urban studies, 30–31, 311
Potts, Deborah, 37, 286–8
pragmatism, 236–8
The Priority of Injustice (Barnett), 238
property-led development, 98, 102
publishing, in urban studies, 30, 385–6

Quand L'Inde s'Urbanise (Zérah), 313

Ragin, Charles, 60, 69, 74, 185, 228, 291
Rancière, Jaques, 293–5
'rapport territorial,' 317
Reading Capital (Althusser), 233
'reciprocal comparison,' 223
regime theory, 12, 64, 67, 71, 85–7, 89–90, 149, 314
'regional assemblages,' 316
regional industrial development, 97
regions in urban scholarship, 29–31
relational comparison, 14, 143, 161–2, 169–70, 173–4, 188, 253
and contexts, 186–191

spatialities of the urban, 191–195
urban neoliberalisation, 171–186
wider processes, 164–171
relational thinking, 143
'repeated instance,' 13, 119–20, 146–153, 156, 159, 162, 165
repetition, 119, 121–2, 124, 152–4, 302n2, 362, 367n22, 367n29
 clothed, 152, 312
 clothed and bare, 126–7, 152
 and conceptualisation, 159
 and differentiation, 132n17
 and origin, 124, 349, 351, 362, 367n22, 367n29,
 and representation, 132n12
'residual traditional-mercantilist' forms, 187
'rethinking urbanism,' 34
re-tracing urban studies, 194
retrospective comparison, 323
'revisable theory claims,' 251
'rhythms of endurance,' 334
'rogue urbanisms,' 132n14
Roy, Ananya, 8, 27, 99, 206, 250, 288, 359–60

Savitch, Hank (and Kantor, Paul), 66, 67, 84–5, 87,-88, 91, 314–5
scale, 251–8
Schmid, Christian, 5, 17, 35–7, 235, 264–6, 267–271, 316–7
 on Lefebvre, 17, 234–5, 264–6
Scott, James, 289
Shared features, 79, 86–7, 156, 257, 272–6
Shatkin, Gavin, 275, 300
Simone, Maliq, 45, 146, 242, 302, 330, 331–7, 342, 356–7, 359–60
'simplified planning zones,' 101
'simultaneity of trajectories,' 38
Singularity, 19, 109, 114, 124, 131n8, 132n15, 155–6, 160n1, 326, 352–3, 362, 363–4n2, 364n7, 368n33, 380
situated theorisation, 210
Slater, David, 93–4
social movement unionism, 291
Social Theory and the Urban Question (Saunders), 244n3
Socialism, 28–9, 67, 91, 140–2

worlding architecture and planning, 140–1
Söderström, Ola, 192–4
South Africa, 29, 117, 259–6, 322–3
 and Brazil, 293–5
 and India, 259–6, 322–3
 and London, 250
Southern
 theory, 31, 32
 scholarship, 206, 338
 south-south, 275
 urban theory, 31
Southern Theory (Connell), 31
Space (spatiality), 4, 6, 38, 49, 62, 114, 161, 192, 211, 250, 252–9, 263, 267–8, 334, 347, 354–5, 362–3, 373–4, 379
 and conjuncture, 252–9
 and comparison, 3, 20–1, 72–5, 107, 120–1, 129, 138, 156, 286
 as compression, 334
 in Deleuze, 122, 325, 362–3
 and 'double consciousness', 176
 and Lefebvre, 38, 256, 267–8, 355
 Massey and, 4, 38, 49, 62, 74, 114, 161, 250
 topologies and, 73, 193, 301–2, 353
 the urban as, 12, 25, 38, 47, 192, 263, 267–8, 286, 379
'spatiotemporalities,' 255
specific/ity, 19, 109, 267–9, 270–1, 307
 urban as, 267–9, 307
'spectral' comparisons, 302
Speculative philosophy, 327, 341, 365n11
 and method, 354–5
'speculative realism,' 341
Spivak, Gayatri, 76, 204, 207–8
Stadtgemeinde, 224–7, 244n7
Stanek, Lukasz, 140–1
'state capitalism,' 275
'state-led' gentrification, 299
state redistributive capacities, 293
strategic essentialism, 27–34
strategic regional imaginations, 31
Strathern, Marilyn, 158–9, 191–2, 202, 204, 262–3, 280, 382
Structural Adjustment Programmes, 117, 172, 178–80
structuration, 169

'subaltern urbanisation,' 313–4
'subject of urban theory', 40–1, 203, 204–217, 228, 356
'submarine relations', 194, 302
'suburbanisation,' 141, 151–2, 308–312, 328n2
Suburban Planet (Keil), 141, 310
sustainable development goals (SDGs), 237, 315
suturing, 336–340
Suturing the City (de Boeck and Baloji), 336–338
Swyngedouw, Eric, 292–9
'syndrome' of neoliberalisation, 173, 183

Tanzania, 78n3, 149
territories, 18–19, 49, 62, 267–8, 307–329, 329–362, 373–4
 assembling, 320–325
 strategic, 27–34
 territorialisations, 312–320
 thinking from, 49, 308–312
 urban territories, 267–8, 312–320
Thatcherite model of loosening planning regulations, 102
Tilly, Charles, 59, 62–3, 146–7, 164–5, 167–9, 271–2
Theodore, Nik, 139, 173–4
Thus Spake Zarathrustra (Nietzsche), 352, 368n31
Todd, Zoe, 205–6
topologies, 73, 129, 193, 301–2, 353
 and comparisons, 129, 301–2
Totality, 14, 110–118, 141, 153, 167, 234–5, 252, 258, 262–4, 326, 339, 350–1
 concrete, 111–4, 127, 153, 234–5, 266–7
 emergent, 166–7
 Stuart Hall, and, 234, 245n9
 Lefebvre and, 110, 234–5, 264–5, 339
 Marxism and, 112
 open, 234, 263–266, 328n4
 'total man', 'total content', 110, 234, 265
 urban and, 132n16, 266–7
Township-Wall (Ole), cover, p.22–4
transcalar territorial networks (TTN), 307, 316
transformative politics, 294

transnational production networks, 97
Trauerspiel, see *On German Tragic Drama* (Benjamin)

UK urban politics, 67, 293
unconceptualised difference, 157
units of comparison, 70–74
universals, 19, 109, 207, 241, 243
 and causality, 68, 69
urban, as a theoretical object, 12, 35–7, 306
urban citizenship, micropolitics of, 293
'urban community,' 224–226, 228
urban comparisons, genetic and generative grounds for, 124–127
urban comparativism, 69–70, 107, 272
Urban Development Corporation (UDC), 102
urban economies, 223, 313
 policy, 85, 90
 globalisation, 72, 190
 liberalisation, 29
urban infrastructures, 138, 318
'urban land nexus,' 192
urban outcomes, see also urban settlements, 4, 35, 168,
urban politics, 75, 84, 101, 157, 275, 276, 295, 314–320, 381
 and urban development, 87, 156–158, 180, 272
 territories of
urban regime, 71, 90, 314
The Urban Revolution (Lefebvre), 264
urban services, 294
urban settlements, 1, 25, 135
urban social movements, 92–3, 115, 291–4, 301, 322
urban spatiality, see also space, urban, 3–5, 6, 74, 267, 373
urban studies, 1–4, 44, 53, 80
 conventional strategies for comparison in urban studies, 57–69
 explosion of, 383–386
 incommensurability in urban studies, 54–57
 institutional change in, 2, 21, 384–6
 traditional object of, 1
urban territories, 307–8, 312–20, 373–4
urban theory, 1, 30, 55, 65, 206, 216, 243, 319, 337

'urbanisation processes', 1, 17, 39, 138–146, 168, 268–270, 299, 316

variation finding comparative method, 64–69, 75, 190
'variegation,' 4, 116, 173–4
variety, and method, 83–91, 328n5
'varieties of capitalism' analyses, 173
'vertiginous inequalities,' 83
'virtuality', 13, 121, 124, 150, 247, 300, 370
  and conceptualisation, 352
  definition, 131n7
  in Deleuze, 122
  Lefebvre, 266, 131n7
  urban as, 7, 120–1, 370

Wacquant, Loïc, 81–3, 229
Waiting for Bus (Dilomprizulike), 22, 304–5

Walton, John, 56, 61, 94–5, 177–9
Wayward Lives (Hartman), 213
Weber, Max, 203–230
  and Chance, 220–1, 230
  and method, 228–9
  Ideal Types, 218–229
welfare state capitalism, 36
'white men' institution, 205
'white tone', 205
'wider' processes, 14, 86, 109, 115–6, 147, 159, 162, 164–171
  contexts, co-constituted, 167
Wirth, Louis, 35, 55, 56
Wu, Fulong, 28, 30, 46, 180, 182, 275–6, 298, 299

Zérah, Marie-Hélène, 313–4
'Zwischenstädte,' 309